The New Psychology Today Reader

Edited by

Robert Epstein, Ph.D.

University Professor, United States International University
Director Emeritus, Cambridge Center for Behavioral Studies
Adjunct Professor of Psychology, San Diego State University

KENDALL/HUNT PUBLISHING COMPANY
4050 Westmark Drive   Dubuque, Iowa 52002

DEDICATION

To Jordan Becerra Epstein
born 8-9, weight same as the date,
with love from Dad,
December, 1998

ACKNOWLEDGMENTS

Copyright on all articles is held by Sussex Publishers, publisher of *Psychology Today* magazine. Permission to reprint articles has been obtained from the authors where appropriate. The original publication dates of the articles, listed by the chapter number in this volume, are as follows:

1. Mr. Behaviorist: A Conversation with B. F. Skinner. Interview by Mary Harrington Hall. **September 1967**

2. The Father of Rogerian Therapy: A Conversation with Carl Rogers. Interview by Mary Harrington Hall. **December 1967**

3. Psychology Cannot Be a Coherent Science, by Sigmund Koch. **September 1969**

4. Re-Examining Freud, by James Hillman, Stephen M. Sonnenberg, Alice Miller, Thomas Szasz, Jerome L. Singer, Paula Caplan, Albert Ellis, Will Gaylin, Robert Jay Lifton, Hans J. Eysenck, Phyllis Chesler, and Rollo May. **September 1989**

5. Self-Fulfilling Prophecy, by Robert Rosenthal. **September 1968**

6. Folk Wisdom, by Robert Epstein. **November 1997**

7. The Think-Drink Effect, by G. Alan Marlatt & Damaris J. Rohsenow. **December 1981**

8. A Love Affair with the Brain: A Conversation with Marian Diamond. Interview by Janet L. Hopson. **November 1984**

9. Right Brain, Left Brain: Fact and Fiction, by Jerre Levy. **May 1985**

10. My Genes Made Me Do It, by Stanton Peele and Richard DeGrandpre. **July 1995**

11. Phantom Limbs, by Ronald Melzack. **October 1970**

12. Educating Your Nose, by William S. Cain. **July 1981**

13. The Psychology of the Step Beyond: A Conversation with J.B. Rhine. Interview by Mary Harrington Hall. **March 1969**

14. Lucid Dreaming: Directing the Action as It Happens, by Stephen P. La Berge. **January 1981**

15. In Search of the Unconscious, by Laurence Miller. **December 1986**

16. The Power of Daydreams, by Eric Klinger. **October 1987**

17. Token Economies: The Rich Rewards of Rewards, by Alan E. Kazdin. **November 1976**

18. Little Brother Is Changing You, by Farnum Gray with Paul S. Graubard and Harry Rosenberg. **March 1974**

19. Fall into Helplessness, by Martin E.P. Seligman. **June 1973**

20. Eyewitnesses: Essential but Unreliable, by Elizabeth F. Loftus. **February 1984**

21. How to...Uh...Remember!, by Gordon H. Bower. **October 1973**

22. Mood and Memory, by Gordon H. Bower. **June 1981**

23. The Seven Frames of Mind: A Conversation with Howard Gardner. Interview by James Ellison. **June 1984**

24. How Sex Hormones Boost—or Cut—Intellectual Ability, by Doreen Kimura. **November 1989**

25. The Differences Are Real, by Arthur Jensen. **December 1973**

26. Differences Are Not Deficits, by Theodosius Dobzhansky. **December 1973**

27. Capturing Creativity, by Robert Epstein. **July 1996**

28. Automated Lives, by Ellen J. Langer. **April 1982**

CONTENTS

Introduction
for Students and Instructors

Not long ago a large, white, somewhat battered volume, sitting on a high shelf that had been untouched and undusted for years, caught my eye. Along the spine were the words *Readings in Psychology Today: Second Edition.*. Because I had recently become an editor for *Psychology Today* magazine, the title—which I must have skipped over a thousand times—had new meaning for me. What could *that* book be, I wondered?

Looking, I'm sure, like the perfect caricature of a doddering professor, I struggled to bring down the book, blew the thick coating of dust off the top edge, and coughed at the cloud that rose up. I turned to the contents and was surprised to find an impressive set of names and titles: Stanley Milgram, whose obedience studies stunned the world; B.F. Skinner, ultimate trainer of rats and pigeons (with whom I had done my doctoral work at Harvard); Carl Rogers, the founder of humanistic psychology (and Skinner's nemesis); Noam Chomsky, the brilliant M.I.T. psycholinguist; Donald O. Hebb, pioneering brain researcher; David McClelland, the achievement-motivation guru; not to mention interviews with Masters and Johnson, the legendary sex researchers; eminent anthropologist Margaret Mead; Harry Harlow, pioneering primate researcher; and Jean Piaget, the dean of developmental psychology. More than 100 articles in all, a veritable treasure-trove of significant articles in psychology and related fields.

As I flipped through the book, marveling at its contents, some long-dormant neural connections began to fire up. *I think I bought this book when I was an undergraduate,* I thought. Sure enough, the publication date was 1972, the year I crossed from sophomore to junior. I still couldn't remember *why* I bought the book, but I remembered enjoying it, and it contained a few marginal notes in my college handwriting. I didn't remember the book from any of my courses, but memory does play tricks, after all. According to the book's unsigned foreword, this was an expanded edition of a volume that had been widely assigned in introductory Psychology courses. It was employed primarily as a friendly companion to the weighty, intimidating "intro psych" text.

What a natural companion book for Introductory Psychology courses, I thought. *Psychology Today* was founded to popularize research and practice in psychology and related fields—to communicate advances in these fields in terms the public could understand and enjoy. Some of its articles were written by journalists, but many were composed by distinguished scholars, researchers, and practitioners in the behavioral sciences and then edited for public consumption. Articles in technical journals, steeped in jargon and statistics, are just about impossible for the novice to understand (and sometimes just about impossible for *professionals* to understand), but *Psychology Today* articles are written for a broad audience of first-timers. What could be more perfect for first-year college students?

You see where this is leading. I had been teaching Introductory Psychology courses since the early 1980s, but as far as I was aware, a *Psychology Today* reader did not exist. Nor did any equivalent readers, as far as I knew. After all, how could there be an equivalent reader? *PT* is, alas, the only magazine of its kind. (What a shame that the public has so little access to legitimate information about mental health and the behavioral sciences.)

Turns out that *Psychology Today* had changed hands in the mid '70s and several times thereafter; it had even been out of print briefly. The *PT* reader disappeared from sheer neglect as the magazine shifted from editor to editor and publisher to publisher. It wasn't that students and instructors didn't like it; the concept had simply gotten lost. When I proposed to the current publisher, John P. Colman, that we revive the *Psychology Today* reader, he was highly supportive.

The Current Volume

Thus began the arduous (but somewhat fun) process of sifting through more than a thousand feature articles and interviews published since the magazine's inception. Working with Holly Parker, an intern at the magazine, and Michelle Osborne, a student at California State University, I selected about 130 articles that I thought might interest today's instructors and students. I then asked twelve experienced psychology professors—including several department chairs and authors of introductory psychology textbooks—and forty-one undergraduates to rate the selections, given the titles, the authors and a brief description of each piece. The ratings allowed me to make the final selection that you see in the pages that follow.

The 61 articles in this volume span the full history of the magazine, from 1967 to the present day. Only eight of them appeared in the 1972 edition. They also span the full range of topics in psychology, from physiology to intelligence to health to love. For convenience, I've organized the articles into eighteen sections that roughly parallel the chapters in contemporary introductory psychology textbooks. I've also included brief introductions to each section, as well as discussion questions at the end of each article. At the end of each section, you'll also find an exercise that's related to one or more of the chapters in that section.

You may be wondering whether students and professors chose the same articles. They did in some cases, and these articles are clearly the stars of the collection (listed here alphabetically by title):

Stars
"Adrenaline Makes the Heart Grow Fonder" (Walster & Berscheid)
"Are You Shy?" (Carducci & Zimbardo)
"Babies: They're a Lot Smarter Than They Look" (Lipsitt)
"Beauty and the Best" (Berscheid & Walster)
"Capturing Creativity" (Epstein)
"College Blues" (Beck and Young)
"Does Personality Really Change After 20?" (Rubin)
"How to…Uh…Remember!" (Bower)
"How We Send Emotional Messages" (Beier)
"Male Brain, Female Brain: The Hidden Difference" (Kimura)
"Marriages Made To Last" (Lauer & Lauer)
"My Genes Made Me Do It" (Peele and DeGrandpre)
"On the Real Benefits of Eustress: A Conversation with Hans Selye"
"Phantom Limbs" (Melzack)
"Play Is Serious Business" (Bruner)
"Right Brain, Left Brain: Fact and Fiction" (Levy)
"Schizophrenia Is a Myth, Born of Metaphor, Meaningless" (Sarbin)
"Self-Fulfilling Prophecy" (Rosenthal)
"The Think-Drink Effect" (Marlatt & Rohsenow)
"The Universal Smile: Face Muscles Talk Every Language" (Ekman)

Three articles—about dreams, orgasms, and Freudian slips—were strongly favored by students but not by faculty:

Student Favorites
"Lucid Dreaming: Directing the Action as It Happens" (La Berge)
"The Orgasm Wars" (Furlow & Thronhill)
"What I Meant to Say" (Motley)

And professors strongly favored several articles that students rejected:

Faculty Favorites
"Differences Are Not Deficits" (Dobzhansky)
"Folk Wisdom" (Epstein)
"The Frontiers of Pharmacology" (Siever)
"A Missionary for Social Psychology: A Conversation with Elliot Aronson"
"Mr. Behaviorist: A Conversation with B. F. Skinner"
"Token Economies: The Rich Rewards of Rewards" (Kazdin)
"Fall into Helplessness" (Seligman)
"A Conversation with Jean Piaget"

The other articles in this collection produced at least moderately strong overall ratings. In only two cases did I include articles that yielded low preference ratings by both faculty members and students:

Editor's Exceptions
"The Differences Are Real" (Jensen)
"The Psychology of the Step Beyond: A Conversation with J. B. Rhine"

I included Arthur Jensen's article on racial differences in intelligence because it didn't make sense to me to include an article that criticizes his position (the one by Theodosius Dobzhansky) without giving Jensen his say. And I included the Rhine interview because, no matter how weak his data, Rhine was a pioneering researcher in an eerie world where few dare to tread.

You may also be wondering about the level of consensus among faculty and students. Professors agreed among themselves much better than I thought they would: The mean preference rating among faculty for all 130 articles was a 4.2 on a possible range of –12 to +12, with moderate variability. (If only we could do that well at faculty meetings!) There was little consensus among students, however, perhaps because they didn't recognize some of the names and terms. The mean student rating was a lowly 0.38 on a possible range of –41 to +41, with fairly high variability. A mean rating of 0 would suggest that positive ratings and negative ratings canceled out completely.

I was somewhat uneasy about including articles and interviews that are decades old, but, with survey results in hand, I came to my senses. The history of psychology is an important part of Introductory Psychology courses, after all, and *Psychology Today* is a crucible of that history. What's more, some of the very oldest articles in this collection—the article on college depression, for example, or the interviews with Piaget, Rogers, Selye, and Skinner—are as interesting now as they were when they were first published. Psychology is still a young science, arguably just over 100 years old. It's not yet a field of dramatic breakthroughs that topple elegant theories, so we can still learn from the pioneers. Perhaps one of you, inspired by an article in this volume, will change that some day.

Acknowledgments

I'm grateful to my colleagues who took the time to complete the survey I utilized to make the final selection of articles: David S. Calverley, Northeastern University: Carl D. Cheney, Utah State University: John D. Cone, United States International University; Russell B. Cooper, United States International University; Gina Grimshaw, California State University San Marcos; Deborah Hickey, National University; Fred Hornbeck, San Diego State University; Karen Guffman, Palomar College; Yoshito Kawahara, Mesa College; Daniel Moriarty, University of San Diego; Peter E. Nathan, University of Iowa; and Miriam Schustack, California State University San Marcos. Special thanks to the students of Dr. Calverley's summer Introductory Psychology class at Northeastern University, as well as to Espen Correll, Rebecca Gloria, and Dennis S. Thompson. Dr. Paul Chance, author of some of my favorite text books and a former editor for *Psychology Today* magazine, offered valuable advice about preparing the volume, as did the indomitable T. George Harris, first editor-in-chief of the magazine. Thanks also to Holly Parker, an intern at *Psychology Today* in New York, who spent the past few months tracking down articles, issues, and authors in expert fashion; to Steven Schmidt, a student at San Diego State University, who helped prepare questions and exercises; to Elva Becerra, Justin Epstein, and Dennis Thompson for help with proofreading; and to Michelle Osborne, a student at California State University San Marcos, who worked at my side during various phases of the book's preparation, patiently correcting my errors. Finally, this volume would not have been possible without the trust and cooperation of John P. Colman of Sussex Publishers and Al Grisanti of Kendall/Hunt.

By the way, many paragraphs ago, you might have asked a very reasonable question: If my old *Psychology Today* reader was published while I was still an undergraduate, and if it was used primarily as a companion text for Introductory Psychology courses, didn't I get the book in that course? I admit that college is a bit of a blur, but I can guarantee you that I did *not* get the book in my Intro Psych course. I went to school during a chaotic time when, ever so briefly, students had Power. We used that Power for various purposes, some noble (like stopping the war in Vietnam) and some ignoble (like sex, drugs, and rock'n'roll). In my case, I used that Power to *skip Intro Psych*, even though I was a psychology major. Here I am, a psychology professor with three degrees in the field, and I've never even taken the basic course.

So where *did* I get that book?

Robert Epstein, Ph.D.
Cardiff by the Sea, California

PART 1

INTRODUCTION TO PSYCHOLOGY

❶ Mr. Behaviorist: A Conversation with B.F. Skinner

❷ The Father of Rogerian Therapy: A Conversation with Carl Rogers

❸ Psychology Cannot Be a Coherent Science, by Sigmund Koch

❹ Re-Examining Freud, by Hilman, Sonnenberg, Miller, Szasz, Singer, Caplan, Ellis, Gaylin, Lifton, Eysenck, Chesler, and May

You're in for a treat in this section, if only to get two different versions of "the duck story"—B. F. Skinner's version, which suggests that Carl Rogers, creator of non-directive therapy, is actually quite directive (even manipulative), and Rogers' version, which subtly makes fun of Skinner's obsession with scientific method. On a more substantive note, you'll also get Skinner's views on behaviorism, conditioning, Freud, programmed instruction, and education. John B. Watson was the actual founder of behaviorism, but, as a result of an indiscretion, Watson left academe for the world of advertising. Young Skinner took up the banner in the 1930s and continued to be behaviorism's most persuasive and visible advocate until his death in 1990. In the interviews that follow, you can contrast Skinner, one of the architects of behaviorism and consummate rat and pigeon experimenter, with Carl Rogers, one of the architects of modern humanism and developer of the "encounter group" that swept through liberal America in the 1960s and 70s. These two individuals could not be more different, and their differences symbolize two very different traditions and perspectives in psychology: the experimental tradition and the clinical tradition.

In the essay that follows, philosopher and psychologist Sigmund Koch argues that psychology is not just splintered in practice but also in principle and that, as a result, it can never be a true science. What, after all, *is* the subject matter of psychology? When you put ideology aside and take a close look at what psychologists actually *do*, this is a difficult question to answer.

The last piece in this section is a collection of statements by various distinguished mental health professionals about the legacy of Sigmund Freud. It was published in *Psychology Today* in 1989 to commemorate the 50th anniversary of Freud's death.

Mr. Behaviorist
A CONVERSATION WITH
B.F. *Skinner*

◆ *Mary Harrington Hall*

Mary Harrington Hall: Would you please explain to me that neat chart above your desk?

B. F. Skinner: I just like to keep some records of what I do. I do my writing and all of my really serious thinking here. And I clock the time. I turn the clock on when I enter and turn it off again when I leave. Whenever the light is burning on the clock up there, that clock is running. When the clock covers twelve hours, I plot a point. I've kept this record for about six or eight years now. I can watch my productivity change during the years. Look at the curve—that flat spot indicates a lecture. My productivity suffers from that, so I avoid lectures. Actually, I'm averaging about three truly productive hours a day. This is my only really creative time. The rest of the day I'm still working, and I don't quit. But I don't do anything very important. I've figured that I average about two minutes of creative time per published word.

Hall: You have certainly caused a lot of discussion about raising children. I understand that your daughter who was the famous Skinner baby is now raising her own "baby in the box."

Skinner: Interestingly, it is the child of our other daughter, the one who was *not* the famous "baby in a box." That phrase is still irksome. It was coined by the *Ladies Home Journal* and could not be less accurate.

I realize in watching my granddaughter how much of the day is given over to contingencies of reinforcement. It is very hard to maintain them, though. How easy it is to do the wrong thing. She starts a little fuss, and you go right over to her. That's the awful thing about raising children. Everything works against you. You are likely to do the wrong thing, especially in an ordinary house. Home is not the place to bring up children: it isn't made for that. You have mighty attractive objects around the house, and then you spank the children for being attracted to them. That's nonsense.

Hall: That's one of the reasons that you designed the air crib, isn't it?

Skinner: Yes, the air crib is nothing but a solution to the problem of physical environment. A child is a very precious possession. What bothers me particularly is that you recognize that when you are talking about whether you are going to use sheets and a blanket or an air crib tonight, but you don't recognize it at all when you ask, what am I doing to this child

> *I've figured that I average about two minutes of creative time per published word.*

> *Remember, the air crib is for the baby, not the parents... The ordinary crib is a small jail.*

to create the behavior that is going to be worthwhile in the future.

The principle of the air crib is really very simple: it solves a very simple problem. Diapers have an obvious function, while all the rest, the blankets and sheets, are just to keep the child warm. And they don't do a very good job: The child gets overheated and the blankets get kicked off and it gets cold and all of that. The air crib—heated, ventilated space—is the obvious solution.

Hall: I've always thought that the volume control on an air crib is a good idea. Once you've done what you can to make your baby comfortable, you can turn down the volume if he cries just for exercise.

Skinner: Remember, the air crib is for the baby, not the parents. The whole point is that this clean, glass-enclosed structure is roomier and healthier than a crib. The baby is more comfortable.

Hall: But it meets with lots of resistance?

Skinner: Well, in the first place it is an area where everybody, mothers in particular, feel they know all about everything. I suppose it took a hundred years to get over believing that you had to keep a child rocking all day long. At one time they had dogs walking on treadmills just to keep the cradle rocking. Now that's disappeared, just as the ordinary crib will probably disappear sometime soon. The ordinary crib is a small jail, if you want to put it that way, with bars. You put the child behind bars. The air crib at least has a clear view without bars. You don't have the feeling that you are preparing the child for a life of crime later on.

Hall: Do you really think the air crib solves the problems of bringing up baby?

Skinner: Not really. It solves only a very simple physical problem. I despair of teaching the ordinary parent how to handle his child. I would prefer to turn child-raising over to a specialist. I just can't believe that an ordinary parent can do a good job. What has happened in the past is that a culture has set up a routine way of handling kids. You spank them for what is wrong; you don't spank them for what is good; and so on. Some of those produce a given type of person. Some produce enterprising persons, other seem to produce lazy persons. But the main point is that we don't have stable cultures any more: so the average parent doesn't know what to do. The books on child care are more confusing than anything else because you can't apply what they recommend: "Go and love your child."

That would be all right, but you can't go and buy three ounces of love at the store. And if the child really isn't lovable, you simply have to fake it. Fake love is probably the worst of all commodities. But I don't really know: that's why I tend to be a Utopian dreamer.

Hall: I'm curious. How were you raised, Fred? Were your parents strict?

Skinner: Yes. I don't think my mother and father ever had any doubts about what I was to be punished for or not. But now we really don't have an on-going culture that gives us any guidance on how to handle people. My parents came from a very strictly defined culture. My mother knew exactly what was right. I can't even remember when I learned what was right or not right, or what I should do or shouldn't do. The rules were right there in the culture: there was never any question. Well, now that's all gone: we have thrown that over, but we have to go on designing from moment to moment to produce a better way.

Hall: Not even religion provides unquestioned rules today.

Skinner: And I don't know whether I want to improve religion or not. I prefer to get rid of it, but until we can get rid of it safely, it may be well to make sure that it functions.

Hall: Until you have a substitute you'd be in terrible danger. And what are you going to replace a religion with?

Skinner: Yes. Well, the whole thing is not to turn the world over in a day. This applies in international politics, too. When you had strict nationalistic lines, territories to be defended, methods of defending them, nationalism, national honor, it was different. Now we don't know. Should we appease, should we threaten? We're asking our statesmen now to use a more

---

And if the child really isn't lovable, you simply have to fake it.

---

creative application of principles that have not gotten into international culture. That's a good, positive need. We don't have time to build a culture so that nations will begin to behave in a consistent way.

Hall: You do get uncertain in a world where you don't even know what an act of war is.

Skinner: Yes. Well, that is the trouble right now. The whole definition of nationalism. A part of this is the fact that many people do begin to feel themselves citizens of the world. Nationalism isn't as strong as it used to be. You have interest beyond your own nation. That upsets everything. When nations are sharply defined, then whether you are at war or not is perfectly clear.

Hall: Do you think that better ways of handling people might be arranged?

Skinner: Well, positive reinforcement seems to offer most of the answers.

Hall: Are you talking about reward learning? Are those the contingencies that you were talking about earlier?

Skinner: Well, I am talking about operant conditioning. People often confuse that with what they refer to as reward learning. Trouble is that specifications in terms of reward and punishment are incomplete. They don't say enough. It is true that people work for rewards: usually a reward means something agreed upon. You do something and you will be rewarded, and so on.

The rewards of a good life are eternal bliss. Now these are contracted rewards, the nature of the situation is that you do this and you will get the following. That isn't involved at all in operant conditioning. Moreover, the point isn't just that hungry rats will work for food or that a sex-starved man will work for sex, and so on. What's fundamentally important—this is very little understood by people outside the field—is what they are actually doing when a reinforcing stimulus occurs.

The whole study of operant conditioning lies in the tricky relationship between what the rat is doing and the moment of truth when the food appears. Oh, some of it is the study of what events are reinforcing and what kinds of behavior can be reinforced, but most of it is the study of the temporal and spatial relations between behavior and its consequences. That is the heart of the matter.

The relationships of importance always involve three things: the situation, call it the stimulus if you like; the behavior, call it the response if you like; and the consequences, the reinforcers. We say that the reinforcers are contingent on behavior in a given situation or that a reinforcer is contingent on a response in the presence of a given stimulus. When those contingen-

Corbis

B. F. Skinner

cies are arranged, the probability of the behavior changes. The behavior becomes more probable in the presence of the stimuli that were present when it was reinforced and less probable when not reinforced, and so on.

Hall: But where exactly does the notion of contingencies come in?

Skinner: That's the whole question of schedules of reinforcement, which is the most important part. You can reinforce every tenth response, every hundredth response, every thousandth response, or you can reinforce a response every minute, every five minutes, and so on. Some of the schedules which are now being studied are extremely complicated and can only be mediated by extremely sensitive apparatus. The most surprising thing is that organisms usually feel these schedules. They respond appropriately to them. That is the heart of the matter. Knowing the contingencies and the history of reinforcement, you can predict the behavior. You can arrange a contingency; you can control the behavior. And of course both prediction and control have widespread im-

plications in human affairs, and in animal affairs, too.

Hall: If you could be remembered for just one contribution to psychology, would that be your analysis of contingencies?

Skinner: Yes, I suppose, if I am limited to just one thing, it would be the whole question of the contingencies of reinforcement arranged by schedules of reinforcement and their role in the analysis of operant behavior. It's a shame. Nobody pays much attention to it at all. It's an extremely interesting and complicated and fascinating field. I think it is my basic scientific contribution.

In fact, I am even now getting a little bit more interested in it, myself, if that is possible. Particularly in the implications of this sort of thing for the design of cultures in general. I have no doubt at all that programmed instruction based on operant principles will take over education. I have no doubt that operant therapy will be very important in the management of psychotics and also in the treatment of neurotics.

Hall: If we're talking about designing cultures, Fred, let's talk about your novel, *Walden Two*. Two generations now have read it, and it's on the required reading list at most schools. I love that book.

Positive reinforcement, properly used, is extremely powerful.

Skinner: I think *Walden Two* has made people stop and look at the culture they have inherited and wonder if it is the last word or whether it can be changed. And even to suggest ways of changing it. I would still put my basic scientific contribution to operant behavior as the analysis of contingencies of reinforcement, but what I really expect to be known for is the application of all this to education, psychotherapy, economics, gov-

ernment, religion, I suppose, and its use in designing a world that will make us into the kind of people we would like to be and give us the things that we could all agree that we want.

Hall: But the society in *Walden Two* is based mainly on positive reinforcement, isn't it? What about punishment, holding down crime, and those strict codes of ethics by which you yourself were brought up?

Skinner: Positive reinforcement, properly used, is extremely powerful. Aversive control (that means punishment mainly and arranging that people do things to get away from or avoid unpleasantness) is immediate and quick and so we use it. But I really think that the use of aversive control has serious, inherent disadvantages. It is used at a terrible cost. That of course doesn't mean that you can change tomorrow.

I always thought, for example, getting back to possible Utopias, that when the Zionist movement took over Israel, it was a terrible mistake for them to emphasize an army. They should have gone in and demonstrated to the world that they could have a culture without any army. What they have got now is just another national culture emerging. Armies compel, they put on pressure, they attempt to control the behavior of other nations with aversive techniques. We say let them do this or that or we will blow you to pieces.

Hall: Now we are talking about the tragedy in international politics. I really don't see acceptance of alternatives to force very soon. Do you?

Skinner: Well it's not only international issues, it's domestic issues, too—the whole business of how you use power and how you use positive reinforcement. Again, it's a matter of the contingencies. Whether you are going to do something either positive or negative, send in food and medical supplies or drop bombs, for example; the important thing is that the behavior of the other country should be contingent on what you are doing to them, so that the other country will do more or less of something you desire.

But I don't get the impression that anyone is paying any attention to this at all. In Vietnam, for example, certainly the only idea is that somehow or other if you make them suffer, they will give up. Well, if you have to use sources of pain, for heaven's sake use them at the right time and in the right way. It's the behavior that's being neglected. If you ask people what kind of world they want to live in, they will mention all the things that are reinforcing to them, such as food, sex, personal relations, nature, music, art, but they won't say what they are going to be doing to get those things.

The analyst would say love is a terribly important thing. He's likely to overlook what you're doing when you're loved. That's the really important thing. That's the whole crucial issue. That's what's wrong with all conceptions of heaven. No one has ever portrayed an interesting heaven. There is music in the streets, gold bricks in the pavement, and what not. But it's a boring existence because nothing is doing. Afterworlds of other cultures are of the same nature. The American Indian isn't much better off. He wants a happy hunting ground, according to song and story. Ridiculous. He doesn't just want food, he wants a happy way to get it.

Well, to get back to the Vietnam business, it isn't really whether you are using money or love or power. It's how you use it. We're

> **No one
> has ever portrayed
> an interesting heaven.**

pouring a tremendous amount of power into Vietnam but the contingencies are absolutely lousy. We are simply not doing things at the right time, properly contingent on the behavior, in order to change the behavior of anyone over there. This is the whole problem.

Hall: You mentioned earlier that our domestic policy suffers from an ignorance of these considerations.

Skinner: Yes, certainly. Here we're going to give large sums of money to the poor. If you just give it to them, you aren't strengthening behavior at all. It is true that you are satisfying certain needs, and that is generally good. They will no longer be hungry; they will no longer be living in filth; that's reasonable, and is the kind of thing one does out of compassion.

But all the money that is going to go into this could be so enormously more effective if it were properly contingent on the kinds of behavior that you want these people to engage in. You might ask the question: Why aren't these people enterprising? Why don't they clean up their own apartment houses, and so on? It isn't that they are unable to live in better surroundings, they just don't do

> **I don't think that you can really
> ever beat down the prejudice
> of the older generation.
> I am convinced now that science
> never progresses by converting.**

whatever it is that makes their surroundings better. And the solution is so very simple: You just have to make what is being done for these people contingent on their doing something.

Hall: Let's get back, if we may, to programmed instruction. This re-

ally has taken hold in a big way in education, hasn't it? But are current teaching machines effective? They bore me.

Skinner: You're right to be bored. It certainly is not because there are no good programs. Oh, you can write terrible programs, and they don't do at all what they are intended to do. But many, many good programs are being written, they are being improved all the time, and fantastic things can be done. It's really just the application of what we know about contingencies of reinforcement to a suitable and efficient method of education.

It's really nothing more than arranging for reinforcing consequences immediately following the behavior of the student in the proper context. But you have to bring the educators around to seeing the advantages, and that takes time.

Hall: They are resistant, the people in education? How typical.

Skinner: Yes, a change of this magnitude takes years. It really takes a new generation—on which we are having quite a considerable impression. I don't think that you can really ever beat down the prejudice of the older generation. I am convinced now that science never progresses by converting.

Among my contemporaries, for example. I can mention only one or two who really very seriously changed their attitudes toward the study of behavior as a result of anything I have ever done or said. That's to be expected, of course. They have invested a great deal in certain lines and you can't expect them to admit that they were wasting their time and have thrown away their life-work.

I would say that, to take a sweeping generalization, almost all the work done with the memory drum is worthless. I mean, they manage to cook up an interesting little problem, but I think in general it's worthless. However, I can't ask people who have worked with memory drums all their lives to admit this or to examine what goes on when somebody looks at a memory drum and tries to memorize something. They just don't want to look too closely at that. They are so afraid that they might find out that they are wrong and not amounting to anything. I suggest that they take a look around and see what is seriously being done in other fields.

Few of the educational psychologists, for example, even know what programming is all about. But the younger people are refreshing; they are looking for what really works, for the wave of the future, the techniques by which you really can manage behavior for the better in a way that actually works. And so when they look at programmed instruction and at the operant treatment of neurotics and psychotics, they see that these things really work, thank goodness.

That's how scientific change comes about, because the young have not been spoiled by miserable histories of reinforcement into running away from possible sources of much greater reinforcement.

Hall: You sound very optimistic about the future of operant conditioning.

Skinner: And justifiably so, I think. You see, as sad as it is to relate, there really isn't very much competition for the allegiance of bright and informed young psychologists. Positive reinforcement really works, and contingencies of reinforcement are really very important, and we are actually very successful in predicting and controlling behavior. These are things you just have to accept.

The young men just entering the field do accept them. They see

that this is where the business is going. To paraphrase President Truman after he defeated Dewey, the competition may feel that this is all too bad and sad and cannot quite figure out how it came about, but it is true and so we will just have to make the best of it.

Hall: What about the rival schools of psychology? They object to operant conditioning on the grounds of dehumanization of mechanization.

Skinner: Well, that's a different issue. I think the main objection to behaviorism is that people are in love with the mental apparatus. If you say that doesn't really exist, that it's a fiction and let's get back to the facts, then they have to give up their first love.

You can't expect a Freudian to say, yes, I will admit that Freud's only contribution was in demonstrating some unusual casual relations between early experience and the present behavior. He loves the superego, the ego, and the id, and the various geographies of the mind and all of that stuff.

I say we can get along without that. In fact, we can get along better without it, because we've misrepresented the facts that Freud discovered.

They won't go along with that. You are asking them to throw away their lifework. Or their only confidence, because they don't really care very much about tracing existence of problems to their environment except to show how the unconscious is causing trouble. They're interested in the mental apparatus. To ask them to give that up would be like asking an engineer to go into sculpture. You may convince him that sculptur-

> *I think the main objection to behaviorism is that people are in love with the mental apparatus.*

> *This Freudian business is dying out, anyway.*

ing is more important than building bridges, but he's a bridge builder. He wouldn't know how to start something over. This Freudian business is dying out, anyway. As for the cognitive seed, that never was anything. They are not doing anything: they are not getting anywhere: and the operant people are.

Take the issue of language, which has lately become the hunting ground of the cognitive people—not that they have been able to find much. I hear that they have come out with the notion of innate ideas, which takes us right back to the dark, mentalistic ages of the 19th century. That's not progress.

Hall: Did your book, *Verbal Behavior*, gain much acceptance in those quarters?

Skinner: Not really, but I am not unhappy about this. I am willing to wait. Verbal behavior apparently has not been understood by the linguist or the psycholinguist.

They have no conception of what I mean by verbal behavior. They made almost no contribution to it, and they apparently are resolved not to make any if they can help it.

In the famous Noam Chomsky review of my book, I suspect you will find what amounts to a hatchet job, although I have never read the review myself. I did read a couple of pages, saw that he missed the point, and I never read the rest. What the psycholinguists miss is any conception of a functional analysis as opposed to a structural analysis of verbal behavior.

Hall: You do have a sweet, succinct way about you. Keep talking.

Skinner: I mean that they try to make sense out of the dependent variable only. They really don't want to look into the situation in which a person is speaking or listening to speech. That would make them psychologists, and they don't want to do it. And so they argue that you don't need to. And then, of course, they try to argue that verbal behavior isn't real behavior, that it goes back to ideas and cognitive processes. They lean very heavily on the mentalistic psychology, and they are going to be let down because there is no such psychology. But as I said earlier, now they are postulating innate ideas, and that is next to worthless, if not a little bit comical. But I am in no real hurry, I have had my say. I am not interested in arguing with them at all. When all their mystical machinery finally grinds to a halt and is laid aside, discarded, then we will see what is remembered fifty or a hundred years from now, when the truth will have all been brought out in the open.

Hall: That takes care of mystical machinery. Where is progress, then?

Skinner: Well, certainly not in mentalism or psychophysics; it's a dead end. You see the old idea was, and still is, as a matter of fact, that you could have a science of mental life. Mental events were going to obey mental laws. All you had to do was find out what those laws are, and you had a life of the mind. This could be scientifically analyzed, perhaps. But what actually happened was that people wanted to find out where the mental events came from, and of course they came from the outside world.

So you study sensation and the relation between the psychic and the physical, and the field is still essentially in that condition. The fact is that a hundred and some years ago they decided that this relation was logarithmic and now they are trying to say that it is a power function. But it is basically unproductive: they believe in a world of sensation, the way that things seem

to be rather than the way things really are.

Hall: Are you cheerier about clinical psychology and psychotherapy?

Skinner Well, they won't get anywhere if they don't get results. And you can't get results by sitting around and theorizing about the inner world of the disturbed. I want to say to those people: get down to the facts. But they seem to be threatened by facts. Operant conditioning—the proper arrangement and management of contingencies of reinforcement—has been fantastically successful with a number of problems of disordered behavior.

Take autistic children, for example. Our success in that area is a real threat, you see, to the people who think that the problem is something about the inner life, or the lack of identity, or alienation, or whatever all those things are that these kids are supposed to be suffering from.

What they are suffering from in fact is very bad schedules of reinforcement. That is something you can change for them, but this is not done. And you really can't expect mentalistic psychologists to do things like that: their approach just simply destines them to inadequacy and failure.

I keep on saying
I've got about five more good years
left, but I have been saying that
for about three years already.

Oh, but they are so sincere. They want to understand the boys, to sit and talk and gain their confidence, and all of this stuff. Meanwhile, there is a very simple way in which you can begin to get them to behave in a very respectable way and to learn the kinds of skills that will give them a chance to be effective citizens.

Take the problem in correctional institutions, for example. One of

our people recently took over one of the buildings in a training school for boys and organized it on the basis of point-reinforcement system. The boys were paid for their work, and they had to buy everything except basics. For free they could get the basic diet and a place to sleep in the dormitory, but anything else they had to buy. And the most points were given for learning something interesting with the help of teaching machines, or without. They got points for learning.

Don't you see, that's the *point*. It made them discover for the first time that they could learn something, and that learning something was valuable. This is a very important thing. Most of them had been convinced by our school systems that they were stupid. They discovered that they really weren't. It's remarkable, surprising, it really works! How very different it is from hand-holding and getting to know the boys.

Hall: You can't slough off people like Carl Rogers and Rollo May and Bruno Bettelheim. They're constructive.

Skinner: Oh, certainly, in certain cases. You know Rogers' technique is to agree with everything everybody says—reinforce support. Have you ever heard the story of Carl Rogers and the duck?

Hall: No, please tell me. Carl is the hero, or victim, of more apocryphal stories than is any other leader in psychology. How fortunate that he has a good disposition.

Skinner: Someone took Carl out duck hunting one morning. It was a bad day, cloudy or something, and hunting was very bad. Toward the very end they were about ready to go home. One duck came in. Carl shot at the duck. At the same time somebody else shot it from down along the shore. The duck fell into the shallow water. Carl walked toward the duck, and the other guy emerged and walked out to get it, too. They met at the duck, Carl looked up at the man and said, "You feel this is your duck." Of course the point of the story is that Carl got the duck. His technique does work, you see.

Hall: I'm going to do an interview with Carl. He's entitled, at this point.

Skinner: You see, Rogers' whole approach is based on the notion that the individual somehow or other has his own salvation within him. And this may not be true. Really it's a matter of the history of reinforcement. Someone brought up in a good old Protestant background probably does have enough behavior to save himself in certain circumstances. But cultures change. Rogers' approach is based on a culture which by and large is coming not to exist any more. This means that he really hasn't gotten at the basic processes.

What would he do, for example, if someone came up with the solution that he had better murder his boss? Rogers isn't going to say, "Oh, you should murder your boss!" and let it go at that. No, he couldn't do it. The only way you can be successful with these things is to get at the basic processes and work with them. It's simply too superficial and dangerous to rely on the previous history of reinforcement—the culture—when that is something that is going to change at least every few generations.

Hall: What do you see surfacing in other areas of psychology that may be of interest in the future?

Skinner: Well, I don't see much of anything interesting going on. The study of sensation is of some interest, but I think primarily as the physiology of how the eye works and how the ear works, the field of perception is not yet up to the level it will reach, though it is an interesting business. But there is not much going on there now.

Some people are working on what conditions lead one to learn to see things in different ways, and that could be fun, if done properly. I have no interest in so-called cognitive psychology. I just don't think there is much there.

Psychological testing, I mark all of that off. Verbal learning, I mark all that off. I just wouldn't look at

---

If I could do it all over again, I'd never teach those pigeons to play Ping-Pong.

---

anything that had to do with the memory drum unless someone suddenly convinced me that someone had something new there. I have never been able to read papers dealing with mazes: once you know something about behavior, it is transparently clear that you simply don't know what's going on in a maze or a jump stand at all.

Hall: Obviously you aren't just the creator of operant conditioning. You are a true believer. Of course you are still hard at work. What does the immediate future hold for you?

Skinner: Well, I may not have too much future personally. I keep on saying I've got about five more good years left, but I have been saying that for about three years already, so I don't know how many good years I have. But I keep in good health, take care of myself, I have always had a lot of things I wanted to do, and I have had quite deliberately to rule out some things which I would have enjoyed.

Three or four years ago I gave up my laboratory. I was still getting grants, as I could now. Grants were hard to get in the old days, but I could get them now. I wanted to turn it over to younger people, and so I said to myself that I have had 35 years of laboratory science, so I will quit. I also have withdrawn pretty much from teaching, but I don't mean to stop working. I spend as much time as I can on creative things. I have always wanted to do a little something worthwhile every day, and the rest of the time is thinking and reading. I have several important books which I want to get out. I think we have put our finger on something of extraordinary importance here—and when we get the truth out, everything will follow these operant rules which we have seen and are still discovering. With them one cannot make a very serious mistake. And since this is where the future of psychology lies, it's well worth the telling.

Hall: If you had your life to live over again, if you were just beginning your career, what would you do differently?

Skinner: Just one thing. I performed one experiment that has never ceased to reverberate. I've been laughed at by enemies and kidded by friends. If I could do it all over again, I'd never teach those pigeons to play Ping-Pong. ◆

Discussion Questions

1. Define operant conditioning.

2. What is an "air crib," and what are various advantages and disadvantages to using this type of crib?

3. What is a contingency of reinforcement?

4. What are Skinner's views on Sigmund Freud?

5. What are Skinner's views on Rogerian therapy?

6. What is positive reinforcement, and what role does Skinner think positive reinforcement should play in society?

7. According to Skinner, which is more effective, reinforcement or punishment? What is his reasoning?

8. What is programmed instruction, and what aspects of Skinner's proposals have become part of modern computer-aided instruction?

9. What are Skinner's views on language, linguistics, and psycholinguistics?

The *Father* of *Rogerian Therapy:*

A CONVERSATION WITH

Carl Rogers

◆ *Mary Harrington Hall*

Mary Harrington Hall: Shall we talk about groups—encounter groups, T-groups, sensitivity-training groups, group therapy? The group phenomenon demands exploration and explanation. And I've wondered...are people drawn toward this intense group experience because they feel loneliness and alienation in our strange society?

Carl Rogers: Of course that's a major reason. Out of the increasing loneliness of modern culture, we have in some social sense been forced to develop a way of getting closer to one another. I think encounter groups probably bring people closer together than has ever been true in history except with groups of people together during crisis. You put men together during war, for instance, and they really know each other to the depths, and so it is in groups. So often someone will say at the end of a group experience: "I just can't believe that I have known you people here better than I know members of my own family, and you know me better than my family knows me."

We have found a way for closeness to develop with amazing rapidity. I think that group work is a far more important social phenomenon than most people realize. Group encounters, by whatever name you call them, are becoming a major force.

Hall: A lot of people in and out of psychology question the useful purpose of such closeness with groups of people who have an experience together for a week or for a weekend, get to know each other's problems and dreams, and then may never see each other again, Carl. Perhaps you're one of the best people in the country to answer this argument. You developed the form of therapy in which the therapist permits himself to become involved with his patient, in a frankly caring relationship with the therapist both permissive and involved. And Rogerian therapy certainly is based on interaction.

Rogers: You're actually putting two questions in a polite way,

---

Group encounters, by whatever name you call them, are becoming a major force. This is a very potent phenomenon. One can't just take it or leave it alone.

Mary. What you're questioning is the *usefulness* and *legitimacy* of the group experience. There is a good deal of argument and furor about the intensive group experience. There have been vituperative articles about how terrible group encounters are, how they take on the Communist brainwashing technique, and such nonsense. You get even more people who think the group experience is simply great. This is a very potent phenomenon.

One can't just take it or leave it alone. You either become involved, in which case group encounter does bring about changes in you, or you can resist it completely. The group experience is not something people remain neutral about.

Hall: Let's differentiate between group therapy and encounter groups.

Rogers: They are really two rather different dimensions. Group therapy is for the person who is already hurting, who has problems, and needs help. Encounter groups are for those who are functioning normally but want to improve their capacity for living within their own sets on relationships. And the leader role is, of course, quite different. One leader must be therapeutic, the other more of a facilitator. Traditional group therapy, with its weekly meeting over a long period, well may be replaced one day by an intensive week or month, or even weekend experience. The intense encounter seems to work wonders in therapy, too.

Hall: You know that I always have been somewhat of a skeptic, or possibly afraid, about the group experience, and thus a questioner of the purpose for people getting together to talk a lot—and cry a lot. But I really want to know: what do people bring home to their daily lives from group encounters?

Rogers: There are so many hundreds and thousands of examples to give. The most common report is that people behave differently with their families and with their colleagues. A school administrator (in a workshop we ran for a California school system not long ago) is typical. She said she *felt* different but was unprepared for how quick her family's response would be. She wrote that her daughters sensed a change in her immediately. Before she had been home a day, she and her

Carl Rogers

daughters had talked over a whole list of things—God, death and hell, menstruation, nightmares, a whole range of things.

Both her 14-year-old and her ten-year-old daughter wanted to be bathed by her, the first time in years they had been so intimate. Finally, the young one said; "What did they teach you at that meeting—how to be nice to kids?" The woman wrote that she replied: "No, I learned how to be myself and found out that was pretty nice." Now, this woman is a teacher. I think she is going to be different with her students, too.

Hall: What about the argument that encounter groups are fine for those who are emotionally stable but may be very upsetting indeed for those with problems—and our number is legion?

Rogers: The possibility of damage concerns me, too, but I think the risk is much, much less than is ordinarily presumed. I did a questionnaire study, a six months' follow-up, of more than 500 people involved in groups which I either led or in which I was responsible. Out of 481 people who responded, only two felt the experience had been more hurtful than helpful. You know, a deep relationship is a very rare experience for anyone, and it always means change.

Hall: How much change and what kind?

Rogers: I think encounter groups help make people more open to experiences that are going on within them, more expressive of their feelings, more spontaneous in their reactions, more flexible, more vulnerable, and probably more genuinely intimate in their interpersonal relationships. Now, I value this type of person, don't you?

Hall: That sounds like the ideal man.

Rogers: Well, there are whole cultures built on exactly the opposite ideal. And many people in our own culture feel also that a person should be contained, disciplined, preferably unaware of his feelings, and should live in terms of a firm set of disciplines that are handed down by someone—God, or someone up there—whomever he looks to as an authority. The person who emerges from encounter groups is likely to be more self-directed and not so easily persuaded by others. I think the absence of open debate about what is the desirable sort of personal development has stirred up misunderstanding and public reaction against the intense-encounter technique.

I think encounter groups help make people more open to experiences that are going on within them, more expressive of their feelings, more spontaneous in their reactions, more flexible, more vulnerable, and probably more genuinely intimate in their interpersonal relationships.

Hall: But, Carl, you can measure attitude change and you can do empirical studies of behavior change, yet you can't measure the essential experience in groups that brings those changes, can you? How can you explain the phenomenon so people will understand?

Rogers: It troubles me, and troubles me deeply, whether we really do know how to have a human science, Mary. Groups are potent, and something very significant is going on. I have gotten increasingly restive about the point you raise, that we can't measure the essential experience that brings about those changes. I feel very perplexed. A lot of my life has been devoted to measuring; I keep being sure it can be done with the group experience, and then failing.

Last year Michael Polanyi, the British philosopher of science, said something I really didn't like at the time, but he may be right. He said we should lay aside the word *science* for the next decade or two and give people the freedom to find out that we need more *knowledge*. He said the word *science* is so wrapped up with the machinery of science that it was stifling rather than helping us at this point, at least in the behavioral sciences. I know that many of us in psychology have gotten so wound up with methodology that we forget to be curious, really. With today's knowledge, we don't know how to study what happened to businessman for whom the encounter experience had an on-going effect for sixteen years. I don't know how to study that. Or why was an intense-encounter experience something a high-school girl told me she had found to be the most important and beautiful experience in her relatively short life?

Hall: You seem to be saying that psychology is groping now toward being a more human science. If that is so, what will happen when you break through?

Rogers: I don't know. The closer one gets to trying to assess the intangible things which probably are most important in personality change, the less are customary instruments being used, and the more suspect are the only instruments that seem to me to make any sense. I think that in those intangibles the only person who can help us out is the person to whom something has happened. We need to get more pictures of what it seems like to the person *inside*, who has experienced the change.

If we adapted Polanyi's suggestion and just said: "Well, science or no science I'm trying to find out something about this," we might have taken a valuable and freeing step. One of the unfortunate things about psychology is that it has tried to make one great leap and become a science like physics. I think we will have to recognize the fact that people observed things, and thought about things, and fiddled around with things a long time before they came up with any of the precise observations which made a science out of physics.

We may have to go back and do much more naturalistic observation, make more of an attempt to understand people, behavior, and the dynamics of things.

Then, perhaps someday, out of that might grow a real psychological science, not an imitation of physics, a human science that should have as its appropriate subject, man. I think the reason so much psychological experimentation is done on rats and cats, and such, is that we realize perfectly that we don't have the tools for understanding human beings.

Hall: But, after all, we do *learn* about humans by animal study.

> ### It troubles me, and troubles me deeply, whether we really do know how to have a human science...

> ### One of the unfortunate things about psychology is that it has tried to make one great leap and become a science like physics. We may have to go back and do much more naturalistic observation. Out of that might grow a real psychological science, not an imitation of physics.

Do you think psychologists have been defensive because psychology is sometimes seen as a stepchild of science?

Rogers: I guess psychologists are about the most defensive professional people around today. We have this terrific fear of looking unscientific. A terrific fear of spinning out wild theories to see how they sound, and a fear of trying them out. We think we must do everything from a *known* base with *known* instruments. Actually, this is *not* the way in which creative scientists, even in the hard sciences, operate. For instance, I think one of the real tragedies of graduate education in psychology is that graduate students in many, many institutions become less and less willing to spout original ideas for fear they will be shot down by their colleagues, and by their professors. This is *not* the way to do things.

Hall: The great intuitive chemists and physicists certainly aren't afraid. They spend a lifetime on hunches, don't they? I'm thinking particularly of one of our mutual close friends, Harold Urey.

Rogers: That's it! They aren't afraid. What psychology needs are ideas that someone dreams up on the basis of hunches and intuition, from experience, or to try to make sense out of some complex set of phe-

> ### I guess psychologists are about the most defensive professional people around today. We have this terrific fear of looking unscientific.

nomena. It may take a lifetime to find out if it was a worthless dream or a really significant pattern of thought. We need that kind of dreaming in psychology, and graduate departments of psychology have no time for dreams. I think they are definitely fearful.

Hall: And maybe it takes someone like you—a former president of the American Psychological Association, a man with every honor his profession and the academic world can bestow—to be so fearlessly critical of his own profession. Or maybe you're impatient to have psychology take that major leap forward to answer your own questions about *why* group encounters do seem to affect people so deeply?

Rogers: Or maybe I'm just used to being involved in controversy? Perhaps all three, Mary. But still, psychology is a defensive profession. I'll give you an example. At a conference last year on "Man and the Science of Man," all the discussions were taped. These were all top scholars. Only three participants refused permission to trust editors to put their taped remarks in shape for future listeners. Two of those three were psychologists. Another example was the dialogue I had in Duluth with B. F. Skinner, the father of operant conditioning, the creator of the modern study of behaviorism. He was unwilling to have the tape of our dialogue transcribed. I thought it was understood in advance that it *would* be transcribed. I call that needlessly fearful.

Hall: By the way, Fred told an interesting anecdote about you in his interview with us in September, Carl.

Rogers: Yes, the ducks. Funny story, but he knows that it's not true. He said I was duck hunting and used the art of gentle agreement to get for myself the duck another man shot. Actually, my brother and I were hunting, we shot at the same time, and tossed a coin to see who got the duck. And I've told Fred I lost the toss. Fred and I actually are friends, you know. He's a marvelous mind. Another friend, Rollo May, whom you rightly labeled in your wonderful interview as "Mr. Humanist," told the story that I once questioned the existence of tragedy by saying that Romeo and Juliet might have been all right with just a little counseling. I probably did say that. I'm more optimistic than Rollo. He is an existentialist—so am I, but my philosophy has more room for hope.

Hall: Your background and Rollo May's are quite similar, though, aren't they?

Rogers: We're both from the rural Midwest. I was a farm boy, he from a small town. This is a good, strong background, you know. He graduated from the Union Theological Seminary. After I graduated in history from the University of Wisconsin, I studied there, and then I went across the street to get my Ph.D. in psychology from Columbia. In 1926, the Seminary was a freewheeling, stimulating place to be. Arthur McGifford, a real scholar, was president. A group of us students decided we didn't have enough chance to talk about issues that really concerned us, so we asked for a seminar which we would run ourselves and for which we would receive credit. Any institution today would drop dead if you made such a suggestion. The Seminary agreed and in many ways it well may have been the very first encounter group, al-

> *The reason so much psychological experimentation is done on rats and cats...is that we realize perfectly well that we don't have the tools for understanding human beings.*

though it was a little more intellectual than most encounter groups as we know them today. Many of us left the Seminary and went into allied fields. I still was very much interested in working with people but I didn't want to tie myself to some particular creed.

I worked for the New York Institute for Child Guidance, and for the Rochester Society for the Prevention of Cruelty to Children before getting into the University life, you know. I earned the glorious sum of $2,900 a year on my first job, with a wife and child to support.

Then, of course, I went to Ohio, to the University of Chicago and to Wisconsin, before I got fed up finally with the restrictions of the academic life, particularly with the frustrations for graduate students, and became a fellow of the Western Behavioral Sciences Institute in Southern California.

Hall: Your book, *Counseling and Psychotherapy*, was published in 1942, Carl, but didn't your major impact come about after *Client-Centered Therapy* was published in 1951?

Rogers: I think so, really. Acceptance came very slowly.

Hall: When did you become interested in groups?

Rogers: My first gropings toward using the intensive-group experience in a constructive way came in 1946, when I was in charge of the University of Chicago's Counseling Center. We had a Veterans Administration contract for training all personal counsellors for returning servicemen and we had to make them into effective counsellors within six-week training programs. They all had Master's degrees, but none of them had done much counseling. We couldn't give them individual counseling, which we

thought would be the best way for them to learn, so we put them together in small groups. It worked very well.

Hall: There was no such thing as encounter groups then, but was there any group therapy?

Rogers: There was some group therapy just beginning. I remember that in about 1945 I told a group of my students that I would be glad to try to conduct a group-therapy program for them, but it would be my first experience. Now, the National Training laboratories in Bethel, Maine, started at about this time, but I was unaware of that.

My groups of personal counsellors and students at Chicago became more and more personal in their discussions and revealed more and more of what was going on within them. It was similar to what goes on in an encounter group today. However, I didn't carry on in this field, partly because I didn't think that group work was a good field for research. I thought that there were enough complexities with the one-to-one-relationship so that we couldn't possibly study a group situation.

Hall: You certainly have changed your mind since that time.

Rogers: Oh, yes, I have certainly revised my opinion. The next time I was closely involved in a group experience was in the autumn of 1950 when I conducted a post-graduate seminar type of therapy held just before the A.P.A. meetings. I remember that for one hour each day I counseled a client in front of a group of twelve. It started off on a somewhat academic basis, but as we got into it, sharing more and more deeply of our personal experiences, our failures, and our difficulties, it became a moving personal experience. All of us left there feeling we had gained deeply. What amazed me was the long, lasting effect from the experience. It was then that I began to realize the potency of group experience.

Hall: Didn't the National Training Laboratories, in Bethel, Maine, begin the sensitivity-training programs for executives, the famous T-Groups, at about the same time you did your first group work at Chicago?

Rogers: At just the time I began putting on summer workshops organized by the Counseling Service Center, I heard that something was going on in the East. Then, one of our members took part in one of the N.T.L. groups, and came back rather unimpressed. We were following different patterns; our groups focused more on the interpersonal relationship and on building a climate where people could express or withhold as much as they wished.

Over the years there has been cross-fertilization, and it is no longer accurate to say we are working two different ways. I conduct N.T.L. workshops every year—Presidents' Lab program for top executives.

Hall: Where does the term T-Group come from, Carl?

Rogers: T-Groups originally were thought of as *Training* groups. I don't think we are in the business of *training*. The term is misleading. I think there still is a different flavor between N.T.L. workshops—and all Eastern approaches—and what is going on in the West.

N.T.L. did the real pioneering in the encounter-group movement, and really have been the prime moving force in the whole thing. They have put on thousands of groups, and they are responsible for getting the business communi-

---

The East Coast shows signs of being an older culture. Their procedures are more rigid, with too much stress on paper credentials.

---

ty involved to the point where the top men in the country attend N.T.L. Presidents' Labs. All groups start from there. What a great thing they did, and yet the West Coast is far more active than is the East, the home of groups.

Hall: Someone once said—me, I think—that the West is on a great group binge. Why is it that groups are more popular on the West Coast? Do you agree with May, who says it's because the West is anti-intellectual?

Rogers: Actually, I think the East Coast shows signs of being an older culture. Their procedures are more rigid, with too much stress on paper credentials. On the West Coast, partly because it is a newer part of the country, partly because the California psychological climate, in particular, is freer, there is more regard for essentials of the work. We've used nonprofessional leaders in groups. N.T.L. would frown on anyone without the proper paper credentials.

Hall: Do you find the West more experimental in its approach to psychology?

Rogers: I certainly do, and I approve. It will be sad if the West settles into a fixed mold. I believe every organization and every profession ought to be upset—put through the mixer—every decade or so, and start again fresh and flexible.

Hall: What makes California especially so different? Is it the fluid population?

Rogers: I cannot account for it. What gives the particularly loose, freewheeling character to the California psychological climate, I don't know. I just know that you can *feel* it.

Ann Roe, a research psychologist, did an extensive study some years ago on 100 creative physical and social scientists who were most highly regarded. Fifteen years later she said that out of the 100, some 70 now live in California—and they aren't retired for the most part—they're still swingers. The great universities are only part of the answer, I think, but an important part.

Hall: Tell me about your Honker group at Cal Tech, Carl. I know that elimination of the grading system for Cal Tech freshmen and sophomores came out of those sessions.

Rogers: I was surprised to be asked by Cal Tech to serve as a consultant on human and education problems, and I decided that if I worked with students, it might cause a student rebellion—so I chose faculty.

We weren't a committee or a group with any legal authority. I didn't want that. We put together top faculty and administration people and I think I was able to

---

I believe every organization and every profession ought to be upset—put through the mixer—every decade or so, and start again fresh and flexible.

---

develop a freer discussion climate than they ever had. We began to take up issues of deep concern, and since they didn't have to arrive at any motions and pass them, they discussed frankly.

Hall: Did the name Honker come from the gabbling of the group?

Rogers: We met first at the Honker Restaurant. The original group met for two years, and finally we had faculty-student groups, and new faculty groups.

We had to break up the original Honkers because the faculty began to fear them as an elite power group. And the new groups were just as effective.

The grading system and a number of good new things just naturally evolved. Most faculty members, incidentally, have never been willing to get off the intellectual level and into the intensive experimental encounter. But there is quite an encounter program now among students.

Hall: You have a grant to do research in the effect of encounter experiences in an educational system, haven't you?

Rogers: We have a two-year Babcock Foundation Grant of $80,000 a year, with an additional $30,000 personal gift from Charles Kettering to see whether the basic encounter group can be an instrument for self-directed change in school systems. Many school systems were interested but I selected the Immaculate Heart College in Los Angeles. It's a marvelous school, and it also certifies about 70 teachers a year, and staffs and supervises eight high schools and 50 elementary schools.

Mary: Carl, I was terribly excited when you told me a year ago that you hoped to do a vertical thing in a school system, starting with administrators in groups, then teachers, parents, and students—and then putting them together. This might end the crashing boredom of most school systems.

Rogers: Well, we've begun now. We've held six weekend workshops, for college faculty, for high-school faculty and student leaders, and for elementary-school principals and teachers. I am hopeful. We'll know in three years.

Hall: What has happened? Are people getting involved?

Rogers: The student councils have asked if our program leaders can meet on a weekly basis to help them iron out interpersonal problems. Lay faculty members have asked for a weekend encounter group for themselves and their spouses. Various departments are asking for encounter groups Everyone is excited. (Sister Mary Corita, the artist and the most joyous soul anywhere, is in the Immaculate Heart Art Department, you know. So you can imagine what a grand place this college is.)

And just as in all school systems, faculty members resisted

> **At Cal Tech, in the Honker Group, we began to take up issues of deep concern, and since they didn't have to arrive at any motions, and pass them, they discussed frankly.**

group encounters with students, but that is working out.

We meet for solid weekends. Groups may meet Friday evening and all day Saturday, then again until Sunday noon. Or perhaps for a very long Saturday till midnight, and then again for a long Sunday.

Hall: All right, let's say I'm a school principal in an encounter group. What is this going to do for the school system?

Rogers: It will affect the system because you are going to be more democratic and more willing to take feedback from your staff, Mary. The teacher I told you about who suddenly was closer to her own daughters had attended one of our Immaculate Heart workshops.

Some people say, "Well, this approach can't change a system." I say it will make systems more open to innovations.

Hall: What do you think frightens people about intense encounter groups?

Rogers: I think many of us live in kind of a precarious balance. We have learned to get along with ourselves and our world in some way, and the possibility that this balance might be upset is always a frightening one. Almost invariably in groups, every person finds the balance is disturbed, or possibly upset, but finds that in a climate of trust he is enormously supported in being *more* himself.

Hal: As you were talking, I thought of the last lines of *Cyrano de Bergerac*. Dying, he reaches for his gaudy hat and says: "My plume, my sacred plume. My pride, my pose, my lifelong masquerade."

Rogers: That moves me. In an encounter group, people learn they really do not need to keep that masquerade. In our last workshop, there was a man who came across as being very competent, very efficient, very self-sufficient. You just felt, here's a guy who really has it made. He has an important job and everything is rosy. It turned out that he is *so* hungry for appreciation and love; he feels he lets other people know that he appreciates them but who in the hell listens to him, or cares about him—nobody. I am thinking of one Navy commander, who appeared to be a complete martinet. We weren't very many days into the workshop before he was telling us some of the personal tragedies that he had in his life, particularly of his son—he felt terrible about what he had helped to do to his son. Then he got to telling about how he was known as a disciplinarian, but that when he was the commander of a ship during the war he got himself in trouble with his officers because of one enlisted man who was always in trouble. This officer felt he was really so much like the bad guy that he couldn't punish him. Others would come up with minor offenses and they got so much time in the brig, and this guy would do horrible things and the officer couldn't bear to punish him because the sailor did things he himself never dared to do. Among the many things that happened during his group experience, he decided to get back and try to rebuild his marriage—I don't know how much success he had in that. When he got back he was going to tell his top staff about the real softy he was inside, and try to loosen up his organization. This is the sort of thing where you see that people *can* change and *do* change and *do* become more human.

Hall: This interview with you leads off a special section on the group phenomenon, Carl. The article following this interview is by a very bright young Harvard psychologist, Tom Cottle, who has experimented with self-analytic groups of Negro and white high-school students just *before* their school integration. He thinks such encounters can greatly ease racial tensions.

Rogers: I'm sure he's right. Group encounters can help end the tragedy of two races which meet fearfully and don't know what to do.

What we need is an enormous effort of the scope of the Manhattan Project. We should call in everyone who has any theoretical contribution to make, everyone who has tried out practical things such as you are describing and such as I have done. We should round up interdisciplinary knowledge that would focus on how tensions can be reduced. Such a project could contribute enormously in the resolving of racial tensions. This approach also could contribute to the resolution of labor and management tensions. I believe it could contribute to the

---

Many of us live in a precarious balance... almost invariably in groups every person finds the balance is disturbed.

---

terrifying problems of international tensions, too.

I would not be in the least afraid to be a facilitator for a massive group program in Watts. I know the tensions and bitterness would be terrific, but the people would be speaking for themselves. And I'm sure we could come to a more harmonious understanding than is possible any other way.

Group encounters can help end the tragedy of two races which meet fearfully and don't know what to do. What we need is an enormous effort of the scope of the Manhattan Project. We should call in everyone who has any theoretical contribution to make, everyone who has tried out practical things. We should round up interdisciplinary knowledge that would focus on how tensions can be reduced.

Hall: Fred Stoller, who with George Boch invented the marathon group you have said *is* effective, has an article in this group section. So does Mike Murphy, president of Esalen Institute. I know you've led workshops there. What do you think of Esalen, Carl? Murphy says you doesn't think you're sold on it.

Rogers: I admire the nerve Mike has. His basic idea is very good.

Living in California has made me realize that there is no sharp dividing line between the cutting edge in psychology and the too far-out hogwash.

Mike is covering the whole spectrum in his Esalen seminars and workshops. We'll look back in ten years and find that some of the things he has sponsored helped start an important trend.

I'm pleased that he has set up a San Francisco headquarters, because I think that his Big Sur place is a little too involved with the sort of hippie culture that has tended to limit the kind of people who participate in seminars there.

Hall: How do you assess your own contributions to psychology?

Rogers: If I have made a contribution it is around the central theme that the potential of the individual—and I would even add, the potential of the group—can be released providing a proper psychological climate is created. And that is an optimistic point of view!

If I, the therapist, can come through to my client as a person who cares about him and understands what he is struggling to express, he gradually will begin to choose healthier directions for himself.

Hall: Your work certainly has emphasized the importance of interpersonal relationships.

Rogers: That is another aspect of whatever contribution I have made. Instead of focusing on the diagnostic or causative elements of behavior. I always have been more concerned with the dynamics of interaction. Not about how a person became what he is, but about how does he change from what he is.

I always have felt psychologically nourished by deep communication with people with whom I was working. I think sometimes people in clinical work apologize if they feel they are getting something out of it. I believe that if a therapist doesn't find particularly deep relationships with people he works with, he shouldn't be either a therapist or working with groups.

This involvement was very true for me when I was doing individual therapy. When I had to give that up because my life was just too hectic, I wondered what would take its place. And soon I found that working intensively with groups—and with individuals in those groups—provided me with the same kind of psychological nourishment.

Hall: For people who criticize the permissiveness of your approach, the way your son and daughter turned out is an answer which must make you and Helen very proud.

Rogers: Well, they have nice families of their own now. Our son, David, is chairman of the Department of Medicine at Vanderbilt University. He was chosen one of the ten outstanding young men in the country for *Life* magazine's issue on the "take-over" generation. He has two daughters and a son.

Our daughter is Mrs. Lawrence Fuchs. Her husband is Professor of American Civilization at Brandeis University and they have three daughters. He organized the Peace Corps in the Philippines. Natalie took her M.A. in psychology with Abe Maslow (present APA presi-

---

My therapeutic point of view threatens many therapists. It is far more satisfying to be the man pulling the strings than to be the man (like me) who provides a climate in which another person can do something.

---

dent). She's very interested in counseling work. She's *good*, too.

Hall: You said you were used to being somewhat controversial, Carl. Where have your battles been?

Rogers: Of course I was very much involved in the battles during the 1930's and '40's in which there were many attempts to stop psychologists from practicing psychotherapy. The last go-around on that was during the 1950's. It's a dead issue now.

Another controversy that somehow hit the clinicians' value sys-

tem—and threatened many therapists—was my confidence in the potentiality of the individual.

It was my publications, based on my conviction and research, which upset many psychologists and psychiatrists. I said the individual can discover his own patterns of capabilities and his maladjustments, and that he can find insight *on his own* and take action to help solve his own problems.

The point of view threatens people who like to be experts. It is far more satisfying to be the man pulling the strings than to be the man who provides a climate in which another person can *do* something. So, there were attacks—there were famous jokes that about how all I did was agree with people.

Hall: That brings up a question. There is a classic Rogers joke...a man in therapy with you is depressed. He says so. You say: "You're *depressed*, aren't you?" He says he feels like jumping out the window in your office, and you say—

Rogers: I *know* the story. My answer, for once and for all time, is that I would not have let him jump out the window. ◆

Discussion Questions

1. Describe the relationship between the client and the therapist in Rogerian Therapy.

2. How does Rogerian therapy differ from other types of therapies?

3. How would Rogers respond if questioned about the usefulness and legitimacy of group therapy?

4. According to Rogers, what is the difference between group therapy and encounter groups?

5. List three ways that people are changed by encounter groups.

6. What are Rogers' thoughts on psychology as science? What does he mean by human science?

7. According to Rogers, how can encounter groups lead to improvements in school systems?

8. What aspect of encounter groups might scare some people?

9. How does Rogers feel racial tensions can be solved?

10. What are Rogers' views on B. F. Skinner and Rollo May?

11. What is the real punch line to the joke at the end of the article? Can you figure it out?

Psychology CANNOT BE A *Coherent* SCIENCE

◆ *Sigmund Koch*

Whether as a "science" or *any* kind of coherent discipline devoted to the empirical study of man, psychology has been misconceived. This is no light matter for me to confess after a 30-year career given to exploration of the prospects and conditions for psychology becoming a significant enterprise.

But the massive 100-year effort to erect a discipline given to the positive study of man can hardly be counted a triumph. Here and there the effort has turned up a germane fact, or thrown off a spark of insight, but these victories have had an accidental relation to the programs believed to inspire them, and their sum total over time is heavily over-balanced by the pseudo-knowledge that has proliferated.

The idolatry of science in our age has insured that this phony knowledge be taken seriously by people everywhere—even by sensitive, creative or sophisticated people. Such "knowledge," when assimilated, is no neutral addition to a person's furniture of confusions. It has an awesome capacity to bias the deepest attitudes of man toward Man, to polarize sensibility.

Indeed, the pooled pseudo-knowledge that is much of psychology can be seen as a congeries of alternate—and exceedingly simple—images, around each of which one finds a dense, scholastic cluster of supportive research, theorizing and methodological rhetoric.

If one is drawn by unassailable scientific argument to the conclusion that man is cockroach, rat or dog, that makes a difference. It also makes a difference when one achieves ultimate certitude that man is a telephone exchange, a servo-mechanism, a binary digital computer, a reward-seeking vector, a hyphen within an S-R

> **My findings over the years suggest that while symptoms may vary, one syndrome is widely evident in modern scholarship. I call it ameaningful thinking.**

process, a stimulation-maximizer, a food, sex, or libido energy-converter, a utilities-maximizing game player, a status-seeker, a mutual ego-titillator, a mutual emotional (or actual) masturbator. And on and on.

If the violence of my apostasy alarms the reader into thinking that I am about to transfer to the humanities, let me relieve him forthwith. In my jaundiced view, the role of the humanities in the teaching of the humanities has not in our century been especially more hygienic than the role of psychology. This has been due partly to direct contagion from the sciences: too many humanists have contracted anywhere from a creeping to a rabid scientism from their

abhorred colleagues in the sciences. In a more fundamental way, pervasive circumstances in culture and history have inflicted the same pathology upon all fields of inquiry.

My findings over the years suggest that while symptoms may vary, one syndrome is widely evident in modern scholarship. I call it *ameaningful thinking* The prefix has the same force as the *a* in words like *amoral*.

Ameaningful thought or inquiry regards knowledge as the result of "processing" rather than discovery. It presumes that knowledge is an almost automatic result of a gimmickry, an assembly line, a methodology. It assumes that inquiring action is so rigidly and fully regulated by *rule* that in its conception of inquiry it often allows the rules totally to displace their human users. Presuming as it does that knowledge is generated by processing, its conception of knowledge is fictionalistic, conventionalistic. So strongly does it see knowledge under such aspects that at times it seems to suppose the object of inquiry to be an ungainly and annoying irrelevance. Detail, structure, quiddity are obliterated. Objects of knowledge become caricatures, if not faceless, and thus they lose reality. The world, or any given part of it, is not felt fully or passionately and is perceived as devoid of objective value. In extreme forms, ameaningful thought becomes obsessive and magical.

On the other hand, *meaningful thinking* involves a *direct perception* of unveiled, vivid relations that seem to spring from the quiddities, particularities of the objects of thought, the problem situations that form the occasions for thought. There is an organic determination of the form and substance of thought by the properties of the object, the terms of the problem. And these are real in the fullest, most vivid, electric, undeniable way. The mind caresses, flows joyously into, over, around, the relational matrix defined by the problem, the object. There is a merging of person and object or problem. It is a fair descriptive generalization to say that meaningful thinking is ontologistic in some primitive, accepting, artless, unselfconscious sense.

For any population, the relative incidence of meaningful or ameaningful thinking will be largely determined by the values that the group places upon either. Such values will, of course, be embedded in the ideologies or rationales of knowledge-seeking behavior dominant in the group and will pervade all institutions and agencies that influence intellectual or scholarly style, habit and sensibility.

Throughout the recent history of the sciences, humanities, and (increasingly) the arts, there is lush and growing evidence of the play of ameaningful thinking. But nowhere is this syndrome so richly and purely exhibited as in those so-called sciences that were created by fiat towards the end of the 19th Century: psychology and the social sciences.

Back in 1935, shortly after having been appalled and insulted by my first few undergraduate courses in psychology, I came upon a book by Grace Adams, *Psychology: Science or Superstition?* The idea that psychology was a congeries of weird insularities was already a cliché, but Grace Adams developed this cliché in so sprightly and compelling a fashion that the field came through to me as, in some perverse way, inviting. So massive an absurdity cried out for redress. Moreover, an absurdity so massive could hardly hold its own against a little clear thinking. Or, so I naively thought.

I did not know then that Clark Hull, the most influential of the neobehaviorists, felt much the same. In one of his early (1935) theoretical papers, "The Conflicting Psychologies of Learning—A Way Out," Hull refers to the Adams book in these words:

"...she points out what we all know only too well—that among psychologists there is not only a bewilderingly large diversity of opinion, but that we are divided into sects, too many of which show emotional and other signs of religious fervor. This emotionalism and this inability to progress materially toward agreement obviously do not square with the ideals of objectivity and certainty which we associate with scientific investigation; they are, on the other hand, more than a little characteristic of metaphysical and theological controversy. Such a situation leads to the suspicion that we have not yet cast off the unfortunate influences of our early associations with metaphysicians. Somehow we have permitted ourselves to fall into essentially unscientific practices."

Hull saw the persisting disagreements among psychologists as centered more on theory than on the results of experiment. His thesis was that there ought not to be such a paradoxical disparity between scientific experiment and scientific theory—that the disparity would not exist if the theory were truly scientific. In this paper, as in others, Hull discussed the "essentials of sound scientific theory" which, of course, recapitulated the schema of a hypothetico-deductive system. He invited contending theorists to axiomize their nebulous thoughts and—in the event that derivations diverging from Hull's ensued—that they arbitrate their differences in the laboratory.

It is now 35 years later, and the theory that Hull so diligently contrived as his answer to the massive absurdity of the "psychologies" is becoming a dim memory even to the few who still work within its tradition. And every judgment, every hope, registered in the remarks of Hull just quoted has been cruelly—indeed, extravagantly—thwarted by history. We are still divided into sects, "many of which show emotional and other signs of religious fervor," but perhaps thrice as many.

Prior to the late 19th Century, there are no precedents in the history of ideas for creating great new fields of knowledge by edict. Sciences won their way to independence by achieving enough knowledge to become sciences. By the late 19th Century, these justly discriminated fields of science had given such food to man's cognitive and material hungers as to make his appetite insatiable. At the same time, inquiry into the nature and trend of science itself began to focus into an apparently wholesome Victorian vision: that of a totally orderly universe, totally open to the methods of science, and a totally orderly science, totally open to the strategems—and wants—of man. It was against this background that psychology was *stipulated* into life.

At the time of its inception, psychology was unique in the extent to which its institutionalization preceded its content and its

> **For any population, the relative incidence of meaningful or ameaningful thinking will be largely determined by the values that the group places upon either.**

> **Sciences won their way to independence by achieving enough knowledge to become sciences.**

methods preceded its problem. Never had thinkers been given so sharply specified an invitation to create, or been so harried by social wish, cultural optimism, and extrinsic prescription into the advance scheduling of ways and means.

The 19th Century program for a science of psychology seems rational enough. It asks man to entertain a huge and wholly open hypothesis: Can the methods of natural science be adapted to the backward studies of man and society: to the analysis of man's experiences, his actions, his artifacts, his values, his institutions, his history, his future?

To entertain such a hypothesis responsibly is no light matter. Madhouses have been populated by responses to lighter intellectual burdens.

No wonder that many inheritors of this awesome challenge have protected themselves from its ravages by reinterpreting the hypothesis as an *a priori* truth. For close to a century now, many psychologists have seemed to suppose that the methods of natural science are totally specifiable and specified; that the applicability of these methods to social and human events is not only an established fact but that no knowledge is worth taking seriously unless it is based on inquiries saturated with the iconology of science. Thus, from the beginning, respectability held more glamor than insight, caution than curiosity, feasibility than fidelity. The stipulation that psychology be adequate to science outweighed the commitment that it be adequate to man.

The 100-year course of "scientific" psychology can now be seen

> **The 100-year course of "scientific" psychology can now be seen to be a succession of changing doctrines about what to emulate in the natural sciences— especially physics.**

to be a succession of changing doctrines about *what* to emulate in the natural sciences—especially physics. Each such strategic doctrine was entertained not as conditional upon its cognitive fruits but functioned rather as a security fetish bringing assurance to the psychologist, and hopefully the world, that he was a scientist. The broad role-playing paradigms regulating 19th Century experimental psychology, and the various phases of behaviorism, succeeded each other not by virtue of differential productivity, but rather because of the dawning recognition that significant problems and segments of subject matter were being evaded—or because of boredom with the old paradigm.

As we proceed through eras of "classical" behaviorism, neo-behaviorism, deflated neo-behaviorism, "liberalized" neo-behaviorism, "subjective" neo-behaviorism, we see successive efforts to salvage an epistemological judgment that condemns an entire "science" to evading, or, at best, misphrasing its subject matter in the interest of enforcing an apparent objectivity. Those who would argue that the behaviorism have

> **The idea that psychology—like the natural sciences on which it is modeled— is a cumulative or progressive discipline is simply not borne out by its history.**

nevertheless been richly productive of research should be reminded that research is not knowledge.

Consider the problem of "learning," which was the central empirical idea of all that effort. Consider the hundreds of theoretical formu-

lations, rational equations, mathematical models of the learning process that have accrued; the thousands of research studies. And *now* consider that there is still no wide agreement on the empirical conditions under which learning takes place, or even on the definition of learning and its relations to other psychological processes or phenomena. Consider also that after all this scientific effort our actual *insight* into the learning process—reflected in every humanly important context to which learning is relevant—has not improved one jot.

The idea that psychology—like the natural sciences on which it is modeled—is a cumulative or progressive discipline is simply not borne out by its history. Indeed, the hard knowledge gained by one generation typically disenfranchises the theoretical fictions of the last. Psychology's larger generalizations are not specified and refined over time and effort. They are merely replaced. Throughout psychology's history as "science," the *hard* knowledge it has deposited has been uniformly negative. Examples of this are myriad; space will permit me to develop only one.

Karl Lashley in 1920 begins a research program designed to provide the physiological underpinnings of Watsonian conditioning theory. To his astonishment, he soon runs into findings utterly at variance with Watsonian or any other then imaginable version of associationism. After 30 years of unrelenting, often brilliant pursuit of the problems suggested by these early findings, we see him concluding:

"This series has yielded a good bit of information about what and where the memory trace is not. It has discovered nothing of the real nature of the engram. I sometimes feel, in reviewing the evidence on the localization of the memory trace, that the necessary conclusion is that learning just is not possible."—Symposium of the Society for Experimental Biology, 1950, *4*, pp. 454–482.

Subsequent developments in biological psychology, made possible in the last 20 years by powerful electrophysiological and other techniques, have had a similar force. As a result of dense piling up of particulate evidence on such matters as graded excitation processes, central feedback to the receptors, "vertical" organization of brain process, etc., the entire earlier history of psycho-physiological theorizing can be seen as hopelessly simplistic. But again, the main *general* contribution is negative knowledge. Indeed, one reading of this knowledge is that the established complexity of the central nervous system is such as to make biological explanation of psychological process an even more remote prospect than Lashley tended to suggest.

Other examples could be derived from the history of Gestalt psychology in its bearing on the critique of Wundtian experimental psychology, structuralism, and, later on, behaviorism; the import of ethological research as a corrective to the unbridled environmentalism of pre-1950 behavior theory and "comparative" psychology; the twists and turns in the allegiances commanded by the diverse behavioristic theories of learning; the complex history of conceptual realignments among general personality theories, and their sub-doctrines concerning psychotherapy.

In some of the foregoing cases—especially biological psychology, the Gestalt contribution to perception, and ethology—there are at least grounds for believing that particular findings are of permanent value. But even these findings give us no purchase on any truly science-like general analysis of the events in their domain. They give us mainly means for destroying older and misconceived analyses.

A century and a quarter ago, John Stuart Mill argued that the backward state of the social sciences could be remedied only by applying to them the methods of physical science, "duly extended, and generalized." His strategy has now been applied in billions of man-hours of research, ardent theoretical thinking, scholarship, writing, planning and administration in hundreds of laboratories by thousands of investigators. (There are over 25,000 members of the American Psychological Association alone.) It has generated a vast literature and attracted generous support. Federal sources alone provided $326 million for "social science" research in 1967.

> *I think it by this time utterly and finally clear that* **psychology cannot be a coherent science,** *or indeed a coherent field of scholarship, in any specifiable sense of coherence that can bear upon a field of inquiry.*

The test of the Millian hypothesis has not been a sleazy one. In my estimation, the hypothesis has been fulsomely disconfirmed. I think it by this time utterly and finally clear that *psychology cannot be a coherent science*, or indeed a coherent field of scholarship, in any specifiable sense of coherence that can bear upon a field of inquiry. It can certainly not expect to become *theoretically* coherent; in fact, it is now clear that no large subdivision of inquiry, including physics, can be.

As for the *subject matter* of psychology, it is difficult to see how it could ever have been thought to be a coherent one under any definition of the presumptive "science"—whether in terms of mind, consciousness, experience, behav-ior, or, indeed, molecule aggregates or transistor circuits. Anything so awesome as the total domain comprised by the functioning of all organisms can hardly be thought the subject matter of a coherent discipline.

But what about "science"? Are the bits and pieces into which psychology falls, in this account, sciences or something else? The core meaning of the word "science" has become connected with a special analytical pattern emerging first in classical modern astronomy, achieving more distinct fruition in Newtonian mechanics and undergoing further differentiation in post-classical physics. Though this analytic pattern has yet to be successfully explicated, no one doubts that it has been implicit in the skills of great physicists. And there is reason to believe the pattern is applicable in aspects of the biological sciences. Whatever the many details that resist specification, this pattern involves the disembedding from a domain of phenomena of a small family of variables that demarcate important aspects of the domain's structure—when the domain is considered as an idealized, monetary static system. Moreover, these variables, by virtue of appropriate internal relations, can be ordered to a mathematical or formal system capable of correctly describing changes in selected aspects of the system as a function of time and/or system changes describable as alterations of the "values" of specified variables. To disembed a family of variables having such properties is no mean feat, even in rather simple natural systems (those, for example, constitutive of pressure-volume relations of a gas), having a highly "closed" character.

There is currently much appreciation of the wide variability of natural systems on some such dimension as "closed-openness" or "weakness-strength" of their boundary conditions (thus, experimental isolability). Nevertheless, insufficient concern has been given to the strong chance that at some critical point of system-openness, boundary-weakness, or mere internal complexity, the definitive analytic pattern may no longer apply. While Ludwig von Bertalanffy and other "systems theorists" have spelled out certain implications for biology that stem from the openness of animate systems, they tend to assume that the empyrean must contain mathematical or logical methods suitable for the analysis of systems of any degree of openness or complexity. I do not think even the empyrean to be that well stocked. Nevertheless, biological psychology is perhaps the one area in which some approximation of the analytic pattern of science can be fruitfully applied.

The 100-year history of "scientific psychology" has proved that most other domains that psychologists have sought to order in the name of "science," and through simulations of the analytical pattern definitive of science, simply *do not* and *can not* meet the conditions for the meaningful application of this analytic pattern.

When I say that designation as "science" only vitiates and distorts many legitimate and important domains of psychological *study*, it is well to understand what I am *not* saying. I am *not* saying that psychological studies should not be empirical, should not strive towards the rational classification of observed events, should not essay shrewd, tough-minded, and differentiated analyses of the interdependences among significant events. I am *not* saying that statistical and mathematical methods are inapplicable everywhere. I am *not* saying that no subfields of psychology can be regarded as parts of science.

I *am* saying that in many fields close to the heart of the psychological studies, such concepts as "law," "experiment," "measurement," "variable," "control," and "theory" do not behave as their homonyms do in the established sciences. Thus the term "science" cannot properly be applied to perception, cognition, motivation, learning, social psychology, psychopathology, personology, esthetics, the study of creativity or the empirical study of phenomena relevant to the domains of the extant humanities. To persist in applying this highly charged metaphor is to shackle these fields with highly unrealistic expectations; the inevitable heuristic effect is the enaction of imitation science.

As the beginning of a therapeutic humility, we might re-christen psychology *and speak instead of* the psychological studies.

As the beginning of a therapeutic humility, we might re-christen *psychology* and speak instead of *the psychological studies.* The current Departments of Psychology should be called Departments of Psychological Studies. Students should no longer be tricked by a terminological rhetoric into the belief that they are studying a single discipline or any set of specialties that can be rendered coherent, even in principle.

There are stronger proposals. William McDougall firmly believed that psychological study was inappropriate for undergraduates. As early as 1942, Heinrich Klüver was cheerfully anticipating "the impending dismemberment of psychology."

The psychological studies already range, as they must, over an immense and disorderly spectrum of human activity and experience. We might well benefit from spin-offs to other disciplines. Much of

what is solid, I tend to think, could best be pursued in association with the germane scientific and humanistic disciplines. Biological psychology could only profit by incorporation within biology. Psycholinguistics should certainly be happening within linguistics. Even now, broad ranges of the psychological studies, as I conceive them—the empirical analysis of art, psychological aspects of history and philosophy, empirical analysis of inquiry—are almost completely bypassed by the psychological studies as they currently exist, and are pursued, when at all, only in the humanities.

Some will think that my analysis of the condition of psychology has focused on behavioral science, and neglected trends in psychology that have fed the humanities. They will think of the psychoanalytic or "depth" psychologies, the return of some to forms of experientialism, the embracement by others of existential alternatives to a behaviorist epistemology, the emergence even of a large grouping called "humanistic psychology."

The depth psychologies, though they arose from a different tradition than did academic psychology, still were a response to a similar configuration of forces in 19th Century culture, and they contain in their very conception assumptions as ameaningful as those at the roots of academic psychology. And humanists characteristically turn to the depth psychologies when they are in search of psychological guidance.

Appreciable numbers of psychologists—clinical psychologists and others involved in a human subject matter—began to flee from behaviorism in the mid '50s. The bases of their protests were varied, and there was at least some diversity in their search for a more significant professional commitment. It was at about this time that

Abraham Maslow, who had long complained about the "means-centeredness" and scientism of psychology, was discovering the apparent promise of existentialism and calling for a "third force" in psychology. Such a group—calling themselves "humanistic psychologists"—soon emerged.

However, I caught up with the "humanistic psychologists" last fall at the annual American Psychological Association meeting in San Francisco. Here scholarly exposition must give way to reportage. On my arrival at the Farimont Hotel, I found in its Victorian lobby a pullulating mass of characters, mainly young, dressed in the assorted output of the Carnaby Streets, the sari sweat-shops, the micro-mini makers and the love-bead mongers of the world. A bit of investigation established that these were members of the Society For Humanistic Psychology, which had been holding its own pre-convention for two days. I learned further that the Society now has some 1,500 members and that there are no professional requirements for membership. The humanistic fervor of the group has been channeled into one activity, variously designated as group therapy, T-group therapy, sensitivity group therapy, syntectics, etc. I had known of the proliferation of forms of group therapy, but had not known that the whole energy of formal "humanistic psychology" is now given to its pursuit.

Before the humanists' own convention disbanded, I did wander into one of their sessions of group-therapy training films. It was confusing. For some reason, about 70 young humanists, mainly ladies, were lying on the floor in an intertwined and palpating mass, quite oblivious of the film (which demonstrated role-playing by two middle-aged and somewhat nasal

therapists; they were acting out a conflict between a husband who wanted to go to the movies and a wife who claimed esthetic anesthesia on account of a runny nose). With curiosity thus reinforced, I attended all the humanists' activities that I could at the APA Convention proper. It was not easy because every humanistic audience spilled over into the corridors, unlike the sullen, spare audiences at the non-humanistic events.

By far the largest audience showed up at a symposium in which Paul Bindrim, the originator of "nude-marathon group therapy," spoke and showed a film. Reprints of a magazine report on Bindrim's "break-through" were made available. Bindrim had won-

---

Dr. Maslow had speculated that with nudity in groups, "people would go away more spontaneous, less guarded, less defensive, not only about the shape of their behinds, but freer and more innocent about their minds as well."

---

dered whether what he calls a man's "tower of clothes" is not only a safeguard for privacy but a self-imposed constraint to keep out people he fears. If so, a man who disrobed physically might be better able to disrobe emotionally. The modest Mr. Bindrim refuses to take sole credit for this hypothesis and wishes to share it with Abraham Maslow. Dr. Maslow had speculated that with nudity in groups, "people would go away more spontaneous, less guarded, less defensive, not only about the shape of their behinds, but freer and more innocent about their minds as well."

Bindrim's methods, for the most part, are the standard devices of group theory. He was enthusiastic at the symposium, however, about a therapeutic intervention of his own inspired coinage that he

calls "crotch-eyeballing." The crotch, he notes, is the focus of many hang-ups. In particular, three classes: (1) aftermath difficulties of toilet training; (2) masturbation guilts; (3) stresses of adult sexuality. Why not blast all this pathology at once! Thus two group members aid in (as Bindrim says) the "spread-eagling" of a third member and the entire company is instructed to stare unrelentingly and for a good long interval at the offending target area. Each group member is given an opportunity to benefit from this refreshing psychic boost. Scientist that he is, Bindrim is unwilling to make a decisive assessment of the benefits until more data are in. But he is encouraged.

Admittedly, Bindrim's is only one of many approaches in group therapy. But all these methods are based on *one* fundamental assumption: that total psychic transparency—total self-exposure—has therapeutic and growth-releasing potential. More generally, they presuppose an ultimate theory of man as socius: man as an undifferentiated and diffused region in a social space inhabited concurrently by all other men thus diffused. Every technique, manipulative gimmick, cherished and wielded by the lovable, shaggy workers in this field is selected for its efficacy for such an end.

This entire, far-flung "human potential" movement is a threat to human dignity. It challenges any conception of the person that would make life worth living, in a degree far in excess of behaviorism. Yet its message is surprisingly akin to that of behaviorism. The "human potential" movement obliterates the content and boundary of the self by transporting it out of the organism—not merely to its periphery, but right out into public, social space. The force of behaviorism is merely to legislate the inner life out of existence for *science*, while allowing the citizen to entertain the illusion, perhaps even the reality, of having one. Even Skinner gallantly acknowledges a world of "private stimulation."

The "human potentialists," however, are saying in effect that a world of *private* stimulations is unhealthy. They generate a militant rhetoric of anti-rigor and are derisive about the "up-tight," whether in scholarship or life. But as fix-it men to the up-hung, they have a passion for the unending collection and elaboration of group engineering *methods*. They have a barrel of them for every type of hang-up. Have hope!

The moral and logic of the foregoing vignette are too obvious. "Humanistic psychology" started as a revolt against ameaning—against nearly a century of constraint by a prejudged Millian hypothesis and 50 years of reductive behaviorism. In no time at all it achieved a conception of human nature so gross as to make behaviorism seem a form of Victorian sentimentality—which perhaps it was. We have come farther than full circle. The resources of ameaning are formidable!

I wish I could offer a constructive and merry coda. I cannot. I am boxed by my own version of the truth. We are, I think, at a grave impasse in the history of scholarship—indeed the history of intelligence. I am sanguine enough to believe it a temporary one. But I

> **The central psychological task is to disembed subtle relational unities within the flux of experience. That, too, is the central task of the humanist.**

have no recipe for its removal. Students everywhere sense this impasse. Their dissidence is their response to the entrenched ameaning about them. Their dissidence is our hope. But *they*, who know not what they do, cannot tell us what to do.

We must do what we can. We who are psychologists or humanists must become for a while not psychologists or humanists, but *men*. Let the teaching of the psychological studies and the humanities be a matter of men exploring the meanings of human experience, actions, and artifacts at their most value-charged reaches, *among* men. Let the teacher be wiser, more able than the student to discriminate finely and value precisely within important segments of human reality. Let him be admirable in *that* sense.

As for the relations between the psychological studies and the humanities, it *should* be more like an identity than any other type of connection. The central psychological task is to disembed subtle relational unities within the flux of experience. That, too, is the central task of the humanist. Let each humanist construct his own psychology. Let each psychologist reconstruct his own humanity.   ◆

Discussion Questions

1. What, according to Koch, is "ameaningful thinking?"

2. How does Clark Hull view the relationship between theory and experiment?

3. Psychology is divided into many different branches or sects. According to Koch, what impact does this have on the science of psychology?

4. Is psychology a scientific practice according to the author? According to you? Explain both answers.

5. According to Koch, why have numerous new paradigms of psychology evolved?

6. How, as Koch sees things, has our understanding of learning changed over the past century?

7. How did John Stuart Mill suggest that psychology could evolve from its backward state? Did it work?

8. Can any psychological specialty be considered a science? Why or why not?

9. Explain the evolution of humanistic psychology. What did it eventually become?

10. Define "crotch hang-ups" and explain their causes.

11. What are Koch's views on humanistic (Rogerian) psychology?

12. Do you think Koch is right in his dismal assessment of psychology? What future do you see for psychology?

Re-EXAMINING
F r e u d

JAMES HILLMAN

Jungian analyst and author of
The Myth of Analysis and *A Blue Fire*,
an anthology of his writings

"Freud's primary emphasis was on the sexual genital life as crucial to life, the human as animal, as an organic-driven creature. Nobody likes that anymore. Freud said that sexual genital life can never be satisfied instinctually. So you're driven and at the same time you cannot be satisfied. That part of Freudian theory hasn't been taken to its fullest consequences. It really locates the human being very deeply in the body and in animal nature. It ties us to the animal world.

Freud was also concerned with civilization. In his book Civilization and Its Discontents, *he points out that one's pathology is not merely a personal or family situation but is tied with the pathology of civilization. And the rectification of pathology involves us in politics. To give a simple example, some of your depression or my depression is due to the terrible rooms we live in and the terrible noise and traffic and so forth. We may also grieve for the destroyed trees and buildings that we grew up with and are fond of. We feel grief and mourning, and those emotions connect us outward to the world. This aspect of Freud has been overlooked, not altogether, but the tremendous focus on childhood has depotentiated the patient as a political being. By emphasizing the child archetypes, the past and the family—we're all abused, abandoned and victims, not political*

beings—both analysts and patients have stepped outside of the political schema. You know, for the last 40 years the most sensitive people have been in analysis and we've become depoliticized. A lot of sensitive people have been studying their abandonment fantasies and have abandoned civilization in a certain way."

STEPHEN M. SONNENBERG

Psychoanalyst and chair of the
Committee on Public Information of
the American Psychoanalytic
Association

"What we can still learn from Freud is what we could always learn from Freud—that most mental activity goes on outside of conscious awareness, that much of the mental pain and anguish that people experience is the result of conflict that is not conscious, and that there is resistance to recognizing that there is unconscious process. Freud also showed us that the cornerstone of any deeply probing treatment, which really respects the autonomy of the individual and the individual's options for growth, works with the resistance and the unconscious conflict.

The lessons of Freud have to be relearned every day by people who are trying to work with the unconscious. The mistake we make is somehow thinking that those basic lessons are learned and ingrained. We need to constantly be reconsidering the nature of unconscious process in ourselves—thinking about it and trying to understand it."

ALICE MILLER

Psychologist and author of
For Your Own Good and
Thou Shalt Not Be Aware

"Do I owe anything to Sigmund Freud, psychoanalyst? Today, I would say: 20 years of blindness toward the reality of child abuse as well as toward the most important facts of my life. In 1896, Sigmund Freud discovered the truth about the repression of childhood traumas and its effects on the adult. Unable to bear this truth, he finally decided to deny his own discovery. One year later, in 1897, he developed the psychoanalytical theory which actually conceals the reality of child abuse and supports the tradition of blaming the child and protecting the parents."

THOMAS SZASZ

Psychiatrist and author of
The Myth of Mental Illness

"We can learn from what he talked about but did not practice—in fact, he systematically lied about it— which is the concept of the absolutely confidential, *totally voluntary, uncoerced conversation with another person, who comes to see you and pays for the service. The conversation should always be paid for; this ensures that the person isn't coming to you for any other reason. But Freud betrayed this concept through his training analysis, through child analysis and through his so-called analysis of his daughter, which was pure existential incest. Freud was like a pope who preached celibacy but didn't practice it."*

JEROME L. SINGER

Professor of Psychology and
Child Study, Yale University

"We all have much to learn about scientific integrity and commitment from

Corbis

Sigmund Freud

Freud's willingness to study his own dreams, reexamine his theories and persist in a lifelong exploration that has stirred the imagination of thousands of thinkers in this century."

PAULA CAPLAN

Professor of Applied Psychology at the Ontario Institute for Studies in Education and author of *Don't Blame Mother: Mending the Mother-Daughter Relationship*

"At his best, before he recanted his correct observation that many women have been sexually abused as children, Freud taught the important lesson that a therapist should listen with care and respect for a long time to what a patient says before presuming to make interpretations. In addition, although his theories about etiology were misguided, he cared enough about female-female relationships to think hard about those relationships, and to make some astute observations about women's tendencies (learned, not biologically based, as we now know) to devalue themselves and other women. This constituted a message that these are important relationships, an attitude all too rarely seen today."

ALBERT ELLIS

President, Institute for Rational-Emotive Therapy in New York City, and author of *A New Guide to Rational Living*

"We can constructively learn from Freud what he first said in 1895 and later, alas, forgot: that "emotional" disturbances are "ideogenic"—that is, importantly related to ideas. We can learn that most of us naturally and easily tend to severely defame our self *(and not merely our* behavior) *when we act imperfectly, and thereby bring about needless "horror," and then unconsciously create—yes, create— defenses (especially denial, rationalization and avoidance) by which we actually perpetuate and aggravate our problems. Freudianism, for all its failings, implies that we innately tie our view of our* self, *our* totality, *to our view of our* achievements *and* performances; *and that unless we scientifically stop such self-poisonous thinking—which psychoanalysts do* not *show us how to do—we will inevitably continue to make ourselves suffer. So we can still learn a great deal about human disturbance from Freud—and then, I hope, efficiently use non-Freudian, rational-emotive and cognitive-behavioral therapy to stop* disturbing *ourselves."*

WILL GAYLIN

Psychoanalyst at the Hastings Institute

"My own sense is to always see our relationship to Freud as paradoxical. We are all speaking Freud—he has influenced our language, perceptions and institutions more than anyone else in the 20th century.

People reject specific ideas of Freud's like castration anxiety and penis envy, thinking of them as fundamental Freud: They are not. The most fundamental aspect of Freud was the concept that all behavior is dynamic. That means that there's not

just one cause for a particular behavior but many. It's like a giant beach ball that 50 people are pushing in every direction: The fact that it moves slightly in one direction is a result of the forces of 20 or 30 pushing one way and slightly fewer pushing the other way. This principle is called the psycho-dynamic principle, the idea that what you do is a result of certain pressure—conscious or unconscious—to do it and certain pressures not to do it.

Freud also showed that behavior is always developmental. Everything we do today must be seen as a result of influences that occurred during our lifetime. Freud truly believed that we don't live in a real world but in a world of our own perception. By that he simply means that it doesn't matter whether you're beautiful or successful or whatever; if you don't feel beautiful, you're not beautiful to yourself.

I have no doubt that Freud's reputation will rest primarily on his contributions to our understanding of normal behavior as distinguished from pathological behavior. He used sick patients to help in understanding the processes of development. Psychoanalysis gave a frame of reference for dynamic psychiatry in general, and it's helping many psychiatrists to become better therapists by helping them understand human motivation."

ROBERT JAY LIFTON

Distinguished Professor of Psychology at the State University of New York, New York City

"We're beyond the point where anyone is either pro-Freud or anti-Freud. I don't see it as a question of holding on to some ideas and getting rid of others but rather of seeing Freud as a great figure who was responsible for one of the great intellectual breakthroughs in our history. We need to read him directly and make use of his insights and the quality of his mind for carrying these ideas further. Then we need to develop new ideas that de-

pend upon Freud but at the same time stray from him, to deal with contemporary issues and, in my view, especially social and historical dimensions."

HANS J. EYSENCK

Professor Emeritus of Psychology at the University of London's Institute of Psychiatry

"I think Freud has been a wholesale disaster for psychology and what we can learn from him is how not to do things.

In psychology as in other sciences one must provide proof for any assertion. Freud intentionally and deliberately refused to look at his cases in comparison with control cases. He never followed them up to see whether in actual fact what he claimed to have been successes were successful. We now know that in fact many of them were not. For instance, the Wolfman Freud claimed to have cured was recently interviewed in Vienna. He ex-

plained that he had been treated throughout his life for the very things Freud said he had cured. Even at the age of 90 he was still suffering from the same symptoms. The claims that Freud made are simply incorrect, and one really cannot pay that much attention to them."

PHYLLIS CHESLER

Psychologist and author of *Women and Madness* and *About Men*; cofounder of the Association for Women in Psychology

"Freud taught us—and this has not been accepted of him here because we're Americans—that life is tragic, that there are real limitations, that everything is a trade-off, that nobody can have a free lunch, that we're not getting out of this alive. He said that there is a life instinct, Eros, but that there is also Thanatos, a death instinct. And there is real death. Freud was a mournful meditator. He was not Dale Carnegie. He didn't say "Read

this book and you're going to be happy and get everything you want." He wasn't saying that, and I don't think that we've picked up his humbling, tragic message."

ROLLO MAY

Author of *Love and Will* and one of the founders of the humanistic movement in psychotherapy

"Freud knew that the 19th century was finished, gone to pieces. The meaning of psychoanalysis gave men and women a new view of life. Freud brought us understanding of depth, death, also our moods, negation of ideas, our fatigue, our sickness. We can still learn from Freud—not mainly from the rules of psychoanalysis, but rather from how he pictured a whole new culture, a culture in which people would be more broadly understood and more broadly human because the unconscious was part of the experience of the 20th century."

Discussion Questions

1. Which aspect of Freudian theory is most fundamental?
2. What is meant by "all behavior is dynamic?"
3. Briefly explain the psychodynamic principle.
4. Discuss various critiques of Freud.
5. Explain the meaning of Thomas Szasz's statement "Freud was like a pope who preached celibacy but didn't practice it."
6. According to Paula Caplan, what did Freud have to say about female-female relationships?
7. According to Freud, why was it important for a patient to pay for services?
8. What message is Will Gaylin conveying in his statement, "My own sense is to always see our relationship to Freud as paradoxical?"
9. Why does Eysenck believe that Freud was "a wholesale" disaster for psychology?

Name: _____

Date: _____

Part 1: Introduction to Psychology

1. I think the behavoristic view espoused by B.F. Skinner is the best way to understand people.

Agree   ①   ②   ③   ④   ⑤   Disagree

2. I think the psychodynamic view espoused by Sigmund Freud is the best way to understand people.

Agree   ①   ②   ③   ④   ⑤   Disagree

3. I think the humanistic view espoused by Carl Rogers is the best way to understand people.

Agree   ①   ②   ③   ④   ⑤   Disagree

Imagine a debate between Skinner and Rogers. Write a dalogue between the two of them with each defending his own theories.

If Sigmund Freud had witnessed this debate, who would he pick as the winner? How would he respond to the points made by Rogers and Skinner?

Who do *you* think won the debate? Which do you think is the better school of thought—behaviorism or humanism? Why?

PART 2
PSYCHOLOGICAL METHODS

5 **Self-Fulfilling Prophecy,** by Robert Rosenthal

6 **Folk Wisdom,** by Robert Epstein

7 **The Think-Drink Effect,** by G. Alan Marlatt and Damaris J. Rohsenow

Behavioral scientists have borrowed some research methods from the physical sciences, but they've also invented many of their own. In the 1800s, Francis Galton, Darwin's first cousin, created new statistical methods to help him study individual differences, and psychologists ever since have been leaders in developing statistical tests to help them discover the complex causes of behavior. In the best scientific tradition, psychologists have also been fanatical about challenging the validity of their own research studies—asking whether the methods are appropriate, whether the results are generalizable, and whether the conclusions are justifiable. In recent decades, Robert Rosenthal of Harvard University has probably been the most persuasive and ingenious regulator of research methodology in the behavioral sciences, and he has also identified subtle behavioral phenomena in the real world. In "Self-Fulfilling Prophecy," the classic article that follows, Rosenthal shows that when people expect certain outcomes—for example, when teachers expect certain students to perform well or poorly, or when experimenters expect certain results in an experiment—they behave in subtle ways to *make* those outcomes occur. Take a close look at Rosenthal's account of rat studies toward the end of his article; can you figure out what's going on?

In the following article, "Folk Wisdom," I ask how well traditional proverbs about behavior, such as "Spare the rod, spoil the child" or "Out of sight, out of mind" measure up to behavioral research. Turns out that some proverbs measure up well, others not so well, and some poorly. But which are which?

In the final article in this section, psychologists G. Alan Marlatt and Damaris J. Rohsenow cite extensive data showing that the mere suggestion that one is drinking alcohol can make one feel drunk—in other words, that drunkenness is in part a "placebo effect." They defend their views using a "balanced-placebo design," which they suggest is a major advance over the usual two-group placebo design. But even the balanced-placebo design contains a significant flaw when it come to alcohol studies. Can you spot it? (Hint: The instructions given to the subjects were not the *only* clues they had about what they were drinking.)

Self-*Fulfilling* PROPHECY

◆ *Robert Rosenthal*

Much of our scientific knowledge is based upon careful observation and recording of events. That the observer himself may have a biasing effect on his observations has long been recognized. There are two basic types of experimenter effects. The first operates without affecting the event or subject being studied. It occurs in the eye, the hand and the brain of the researcher. The second type is the result of the *interaction* between the experimenter and the subject of the experiment. And when the research deals with humans and animals, as it does in the behavioral sciences, this interaction actually can alter the responses or data that are obtained.

Quite unconsciously, a psychologist interacts in subtle ways with the people he is studying so that he may get the response he expects to get. This happens even when the person cannot see the researcher. And even more surprisingly, it occurs when the subject is not human but a rat.

If rats became brighter when expected to by their researcher, isn't it possible that children become brighter when their teachers expect them to be brighter?

Lenore Jacobson, of the South San Francisco Unified School District, and I set out to see if this is so. Every child in an elementary school was given an intelligence test, a test described by us as one that would predict "intellectual blooming."

The school was in a lower socioeconomic neighborhood on the West Coast. There were three classrooms for each grade—one for children of above average ability, one for average ability, and one for below average ability. About 20 percent of the children in each classroom were chosen at random to form the experimental group. The teachers were given the names of this group and told that these children had scored high on the test for intellectual blooming and would show remarkable gains in intellectual development during the next eight months.

In reality, the only difference between these children and their classmates was *in the minds* of their teachers.

At the end of the school year, all the children were again given the same I.Q. test. In the school as a whole, the children who had been designated as "bloomers" showed only a slightly greater gain in verbal I.Q. (two points) than their classmates. However, *in total* I.Q., the experimental group gained four points more on the average than their counterparts did, and in reasoning I.Q., the average gain was seven points more.

Usually, when educational theorists talk of improving scholastic achievement by improving teacher expectations, they are referring to children at the lower levels of achievement. It was interesting to find that teacher expectations affected children at the highest level of achievement as much as it did children at the lowest level.

At the end of the school year, we asked the teachers to describe the classroom behavior of all their pupils. The children in the group designated as the bloomers were seen as more interesting, more curious, and happier. The teachers also found "blooming" children slightly more appealing, better adjusted, and more affectionate, and with less need for social approval.

Many of the other children in the classes also gained in I.Q. during the year, but teachers reacted negatively to *unexpected* improvement. The more the undesignated children gained in I.Q. points, the more they were regarded as *less* well-adjusted, *less* interesting, and *less* affectionate. It appears that there may be hazards to unpredicted intellectual growth—at least in the eyes of the teacher. This is particularly true of children in the low-ability groups.

The effects of teacher expectation were most evident in reasoning I.Q. gains. But only the girls in the group designated as "bloomers" showed greater gains than the rest of the class. The boys designated as bloomers actually gained less than their classmates. Partly to check this finding, Judy Evans and I repeated the experiment with schoolchildren in a small Midwestern town. The chil-

If rats became brighter when expected to by their researcher, isn't it possible that children become brighter when their teachers expect them to be brighter?

The children in the group designated as the bloomers were seen as more interesting, more curious, and happier.

© 1998 PhotoDisc, Inc.

dren here were from substantial middle-class families.

Again we found that teacher expectations affected reasoning I.Q. gains in the pupils. However, this time it was the boys who tended to show greater gains than girls. These results underline the effects of teacher expectations, but they also indicate the complexity of these effects as a function of the pupil's sex, social status, and very likely other variables as well.

In another study, conducted by Lane K. Conn, Carl N. Edwards, Douglas Crowne and me, we selected an East Coast school with upper-middle-class pupils. This time we also measured the children's accuracy in judging the emotion conveyed in tone of voice. The children who were more accurate in judging the emotional tone of an adult female's voice benefited most from favorable teacher expectations. And in this school, both the boys and girls who were expected to bloom intellectually showed greater reasoning I.Q. gains than their classmates.

W. Victor Beez of Indiana University conducted an experiment in 1967 which sheds some light on the phenomenon of teacher expectancy.

His pupils were 60 preschoolers from a summer Head-Start program. Each child had one teacher who taught him the meaning of a series of symbols. Half of the teachers were led to expect good symbol learning, and the other half were led to expect poor learning.

Nearly 77 percent of the children designated as good intellectual prospects learned five or more symbols. Only 13 percent of the children designated as poor prospects learned five or more symbols. A researcher from the outside who did not know what the teachers had been told about the children's intellectual prospects assessed the children's actual performance.

What happened in this study was that the teachers with favorable expectations tried to teach more symbols to their pupils than did teachers who had unfavorable expectations. This indicates that the teacher's expectations may not only be translated into subtle vocal and visual nuances, but also may

> ***If the expectancy effect occurs in the laboratory and in the classroom, then it is not surprising to find it occurring in everyday life.***

cause dramatic alterations in teaching style. Surprisingly, however, even when the amount of teaching was held constant, the children who were expected to learn more did learn more.

Teacher expectancy effects are not limited to the teaching of intellectual tasks. Recent research reported by J. Randolph Burnham and Donald M. Hartsough of Purdue University indicates that the teaching of motor skills also may be affected by teacher expectations. At a camp for underprivileged children from the Philadelphia area, Burnham administered a test to nonswimmers that ostensibly would predict psychological readiness to swim. He then randomly selected children from various age groups and gave their names to the waterfront counselors as those who were "ready" to swim. He found that the children designated as "ready' tended to pass more of the tests in the Red Cross beginning swimmer's course than the average for their peer group.

If the expectancy effect occurs in the laboratory and in the classroom, then it is not surprising to find it occurring in everyday life. Your expectation of how another person will behave often may become a self-fulfilling prophecy. We know that nonverbal and unintentional communication between people does take place. What we don't know is *how* such communication occurs [see Communication Without Words, page 52]. Further research on the interaction of the experimenter and the subject may eventually teach us more about dyadic interactions in general.

The interaction of experimenter and his subject is a major source of knowledge in the behavioral sciences. Until recently, however, this interaction has been an uncontrolled variable in psychological research. But the demonstration of experimenter effects does not necessarily invalidate a great deal of behavioral research. It does mean, however, that we must take extra precautions to reduce "expectancy" and other unintended effects of the experimenter.

Just what does a behavioral scientist unintentionally do in gathering his data so that he unwittingly influences his subjects' responses? This question must be answered satisfactorily if we want to have dependable knowledge in the behavioral sciences.

In our research, we have distinguished five categories of interactional effects between the experimenter and his subjects, the *Biosocial, Psychosocial, Situational, Modeling* and *Expectancy Effects.*

Biosocial Effects

The sex, age and race of investigators all have been found to affect the results of their research. It is tempting to assume that the subjects simply are responding to the biosocial attributes of the investigator. But the investigator himself, because of sex, age or race, may respond differently to male or female, young or old, white or

© 1998 PhotoDisc, Inc.

Negro subjects. And even a slight change in behavior alters the experimental situation.

Our evidence suggests, for example, that male and female experimenters conduct the same

---

What happens to the experimenter during the course of his experiment can influence his behavior, and changes in his behavior may lead to changes in the subjects' responses.

---

experiment quite differently. The different results they obtain are not due to any error as such, but may well be due to the fact that they have unintentionally conducted different experiments.

In one study of the effect of the characteristics of subjects on the experimenter, the interaction between experimenters and subjects was recorded on sound film. Only 12 percent of the investigators smiled even a little at male subjects, but 70 percent smiled at female subjects. These smiles may well have affected the results of the experiment. It may be a heartening finding to know that chivalry is not dead, but as far as methodology is concerned it is a disconcerting finding. In general, the experimenter treated his male subjects and female subjects differently, so that, in a sense, men and women really were not in the same experiment at all.

Moreover, when we consider the sex of both the experimenter and the subject, other interaction effects emerge. In the study recorded on film, we found that the experimenters took more time to collect some of their data from subjects of the opposite sex than from subjects of the same sex.

The age of the investigator may also affect the subject's response. Studies suggest that young subjects are less likely to say "unacceptable" things to much older investigators, indicating that an

"age-barrier" may exist in at least some behavioral studies.

The skin color of the investigator also may affect response, even when the response is physiological.

A number of studies have found that Negroes tend to control their hostility more when contacted by a white rather than a Negro experimenter and give more "proper" responses to white than black interviewers.

Psychosocial Effects

Experimenters are people, and so they differ in anxiety, in their need for approval, in personal hostility, authoritarianism, status and in personal warmth. Experimenters with different personalities tend to get different responses from their experimental subjects. For example, researchers higher in status—a professor as compared to a graduate student, or a captain as compared to a corporal—tend to obtain more responses that *conform* to the investigator's suggestions. And investigators who are warmer toward people tend to obtain more *pleasant* responses.

Situational Effects

Investigators experienced in conducting a given experiment usually obtain responses different from those of less experienced investigators. This may be because they behave differently. Also, experimenters who are acquainted with the people in the experimental group get results that differ from those obtained by researchers who have never met their subjects before.

What happens to the experimenter during the course of his experiment can influence his behavior, and changes in his behavior may lead to changes in the subjects' responses.

For instance, if the first few subjects respond as expected (*i.e.,* confirming the experimenter's hypothesis), the behavior of the researcher alters, and he influences subsequent subjects to respond in a way that supports his hypothesis.

Modeling Effects

Sometimes before an experimenter conducts a study, he first tries out the task he will have his research subjects perform. For example, if the task is to rate a series of 10 photos of faces according to how successful or unsuccessful the person pictured appear to be, the experimenters may decide to rate the photos themselves before contacting their subjects. Though evidence is not yet definite, it appears that at least sometimes the investigator's own ratings become a factors in the performance of his subjects. In particular, when the experimental stimuli, such as photos, are ambiguous, the subjects' interpretation may agree too often with the investigator's interpretation, even though the latter remains unspoken.

Some expectation of how the research might turn out is virtually a constant factor in all scientific experiments. In the behavioral sciences, this expectancy can lead the investigator to act unconsciously in such a way that he affects the responses of his subjects. When the investigator's expectancy influences the responses in the direction of what the investigator expects to happen, we can appropriately regard his hypothesis as a *self-fulfilling prophecy.* One prophesies an event, and the expectation of the event then changes the behavior of the prophet in such a way as to make the prophesied event more likely.

In the history of psychology, the case of *Clever Hans* is a classic example of this phenomenon. Hans was a horse owned by a German mathematics instructor named Von Osten. Hans could perform difficult mathematical calculations, spell, read and solve problems of musical harmony by tapping his foot.

A panel of distinguished scientists and experts on animal behavior ruled that no fraud was involved. The horse was given no cues to tell him when to start or when to stop tapping his foot.

But, of course, there *were* cues. In a series of brilliant experiments reported in 1911, Oskar Pfungst showed that Hans could answer questions only when the questioner himself knew the answers and when the horse could see the questioner. Finally, Pfungst learned that a tiny forward movement of the experimenter's head was the signal for Hans to start tapping. A slight upward movement of the head, or even a raised eyebrow, was the signal for the horse to stop tapping.

Hans's questioners expected him to give the right answers, and their expectation was reflected in their unwitting signals to start and stop tapping. The horse had good eyesight, and he *was* a smart horse.

© 1998 PhotoDisc, Inc.

Self-fulfilling Prophecies

To demonstrate experimenter effects in behavioral research, we must have at least two groups of experimenters with different expectations. One approach is to take a survey of investigators in a certain area of research and ask those with opposite expectancies to conduct a standard experiment. But the differences in the results could be due to factors other than expectancy, and so a better strategy is required.

Rather than trying to find two groups of experimenters with different expectations, we could *create* such groups. In one experiment, we selected 10 advanced undergraduate and graduate students of psychology as our researchers. All were experienced in conducting research. Each was assigned a group of 20 participating students as his subjects. The experiment consisted of showing 10 photographs of people's faces one at at time to each subject. The participant was to rate the degree of success or failure reflected in the facial expression of the person in the photo. Each of the faces could

be rated from −10 (extreme failure) to +10 (extreme success). The faces in the photos were actually quite neutral, and on the average the total ratings should have produced a numerical score of zero.

All 10 experimenters had identical instructions to read to their subjects, and they also had identical instructions on how to conduct the experiment. They were specifically cautioned not to deviate from these instructions.

Perhaps a new profession of fulltime experimenters could be developed, who would perform others' experiments without becoming involved in setting up a hypothesis or interpreting the results.

Finally, we informed our researchers that the purpose of the experiment was to see how well they could duplicate results which were already well-established. We told half of the experimenters that the "well-established" finding was that people rated the faces in the

photos as successful (+5). And we told the other half that people rated the faces in the photos as unsuccessful (-5). And thus informed, they began their research.

The results were clear-cut. Every researcher who was led to expect that the photographed people were successful obtained a higher average rating of success from his group than did any experimenter who expected low-success ratings.

We repeated this experiment twice with different groups with the same results. Research in other laboratories has shown much the same thing. Although not every experiment showed a significant effect, probability that results of all these experiments occurred by chance is less than one in a thousand billion.

Having found that what the experimenter expects to happen can affect the outcome of his research, we then began to look for some clues as to *how* the experimenter unwittingly communicates his expectancy to his subjects.

Through the use of accomplices who acted as subjects in an experiment, we learned how the responses of the first few subjects affected the experimenter's behavior to subsequent subjects. If the responses of the first few subjects confirmed the experimenter's hypothesis, his behavior to subsequent participants somehow influenced them also to confirm his hypothesis. But when the "planted" accomplices contradicted the expectations of the experimenter, the following subjects were affected by the experimenter's behavior so that they, too, tended to disconfirm his hypothesis. It seems, then, that the early returns of data in behavioral research can affect and possibly shape the final results.

© 1998 PhotoDisc, Inc.

Reverse Effects

In some of our experiments, when we offered too-obvious incentives or too-large rewards to investigators to bring in "good" data, the expectancy effect was reduced, and in some cases even reversed. Both the autonomy and the honesty of the researchers may have been challenged by the excessive rewards offered. It speaks well for the integrity of our student-researchers that they would not be bribed. In fact, they tended to bend over backwards to avoid the biasing effect of their expectation. But they often bent so far backward that the results of their experiments sometimes were the opposite of what they had been told to expect.

The process by which an experimenter unintentionally and covertly communicates instructions to his subjects is very subtle. For six years we have studied sound films of research interviews in an attempt to discover the cues that the experimenter unwittingly gives to the subject, and for six years we have failed, at least partly.

We know, however, that visual cues *are* important. Placing a screen between the investigator and the person he is interviewing reduces the investigator's influence on the results. But the expectancy effect is not eliminated completely, indicating that auditory cues are also important.

This was dramatically demonstrated by John G. Adair and Joyce Epstein of the University of Manitoba in their tape recording experiment. They first duplicated the expectation effects study in which 10 photographs of people's faces are rated successful or unsuccessful. Half of the investigators were told to expect a success response and half a failure response. Adair and Epstein tape-recorded each of the sessions. The result matched those of the original studies.

Next, with a new group of subjects a second experiment was conducted. But instead of having live investigators, the subjects listened to the tape-recording of an investigator reading the standard instructions to the previous group. Again the results were much the same. Self fulfilling prophecies, it seems, can come about as a result of the prophet's voice alone. Since in the experiment all prophets read standard instructions, self fulfillment of prophecies may be brought about by the tone in which the prophet prophesies.

Early in our research on self-fulfilling prophecies, we thought that some form of operant conditioning might be the explanation. It could be that when the investigator obtained a response consistent with his expectations, he would look more pleasant, or smile, or glance at the subject approvingly. The investigator could be entirely unaware of these reinforcing responses. We analyzed many experiments to see if this type of operant conditioning was present. If indeed it was, then the subject's responses should gradually become more like those expected by the investigator—there would be a "learning curve" for subjects.

But no learning curve was found. On the contrary, it turned out that the first responses of the subject were about as much affected by the investigator's expectations as the last responses.

Further analysis revealed that while there was no learning curve for the subjects, there seemed to be a learning curve for the investigators. As the investigator interviewed more and more subjects, the expectancy effect grew stronger. It appeared possible that the subject's response was the reinforcing event. The subjects, then, may quite unintentionally shape the investigator's behavior. So not only does the experimenter influence his subjects to respond in the expected manner, but the subjects may well influence the experimenter to behave in a way that leads to fulfillment of his prophecies.

Perhaps the most significant implication of this research is that human beings can engage in highly effective and influential unintended communication with one another—even under controlled laboratory conditions.

But do expectancy effects occur when the experimental subjects are not human? We designed a study to find out. Twelve experimenters were each given five rats that were to be taught to run a maze with the aid of visual cues. Six of the experimenters were told that their rats had been specially bred for maze-brightness; the other six were told that their rats had been bred for maze-dullness. Actually, there was no difference between the rats.

At the end of the experiment, researchers with "maze-bright" rats found superior learning in their rats compared to the researchers with maze-dull rats.

A second experiment made use of the special training setup designed by B.F. Skinner of Harvard. Half the researchers were led to believe that their rats were "Skinner box bright" and half were told that their rats were "Skinner box dull." Initially, there were not really such differences in the rats, but at the end of the experiment the allegedly brighter animals *were* really brighter, and the alleged dullards *really* duller.

How can we reduce the expectancy effect in behavioral research?

One way is to design procedures that enable us to assess whether the expectancy effects have altered the results of an experiment. In addition, the experimenter could employ investigators who have not been told the purpose of the study, or automated data-collection systems could be used.

Perhaps a new profession of fulltime experimenters could be developed, who would perform others' experiments without becoming involved in setting up a hypothesis or interpreting the results. Precedents for such professionals are found in both medical research and public-opinion surveys.

Dependable Knowledge

Because of the general nature of expectancy and other experimenter effects, it would be desirable to use more experimenters for each study than we presently use. Having a larger number of returns we could assess the extent to which different experimenters obtained different results, and in any area of psychological research this is worth knowing.

To the extent that we hope for dependable knowledge in the behavioral sciences, we must have dependable knowledge about the psychological experiment and the interaction of experimenter and subject.

Scientists have long employed control groups in their experiments. Usually the experimental group receives some kind of treatment while the control group receives no treatment. To determine the extent of the expectancy effect, we could add two special "expectancy control" groups to the experiment. In one of these special groups, the investigator would be told that the groups subjects had received some treatment, when in fact it had not. The experimenter in the other group would be told the subjects had not received treatment when in fact it had. Such a research design would permit us to assess the magnitude of the effect of experimenter's expectancy.

To the extent that we hope for dependable knowledge in the behavioral sciences, we must have dependable knowledge about the psychological experiment and the interaction of experimenter and subject. We can no more hope to acquire accurate information for our disciplines without understanding the experimenter effect than astronomers or zoologists could hope to acquire accurate information without understanding the effects of their telescopes and microscopes.

And behavioral scientists, being as scientifically self-conscious a group as they are, may one day produce a psychology of those psychologists who study psychologists.

Then, in the laboratory, in the classrooms, in every sector of our lives we will come closer to understanding the effect of a smile.

◆

Discussion Questions

1. What are the two types of experimenter effects?

2. Describe teacher expectancy effects.

3. List and describe the five interactional effects that can occur between experimenter and participants.

4. Describe the case of Clever Hans.

5. Describe the learning curve. Did the author find that it related to the experimenters or to the participants?

6. How can we reduce expectancy effects in research?

7. Looking at your life, how do you think that expectancy effects have influenced your behavior? In what areas of your life?

FOLK *Wisdom*

◆ *Robert Epstein*

The table next to me at Filipi's restaurant was a noisy one. Two men and two women in their 20s and 30s were arguing about a relationship issue. One of the men—call him Male #1—would soon be leaving the country for six months. Would the passion he shared with his beloved survive? The exchange went something like this:

Female #1 (probably the girlfriend): "When you really love someone, being apart makes you care even more. If someone is good to you, you sometimes take that for granted when the person is around every day. But when he's gone, all that good treatment is gone, too, and you realize just how much you had. You really start to yearn for him."

Male #2 (looking lustfully at Female #1, even though he seemed to be with the other woman): "That's right. The same thing happens when your parents die. You really start to miss and appreciate them. You even rewrite the past, forgetting the bad things and focusing on the good times and the kindness they showed you."

Female #1 (starting to look lovingly at Male #2): "Exactly. Everyone knows that absence makes the heart grow fonder."

Then Male #1, the one probably on his way to Thailand, spoke up. "Well, but…" He faltered, thinking hard about going on. All eyes were on him. He took a deep breath.

And then he said, slowly and deliberately, "But don't we also say, 'Out of sight, out of mind'?"

This was not good for anyone's digestion. Female #1's face turned the color of marinara sauce. Male #2 smiled mischievously, presumably imagining himself in bed with Female #1. Female #2 looked back and forth between her date and Female #1, also apparently imagining them in bed together. And Male #1, not wanting to face the carnage, lowered his eyes and tapped out a strange rhythm on the table top with his fork. Was he thinking about the classy Thai brothels he had read about on the Internet?

Truth or Poppycock

"Absence makes the heart grow fonder" and "Out of sight, out of mind" are examples of folk wisdom—folk psychology, you might say. All cultures pass along wisdom of this sort—sometimes in the form of proverbs; sometimes through songs (remember Paul Simon's "Fifty Ways to Leave Your Lover"?), rhymes (Mother Goose), or stories (Aesop's fables); sometimes through laws and public information campaigns ("Stay alive, don't drink and drive"); and always through religion ("Do unto others as you would have them do unto you").

But folk wisdom is an unreliable, inconsistent kind of wisdom. For one thing, most proverbs coexist with their exact opposites, or at least with proverbs that give somewhat different advice. Does

absence truly make the heart grow fonder, or are loved ones out of mind when they're out of sight? And isn't variety the spice of life? (If Male #1 had come up with *that* one, he might have been murdered on the spot.)

Do opposites attract, or do birds of a feather flock together? Should you love the one you're with, or would that be like changing horses in midstream? We all know that he who hesitates is lost, but doesn't haste make waste, and isn't patience a virtue, and don't fools rush in, and aren't you supposed to look before you leap?

And, sure, money is power, but aren't the best things in life supposed to be free? And since time is money, and money is power, and power corrupts, does that mean time also corrupts? Well, maybe so. After all, the Devil finds work for idle hands.

I've only covered a few well-known proverbs from the English-speaking world. Each culture passes along its own wisdom, which is not always meaningful to outsiders. In India, for example, people say, "Call on God, but row away from the docks," and Romanians advise, "Do not put your spoon into the pot that does not boil for you." In Bali they say, "Goodness shouts and evil whispers," while in Tibet the message is, "Goodness speaks in a whisper, but evil shouts."

You get the idea. Proverbs that relay wisdom about how we're supposed to live do not necessarily supply useful or reliable advice. In fact, proverbs are sometimes used merely to justify what we already do or believe, rather than as guidelines for action. What's more, we tend to *switch* proverbs to suit our current values and ideals. A young man might rationalize risky action by pointing out that "You only live once"; later in life—if he's still around—he'll probably tell you, "Better safe than sorry."

Is the situation hopeless? Can we glean any truths at all from the wisdom of the ages?

The behavioral sciences can help. Science is a set of methods for testing the validity of statements about the world—methods for getting as close to "truth" as we currently know how to get. Psychologists and other scientists have spent more than a century testing the validity of statements about human behavior, thinking, and emotions. How well does folk psychology stand up to scientific inquiry? What do we find when we test a statement like "Absence makes the heart grow fonder"? If, as I do, you sometimes rely on folk wisdom to guide your actions or teach your children, this is a question well worth considering.

Here's how five common proverbs measure up to behavioral research.

Confession is Good for the Soul

Psychologists don't study the soul, of course. But says psychologist James W. Pennebaker, Ph.D., "If we define 'soul' loosely as who you are, how you feel about yourself, and how healthy you are, then confession *is* good for the soul." Pennebaker, a researcher at the University of Texas at Austin, is one of several behavioral scientists who have looked carefully at the results of "self-disclosure"—talking or writing about private feelings and concerns. His research suggests that for about two-thirds of us, self-disclosure has enormous emotional and physical benefits. Pennebaker's newly revised book, *Opening Up: The Healing Power of Expressing Emotion*, summarizes 15 years of compelling research on this subject.

Self-disclosure, as you might expect, can greatly reduce shame or guilt. In fact, studies of suspected criminals showed that they acted far more relaxed after confessing their crimes—despite the fact that punishment now awaited them. Self disclosure may also provide the power behind talk therapy. "The fact that self-disclosure is beneficial," says Pennebaker, "may explain why all forms of psychotherapy seem to be helpful. Whether the therapy is behavioral or psychoanalytic, in the beginning the clients tell their stories."

Perhaps most intriguing are the physical effects of "confession." Pennebaker has found that self-disclosure may actually boost the immune system, spurring production of white blood cells that attack invading microorganisms, increasing production of antibodies, and heightening the body's response to vaccination.

But what about those other proverbs that advise us to keep our mouths shut? "Let sleeping dogs lie." "Least said is soonest mended." "Many have suffered by talking, few by silence." Can self-disclosure do harm? According to Pennebaker, self-disclosure is not likely to be beneficial when it's forced. University of Notre Dame psychologist Anita Kelly, Ph.D., has suggested,

> *...self-disclosure may actually boost the immune system, spurring production of white blood cells that attack invading microorganisms, increasing production of antibodies, and heightening the body's response to vaccination.*

moreover, that revealing secrets may be harmful if the confidant is likely to be judgmental. And a 1989 study conducted by Maria Sauzier, M.D., of Harvard Medical School, showed that people often regret disclosures of child abuse. Sauzier found that nearly half of the parents whose children had disclosed sexual abuse (usually to the other parent or a therapist) felt that both the children and the families were harmed by the disclosures. And 19 percent of the adolescents who confessed that they had been abused regretted making the disclosures. In general, however, confession seems to be a surprisingly beneficial act.

All Work and No Play Makes Jack a Dull Boy

To me, the most frightening scene in the movie *The Shining* was the one in which actress Shelley Duvall, concerned that her husband (Jack Nicholson) was going crazy, approached the desk at which he had spent several months supposedly writing a novel. There she found hundreds of pages containing nothing but the sentence, "All work and no play makes Jack a dull boy" typed thousands of times on a manual typewriter. I've always wondered who did all that typing! And I've also wondered about the truth of the proverb. Once again, we're also faced with contradictory bits of folk wisdom that urge us to work until we drop: "Rest makes rusty." "Labor warms, sloth harms." "Labor is itself a pleasure."

Is too much work, without the balance of leisure activity ("play"), actually harmful? Research suggests that the answer is yes, with one possible exception: if you love your work—in other words, if you've been able to make your *avocation* your *vocation*—then work may provide you with some of the benefits of play.

In the 1940s, anthropologist Adam Curle pointed out that the distinction between work and leisure seems to be an unfortunate product of modern society. In many traditional cultures, he wrote, "there is not even a word for work." Work and play "are all of a piece, " part of the integrated structure of daily living. But modern society has created the need for people to earn a living, an endeavor that can be difficult and can easily get out of hand. Hence, the modern pursuit of "leisure time" and "balance"—correctives for the desperate measures people take to pay their bills.

Study after study confirms the dangers of overwork. It may or may not make you a dull person, but it clearly dulls your mind. For example, recent research on fire fighters by Peter Knauth, Ph.D., shows that long work shifts increase reaction time and lower alertness. And studies with emergency room physicians show that overwork increases errors and impedes judgment. Indeed, a Hollywood cameraman, coming off an 18-hour work shift, made news recently when he lost control of his car and died in a crash.

Conversely, leisure activities have been shown in numerous studies by researchers Howard and Diane Tinsley, Virginia Lewis, and others, to relieve stress, improve mood, increase life satisfaction, and even boost the immune system.

Curiously, the hard-driven "type A" personalities among us are not necessarily Dull Jacks. According to a recent study of more than 300 college students by Robert A. Hicks, Ph.D., and his colleagues, type-A students claim to engage in considerably more leisure activities than their relaxed, type-B counterparts. Type As may simply live "more intensely" than type Bs, whether they're on the job or goofing off.

The distinction between work and play is, to some extent, arbitrary. But it's clear that if you spend too much time doing things you don't want to do, your performance, health, and sense of well-being will suffer.

© 1998 PhotoDisc, Inc.

Boys Will Be Boys

The widely held (though politically incorrect) belief that boys are predisposed from birth to feel, learn, and perform differently from girls is strongly supported by research. For example, boys are, on average, considerably more aggressive than girls. They are left-handed more frequently than girls and tend to be better at math and at spatial rotation tasks. Girls, meanwhile, may perform certain kinds of memory tasks better. They also start talking earlier than boys, and, at the playground, they're more likely to imitate boys than boys are to imitate girls. And boys tend to listen more with their right ear, while girls tend to listen with both ears equally. These findings generally hold up cross-culturally, which suggests that they are at least somewhat independent of environmental influences. Upbringing plays an important role in gender differences, of course— even in the first days after birth, parents treat boy babies differently from girls—but converging evidence from psychology, neuroscience, and evolutionary biology suggests that many gender differ-

ences are actually programmed from birth, if not from conception.

Since the brain is the mechanism that generates behavior, where we find behavioral differences, we should also find neurological differences. Indeed, recent research suggests a host of differences between male and female brains. For example, although, on average, male brains are larger than female brains, the hemispheres of the brain seem to be better connected in females, which may help explain why females are more sensitive and emotional than males.

Behavior is also driven by hormones. Here, too, there are significant gender differences. From birth, testosterone levels are higher in males, which helps to account for males' aggressiveness. June Reinisch, Ph.D., then at Indiana University, studied boys and girls whose mothers had been exposed to antimiscarriage drugs that mimic testosterone. Not surprisingly, she found that these children of both sexes were considerably more aggressive than their counterparts with normal testosterone levels. But even among the exposed children, the boys were more aggressive than the girls.

Rating the Proverbs

Here's a quick rundown on how well some other common proverbs measure up to research findings:

***** looks good

**** some evidence supports it

***not clear

** some evidence casts doubt

* scrap heap

"Once bitten, twice shy." Behind almost every dog or cat phobia, there's a bite or scratch. *****

"Practice makes perfect." Even the brain-injured can often learn new material with sufficient repetition. ****

"Misery loves company." Depressed people often shun company, which unfortunately is part of the problem. **

"Two heads are better than one." Teams or groups typically produce better solutions than individuals do. ****

"Cold hands, warm heart." Cold hands, poor circulation. See your physician. *

"Every cloud has a silver lining." Not really, but therapy techniques like cognitive restructuring can get you to think so, and that can get you through the day. ***

"Old habits die hard." When we fail at a task, we tend to resort to old behavior patterns, even those from childhood. ****

"You can't teach an old dog new tricks." You'll feel better, think more clearly, and may even live longer if you keep learning throughout life. **

"Familiarity breeds contempt." People tend to like what's familiar. *

"Blood will tell." For better or worse, genes really do set limits on both physical characteristics and behavior. ****

"A woman's place is in the home." Only when artificial barriers keep her there. *

"When the cat's away, the mice will play." Kids and employees tend to slack off when their parents or supervisors are out of sight. ****

"There's no accounting for tastes." Until you look at upbringing, biochemistry, evolutionary influences, and so on. **

So boys will indeed be boys (and, by implication, girls will be girls). But this is only true "on average." Male and female traits overlap considerably, which means that a particular male could be more emotional than most females and a particular female could be better at math than most males. To be fair, you have to go case by case.

Early to Bed, and Early to Rise, Makes a Man Healthy, Wealthy, and Wise

This proverb, often attributed to Ben Franklin, actually seems to have originated in the late 1400s, and Franklin may have lifted it from a collection of adages published in 1656. Historical trivia aside, research on sleep suggests that the proverb gives sound advice—but only because our culture is out-of-synch with the biology of nearly half the population.

Here's how it works: it's long been known that the body has natural rhythms. Those that occur on a 24-hour cycle are called "circadian" and include cycles of temperature change, wakefulness, and eating. For most people, these cycles are highly resistant to change. This much you probably have heard, but what you might not know is that there are two distinctly different circadian rhythm patterns. "Larks"—who show what researchers call "morningness" (honest!)—are people whose cycles peak early in the day. Not surprisingly, larks awaken early and start the day strong. "Owls"—people inclined toward "eveningness"—peak late in the day. In both cases, the peaks are associated with better performance on memory tasks, quicker reaction times, heightened alertness, and cheerful moods. Some people are extreme larks or owls, others are moderates, and a few fit neither category.

There's a problem here, especially if, like me, you're an extreme owl. The trouble is that many important human activities—business meetings, job interviews, weddings, classes, and so on—are conducted during daylight hours, when larks have a distinct advantage. Not surprisingly, owls spend much of their time griping about how out-of-synch they seem to be.

A 1978 study of college students by Wilse B. Webb, Ph.D., and Michael H. Bonnet, Ph.D., of the University of Florida, paints a grim picture for people like me: "Larks reported waking up when they expected to, waking up feeling more rested, and waking up more easily than the owls." Larks also reported having "fewer worries" and getting "more adequate sleep," and they awakened feeling physically better than owls. The differences were even greater, moreover, when owls tried to adapt to the lark sleep pattern. What's more, these problems can impair not only owls' sense of restedness but also their bank account; a study of Navy personnel suggests that people who sleep well make considerably more money than people who sleep poorly.

The long and short of it is that if your biorhythms allow you easily to "go to bed with the lamb and rise with the lark" (another old proverb), you may indeed end up with more money, better health, and more life satisfaction—but only because your internal clock is more in-synch with the stock exchange.

Spare the Rod and Spoil the Child

A recent headline in my local newspaper proclaimed, "Spanking Backfires, Latest Study Says." I cringe when I see stories like this, because I believe they ultimately harm many children. People have come to confuse discipline with "abuse," which is quite a different beast. "Discipline"—whether in the form of "time outs," reprimands, or spankings—is absolutely necessary for parenting. Extensive research by psychologist Diana Baumrind, Ph.D., and others, has shown that permissive parenting produces children who can't handle independence and are unable to behave in a socially responsible manner. A great many social problems that we face today may be the inadvertent product of a generation of well-meaning, misinformed, overly-permissive parents.

However, if all you provide is discipline, without affection and emotional support—the "authoritarian" parenting style—you can damage your children. Offspring of authoritarian parents tend to be hostile and defiant, and, like the victims of permissive parents, they too have trouble with independence.

The most effective parenting style involves both a high level of discipline and ample affection and support. That's the best approach for producing children who are self-reliant, socially responsible, and successful in their own relationships, research shows.

In a recent anti-spanking study, published in 1997 by University of New Hampshire sociologist Murray Straus, Ph.D., children between the ages of 6 and 9 who were spanked more than three times a week displayed more misbehavior two years later. Doesn't this show that spanking causes misbehavior? Not at all. Correlational studies are difficult to interpret. Perhaps without those spankings, the kids would have been even worse off. It's also possible that many of these spankings were unnecessary or excessive, and that it was this inappropriate discipline that sparked the later misbehavior.

Conversely, at lest eight studies with younger kids show that spanking can indeed improve behavior. The age of the child, in fact, is probably important. Children under the age of six seem to regard spanking as a parent's right. But older kids may view it as an act of aggression, and in such cases spanking's effects may not be so benign.

Punishment, verbal or physical, applied in moderation and with the right timing, is a powerful teaching tool. It should not be the first or the only tool that a parent uses, but it has its place.

Truth à la Carte

But what about the restaurant debate? Does absence make the heart grow fonder or not? Alas, not enough research has been conducted to shed much light on this question. We do know that "out of sight, out of mind" is true when we're fresh from the womb; young babies will behave as if a toy has vanished into thin air when the toy is moved out of sight. But our memories quickly improve. Research conducted by Julia Vormbrock, Ph.D., and others, shows that children grow more fond of their caregivers when they're separated from them—at least for a few days. After two weeks of separation, however, most children become "detached," reports Vormbrock.

Psychologist Robert Pelligrini, Ph.D., once asked 720 young adults about separation, and two-thirds said that "absence makes the heart grow fonder" seemed more true than "out of sight, out of mind." A poll, however, doesn't tell us much about the truth of the matter. To settle things, we'll need an experiment. Hmmm. First we'll need 100 couples, whom we'll give various tests of "fondness." Then we'll assign, at random, half of the couples to a Control Group and half to an Absence Group. Next we'll separate the partners in each couple in our Absence Group by, say, 1,000 miles for six months—somehow providing jobs, housing, and social support for every person we relocate. Finally, we'll re-administer our fondness tests to all 100 couples. If we find significantly greater levels of fondness in the separated couples than in the unseparated couples, we'll have strong support for the idea that absence makes the heart grow fonder.

Any volunteers? What? You would never subject yourself to such an absurd procedure? Well, fortunately, no one would ever conduct such research, either.

Discussion Questions

1. Why is folk wisdom unreliable?

2. What are the physical effects of confession according to James W. Pennebaker?

3. What is the exception to the rule that too much work is harmful?

4. What are two typical circadian rhythm patterns? Which type is most advantageous, and why?

5. What is the most effective parenting style, and why?

6. Think of a proverb that you know and design an experiment that you think would be able to test the validity of that proverb.

The **Think-*Drink*** Effect

◆ *G. Alan Marlatt and Damaris J. Rohsenow*

We know him and try to avoid him at parties: the fellow who after a few drinks suddenly turns into a pawing letch or a would-be Sugar Ray. The belief that people become sexually aroused or aggressive after drinking is deeply entrenched, so much so that we suspect the lout at the party is just using alcohol as an excuse. He's not really that far gone.

Before reading on, ask yourself what your own beliefs are about how alcohol affects you. Does it make you feel more sociable and extroverted, or more withdrawn? Do you believe alcohol makes you feel more relaxed? More or less sexually aroused? More prone to angry outbursts?

We now have the first solid evidence that psychological processes have as much—or more—to do with some drinking behaviors than do the physical effects of alcohol. In a series of experiments with a unique "balanced placebo" design, psychologists have shown that people will act in certain stereotypical ways when they drink, even if they are drinking tonic water but have been told they are drinking vodka and tonic. In other words, the think-drink effect is as dramatic as a placebo's seemingly miraculous curative power.

The studies strongly suggest that cognitive processes—our beliefs about how people are supposed to act when drinking—influence our reactions to alcohol in ways we have previously failed to acknowledge. For example:

◆ Men who believe they have been drinking alcohol become less anxious in social situations even when they have not been drinking the real thing. Women, strangely, become more anxious. But both types of response are determined by expectations (beliefs, hopes, and fears) about what happens when people drink.

◆ Many experts believe alcoholics develop a craving for liquor after just one or two drinks because a small amount of alcohol triggers a physiologically based addictive mechanism. However, studies show alcoholics experience the same craving after one or two placebo drinks. Even more surprising, alcoholics report little or no craving when they are given drinks containing alcohol that they believe are non alcoholic.

◆ Men become more aggressive in laboratory situations when they are drinking only tonic but believe that it contains vodka. They also become relatively less aggressive when they think they are drinking only tonic water, even though their drinks actually contain vodka.

◆ Men also tend to become more sexually aroused when they believe they are drinking the real thing—even when they're not. Women report feeling more aroused when they believe they have been drinking alcohol, but curiously, a measure of their vaginal blood flow shows that they are physically becoming less aroused.

Mental Set and Setting

Observers of various drug subcultures have frequently mentioned the role played by expectancy (mental set) and situational factors (setting) in a "high." Andrew Weil, in his pioneering book *The Natural Mind,* suggested that marijuana users did not need the substance to get high. "Pharmacologists do not understand," Weil wrote, "that all psychoactive drugs are really active placebos since the psychic effects arise from consciousness, elicited by set and setting, in response to physiological cues. Thus, for most marijuana users, the occasion of smoking a joint becomes an opportunity or excuse for experiencing a mode of consciousness that is available to everyone all the time, even though many people do not know how to get high without using a drug."

Because of our exposure to drinking models presented both in real life and in the media, we have come to expect that people will sometimes do things under the influence of alcohol that they would never do otherwise. Alcohol is frequently consumed in relaxed, convivial settings in which sexual advances, for example, are appropriate. In this sense, alcohol acts as a cue for sexual behavior. The cue effects are the same regardless of the pharmacological properties of alcohol, as long as the people in-

© 1998 PhotoDisc, Inc.

volved believe they are really drinking liquor.

Very little attention was paid to mental set and setting in early investigations of alcohol and other drug use by humans. Traditional placebo-drug studies were not able to isolate the pharmacological effects of a drug that were independent of expectancy. In a typical experiment, subjects were divided into two groups: expect drug/receive drug and expect drug/receive placebo. Since expectations could pay a part in both of the conditions—all subjects expected the real drug—the chemical effects alone could not be measured with any certainty.

John Carpenter of Rutgers University first suggested the use of an "anti-placebo" procedure, in which both the placebo and the active drug could be administered under conditions in which the subject expects to receive an inert substance. Thus the traditional two-group design was expanded in the 1960s to include four alternatives: expect drug/receive drug; expect drug/receive placebo; expect placebo/receive drug; and expect placebo/receive placebo. Using this balanced-placebo method, investigators for the first time could separate out the inde-

pendent effects of psychological processes (beliefs about whether the substance ingested is active or inert) from the pharmacological properties of the drug (whether it is actually active).

In the early 1970s, researchers in our lab at the University of Wisconsin and another group at Western Michigan University independently rediscovered the balanced-placebo design and applied it to studies of drinking. In these experiments, we have tried to control not only for the subjects' expectancies but for possible investigator biases. To prevent the researcher from subtly influencing the results, we have employed a double-blind strategy in which neither the researcher nor his subjects know who is drinking alcohol and who is not until the data have been compiled.

We tried to choose a drink for our studies that most people would already be familiar with, but one that could not easily be distinguished from a placebo drink. Pilot testing revealed that drinkers could tell a mixture of one part vodka to five parts tonic water with no more than 50 percent accuracy, or chance odds. (The method works best when drinks are chilled and a squirt of lime juice is added, both of which make it harder to detect the vodka taste.) Most of the studies reviewed employed these beverages.

We also had an ethical dilemma to resolve. The balanced-placebo design requires that some subjects drink alcohol after being told they will be given a nonalcoholic drink. But informed consent dictates that they know they may be drinking alcohol since it may affect their physical and psychological functioning. Accordingly, we informed all subjects beforehand that they might be receiving alcohol as part of the procedure. Later on, an assistant of the researcher's tells each that he or she has been randomly assigned to either the group that

will receive vodka or the group that will not; at this stage of the study, of course, some subjects are being deceived.

At the time that we first employed this strategy, the teams at Wisconsin and Western Michigan were both investigating the so-called loss-of-control drinking of alcoholics. According to many authorities, the alcoholic has great difficulty in stopping after one or two drinks. Just a little alcohol is enough to trigger an addictive mechanism that produces craving and an involuntary "loss of control," or inability to moderate further drinking, from this point of view. (Thus, most treatment programs insist upon total abstinence.)

If it is true that alcoholism is a purely physical addiction, then behavioral therapy and other approaches to training the alcoholic to drink moderately are doomed to failure. It was thus essential to test this proposition. We asked a

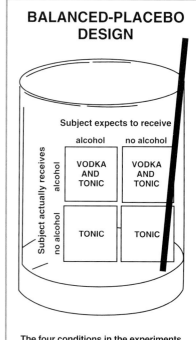

BALANCED-PLACEBO DESIGN

	Subject expects to receive	
	alcohol	no alcohol
Subject actually receives — alcohol	VODKA AND TONIC	VODKA AND TONIC
no alcohol	TONIC	TONIC

The four conditions in the experiments. The expect-no-alcohol/receive-alcohol condition is uniquely able to isolate purely physiological effects of alcohol on behavior.

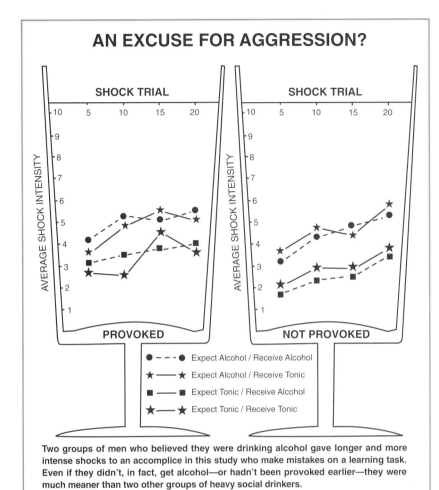

AN EXCEPTION FOR AGGRESSION?

Two groups of men who believed they were drinking alcohol gave longer and more intense shocks to an accomplice in this study who make mistakes on a learning task. Even if they didn't, in fact, get alcohol—or hadn't been provoked earlier—they were much meaner than two other groups of heavy social drinkers.

group of male alcoholics and a matched set of social drinkers to participate in a "taste-rating task" in which they would compare the taste properties of either alcoholic or nonalcoholic beverages. The alcoholic men in the study consisted of volunteers who had resumed drinking after leaving a hospital-treatment program for alcoholism. What we were really trying to measure in the experiment was the impact of expectancy on how much both groups would drink and whether alcoholics would drink more than social drinkers in the expect-alcohol condition.

We divided the 32 social drinkers and 32 alcoholics into the four conditions of the balanced-placebo method (see chart above). Subjects in the two expect-alcohol conditions were led to believe they would be comparing three brands

of vodka, while those in the two expect-no-alcohol groups were told they would be comparing three brands of tonic water. Three full decanters were placed in front of each subject, who was then instructed to sample them on an ad-lib basis in order to make his ratings. Half the subjects in the expect-alcohol condition were actually given vodka and tonic; half of those in the expect-no-alcohol condition also received vodka and tonic. The rest of the subjects were given tonic water.

The results showed that expectancy was the main influence on the total amount consumed by both social drinkers and alcoholics. Subjects who thought they were sampling decanters with vodka and tonic drank significantly more (and later estimated that their drinks contained more alco-

hol than they actually did) than did subjects who expected only tonic water—regardless of the actual presence or absence of alcohol in their drinks.

For some of the alcoholic subjects the effects were striking. Since our volunteers were required to abstain from alcohol for at least eight hours prior to their appointment in the lab (and had to show a zero reading on our breath-analysis test to prove their sobriety), some of them arrived with the "shakes" and reported craving alcohol. After the drinking session, one of the men in the expect-alcohol/receive-tonic condition began acting in an intoxicated manner, stumbling around the room and trying to make a date with our female research assistant. Several other men in the expect-tonic/receive-vodka group still showed tremor and described a strong desire for alcohol, even after consuming the equivalent of double vodkas.

Aggression

Using the balanced-placebo design, experimenters have also shown that people's beliefs about drinking have a lot to do with some drinkers' aggressive behavior. That there is a link between alcohol consumption and aggressiveness has been well established by previous studies. But investigators have offered two competing explanations. The first proposes that an aggressive drive exists in human beings but that its expression is normally inhibited by anxiety, guilt, or social restraints. Alcohol is assumed to disinhibit the aggressive motivation, presumably by its effect on the higher cortical centers and a corresponding reduction in fear about the consequences of aggression.

The second explanation assumes that alcohol has an overall energizing effect on the general activity level of the organism and that drinking will increase the probability of aggressive fantasies and expression of "power needs."

A third theory, neglected by researchers but familiar from our opening example, suggests that alcohol may provide a culturally accepted excuse for engaging in behaviors that are normally unacceptable—including aggression.

The one balanced-placebo study published so far supports this alternative explanation. In the experiment conducted by Alan Lang and others from our research team, 96 men who were described as heavy social drinkers were given either plain tonic or vodka and tonic (to a blood-alcohol concentration of .10 percent, the legal limit of intoxication in most states), and each was given one of two sets of instructions (expect-alcohol or expect-no-alcohol), in accord with the balanced-placebo design. After drinking their beverages, half of the 96 subjects were purposely provoked by a confederate of the experimenters posing as another subject, who criticized the real subjects' performance on a difficult task of physical coordination by making series of sarcastic and belittling remarks. The other half were not provoked. As a way of measuring aggressiveness, all were asked to engage in a learning experiment in which they were able to give shocks of varying intensity and duration to the same confederate when he made mistakes on a decoding task. (As in other such experiments, the confederate appeared to be pained but was not actually receiving the shocks.)

The results (see the chart on previous page) were clear-cut. Both provoked and unprovoked men who believed they had consumed alcohol were more aggressive—that is, gave shocks that were significantly more intense and of longer duration to the con-

federate than did those who believed what they had been drinking was tonic water—regardless of the actual content of the drinks. On the other hand, we also found that expectancy had little to do with a person's reaction time. In the aggression task, we also measured how long each of the men took to respond to the confederate's responses on the decoding task. Regardless of expectancy, those who consumed alcohol were significantly slower in responding to the confederate's signals.

Two experiments identical in design show, however, that whether alcohol stimulates or calms the drinker, expectancy plays a large role.

This finding suggests that expectancies have a strong influence only when people have well-defined beliefs about the effects of alcohol. It is likely that many of us already have fixed beliefs about how alcohol influences social behavior, while we may have few or no set expectations about how it affects such things as reaction time.

Anxiety

Research on the relationship between anxiety and drinking is more contradictory. Most studies have been aimed at testing the notion that alcohol reduces tension, possibly by depressing or tranquilizing the nervous system. Drinking is thus reinforced—further encouraged—by the release from tension. This theory and its corollary, that people drink more when they are anxious, have become part of the cultural folklore about alcohol.

Previous studies have shown every possible result, some supporting the tension-reduction theory and others showing that alcohol may, under certain cir-

cumstances, increase arousal or tension. Two experiments identical in design show, however, that whether alcohol stimulates or calms the drinker, expectancy plays a large role.

Terence Wilson and David Abrams at Rutgers University investigated the effect of alcohol on social anxiety and physiological arousal in both males and females. Their experiments used the balanced-placebo design. In the first study, Wilson and Abrams gave men who were moderate social drinkers a drink containing tonic or vodka and tonic, with instructions either to expect alcohol or to expect no alcohol. To test social anxiety, they asked the men to try to make a favorable impression on a woman who was an accomplice of the researchers and offered the men little encouragement.

Previous research had established that heart rate is a reliable way to identify people who are anxious in social situations. Wilson and Abrams found that men who believed they had been drinking liquor (whether they had or not) tended to have slower heart rates when trying to impress the woman than did the men who thought they had drunk only tonic water. In other words, the men who thought they were drinking vodka were less anxious than the others.

A group of women had exactly the opposite reaction in a follow-up study. The women became more aroused, not calmer, but again, expectancy shaped their response. This experiment was identical to the one Wilson and Abrams did with men (the women were asked to try to impress a male confederate who acted cool toward them). In this situation, the women who were told they were drinking alcohol had significantly faster heart rates, along with increased skin conductivity—both signs of increased anxiety—than the women who thought they were drinking just tonic.

There are two possible explanations for their reactions. The women in the study had less drinking experience than the men did and may thus have been more wary about the effect of alcohol on their behavior. In fact, several of them commented that they felt the need to monitor their behavior closely after drinking; unlike the men, they may have been anxious about their ability to exert self-control after drinking, or they may have felt that the male confederate would disapprove of their drinking as "unfeminine." These findings highlight the fact that women generally have different past experiences with alcohol and therefore have different expectancies about the effects of drinking.

Sexual Arousal

The effects of alcohol on human sexual arousal have been debated for centuries. No less an authority of human behavior than Shakespeare wrote that drinking "provokes the desire, but it takes away the performance" (*Macbeth*, Act II, Scene 3). Ogden Nash expressed a more contemporary view: "Candy is dandy/But liquor is quicker." The verdict of behavioral scientists so far differs for the sexes: men seem to be physically turned on by alcohol, while women are turned off. But again, both responses may be determined by beliefs about drinking.

Three studies of men have been conducted using the balanced-placebo design. In the first two studies, a strain gauge was used to measure penile tumescence (which has proven a more reliable measure of arousal than self-report). In the first experiment, Terence Wilson and David Lawson assigned male social drinkers to one of the two expectancy conditions, in which they were led to believe they were drinking either vodka

© 1998 PhotoDisc, Inc.

and tonic or tonic only. To convince them of what they had been drinking, all were given accurate or false information on blood-alcohol levels after a breath-analysis test. Then, all the subjects watched films that portrayed both heterosexual and homosexual scenes.

Alcohol itself had no effect on tumescence. But men who believed they had consumed vodka became significantly more aroused watching the films, in comparison with those who thought they were drinking only tonic—regardless of the actual alcohol content of the drinks.

In a second study, Daniel Briddell and his colleagues at Old Dominion University replicated these results, but with a twist. In this experiment, male subjects were exposed to taped materials that depicted heterosexual intercourse or deviant activities such as rape or aggression. Oddly, the men who believed they were drinking alcohol were significantly more aroused by deviant sexual stimuli than those who thought what they were drinking was nonalcoholic. But there was no significant difference in arousal in response to the

tape portraying normal sex.

Finally, in a third study conducted by Alan Lang, now at Florida State University, male subjects, after drinking their beverages, viewed erotic slides that varied in sexual content and were then asked to rate how stimulating they were. They rated the slides as more sexually stimulating if they believed they had been drinking alcohol, whether there was vodka in the drink or not. This effect was most pronounced for men who had high scores on a sex-guilt inventory. Taken together with the results showing greater arousal to deviant sexual stimuli by men who believed they had consumed alcohol, Lang's findings suggest that men whose normal sexual response is inhibited by sexual guilt or social restraints will show the greatest disinhibition effect when they believe they are drinking alcohol. There is an important personal payoff in this process, since the men can absolve themselves of responsibility for their actions by blaming alcohol for their disinhibited behavior.

Most people suspect that men and women differ in their expectancies about the effects of alcohol on sexual responsiveness. These differences were clearly demonstrated in research conducted by Wilson and Lawson, who did a study with women that was similar in design to the one they had done with men. After receiving their drinks and instructions in accordance with the balanced-placebo design, the women viewed films with heterosexual and homosexual activity or one with neutral content. Each woman's sexual arousal was monitored physiologically by the use of a photoplethysmograph, a device that assesses changes in vaginal blood flow. In this case, the two groups of women who actually drank alcohol showed significantly reduced sexual arousal during the film regardless of whether they *believed* they were drinking alcohol. However in this and in a related study, women who believed they had been drinking alcohol generally gave self-reports indicating increased arousal.

Thus women who think they have been drinking experience sexual arousal subjectively—but not objectively. Expectations do not seem to play a role in their actual physical response. Wilson and Lawson offer a number of possible explanations for the differing male and female reactions. They speculate that women may simply be more vulnerable to the physical effects of alcohol and/or have had different past drinking experiences than men. It also seems possible that women may be less accurate than men in interpreting signs of sexual arousal that arise from within their own bodies. Men, on the other hand, may have stronger beliefs about alcohol's effect on enhancing sexual arousal and/or may exert greater voluntary control over their sexual arousal.

Mood and Motor Abilities

We cannot say, of course, that alcohol itself has no impact at all on our minds and bodies apart from our beliefs about it. It clearly does. With more complicated motor and cognitive behaviors, studies show little or no effects of expectancy (as in memory tests or other complex cognitive tasks). Research conducted by investigators at Vanderbilt University showed that when one group of subjects was asked to perform a pursuit rotor task (a demanding test of motor coordination) 30 minutes after drinking alcoholic or placebo drinks, their performance was significantly impaired only when

> *Research has shown, for example, that the effect of drinking on mood is very different depending on whether the drinker is alone or is interacting with others in a social situation.*

they had consumed alcohol. However, on a second test in which subjects had to divide their attention between two complex cognitive tasks, both those who believed they were drinking alcohol and those who were actually drinking it made more errors than other subjects. Thus, in this task, the subjects' motor performances were disrupted by a belief that alcohol had been consumed as well as by actual consumption of alcohol.

Again, the existence of strong prior beliefs about the effects of alcohol may underlie these findings. Most people would seem to be relatively uncertain about how alcohol affects specific motor abilities. Furthermore, other research suggests that when people expect to perform a complicated task after drinking alcohol (such as driving a car home from a party), they will attempt to compensate for whatever loss of skill may ensue by devoting extra care and attention to the task.

The studies also suggest that expectancy effects are strongest for behaviors that are believed to be positive or desirable for the drinker, like reduced anxiety, increased assertiveness, or behaviors that are associated with some form of immediate gratification, such as sexual or aggressive acting-out. On the other hand, making errors in carrying out a complicated cognitive or motor act (driving, for example) would not be considered desirable, and drinking would thereby not exert the same reinforcing effect with these behaviors.

Expectancy effects seem to be relatively weak or absent altogether for the mood states that accompany drinking. In balanced-placebo studies, people have been asked to report their feelings on mood checklists both before and after drinking. Moderate and heavy drinkers have reported some changes in mood after actually drinking alcohol—they may get happier, say, or more depressed—but expectancy manipulations exert little or no effect in these experiments. The studies, by their very nature, may make it easier for people to see through the balanced-placebo deception. Since subjects are asked to be introspective, to closely monitor their feelings, they may also notice subtle physical changes (or their absence) that are usually associated with alcohol consumption.

Setting factors also exert an important influence on alcohol's effect on mood states, further complicating the interpretation of these findings. Research has shown, for example, that the effect of drinking on mood is very different depending on whether the drinker is alone or is interacting with others in a social situation. Solitary drinkers describe the effects of alcohol primarily in terms of physical symptoms (feeling dizzy or numb), in contrast with drinkers in the social setting, who describe the effects as psychological or interpersonal in nature (feeling more extraverted or friendly), even though the same amount of alcohol is consumed by all subjects.

It is clear from this research, all of which has been conducted within the past decade, that cognitive processes exert a powerful influence on our drinking behavior—both in the beliefs that we hold about the expected effects of alcohol and the attributions we make about alcohol as an agent that enhances certain behaviors or "disinhibits" the expression of others. More than 25 published studies that use the balanced-placebo design have replicated the expectancy effect with a variety of social and affective responses that were previously thought to be influenced primarily by the physiological or chemical properties of alcohol itself. Considerable research needs to be done in order to identify the underlying mechanisms of the placebo effects we have described in this article.

Early indications suggest that classical conditioning may play a role in this process: just as Pavlov's dogs learned to salivate at the sound of a bell that had been previously associated with a food reward, so the experienced drinker may achieve a conditioned high when presented with the signal or cue properties (sight, smell, taste, and so on) of a drink, regardless of whether the drink actually contains alcohol.

In addition, another important component would seem to be the attributions we make about alcohol as the "cause" of certain behaviors ("I wasn't myself..."). The ingestion of alcohol itself seems to produce little more than an indefinite or ambiguous physiological reaction, an amorphous change in mood, at least at the dose levels most social drinkers are accustomed to. The interpretation or "framing" of this diffuse reaction appears to be more influenced by our prior beliefs, the drinking environment, and personal payoffs than by the physical effects of alcohol. ◆

Discussion Questions

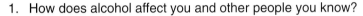

1. How does alcohol affect you and other people you know?

2. Do you think that your behavior could be influenced merely by the belief and not from the alcohol itself? Why or why not?

3. Describe the balanced-placebo research design? Why, according to the authors, is this superior to the traditional placebo design?

4. Even the balanced-placebo design may falsely suggest a placebo effect for alcohol. Please explain.

5. What did this article suggest about the belief that alcoholism is a purely physical addiction?

6. What are the three explanations for increased aggression resulting from consumption of alcohol? Which one is supported by this research?

7. If this study were mandatory reading for all college freshmen, do you think it would change their drinking behavior? Would it change their beliefs about the effects of drinking? Why or why not?

Exercises

Name: _____

Date: _____

Part 2: Psychological Methods

1. I have frequently experienced the placebo effect.

Agree   (1)   (2)   (3)   (4)   (5)   Disagree

2. I have observed the placebo effects of alcohol on friends or family members.

Agree   (1)   (2)   (3)   (4)   (5)   Disagree

3. I live by certain proverbs or adages and believe they are true.

Agree   (1)   (2)   (3)   (4)   (5)   Disagree

List three of your own favorite proverbs or axioms—ones that you live by and believe to be true. Then design an experiment to test the validity of each proverb.

You are head of the Federal Drug Administration, and you have been called to testify before Congress about anti-depressants. You have evidence that these medications are effective primarily as placebos, and some people are insisting that you ban their sale. What is your testimony?

PART 3
BIOLOGY UNDERLYING BEHAVIOR

◆ **⑧ A Love Affair with the Brain: A Conversation with Marian Diamond**

◆ **⑨ Right Brain, Left Brain: Fact and Fiction,** by Jerre Levy

◆ **⑩ My Genes Made Me Do It,** by Stanton Peele and Richard DeGrandpre

New psychology students are often surprised to learn—and sometimes *alarmed* to learn—that psychologists study biological mechanisms like the sense organs and the brain and that they are sometimes concerned with genetic and evolutionary determinants of behavior. Isn't that what *biologists* do? Don't psychologists just listen to people who lay on sofas talking about their problem?

Clinical psychologists spend most of their time counseling patients, but *experimental* psychologists conduct a wide variety of research to try to *understand* behavior, both normal and abnormal, in all its aspects. What we do and think and feel is determined by what we've learned in life ("nurture") and also by our genes and the physical systems that underlie behavior ("nature"). So psychology as a comprehensive science of behavior overlaps with biology quite a bit, and many psychologists call themselves *biopsychologists* or *neuroscientists* for that reason.

The first article in this section is an informative interview with neuroscientist Marian Diamond of the University of California at Berkeley, whose pioneering studies with rats have shown how remarkably responsive brain anatomy can be to environmental influences. Enriched environments, for example, increase the complexity of tissue in the area of the brain that governs thinking (the "cortex"), and impoverished or stressful environments can shrink critical areas of the brain.

The next article, "Right Brain, Left Brain: Fact and Fiction," by biopsychologist Jerre Levy, is especially important. Levy debunks one of the most well-entrenched myths of our time: that the two halves of our brain perform radically different functions and that people can learn to "use" one side or the other. In fact, the two halves of our brain are connected by a rather large structure called the *corpus callosum*, the hemispheres function together continuously, and one certainly cannot learn to "use " one side or the other. The popular assertions that creativity or language are located exclusively in one hemisphere or the other are without merit. Alas, "pop psych"—the informal psychological teachings espoused by literature and the media—is often out-of-sync with the real science, and no one has yet found a way to solve this problem.

Finally, in "My Genes Made Me Do It," psychologists Stanton Peele and Richard DeGrandpre offer a balanced, reasoned approach to what is often called the nature-nurture controversy. We sometimes attribute human characteristics (e.g., aggression or schizophrenia or intelligence) exclusively to heredity or environment, or we assign percentages to the contributions each has made. But *all* human characteristics are the joint result of *both* heredity and environment; it's misleading to say they make separate contributions. I find it helpful to think about their relationship this way: Genes set limits on what we can be; they create a *range of reaction*, larger for some characteristics (like weight or aggressiveness) and smaller for other characteristics (like height or schizophrenic illness). But where we end up in that range is determined by our experience.

A Love Affair *with the* **Brain:**

A CONVERSATION WITH

Marian *Diamond*

◆ *Janet L. Hopson*

Janet L. Hopson: Many people would have been shocked at seeing a disembodied brain, and yet it fascinated you. Why?

Marian Diamond: It's because that mass of protoplasm has the capacity to think. We still don't understand what thinking is. But to this day, it fascinates me when I meet people and I imagine the brains inside their skulls. No other organ can store information for 100 years to the degree the brain can. With the intricacies and original creation of ideas that come from the human brain, it is unquestionably the most esoteric functional mass on Earth.

Hopson: When you began trying to change an animal's brain by changing its environment, did most biologists believe such changes were possible?

Diamond: No. The general conception in the 1960s, and of course before, was that the brain did not change—that it was a stable structure—and after it developed, it retained its size and eventually decreased. Nutritionists, for example, never included the head in their studies because they felt the brain was so stable.

Hopson: Considering that background, wasn't it a somewhat radical notion to look for environmentally induced changes?

Diamond: There's actually a logical history behind it. Back in the 1920s, Richard Tryon, of the University of California at Berkeley, noticed that some rats ran mazes

better than other rats. He bred those rats and developed a "maze-bright" strain of rats. Almost 35 years later, it was David Krech and Melvin Calvin of Berkeley, walking in the hills of Norway one day, who wondered, "If the rats run mazes differently, could their brain chemistry be different?" Krech came back to California and, working with Mark Rosenzweig and Edward Bennett, showed that there was a chemical difference between these strains of rats.

Hopson: How did you get involved in this work?

Diamond: I was at Cornell in the late 1950s and read their paper in *Science*. I thought, that's what I've

---

The human brain is unquestionably the most esoteric functional mass on earth.

---

been waiting for! I came out and joined the team, and this whole enrichment project grew out of that original brain chemistry experiment. Since there was a chemical difference, we wondered whether you could change that chemistry and structure by designing the environment a different way.

Hopson: And you found that you could?

Diamond: Yes. We found that by placing young rats in an enriched environment, we could change the chemistry and structure of the outer layers of the brain, the cor-

tex. After autopsies, we could actually measure an increase in cortical thickness. We later learned we could bring about such changes in only four days.

Hopson: How did you know how to enrich a rat's environment?

Diamond: Donald Hebb in Montreal pioneered the idea of an enriched environment with a bigger cage and playmates. Then you added almost anything—wheels, ladders, blocks—any object the animals can explore. They climb on them, sniff them, crawl under them, explore with their whole sensory mechanism.

Hopson: Why does exploring lead to an enlarged cortex?

Diamond: We really don't know what the crucial factors are in inducing the changes. But we know that the cortical thickening is not just the result of a motor response, because if the animals are placed in running wheels alone, they do not experience the cortical change.

Hopson: What does thickening the cortex actually mean?

Diamond: See that picture over there with all the dots? That is one square millimeter of brain tissue that we've blown up to poster size so we can count the cells and find out if a particular area is changing in cortical depth. If it is, we find that the neurons have increased in area but not in number. The glial, or support, cells have divided. The dendrites have grown. There is an increase in dendritic spines. And the post-synaptic thickening has increased in length. So, in other words, every part of the nerve cell has enlarged, and there has been an increase in the number of support cells.

Hopson: Is there proof that rats with cortical thickening are any smarter?

Diamond: They've been exposed to mazes in many laboratories, and they do run a better maze.

Hopson: Are there measures other than maze running?

OF RATS AND CAGES

If you want your rats to have bigger brains, raise them in a fancy cage with a lot of friends and toys to play with. The enriched condition (cage at far right) contains three mothers with three pups each and a variety of toys for them to explore and play with. The impoverished condition consists of one mother with her three pups living in a smalll cage with no toys.

Diamond and her colleagues find that the cerebral cortex of the brains of rats raised in the enriched cages is as much as 16 percent thicker than that of rats from the impoverished environment. This transverse section of a rat brain shows the areas of the cerebral cortex that are measured for thickness.

CEREBRAL CORTEX   HIPPOCAMPAL REGION

Diamond: Most researchers measure rat intelligence with maze running—perhaps it's a limitation of us investigators, but maze running does give you a baseline to compare with other rats, and other researchers can know exactly how well the enriched rats have done.

Hopson: What was the impact of your enrichment work?

Diamond: The new idea that the brain is measurably responsive to the environment has been applied with brain-injured people, giving us more hope for the recovery of brain function. And it's helped us to understand the potential of early training. Some teachers and school principals have even told me that it changed their whole view of education.

Hopson: After "enriched rats" grow up and reproduce, do their pups have larger brains?

Diamond: We've been studying this question recently, and we found that rat pups from the enriched parents have increased body weight at birth, but the cortex does not show significant change. Then we wondered if we would see cortical differences when those pups grew up. And we did!

Hopson: Were the pups kept in a standard cage?

Diamond: Yes—no direct enrichment. But their brains were still bigger as adults. We're up to the third generation and the brains are still enlarged, all because the pups coming from enriched parents have greater body weights. We've got the data and how we have to figure out what they mean.

Hopson: And now you are studying brain changes in aging rats?

Diamond: Yes. We are giving the same type of environment to older animals and taking the same type of measurements. We are looking for a normal development and aging curve.

Hopson: And what have you found?

Diamond: We worked with extremely old animals. We kept them in a standard cage until they were 766 days old.

Hopson: What would that be in human years?

Diamond: The rat has the potential to live 1,000 days, and the human being has the potential to live 100 years. So at 766 days, when we moved some rats to enriched environments, we were three-quarters of the way through the animals' lives. We added to this experiment the fact that we held the animals as we changed their cages and gave them a little tender loving care. We found that when they were exposed to an enriched environment between 766 and 904 days of age, even these very old rats showed thickening of the cerebral cortex.

Hopson: Is there a connection between longevity and enrichment?

Diamond: Actually, there was a peculiar incident at 900 days. We lost one of the enriched animals, and then in the next three days we lost two more. Yet none of the animals in the control group—the ones we kept in standard cages—had died. We decided to stop the experiment right then and there. And we asked ourselves, "Why did we start losing them in the enriched condition?" My son, who is an architect and interested in housing for the elderly, finds that many of these people find group living stressful. They like some isolation, but they also like the opportunity to come together when they want to. So in our next aging experiment, we'll have a community playroom for the enriched rats but also have radiating side rooms with isolation compartments.

Hopson: You've shown that the cortex can thicken even in old rats, and yet there is a common belief that we lose brain cells as we age.

Diamond: In a nonenriched environment, the normal rat brain does decrease in size with age, but it is not necessarily losing brain cells. It is just the dendrites coming down so the cells get more compact.

Hopson: "Coming down"?

Diamond: When I lecture, I show my hand—my palm is the cell body and my fingers are the dendrites. With use, you can keep those dendrites out there, extended, but without stimulation, they shrink down. It's quite simple: You use it or lose it.

Hopson: What are the implications of this work on the aging brain?

Diamond: For researchers, I think it's terribly important that they pay attention to how they house their animals. So much of aging research is done on isolated animals. Is this normal aging? Until they have stimulating environments, it's not necessarily the normal lifestyle span of the animal. For peo-

ple's lives, I think we can take a more optimistic view of the aging brain.

Hopson: What would enrichment be for an older person?

Diamond: That depends on the individual, since no two human brains are alike Some people like to do crossword puzzles. Some go back to school. Some like to visit neighbors. The main factor is stimulation. The nerve cells are designed to receive stimulation. And I think curiosity is a key factor. If one maintains curiosity for a lifetime, that will surely stimulate neural tissue and the cortex may in turn respond.

Hopson: Is there any way to determine the effects of environment on the size and structure of a person's brain?

Diamond: I think some day we will have better records than we do today on the health of the indi-

---

I found that people who use their brains don't lose them.
It was that simple.

---

vidual—mental health as well as physical health—and when we get the human brains in the laboratory, we'll be able to correlate the structure and function with the environment people had.

Hopson: Would that involve doing some kind of brain anatomy?

Diamond: Very definitely. That's what all these file folders are—bits of data on human brains.

Hopson: Where did those brains come from?

Diamond: People donate their brains—it's a form of immortality, because everything we learn from their brains is imbedded in somebody else's brain. So many people are willing to donate their brains. It is amazing. I'll be in a bookstore and somebody will say, "I've heard that you don't have enough female brains. Would you like

mine? Let's have tea and discuss it." I was out to dinner just the other night with people who asked if I would like their brains. And there is a musician in Santa Cruz who wants me to have his brain when he dies because he is convinced it is different from those of nonmusicians.

Hopson: I understand you did a series of interviews of active elderly people.

Diamond: Yes. I looked for people who were extremely active after 88 years of age. I found that the people who use their brains don't lose them. It was that simple. These people were interested in their professions even after retirement. They kept healthy bodies. They drank milk and ate an egg each day—that was one common denominator that goes against the prevailing thought today. And other denominators were activity, and love of life and love of others and being loved. Love is very basic.

Hopson: Did you learn anything from the interviews that gives you ideas for future directions?

Diamond: I think we need to combat the negative attitude towards the aged, the idea that they can't learn and that we must keep retiring them. I prefer to think of retirement as changing, going in another direction, not removing yourself from life or work altogether.

I was asked to speak at Bell Labs recently. I went hoping that by knowing the potential of the brain to be active at any age, they would treat the older workers with greater dignity. I think it is absolutely essential. And then, to phase them out gradually without losing their potential instead of stopping all these marvelous people at the peak of their careers. To provide dignity at any age is our goal.

Hopson: There's another area of your work with important human implications—the structural difference between male and female brains. Could you summarize those studies?

Diamond: Essentially, we've found that in the male rat, the right hemisphere—that is, the right cerebral cortex—is thicker than the left. We find that it's this way at birth and continues throughout the lifetime of the animals.

Hopson: Do you know why the male shows dominance of the right cortex?

Diamond: We truly wish we knew. We decided to ask the obvious, "How does testosterone, the male hormone, influence the development of one particular side?" So we took the testes out of rats at birth and waited for three months. We found that the anterior two-thirds of the cortex reversed, and developed greater left dominance, but that the posterior one-third remained right-greater-than-left. So it appears that the male's posterior or visual-spatial cortex is what we might call "hard-wired." It's not as easily influenced by the testosterone as is the rest. That surprised us.

Hopson: Why?

Diamond: Because, in the female, we find that the left cortex is significantly thicker than the right. And if we remove the female rat's ovaries at birth, her whole cortex shifts to right dominance over left, especially in the visual-spatial area. In other words, she gets a male pattern. We thought if we took out the testes in males, we'd get a complete reversal to the other picture, but we didn't.

Hopson: Are the right-left differences true for other parts of the brain?

Diamond: If you look at the hippocampus, which we're doing right now, we find that in the male, it is 8 percent greater on the right side than on the left at birth, but it drops to a nonsignificant level of difference later in life. In the female, the left side of the hippocampus is greater than the right, and when she becomes sexually mature, that difference becomes strongly evident. What we're finding is not only that dendrites and thickness change in the cortex, but that brain symmetry patterns change at different stages in the lives of males and females.

Hopson: Would there be an evolutionary advantage to these male-female brain differences?

Diamond: Well, let's consider the female. We autopsied mother rats right after they had given birth, and found that during pregnancy their cortex had grown. And not only mothers raised in enriched environments: Even in females from impoverished environments, the cortex had grown. It would make sense, in evolutionary terms, for the female to be at her optimum behavioral capacity during and after pregnancy. It would help her to prepare for and protect her young.

Hopson: What do these rat brain differences mean for our understanding of human behavior?

Diamond: The results provide baselines for studies on human brains. Several studies show that men are more visually and spatially oriented and women more language oriented. But of course we all know that there are excellent female architects and men who are linguists. There are ranges in basic patterns of behavior as well as changes due to the environment. Men and women will have more tolerance for each other as we learn about our brain similarities and differences.

Hopson: You have also written about a connection between the cortex and the immune system. Aren't female mammals considered to have a more active immune system?

Diamond: Yes, and they have the larger left cortex. A group of French researchers has just found evidence that the left cortex is involved with controlling the immune system.

Hopson: You have suggested that breast cancer may be a model for this.

Diamond: Yes, I think there are reasons to believe that in some individuals breast cancer may develop from six to eight months after severe emotional distress. I was losing my friends and relatives with stress followed by breast cancer, and after five of them in a row, I saw a possible connection.

Hopson: If people know they've had a period of stress, what could they do to prevent a problem later?

Diamond: If the immune system is controlled by the cortex, biofeedback might help. It gets back to Norman Cousins and his theory of laughter and healing. So many people have a common-sense notion that if you have a positive attitude about your body and your life, you're not subject to disease. And the minute you get a negative attitude toward them, disease somehow begins to manifest itself. People have spoken in generalities about this, and we're trying to find a mechanism.

Hopson: What is next in your professional future?

Diamond: I'd like to write up 20 years of research on environmental effects on the brain. We've got file cabinets filled with data that haven't been touched—I'd just take a leave of absence and bring it all together.

Hopson: How about your personal future? What do you hope to be doing by age 88?

Diamond: Eighty-eight is a long way off. And right now, I'm just trying to keep up with my work, be a decent professor. But I'm sure I'll still be learning, teaching and creating somewhere, somehow—perhaps learning more about how the brain can continue to improve our environment, not only how the environment improves the brain.   ◆

Discussion Questions

1. What is an "enriched environment"?

2. How does an enriched environment influence nerve cells and the support cells of the brain?

3. What are the age ranges during which an enriched environment can be effective?

4. Is the phrase, "You can't teach an old dog new tricks," correct? Why or why not.

5. What is the main physical difference between female and male brains?

6. Regardless of environment, what does pregnancy do to the brains of female rats?

7. Why do women have stronger immune systems than men do?

8. As a parent, how would you manipulate the environment to promote brain development in your children? List at least three ways and explain how each might help.

9. List the activities you would engage in throughout life that would help to maintain or increase your brain power.

Right Brain, **Left** Brain:

FACT AND FICTION

◆ *Jerre Levy*

I guess I'm mostly a right-brain person...my left side doesn't work long enough for me to figure it out," concludes a character in a *Frank and Ernest* cartoon. "It's tough being a left-brained person...in a right-brained world, " moans a youngster in the cartoon *Wee Pals*, after perusing a tome on the "psychology of consciousness."

The notion that we are "left brained" or "right brained" has become entrenched in the popular culture. And, based on a misinterpretation of the facts, a pop psychology myth has evolved, asserting that the left hemisphere of the brain controls logic and language, while the right controls creativity and intuition. One bestselling book even claimed to teach people how to draw better by training the right brain and bypassing the left. According to the myth, people differ in their styles of thought, depending on which half of the brain is dominant. Unfortunately, this myth is often represented as scientific fact. It is not.

As a researcher who has spent essentially her whole career studying how the two hemispheres relate to one another and to behavior, I feel obliged to set the record straight on what is known scientifically about the roles of the hemispheres. As it turns out, the brain's actual organization is every bit as interesting as the myth and suggests a far more holistic view of humankind.

People's fascination with relating mental function to brain organization goes back at least to Hippocrates. But it was René Descartes, in the 17th century, who came up with the notable and influential notion that the brain must act as a unified whole to yield a unified mental world. His specific mental mapping was wrong (he concluded that the pineal gland—now known to regulate biological rhythms in response to cycles of light and dark—was the seat of the soul, or mind). But his basic premise was on the right track and remained dominant until the latter half of the 19th century, when discoveries then reduced humankind to a half-brained species.

During the 1860s and 1870s, Paul Broca, a French neurologist, and Karl Wernicke, a German neurologist, reported that damage to the left cerebral hemisphere produced severe disorders of language, but that comparable damage to the right hemisphere did not. Neurology was never to be the same.

Despite their generally similar anatomies, the left and right cerebral hemispheres evidently had very different functions. Language appeared to be solely a property of the left side; the right hemisphere, apparently,was mute. The scientific world generalized this to conclude that the left hemisphere was dominant not only for language but for all psychological processes. The right hemisphere was seen as a mere relay station. Since each

half of the brain is connected to and receives direct input from the opposite side of the body, the right hemisphere was needed to tell the left hemisphere what was happening on the left side of space and to relay messages to muscles on the body's left side. But the right hemisphere was only an unthinking automaton. From pre-19th century whole-brained creatures, we had become half-brained.

From the beginning, there were serious difficulties with the idea that the left hemisphere was the seat of humanity and that the right hemisphere played no role in thinking. In the 1880s, John Hughlings Jackson, a renowned English neurologist, described a patient with right-hemisphere damage who showed selective losses in certain aspects of visual perception—losses that did not appear with similar damage of the left hemisphere. He suggested that the right hemisphere might be just as specialized for visual perception as the left hemisphere was for language.

From the 1930s on, reports began to confirm Hughlings Jackson's findings. Patients with right-side damage had difficulties in drawing, using colored blocks to copy designs, reading and drawing maps, discriminating faces and in a variety of other visual and spatial tasks. These disorders were much less prevalent or serious in patients with left-himisphere damage.

The investigators, quite aware of the implications of their findings, proposed that although the left hemisphere was specialized for language, the right hemisphere was specialized for many nonlinguistic processes. Nonetheless, these were voices in the wilderness, and their views hardly swayed the general neurological community. Until 1962, the prevalent view was that people had half a thinking brain.

Beginning in the early 1960s, Nobel prize winner Roger W. Sperry and his colleagues and stu-

Funny But Fallacious

Frank and Ernest

I GUESS I'M MOSTLY A RIGHT-BRAIN PERSON... MY LEFT SIDE DOESN'T WORK LONG ENOUGH FOR ME TO FIGURE IT OUT.

THAVES

© 1998 Tom Thaves

dents demonstrated certain unusual characteristics in patients who, to control intractable epileptic seizures, had undergone complete surgical division of the corpus callosum, the connecting bridge between the two sides of the brain. These patients, like split-brain animals that Sperry had studied, couldn't communicate between the cerebral hemispheres. An object placed in the right hand (left hemisphere) could be named readily, but one placed in the left hand (nonverbal right hemisphere) could be neither named nor described. But these same patients could point to a picture of the object the left hand had felt. In other words, the right hemisphere knew what it felt, even if it could not speak.

Outside the laboratory, the split-brain patients were remarkably normal, and within the laboratory, each cerebral hemisphere seemed to be able to perceive, think and govern behavior, even though the two sides were out of contact. In later split-brain studies, a variety of tasks were devised to examine the specialized functions of each hemisphere. These showed that the right hemisphere was superior to the left in spatial tasks but was mute and deficient in verbal tasks such as decoding complex syntax, short-term verbal memory and phonetic analysis. In brief, the split-brain studies fully confirmed the inferences drawn from the ear-

lier investigations of patients with damage to one hemisphere.

These findings were further expanded by psychologist Doreen Kimura and others, who developed behavioral methods to study how functions of the hemispheres differed in normal people. These involved presenting visual stimuli rapidly to either the left or right visual fields (and the opposite hemispheres). Normal right-handers were more accurate or faster in identifying words or nonsense syllables in the right visual field (left hemisphere) and in identifying or recognizing faces, facial expressions of emotion, line slopes or dot locations in the left visual field (right hemisphere).

Another method was "dichotic listening," in which two different sounds were presented simultaneously to the two ears. The right ear left hemisphere) was better at identifying nonsense syllables, while the left ear (right hemisphere) excelled at identifying certain nonverbal sounds such as piano melodies or dog barks.

By 1970 or soon thereafter, the reign of the left brain was essentially ended. The large majority of researchers concluded that each side of the brain was a highly specialized organ of thought, with the

right hemisphere predominant in a set of functions that complemented those of the left. Observations of patients with damage to one side of the brain, of split-brain patients and of normal individuals yielded consistent findings. There could no longer be any reasonable doubt: The right hemisphere, too, was a fully human and highly complex organ of thought.

It was not long before the new discoveries found their way into the popular media and into the educational community. Some mythmakers sought to sell the idea that human beings had neither the whole and unified brain described by Descartes, nor the half brain of Broca and Wernicke, but rather two brains, each devoted to its own tasks and operating essentially independently of the other. The right hemisphere was in control when an artist painted a portrait, but the left hemisphere was in control when the novelists wrote a book. Logic was the property of the left hemisphere, whereas creativity and intuition were properties of the right. Further, these two brains did not really work together in the same person. Instead, some people thought primarily with the right hemisphere, while others thought primarily with the left. Finally, given the presumed absolute differences between hemispheres, it was claimed that special subject matters and teaching strategies had to be developed to educate one hemisphere at a time, and that the standard school curriculums only educated the "logical" left hemisphere.

Notice that the new two-brain myth was based on two quite separate types of scientific findings. First was the fact that split-brain patients showed few obvious

> *A myth:
> the left hemisphere
> controls logic
> and language,
> the right controls
> creativity and intuition.*

© 1998 PhotoDisc, Inc.

symptoms of their surgery in everyday life and far greater integrity of behavior than would be seen if two regions within a hemisphere had been surgically disconnected. Thus, it was assumed that each hemisphere could be considered to be an independent brain.

Second, a great deal of research had demonstrated that each hemisphere had its own functional "expertise," and that the two halves were complementary. Since language was the specialty of the left hemisphere, some people concluded that any verbal activity, such as writing a novel, depended solely on processes of the left hemisphere. Similarly, since visual and spatial functions were the specialties of the right hemisphere, some people inferred that any visuospatial activity, such as painting portraits, must depend solely on processes of that hemisphere. Even if thought and language were no longer synonymous, at least logic and language seemed

to be. Since intuitions, by definition, are not accessible to verbal explanation, and since intuition and creativity seemed closely related, they were assigned to the right hemisphere.

Based, then, on he presumed independent functions of the two hemispheres, and on the fact that they differed in their specializations, the final leap was that different activities and psychological demands engaged different hemispheres while the opposite side of the brain merely idled along in some unconscious state.

The two-brain myth was founded on an erroneous premise: that since each hemisphere was specialized, each must function as an independent brain. But in fact, just the opposite is true. To the extent that regions are differentiated in the brain, they must integrate their activities. Indeed, it is precise-

In the late 19th century we went from being whole-brained creatures to half-brained.

ly that integration that gives rise to behavior and mental processes greater than and different from each region's special contribution. Thus, since the central premise of the mythmakers is wrong, so are all the inferences derived from it.

What does the scientific evidence actually say? First, it says that the two hemispheres are so similar that when they are disconnected by split-brain surgery, each can function remarkably well, although quite imperfectly.

Second, it says that superimposed on this similarity are differences in the specialized abilities of each side. These differences are seen in the contrasting contributions each hemisphere makes to all cognitive activities. When a person reads a story, the right hemisphere may play a special role in decoding visual information, maintaining an integrated story structure, appreciating humor and emotional content, deriving meaning from past associations and understanding metaphor. At the same time, the left hemisphere plays a special role in understanding syntax, translating written words into their phonetic representations and deriving meaning from complex relations among word concepts and syntax. But there is no activity in which only one hemisphere is involved or to which only one hemisphere makes a contribution.

Third, logic is not confined to the left hemisphere. Patients with right-hemisphere damage show more major logical disorders than do patients with left-hemisphere damage. Some whose right hemisphere is damaged will deny that their left arm is their own, even when the physician demonstrates its connection to the rest of the body. Though paralyzed on the left side of the body, such patients will often make grandiose plans that are im-

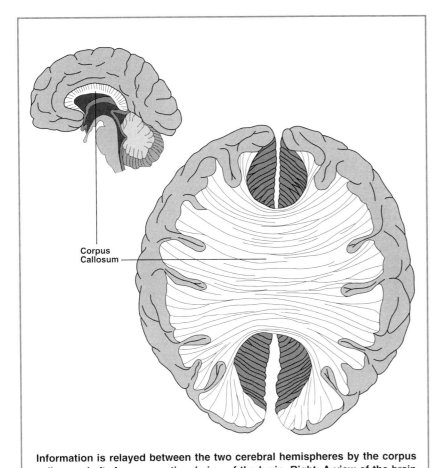

Information is relayed between the two cerebral hemispheres by the corpus callosum. Left: A cross-sectional view of the brain. Right: A view of the brain from above, with the gray matter removed.

Finally, what of individual differences? There is both psychological and physiological evidence that people vary in the relative balance of activation of the two hemispheres. Further, there is a significant correlation between which hemisphere is more active and the relative degree of verbal or spatial skills. But there is no evidence that people are purely "left brained" or "right brained." Not even those with the most extremely asymmetrical activation between hemispheres think only with the more activated side. Rather, there is a continuum. The left hemisphere is more active in some people, to varying degrees, and verbal functioning is promoted to varying degrees. Similarly, in those with a more active right hemisphere, spatial abilities are favored. While activation patterns and cognitive patterns are correlated, the relationship is very far from perfect. This means that differences in activation of the hemispheres are but one of many factors affecting the way we think.

In sum, the popular myths are misinterpretations and wishes, not the observations of scientists. Normal people have not half a brain nor two brains but one gloriously differentiated brain, with each hemisphere contributing its specialized abilities. Descartes was, essentially, right: We have a single brain that generates a single mental self.

possible because of paralysis and will be unable to see their lack of logic.

Fourth, there is no evidence that either creativity or intuition is an exclusive property of the right hemisphere. Indeed, real creativity and intuition, whatever they may entail, almost certainly depend on an intimate collaboration between hemispheres. For example, one major French painter continued to paint with the same style and skill after suffering a left-hemisphere stroke and loss of language. Creativity can remain even after right-hemisphere damage. Another painter, Lovis Corinth, after suffering right-hemisphere damage, continued to paint with a high level of skill, his style more expressive and bolder than before. In the musical realm, researcher Harold Gordon

found that in highly talented professional musicians, both hemispheres were equally skilled in discriminating musical chords. Further, when researchers Steven Gaede, Oscar Parsons and James Bertera compared people with high and low musical aptitude for hemispheric asymmetries, high aptitude was associated with equal capacities of the two sides of the brain.

Fifth, since the two hemispheres do not function independently, and since each hemisphere contributes its special capacities to all cognitive activities, it is quite impossible to educate one hemisphere at a time in a normal brain. The right hemisphere is educated as much as the left in a literature class, and the left hemisphere is educated as much as the right in music and painting classes.

Discussion Questions

1. Who developed the idea that the brain worked as one entire entity?

2. Which side of the brain is most specialized for language?

3. Which perception is most specialized in the right side of the brain?

4. What part of the brain connects the two hemispheres?

5. Explain the events that led to the belief that the brain was two separate organs.

6. Do split-brain people function normally? Why or why not?

7. List all of the activities to which only one side of the brain contributes.

8. What type of brain dominance do the best musicians have?

9. What's wrong with the popular notion about the left-brain/right-brain distinction?

My *Genes* Made Me Do *IT*

◆ *Stanton Peele and Richard DeGrandpre*

Just about every week now, we read a newspaper headline about the genetic basis for breast cancer, homosexuality, intelligence, or obesity. In previous years, these stories were about the genes for alcoholism, schizophrenia, and manic-depression. Such news stories may lead us to believe our lives are being revolutionized by genetic discoveries. We may be on the verge of reversing and eliminating mental illness, for example. In addition, many believe, we can identify the causes of criminality, personality, and other basic human foibles and traits.

But these hopes, it turns out, are based on faulty assumptions about genes and behavior. Although genetic research wears the mantle of science, most of the headlines are more hype than reality. Many discoveries loudly touted to the public have been quietly refuted by further research. Other scientifically valid discoveries—like the gene for breast cancer—have nonetheless fallen short of initial claims.

Popular reactions to genetic claims can be greatly influenced by what is currently politically correct. Consider the hubbub over headlines about a genetic cause for homosexuality and by the book *The Bell Curve*, which suggested a substantial genetic basis for intelligence. Many thought the discovery of a "gay gene" proved that homosexuality is not a personal choice and should therefore not lead to social disapproval. *The Bell Curve*, on the other hand, was attacked for suggesting differences in IQ measured among the races are inherited.

The public is hard pressed to evaluate which traits are genetically inspired based on the validity of scientific research. In many cases, people are motivated to accept research claims by the hope of finding solutions for frightening problems, like breast cancer, that our society has failed to solve. At a

> **At a personal level, people wonder about how much actual choice they have in their lives. Accepting genetic causes for their traits can relieve guilt about behavior they want to change, but can't.**

personal level, people wonder about how much actual choice they have in their lives. Accepting genetic causes for their traits can relieve guilt about behavior they want to change, but can't.

These psychological forces influence how we view mental illnesses like schizophrenia and depression, social problems like criminality, and personal maladies like obesity and bulimia. All have grown unabated in recent decades. Efforts made to combat them, at growing expense, have made little or no visible progress. The public wants to hear that science can help, while scientists want to prove that they have remedies for problems that eat away at our individual and social well-being.

Meanwhile, genetic claims are being made for a host of ordinary and abnormal behaviors, from addiction to shyness and even to political views and divorce. If who we are is determined from conception, then our efforts to change or to influence our children may be futile. There may also be no basis for insisting that people behave themselves and conform to laws. Thus, the revolution in thinking about genes has monumental consequences for how we view ourselves as human beings.

The Human Genome Project

Today scientists are mapping the entire genome—the DNA contained in the 23 human chromosomes. This enterprise is enormous. The chromosomes of each person contain 3 billion permutations of four chemical bases arrayed in two interlocking strands. This DNA may be divided into between 50,000 and 100,000 genes. But the same DNA can function in more than one gene, making the concept of individual genes something of a convenient fiction. The mystery of how these genes, and the chemistry underlying them, cause specific traits and diseases is a convoluted one.

The Human Genome Project has, and will continue to, advance our understanding of genes and suggest preventive and therapeutic strategies for many diseases. Some diseases, like Huntington's, have been linked to a single gene. But the search for single genes for complex human traits, like sexual orientation or antisocial behavior, or mental disorders like schizophrenia or depression, is seriously misguided.

Most claims linking emotional disorders and behaviors to genes are *statistical* in nature. For example, differences in the correlations in traits between identical twins (who inherit identical genes) and fraternal twins (who have half their genes in common) are examined with the goal of separating the role of environment from that of genes. But this goal is elusive. Research finds that identical twins are treated more alike than fraternal twins. These calculations are therefore insufficient for deciding that alcoholism or manic-depression is inherited, let alone television viewing, conservatism, and other basic, everyday traits for which such claims have been made.

The Myth of Mental Illness

In the late 1980s, genes for schizophrenia and manic-depression were identified with great fanfare by teams of geneticists. Both claims have now been definitively disproved. Yet, while the original announcements were heralded on TV news and front pages of newspapers around the country, most people are unaware of the refutations.

In 1987, the prestigious British journal *Nature* published an article linking manic-depression to a specific gene. This conclusion came from family linkage studies, which search for gene variants in suspect sections on the chromosomes of families with a high incidence of a disease. Usually, an active area of DNA (called a genetic marker) is observed to coincide with the disease. If the same marker appears only in diseased family members, evidence of a genetic link has been established. Even so, this does not guarantee that a gene can be identified with the marker.

One genetic marker of manic-depression was identified in a single extended Amish family. But this marker was not apparent in other families that displayed the disorder. Then, further evaluations placed several members of the family without the marker in the manic-depressive category. Another marker detected in several Israeli families was subjected to more detailed genetic analysis, and a number of subjects were switched between the marked and unmarked categories. Ultimately, those with and without the putative markers had similar rates of the disorder.

Other candidates for a manic-depression gene will be put forward. But most researchers no longer believe a single gene is implicated, even within specific families. In fact, genetic research on manic-depression and schizophrenia has rekindled the recognition of the role of environment in emotional disorders. If distinct genetic patterns can't be tied to the disorders, then personal experiences are most likely crucial in their emergence.

Epidemiologic data on the major mental illnesses make it clear that they can't be reduced to purely genetic causes. For example, according to psychiatric epidemiologist Myrna Weissman, Ph.D., Americans born before 1905 had a 1 percent rate of depression by age 75. Among Americans born a half century later, 6 percent become depressed by age 24! Similarly, while the average age at which manic-depression first appears was 32 in the mid 1960s, its average onset today is 19. Only social factors can produce such large shifts in incidence and age of onset of mental disorders in a few decades.

Genes and Behavior

Understanding the role of our genetic inheritance requires that we know how genes express themselves. One popular conception is of genes as templates stamping out each human trait whole cloth. In fact, genes operate by instructing the developing organism to produce sequences of biochemical compounds.

In some cases, a single, dominant gene *does* largely determine a given trait. Eye color and Huntington's disease are classic examples of such Mendelian traits (named after the Austrian monk, Gregor Mendel, who studied peas). But the problem for behavioral genetics is that complex human attitudes and behavior—and even most diseases—are not determined by single genes.

Moreover, even at the cellular level, environment affects the activity of genes. Much active genetic material does not code for any kind of trait. Instead it regulates the speed and direction of the expression of other genes; it modulates the unfolding of the genome. Such regulatory DNA reacts to conditions inside and outside the womb, stimulating different rates of biochemical activity and cellular growth. Rather than forming a rigid template for each of us, most genes form part of a lifelong give-and-take process with the environment.

> *Genetic research on manic-depression and schizophrenia has rekindled the recognition of the role of environment in emotional disorders.*

The inextricable interplay between genes and environment is evident in disorders like alcoholism, anorexia, or overeating that are characterized by abnormal behaviors. Scientists spiritedly debate whether such syndromes are more or less biologically driven. If they are mainly biological—rather than psychological, social, and cultural—then there may be a genetic basis for them.

Therefore, there was considerable interest in the announcement of the discovery of an "alcoholism gene" in 1990. Kenneth Blum, Ph.D., of the University of Texas, and Ernest Noble, M.D., of the University of California, Los Angeles, found an allele of the dopamine receptor gene in 70 percent of a group of alcoholics—these were cadavers—but in only 20 percent of a non-alcoholic group. (An allele is one form of gene.)

The Blum-Noble discovery was broadcast around the country after being published in the *Journal of the American Medical Association* and touted by the AMA on its satellite news service. But, in a 1993 *JAMA* article, Joel Gelernter, M.D., of Yale and his colleagues surveyed all the studies that examined this allele and alcoholism. Discounting Blum and Noble's research, the combined results were that 18 percent of non-alcoholics, 18 percent of problem drinkers, and 18 percent of severe alcoholics *all* had the allele. There was simply no link between this gene and alcoholism!

Blum and Noble have developed a test for the alcoholism gene. But, since their own data indicate that the majority of people who have the target allele are not alcoholics, it would be foolhardy to tell those who test positive that they have an "alcoholism gene."

The dubious state of Blum and Noble's work does not disprove that a gene—or set of genes— could trigger alcoholism. But scientists already know that people do not inherit loss-of-control drinking whole cloth. Consider this: Alcoholics do not drink uncontrollably when they are unaware that they are drinking alcohol—if it is disguised in a flavored drink, for example.

A more plausible model is that genes may affect how people ex-

perience alcohol. Perhaps drinking is more rewarding for alcoholics. Perhaps some people's neurotransmitters are more activated by alcohol. But although genes can influence reactions to alcohol, they cannot explain why some people continue drinking to the point of destroying their lives. Most people find orgasms rewarding, but hardly any engage in sex uncontrollably. Rather, they balance their sexual urges against other forces in their lives.

Jerome Kagan, Ph.D., a Harvard developmental psychologist, was speaking about more than genes when he noted, "we also inherit the human capacity for restraint."

Of (Fat) Mice and Men

Public interest was aroused by the 1995 announcement by Rockefeller University geneticist Jeffrey Friedman, M.D., of a genetic mutation in obese mice. The researchers believe this gene influences development of a hormone that tells the organism how fat or full it is. Those with the mutation may not sense when they have achieved satiety or if they have sufficient fatty tissue, and thus can't tell when to stop eating.

The researchers also reported finding a gene nearly identical to the mouse obesity gene in humans. The operation of this gene in humans has not yet been demonstrated, however. Still, professionals like University of Vermont psychologist Esther Rothblum, Ph.D., reacted enthusiastically: "This research indicates that people really are born with a tendency to have a certain weight, just as they are to have a particular skin color or height."

Actually, behavioral geneticists believe that less than half of total

Rather than forming a rigid template for each of us, most genes form part of a lifelong give-and-take process with the environment.

weight variation is programmed in the genes, while height is almost entirely genetically determined. Whatever role genes play, America is getting fatter. A survey by the Center for Disease Control found that obesity has increased greatly over the last 10 years. Such rapid change underlines the role of environmental factors, like the abundance of rich foods, in America's overeating. The CDC has also found that teens are far less physically active than they were even a decade ago.

Certainly people metabolize food differently and some gain weight more easily than others. Nonetheless, anyone placed in a food-rich environment that encourages inactivity will gain weight, whatever fat genes the person has. But, in nearly all environments, highly motivated people can maintain lower weight levels. We thus see that social pressure, self-control, specific situations—even seasonal variations—combine with physical make-up to influence diet and determine weight.

Accepting that weight is predetermined can relieve guilt for overweight people. But people's belief that they cannot control their weight can itself contribute to obesity. No test will ever be performed that can tell you how much you must weigh. Personal choices will always influence the equation. And anything that inspires positive efforts at weight control can help people lose weight, or avoid gaining more.

The case of obesity—along with schizophrenia, depression, and alcoholism—raises a striking paradox. At the same time that we now view these conditions as diseases that should be treated medically, their prevalence is growing precipitously. The very reliance on drugs and other medical treatments has created a cultural milieu that seeks external solutions for these problems. Relying on external solutions may itself be exacerbating matters; it may be teaching us a helplessness that is at the root of many of our problems. Instead of reducing the incidence of these problems, this seems to have fueled their growth.

Harnessing Discoveries

In 1993, the gene that determines the occurrence of Huntington's disease, an irreversible degeneration of the nervous system, was discovered. In 1994, a gene was identified that leads to some cases of breast cancer. Utilizing these discoveries, however, is proving more difficult than anticipated.

Finding a gene for breast cancer was cause for elation. But of all of the women with breast cancer, only a tenth have family histories of the disease. Furthermore, only half of this group has the gene mutation. Scientists also hoped that breast cancer victims without family histories would show irregularities at this same site on the DNA. But only a small minority do.

The section of the DNA involved in inherited breast cancers is enormously large and complex. There are probably several hundred forms of the gene. The task of determining which variations in the DNA cause cancer, let alone developing therapies to combat the disease, is tremendous. Right now, women who learn that they have the gene defect know they have a high (85 percent) likelihood of developing the disease. But the only decisive response available to them is to have their breasts removed before the disease appears. And even this does not eliminate the possibility of cancer.

The failure to translate genetic discoveries into treatments has also been true for Huntington's disease. Scientists have been unable to detect how the flawed gene switches on dementia and palsy. These difficulties with a disease created by an individual gene

show the monumental complexity involved in unraveling how genes determine human traits.

When a distinct gene is not involved, linking genes to traits may well be an absurdity. Any possible link between genes and traits is exponentially more complex with elaborate behavior patterns like over drinking, personality characteristics like shyness or aggressiveness, or social attitudes such as political conservatism and religiousness. Many genes might be involved in all such traits. It is impossible to separate the contributions environment and DNA make to attitudes and behaviors.

Behavioral Genetics: Methods and Madness

The research discussed so far searches for genes implicated in specific problems. But research relating behavior and genetics rarely involves actual examination of the genome. Instead, psychologists, psychiatrists, and other non geneticists calculate a heritability statistic by comparing the similarity in behaviors among different sets of relatives. This statistic expresses the old nature-nurture division by representing the percentage of a behavior due to genetic inheritance versus the percentage due to environmental causes.

Such research purports to show a substantial genetic component to alcoholism. For example, some studies have compared the incidence of alcoholism in adopted children with that of their adoptive parents and with their natural parents. When the similarities are greater between the offspring and absent biologic parents, the trait is thought to be highly heritable.

But children are often adopted by relatives or people from the same social background as the parents. The very social factors related to placement of a child—particularly ethnicity and social class—are also related to drinking

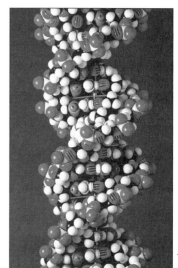

© 1998 PhotoDisc, Inc.

problems, for example, thus confusing efforts to separate nature and nurture. A team led by University of California sociologist Kaye Fillmore, Ph.D., incorporated social data on adoptive families in the reanalysis of two studies claiming a large genetic inheritance for alcoholism. Fillmore found that the educational and economic level of the receiving families had the greater influence, statistically erasing the genetic contribution from the biological parents.

Another behavioral genetics methodology compares the prevalence of a trait in monozygotic (identical) twins and dizygotic (fraternal) twins. On average, fraternal twins have only half their genes in common. If the identical twins are more alike, it is believed that genetic inheritance is more important, because the two types of twins are supposedly brought up in identical environments. (To eliminate the confounding influence of gender differences, only same-sex fraternal twins are compared.)

But if people treat identical twins more similarly than they treat fraternal twins, the assumptions of the heritability index dissolve. Much research shows that physical appearance affects how parents, peers, and others react to a child. Thus, identical twins—who more closely resemble one another—will experience a more similar environment than fraternal twins. University of Virginia psychologist Sandra Scarr, Ph.D., has shown that fraternal twins who resemble one another enough to be *mistaken* for identical twins have more similar personalities than other such twins.

Heritability figures depend upon a number of factors, such as the specific population being studied and where. For example, there will be less variation in weight in a food-deprived environment. Studying the inheritance of weight in deprived settings rather than an abundant food environment can greatly influence the heritability calculation.

Heritability figures in fact vary widely from study to study. Matthew McGue, Ph.D., and his colleagues at the University of Minnesota calculated a zero heri-tability of alcoholism in women, while at the same time a team led by Kenneth Kendler, M.D., at Virginia Medical College calculated a 60 percent heritability with a different group of female twins! One problem is that the number of female alcoholic twins is small, which is true of most abnormal conditions we study. As a result, the high heritability figure Kendler's team found would be reduced to nothing with a shift in the diagnoses of as few as four twins.

Shifting definitions also contribute to variations in the heritability measured for alcoholism. Alcoholism may be defined as any drinking problems, or only physiological problems such as DTs, or various combinations of criteria. These variations in methodology explain why heritability figures for alcoholism in different studies vary from zero to almost 100 percent!

The Inheritance of Homosexuality

In the debate over homosexuality, the data supporting a genetic basis are similarly weak. One study by Michael Bailey, Ph.D., a Northwestern University psychologist, and Richard Pillard, M.D., a psychiatrist at Boston University, found that about half the identical twins (52 percent) of homosexual brothers were homosexual themselves, compared with about a quarter (22 percent) of fraternal twins of homosexuals. But this study recruited subjects through ads in gay publications. This introduces a bias toward the selection of overtly gay respondents, a minority of all homosexuals.

Moreover, other results of their study do not support a genetic basis for homosexuality. Adopted brothers (11 percent) had as high a "concordance rate" for homosexuality as ordinary brothers (9 percent). The data also showed that fraternal twins were more than twice as likely as ordinary brothers to share homosexuality, although both sets of siblings have the same genetic relationship. These results suggest the critical role of environmental factors.

One study that focused on a supposed homosexual gene was conducted by Dean Hamer, Ph.D., a molecular biologist at the National Cancer Institute. Hamer found a possible genetic marker on the X chromosome in 33 of 40 brothers who were both gay (the number expected by chance was 20). Earlier Simon LeVay, M.D., a neurologist at the Salk Institute, noted an area of the brain's hypothalamus that was smaller among gay than heterosexual men.

Although both these findings were front-page stories, they provide quite a slender basis for the genetics of homosexuality. Hamer did not check for the frequency of the supposed marker in heterosexual brothers, where it could conceivably be as prevalent as in gay siblings. Hamer has noted that he doesn't know how the marker he found could cause homosexuality, and LeVay likewise concedes he hasn't found a brain center for homosexuality.

But for many, the politics of a homosexual gene outweigh the science. A genetic explanation for homosexuality answers bigots who claim homosexuality is a choice that should be rejected. But to accept that non-genetic factors contribute to homosexuality does not indicate prejudice against gays. David Barr, of the Gay Men's Health Crisis, puts the issue this way: "It doesn't really matter why people are gay....What's really important is how they're treated."

Everyday Psychological Traits

By assigning a simple percentage to something very complex and poorly understood, behavioral geneticists turn heritability into a clear-cut measurement. Behavioral geneticists have employed these same statistical techniques with ordinary behaviors and attitudes. The resulting list of traits for which heritability has been calculated extends from such well known areas as intelligence, depression, and shyness to such surprising ones as television viewing, divorce, and attitudes like racial prejudice and political conservatism.

Such heritability figures may seem quite remarkable, even incredible. Behavioral geneticists report that half of the basis of divorce, bulimia, and attitudes about punishing criminals is biologically inherited, comparable to or higher than the figures calculated for depression, obesity, and anxiety. Almost any trait seemingly yields a minimum heritability figure around 30 percent. The heritability index acts like a scale that reads 30 pounds when empty and adds 30 pounds to everything placed on it!

Believing that basic traits are largely predetermined at birth

could have tremendous implications for our self conceptions and public policies. Not long ago, an announcement of a government conference, for example, suggested that violence could be prevented by treating with drugs children with certain genetic profiles. Or parents of children with an alcoholic heritage may tell the children never to drink because they're destined to be alcoholics. But such children, in expecting to become violent or drink excessively, may enact a self-fulfilling prophecy. Indeed, this is known to be the case. People who believe they are alcoholic drink more when told a beverage contains alcohol—even if it doesn't.

Believing the heritability figures developed by behavioral geneticists leads to an important conclu-

Is there a connection between the increase in depression and other emotional disorders in 20th-century America and our outlook as a society? If so, then the growing belief that our behavior is not ours to determine could have extremely negative consequences.

sion: Most people must then be overestimating how much daily impact they have on important areas of children's development. Why ask Junior to turn off the TV set if television viewing is inherited, as some claim? What, exactly, can parents accomplish if traits such as prejudice are largely inherited? It would not seem to matter what values we attempt to convey to our children. Likewise, if violence is mostly inbred, then it doesn't make much sense to try to teach our kids to behave properly.

From Fatalism to Depression

The vision of humanity generated by statistical research on be-

havioral genetics seems to enhance the passivity and fatalism many people are already saddled with. Yet evidence gathered by University of Pennsylvania psychologist Martin Seligman, Ph.D., and others indicates that "learned helplessness"—or believing one can't influence one's destiny—is a major factor in depression. The opposite state of mind occurs when people believe they control what happens to them. Called self-efficacy, it is a major contributor to psychological well-being and successful functioning.

Is there a connection between the increase in depression and other emotional disorders in 20th-century America and our outlook as a society? If so, then the growing belief that our behavior is not ours to determine could have extremely negative consequences. As well as attacking our own sense of personal self-determination, it may make us less able to disapprove of the misbehavior of others. After all, if people are born to be alcoholic or violent, how can they be punished when they translate these dispositions into action?

Jerome Kagan, whose studies provide a close-up of the interaction of nature and nurture and how it plays out in real life, worries that Americans are too quick to accept that behavior is predetermined. He has studied the temperaments of infants and children and found distinctive differences from birth—and even before. Some babies are outgoing, seemingly at home in the world. And some recoil from the environment; their nervous systems are overly excitable in response to stimulation. Do such findings mean children born with a highly reactive nervous system will grow into withdrawn adults? Will extremely fearless children grow into violent criminals?

In fact, less than half of the reactive infants (those who more frequently fret and cry) are fearful children at the age of two. It all depends on the actions parents take in response to their infant.

Kagan fears people may read too much into children's supposedly biological dispositions, and make unwarranted predictions about how they will develop: "It would be unethical to tell parents that their three-year-old son is at serious risk for delinquent behavior." People who are more fearful or fearless than average have choices about the paths their lives will take, like everyone else.

Nature, Nurture: Let's Call the Whole Thing Off

How much freedom each person has to develop returns us to the issue of whether nature and nurture can be separated. Thinking of traits as being either environmentally or genetically caused cripples our understanding of human development. As Kagan puts it, "To ask what proportion of personality is genetic rather than environmental is like asking what proportion of a blizzard is due to cold temperature rather than humidity."

A more accurate model is one in which chains of events split into further layers of possible paths. Let's return to alcoholism. Drinking produces greater mood change for some people. Those who find alcohol to serve a strong palliative function will be more likely to use it to calm themselves. For example, if they are highly anxious, alcohol may tranquilize them. But even this tranquilizing effect, we should recognize, is strongly influenced by social learning.

Among drinkers who are potentially vulnerable to alcohol's addictive effects, most will nonetheless find alternatives to drinking to deal with anxiety. Perhaps their social group disapproves of excessive drinking, or their own values strongly rule out drunkenness. Thus, although people who find that alcohol redresses their anxiety are more likely to drink addictively than others, they are not programmed to do so.

Mirror, Mirror

The goal of determining what portion of behavior is genetic and environmental will always elude us. Our personalities and destinies don't evolve in this straightforward manner. Behavioral genetics actually shows us how the statistical plumbing of the human spirit has reached its limits. Claims that our genes cause our problems, our misbehavior, even our personalities are more a mirror of our culture's attitudes than a window for human understanding and change. ◆

◆ Discussion Questions

1. Why do people want to find the answers to their problems in their genes?

2. What is a disease linked to a single gene? Has this knowledge led to a cure for this disease? Explain.

3. Why are twins used in genetic studies, and what is the difference between fraternal and identical twins?

4. Can mental illnesses be linked strictly to genetic causes? If not, what are their causes?

5. What is an allele?

6. Genetics may play some role in weight, but what plays a more important role?

7. Compare the different methods used by psychologists and geneticists to determine the relationship of genes to disorders.

8. What factors can confound the results of twin studies?

9. About 52 percent of identical twins of homosexual brothers are also homosexual. If genes was the only factor involved in gender preference, what would the percentage be?

10. Explain how behavioral geneticists have linked television viewing to genetics.

11. What is the nature-nurture controversy, and how would you resolve it?

Name: _____

Date: _____

Part 3: Biology Underlying Behavior

1. I am primarily left-brained.

   Agree   ① ② ③ ④ ⑤   Disagree

2. I believe that most human behavior is determined by heredity.

   Agree   ① ② ③ ④ ⑤   Disagree

3. With the right stimulation, brain functioning can be vastly improved.

   Agree   ① ② ③ ④ ⑤   Disagree

Design a lifestyle plan for a retirement home that might promote productiveness and intellectual maintenance for the elderly.

Design a plan for a childcare center that might promote optimal neurological development.

Are you left-brained or right-brained? What's your *evidence*? Design a plan to strengthen part of your brain that you're currently not using, and be sure to include a *test* to determine whether or not your plan has worked! (Good luck!)

Part 4

Sensation and Perception

- **①** **Phantom Limbs,** by Ronald Melzack

- **②** **Educating Your Nose,** by William S. Cain

- **③** **The Psychology of the Step Beyond: A Conversation with J.B. Rhine**

A professor I had in college insisted that sensation and perception—or "S&P," as we say in the profession—was by far the most important part of psychology. I thought this assertion was very odd. How could such an obscure area, which I had never even heard of before I took psychology courses, be so important? Over the years, I've come to have increasing respect for this somewhat esoteric branch of the field. The sense organs are, after all, our only pathways to the world outside our bodies, so experience can impact us only through our sensory systems. Even more intriguing, as a result of our experience, we *interpret* the signals that our sense organs provide; young children react to their mirror images as if they're seeing other children, but older children recognize their own reflections. In other words, we add meaning to sensation, a process called "perception."

In "Phantom Limbs," a classic article by pioneering neuroscientist Ronald Melzack, a fascinating perceptual anomaly—the apparent sensations some people continue to have after a limb has been amputated—leads to an intriguing theory of pain. In "Educating Your Nose," researcher William S. Cain suggests that our ability to discriminate odors depends on how and whether we have learned to name them—another example of how experience alters perception. Without special training, apparently, women have a keener sense of smell than men do, but here Cain reaches the surprising conclusion that men are trainable.

The last article in this section is a 1969 interview with former Duke University professor J.B. Rhine, pioneering researcher in the bizarre realm called "parapsychology," which includes both psychokinesis—the supposed ability to move objects by thought alone—and extra-sensory perception—the supposed ability to perceive events or object through sources other than the five senses. For more than 40 years, Rhine used scientific methodology to analyze parapsychological phenomena, and he claimed repeatedly to have demonstrated the existence of such phenomena. Alas, the mainstream scientific community consistently found fault with his work. See for yourself what Rhine has to say, especially about a mind-reading horse!

Phantom
Limbs

◆ *Ronald Melzack*

In 1956 I was privileged to attend the late Dr. W.K. Livingston's pain clinic at the University of Oregon Medical School. Among the patients was a Mrs. H., a remarkable woman of about 70. Because of persistent circulation problems and, finally, gangrene, she had just undergone amputation of both legs above the knees.

After the amputations, Mrs. H. could still "feel" the missing portions of her legs. At unpredictable intervals she suffered excruciating pain in both phantom limbs—intense pain that made her scream out in helpless agony.

Despite her suffering, Mrs. H. tried to maintain a happy home for her devoted husband, continued many of her household activities, and occasionally painted pictures to amuse herself. The pain persisted.

In 1958 I suggested to Mrs. H. that she try painting with a long brush strapped to one of her stumps. She soon showed remarkable talent and dexterity. Gradually her pain decreased to tolerable levels—perhaps because painting distracted her, but more likely because her use of the stump muscles evoked increased levels of sensory input.

In the majority of cases, an amputee reports feeling a phantom limb almost immediately after surgery. He describes the limb as having a definite shape. It moves through space the way a normal limb would when he walks, sits or stretches out in bed. At first the phantom limb feels perfectly normal in size and shape—so much so that the amputee may reach out for objects with a phantom hand, or try to get out of bed by stepping onto the floor with a phantom leg. Amputees also report that they can clench missing fists and even try to scratch missing fingers that itch.

As time passes, however, the limb begins to change shape. The leg or arm becomes shorter, and may even fade away altogether, so that the phantom foot or hand seems to be hanging in midair. Sometimes the limb slowly telescopes into the stump until only a hand or foot remains at the stump. Over the years the phantom may become less distinct and disappear. If the patient wears an artifi-

> *The study of phantom-limb pain can teach us much about pain in general, and it forces us to take a second look at many accepted theories of pain.*

cial limb, however, the phantom usually remains vivid and may correlate perfectly with the movement and shape of the artificial limb.

An amputee generally reports a tingling sensation in the phantom limb, but many also report other sensations, such as pins-and-needles (which we all feel when we block a limb's circulation), warmth or coldness, heaviness, and many kinds of pain.

About 30 percent of amputees report pain in phantom limbs. Fortunately the pain usually tends to decrease and eventually to disappear. In about five to 10 percent of the amputees however, the pain is severe, and may even become worse over the years. While the pain usually starts just after the surgery, sometimes it does not appear until weeks, months, or years have passed.

The pain may be occasional or continuous, but it is felt in definite parts of the phantom limb. A common complaint, for example, is that the phantom hand is clenched, fingers bent over the thumb and nails digging into the palm of the hand, so that the whole hand is tired and painful. Sometimes the pain is described as shooting, burning, or crushing.

Phantom-limb pain is more likely to develop in a patient who had pain in the limb before it was amputated. Even minor pains associated with a limb may continue. Thus, a patient who suffered from a bunion on the day that he lost his leg in an accident reported that he could still feel the bunion on the side of his phantom foot.

The study of phantom-limb pain can teach us much about pain in general, and it forces us to take a second look at many accepted theories of pain. For example, phantom-limb pain continues for more than a year after onset in about 70 percent of patients. It endures long after the injured tissues have healed, even when the stump itself is perfectly formed and not painful or sensitive.

Sometimes *trigger zones* develop—spots that, when touched, produce intense pains in the phantom limb. Trigger zones may appear in the stump, but they may also develop at distant areas such as the head or the opposite, healthy limb. Sometimes a pain in another part of the body, such as the heart, may evoke intense pain in a phantom limb, even one that in 25 years or more had never produced pain.

Once phantom-limb pain is under way, almost any kind of stimulus will make it worse. Even gentle brushing of sensitive areas can evoke severe, prolonged pain. Paradoxically, increased sensory input may sometimes bring relief. Salt solution injected into the tissue around an amputee's spine produces a sharp, localized pain that radiates into the phantom limb. It lasts only about 10 minutes yet it may produce dramatic relief for hours, weeks, sometimes indefinitely.

On the other hand, *decreasing* the sensory input is a more reliable method of relief. Local anesthetic in the stump tissues or nerves may stop the pain for days, weeks, sometimes permanently. Anesthesia can also change the pain without reducing it: one subject who had painful phantom toes said he could barely feel his toes after an injection of anesthetic into the tissues near the spine. But now he had pain in his phantom heel, a pain that persisted for more than two months.

Traditional theories of pain cannot easily explain phantom-limb pain. For example, many theorists say that pain is merely the result of stimulation of pain receptors in the skin—but they have a hard time finding pain receptors in a foot that isn't there.

These theorists may then look at the severed ends of the nerves at the stump and claim that big-toe pain is the result of stimulating the end of the pain nerve that *would* be coming from the big toe if the leg were intact. They may point out that pressure on tender neuromas, the abnormal neuron growths in

damaged nerves at the stump, can evoke severe, prolonged pain. But how can this theory explain a trigger point that develops on the other leg? And phantom-limb pain can occur spontaneously, or it can be triggered by vibration or by light touch, which are too weak to stimulate pain receptors.

Besides, the peripheral nerves can be cut completely—without stopping the pain. Even when the dorsal roots are severed in a rhizotomy, which cuts off the only sensory-input path into the spinal cord, the pain may persist. One recent neurosurgical text describes the case of Henry B., who suffered agonizing, stabbing pains in the phantom fingers that protruded from his upper-arm stump. Physicians cut the dorsal roots that carried all sensory information from his chest to his brain. After the surgery he could feel nothing from his shoulders to his navel, but the pain persisted in his phantom fingers, sharp as ever.

We can therefore rule out irritation at the stump as a major cause of pain. Mild irritation certainly can contribute to the pain—anesthetizing the area can sometimes

---

Many theorists say that pain is merely the result of stimulation of pain receptors in the skin— but they have a hard time finding pain receptors in a foot that isn't there.

---

bring dramatic relief—but it is not the whole story.

Since cutting sensory nerves often does not work, some theorists attempt to salvage the specific-receptor theory with another hypothesis. It is assumed that pain fibers travel through the sympathetic ganglia—part of the autonomic nervous system that controls such body functions as blood flow and digestion. Part of the reason for this belief is that the stump shows abnormal sympa-

thetic signs such as excessive sweating. It is also known that some autonomic functions such as urination or orgasm can induce phantom-limb pain. Sympathectomy, cutting the sympathetic ganglia, should relieve the pain.

Sympathectomy does relieve some kinds of pain, but, unfortunately, not phantom-limb pain: fewer than 10 percent of cases report complete pain relief one to four years after surgery. In the few successful cases it probably works by cutting down the total amount of activity entering the spinal cord. Sensory nerves from the stomach, blood vessels and other deep tissues converge into some of the same spinal-cord cells that receive inputs from the skin. Together these impulses produce the nerve-impulse patterns that eventually lead to the sensation of pain. Cutting the sympathetic ganglia cuts down on the total amount of activity in these spinal cells, and would therefore reduce the pain.

Surgeons have tried almost every conceivable operation to relieve phantom-limb pain. Results have been discouraging. As Sydney Sunderland wrote: "Operations have been performed for pain at nearly every possible site in the pathway from the peripheral receptors to the sensory cortex, and at every level the story is the same—some encouraging results, but a disheartening tendency for the pain to recur."

Some dismiss the whole dilemma by proposing that phantom-limb pain is psychological. The pain, they say, is simply a manifestation of pathological personal need. In support of this view, they note that pain is often triggered by emotional disturbance, and is sometimes diminished by psychotherapy, hypnosis, or simple distraction. Patients suffering from phantom-limb pain are often anxious and have worrisome social adjustments. Indeed, the intense, unrelenting pain may itself produce marked withdrawal, paranoia and other personality changes.

It is clear that all phantom-limb pain cannot be ascribed to psychological factors. Anesthetics injected into the wrong nerve will not relieve the pain, but, injected in the right nerve in the same patient, they may have dramatic effect. Moreover, reliable studies have shown that patients with phantom-limb pain do not have greater incidence of neurosis than amputees who do not have pain. Emotional problems undoubtedly contribute to the pain, but they are not the major cause.

If the pain is not strictly psychological, and if we cannot assume that there are specialized nerve fibers that carry pain to the brain, then other theories of pain must be considered. One of these

other approaches is the pattern theory of pain, which assumes that it is the pattern and frequency of nerve impulses, carried by non-specialized fibers, that the brain interprets as pain.

W. K. Livingston proposed that there might be self-sustaining *reverberatory circuits* in the spinal cord—closed loops of nerve fibers in which one fiber stimulates another, which in turn stimulates others that eventually restimulate the first, and so on. These reverberatory circuits would send volleys of nerve impulses up the spinal cord, and the brain would interpret them as pain.

Such circuits might be started by the initial injury to the limb, or even by the amputation itself. After that, even minor irritations of the skin or nerves would feed into the circuits to keep them abnormally disturbed over a period of years. Impulses that would or-

dinarily be interpreted as touch may then stimulate the neuron pools to send more impulses to the brain, resulting in still more pain, pain that will persist even after the touch stimulus is gone.

Once the abnormal spinal-chord activity has become self-sustaining, removal of the source of stimulation may not stop it. Since the source of the persistent pain is in the spinal cord itself, this would explain why traditional surgery—neurectomy, rhizotomy, sympathectomy—may have little effect.

If Livingston is correct, it would appear that in order to cure phantom-limb pain, we would have to cut fibers in the spinal cord itself, somewhere between the reverberatory circuit and the brain.

These pathways *have* been cut by optimistic surgeons, at nearly every level from the spinal cord to the thalamus, sometimes on both sides and at successively higher

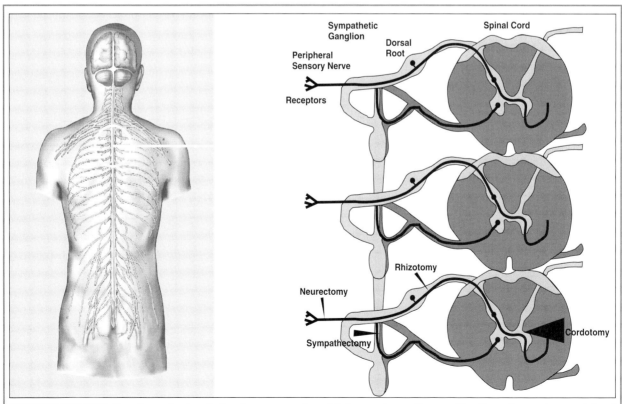

SURGERY FOR PAIN. To relieve phantom-limb pain, surgeons have tried several operations: cutting the pathways from peripheral receptors (neurectomy), the dorsal roots (rhizotomy), the sympathetic ganglia (sympathectomy), even the spinal cord itself (cordotomy). These operations relieve some types of pain, but are discouragingly ineffective with phantom-limb pain.

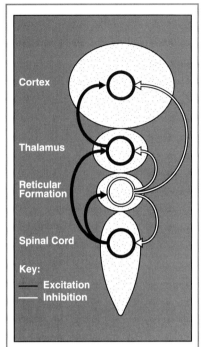

EXCITATION AND INHIBITION.
A schematic diagram of the major projections and interactions in the skin sensory system. Large and small fibers from a limb activate a neuron pool in the spinal cord, which excites higher areas. The reticular formation inhibits activity at all levels. When sensory fibers are destroyed after amputation, the inhibitory influence decreases. This results in sustained activity at all levels that can be triggered repeatedly by the remaining small fibers.

levels—yet pain often returns. Indeed, new pains may arise to make the patient even more miserable than before.

Working with several colleagues—Kenneth Casey, Bernardo Dubrovsky and Karl Konrad—I have made some discoveries with cats that suggest a new approach to the problem. Gentle rubbing of the skin of a normal cat for 10 or 15 seconds produces short-lasting changes in the electrical activity of the sensory system in the brain. In anesthetized cats, the same brief stimulation may produce changes in the brain that last 10, 15, even 30 minutes.

Apparently there is a natural inhibiting influence that normally shuts off the brain activity as soon as a stimulus is removed. Moderate anesthesia removes this inhibiting force so that a stimulus that usually has only momentary

effects may produce persistent activity. The mechanism for this long-lasting activity might be a group of nerve fibers similar to Livingston's proposed reverberatory circuits. In fact, Sir John Eccles and other physiologists have found evidence for a simple two-neuron closed loop that can produce sustained rhythmic activity for prolonged stretches of time.

These observations allow us to propose a model to explain at least some of the phenomena of phantom-limb pain. Nerves from a limb contain fibers that activate pools of neurons in the spinal cord. Some of these fibers are relatively large and conduct impulses quickly; other fibers are small and conduct impulses more slowly. We know that after a limb is amputated about half of the cut nerve fibers still in the stump die. The rest regenerate and grow into the stump tissues. These fibers are usually small and slow-conducting.

Thus, stimulation of the stump tends to produce synchronous volleys in the small fibers, rather than the complex, dispersed patterns seen in a normal nerve that contains the full range of fiber sizes.

The sensory neurons in the spinal cord project upward to the thalamus and cortex of the brain, of course, but they also send impulses to the reticular formation in the brainstem. On receiving these impulses, the reticular formation acts primarily to inhibit nerve transmission in the spinal cord, the thalamus and the cortex—at all the levels of the sensory system.

Since the inhibitory influence of the reticular formation is partly maintained by sensory inputs from the skin, any decrease in the number of sensory fibers from an area would mean that there would be less inhibition at all levels of the sensory pathway from the spinal cord to the brain. Consequently, inputs from the skin or deeper tissues would tend to produce sustained, uninhibited activity in

neuron pools in the spinal cord, thalamus and cortex.

Even if this activity stopped spontaneously, the volleys of impulses from the remaining small fibers at the stump would again reactivate it. These neuron pools have widespread connections, and it would be only a matter of time before the sustained, rhythmic activity would spread to adjacent areas of the nervous system. The pain-signaling pathways in the spinal cord could be cut, but activity patterns in the thalamus and cortex would continue: the pain would persist. Indeed, some cells in the thalamus and cortex have very large sensory fields, sometimes half or more of the body surface, so that stimuli from distant skin areas could cause sustained activity at these levels. This could explain how trigger zones can develop far from the stump.

This model is, of course, highly speculative. However, it can explain many facts of phantom-limb pain. For example, an anesthetic injection of several hours' duration would block all sensory input from an area; it would stop the sustained activity and would bring relief from pain. The relief would sometimes outlast the anesthesia, because as the anesthesia wears off a certain amount of time would be required before the sustained activity could spread to a sufficiently large number of neurons within the pool. Moreover, while the patient is relieved of pain he would be able to use the stump. This would produce patterned, temporally dispersed activity that would be out of phase with the rhythmically firing neuron pools and would disrupt their activity. Massive, continuous inputs, such as those produced by salt-solution injection, could bring relief by interrupting the rhythmic activity and also by raising the level of inhibition. In contrast, cutting a sensory pathway in the spinal cord would decrease the inhibition still further and would tend to enhance rather than decrease the pain.

The model also proposes new approaches to the relief of phantom-limb pain. It suggests a search for drugs that enhance the inhibiting influences of the reticular formation. It also proposes that sensory inputs of moderate or high intensities, applied to widespread areas of the body, should increase inhibitory levels and decrease pain. Because the reticular formation is also influenced from above, by activity in the cortex, it also suggests that manipulation of psychological attitudes toward pain may have powerful effect. ◆

Discussion Questions

1. What is the phantom limb phenomenon?

2. How is this phenomenon usually explained?

3. What are trigger zones, and where are they located?

4. What are the reverberatory circuits suggested by W.K. Livingston?

5. Describe the model of pain that Melzack proposes to try to account for the phantom limb phenomenon.

6. Have you ever had any perceptual experiences similar to the phantom-limb phenomenon? If so, what happened, and how might you account for it in terms of neural processes?

Educating *Your* **Nose**

◆ *William S. Cain*

If you want to frustrate your friends, give them 10 common substances to smell. They will most likely "block" on the names of at least a few. They may be able to describe the odor in general terms—sweet, woody, fruity, solventlike. Their descriptions may show that they know something about the smells—whether an odor comes from an edible or inedible source, for example. But the exact identity of the origin of the smell will probably elude them.

When it comes to identifying odors, people are strangely inconsistent and often imprecise. When exposed to a smell whose origins are not obvious, they may feel on the verge of identifying it—"it's on the tip of my tongue"—but they often cannot come up with the name without prompting.

Among those most frustrated by the hit-or-miss nature of odor identification are neurologists, who frequently use tests of olfaction in diagnosing patients with head injuries, chronic allergies, certain viral illnesses, and other disturbances. On the other hand, manufacturers of synthetic flavorings take advantage of our general inability to distinguish between odors and their labels, knowing that consumers will often accept even a copy of a natural flavor if the label on the container causes them to "find" the intended odor in the product.

For more than a decade, experimental psychologists believed that the typical person, when tested, could identify no more than about 16 substances by their odors. More recent experiments at the John B. Pierce Foundation Laboratory at Yale challenge this belief. We have now demonstrated that people can improve their ability to identify odors through practice. More specifically, they can improve it through various cognitive interventions in which words are used to endow odors with perceptual or olfactory identity.

The role of cognition in virtually all aspects of chemosensory experience has long been neglected. The sensation of smell is not simply a physiological response to a stimulus. The labels we give to odors not only help us to remember them, but as perfume manufacturers have discovered, they may even influence how we perceive them.

When cognitive limitations are circumvented, we have found, most people can identify a large number of objects by smell. The crucial importance of cognitive processes for smell may help to explain why some elderly people are not as good at identifying odors as the young and why women can generally name more odors than men. (For this reason, we usually use women as subjects in our research).

Learning the Language of Smell

Although the connection between odor and cognition has largely escaped notice until recently, a few scientists did develop ambitious schemes in the past for classifying smells (see the box on page 50). But the language of their classification schemes is incompatible with the way ordinary people identify smells. Rather than describe an odor with a series of adjectives—say, *fruity, fishy,* or *musky*— most people automatically describe it in terms of the object from which it arises. That seems entirely reasonable, since outside the laboratory odors are identified initially through a congruity of sight and smell. Objects that look different tend to smell different. Objects that look the same tend to smell the same. The same motive that drives people to apply different terms to the objects apple, banana, and lemon drives them similarly to apply different names to odors. Once attached to odors, the names form the only acceptable categorization: names define odors, locate them in relation to other odors, and even give them an internal "address" for retrieval from memory storage.

If the words that people attach to odors reflect both how and how well an odor is encoded, then perhaps an externally endowed name can manipulate both the odor experience and its subsequent identifiability. Such manipulations cannot be entirely arbitrary if they are to work. They must make sense in terms of whatever partial knowledge the participants already possess. The simplest example of modifiability seems to lie in the ability of a name to transform a smell from the vague to the clear. When presented with an object to smell, people may fail to identify

> **When it comes to identifying odors, people are strangely inconsistent and often imprecise.**

it exactly but may decide that it smells somewhat fishy, somewhat goaty, and somewhat oily. If asked to remember this personally generated label—*fishy-goaty-oily*—for subsequent use, most people have difficulty. If, however, people are told the true name, or realize it spontaneously, the sensation takes on a new clarity. Knowledge that the fishy-goaty-oily smell actually comes from leather typically transforms the odor impression into that of leather.

Just how many odor categories can a person keep straight? The answer has ranged from just a few to many, depending upon experimental circumstances that in retrospect have less to do with olfaction than with cognition.

The experiment that led to the rather low estimate of 16 identifiable smells asked subjects to identify many unfamiliar odors. After seeing how many odors the subjects could name initially, the researchers then attempted to

improve that ability through repeated tests. The participants were allowed to choose labels that were meaningful to them (*like fishy-goaty-oily*) rather than the chemical names for some of the obscure odors used in the experiment.

After considerable practice, subjects reached their peak performance, called the "channel capacity" for odor quality, or the maximum number of odors they could identify. Though not apparent at the time, the personally cho-

The Grand Classifiers of Smell

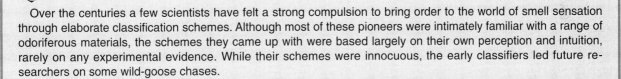

Over the centuries a few scientists have felt a strong compulsion to bring order to the world of smell sensation through elaborate classification schemes. Although most of these pioneers were intimately familiar with a range of odoriferous materials, the schemes they came up with were based largely on their own perception and intuition, rarely on any experimental evidence. While their schemes were innocuous, the early classifiers led future researchers on some wild-goose chases.

The great 18th-century botanical and medical taxonomist Linnaeus, history's most compulsive classifier, decided that the odor world comprised seven categories: (1) aromatic, (2) fragrant, (3) ambrosial (musky), (4) alliaceous (garlicky), (5) hircine (goaty), (6) repulsive, and (7) nauseous. His successors in the 19th and 20th centuries kept the Linnaean tradition strongly alive by refining his system, devising new ones, and arguing about which was best. The Dutch physiologist Hendrik Zwaardemaker's adoption of the Linnaean class of aromatic odors at the turn of the 20th century provides a good illustration of how these categories were refined by various theorists, most of whom were headed for obscurity: "This group comprises the aromatic odors of Linnaeus, the series 3 and 4 of Fourcroy, the camphors and the volatile acids of Lorry, the first, fourth, and fifth groups of Froehlich, and finally the spicy, caryophyllaceous, camphorous, santalaceous, citronous, herbaceous, menthaceous, anis- and almondlike series of Rimmel." Zwaardemaker settled on five subclasses of aromatic odors. He went on to refine other Linnaean classes as well.

There is nothing wrong with erecting odor classification systems. They can be particularly useful for perfumers, chemists, and others who need to describe the odors of newly synthesized chemicals and product ingredients. In fact, when applied to a specific substance like beer, they can be quite important for quality control (see chart on following page).

A problem arises, however, when the classifiers believe that a given scheme embodies reality, and that they have in one respect or another uncovered sensory building blocks. For Zwaardemaker, the classification system lay at the heart of olfactory physiology. Such mistaken beliefs have given rise to entire theories of olfaction. These included such passing fictions as distinct sites for classes of "minty" and "floral" odors.

The theories generated some research, but virtually no understanding of olfactory functioning. Why? Because the analysis of odor quality into fundamentals reflects the cognitive structure of the analyzer more accurately than it does any basic element of olfaction. Unlike taste research, which has shown that sensations such as sweet and sour function independently to some extent, olfaction researchers have yet to demonstrate that smells in different "categories" are functionally distinct.

For lack of a better insight, some experts have wasted years in pursuit of the Holy Grail of a perfect olfactory classification scheme. And they still failed to recognize that the experience of smell itself depends on the words available to describe it.

sen labels probably offered them little advantage. Experiments in our lab show that the formation of new associations between words and odors proceeds at a painfully slow pace. Thus the low figure of 16 identifiable odors probably has more to do with the difficulty of learning names for unfamiliar odors than it does with the subjects' actual channel capacity.

For more than a decade, researchers believed that the average person could identify no more than 16 odors.

In our studies at the Pierce Foundation Laboratory, we decided to use only everyday objects that would have strong associations with sights, smells, and names learned over a period of years. We chose 80 substances that we felt virtually every American adult could identify. The substances included meat (liverwurst), fish (sardines), fruits (orange), spices (ginger), snacks (potato chips), condiments (barbecue sauce), beverages (beer), confections (caramel), household products (shoe polish), medical products (Band-Aids), raw materials (clay), personal products (baby powder), and other common items (leather, pencil shavings, crayons). When asked to smell them one at a time, participants (young women wearing blindfolds) could, on the average, accurately identify 36 of them.

But on the average, they could *not* correctly name the remaining 44 odors, although they seemed to "know" many of them (or, at least, they often indicated as much). They came close to a correct identification of 18 of the 44, but they were further off the mark for the other 26. Failure to identify, then, looked in part like failure to retrieve the correct label, even though an association between odor and label already existed in memory. The probability that an odor would precipitate a tip-of-the-tongue experience varied from substance to substance even for

substances of equal familiarity. For instance, most participants found the odors from burnt paper, prune juice, and vinegar all highly familiar, but they gave more incorrect responses for prune juice.

This initial test of identification was only the beginning of our experiment. Next, we wanted to find out whether people could improve their ability to identify odors with the help of corrective feedback on labels. After the initial inspection of the 80 substances, we asked participants to apply their own labels, right or wrong, on five subsequent occasions two to three days apart. On each of those occasions, participants received corrective feedback

with their original label. If a person first called beer by the name *wine*, then any subsequent response other than *wine* would lead to the feedback "You called that wine." This exercise allowed us to see whether an objectively poor label that came spontaneously from a participant's repertoire served as well as or worse than an objectively good label. The self-generated labels were usually worse. If, for instance, a person had first called a lemon by the name *lemon* (a direct hit), she stood about an 85 percent chance of using *lemon* correctly on the next round of testing. If she had first called lemon by the name *lime* (a near miss), then she stood about a 60 percent chance of calling it *lime* on the next round. If she had first called it *fruit* (a far miss), then she later stood only about a 30 percent

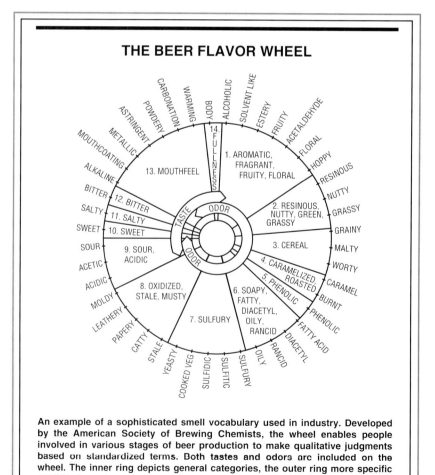

THE BEER FLAVOR WHEEL

An example of a sophisticated smell vocabulary used in industry. Developed by the American Society of Brewing Chemists, the wheel enables people involved in various stages of beer production to make qualitative judgments based on standardized terms. Both tastes and odors are included on the wheel. The inner ring depicts general categories, the outer ring more specific qualities in each category.

chance of calling it *fruit* (see graph).

This outcome made us wonder if the original label reflected how well a participant had initially encoded the odor in memory. Saying the word *fruit* for the highly familiar substance lemon implies vague encoding of the odor during the inspection period, that is, failure to register the odor as itself. Even with corrective feedback, the probability that the same vaguely encoded stimulus would evoke the same response, fruit, was quite low. Nevertheless, corrective feedback did appear to help to some degree. Participants made steady, session-by-session progress with all types of labels, even poor ones.

We discovered that progress in spite of poor associations could be explained by something else. In another experiment, we allowed participants to change a label whenever it seemed desirable. The experiment revealed that in our previous studies, participants had apparently not improved the association between an odor and a poor label, but had sometimes realized that other labels were better and from then on had used them as mental reminders. Later interviews revealed the strategy again and again: "I eventually realized that what I had called 'wood' was actually maple syrup. After that, it was easy to remember to say 'wood' whenever I smelled maple syrup." Thus, only better labels led to better performance, including many cases in which a participant switched from a far miss to a near miss. Each improvement of label brought with it a sharp increase in the probability of success on that substance in the next test session two to three days later. A switch from a far miss to a direct hit carried a larger chance of success than a switch to a near miss.

Psychophysical experiments on quality discrimination and on

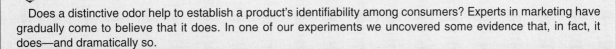

The Smell of Success in Marketing

Does a distinctive odor help to establish a product's identifiability among consumers? Experts in marketing have gradually come to believe that it does. In one of our experiments we uncovered some evidence that, in fact, it does—and dramatically so.

We wanted to compare people's impression of how easy it is to identify the common products on our list with how easy it actually is. A group of 103 women were given the names of 80 products and asked to rate them on a 4-point scale according to how easy they thought it would be to identify them. Then we asked a different group (a dozen women) to actually identify each of the items on the list; they were tested five items each and the results were averaged.

The top 10 in expected and actual identifiability are shown at right. Five of the top 10 in the right column have odors unique to a particular brand. Invariably, when identifying these substances, the participants mentioned the brand name. Thus, they did not say just baby powder, but Johnson's baby powder—and the same for Crayola crayons, Ivory soap, Vicks VapoRub, and Bazooka bubble gum. We included the specific products in the test because we suspected they were brand-leaders in their respective categories; but we hardly expected that they would be more easily identified than such generic items as orange, vinegar, lemon, ammonia, and peanut butter.

Expected Identifiability

1. Ammonia
2. Coffee
3. Mothballs
4. Perfume (brand not specified)
5. Orange
6. Lemon
7. Bleach
8. Vinegar
9. Nail-polish remover
10. Peanut butter

Actual Identifiability

1. Johnson's baby powder
2. Chocolate
3. Coconut
4. Crayola crayons
5. Mothballs
6. Ivory soap (bar)
7. Vicks VapoRub
8. Bazooka bubble gum
9. Coffee
10. Caramel

odor thresholds have failed to support the assertion that women have a keener sense of smell than men. But our own studies have demonstrated that women actually make better use of their sense of smell.

We asked 102 men and 103 women how well they thought the typical person could identify each of the 80 items in our substance set. The respondents rated identifiability on a 4-point scale ranging from excellent to poor. Men and women agreed in their evaluations to a remarkable degree. We also asked them to guess whether each item could be identified better by men or by women. Again, the two groups agreed. With the exception of about 16 stereotypically "male" substances, such as beer, cigar butts, machine oil, and pine shavings, the two groups felt that women would do better. In addition to the "female" analogues of the stereotypically "male" items

(Ivory soap, nail-polish remover, bleach, and baby powder), there was agreement that women would more accurately identify most foods. About 85 percent of the respondents felt that women would be better at naming a group of spices, including vanilla extract, oregano, nutmeg, ginger, garlic powder.

Clearly those substances will have a more distinct identity to someone who prepares food than to someone who only eats it. Yet about 80 percent of our respondents also predicted that women would be better than men at identifying common fruits and confections, and about 65 percent predicted women would be better at identifying odors of snack foods, luncheon meats, fish, and condiments.

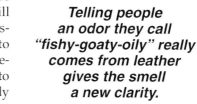

Telling people an odor they call "fishy-goaty-oily" really comes from leather gives the smell a new clarity.

Their intuitions turned out to be correct. In an actual experiment women indeed outperformed men, even on most of the stereotypically male items. Men managed to avoid a shutout by exhibiting marginal superiority on seven items: bourbon, Brut aftershave, Crayola crayons, horseradish, rubbing alcohol, soap and Vicks VapoRub (see the graph below). It appears that women can retrieve the names of odors more readily at the outset, can employ their own labels better, and can even use true (correct) labels supplied by the experimenter to better advantage.

It seems unlikely that women's superiority in odor identification is primarily an expression of a biological advantage; we think it reflects different experience. Rather than learn about odors incidentally, as men do, women usually learn about them more directly and deliberately. Some people are better at olfactory information processing than others, and a person's ability probably depends on biological factors that have less to do with gender than with intelligence and a variety of other factors, such as age, occupation, hobbies, and cultural priorities. Still, a combination of those factors, in America at least, somehow leads to female superiority.

But it seems that with appropriate training men can eventually manage to catch up with women. If the true label contributes to odor encoding and can be more easily recalled subsequently, can performance in the identification experiment be enhanced by merely reminding participants of the label? We thought it might. Replacing a personally generated but perhaps inadequate name with the true name, we reasoned, should

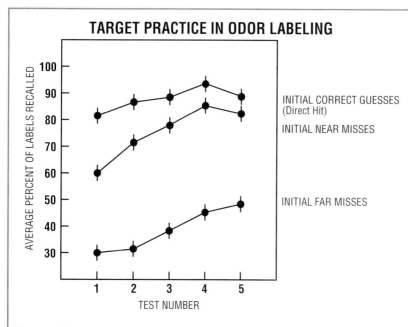

TARGET PRACTICE IN ODOR LABELING

INITIAL CORRECT GUESSES (Direct Hit)

INITIAL NEAR MISSES

INITIAL FAR MISSES

An experiment showing that the more accurate people are in labeling an odor, the easier it is for them to remember the original label in connection with that odor. After a trial run, the preliminary guesses of 12 subjects on each of 80 odors were divided into direct hits (correct names, say lemon), near misses (lime), and far misses (a generic term—fruit, or a vague association—"the hall closet"). In five later tests, subjects who scored direct hits were able to use those labels with 90 percent accuracy. The near misses were remembered with 80 percent accuracy. The far misses improved over time, but were still much harder to remember than the more accurate labels.

WOMEN'S KEENER SENSE OF SMELL

Outcome of an experiment that tested 22 men and 24 women on learning 80 odors, over a period of 10 days. After a trial run, subjects were told the names of some of the odors. The ability of both men and women to come up with the correct names improved over time. But on the average, women correctly identified more items on the initial test and maintained their advantage in four later trials.

impart definition to the stimulus, allowing the best possible encoding and permitting excellent retrieval.

That is exactly what happened in a later experiment. We first reminded participants of the labels for the 80 common substances during an initial phase. After that, our subjects had an average of 78 percent correct on their first test, and by the fifth test their accuracy had climbed to 94 percent. By that time, they could identify odors up to the limit of their discriminative capacity. This outcome implies that with appropriate help in encoding and retrieval, people can identity as many substances as they can discriminate and for which they possess well-learned names—presumably hundreds and perhaps even thousands.

Susan Schiffman, a psychologist at Duke University, and Claire Murphy, a psychologist at Monell Chemical Senses Center in Philadelphia, have discovered that older people are often unable to identify the flavors of foods accu-

rately. Their inability hinges on smell rather than taste and perhaps more on impaired cognitive processing than on sensory disability. Older people commonly suffer from an inability to encode stimuli, remember names, or use verbal mediation. And all three abilities play a role in successful odor identification.

We asked young women (average age, 18) and healthy, active older women (average age, 76) to identify odors in a set of 40 substances. Before participating, all candidates passed a test designed to eliminate those with sensory impairment. Half of the older people failed, showing that sensory deficits are quite common. In addition, older people who had passed the screening test still showed marked deficits in odor identification, whether they used their own or experimenter-supplied labels.

The older women gave poorer labels than the young women, an outcome that in itself would lead

us to anticipate poorer performance in subsequent testing. The disparity between the two age groups on the basis of label quality alone actually exceeded our expectation and seemed due, in large measure, to the older women's inability to benefit from corrective feedback given for their own labels. That led us to wonder whether the older people would profit at all from prompting with the true names. When told the true names during the inspection period, the younger women performed much like the young women in the previous study, eventually getting more than 90 percent right. The older women were less successful, but improved somewhat over time, finally getting about 50 percent correct.

Odor Testing and Disabilities

Our research on the importance of cognition for odor identification has already had important practical benefits. We have, for example, designed a new neurological test for smell that is more accurate than older versions in assessing sensory functioning.

In the past, neurological tests for smell were so poorly designed that physicians were instructed to accept as normal those who could recognize and name about five odors quickly, those who could recognize odors but not name them, and even those who could detect odors and distinguish among them but could neither recognize nor name them. The tests had less to do with sensory ability than with cognitive ability, but only the former is really important for early detection of frontal brain tumors and some hormonal disorders.

Our experiments suggested that, in neurological tests, the use of highly familiar substances and clues to their names would help patients retrieve odor names and eliminate the confusion between cognition and sensory ability. We gave patients a list containing the names of 11 test substances: Johnson's baby powder, Juicy Fruit gum, chocolate, cinnamon, coffee, leather, mothballs, peanut butter, potato chips, Ivory soap, and wintergreen. Those substances had in the past proven to be highly identifiable. The list also contained the names of "distractor" items: burnt paper, garlic, ketchup, orange, black pepper, rubber, sardines, spoiled meat, tobacco, turpentine, and wood shavings. Some of the distractors were included to detect people who have a smell disorder called parosmia, which distorts their sense of smell.

The procedure has worked extremely well in testing patients ranging from under 10 to over 65 years of age. In comparison with other criteria—a somewhat cumbersome clinical judgment derived from a lengthy questionnaire—our odor-identification test has so far not misclassified a single patient. Patients deemed by our criteria to have normal olfaction have scored, on the average, well above 90 percent on our identification task. Patients deemed hyposmic (having a weak sense of smell) or anosmic (with virtually no sense of smell) have performed very poorly.

Our experiments have taught us that the sense of smell can seem either deficient or surprisingly proficient, depending on how we ask the simple question "Do you know what this smell is?" It can appear deficient when we are groping for names of new smells or sometimes even when we seek to retrieve the names of old smells. It can appear remarkably proficient when, with a little prompting if necessary, we manage to enlarge the number of smells people can identify.

That makes us optimistic about the latent talent we all have for odor identification and gives researchers the incentive to look at the talent of special groups, such as young children, people with appetite disorders (anorexia or obesity), and people with loss of sight or hearing. With some idea of the odor-identification talent that normal people possess, we can feel more kinship with the blind deaf-mute Julia Brace who, according to William James, was "employed in the Hartford Asylum to sort the linen of its multitudinous inmates, after it came from the wash, by her wonderfully educated sense of smell."   ◆

Discussion Questions

1. What might labeling an odor accomplish for us?

2. Describe an experiment that suggests that people can identify only as many odors as they can name.

3. What are possible reasons why older people are unable to identify the flavors of foods?

4. How is cognition related to the sense of smell?

5. Discuss sexual differences in the sense of smell. How can men be trained to identify odors more accurately?

6. What do the authors mean by "the latent talent we all have for odor identification"?

The **Psychology** *of the*
Step Beyond:
A CONVERSATION WITH
J. B. Rhine

◆ *Mary Harrington Hall*

Mary Harrington Hall: Remember the campfire song—"My Grandfather's Clock was too large for the shelf, So it stood 90 years on the floor; It was taller by half than the old man himself, Tho' it weighed not a pennyweight more. It was bought on the morn' of the day that he was born, And was always his treasure and pride; But it stopped short never to go again When the old man died."

J. B. Rhine: That's a good old parapsychological song!

Hall: Could I stop a clock?

Rhine: You probably could, if you really wanted to, but you undoubtedly wouldn't want to.

Hall: Oh, I don't know. But I didn't do too well in controlling the fall of the dice in your laboratory. That's the same principle—psychokinesis—in which one can affect the physical environment, isn't it?

Rhine: Yes. We've collected all the reports we can get of unaccountable physical happenings. The picture of a boy that fell from the wall of his home when his ship sank in a far-off sea. The vase—a wedding gift—that suddenly cracked and shattered when a marriage ended. The simultaneous stopping of two timepieces when a man died—one, a watch in his pocket; the other, a clock in his room.

Hall: But it's impossible to get enough people to die voluntarily and to stop clocks for scientific purposes. So you can't check out such reports, really.

Rhine: We shift the problem over to moving other objects—letting dice or balls roll down a chute and having people try to control the numbers that come up on dice or the lie of the balls at the bottom of the chute. If a person can control this, there is nothing to stopping a clock that would involve any other principle. And, yes, we have been able to verify experimentally this kind of psychokinesis in scores of the experiments.

Hall: The control of moving objects is just one form of parapsychology. You started the real pioneer work in parapsychology, right here when you were in the psychology department at Duke. What are the various parts of parapsychology—or psi as you call it?

Rhine: If you drew a map of Psi-Land, it would be a circular country made up of six states. Half would be in the domain of psychokinesis, which we call PK. The other half would be the realm of extrasensory perception.

The telepathic type of ESP is most readily accepted and believed, but also is the most difficult to investigate under strict experimental conditions. It wasn't until 1940 that the first pure telepathy experiment was conducted.

Hall: Why so long?

Rhine: It's so easy to contaminate telepathy with clairvoyance.

Hall: You mean I'd be aware about some *thing* instead of some *thought*, and so I'd foul up the research?

Rhine: Right. Clairvoyance indicates awareness of objective events, not thoughts. It is much simpler to test than telepathy, by the way. Examples in real life are frequent—like the awareness of the death of a friend miles away.

The final form of ESP is precognition, which is the awareness of future events. It can be experienced as intuition or hallucination or as dreams, but I think that it occurs most often in dreams.

Hall: A lot of top-drawer people now accept ESP. But you keep trying to verify all these phenomena *scientifically*. I don't see how—or even why—you can expect scientific measurement of the many strange, special dimensions of human communication.

Rhine: Because the challenge and the need are there, Mary. People will not accept things without proof.

Hall: You've extended ESP research to include animals too. I think my dog, Sam, probably is clairvoyant. And we people all think that we have had great moments of clairvoyance.

Rhine: We can't say that *everyone* has any kind of ESP until we demonstrate it. And the demonstration depends upon who tests people, on the conditions, on their preparation, on so many variables. But we haven't found limits in anyone that would spoil our working hypothesis that ESP is a potential in the human species. It's like talking about a

> *...if a man criticizes us honestly, I know that he just has his windows cut to a certain size and can't see any farther.*

J. B. Rhine

sense of humor or an appreciation of beauty.

Hall: How *much* appreciation and how *much* humor, and how much ESP? And—in your work—how much doubt and how much criticism have you absorbed?

Rhine: I have never felt bitter or defeated. It's true that we have had to fight our way into the field of science over the critics. But if a man criticizes us honestly, I know that he just has his windows cut to a certain size and can't see any farther.

Hall: Have you ever convinced a critic by redoing an experiment to meet his objections? Or by doing anything?

Rhine: Of course not. And our experimental standards are above those in most of psychology. They have to be. We use a higher standard of significance; we repeat all significant work before we report it; we conduct all crucial work as a double blind experiment. Our *Journal of Parapsychology* may well be the only scientific journal that insists that all articles be read for mathematical accuracy by two mathematicians.

Years ago, when some psychologists attacked our work on mathematical grounds, the president of the Institute for Mathematical Sta-

tistics announced that if our experiments were criticized, then criticism would have to be on other than mathematical grounds.

Engineers, particularly those in electronics and astronautics, have been a great help, too. They are very strong and secure so they aren't embarrassed to be caught looking into something new. Engineers aren't afraid of being too far out, but of being too far behind.

Hall: Just a minute. You're saying psychology is not that secure a discipline.

Rhine: That's about it. And so parapsychology is treated like a ragged little urchin tagging along, an urchin psychology doesn't want to be photographed with.

Hall: I think the many mediums and the thousands of charlatans who pretend to have communication with the dead may have turned people off on your sincere parapsychology convictions.

Rhine: Of course. And we've had our problems steering a course between the charlatans and the overcredulous on one hand, and the overskeptical on the other.

The work here would have been nothing without my wife. We have always worked together in parapsychology. Louie keeps my thoughts alive.

Hall: Louisa has a great sense of humor, too. Which helps smooth the rough edge of controversy.

Rhine: Louie is just finishing her new book. It is called *Mind Over Matter*. It is the first story of psychokinesis.

> *...we've had our problems steering a course between the charlatans and the overcredulous on one hand, and the overskeptical on the other.*

Hall: What's this new physical action on plants Louisa was mentioning? It sounds like the ultimate in green thumb research.

Rhine: This form of psychokinesis involves live targets. We give

plants the Galvanic Skin Response test of skin resistance. Then we find someone with a green thumb and set up two plants before the person. The plants are screened so the subject can't breathe on them, and one is the target plant. The subject concentrates on the plant for short periods, trying to activate it or to impress it in some way.

Hall: Starting a plant. It's the reverse of trying to stop a clock!

Rhine: We attach a sensitive apparatus—a polygraph—to the plants to register the electrical current that flows through the leaf epidermis. Now if this current fluctuates greatly when a person concentrates on the plant, then the subject has made a hit. If there is only the slight, normal fluctuation, the subject has no effect, of course.

Hall: Wow!

Rhine: We are making progress. Bob Brier, who's in charge of this series at our institute, reports effects that are moderately positive but not yet completely conclusive. Next year we'll know more.

Hall: That reminds me of a book that was published a few years ago, *The Power of Prayer on Plants*. People who prayed over plants to make them grow.

Rhine: That was Franklin Loehr's book. We had nothing to do with his experiments, although he got the idea for his test at our Duke laboratory. We did train one of his workers for him. We help any sincere researcher to organize his thinking so it can be tested—and then help him develop a method that will test it.

PK work similar to that of Loehr's was done in Canada at McGill University, with much better controls. Using a man who believes he has the power to heal, Dr. Bernard Grad reported successful effects on plant growth.

Hall: If all this is so, that would leave only one kind of PK unvalidated—the kind that supposedly would let me, through my mental powers, wing a cup across the room.

Rhine: There are a few people working on static matter, too. Some have tried to influence a cloud chamber or the rate of flow in an hourglass, or the speed at which certain tablets dissolve. We're always ready to listen to all claims.

But most of our work has been done with moving targets, such as dice, balls and discs. Some have tried PK in the microphysical particle field. There has been evidence developed at Strasbourg University that PK can be made to modify the number of particles that will be picked up from radioactive material.

Hall: That's sophisticated action. ESP is easier than molecular modulation.

Rhine: Most of the work we've done in ESP is pretty elementary, and the general audience for parapsychology today is sophisticated. When my daughter talked to a class of seventh graders a few days ago, they asked her questions she would have expected from a college group.

Hall: That's what I mean—why keep trying to fight a battle already won?

Rhine: Oh, that period is past. We still need to be cautious, but the interest today is in new findings—like psi-missing.

Hall: You mean there is *negative* ESP? Then the psychology of the loser would involve negative ESP.

Rhine: It's the equivalent of the turning of luck on a man who has been winning at a crap table. Instead of winning consistently—at rates far above the laws of chance—suddenly he is a constant loser.

Several factors appear to result in psi-missing. Suppose, during an experiment here, a young man is scoring well, so we keep him

working and make him late for a date he is too polite to tell us about. At the very least, his attention wanders. Invariably his score will drop just as far below chance as it had been above.

Another factor is belief or disbelief in ESP. A psychologist in New York discovered that if she had subjects first record whether or not they believed in ESP, a breakdown of the data would show that believers averaged above the laws of change on their scores and nonbelievers averaged just as far below chance.

Hall: I wonder if that's why I did so badly in your PK test.

Rhine: Well, you weren't very serious. Boredom, fear, disbelief all appear to operate in psi reactions. And what we get is ESP working in reverse.

It operates so strongly that if you see someone giving a performance of ESP on stage or on television, you can be pretty sure it's not on the level. There is so much strain in giving a high-percentage performance—and that strain will interfere and result in psi-missing, your negative ESP, even for someone who is used to stage appearances.

Hall: What about people like Jeane

Marjorie was supposed to produce ectoplasm, but it looked like something she had smuggled in from the butcher shop.

Dixon, the lady who writes the best sellers predicting the future?

Rhine: Lots of people predict things. She happens to have a good press agent. But let me answer impersonally. Unless prophecies are carefully recorded in advance of fulfillment and checked by responsible, trained scientists, they should not be taken seriously.

Hall: Let's talk international ESP. To understate the case, Europe is more receptive to parapsychology

than the Untied States is. But what about Iron Curtain countries?

Rhine: I haven't heard of well-designed psi research in Russia in the last 30 years. And we've had lots of contact with researchers behind the Iron Curtain.

Hall: Isn't it possible that there is work going on that you don't know about?

Rhine: Entirely possible, but we would hardly expect secrecy at this stage. A little boasting would be more like it.

In 1966, the Russian magazine, *Science and Religion*, devoted an issue to parapsychology. All but two of the scientists who contributed were favorable to the idea. The editorial position was that development of parapsychology would bring the spirit of scientific inquiry to the supernatural claims of religion.

Hall: Nullifying the need for a deity?

Rhine: That's just what they meant. Most Russians who have expressed themselves on parapsychology are sure that psi results must come from some unknown physical energy. They don't recognize the existence of anything else but physical reality. But then, that party-line position is not different from the academic line in our country. Albert Einstein said that if ESP is not related to space-time, it must be wrong.

Hall: And if it isn't physics, it must be supernatural?

Rhine: I've heard that dozens and dozens of times. But we don't want parapsychology as supernatural and we can't have it as physics. It must be something else.

Man is not completely describable in physical terms; physical terms can't possibly deal with knowing a future event.

Hall: Oh, now, no one describes man in just physical terms any more. But speaking of future events, how can anyone *know* something before the fact?

Rhine: I can't conceive how precognition can occur. But occur it does. And it doesn't bother me that it's inexplicable at this point. The explanations never come first in science. First comes the unexplainable phenomenon. Then with hard work, ultimately you may get an explanation.

Hall: That could be light years away.

Rhine: I wonder if perhaps the greatest gap in our conception of nature is not right here in this constant interchange of simultaneously talking and gesturing and thinking together. There is something distinctive about consciousness and something distinctive about the matter outside of it. Communication is a bridging operation, and we have no idea about such bridging for consciousness any more than for precognition.

Hall: Why not just relax and enjoy it. Try philosophy.

Rhine: I considered philosophy at the outset, but I came to realize that there is no empirical approach to philosophy as it has been set up in the universities. It doesn't lend itself to approaching problems of natural occurrence.

I don't see a place for a philosopher here at the Institute. But on the other hand, I see a definite need to keep in touch with certain sections of philosophy—logic, the logic of science, the philosophy of science.

Hall: And religion is not an inquiring field? Really?

Rhine: There are no laboratories in the seminaries. But some day religion will come to the laboratory.

A religious attitude tends to make people more favorable toward the idea of parapsychology. They are ready to think that something miraculous can happen. Every theology in the world implies extrasensory perception and psychokinesis. You can't have what is called supernatural without it.

Hall: You've been trying to understand ESP and PK for more than 40 years. Your father was a farmer and you became a botanist. How did you become interested in the field of parapsychology?

Rhine: My father was tremendously curious. He was the only farmer in the valley with a library.

...we haven't found limits in anyone that would spoil our working hypothesis that ESP is a potential in the human species.
It's like talking about a sense of humor or an appreciation of beauty.

He would buy a book from every book salesman who knocked at the door. And I read those books.

Hall: He farmed for your wife's father, didn't he? I know she came from a strictly no-nonsense Mennonite family.

Rhine: By the time Louie and I married and came to the University of Chicago in 1920, our religion had crumbled. I had considered being a minister, you know. But once we were confronted with the physical-chemical view of the universe, theology just didn't fit. We thought the scientific approach was the only way to solve problems. Yet we couldn't see how this approach could fully explain man.

Hall: This was just about the time of the Scopes monkey trial,

---

...if you see someone giving a performance of ESP on stage or on television, you can be pretty sure it's not on the level.

---

wasn't it? Maybe that's what keeps you trying to use the scientific method.

Rhine: One of the scientists at the University went down to testify in that trial, and William Jennings Bryan lectured on the Chicago campus. It was a time of tremendous ferment.

Louie and I both took all three of our degrees in botany, with the idea of going into forestry and getting away from it all. Without realizing it, we were fleeing from the ideas of our homes, our schools and our cultures.

Hall: Your college days were during a time of change and upheaval in American psychology. The Watsonian rebellion was in full swing.

Rhine: But the important event for us was the arrival of William McDougall at Harvard. He was a Scot who held out for a big psychology—a William James psychology. He was interested in psychical research, in hypnosis, in the Lamarckian hypothesis. He drove the psychologists at Harvard into corners.

Hall: And up the walls.

Rhine: And he was never afraid—no matter how unpopular his ideas. We read some of McDougall's writings in the library at Chicago and went to do graduate study with him at Harvard. But when we got to Cambridge, he and his family were about to leave for a trip around the world. And we were alone in Cambridge.

Hall: You must have been scared. Cambridge then and now can be devastating.

Rhine: It was disappointing. While McDougall was traveling, I studied with E.G. Boring and Morton Prince. And I did some work at the Boston Society for Psychical Research, headed by Walter Franklin Prince. It was time well spent.

When McDougall ended his trip, he began teaching at Duke. And once again we followed him.

Hall: Successfully this time, I hope.

Rhine: He opened the laboratories at Duke to me and offered me a job. Like William James, he felt that the claims of spiritualists were worth investigating.

Louie and I had worked with mediums in Boston, trying to see if there was validity to their claims. We exposed one medium, Marjorie, whom we caught in trickery. Marjorie was reported to produce ectoplasm, but it looked like something she had smuggled in from the butcher shop.

Hall: I know you don't believe in ectoplasm, but maybe some mediums are for real. Maybe they have phony trances but real ESP.

Rhine: Oh, yes. McDougall asked me to work with the medium Eileen Garrett. We studied her mediumship and tested her ESP ability at the same time. She was able to get results in her trances through heavy doors and heavy walls. She didn't have to be in the same room with the person asking the question. We were asking her to identity markings on cards, and we discovered that she had given us more information about the cards than about spiritistic questions. We had no way of knowing whether we were dealing with spirit communication or with ESP. If she could guess the cards, why couldn't she get the information by telepathy?

That's when we began to back away from the problem of postmortem survival and turn to things we could do experimentally with living people.

No way has been found to prove spirit survival through mediums. That's a dead end—at least as far as present knowledge goes, but it will long be exploited, I'm afraid.

Hall: And your laboratory experiments in ESP date from when you came to Duke in 1927?

Rhine: At duke we gradually developed new methods to test for the existence of psi, and we followed up each report of people with some special ability. We even took McDougall with us to see a mindreading horse.

Hall: I once knew a talking dog, Argo. He tapped out words. It was hard to figure what he was saying when the words were long.

Rhine: That's something else. The horse I knew was a restless, poorly trained four-year-old filly. The al-

---

Parapsychology is treated like a ragged little urchin tagging along, an urchin psychology doesn't want to be photographed with.

---

phabet was stretched out before her with number blocks behind it. She spelled out answers by touching her nose to the blocks. The woman who owned the horse used what could well have been sensory cues. She kept up a running chatter and moved and tapped the stall with a crop. We couldn't make out any system or code.

Hall: Did you ask that horse any questions?

Rhine: The person asking a question had to write down the answer on a tablet. We figured that perhaps the woman could decipher the answer by the movement of the long pencil or by the sound it made on the tablet.

We asked the horse to tell us the number on a coin we held. I wrote down the answer slowly and softly with a short pencil. To our surprise, the horse was successful.

Hall: Then did you test the horse in different ways?

Rhine: We tested that horse every way we could. We screened the owner from the horse with a piece of cardboard. We stopped writing the target down in advance. The horse would still get results, something like six times out of 10. The results suggested telepathic exchange from man to animal. We published our findings in the *Journal of Abnormal and Social Psychology*, but nobody ever followed up on our study.

Hall: And I also wonder what happened to Argo the talking dog.

Maybe his paws got tired. But tell me, what was your first laboratory work here in Durham? You were the darling of Duke for a long time.

Rhine: When we abandoned the work on spirit communication, we chose to investigate clairvoyance.

It is simple, direct, and requires little planning. All you need to do is to hide something and see if the person who claims to be clairvoyant can find it. We designed our deck of ESP cards for these experiments.

Hall: Thats the five-suited deck of geometric figures—stars and circles and wavy lines. how many cards are in the deck?

Rhine: Twenty-five. And by pure chance, you should be able to guess five. By simplifying our tests, by encouraging our subjects, by using hypnosis at times, we found that there were always some students who scored consistently better than chance.

Then at last we found a man who hardly ever failed to do well, no matter what kind of conditions we used—screens, hidden cards, separate buildings.

Hall: This must have been the famous case of Hubert Pearce.

Rhine: After we had worked with him on clairvoyance, we switched to precognition—with equally impressive results. And with precognition there is no chance for sensory clues.

Hall: What happened to Pearce?

Rhine: He had problems in a love affair, and his psi ability completely disappeared. Today he is a Methodist minister in Kansas City. He has tried and tried, but he has never again scored above chance. It's a strange thing. We've never found a person of extraordinary psi ability who did not later lose that ability.

Hall: That may be because it is easier to have grace under pressure than grace under test conditions.

Rhine: In 1934, we published a modest little monograph describing our first six years of experimentation. We concluded that we had, indeed, found ESP in some carefully controlled experimental tests.

Hall: And then all hell broke loose.

Rhine: The science editor of the *New York Times* devoted his Sunday column to our findings. We had requests from magazines and from publishers for more material. All the world appeared to have been waiting for something like this. Public response was overwhelming. And that has been both our advantage, and the basis of our trouble.

Hall: Cold winds can blow through the groves of academe.

Rhine: We soon found that out. There was even a national radio program on ESP. I was on a committee of psychologists to see that it was kept on a scientific level, but we resigned after only a month. We found that the studio really ran the show, and the scientific standards were not all they might have been.

Hall: You were had.

Rhine: It was worse than that. We were given assurances that were not kept. Too late we saw what the notoriety was doing.

At last, in 1935, we set up the Parapsychology Laboratory separate from the Department of Psychology so the psychologists wouldn't be blamed for what we were doing.

Hall: I know that a change in Duke administration cost you the early strong university backing. But when did you finally separate from the University?

Rhine: In 1965, at the maximal retirement age. After the lab was set up, we became increasingly independent from the department of psychology. I had asked to be relieved of half my teaching load as soon as we had our own lab. Then, in 1950, I asked to be freed entirely for research. For 15 years, from 1950 to 1965, we were an indepen-

dent center on the campus, partially supported by the University. We were well treated and there was a friendly spirit toward us on the campus. There still is, and for this I am deeply grateful.

Hall: Speaking of things that get turned off, have you studied the effects of drugs on ESP?

Rhine: Only a little. We haven't done justice to the physiological side, because of lack of money and personnel. It's expensive research.

We're trying to understand some of those things in the universe that don't fit into the recognized laws...

Very early, we tried some experiments using sodium amytal as a narcotic and caffeine as a stimulant. We manipulated scoring levels by depressing them with a double dose of amytol, and by raising them with caffeine tablets. But we've done only a few exploratory experiments.

Hall: And what would it prove anyway. I wonder, though, what the hallucinogenic drugs would do to psi ability. ESP with LSD! I can just see it on a poster.

Rhine: We haven't gone into the hallucinogens at all. We don't think that just because ESP is an unknown that we must combine it with another unknown. Two unknowns don't very often produce a known, you know.

Here and at a few other places, measurements of skin resistance, blood volume and brain waves are attempts to learn if there are physiological accompaniments to ESP. Nobody has any introspective inkling when ESP and PK occur.

Hall: And have physiological tests turned up any measurable differences? What about turning on the alpha brain waves—Joe Kamiya at Langley Porter has actually taught people to control their alpha waves.

Rhine: The only clue so far is that subjects seem to get their best results within a certain range of alpha rhythm. Each person seems to have his own individual amount of alpha rhythm that accompanies his successful ESP trials.

Hall: Has the government ever been interested in your research?

Rhine: We've been called in a couple of times to deal with something that obviously was a fraud. And we showed that fraud it was. We did have two series of contracts with the government years go. We did some good work for them in directions that have not been followed up. And we can't follow it without more financial help than we have now. The work is lost because the government is doing nothing with it. And some of it we can't talk about because it's classified. We're not enthusiastic about getting any more government contracts. We don't like to have our work buried.

Hall: Is Sara Feather the only one of your children to follow you in your work in ESP?

Rhine: Yes, so far. Sally has become Acting Director of the Institute since I retired. She got her Ph.D. in psychology here at Duke.

Betsy lives with us and breeds poodles. Rosemary is married to a member of the music department faculty at Western Carolina. And Robert, our only son, works for General Motors in Belgium.

Hall: It must give you real satisfaction to look back over your years of work here and realize that you were the pioneer student of parapsychology under controlled experimental conditions.

Rhine: Yes, life has been good to me—to us. We're trying to understand some of those things in the universe that don't fit into the recognized laws, but which are valid and indicate by their recurrence

that there is an underlying lawfulness. It has been slow work, but that is the way of science.
Hall: Somebody has to take that lonely step out into the night.

Rhine: If you have people to hold your hand and to go along with you, it makes it all much easier.
Hall: You've taken one of those brave steps. If no one is willing to

do that, all the lights would eventually go out. ◆

Discussion Questions

1. What is psychokinesis?
2. What is the difference between clairvoyance and telepathy?
3. What, according to Rhine, is "psi-missing"?
4. What are the factors that appear to result in psi-missing?
5. According to Rhine, which brain waves accompany psi?
6. How does Rhine respond to his many critics?
7. What does Rhine have to say about the parapsychological abilities of animals?
8. What are your thoughts on parapsychology? Do you believe in any of it? Why or why not?
9. If you believe in parapsychological phenomena, what is your evidence?
10. Are you or anyone you know capable of psychokinesis or ESP? How do you know?

Exercises

Name: _____

Date: _____

Part 4: Sensation and Perception

1. I believe in ESP.

Agree	(1)	(2)	(3)	(4)	(5)	Disagree

2. I have had strange perceptual experiences that cannot be explained by science.

Agree	(1)	(2)	(3)	(4)	(5)	Disagree

3. The sense organs provide me with an accurate picture of the world around me.

Agree	(1)	(2)	(3)	(4)	(5)	Disagree

Have you ever had any strange perceptual experiences? What were they? How might a superstitious layperson interpret such experiences? How might various psychologists, such as Ronald Melzack or J. B. Rhine, interpret such experiences?

Working with your roommates, family members, or classmates, replicate one of the experiments described in "Educating Your Nose." Can you confirm that females outperform males? Can you improve people's ability to discriminate odors?

PART 5

STATES OF CONSCIOUSNESS

14 **Lucid Dreaming: Directing the Action as It Happens,**
by Stephen P. La Berge

15 **In Search of the Unconscious,** by Laurence Miller

16 **The Power of Daydreams,** by Eric Klinger

"Consciousness" corresponds to what most people think of as awareness. When we are aware of—in other words, when we can *observe* or *respond to*—our own thoughts and behavior, properties of our bodies, and properties of our surroundings, we are said to be fully conscious. The term "states of consciousness" refers to varying degrees of responsivity. For example, if we are aware only of our thoughts but not of our bodies or our surroundings—which might be the case if we are meditating or daydreaming—we would be said to be in a special state of consciousness. Movies like "Altered States" make states of consciousness seem mystical and other-worldly, but they're actually fairly straightforward. Because we can have perceptual experiences in the absence of sensation, we can "fantasize," "imagine," "envision," "dream," and so on, as long as our immediate environment allows; real sensory experience can easily overwhelm the purely perceptual kind. If we are unresponsive even to our own thoughts, we are said to be "unconscious." I don't mean to imply that consciousness is a simple matter, but I don't think it's nearly as complicated or mysterious as most people (including most psychologists) think it is.

That aside, in "Lucid Dreaming," Stephen P. LaBerge suggests that it is possible to control one's dreams. His work is a good example of a little-used but somewhat-respected research methodology called "self-experimentation." In other words, he serves as his own research subject in many of his experiments. In Miller's "In Search of the Unconscious," modern neuroscientific evidence is offered that suggests a physical basis for Freud's concept of the unconscious—or at least Miller shows us that stimuli can affect our behavior even when we're not aware of them. Finally, University of Minnesota psychologist Eric Klinger suggests that the common daydream can be useful for overcoming boredom, increasing sexual pleasure, boosting creativity, and other purposes.

LUCID *DREAM*ING:
Directing the **A**ction
As It HAPPENS

◆ *Stephen P. La Berge*

"I am in the middle of a riot in the classroom. Everyone is running around in some sort of struggle. Most of them are Third World types, and one of them has a hold on me—he is huge, with a pockmarked face. I realize that I am dreaming and stop struggling. I look him in the eyes and, while holding his hands, speak to him in a loving way, trusting my intuition to supply the beautiful words of acceptance that flow out of me. The riot has vanished, the dream fades, and I awaken feeling wonderfully calm."

We do not usually question the reality of our dreams until after we have awakened. But it is not always so. That we sometimes dream while knowing that we are dreaming has been known since the time of Aristotle. During such "lucid dreams," the dreamer's consciousness seems remarkably wakeful. The lucid dreamer can reason clearly, remember freely, and act volitionally upon reflection, all while continuing to dream vividly. As in the dream above, which I had a little more than two years ago, the dreamer may take an active hand in resolving the dream's conflict and in bringing the plot to a satisfactory conclusion.

Unlike researchers who have gotten people to change the outcome of their dreams through discussions beforehand (see Happy Endings for Our Dreams, by Rosalind Cartwright, *Psychology Today*, December 1978), I have found that the dreamer can change the dream from within—while it is in progress. For example, even while I was dreaming about the thug assaulting me, I felt on another level that he represented an aspect of my own personality I was actively denying. I wanted to make peace with that part of me and was able to do so, consciously, in the course of the dream.

In a personal experiment, I discovered that it is possible to enhance one's capacity for lucid dreaming. For three years, I recorded all the lucid dreams that I could recall—a total of 389. Experimenting with a variety of autosuggestion techniques, I was able to increase the frequency of lucid dreams almost fourfold, to a peak of as many as 26 dreams a month.

---

*During "lucid dreams",
we are remarkably wakeful—
even though still asleep.
We may be able to reason clearly,
remember freely,
signal that we are conscious,
and may even change the plot
if we so choose. But it takes training.*

Because of the vagueness and inefficiency of such techniques, it took me almost two years to work out a method that was fully effective. But toward the end of my ex-

periment, in the third year, I was able to produce lucid dreams virtually at will.

People can not only train themselves to dream lucidly but may also be able to signal laboratory researchers that they are having the dreams. My colleagues at the Sleep Research Center at Stanford University and I have already demonstrated in one study that use of prearranged signals is possible. We were able to verify the occurrence of lucid dreams during rapid eye movement (REM) sleep for subjects who signaled that they knew they were dreaming. The signals consisted of particular dream actions that had observable concomitants and were performed in accordance with presleep agreements. We believe that such experiments can provide a new model for dream research. In the view of Charles Tart, a psychologist at the university of California, Davis, they may lead to "an era of deliberate and controlled phenomenological and scientific exploration of dreaming...which promises great excitement as well as great significance."

MILD: A Technique for Lucid Dreaming

Lucid dreaming has been treated more often as a mysterious talent than as a learnable skill. What little has been written consists largely of reports of lucid dreams, with few hints on how the ability might be cultivated. One exception is the book *Creative Dreaming*, in which psychologist Patricia Garfield describes a very simple method of autosuggestion: before going to sleep, she would tell herself, in effect, "Tonight I *will* have a lucid dream." Garfield, who has experimented with the technique for several years, reports having had an average of four or five lucid dreams per month. Her results indicate that autosuggestion might be a starting point for a method of deliberately inducing lucid dreams.

Long before my study, I had had occasional lucid dreams. At the age of five, I can remember having a series of such dreams, which I would intentionally redream on successive nights. I vividly recall one of the dreams, in which I was underwater for too long and suddenly became fearful of drowning, but then I recalled that in the dream series, I had always been able to breathe underwater. The next lucid dream I can recall did not occur until 20 years later; for several years after that, however, I had an average of less than one a month, but I found lucid dreams sufficiently intriguing to persuade me to study the phenomenon, starting in 1977, for a Ph.D. thesis at Stanford.

During the first year and a half of the study, I experimented with Garfield's autosuggestion technique. I achieved essentially the same results she did, averaging about five dreams a month. (See graph at right.)

By the end of Phase I, I had observed two presleep psychological factors that were associated with the later occurrence of lucid dreams. The first and most obvious was motivation. During Phase I, there were two months during which I reported, respectively, two and three times more lucid dreams than the average for the rest of this period. During the first month (marked A on the graph), I was preparing a dissertation proposal in connection with the study, and during the second (B on the graph), I was attempting to have lucid dreams in the sleep laboratory. During both months, I was thus challenged to demonstrate the feasibility of a scientific study of lucid dreaming.

> *As a child, I dreamed I was drowning. Then I remembered I was able to breathe underwater in such dreams.*

Gradually, more self-observation led to the realization of a second psychological factor: the presleep intention to *remember* to be lucid during the next dream. This clarification of intention was accompanied by an immediate increase in the monthly frequency of lucid dreams (Phase II). Further practice and procedural refinements led within a year to a method that could reliably induce lucid dreams. The method is based on our ability to remember to perform future actions. One does this by forming mental associations between what one wants to remember to do and the future circumstances in which one in-

tends to act. The associations are most readily formed by the mnemonic device of visualizing oneself doing what one intends to remember. It is also helpful to verbalize the intention: "When such and such, do thus and so." What I call the mnemonic induction of lucid dreams (MILD) procedure goes as follows:

1. During the early morning, I awaken spontaneously from a dream.
2. After memorizing the dream, I engage in 10 to 15 minutes of reading or any other activity demanding full wakefulness.
3. Then, while lying in bed and returning to sleep, I say to myself, "Next time I'm dreaming, I want to remember I'm dreaming."

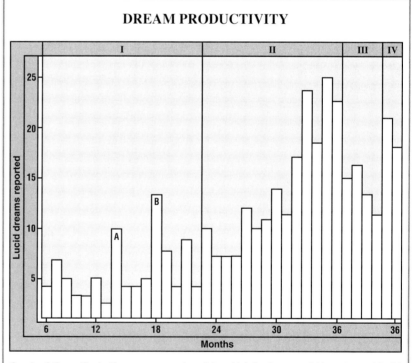

DREAM PRODUCTIVITY

Graph of the author's three-year experiment in which he increased his output of lucid dreams almost fourfold. In Phase I, he is using a simple autosuggestion technique (telling himself, "Tonight I *will* have a lucid dream"); his best performances are associated with strong motivation while (A) preparing a dissertation proposal on lucid dreams and (B) trying to induce the dreams in the sleep lab. In Phase II, he develops a more sophisticated mnemonic method (MILD), cultivating various ways of *remembering* to dream lucidly when he sleeps. After reaching a peak of 26 dreams in one month, he is no longer practicing MILD regularly in Phase III, and his output falls off. He regains stride in Phase IV, when he resumes the MILD exercises while engaged in a dream-signaling study.

4. I visualize my body lying asleep in bed, with rapid eye movements indicating that I am dreaming. At the same time, I see myself as being in the dream just rehearsed (or in any other, in case none was recalled upon awakening) and realizing that I am in fact dreaming.

5. I repeat steps 3 and 4 until I feel my intention is clearly fixed.

Using the MILD technique (during Phase IV and the last four months of Phase II), I had an average of 21.5 lucid dreams per month, with as many as four in one night. Afterward, I discontinued regular practice of MILD during a four-month withdrawal period (Phase III), resulting in a decline that was reversed during the last two months (Phase IV), when I used MILD to produce lucid dreams for the laboratory study I will describe later.

It seemed to me that I could stimulate lucidity whenever I wanted to during REM sleep, which normally occurs about every 90 minutes, four or five times a night, and produces our richest dreams. Although I could successfully induce the dreams in the first REM period of the night, the procedure was most effective during the early morning—in the last stages of REM sleep, when dreams are copious—and after awakening from a previous dream.

Interestingly, certain waking activities during the hours of sleep have been claimed to stimulate lucid dreaming. Garfield, for example, found that in her case "sexual intercourse during the middle of the night was often followed by a lucid dream" if she returned to sleep. Gregory Scott Sparrow, a counselor in Virginia Beach, reports having lucid dreams when

he goes to sleep after meditating early in the morning. Others have told of having the dreams after reading or writing early in the morning.

The diversity of these stimuli (all of which were confirmed by my own experiences) suggests it is not the particular behavior that is important but the *wakefulness* required for it.

We can probably further refine techniques for training people to dream lucidly. So far, MILD has not been tested in a formal lab setting; only three other lucid dreamers besides myself have reported using it successfully. Because it is based on a universal cognitive skill, though, I believe MILD will prove to be generally useful.

But other approaches might be profitably explored. One is the use of hypnosis. On three occasions I was hypnotized and given a posthypnotic suggestion to have a lucid dream; after going to sleep, I did indeed have such a dream two out of the three times.

Another possible method of stimulating lucid dreams might be

> *Lucid dreaming provides a convenient escape for those who choose to avoid dealing with conflicts arising in dreams.*

to provide lab subjects with an external cue while they are sleeping. Other investigators have found that subjects hearing tape recordings of their own voices during REM sleep have dreams that are more assertive, active, and independent. While sleeping in the lab, I had a tape recording of my voice played during REM periods, reciting, "Stephen, you're dreaming." Both times I incorporated the sentence into dreams that I was having and became lucid, but on each occasion I awoke almost immediately.

Messages from the Dream World

Although many people report being able to dream lucidly, how can we prove empirically that they achieve a kind of consciousness during those dreams? In the absence of experimental data, contemporary dream researchers have questioned whether these experiences occur during sleep or during brief periods of hallucinatory wakefulness. Further, if lucid dreamers really are asleep, how can we arrange for them to signal the laboratory researcher when they are having the dreams?

We know that actions in dreams sometimes have shown good correlations with polygraphically recorded eye movements and muscle activity. For example, if a dog is chasing a ball down the street in a dream, the dreamer's eyes have been observed to move rapidly, as if he were following the action. Similarly, body movements in dreams have been known to be accompanied by electrical changes in the muscles of the dreamer. Thus, it seems plausible that lab subjects might be able to signal by carrying out particular dream actions that have observable correlates.

Previous experiments have shown that sleeping subjects are sometimes able to produce behavioral responses while dreaming. One of the most recent studies was done by Rosalind Cartwright at Rush University and Judith Brown, one of her students, who instructed groups of subjects to press microswitches if they began to dream during sleep; the researchers found that when these subjects were awakened, they were more likely to remember dreaming if they had pressed the switches. However, since according to Cartwright the subjects were not conscious of making the responses, these studies do not provide evidence of voluntary action (and thus reflective consciousness) during sleep.

In our study at the Stanford Sleep Center, I was one of four subjects claiming proficiency as lucid dreamers who were studied for a total of 27 nights. We were all hooked up each night to standard apparatus that records eye movements, brain waves, and muscle tension in the chin as well as the wrists (for signaling). The four of us—two men and two women—attempted to follow a prearranged procedure of signaling whenever we became aware we were dreaming. A variety of signals were used, generally consisting of a pattern of upward eye movements and left and right fist clenches. Although

we were allowed to perform each of the prearranged signals when the machinery was being calibrated, we did not otherwise practice while awake.

After each lucid dream we were to awaken and make a detailed report. In the course of the study, 27 lucid dreams were reported subsequent to awakening from various stages of sleep. The four of us reported signaling during 22 of the dreams. After each nights recording, the reports mentioning signals were submitted, along with the respective polysomnograms, to a judge *who was not informed of the times of the the reports.* (The judge was experienced in scoring polygraph records but had no association with the experimenters.)

In 16 cases, the judge was able to select the appropriate 30-second periods on the basis of a correspondence between reported and observed signals. But what might account for the judge's lack of success in blind-matching six of the 22 instances of signaling? We inspected the recordings that immediately preceded each of those signals and found that in most cases, the signals were not strong enough to rise above the level of background "noise"—random activity of the muscles—in the recordings. However, the judge identified no signals from the recordings that had not, in fact, been reported by the four subjects.

The most complex signal, which I performed successfully on two occasions, consisted of a single upward eye movement, followed by a series of left (L) and right (R) dream fist clenches, in the order LLL, LRLL. (See chart at left.) This sequence is equivalent to my initials in Morse code (LLL being three dots, or S; and LRLL being a dot-dash-dot-dot sequence, or L).

All signals during lucid dreams occurred at times of unambiguous REM sleep. However, the occasional but normal appearance during REM sleep of alpha rhythm (a brain wave usually associated with wakefulness) raises the possibility that lucid dreaming could occur during momentary partial arousals, or microawakenings. Nevertheless, alpha rhythm need not be present during lucid-dream signals. Furthermore, some of the lucid dreams were several minutes long, ruling out any explanation based on brief intrusions of wakefulness.

Were the subjects really asleep when the signals were sent? If the criterion of being awake is whether the person perceives the external world, then the subjects were not, in fact, awake. Although we knew we were in the laboratory, that knowledge was a matter of

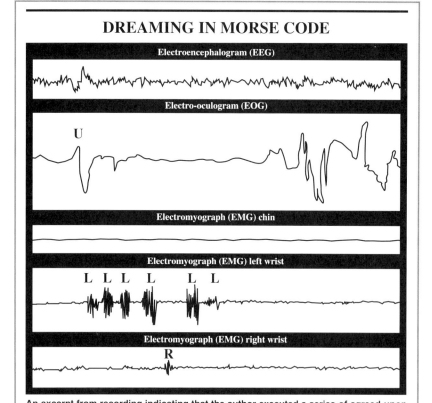

DREAMING IN MORSE CODE

Electroencephalogram (EEG)

Electro-oculogram (EOG)

U

Electromyograph (EMG) chin

Electromyograph (EMG) left wrist

L L L L   L L

Electromyograph (EMG) right wrist

R

An excerpt from recording indicating that the author executed a series of agreed-upon signals while dreaming. When having a lucid dream, he was to carry out actions in it that required a sharp upward eye movement (U on the EOG line) and a series of fist clenches, LLL, LRLL—Morse code for the author's initials, S. L.—picked up on the EMGs as changes in muscle tension. About 20 seconds after this sequence, the author woke up; he said he had indeed been having a lucid dream and had performed the signals. (The erratic eye movements in the excerpt, the low-voltage mixed-frequency EEGs, and the low-amplitude chin EMGs confirm the author was in a phase of REM sleep.)

memory, not perception; upon awakening, all four of us reported having been totally in the dream world and not in sensory contact with the laboratory environment in which we slept.

Was it possible that we were really awake but just not paying attention to the environment (as, for example, when a person is reading or absorbed in daydreaming)? All four of us tended to report that we were conscious of the *absence* of sensory input from the external world. These subjective accounts are, moreover, corroborated by the physiological measures.

The study suggests that under certain circumstances, dream cognition during REM sleep can be much more reflective and rational than was previously assumed. If further experiments confirm that it is indeed possible for lucid dreamers to intentionally signal while they dream, we may soon have a technique for exploring the timing, sequences, and content of dreams with first-hand data from within the dreamers world itself.

The Experience of Lucid Dreaming

In lucid dreams, the realization that one is dreaming may either be gradual or relatively sudden. In the following dream, consciousness comes slowly, under prodding by one of the characters: "I am crossing a bridge over an abyss. When I look into the depths I am afraid to continue. My companion, behind me, says, 'You know, you don't *have* to go this way. You can go back the way you came,' and he points back down an immense distance. But then it occurs to me that if I became lucid I would not need to fear the height. As I realize that I *am* dreaming, I'm able to master my fear—I cross the bridge and awaken."

What happens in lucid dreams has real significance for the dreamer. Though the events that appear to take place in dreams are illusory, our *feelings* in response to dream content are real. So when we are fearful in a dream and realize that it is a dream, the fear doesn't vanish automatically. We still have to deal with it; were it not so, lucid dreams would have no useful connection with our waking lives.

The lucid dreamer does not wish to leave the dream world by awakening, but to awaken within the dream.

We could compare the nonlucid dreamer to a small child terrified of the dark. The child really believes there are "monsters" lurking in the shadows. The lucid dreamer would perhaps be an older child—still afraid of the dark, yet no longer believing that there are monsters out there.

For the naive dreamers, lucidity is most likely to be precipitated by anxiety. But it may also be brought on by embarrassment or delight— or by some bizarre element that suddenly intrudes in the dream. As an example of an anomaly that clarifies the dream consciousness, here is another of my lucid dreams:

"I am walking down a street when I notice a new church—a mosque, in fact, so vast and impressive that I realize that I'm dreaming. As I approach it with great interest, its huge window blasts forth the theme from *Close Encounters of the Third Kind* in organ tones that shake the street beneath my feet. I am thrilled with the realization that it is a spaceship in disguise. Now fully lucid, with great expectation, I walk up the steps and into the blinding light of the door. But here memory fails."

Dreams have long held the reputation of being an important source of cultural, scientific, and artistic innovation. Is it not possible that the fantastic but unreliable creativity of the dreaming state could be brought under conscious control? In the following lucid dream, I seem to have played the piano much more creatively than in the waking state:

"I have not been doing too well in a high school mechanical drawing class. After it, I am sitting listening to a lecture in a large room filled with students. Somehow, as the teacher is saying something or demonstrating at the piano, I remember I'm dreaming. I get up and consider what to do. I walk up to the teacher at the piano as if I were an expected guest artist and sit down to play. I think of playing something out of a book of music, but I find that my vision is too weak. So, I improvise a fantasy in F-sharp minor, starting out prosaically enough but building up to a terrific climax. The truth of the music has, however, made most of the audience flee. But *I* feel satisfied as the dream fades with the last chord."

In contrast, the lucid dreamer's power to control dream content can sometimes become a problem—when, for instance, the person becomes just lucid enough to realize that he or she has the power to awaken or otherwise avoid an unpleasant dream experience instead of resolving the conflict. I became aware of this problem in myself in an early lucid dream:

"I am escaping down the side of a skyscraper, climbing like a lizard, when I realize that I'm dreaming and can fly away. As I do so, the dream fades into a scene in which [a certain teacher] comments on my dream: 'It was good that Stephen realized he was dreaming and could fly, but too bad that he failed to see that since it was a dream, there was no need to escape.'"

The Awakened Dreamer

There is an important issue that we have so far neglected to raise—the symbolic significance of lucid dreams. What does it mean to dream while knowing we are dreaming?

We may generalize from what Freud said of Hervey de Saint-Denys, a famous lucid dreamer of the 19th century: "It seems as though in [the lucid dreamer's] case the wish to sleep [has] given way to another...wish, namely to observe his dreams and enjoy them." And why not! Dreams could be the magic theater of all possibilities and a workshop of creativity and growth. Yet too often we use them to play out repetitious melodramas and confine ourselves by habit to a prison of self-limitation. Lucid dreaming presents a way out of this sleep within our sleep, allowing us to take responsibility for dream and waking lives that we have created.

But there is more significance to lucid dreaming than that. If you were asked, "Are you awake *now*," you would doubtless reply, "Certainly." However, feeling certain that we are awake provides no guarantee that we *are* awake. When Samuel Johnson kicked a stone as if to say, "We *know* whats real," he was expressing this sense of certainty. Yet Johnson could have been dreaming he kicked a stone and felt the same. The illusory sense of certainty about the completeness and coherence of our lives leads us to what William James described as a "premature closing of our accounts with reality."

Finally, in my opinion, the real significance of lucid dreams is that they guide us to higher levels of consciousness, for they suggest what it would be like to discover that we are not yet fully awake. Consider the following analogy: as the state of ordinary dreaming is to lucid dreaming, so the ordinary waking state is to the fully awakened state. Taken in this sense, the lucid dreamer's wish might be to transcend his or her level of limited awareness.

The lucid dreamer does not wish to leave the dream world by awakening but rather, to awaken within the dream. A slogan suggests itself: "Be *in* the dream but not *of* it."   ◆

◆ Discussion Questions

1. What is lucid dreaming?

2. Can dreams be controlled? If so, how?

3. What is the autosuggestion technique and how effective is it?

4. Describe two pre-sleep factors that are linked to lucid dreaming.

5. What is MILD?

6. Explain the procedure required for MILD to be effective.

7. How effective is MILD at producing lucid dreams?

8. At which part of the night is it easiest to have lucid dreams?

9. Define REM sleep.

10. What other methods have been useful in eliciting lucid dreams?

11. Describe the methods used by researchers to determine if someone is having a lucid dream.

In *Search* of the
Unconscious

◆ *Laurence Miller*

Is Freud outdated? In an era when neuroscientists are mapping the chemical pathways of the brain, probing the microsecrets of the neural synapse, computer analyzing human brain-wave patterns and quantifying the cognitive effects of cerebral injury, Freud's grand system of theory and therapy may appear imminently doomed to the status of historical curiosity. With the advance in scientific understanding of behavior, some have argued, notions such as the unconscious, dream interpretation and the importance of sexuality may be so much psychological baggage. "Psychoanalysis, born amid doubt in 1900," says J. Allan Hobson, Harvard Medical School professor of psychiatry, "could well be dead by the year 2000."

But Hobson's prediction may be a bit premature. The brain and behavioral sciences, far from sounding the death knell of psychoanalytic theory and practice, may instead be rallying to Freud's support. Witness the recent profusion of books, professional conferences, scientific papers and popular accounts, all speaking to the potential rapprochement between psychoanalysis and research in the basic neurosciences. Freud himself predicted that his provisional ideas about human psychology would some day find a basis in human biology. Today, a century after the first psychoanalyst opened up his practice in Vienna, the tools, techniques and concepts of the human neurosciences are being used to examine scientifically such fundamental Freudian concepts as the unconscious mind, repression, dream symbolism, sexuality and the development of neurotic symptoms.

A good example of such research is the study of neurosurgery patients carried out by Benjamin Libet and his associates at the university of California School of Medicine. They have shown that a weak electrical pulse delivered either to the hand or to the exposed sensory cortex re-

> *The brain, by allowing a brief interval for its preconscious mechanisms to analyze thoughts and feelings, is able to repress them if they are too unpleasant.*

quires about a half-second of processing time in the brain to reach consciousness. But interestingly, when the pulse is delivered to the hand the patient becomes conscious of the stimulus at the same instant it was delivered, not a half-second later. In other words, some brain mechanism must be "correcting" for the half-second processing delay in the case of natural sensory stimulation, so that subjectively, we regard our perception of an experience as occurring at the same time as the experience itself, not a half-second later.

According to Rockefeller University neuroscientist Jonathan Winson, the one-half second it takes for a sensation to make its way into consciousness provides a possible neurophysiological basis for Freud's notion of repression, the mental burying of disturbing thoughts out of normal awareness; the brain, by allowing a brief interval for certain preconscious mechanisms to analyze thoughts, feelings and memories, is able to repress them if their content is too unpleasant.

Others agree. "Libet's work has enormous implications for understanding unconscious processes," says Howard Shevrin of the University of Michigan Medical Center. Shevrin's own work has involved the study of subliminal perception—the information processing that goes on just below the threshold of conscious awareness. Shevrin uses a technique called "evoked potential" (EP) recording, in which the patters of brain-wave activity accompanying particular kinds of input are recorded by the electroencephalograph (EEG) and analyzed. In a typical experiment, someone is presented with two kinds of visual stimuli for intervals too brief to register in conscious awareness. The first consists of a "meaningful" picture, such as a fountain pen pointed at a person's knee; the second is a similar, but more abstract and less meaningful, arrangement of shapes. After each presentation, the person is asked to relate all the words that come to mind.

The results have typically shown that the meaningful stimulus—the pen-knee combination, for example—produces a greater degree of brain activity as recorded by the EP, even though the person denies having seen anything. This suggests that a more intrinsically interesting or meaningful stimulus elicits more attention and mental processing, even if this attention and mental processing are "unconscious."

How do such findings bolster psychoanalytic theory? Freud hypothesized that during early child development, mental life is dominated by a style of nonrational, impulse-oriented thought, which he called "primary process." Only later, he theorized, does this style of thinking give way to the logical, planning-oriented and judgmental "secondary process" thinking necessary for dealing with the demands of reality. Residue of this early primary-process thinking can show up in adult life in the form of dreams and in some of the delusions and hallucinations of madness.

The verbal associations elicited by the subliminal pen-knee stimulus in Shevrin's experiments have been of several types, some relating conceptually to the stimulus, such as "ink" and "paper," or "leg" and "bone," others relating more to simple sound-associations, such as "pennant," happen," or "neither," "any." And Shevrin has found that different types of brain activity are connected with sound associations and conceptual associations—expressions, he believes, of primary- and secondary-process thinking, respectively.

Further, Shevrin has found that people who characteristically show a tendency to keep unpleasant thoughts, feelings and experiences out of conscious awareness—called "repressers"—typically show less brain activity in response to meaningful stimuli and make fewer associations. Since the stimuli are presented too quickly to register in consciousness, this must mean that the repressers are perceiving the stimuli at least well enough for some unconscious evaluative process to keep them out of awareness. What brain mechanisms might account for this?

Neuropsychological studies have shown that for most people the left hemisphere is specialized for language and for sequential, logical analysis and problem-solving. It is good at perceiving details and particulars and making literal, descriptive interpretations of things. By contrast, the right hemisphere is specialized for spatial processing and the synthesis of

> **Neuropsychological studies have shown that for most people the left hemisphere is specialized for language and for sequential, logical analysis and problem-solving.**

images and forms; it is more intuitive, emotional and inferential and generally takes a more symbolic and associational approach to information processing.

David Galin of the Langley Porter Neuropsychiatric Institute regards certain aspects of right-hemisphere functioning as congruent with Freudian primary-process thinking. The right hemisphere, according to Galin, reasons in a nonlinear style rather than by syllogistic logic. Conversely, other neuropsychologists have associated the faculty we call rationality with the logical, verbal and analytical cognition of the left hemisphere—a form of thought similar to Freudian secondary-process thinking.

> **The right hemisphere is specialized for spatial processing and the synthesis of images and forms; it is more intuitive, emotional and inferential and generally takes a more symbolic and associational approach to information processing.**

Normally, the two hemispheres work together so that a person's perception and consciousness form a unitary whole. But in some peo-

ple, intractable neurological conditions require that the main cerebral "commissures," the fiber pathways connecting the two hemispheres, be surgically severed. These so-called "split-brain" patients sometimes show a curious dissociation of perception and thinking, especially under certain experimental conditions. For example, an erotic visual image flashed to the right hemisphere elicits emotional sin of embarrassment, but the person is unable to describe what was seen. The right hemisphere is processing the image and emotional content of the message, but this information cannot be communicated to the left hemisphere for verbal analysis and labeling. The person can't articulate—either to himself or the experimenter—what is causing the embarrassment. For all intents and purposes, this information is "unconscious."

Psychoanalyst Klaus Hoppe of the University of California, Los Angeles, School of Medicine postulates that one effect of surgical commissurotomy is to interrupt the normal preconscious stream of thought between the two hemispheres. This allows right-hemisphere primary-process thinking to go on, unaccounted for and uninterpreted by the analytic left hemisphere. To explain the similar lack of self-awareness seen in many neurotic, but neurologically intact, individuals, Hoppe hypothesizes the existence of a "functional commissurotomy," which may serve as the cerebral foundation for the concept of repression. Such a psychological impairment would account for the inability of some neurotic patients to develop fresh insights into their feelings, motives and behavior.

Working with neurosurgeon Joseph Bogen of the University of

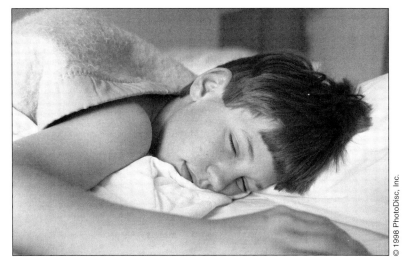

Southern California, Hoppe studied a group of 12 split-brain patients using what is called a psychosomatic questionnaire, which has been used to measure the symptoms seen in a type of psychoanalytic patient called alexithymic. Alexithymia refers to the bland, emotionless, fantasy-poor and virtually dreamless mental style of these overly repressed patients who typically show a marked tendency to develop psychosomatic symptoms. It's as if the physical symptom serves to express the feelings and conflicts that the alexithymic can't consciously get in touch with or verbalize in therapy.

The results of the psychosomatic questionnaire for the split-brain patients were similar to those obtained from diagnosed alexithymics, suggesting that there may be a relationship between the effects of surgical commissurotomy and the thinking style of overly repressed psychoanalytic patients. Are alexithymics and their split-brain counterparts similar to repressers?

Of course, most of us are neither alexithymic nor commissurotomized. Yet we all carry around little pockets of memories, feelings and fantasies of which we may not

be fully aware, but which nevertheless may insidiously influence our perceptions and actions. Galin has some thoughts about how such a condition may develop. Suppose, he says, that a mother gives her child a positive verbal message ("what a good boy") but at the same time speaks in an angry tone and scowls. Since the pathways connecting the brain's two hemispheres are developmentally immature in young children, and the hemispheres are still highly specialized for either emotional or verbal processing, each hemisphere perceives and interprets independently the different aspects of the mother's message. The left hemisphere processes and responds to the positive verbal message, while the negative emotional connotation percolates simultaneously in the right hemisphere.

Then, in future situations in which an authority figure gives an inconsistent message, the individual may find himself experiencing all the raging emotions of an intense conflict—but without knowing why. Because of the early lack of interhemispheric communication, the conflictual material has remained, in effect, "repressed."

Is there any evidence that this kind of primary-process thinking can be traced to right-hemisphere activity? This brings us back to dreaming. Michael Stone of Cornell University suggests that the right hemisphere may contribute to the special, visual, surrealistic and symbolic aspects of dreams. Others, like Bogen, see the right hemisphere as the source of certain kinds of dream material. Commissurotomy patients frequently report fewer dreams than before the operation, suggesting to Bogen that dream material elaborated in the right hemisphere is no longer available for conscious recognition by the left.

Several studies and case reports have found that loss or reduction of subjective dreaming is more likely to occur following right-hemisphere injury than left-hemisphere damage. Yet one EEG sleep study of a supposedly "dreamless" patient born without the main cerebral commissure showed that he exhibited a normal amount of REM sleep. This suggests that right-hemisphere dream elaboration was in fact occurring but was not being communicated to the left, where it could be comprehended and reported.

Paul Bakan of Simon Fraser University notes that during REM sleep the right hemisphere is more active than the left. He hypothesizes that during REM sleep the connections between the two hemispheres are somehow reduced, allowing the right hemisphere more autonomy of functioning. Certain types of mental illness, such as schizophrenia, represent in part a "spillover" of dream-like primary-process thinking into waking consciousness, according to Bakan.

Sexuality is a prominent dream theme and, of course, a central theme in the Freudian psychic drama. If dreaming, including sexual dreaming, can be conceptualized as a predominantly right-hemisphere function, what about sexual responses in general? In an experiment done in the lab of Leonide Goldstein of the Robert Wood Johnson Medical School in New Jersey, male and female volunteers masturbated to orgasm while their brain activity was monitored by EEG. In addition, a few were asked to fake an orgasm. Real, but not feigned, orgasms were associated with increased right-hemisphere activity. This further suggests a major role for the right hemisphere in handling the expression of basic drives, a finding consistent with Freud's emphasis on the importance of sexuality in human development and behavior.

Much of Freud's early data on the unconscious came from the study of hypnosis. Could this, too, be a lateralized function? Studies by Bakan and others have indicated that lateral eye movements, or LEMs, may be a way of assessing hemisphere dominance for certain types of psychological processes. For example, while reflecting on the answer to a question, most people's eyes characteristically flit either to the right or the left, and any given individual makes about 75 percent of LEMs in one or the other direction. Since direction of eye movement indicates activation of the opposite hemisphere, left-movers can be characterized as right-hemisphere-dominant and right-movers as left-hemisphere-dominant.

Bakan administered the Stanford Hypnotic Susceptibility Scale to a group of college students who were also assessed for LEM direction. The results showed that left-movers were more hypnotizable and more likely to report clear visual imagery. To Bakan this suggests that hypnotizability, like dreaming, is a process that relies heavily on the right hemisphere.

LEM research has been used to study another aspect of Freudian theory, the idea that repression may lead to the development of psychosomatic symptoms. Raquel and Ruben Gur of the University of Pennsylvania studied the rela-

---

The right hemisphere may contribute to the surrealistic and symbolic aspects of dreams.

---

tionship between LEM direction, the tendency to use psychological defense mechanisms as measured by the Defense Mechanism Inventory and the presence of psychosomatic symptoms in a group of college undergraduates. They found that left-movers characteristically used defense mechanisms such as denial, repression and reaction formation—disguising an unwanted thought or feeling with the opposite thought or feeling—while right-movers used more projection and turning against others. And left-movers reported more psychosomatic symptoms.

Sandor Ferenczi, one of the early Freudian followers, postulated that the left side of the body is more accessible to unconscious influences than the right. More recently, studies have documented that "hysterical" conversation symptoms—physical symptoms of

psychological origin—tend to occur more frequently on the left side of the body (served by the right hemisphere), even in left-handers. Also, the so-called *la belle indifférence*—paradoxical unconcern for seemingly "serious" conversion symptom such as paralysis—observed in some hysterics by clinicians from Freud's day to the present, bears a striking clinical resemblance to the syndrome of anosognosia, or denial of illness, that frequently occurs after organic right-hemisphere injury.

What this research on consciousness and hemisphericity suggests is that the cerebral mechanisms underlying our hidden motives may be similar to the more well-known neurological underpinnings of language, spatial reasoning and memory. And if the foundations in the brain are similar, then the tools and techniques may indeed be applicable to the study of our most fundamental selves.

So, the verdict for psychoanalysis? On balance, the general consensus seems positive. "That psychoanalysis will be blown over by increased research is wishful thinking" on the part of the skeptics, says Shevrin, who perceives a "quiet revolution" in the direction of scientific psychoanalysis, particularly with regard to such concepts as the unconscious mind and the influence of early experience on later personality and behavior.

"The laboratory and the consulting room do seem to be sharing at least a common wall," he concludes, "which may in fact turn out to have a door in it." ◆

Discussion Questions

1. Explain the neurological process that may explain Freud's theory of repression.

2. How do scientists test the theory that people recognize things that they are not consciously aware that they are seeing?

3. What, according to Miller, are the specialties of the hemispheres of the brain?

4. Name and explain the two types of thinking described by Freud.

5. If a gruesome picture of a decapitated man were displayed in the left field of vision of someone with a split brain, how might he or she respond? Why?

6. What psychological disorders yield symptoms similar to those displayed by split-brain individuals?

7. According to Miller, which part of the brain dreams, and which part brings the dreams to consciousness?

8. Which part of the brain, according to Miller, is more active during orgasm, and how does this support Freud's theory?

9. Explain what an LEM is. How are LEMs used in neurological research?

10. What are "left movers" and "right movers?"

11. According to the author, which part of the brain is associated with conscious thought, and which part is associated with unconscious thought?

The POWER of DAYDREAMS

◆ *Eric Klinger*

A young woman sits in a laboratory surrounded by electronic equipment, lulled by the drone of a tape-recorded narration. She finds herself imagining a man's hand touching her—a welcome thought. She savors it, experiences it in great detail, feels the warmth of his hand on her body. She thinks of her contentment during the act of sex. Meanwhile, the tape keeps droning, the polygraphic pens keep recording. There are two worlds here, side by side in striking contrast.

We know about her daydream because shortly thereafter the tape stopped and a beep signaled her to report her thoughts. The tape was not about sex and the laboratory was chillingly unromantic, but the woman had created her own mental world and inhabited it briefly—as most of us do, often many times a day.

Daydreaming is so commonplace that we usually think little about what it is, why we do it, how it affects us or what sets off the particular content of our fleeting excursions away from the here and now. But it's an important, intriguing—and for psychologists, challenging—part of our mental life.

Our minds constantly flit from one thought to another and one type of daydream to another. Indeed, the types are so varied that there is still no definition of daydreaming that all researchers agree upon. But psychologists usually label thoughts as daydreams if they are about something apart from the person's immediate situation, are spontaneous and are fanciful (with things happening in ways that are contrary to reality). I view daydreams broadly in my own studies: They include reactions to what is happening outside or inside us; fantasies about ordinary, everyday things as well as extravagant flights of fancy; daydreams that are spontaneous as well as those we plan.

Mind-wandering is perhaps the most obvious form of daydreaming. We regularly take at least brief

> **Most daydreams are about ordinary, everyday events: paying the rent, getting your hair done, dealing with somebody on your job, solving a problem with your spouse or special friend.**

side trips into our own imagery and memories even as we read or listen, and occasionally the side trips go on and on. They are sometimes set off by sensations from the world around us, but often their origins seem completely internal: "For five seconds I could picture myself…I'm not sure why…it didn't come from the reading…filling up my snowmobile with gas in back of a station like I've done many times before…And then after I'd fill it up I almost got…kind of like a power feeling. Now I'm ready to go.

Nothing's going to stop me…I see myself just clippin' along."

While doing something that requires little attention, our minds often wander into a review of the past or rehearse what is coming up. We imagine ourselves in interviews, on dates, at parties, in bed—experiences we've had and those we might have. Daydreams usually involve emotion of some kind. Sometimes those imagined events are deeply gratifying: "I was thinking about the last time I went to a concert with my girlfriend—it was down at the stadium—and…how good I thought the concert was." Sometimes they are frightening, enraging or embarrassing: "I was thinking about my girlfriend—she came up last night—and the mix-up that occurred because I thought she was supposed to be coming up on Thursday."

Most daydreams are about ordinary, everyday events: paying the rent, getting your hair done, dealing with somebody on your job, solving a problem with your spouse or special friend. This kind of semi-automatic thought flow is very functional. Even though daydreams occur while you are shaving or ironing or walking to the store, planning and problem-solving just naturally happen. Our daydreams serve as reminders, keeping us aware of important things ahead.

Surprisingly few daydreams are out-and-out self-gratifications, the kind of grandiose fantasies that Freud considered "wish fulfillment" and that humorist James Thurber caught so accurately in *The Secret Life of Walter Mitty* (see "The Ultimate Daydreamer: An Episode from *The Secret Life of Walter Mitty*," this article).

Most of the daydreams I've mentioned happened spontaneously, but people sometimes start daydreams deliberately. They may use daydreams to arouse themselves sexually, both for masturbation and during sex with partners (see "What About Sexual Daydreams?" this article). Soldiers going into battle sometimes whip themselves into fury by imagining their enemies' hateful deeds. Workers in boring jobs often use daydreams to keep themselves stimulated and awake. In studying lifeguards and truck drivers, for example, I found that over 80 percent occasionally launch into vivid daydreams deliberately to ease the boredom.

> *I've found that more than 80 percent of lifeguards and truck drivers daydream at times to ease their boredom.*

What people daydream about differs sharply from one person to the next, but a number of studies, including my own, have shown there are some overall patterns. In one study, I had student volunteers wear beepers during the day. When the beep sounded at irregular intervals, the students recorded what they had just been thinking. I found that about two-thirds of all thoughts—including daydreams—focus on the person's immediate situation and tasks. Most of the rest dwell on everyday tasks, past and future, and relationships.

Despite the common belief that daydreams are often romantic, sexual and violent, it is simply not so. Although most people do have such daydreams at times, these make up a very small proportion of the total. In various samples, and with various measures, a number of studies, including my own, have shown that explicitly sexual thoughts and daydreams made up at most 5 percent of the total. Violent daydreams were also uncommon, ranging from under 1 percent to 9 percent.

Just as there are many kinds of daydreams, there are also many kinds of daydreamers. Twenty years ago, psychologist Jerome L.

Singer of Yale University—the most influential pioneer of modern day-dream research—and psychologist John S. Antrobus of the City College of New York developed a daydream questionnaire called the Imaginal Processes Inventory (IPI). By now thousands of adults of all ages have taken it, and dozens of investigators have analyzed their responses. Psychologists Leonard Giambra of the National Institute on Aging and George Huba of Western Psychological Services in Los Angles have found, using the IPI, that daydreamers consistently differ from one another in three main ways: how many vivid, enjoyable daydreams they have; how many guilty or fear-ridden daydreams they have; and how distractible they are—how well they can control their attention.

These daydreaming styles match the three major dimensions of personality identified by University of Minnesota psychologist Auke Tellegen. He found that people differ systematically in how much positive and negative emotion they experience and how much they conform to society's rules. People who have many guilty or fearful daydreams, for example, also have many negative feelings in their real lives. Steven Starker, chief psychologist at the Veterans Administration Medical Center in Portland, Oregon, has shown that they also suffer more from sleep disturbances.

> *Despite the common belief that daydreams are often romantic, sexual and violent, it is simply not so.*

Although you might expect men's and women's daydreams to be quite different, they are remarkably similar in frequency,

vividness, spontaneity and realism. The differences usually reflect contrasts in women's and men's concerns and stereotypical roles in our society. As sex roles converge, the daydreams of men and women are likely to converge, too.

What triggers daydreams and determines their content is still a question. We are beginning to find some answers through the kind of laboratory research mentioned at the beginning of the article, in which individuals listen to a tape recording and periodically report their thoughts. Actually, we simultaneously played two different taped excerpts of a story or verse, one to each ear. The listeners were free to shift their attention between the two or let their minds wander.

We discovered that we could change what they thought about by changing the wording of the tapes. The most effective words were those that subtly reminded the listener of a "current concern," an unmet goal to which the person was committed. This could be something as trivial as remembering to buy bananas or as serious as a love relationship, a corporate merger or recovery from a coronary.

For the woman we first described, who was concerned about her relationship with her boyfriend, we played simultaneously a tape that subtly touched on that concern and another that was irrelevant. For another person in our study, who wanted to be a counselor, social worker or someone in one of the other helping professions, the relevant tape contained occasional brief passages with descriptions of people in need of help.

Passages designed to remind people gently of their current concerns influenced listeners' thoughts much more reliably than did irrelevant material. Not only did the passages trigger some of the daydreams described above, but the listeners also paid more attention to these concern-related passages and were much more likely to remember them later.

These results suggest that daydreams pop into our heads when we bump into a cue—such as words or pictures from the outside world or from our own thought stream—that reminds us of a current concern. We then notice the cue, store it in memory and start

thinking or daydreaming about that concern.

This process seems to be largely automatic. When my colleagues and I did similar experiments with people who were sleeping, concern-related words influenced what they dreamed about much more reliably than did neutral words. Other researchers have since confirmed the strong association between daydreams and current concerns. Psychologists Steven Gold at Western Carolina University and Loriann Roberson of New York University separately

found that about two-thirds of the daydreams and other thoughts they studied were linked to current concerns.

While a psychology graduate student at the University of Minnesota, Jason Young asked people to concentrate on the middle of a television screen and decide quickly whether what occasionally appeared there was or was not a word. The left side of the screen was filled with computer-related words that the viewers were instructed to ignore. Every so often, however, one of these words relat-

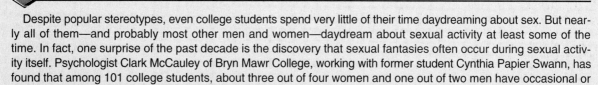

What About Sexual Daydreams?

Despite popular stereotypes, even college students spend very little of their time daydreaming about sex. But nearly all of them—and probably most other men and women—daydream about sexual activity at least some of the time. In fact, one surprise of the past decade is the discovery that sexual fantasies often occur during sexual activity itself. Psychologist Clark McCauley of Bryn Mawr College, working with former student Cynthia Papier Swann, has found that among 101 college students, about three out of four women and one out of two men have occasional or frequent sexual fantasies during sex with partners.

People have an enormous range of fantasies during sex, but the most common is of having sex with someone other than the actual partner. This may be someone known to the fantasizer or an imaginary romantic lover. The fantasizer may replay sexually exciting scenes from films or books. Common themes include imaging the fantasy partner's particular body parts, being in a more romantic setting, having oral or other sex with the imaginary lover, having more than one partner at a time, being tied up by the partner or forcing the other person into sex.

These fantasies are not substitutes for enjoying the act itself, nor do they interfere with sexual enjoyment. On the contrary; on average, the people who most often engage in such fantasies during sex seem to enjoy sex as much as or more than other people and seem to be as sound psychologically. They simply use sexual fantasy as a way to enhance their sexual pleasure.

Questionnaires have unearthed a few gender differences in sexual fantasy. McCauley and Swann found that, during sexual activity, men usually daydream more about real events, past and present, whereas women daydream more about purely imaginary situations. This is true for masturbation as well as sex with others.

A number of investigators have also found that, when fantasizing during sex, men are generally more likely than women to envision themselves as the more active partner in a sexual encounter. This difference, of course, reflects cultural stereotypes. Surprisingly, a substantial proportion of both men and women fantasize that they are being raped or, less commonly, raping someone else. In a study of 230 college students by psychologist David Sue at Western Washington University in Bellingham, Washington, 36 percent of the women and 21 percent of the men reported at least occasional fantasies of being forced to have sex. Sixteen percent of the women and 24 percent of the men reported at least occasional fantasies of forcing others.

In most of these fantasies, both the aggressor and the passive partner are imagined as passionately turned on by the experience—a far cry from the facts of real rape, in which the rapist acts more out of anger or lust for power than out of sexual passion and the victim is too terrified and revolted to respond sexually. Fortunately, most people who are turned on by idealized rape scenes know the difference between their fantasies and reality, and do not try to realize their fantasies in the real world.

The Ultimate Daydreamer: An Episode from *The Secret Life of Walter Mitty*

Walter Mitty stopped the car in front of the building where his wife went to have her hair done. "Remember to get those overshoes while I'm having my hair done," she said. "I don't need overshoes," said Mitty. She put her mirror back into her bag. "We've been all through that," she said, getting out of the car. "You're not a young man any longer." He raced the engine a little. "Why don't you wear your gloves? have you lost your gloves?" Walter Mitty reached in a pocket and brought out the gloves. He put them on, but after she had turned and gone into the building and he had driven on to a red light, he took them off again. "Pick it up, brother!" snapped a cop as the light changed, and Mitty hastily pulled on his gloves and lurched ahead. He drove around the streets aimlessly for a time, and then he drove past the hospital on his way to the parking lot.

…"It's the millionaire banker, Wellington McMillan," said the pretty nurse. "Yes?" said Walter Mitty, removing his gloves slowly. "Who has the case?" "Dr. Renshaw and Dr. Benbow, but there are two specialists here, Dr. Remington from New York and Mr. Pritchard-Mitford from London. He flew over." A door opened down a long, cool corridor and Dr. Renshaw came out. He looked distraught and haggard. "Hello, Mitty," he said. "We're having the devil's own time with McMillan, the millionaire banker and close personal friend of Roosevelt. Obstreosis of the ductal tract. Tertiary. Wish you'd take a look at him." "Glad to, " said Mitty.

In the operating room there were whispered introductions: "Dr. Remington, Dr. Mitty. Mr. Pritchard-Mitford, Dr. Mitty." "I've read your book on streptothricosis," said Pritchard-Mitford, shaking hands. "A brilliant performance, sir." "Thank you," said Walter Mitty. "Didn't you know you were in the States, Mitty," grumbled Remington. "Coals to Newcastle, bringing Mitford and me up here for a tertiary." "You are very kind," said Mitty. A huge, complicated machine, connected to the operating table, with many tubes and wires, began at this moment to go pocketa-pocketa-pocketa. "The new anesthetizer is giving way!" shouted an interne. "There is no one in the East who knows how to fix it!" "Quiet, man!" said Mitty, in a low, cool voice. He sprang to the machine, which was now going pocketa-pocketa-queep-pocketa-queep. He began fingering delicately a row of glistening dials. "Give me a fountain pen!" he snapped. Someone handed him a fountain pen. He pulled a faulty piston out of the machine and inserted the pen in its place. "That will hold for ten minutes," he said. "Get on with the operation." A nurse hurried over and whispered to Renshaw, and Mitty saw the man turn pale. "Coreopsis has set in," said Renshaw nervously. "If you would take over, Mitty?" Mitty looked at him and at the craven figure of Benbow, who drank, and at the grave, uncertain faces of the two great specialists. "If you wish," he said. They slipped a white gown on him; he adjusted a mask and drew on thin gloves; nurses handed him shining...

"Back it up, Mac! Look out for that Buick!" Walter Mitty jammed on the brakes. "Wrong lane, Mac," said the parking-lot attendant, looking at Mitty closely. "Gee. Yeh," muttered Mitty. He began cautiously to back out of the lane marked "Exit Only."
—*Excerpted from* The Secret Life of Walter Mitty *by James Thurber*

ed to the viewers' current concerns. When such words appeared, it took viewers longer to decide about the words they were supposed to watch. They apparently couldn't help being distracted by something related to their current concerns.

Such findings raise the question of why some concerns influence our thoughts and daydreams more than others. When we asked people to list and rate the things they had been thinking about, they reported spending the most time of what was most valuable to them, what had the greatest overall likelihood of success and what required action soon. They thought particularly often about things that posed some challenge, such as a troubled relationship. Something routine, no matter how important, received very little thought.

Value, anticipation, threat, frustration—these aspects marked the concerns whose cues grabbed people's attention. It began to look as if emotion was another key to influencing thought. West German psychologist Michael Bock and I tested this idea indirectly by asking students to perform various tasks with groups of words, such as rating them on their length or abstractness. We then asked them, unexpectedly, to recall as many of the words as they could. They did much better on those that were emotionally loaded for them and more related to their current concerns. On closer examination, we found that they were particularly likely to remember emotionally arousing words, regardless of their association with current concerns. Words that were associated with a current concern but not very emotionally arousing were usually forgotten. Emotionally evocative cues indeed have an edge in influencing our mental processes.

In a way, emotion and current concerns are intertwined with one another and with our daydreams. Our joys, fear, angers, disappoint-

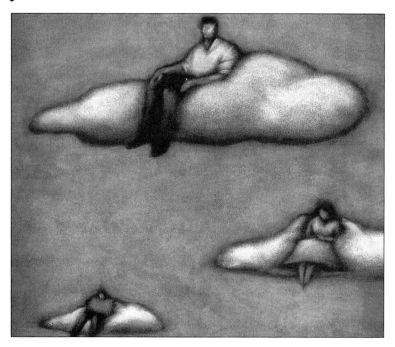

ments and depressions are mostly reactions to how well we are achieving our various goals. We experience most of those emotions precisely because we have become committed to a particular people, achievements and life-styles. Our commitments to goals and our concerns about reaching them control much of our emotional life, and through that, our daydreams.

But, as we have seen, cues may have emotional significance for reasons besides current concerns. First, we seem to have inborn emotional reactions to some kinds of sensations, such as that of falling. Second, once we learn to react emotionally to something, we continue for a time to react to it emotionally. If you have just had a marvelous time at Glacier National Park, for awhile anything associated with the experience will continue to evoke memories and daydreams about the park, accompanied by pleasant feelings.

While daydreams usually draw on the daydreamer's ideas of how people normally act, they lack some of reality's constraints. The employee who is too intimidated to tell off his boss at work may give her an earful in his daydreams. And the boss may react in the daydream in a way that is unlikely in real life. Yet, how they both behave is likely to conform to the daydreamer's notion of "possible worlds." Even the most fan-

---

For many years, daydreaming was in disrepute. It was associated with laziness and even craziness.

---

ciful daydreams seem to be elaborations of thoughts about immediate and longer-range goals and wishers, a kind of personal brain-storming that tries out improbable plans and solutions for particular concerns.

Sometimes, however, people seem to daydream the impossible

spontaneously. A daydreamer might imagine escaping a predicament by literally flying away. Daydreams of this kind seem different from anything in the daydreamer's experience, but they are not; in such fantasies daydreamers combine their observations (in this case, of birds) with their experience of themselves. This fusion of normally separate components, often encountered in dreams, is the essence of creative insight. Combining the uncombinable is generally impossible in the everyday world, but there is nothing besides habit and limited imagination to prevent it in daydreaming.

For many years, daydreaming was in disrepute in the Western world. It was associated with laziness, and Freud's theories described it as infantile and neurotic. Since popular notions of schizophrenia emphasized schizophrenics' difficulty distinguishing between fantasy and reality, people believed that such mentally ill people had retreated into their daydreams. Accordingly, some midcentury educational psychologists cautioned against letting children daydream, lest they slide into neurosis and even psychosis.

But current research indicates that the old notions about daydreams are completely wrong. There is no evidence that any amount of daydreaming can make a person schizophrenic or bring on any other psychological disorder. Most studies reveal no significant differences between schizophrenics and others in daydreaming or other imagery. Investigators such as Starker have shown that schizophrenics do not daydream more often or have more vivid daydreams than other people do. And when psychologists Sheryl Wilson and Theodore X. Barber studied people who were easily hypnotized, they found that although the people enjoyed daydreaming much more than others did, there was nothing especially unstable about them.

Indeed, other evidence shows that people who are given to fantasy may even have special psychological strengths. Psychologist Roni Beth Tower found that "in general, imaginative children [those who pretend easily and comfortably] are more lively, concentrate better, are more attractive to others, tolerate frustration better, tend to show less fear, are more alert and generally joyful."

Israeli high school students who scored high on the daydreaming scale of the IPI were more empathic than were low scorers. According to E. Barbara Hariton, a clinical psychologist in New York who studied with Singer, women who fantasize frequently during sexual intercourse with their mates are just as well adjusted as others and enjoy sex perhaps somewhat more. In sum: Frequent and fanciful daydreamers are clearly no worse off psychologically—and possibly better off—than those who daydream less.

Although daydreaming itself is not harmful, some daydreams may be bad for some individuals, since daydreams can be rehearsals and can carry over into action. People with phobias who dwell on their fears, such as someone with a strong fear of flying who keeps imagining taking off and then crashing, may conceivably strengthen their phobias. Depressed individuals who keep ruminating about their miseries without taking constructive action may prolong their depressions. And, although the issue is far from settled, it's possible that rapists who rehearse their rapes in fantasy may increase their readiness to commit such crimes.

Some people do daydream too much, or at least more than they would like, but such fantasies are symptoms of a problem, not the problem itself or its cause. Excessive daydreaming most likely indicates frustration in reaching the daydreamer's main life goals, such as establishing meaningful relationships and finding occupational success. It may even be a way of bringing some peace of mind or gratification to an otherwise dismal existence. The answer is to get help in changing the real-life situation.

The fact that people who daydream more than average (but not excessively) often seem to have above-average psychological strengths suggests that daydreaming can actually be helpful. We have already seen that playing over one's current concerns serves as a reminder of important events and problems; it provides an arena for reviewing and learning from the past and rehearsing and refining future behavior. In addition, many important creative works, including Mozart's symphonies, Nietzsche's *Thus Spake Zarathustra* and Poincaré's mathematical invention of Fuchsian Functions, originated in daydreaming or daydream-like states.

Psychotherapists and behavior therapists alike have turned to guided daydreams as a way of helping clients work through major personal problems. Los Angeles psychologist Joseph E. Shorr, for example, has developed extensive tactics for using mental imagery to diagnose clients and help them reach key personal insights. There's also evidence that practicing physical or social skills in fantasy, such as the visualization Greg Louganis uses before his spectacular high dives, can improve performance later.

Our brains seem to be built to daydream—to create images that reflect our inner psychological selves in action. Researchers such as psychologist Ronald Finke have shown that when we create visual images in our minds, we activate some of the same brain mechanisms used in perceiving the world around us. Studies by Edmund Jacobson, the psychologist who developed the technique of progressive relaxation early in this century, indicate that movement images share some of the brain and body mechanisms used by actual movement. And other research has revealed that mental images carry emotions with them and are linked to daydreamer's motivational state.

These broad connections suggest to me that images represent the internal working of the daydreamer's whole psychological structure, free from the real-world constraints of sensation and movement. And, in the same way, images in daydreams represent the daydreamer's core psychological processes in action.

Daydreaming seems to be a natural way to use brain power efficiently. Daydreams usually start spontaneously when what we are doing requires less than our full attention: Our brains move our conscious attention automatically away from the here and now to work over other concerns. Daydreaming keeps our mind active while helping us to cope and create.   ◆

Discussion Questions

1. Give three definitions of daydreaming: your perspective, the author's perspective, and the typical psychologist's perspective.

2. What role does reality play in daydreams? In fantasies?

3. How do planning and problem solving relate to daydreams?

4. Can daydreams be useful? If so, how? If not, why not?

5. What percent of daydreams are sexual?

6. What are the differences between the daydreams of men and women?

7. Explain how daydreams are related to personality.

8. Can outsiders (such as experimenters) manipulate the content of a daydream?

9. What has the greatest influence on the content of daydreams?

10. Has daydreaming helped you in some way? If so, how?

11. Have you ever been reprimanded for daydreaming? When, and why? What effect, if any, might social disapproval have on daydreaming?

Exercises

Part 5: States of Consciousness

1. I believe that my dreams have definite meaning.

Agree   ①   ②   ③   ④   ⑤   Disagree

2. I believe that dreams can predict future events.

Agree   ①   ②   ③   ④   ⑤   Disagree

3. The unconscious mind exists and is an important part of human functioning.

Agree   ①   ②   ③   ④   ⑤   Disagree

For the next three days, write down a brief description of all your dreams and daydreams. List related items into categories in the space below.

What patterns, if any, do you see in the content of your dreams and daydreams?

Which items listed above are sources of useful information or ideas? Explain how recording your dreams and daydreams might help you in everyday life.

PART 6

LEARNING

Three types of processes—classical conditioning (first studied by Ivan Pavlov early in the 1900s), operant conditioning (studied crudely by Edward Thorndike in the late 1800s and expertly by B.F. Skinner and others during much of the twentieth century), and observational learning (which everyone knows is important but hardly anyone studies)—are essential for human learning. Research on classical (or "Pavlovian") conditioning shows us that we respond very differently to boring stimuli (like the sound of the bell) after they have been paired with biologically-important stimuli (like ice cream being transported by the neighborhood ice cream truck). Research on operant conditioning shows us how the consequences of behavior (like praise or criticism or money) affect subsequent behavior. And research on observational learning (such as it is) shows us that we can learn from others just by watching them and listening to them (like when we take a class!).

Without doubt, it has been research on operant conditioning that has led to the greatest number of practical applications, including advances in education, computer-aided instruction, business and industry, pharmacology, and therapy. In "Token Economies: The Rich Rewards of Rewards," Alan E. Kazdin talks about the many benefits of one application of operant conditioning research, the "token economy," a technique used for both management and training purposes in a variety of institutional settings. The token economy is now virtually universal in facilities serving emotionally-disturbed, developmentally-disabled, autistic, psychotic, and other impaired individuals. One could argue, of course, that even normal people march in step to tokens—that our entire economy is one giant token system, with coins and bills as tokens.

Legend has it that some of Skinner's students once conspired to use operant conditioning techniques to alter his lecturing behavior. They paid attention to his lecturing only when he walked toward one side of the stage. Within minutes, he was hovering so close to the edge that he nearly fell off. So it seems that even the behavior of authority figures is affected by its consequences. In "Little Brother Is Changing You," we learn about a remarkable program in which troublesome youths use operant conditioning techniques to alter the behavior of teachers, parents, and peers in constructive ways. Finally, in "Fall into Helplessness," distinguished researcher Martin Seligman explains how a history of conditioning might account for many cases of clinical depression.

Token ECONOMIES: The RICH *Rewards* of REWARDS

◆ *Alan E. Kazdin*

For about 15 years, token economies have been used by the staffs of mental hospitals, prisons, and schools for the retarded to change the behavior of their charges. Whether the tokens are coins, tickets, points, check marks, stars, or cards, patients, prisoners, and students earn them for specific behavior and use them, like money, to purchase other rewards.

Under such a system, mental patients become less apathetic, prisoners become cooperative, and retarded children learn to care for themselves. But token economies are no longer confined to the walls of institutions. Radical new developments have brought them into the community, where they are helping clear litter from the landscape, reduce public consumption of electricity, recycle waste, and encourage the use of mass transit.

Contemporary token economies can be traced to B.F. Skinner's development of operant conditioning. Years of work with rats and pigeons established the basic principles behind the systems. The key to the token economy is positive reinforcement, which indicates that—for pigeons or people—behavior that is rewarded is likely to be repeated.

Tokens provide powerful reinforcement, because they can be exchanged for so many other things. For example, in a psychiatric hospital a patient might earn tokens for attending therapy, dressing himself, socializing with the other patients, and keeping up with current events. He could exchange the tokens for extra snacks, admission to movies or social functions, special dining privileges, or commodities at a hospital store.

Punishment sometimes plays a role in these economies. A patient who engages in undesirable behavior may forfeit some of the tokens he has earned.

In 1961, Teodoro Ayllon and Nathan Azrin developed the first token economy in a mental institu-

> **The key to the token economy is positive reinforcement, which indicates that—for pigeons or people—behavior that is rewarded is likely to be repeated.**

tion, Anna State hospital in Illinois. Patients earned coins for bathing, brushing their teeth, making their beds, and working at jobs that kept the hospital running. Their tokens could rent private rooms in the hospital, reserve private sessions with a psychologist, let them attend church, or see a movie. The program was extremely successful and showed the powerful effects that tokens exert on patients' behavior in a hospital setting.

Another influential token economy began at the University of Washington, where Montrose M. Wolf, Sidney Bijou, and Jay Birnbrauer developed a system at Ranier School for getting retarded children to work at academic tasks. The program, developed in 1962, gave students tokens and approval for applying themselves to reading, writing, and arithmetic as well as for mastering such practical skills as telling time. The children's academic performance improved markedly.

Silver Medals

Although contemporary token economies derive directly from operant conditioning, full-fledged token economies were in existence more than 150 years ago. In England in the early 1800s, Joseph Lancaster developed a system to teach masses of poor children by using other students as classroom monitors. Children could earn plaques, badges, or tickets for reciting their lessons to monitors. These tokens could be exchanged for other rewards. Some hard-working students proudly displayed large silver medals on chains around their necks. Lancaster's system, which provided inexpensive education by using student teachers, was adopted widely throughout Great Britain, Europe, Russia, South America, Asia, the United States, and Canada. As rote memorization fell out of favor and education became more individualized, the programs died out.

Another early 19th-century token economy was devised by Alexander Maconochie, whose aim was to rehabilitate prisoners at Norfolk Island, Australia. Maconochie's system converted criminal sentences into marks that individuals had to earn to obtain release. Prisoners earned marks for working within the prison. Maconochie's system, which contrasted sharply with the brutal penal methods of the time, never caught on in the way that Lancaster's system did.

The economies of Lancaster and Maconochie used principles and techniques that have been studied scientifically only within the last few years. But by the late 1960s and early 1970s, token economies based on the Anna State Hospital and Ranier School systems had spread. Most programs were used with psychiatric patients, the mentally retarded, and schoolchildren, but some delinquents, convicts, drug addicts, alcoholics, geriatric residents, and stutterers also found themselves responding to tokens.

Although token economies focus on well-developed, easily observed responses to specific situations, the programs often lead to wider changes. For example, reinforcing psychiatric patients for taking care of themselves and keeping the ward running may result in broad changes, as such patients become more cooperative, socialize more with other patients and staff, are able to spend more time away from the hospital, seem more cheerful and outgoing, seem less depressed, engage in less bizarre talk and screaming. Moreover, patients participating in token economies tend to be released from hospitals much sooner than patients given traditional hospital care.

Outside the Walls

Token economies are also effective outside hospital walls. For example, in Achievement Place, a program for delinquent youths in Lawrence, Kansas, adolescents live in a home supervised by a resident couple. Tokens reinforce the youths for such things as speaking, studying, cleaning their rooms, saving money, accepting criticism gracefully, and keeping up on current events. Besides these specific changes, the youths increase their self-concepts and their desire to achieve, and begin to feel that they are masters of their fate.

The immediate effect of token economies is well-documented. We know much less about their long-term effects. Few studies have followed people treated in a token economy, but its use in psychiatric hospitals has been followed by an increase in the discharge of patients and a decrease in their readmission; in facilities for delinquents, by a decrease in the adolescents' contacts with the law and the courts; and in schools, by students' improvement in achievement and an increase in intelligence-test scores.

There is a clear difference in status between the managers of a token economy and those whose behavior is to be changed.

No matter how diverse the situation, traditional economies share common features. First, there is a clear difference in status and authority between the people who administer the program and the people whose behavior is changed. The latter have little say.

Second, treatment focuses on the behavior of the person considered to be deviant: the patient, delinquent, student, hyperactive child, or prisoner.

Third, tokens have been restricted largely to traditional institutions such as hospitals, prisons, and schools. Implementing programs in such settings is simple because the clients are captive. They live in a controlled environment, which makes it easy to see that they are reinforced at proper times.

All these traditional features are changing, so that token economies are becoming increasingly democratic, switching their focus from the person who is considered deviant to those who may influence his behavior, and moving from corrective institutions to the world outside.

Who Gives the Token?

When only staff members deliver tokens to residents, a patient or prisoner may behave appropriately but fail to get his tokens because no staff member was there to see him. Further, if a patient's unobserved behavior goes unrewarded, he will soon learn to behave properly only when a staff member is there to hand him a token.

Many programs get around this problem by having other patients, prisoners, or students give tokens or take them away, according to an agreed-upon schedule. At Achievement Place, delinquent youths are effective and enthusiastic in rewarding—and punishing—their peers. To ensure that the youth administrators give tokens for desirable performance, and only then, and that they take away tokens only for specified misbehaviors, such as not doing an assigned job on time, the tokens they get depend upon how well they do their jobs. In some programs, peers also help determine how tokens are earned, lost and spent, as well as how to handle infractions of the program's rules.

Although token economies focus on well-developed, easily observed responses to specific situations, the programs often lead to wider changes.

Peers can help develop desired behavior in other ways. One effective procedure calls for peers to share the consequences that are earned by others. For example, when one or more students earn tokens for their behavior, the entire class divides them. This leads the class members to encourage and support appropriate behavior. Such an arrangement restructures the social situation so that peers notice and praise any improvement in behavior.

Another way to involve peers in the program is to give rewards on the basis of group behavior. When the behavior of the entire ward of patients or classroom of students determines the number of tokens that are earned, patients or students monitor each other to make sure that the group behaves properly. In this sort of token program, changes in individual behavior may come from the knowledge that peers are watching and from their words of encouragement or scorn rather than from the tokens themselves.

When peers give rewards, side effects often appear. Some studies indicate that when peers either dole out the tokens or share in the tokens of the group, there is more social interaction and the students or patients behave altruistically toward each other. Occasionally, the changed behavior that emerges during a peer-administered token economy lasts longer after the program ends than does behavior that changed under a staff-administered program.

Another development involves teaching individuals to give themselves tokens. Most self-reinforcement programs are run in elementary-school classrooms. Students give themselves tokens for working on their assignments and for paying attention to the teacher. The teacher generally administers the program in the beginning to show the children what is expected and what behavior is to be rewarded. Then the children take control. As expected, if children are never checked, they tend

to become lenient in dealing themselves tokens. But occasional praise from the teacher or bonus tokens for taking their rewards only at appropriate times usually maintains their honesty.

Patients may give therapists money, then earn it back by meeting certain standards. This works well with obesity.

Individuals can also help determine the standards that earn tokens and the rewards for which the tokens can be exchanged.

Allowing clients a major role in their own treatment may be valuable. People seem to prefer programs over which they have some control. Individuals can also reinforce themselves no matter where they happen to be so that broad changes in behavior occur that would be difficult to accomplish in programs that rely solely on staff members. Finally, giving individuals control over a program guards against coercive, unfair, or unethical practices.

Who Gets the Token?

In traditional programs, the rewards go to the people for whom the hospital, prison, or school was established. But changes in the clients' behavior may depend upon the actions of the staff. The things they do—or fail to do—may have a great impact on their charges.

For this reason, token economies have recently been established to reward or punish the behavior of the hospital staff or the teachers. In many hospitals, aides get money, trading stamps, certificates, or extra work breaks for behaving appropriately toward the patients. They may earn tokens for initiating conversation with patients, for responding to the patients' actions, or for ignoring the patients when they behave bizarrely. (Behavior such as temper tantrums in children or incoherent talk in mental patients

will often disappear if it is ignored. Paying attention to such behavior, whether by spankings or scoldings or solicitous attention, may reinforce the tantrums or the wild speech.)

Where such programs have been instituted, the behavior of both staff and patients has changed markedly. Incentives for staff performance smoothly restructure the manner in which the aides behave toward the patients. As the patients respond to the new staff demeanor, their own behavior changes without additional rewards.

In a restricted setting, such as a hospital or a school, clients have little choice but to participate in the token economy or lose all hope of its limited rewards. Because of this close control, many have questioned whether it is possible to use token economies in relatively free situations. Recently, however, tokens have made their way into diverse areas with some success.

Tokens in the Home

Token programs are used regularly in outpatient treatment with both children and adults. Parents of child clients learn to use tokens to get their children to complete chores, to do their homework, to comply with instructions, and to cooperate with their brothers and sisters. When adults are the clients, spouses may use tokens with each other to encourage conversation, to control excessive talk, or to cut alcohol or cigarette consumption.

Money, the basic token in the national economy, is often used to reinforce individuals in outpatient therapy. In many studies, patients give therapists money at the outset of treatment, and they may earn it back by meeting certain standards. This procedure is especially successful in cases of obesity. Overweight clients earn back their money by losing pounds, by adhering to a diet, or by exercising regularly. Any unearned money is forfeited at the end of treatment.

Probably the greatest change in the use of tokens has come in community programs. Most programs focus on behavior that has social and environmental impact on the community, and the token economy generally covers a single community problem. Tokens have successfully cut down on litter and energy consumption and have stepped up the recycling of waste material and the use of mass transit.

Each type of program has been tried in a variety of settings. For example, anti-litter programs have been conducted in zoos, grocery stores, movie theaters, national campgrounds, city neighborhoods, schools, and athletic stadiums. Projects designed to increase the recycling of paper have been carried out on college campuses, in grocery stores, and apartment complexes.

One timely application of tokens has been to alter patterns of energy consumption. For decreasing their use of electricity, gas, or oil, families get small monetary incentives or points they can exchange for rewards they select. Sometimes the rewards center on a single kind of energy consumption, such as decreasing the use of heat, air conditioning, dishwashers, or automobiles.

One city increased the use of its buses by giving passengers a token each time they rode the bus. The tokens could be saved and exchanged for coffee, pizza, beer, or free bus rides.

Tokens have been used in industry to develop job-related behavior by reinforcing punctuality, regular attendance, and completion of specific tasks. The incentives generally are money. Monetary incentives also have been used to find jobs for the unemployed. In Illinois, each person who told the employment agency about a job opening got $100 if

that job was filled by one the the agency's clients.

Token reinforcement has been incorporated into basic-training programs in some army camps. Recruits earn points for their performance at inspections, training formations, their proficiency in combat tactics, and so on. They can exchange the points for overnight passes, recreational opportunities, and even for promotion.

Slipping into Old Habits

These widespread advances present only part of the picture. The token economy faces unresolved issues and some uncertainty about its future.

Many critics charge that once a program ends, people slip back into their old ways of behaving. Unfortunately, the critics are often right. At first, investigators assumed that when appropriate behavior, such as studying or interacting with others, was developed, it would endure. The natural reinforcements of success, good grades, or social contacts would insure its continuation. But this appears to be the exception, not the rule.

Once the token economy has changed behavior, specific techniques must be used to make temporary gains permanent.

Even behavior that seems to be important for everyday functioning does not continue after a program is withdrawn. Thus, although token economies will keep a hospital ward, a prison, or a classroom running smoothly, in most cases they fail to change behavior permanently. And when a client leaves the hospital or school and enters an environment where no tokens appear for good behavior, he falls into old behavior patterns.

Studies conducted in the last few years indicate that, once the

token economy has changed behavior, specific techniques must be used to make sure that the gains will be carried over to new settings. At the Pennsylvania State University, Russell Jones and I used such a procedure to keep student behavior in a special-education elementary classroom at a high level after ending a token economy. After tokens had improved the students' behavior, these reinforcements were gradually phased out. To keep the children working at their new level, we encouraged them to reward each other at the close of the day by applauding each of the students who had done especially well. We also instituted special classroom activities, such as movies, ice cream, or extra recesses, that rewarded the whole class on the basis of each student's performance. We had shifted from the artificial reinforcement of tokens to natural events such as attention and class activities. By making the shift gradually, the gains in student behavior remained. Twelve weeks later, when the term ended, the children were still performing as well as they had under the token economy.

Another way to avoid backsliding is to develop desired behavior in many different situations and have may different people reward it. This way the new behavior does not become confined to specific settings and certain people. For example, teachers, peers, and parents can reinforce the same behavior by giving tokens in the classroom, on the playground, and at home. When the program ends, the chances are improved that the child's new behavior will remain and will transfer to new settings.

Tokens and the Courts

In the late 1960s, the courts stepped in and ruled that some programs violated prisoners' rights.

Some feared that, no matter how effective token economies might be, their use would soon be prohibited.

Such fears proved groundless. Recent court decisions regarding the treatment of the mentally ill, the retarded, delinquents, and prison inmates certainly have had a direct bearing upon token economies, but few of the programs found themselves put out of business by the rulings. The new democratic practices, developed without judicial pressure, had already changed the look of most token programs.

A major legal issue pertains to the use of an institution's amenities as positive reinforcement. In the case of *Wyatt v. Stickney*, the court noted that the institutionalized patient has the right to many of the events and activities that formed the core of many token economies. For example, according to this ruling the patient is entitled to a comfortable bed, a closet or locker for personal belongings, a nutritionally balanced meal, the right to receive visitors, to wear his own clothes, to attend religious services, to be outdoors, and to visit with the opposite sex.

Many token economies in mental hospitals and prisons regarded some of these as privileges and required that patients or prisoners purchase them with earned tokens. Some harsh prison programs, for example, took away razor blades, tobacco, combs, soap, and Bibles from prisoners and required them to exchange earned tokens for even minimal comforts.

If token economies are to survive in institutions, new and desirable items must be added to the economy's environment. In some prisons, such items have been found. Inmates can exchange their tokens for trading stamps and purchase items from redemption catalogs. Or they may trade tokens for the right to go fishing or to visit with prisoners of the opposite sex.

Ingenious administrators have gone further. Other possible rein-

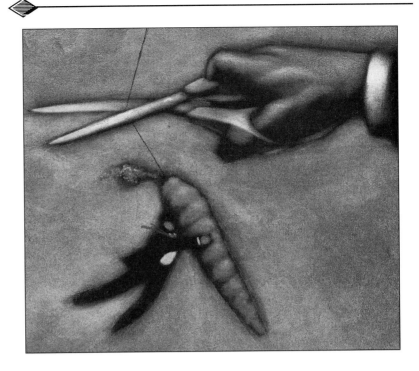

forcements include extra opportunities to engage in activities, such as using the phone or writing letters, that present rules make available on only limited occasions. In general, investigators will have to become increasingly creative in selecting rewards to back up tokens.

The court has also intervened in the kinds of behavior that may earn tokens. Although most of the behavior altered in token economies has not been controversial, the court has forbidden having institutionalized residents work for the benefit of the institution. Work within an institution frequently helps overcome patient apathy, but the court believes, rightly, that patients are often exploited. Patients can be coerced into work in order to earn tokens and receive other privileges. Patients ready for release might be kept because of their economic value to the hospital. In several decisions, the courts have ruled that patients can work on hospital jobs only if their work is voluntary and

if they receive the minimum wage. Work that does not maintain the hospital operation or, like vocational training, that has a clear therapeutic value is expected. Many token programs have focused on hospital jobs to increase patient activity; they must now find other methods.

Other legal issues also have implications for institutional treatment: the right of patients to receive treatment, the right to refuse it, and informed consent. These issues transcend the use of token economies and their resolution may influence the general nature of institutional treatment. The courts' scrutiny of patient and inmate rights may lead to an insistence on the accountability of all treatment programs. While this might create difficulties for traditional therapies, such insistence could eventually benefit token economies and other behavior-modification programs that can show consistent improvement in the patients they treat.

Discussion Questions

1. What is the key principle of token economies?

2. From what learning theory are token economies derived?

3. Why is it important to have non-authority figures hand out the rewards?

4. List some ways that peers are used in a token economy.

5. List and describe some ways that token economies have been applied in the community.

6. What are some techniques to insure that the behavior change created by the token economy will carry over to new settings?

7. Think of an area in which you or someone you know would like to improve. How could you use a token economy to help?

Little **Brother IS** *Changing* **You**

◆ *Farnum Gray with Paul S. Graubard and Harry Rosenberg*

Jess's eighth-grade teachers at Visalia, California, found him frightening. Only 14 years old, he already weighed a powerful 185 pounds. He was easily the school's best athlete, but he loved fighting even more than he loved sports. His viciousness equaled his strength: he had knocked other students cold with beer bottles and chairs. Jess's catalog of infamy also included a 40-day suspension for hitting a principal with a stick, and an arrest and a two-and-a-half-year probation for assault.

Inevitably, Jess's teachers agreed that he was an incorrigible, and placed him in a class for those with behavioral problems. Had they known that he had begun secret preparations to change *their* behavior, they would have been shocked.

The New Jess

His math teacher was one of the first to encounter his new technique. Jess asked for help with a problem, and when she had finished her explanation, he looked her in the eye and said, "You really help me learn when you're nice to me." The startled teacher groped for words, and then said, "You caught on quickly." Jess smiled, "It makes me feel good when you praise me." Suddenly Jess was consistently making such statements to all of his teachers. And he would come to class early or stay late to chat with them.

Some teachers gave credit for Jess's dramatic turnaround to a special teacher and his rather mysterious class. They naturally assumed that he had done something to change Jess and his "incorrigible" classmates.

Rather than change them, the teacher had trained the students to become behavior engineers. Their parents, teachers and peers in the farm country of Visalia, California, had become their clients.

A Reward System

Behavior engineering involves the systematic use of consequences to strengthen some behaviors and to weaken others. Jess, for example, rewarded teachers with smiles and comments when they behaved as he wanted; when they were harsh, he turned away.

People often call reward systems immoral because they impose the engineer's values upon those he conditions. But the Visalia Project turns things around, according to Harry Rosenberg, head of the project and the Director of Special Education for the school district. "The revolutionary thing here is that we are putting behavior-modification techniques in the hands of the learner. In the past, behavior modification has been controlled more-or-less by the Establishment. It has been demanded that the children must change to meet the goodness-of-fit of the dominant culture. We almost reverse this, putting the kid in control of those around him. It's kind of a Rogerian use of behavior modification."

Rosenberg was born and reared in Visalia and has been teacher and principal in a number of schools in that area. He began using behavior modification nine years ago, and he has kept experimentation going in the district with modest grants, mostly Federal. His proposals have emphasized that Visalia is an isolated district that, to avoid provincialism, needs contact with innovative educators from around the country. The grants have paid a variety of consultants to work with Visalia schools over the years.

Reinforcing Opponents

The idea of training kids as behavior engineers arose from a single incident with a junior-high-school student. He was in a behavior-modification program for the emotionally disturbed. His teacher told Rosenberg that although the boy was responding fairly well to the class, he was getting into fights on the playground every day. As they discussed ways of helping the boy, the teacher suggested that they identify the kids with whom he was fighting and teach him to reinforce those kids for the behaviors that he wanted. The process worked.

Rosenberg mentioned the incident to Paul Graubard of Yeshiva University who was a consultant to the district. The incident intrigued him and he thought that training students as behavior engineers could have widespread implications in education, answering some philosophical objections to the use of behavior modification in schools.

Rosenberg had long believed that many students who were segregated in special-education classes should be reintegrated into regular classes. Graubard agreed. He designed an experiment to help children diagnosed as retardates, or as having learning or be-

135

havior problems, change their teachers' perceptions of them. This, predicted Graubard, would enable the child to be reintegrated into regular classes.

Special Classes: Incorrigibles and Deviants

For the pilot project, Rosenberg selected a local junior high school with an unfortunate but accurate reputation. It was the most resistant in the district to the integration of special-education students; it had a higher percentage of students assigned to special classes than any other in the district. Classes for those labeled incorrigible held 10 percent of the school's 450 students; Rosenberg saw this as a disturbing tendency to give up on pupils too easily. He also found that minority children were more likely to be labeled incorrigible or tagged with some other form of deviancy. Directives from the principal and supervisors to treat all children alike regardless of race or ability had failed. To make matters worse, the school also had the highest suspension and expulsion rates in the district.

Graubard and Rosenberg selected seven children, ages 12 to 15, from a class for children considered incorrigible, to be the first behavior engineers. Jess and one other child were black, two were white, and three were Chicanos. A special-education teacher gave the seven students instruction and practice in behavior modification for one 43-minute class period a day. He then moved them into regular classes for two periods each day. The teachers of these classes became their clients. The teachers ranged in age from 26 to 63, and had from two to 27 years of teaching experience.

© 1998 PhotoDisc, Inc.

Shaping Teachers' Behavior

Stressing the idea that the program was a scientific experiment, the special teacher required each student to keep accurate records. During the experiment, they were to record daily the number of both positive and negative contacts with their clients. The students would not try to change the teachers' behavior during the first period; instead, they would keep records only to determine the norm. For the next phase, the stu-

Learning to praise teachers with sincerity was difficult for the children. They were awkward and embarrassed at first, but they soon became skillful.

dents were to work at shaping the teachers' behaviors and to continue to keep records. For the last phase the students were not to use any of the shaping techniques.

Rosenberg had estimated that record-keeping could begin after two weeks of training students to recognize and to record teachers' positive and negative behavior. But this preliminary training took twice as long as he expected. While the students quickly learned to score negative behavior, they were seldom able to recognize positive behavior in their teacher-clients. Without the knowledge of the teachers or of the student-engineers, trained adult aides also kept records of teacher behavior in classes. Rosenberg compared their records to those of the students to determine accuracy; he found that the aides recorded substantially more instances of positive teacher behavior than did the students. For example, an aide reported that a teacher had praised a child, but the child reported that the teacher had chewed him out. Rosenberg determined through closer monitoring that the aides were more accurate. He speculated that students were unable to recognize positive

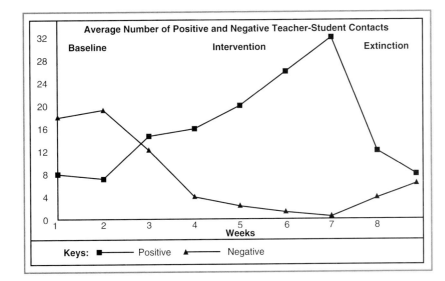

Average Number of Positive and Negative Teacher-Student Contacts

Baseline | Intervention | Extinction

Weeks

Keys: ■——— Positive ▲——— Negative

teacher behavior because they were accustomed to failure and negative treatment.

The student learned to identify positive teacher behavior accurately by role playing and by studying videotapes. This eventually brought about a high correlation between their records and those kept by adult teacher aides.

Building a New Smile

Rosenberg and Graubard taught the students various reinforcements to use in shaping their teachers' behavior. Rewards included smiling, making eye contact, and sitting up straight. They also practiced ways of praising a teacher, for example, saying, "I like to work in a room where the teacher is nice to the kids." And they learned to discourage negative teacher behavior with statements like, "It's hard for me to do good work when you're cross with me."

Each student studied techniques for making himself personally more attractive. One of the hardest tasks for Jess, for example, was learning to smile. Through use of a videotape, he learned that instead of smiling at people, he leered at them menacingly. Although he thought the process was hilarious, he practiced before the

camera, and eventually developed a charming smile.

Learning to praise teachers with sincerity was difficult for the children. They were awkward and embarrassed at first, but they soon became skillful. Rosenberg said that the teachers' responses were amazing, and added that "the nonverbal cues make the difference between being a wise guy and being believable. They had to *sincerely* mean it so it would be accepted by the teacher as an honest

statement of a kid's feelings, not as smarting off." Besides learning to praise and to discourage teachers, they also learned to make small talk with them. This was a new skill for these student and, after considerable training, they excelled at it.

Ah Hah!

The students enjoyed using a device that Fritz Redl, a child psychologist, has called "the Ah-Hah reaction. "When a pupil was sure that he already understood a teacher's explanation, he would say that he did not understand. When the teacher was halfway through a second explanation, the pupil would exclaim, "Ah hah! Now I understand! I could never get that before." Unlike some of the other reinforcements used, this one does not directly help the teacher improve his teaching, and it is less than honest. But it does encourage the teacher to like the student who gave him feeling of accomplishment, and it is hoped, will lead to a better relationship between them.

Rosenberg recorded the results of the project on a graph. It showed that during each of the five weeks of shaping, the number of positive comments from teachers increased while the number of negative comments decreased. The seven students in Jess's group felt that they had succeeded in engineering their teachers' behavior more to their liking. The "extinction" period proved to be a good indicator of the effects of this engineering. During those two weeks, there was a sharp drop in positive comments, but a marked rise in negative comments. The engineering had indeed caused the changes in teacher behavior. As the extinction period showed, the teachers were like other people. Most were backsliders and they needed persistent reinforcement to maintain their new behavior.

When the project was over, the students resumed conditioning of the teachers, but they no longer kept formal records. Positive behavior increased once again, they reported; and in many cases, the negative comments ceased entirely. Rosenberg stressed the importance of requiring the children to keep data while teaching them reinforcement techniques. Projects that do not require data have failed. A student's success with a full, formal project, on the other hand, increases his ability to continue informal use of the behavior-engineering techniques that he has learned.

Who Really Changed?

The teacher-clients were enthusiastic about the project, and Rosenberg reported that so far, none had expressed hostility or displeasure. Some teachers did

---

"We can teach kids systematically how to make friends, how to get along with other students," Rosenberg said. "If they're being teased, we can teach them how to extinguish that permanently. If they're getting in fights, we can teach them to use basic learning principles to get the same thing they were trying to get by fighting."

---

question the right of aides to observe and to record their teaching methods. But Rosenberg pointed out that it was "justified by the necessity for scientific validation of the procedure." He assured them that the district did not use data from the project for evaluation of their abilities, and so, it would not affect their careers. When he explained the project to teachers afterwards, two or three said that it did change them. They admitted that they had become more positive toward their engineers. It is interesting to note, however, that most teachers tended to think of the projects as having changed the *children* rather than themselves.

Children, especially those in special-education classes, often suffer feelings of impotence when they encounter the school environment. The crucial goal of the project was to instill within the student a feeling of power, the ability to control the controllers, i.e., his teachers and the school. As a result of their training in behavior engineering, the students reported feeling more power in their relationships with their teachers and the school than ever before. And with that feeling of power came a new feeling of self-confidence.

Parents as Clients

When children shape the behaviors of their parents, procedures are much the same as they are in the teacher-training projects. One difference, however, is that Rosenberg first asks the parents to let him work with the child. He does not tell them, though, that their children will be shaping them.

After the parents grant permission, the student decides what he wants to change in their behavior. Then, Rosenberg or a special teacher will help him to design a project to bring about that change. After the child completes his project, Rosenberg talks with the parents in their home, and tells them what the child has been trying to accomplish. For example, one girl's mother seldom had meals on time, nor did she wash or iron the girl's clothes. Through systematic use of praise and other conditioning techniques, the girl made her mother into a much better homemaker. After more than a year, the mother had maintained her improvement and gained new self-respect.

Rosenberg cited other examples of adolescents who have shaped their parents to be less restrictive. But the critical result of each of these parent-shaping projects was the parents' increased awareness of their child's needs as a person. One father said that the project had really helped them with their child; for the first time the child talked to them about the different ways that they could help him.

Switch, Don't Fight

Since children have problems with each other as well as with adults, the students at Visalia have used the same conditioning on their classmates.

"We can teach kids systematically how to make friends, how to get along with other students," Rosenberg said. "If they're being teased, we can teach them how to extinguish that permanently. If they're getting in fights, we can teach them to use basic learning principles to get the same thing they were trying to get by fighting."

He cited the example of Peggy, an attractive, intelligent girl who nevertheless encountered extreme problems in school. Her sixth-grade teachers sent her to the office frequently, and she was unable to make friends with the other students, whose hostility towards her made her miserable. She was gifted academically, but apparently

because of her unhappiness in school, she had never achieved even an average report card.

The special teacher helped her to design and to carry out a project to change her classmates' attitudes towards her. She was

---

Rosenberg estimates that the students are doing about as well in exercising control over human behavior as professionals who charge 50 dollars an hour.

---

spectacularly successful. She spoke of the experience later: "They told me it was a scientific experiment, but I really didn't know what that meant. At first I was confused, and I really didn't think it would help me. But then I thought I might as well try it. At least I would get out of the classroom for part of the time."

The teacher asked Peggy to name three people whom she would like to have as friends. She named Arthur, Elwyn and Doris, all of whom frequently insulted her. For two weeks, she and her teacher recorded both positive and negative contacts with them. Then they discussed how they could increase the number of nice things that those students said to her. She began to apply the behavior-modification theory and techniques that her teacher had taught her. "I ignored Doris if she said anything bad to me. But when she said anything nice to me, I'd help her with her work, or compliment her, or sit down and ask her to do something with me. She's been increasing saying the nice things about me and now we can ride on the bus together, and she'll sit by me in the class. I'll tell you that really helps me a lot."

She engineered Elwyn's behavior in much the same manner; she would turn her back on him whenever he said something bad to her. But the first time he walked

past her without saying something bad, she gave him a big smile and said, "Hi, Elwyn, how are you today?" After he recovered from his initial shock at Peggy's overtures, he eventually became her friend.

Arthur proved to be a much tougher subject than the other two. As Peggy stated, "He calls *everybody* names. I don't think anybody likes Arthur." She attempted to ignore him whenever he called her names, but with Arthur, this tactic was unsuccessful. If the other children laughed, it just gave Arthur more encouragement. As she discussed her shaping of Arthur, Peggy showed her grasp of behavior learning theory. She realized that the reward of the other children's laughter far outweighed her attempts to extinguish Arthur's teasing by ignoring it. They, not she, were reinforcing Arthur. She came up with a clever solution. "If Arthur was standing around with some kids, I tried to stay away from him. I'd wait until Arthur was by himself, and then I'd walk up to him, say "Hi" and smile. He just didn't know what to do! The first time, though, he still called me a name, because he thought I was being mean to him...I'd never said anything nice to Arthur...hardly anybody ever does. I guess the only way [he] ever gets anybody's attention is by calling people names...being mean, and fighting."

Arthur was a small sixth-grader and apparently, his stature caused him a great deal of self-consciousness. Peggy continued her positive reinforcement of Arthur, who is now friendly and no longer calls her names.

Peggy's social difficulties disappeared with dramatic speed as she made use of behavior-modification techniques. The teachers who once reported her attitude as disagreeable, now found her charming and delightful. Her grade average rose to B, and the following year, she was elected president of the seventh grade.

Gifted Students

Rosenberg also instructed a class of gifted children in the use of behavior engineering; each child chose as a client a classmate, an adult, or a sibling. The children met frequently to discuss ways of handling problems and to report on the progress of their projects.

One student related how he had modified the disruptive behavior of a fellow math student. "I compliment him when he's not disruptive, and when he is, I say things to him like,'You know, you could be a real bright student, and I like you a lot more when you don't disrupt the class.' He doesn't do it so much now, and he makes good grades."

One student was near despair over her efforts to change a teacher who, the other students agreed, was a difficult person. This teacher seemed impervious to any type of conditioning tech-

nique. "His latest thing is to send everybody out to sit under a table," she reported. "The first minute you open your mouth, he sends you out, and he doesn't really give you a chance." She had tried unsuccessfully to tell him that she was not learning math while sitting under the table, or she would apologize for saying something she should not have. But his response was usually, "You're not sorry, you're *ignorant*," or "You're a knothead!"

The special-education teacher asked the girl to name the behavior she most wanted to change. "Sending me out without a chance," the girl replied. "That's what bothers me most. I'm out in the *first ten minutes* of the class!"

The special teacher then suggested that she say to the problem teacher, "I'd really appreciate it if you'd give me a warning before sending me out of the room, because I have trouble about talking anyway." It was necessary for her to repeat this several times, but it wasn't long before the teacher stopped sending kids out of the room.

© 1998 PhotoDisc, Inc.

Dignity and Worth

In *Beyond Freedom and Dignity*, B.F. Skinner points out that "Any evidence that a person's behavior may be attributed to external circumstances seems to threaten his dignity or worth. We are not inclined to give a person credit for achievements over which he has no control."

The people at Visalia are very concerned with maintaining the dignity of their clients. They believe that dignity is lost if the reinforcements given in behavior engineering are insincere. The individual must feel that he has earned rewards by his own actions, not because the engineer is using a technique. Otherwise the gesture lacks dignity and worth.

A junior-high-school boy drew agreement from his fellow students when he said, "If the person knows you're doing it, it won't work. At least not very well. He'll figure, 'Oh, he's trying to do it on me. He's not going to change the way I am!'" The boy cited his little brother as an example. He was trying to condition him not to curse, but the child found out about the conditioning techniques, and said, "Oh, you dumb little psychologist!"

Sincerity is also an integral part of instruction in behavior engineering. Rosenberg recalled with amusement that the teachers working with him on the experiment have at times doubted each other's sincerity. "One person compliments another, who says, 'You're just reinforcing me!' And the response is, 'Oh the hell if I am! I really mean it.' With the kids, and with our own staff," Rosenberg said, "we've had to continually stress being sincere. You should really want the other person to change."

Many of the teachers felt that the engineering by the students created a more positive working environment; it eliminated the ever-present cutting and sarcasm. It also eliminated the meanness that is so often characteristic of junior-high-school students, according to a humanities teacher. He found that children of that age often conform by being meaner than they would really like to be. "I feel these projects are very effective in giving kids an *excuse* to be positive. At this age, that seems very helpful to them."

The Visalia project revived the issue of whether it is *moral* for people to condition each other. Certainly, behavior engineering could appear to be a harbinger of *A Clockwork Orange*, or *Brave New World*. But Rosenberg, Graubard, and other behaviorists believe that people are always conditioning each other, and that often, in their ignorance, they strengthen behaviors that no one wants. Proponents believe that to make really *constructive* changes in behavior, people should be conscious of what they are doing.

Future Projects

Rosenberg envisions another three or four years of research on this project before its techniques are disseminated in the school district. The current research is to provide information for the effective matching of the student with the technique for behavioral conditioning. In the future, this "prescription" will aid the counselor in helping the student.

Additional experiments planned will compare the teacher-training effectiveness of a single child to that of two or three children working as a team. And in some projects, teachers will know that the students are trying to change them. In this instance, Rosenberg wants to find out if that will make a difference in the effectiveness of the conditioning.

Having students train teachers is inexpensive and effective. Since the students spend more time with their teachers than does any professional supervisor, they have more opportunity to change them. Students also have the most to gain or to lose from the quality of teaching. Rosenberg estimates that the students are doing about as well in exercising control over human behavior as professionals who charge 50 dollars an hour. ◆

Discussion Questions

1. What is "behavior engineering?"

2. In the studies by Graubard and Rosenberg, how did the students change the behavior of the teachers? What did the students use as reinforcers and punishers?

3. What is the "Ah hah!" technique? What did it accomplish? What is the negative aspect of this technique?

4. What was the goal of this project in the school environment? Was it accomplished?

5. Why is sincerity so important in behavioral engineering?

6. What is the moral issue surrounding behavioral engineering? What are the arguments in favor of it? What is your position?

7. Think of a way that you could use behavioral engineering to modify the behavior of those around you. Describe the situation, rewards, and punishments that you would use.

Fall *Into* **HELP**LESSNESS

◆ *Martin E. P. Seligman*

Depression is the common cold of psychopathology, at once familiar and mysterious. Most of us have suffered depression in the wake of some traumatic event—some terrible loss—in our lives. Most of these depressions, like the common cold, run their course in time.

Serious forms of depression afflict from four to eight million Americans. Many of these depressive Americans will recover. Some of them won't; they'll just give up, becoming like T.S. Eliot's hollow men, a "...shape without form, shade without color. Paralyzed force, gesture without motion..." Many of those who are hospitalized will simply turn their heads to the wall. Others, at least one out of 200, will take their own lives. Yet we know there are some individuals who *never* succumb to depression, no matter how great their loss.

The *Wall Street Journal* has called depression the "disease of the '70s," and perhaps it is part of the character of our times. It is not a new malady, however. Physicians have been describing depression since the days of Hippocrates; he called it melancholia. The 2,500 years since Hippocrates have added little to our knowledge of the cure and prevention of depression. Our ignorance is due not to lack of research on the problem, but, I believe, to a lack of clearly defined and focused theory. Without a theory to organize what is known about the symptoms and cause, predictions about the cure and prevention of depression are at best haphazard.

A Cogent Theory

I think such a theory is possible and my belief is based on the phenomenon known as "learned helplessness." There are considerable parallels between the behaviors that define learned helplessness and the major symptoms of depression. In addition, the types of events that set off depression parallel the events that set off learned helplessness. I believe that cure for depression occurs when the individual comes to believe that he is not helpless and that an individual's susceptibility to depression depends on the success or failure of his previous experience with controlling his environment.

So the focus of my theory is that if the symptoms of learned helplessness and depression are equivalent, then what we have learned experimentally about the cause, cure and prevention of learned helplessness can be applied to depression.

> **The Wall Street Journal has called depression the "disease of the '70s," and perhaps it is part of the character of our times.**

Inescapable Shock

A few years ago, Steven F. Maier, J. Bruce Overmier and I stumbled onto the behavioral phenomenon of learned helplessness while we were using dogs and traumatic shock to test a particular learning theory. We had strapped dogs into a Pavlovian harness and given them electric shock—traumatic, but not physically damaging. Later the dogs were put into a two-compartment shuttlebox where they were supposed to learn to escape shock by jumping across the barrier separating the compartments.

A nonshocked, experimentally naive dog, when placed in a shuttlebox, typically behaves in the following way: at the onset of the first electric shock, the dog defecates, urinates, howls, and runs around frantically until it accidentally scrambles over the barrier and escapes the shock. On the next trial, the dog, running and howling, crosses the barrier more quickly. This pattern continues until the dog learns to avoid shock altogether.

But our dogs were not naive. While in a harness from which they could not escape, they had already experienced shock over which they had no control. That is, nothing they did or did not do affected their receipt of that shock. When placed in the shuttlebox, these dogs reacted at first in much the same manner as a naive dog, but not for long. The dogs soon stopped running and howling, settled down and took the shock, whining quietly. Typically, the dog did not cross the barrier and escape. Instead, it seemed to give up. On succeeding trials, the dog made virtually no attempts to get away. It passively took as much shock as was given.

After testing alternative hypotheses, we developed the theory that it was not trauma per se (electric shock) that interfered with the dog's adaptive responding. Rather, it was the experience of having *no control* over the trauma. We have found that if animals can control shock by any response—be it an active or a passive one—they do not later become helpless. Only those animals who receive uncontrollable shock will later give up. The experience in the harness had taught the dog that its responses did not pay, that his actions did not matter. We concluded that the dogs in our experiments had learned that they were helpless.

Our learned-helplessness hypothesis has been tested and confirmed in many ways with both animal and human subjects. Tests with human beings revealed dramatic parallels between the behavior of subjects who have learned helplessness and the major symptoms exhibited by depressed individuals.

Reactive Depression

Depression, like most clinical labels, embraces a whole family of disorders. As a label it is probably no more discriminating than "disease of the skin," which describes both acne and cancer. The word "depressed" as a behavioral description explicitly denotes a reduction or depression in responding. The reactive depressions, the focus of this article, are most common. As distinguished from process depression, reactive depression is set off by some external event, is probably not hormonally based, does not cycle regularly in time, and does not have a genetic history. The kind of depression experienced by manic depressives is process depression.

Some of the events that may set off reactive depression are familiar to each of us: death, loss, rejection by or separation from loved ones, physical disease, failure in work or school, financial setback and growing old. There are a host of others of course, but those capture the flavor. I suggest that what all these experiences have in common—what depression is—is the belief in one's own helplessness.

Goodies from the Sky

Many clinicians have reported an increasing pervasiveness of depressions among college students. Since this is a generation that has been fused with more reinforcers—more sex, more intellectual stimulation, more buying power, more cars, more music, etc—than any previous generation why should they be depressed? Yet the occurrence of reinforcers in our affluent society is so independent of the actions of the children who receive them, the goodies might as well have fallen from the sky. And perhaps that is our answer. Rewards as well as punishments that come independently of one's own effort can be depressing.

We can mention success depression in this context. When an individual finally reaches a goal after years of striving, such as getting a Ph.D. or becoming company president, depression often ensues. Even the disciplined astronaut, hero of his nation and the world, can become depressed after he has returned from walking on the Moon.

From a learned-helplessness viewpoint, success depression may occur because reinforcers are no longer contingent on present responding. After years of goal directed activity, a person now gets his reinforcers because of who he *is* rather than because of what he is *doing*. Perhaps this explains the number of beautiful women who become depressed and attempt suicide. They receive abundant positive reinforcers not for what they do but how they look.

Symptoms in Common

Consider the parallels between depression and learned helplessness: the most prominent symptom of depression, passivity, is also the central symptom of learned helplessness. Joseph Mendels describes the slowdown in responding associated with depression: "…Loss of interest, decrease in energy, inability to accomplish tasks, difficulty in concentration, and the erosion of motivation and ambition all combine to impair efficient functioning. For many depressives the first signs of illness are in the area of their increasing inability to cope with their work and responsibility… Aaron T. Beck describes "paralysis of the will" as a striking characteristic of depression:

"…In severe cases, there often is complete paralysis of the will. The patient has no desire to do anything, even those things which are essential to life. Consequently, he may be relatively immobile unless prodded or pushed into activity by others. It is sometimes necessary to pull the patient out of bed, wash, dress and feed him…"

© 1998 PhotoDisc, Inc.

Experiments in learned helplessness have produced passivity in many kinds of animals, even the lowly cockroach, and in human subjects. Donald Hiroto subjected college students to loud noise. He used three groups: group one could not escape hearing the loud noise; group two heard the loud noise but could turn it off by pressing a button; group three heard no noise.

In the second part of the experiment, Hiroto presented the students with a finger shuttlebox. Moving one's fingers back and forth across the shuttlebox turned off the loud noise. The students in group two, who had previously learned to silence the noise by pushing a button, and those in group three, who had no experience with the loud noise, readily learned to move their fingers across the shuttlebox to control the noise. But the students in group one, whose previous attempts to turn off the noise had been futile, now merely sat with their hands in the shuttlebox, passively accepting the loud noise. They had learned that they were helpless.

Hiroto also found out that "externals" were more susceptible to learned helplessness than "internals." Externals are persons who believe that reinforcement comes from outside themselves; they believe in luck. Internals believe that their own actions control reinforcement.

Born Losers

Depressed patients not only make fewer responses, but they are "set" to interpret their own responses, when they do make them, as failures or as doomed to failure. Each of them bears an invisible tattoo: "I'm a Born Loser." Beck considers this negative cognitive set to be the primary characteristic of depression:

"...The depressed patient is peculiarly sensitive to any impediments to his goal-directed activity. An obstacle is regarded as an impossible barrier, difficulty in dealing with a problem is interpreted as a total failure. His cognitive response to a problem or difficulty

> *Depressed patients not only make fewer responses, but they are "set" to interpret their own responses, when they do make them, as failures or as doomed to failure. Each of them bears an invisible tattoo: "I'm a Born Loser."*

is likely to be an idea such as 'I'm licked,' 'I'll never be able to do this,' or I'm blocked no matter what I do'..."

This cognitive set crops up repeatedly in experiments with depressives. Alfred S. Friedman observed that although a patient was performing adequately during a test, the patient would occasionally reiterate his original protest of "I can't do it," "I don't know how," etc. This is also our experience in testing depressed patients.

Negative cognitive set crops up in both depression and learned

helplessness. When testing students, William Miller, David Klein and I found that depression and learned helplessness produced the same difficulty in seeing that responding is successful. We found that depressed individuals view their skilled actions very much as if they were in a chance situation. Their depression is not a general form of pessimism about the world, but pessimism that is specific to their own actions. In animal behavior this is demonstrated by associative retardation: animals don't catch on even though they make a response that turns off shock; they have difficulty in learning what responses produce relief.

Maier and I found in separate experiments, that normal aggressiveness and competitiveness become deficient in the subjects who have succumbed to learned helplessness. In competition, these animals lose out to animals who have learned that they control the effects of their responses. Further, they do not fight back when attacked.

Depressed individuals, similarly, are usually less aggressive and competitive than nondepressed individuals. The behavior of depressed patients is depleted of hostility and even their dreams are less hostile. This symptom forms the basis for the Freudian view of depression. Freud claimed that the hostility of depressed people was directed inward toward themselves rather than outward. Be this as it may, the *symptom* corresponds to the depleted aggression and competitiveness of helpless dogs and rats.

The Balm of Time

Depression also often dissipates with time. When a man's wife dies he may be depressed for several days, several months, or even several years. but time usually heals.

One of the most tragic aspects of suicide is that if the person could have waited for a few weeks, the depression might well have lifted.

Time is also an important variable in learned helplessness. Overmier and I found that the day after they received one session of inescapable shock, dogs behaved helplessly in the shuttlebox. However, if two days elapsed between the inescapable shock and testing, the dogs were not helpless, their helplessness, like the widower's depression had run its course. Unfortunately, helplessness does not always respond so well to the elixir of time. We found that multiple sessions of inescapable shock made the animals' learned helplessness virtually irreversible. We also found that animals that had been reared from birth in our laboratories with a limited history of controlling reinforcers also failed to recover from learned helplessness over time.

Often when we are depressed, we lose our appetites and our zest for life. Jay M. Weiss, Neal L. Miller and their colleagues at Rockefeller University found that rats that had received inescapable shock lost weight and ate less than rats who had been able to escape from shock. In addition, the brains of the rats subjected to inescapable shock are depleted of norepinephrine, an important transmitter substance in the central nervous system. Joseph J. Schildkraut and Seymour S. Kety have suggested that the cause of depression may be a deficiency of norepinephrine at receptor sites in the brain. This is because reserpine, a drug that depletes norepinephrine, among other things, produces depression in man. Moreover, antidepressant drugs increase the brain's supply of norepinephrine. Therefore, there may be a chemical similarity between depression and learned helplessness.

Weiss found that rats subjected to uncontrollable shock got more stomach ulcers than rats receiving no shock or shock they could control.

No one has done a study of ulcers in depression, so we don't know if human experience will correspond to ulceration in helpless rats. However, anxiety and agitation are sometimes seen along with depression. It is my speculation, however, that anxiety persists as long as the depressed person believes there might still be something he can do to extract himself from his dilemma. When he finally comes to believe that no response will work, depression wholly displaces anxiety.

The Chances for Cure

As arrayed above, there are considerable parallels between the behaviors which define learned helplessness and the major symptoms of depression. We have also seen that the cause of learned helplessness and reactive depression is similar: both occur when important events are out of control. Let me now speculate about the possibility of curing both.

In our animal experiments, we knew that only when the dog learned to escape the shock, only when it learned that it could control its environment, would a cure for its learned helplessness be found.

At first, we could not persuade the dog to move to the other side of the box, not even by dropping meat there when the dog was hungry. As a last resort, we forcibly dragged the dog across the barrier on a leash. After much dragging, the dog caught on and eventually was able to escape the shock on its own. Recovery from helplessness was complete and lasting for each animal. We can say with confidence that so far only "directive therapy"—forcing the animal to see that it can succeed by responding—works reliably in curing learned helplessness. However, T.R. Dorworth has recently found that electroconvulsive shock breaks up helplessness in dogs. Electroconvulsive shock is often used as a therapy for depression and it seems to be effective about 60 percent of the time.

Although we do not know how to cure depression, there are therapies that alleviate it, and they are consonant with the learned help-

		Learned Helplessness	Depression
SYMPTOMS		1 passivity 2 difficulty learning that responses produce relief 3 lack of aggression 4 dissipates in time 5 weight loss and undereating, anorexia, sexual deficits (?) 6 norepinephrine depletion 7 ulcers and stress	1 passivity 2 negative cognitive set 3 introjected hostility 4 time course 5 loss of libido 6 norepinephrine depletion 7 ulcers(?) and stress 8 feelings of helplessness
CAUSE		learning that responding and reinforcement are independent	belief that responding is useless
CURE		1 directive therapy forced exposure to responding producing reinforcement 2 electroconvulsive shock 3 pharmacological agents (?) 4 time	1 recovery of belief that responding produces reinforcement 2 electroconvulsive shock (?) 3 pharmacological agents (?) 4 time
PREVENTION		inoculation with mastery over reinforcement	inoculation (?)

lessness approach. Successful therapy occurs when the patient believes that his responses produce gratification, that he is an effective human being.

Against the Grain

In an Alabama hospital, for instance, E.S. Taulbee and H.W. Wright have created an "antidepression room." They seat a severely depressed patient in the room and then abuse him in a simple manner. He is told to sand a block of wood, then is reprimanded because he is sanding against the grain of the wood. After he switches to sanding *with* the grain, he is reprimanded for sanding with the grain. The abuse continues until the depressed patient gets angry. He is then promptly led out of the room with apologies. His outburst, and its immediate effect on the person abusing him, breaks up his depression. From the helplessness viewpoint, the patient is forced to vent his anger, one of the most powerful responses people have

for controlling others. When anger is dragged out of him, he is powerfully reinforced.

Other methods reported to be effective against depression involve the patient's relearning that he controls reinforcers.

Expressing strong emotions is a therapy that seems to help depressed patients, as self-assertion does. In assertive training, the patient rehearses asserting himself and then puts into practice the responses he has learned that bring him social reinforcers.

Morita therapy puts patients in bed for about a week to "sensitize

We could get severely depressed patients to give extemporaneous speeches, with a noticeable lifting of their depression.

them to reinforcement." Then the patients progress from light to heavy to complicated work.

The Lift of Success

Other forms of graded-task assignments also have been effective.

Elaine P. Burgess first had her patients perform some simple task, such as making a telephone call. As the task requirements increased, the patient was reinforced by the therapist for successfully completing each task. Burgess emphasized how crucial it is in the graded-task treatment that the patient succeed.

Using a similar form of graded-task assignment, Aaron Beck, Dean Schuyler, Peter Brill and I began by asking patients to read a short paragraph aloud. Finally, we could get severely depressed patients to give extemporaneous speeches, with a noticeable lifting of their depression. What one patient said was illuminating: "You know, I used to be a debater in high school and I had forgotten how good I was."

Finally, there is the age-old strategy adopted by individuals to dispel their own minor depressions: doing work that is difficult but gratifying. There is no better way to see that one's responses are still effective. It is crucial to succeed. Merely starting and giving up only makes things worse.

Dramatic successes in medicine have come more frequently from prevention than from treatment, and I would hazard a guess that inoculation and immunization have saved more lives than cure. Surprisingly, psychotherapy is almost exclusively limited to curative procedures, and preventive procedures rarely play an explicit role.

In studies of dogs and rats we have found that behavioral immunization prevents learned helplessness. Dogs that first receive experience in mastering shock do not become helpless after experiencing subsequent inescapable shock. Dogs that are deprived of natural opportunities to control their own rewards in their development are more vulnerable to

helplessness than naturally immunized dogs.

The Masterful Life

Even less is known about the prevention of depression than about its cure. We can only speculate on this, but the data on immunization against learned helplessness guide our speculations. The life histories of those individuals who are particularly resistant to depression or who are resilient from depression may have been filled with mastery. Persons who have had extensive experience in controlling and manipulating the sources of reinforcement in their lives may see the future optimistically. A life without mastery may produce vulnerability to depression.

Adults who lost their parents when they were children are usually susceptible to depression and suicide.

A word of caution is in order. While it may be possible to immunize people against debilitating depression by giving them a history of control over reinforcers, it may be possible to get too much of a good thing. The person who has met only success may be highly susceptible to depression when he faces a loss. One is reminded, for example, of the stock market crash of 1929: it was not the low-income people who jumped to their deaths, but those who had been "super-successful" and suddenly faced gross defeat.

One can also look at successful therapy as preventative. After all, therapy usually does not focus just on undoing past problems. It also should arm the patient against future depressions. Perhaps therapy for depression would be more successful if it explicitly aimed at providing the patient with a wide repertoire of coping responses. He could use these responses in future situations where he finds his usual reactions do not control his reinforcements. Finally, we can speculate about child rearing. What kind of experiences can best protect our children against the debilitating effects of helplessness and depression? A tentative answer follows from the learned helplessness view of depression: to see oneself as an effective human being may require a childhood filled with powerful synchronies between responding and its consequences.

Discussion Questions

1. Define learned helplessness.

2. In the experiment described, what interfered with the dog's adaptive responding?

3. What is Seligman's definition of depression?

4. How are learned helplessness and reactive depression similar?

5. What is the primary characteristic of depression?

6. Describe how norepinephrine is related to learned helplessness and depression.

7. Why is anger helpful in combating depression?

8. When you find yourself depressed, what do you do to snap yourself out of it? How have you learned to alleviate your depression?

Exercises

Name: _____

Date: _____

Part 6: Learning

1. I agree with Seligman's "learned helplessness" theory of depression.

2. Much of my behavior can be explained by the rewards and punishments I've received during my life.

3. I have one or more fears which came about because of classical conditioning I experienced long ago.

Conspire with fellow students to modify the behavior of your instructor using positive reinforcement. For example, make eye contact with your instructor only after he or she raises a hand high in the air or bangs on the table. Keep a tally (below) of the behaviors before you begin your procedure (this is your "baseline" observation period) and after you have begun your procedure (this is your "treatment" phase). Were you successful?

Can behavior modification techniques be used on oneself? How might you use such techniques on yourself to help you achieve your personal goals?

PART 7

MEMORY

20 ◆ Eyewitnesses: Essential but Unreliable, by Elizabeth F. Loftus

21 ◆ How to...Uh...Remember!, by Gordon H. Bower

22 ◆ Mood and Memory, by Gordon H. Bower

Memory is probably the most thoroughly-researched topic in all of psychology. The first experimental treatise on memory was published in Germany in 1885 by Hermann Ebbinghaus. In systematic fashion, Ebbinghaus memorized and then tried to recall thousands of lists of nonsense syllables, varying the delay times and the lengths of the lists. He discovered that forgetting was a very orderly process—at least the forgetting of nonsense syllables! Basically, the longer the list or the longer the delay, the poorer the recall (no surprises here). Since then thousands of related studies have been published, further demonstrating the orderliness of memory and forgetting, at least when simple stimuli are utilized.

A very different type of research on memory was conducted by the English psychologist, Sir Frederick Bartlett. In his 1932 book, *Remembering*, Bartlett reported on how well people remembered unusual stories after varying lengths of time, even after years had passed. He found that memory was very much a *constructive* process—even an *imaginative* one—in which people's experiences become interwoven with the few details they can actually recall. Ebbinghaus had used arbitrary, simplistic stimuli in his studies, whereas Bartlett employed rich, complex material more like the information we're exposed to in everyday life. Research using rich, natural stimuli repeatedly confirms Bartlett's observations: that human memory is constructive, imprecise, and easily influenced by experience.

Which brings us to Elizabeth F. Loftus, one of contemporary psychology's most gifted memory researchers. Her illuminating studies on eyewitness testimony are not only scientifically interesting; they also have immense practical value. As you might expect, she has shown that eyewitness testimony is...yes, that's right, constructive, imprecise, and easily influenced by experience. In recent years, she has helped teach the courts and the public about the unreliability of memories that have supposedly been "repressed" and later "recovered" by hypnotists or therapists. Directly or indirectly, she has rescued many innocent people from prison.

Following Loftus' article are two classic pieces by Stanford University's Gordon H. Bower, also a towering figure in the world of memory research. In "How to...Uh...Remember!," Bower reveals a variety of techniques for improving one's memory, and in "Mood and Memory," he talks about a phenomenon called "state-dependent learning." Just be sure not to read that last piece when you're drunk, because, if Bower is right, you'll have to get drunk again in order to remember it.

EYEWITNESSES:
Essential *but Unreliable*

◆ *Elizabeth F. Loftus*

The ladies and gentlemen of William Bernard Jackson's jury decided that he was guilty of rape. They made a serious mistake, and before it was discovered, Jackson had spent five years in prison. There he suffered numerous indignities and occasional attacks, until the police discovered that another man, who looked very much like Jackson, had committed the rapes.

If you had been on the jury, you would probably have voted for conviction too. Two women had positively identified Jackson as the man who had raped them in September and October of 1977. The October victim was asked on the witness stand, "Is there any doubt in your mind as to whether this man you have identified here is the man who had the sexual activity with you on October 3, 1977?" She answered "No doubt." "Could you be mistaken?" the prosecutor asked. "No, I am not mistaken," the victim stated confidently. Jackson and other defense witnesses testified that he was home when the rapes occurred. But the jury didn't believe him or them.

This is just one of the many documented cases of mistaken eyewitness testimony that have had tragic consequences. In 1981, Steve Titus of Seattle was convicted of raping a 17-year-old woman on a secluded road; the following year he was proven to be innocent. Titus was luckier than Jackson; he never went to prison. However, Aaron lee Owens of Oakland, California, was not as fortunate. He spent nine years in a prison for a double murder that he didn't commit. In these cases, and many others, eyewitnesses testified against the defendants, and jurors believed them.

One reason most of us, as jurors, place so much faith in eyewitness testimony is that we are unaware of how many factors influence its accuracy. To name just a few: what questions witnesses are asked by police and how the questions are phrased; the difficulty people have in distinguishing among people of other races; whether witnesses have seen photos of suspects be-

> *One reason most of us, as jurors, place so much faith in eyewitness testimony is that we are unaware of how many factors influence its accuracy.*

fore viewing the lineup from which they pick out the person they say committed the crime; the size, composition and type (live or photo) of the lineup itself.

I know of seven studies that assess what ordinary citizens believe about eyewitness memory. one common misconception is that police officers make better witnesses than the rest of us. As part of a larger study, my colleagues and I asked 541 registered voters in Dade County, Florida, "Do you think that the memory of law enforcement agents is better than the memory of the average citizen?" Half said yes, 38 percent said no and the rest had no opinion. When A. Daniel Yarmey of the University of Guelph asked judges, lawyers and policemen a similar question, 63 percent of the legal officials and half the police agreed that "The policeman will be superior to the civilian" in identifying robbers.

This faith in police testimony is not supported by research. Several years ago, psychologists A.H. Tinker and E. Christopher Poulton showed a film depicting a street scene to 24 police officers and 156 civilians. The subjects were asked to watch for particular people in the film and to report instances of crimes, such as petty theft. The researchers found that the officers reported more alleged thefts than the civilians but that when it came to detecting actual crimes, the civilians did just as well.

More recently, British researcher Peter B. Ainsworth showed a 20-minute videotape to police officers and civilians. The tape depicted a number of staged criminal offenses, suspicious circumstances and traffic offenses at an urban street corner. No significant differences were found between the police and civilians in the total number of incidents reported. Apparently neither their initial training nor subsequent experience increases the ability of the police to be accurate witnesses.

Studies by others and myself have uncovered other common misconceptions about eyewitness testimony. They include:

◆ *Witnesses remember the details of a violent crime better than those of a nonviolent one.* Research shows just the opposite: The added stress that violence creates clouds our perceptions.

◆ *Witnesses are as likely to underestimate the duration of a crime as to overestimate it.* In fact, witnesses almost invariably think a crime took longer than it did. The more violent and stressful the crime, the more witnesses overestimate its duration.

◆ *The more confident a witness seems, the more accurate the testimony is likely to be.* Research suggests that there may be little or no relationship between confidence and accuracy, especially when viewing conditions are poor.

© 1998 PhotoDisc, Inc.

The unreliability of confidence as a guide to accuracy has been demonstrated outside of the courtroom, too; one example is provided by accounts of an aircraft accident that killed nine people several years ago. According to *Flying* magazine, several people had seen the airplane just before impact, and one of them was certain that "it was heading right toward the ground, straight down." This witness was profoundly wrong, as shown by several photographs taken of the crash site that made it clear that the airplane hit flat and at a low enough angle to skid for almost 1,000 feet.

Despite the inaccuracies of eyewitness testimony, we can't afford to exclude it legally or ignore it as jurors. Sometimes, as in cases of rape, it is the only evidence available, and it is often correct. The question remains, what can we do to give jurors a better understanding of the uses and pitfalls of such testimony? Judges sometimes give the jury a list of instructions on the pitfalls of eyewitness testimony. But this method has not proved satisfactory, probably because, as

Despite the inaccuracy of eyewitness testimony, we can't afford to exclude it legally.

studies show, jurors either do not listen or do not understand the instructions.

Another solution, when judges permit, is to call a psychologist as an expert witness to explain how the human memory works and describe the experimental findings that apply to the case at hand. How this can affect a case is shown by a murder trial in California two years ago. On April 1, 1981, two young men were walking along Polk Street in San Francisco at about 5:30 in the evening. A car stopped near them, and the driver, a man in his 40s, motioned one of the men to get in, which he did. The car drove off. Up to this point, nothing appeared unusual. The area was known as a place where prostitutes hang out; in fact, the young man who got in the car was there hustling for "tricks." Three days later, he was found strangled in a wooded area some 75 miles south of San Francisco.

Five weeks later, the victim's friend was shown a six-person

photo lineup and picked out a 47-year-old I'll call D. The quick selection of D's photograph, along with the strong emotional reaction that accompanied it (the friend became ill when he saw the photo), convinced the police that they had their man. D was tried for murder.

At his trial, the defense lawyer introduced expert testimony by a psychologist on the factors that made accurate perception and memory difficult For example, in the late afternoon of April 1, the witness had been using marijuana, a substance likely to blur his initial perceptions and his memory of them. Furthermore, just before viewing the lineup, the witness had seen a photograph of D on a desk in the police station, an incident that could have influenced his selection. During the five weeks between April 1 and the time he saw the photographs, the witness had talked about and been questioned repeatedly about the crime, circumstances that often contaminate memory.

In the end, the jury was unable to reach a verdict. It is difficult to assess the impact of any one bit of testimony on a particular verdict. We can only speculate that the psychologist's testimony may have made the jury more cautious about accepting the eyewitness testimony. This idea is supported by recent studies showing that such expert testimony generally increases the deliberation time jurors devote to eyewitness aspects of a case.

Expert testimony on eyewitness reliability is controversial. It has its advocates and enemies in both the legal and psychological professions. For example, several judicial arguments are used routinely to exclude the testimony. One is that it "invades the province of the jury," meaning that it is the jury's job, not an expert's, to decide whether a particular witness was in a position to see, hear and remember what is being claimed in court. Another reason judges sometimes exclude such testimony is that the question of eyewitness reliability is "not beyond the knowledge and experience of a juror" and thus is not a proper subject matter for expert testimony.

In virtually all the cases in which a judge has prohibited the jury from hearing expert testimony, the higher courts have upheld the decision, and in some cases have driven home the point with negative comments about the use of psychologists. In a recent case in California, *People v. Plasencia*, Nick Plasencia Jr. was found guilty of robbery and other crimes in Los Angeles County. He had tried to introduce the testimony of a psychologist on eyewitness reliability, but the judge refused to admit it, saying that "the subject matter about which (the expert) sought to testify was too conjectural and too speculative to support any opinion he would offer." The appellate court upheld Plasencia's conviction and made known its strong feelings about the psychological testimony:

"Since our society has not reached the point where all human conduct is videotaped for later replay, resolution of disputes in our court system depends almost entirely on the testimony of witnesses who recount their observations of a myriad of events.

"These events include matters in both the criminal and civil areas of the law. The accuracy of a witness's testimony of course depends on factors which are as variable and complex as human nature itself.... The cornerstone of our system remains our belief in the wisdom and integrity of the jury system and the ability of 12 jurors to determine the accuracy of witnesses' testimony. The system has served us well....

"It takes no expert to tell us that for various reasons, people can be mistaken about identity, or even the exact details of an observed event. Yet to present these commonly accepted and known facts in the form of an expert opinion, which opinion does nothing more than generally question the validity of one form of traditionally accepted evidence, would exaggerate the significance of that testimony and give a 'scientific aura' to a very unscientific matter.

> *The cornerstone of our system remains our belief in the wisdom and integrity of the jury system and the ability of 12 jurors to determine the accuracy of witnesses' testimony.*

THE INVESTIGATION

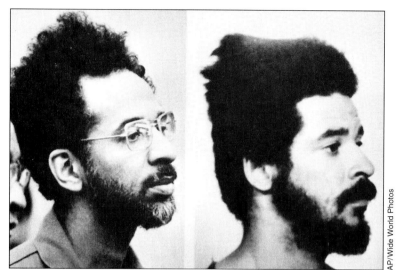

AP/Wide World Photos

The wrong man: William Jackson, right, was imprisoned for five years for two rapes actually committed by Dr. Edward Jackson Jr., left.

"The fact remains, in spite of the universally recognized fallibility of human beings, persons do, on many occasions, correctly identify individuals. Evidence that under contrived test conditions, or even in real-life situations, certain persons totally unconnected with this case have been mistaken in their identification of individuals is no more relevant than evidence that in other cases, witnesses totally unconnected with this event have lied.

"It seems beyond question that the identifications in this case were correct. We find no abuse of discretion in the trial court's rejecting the proffered testimony."

Quite the opposite view was expressed by the Arizona Supreme Court in *State v. Chapple*. At the original trial, defendant Dolan Chapple had been convicted of three counts of murder and two drug-trafficking charges, chiefly on the testimony of two witnesses who identified him at the trial. Earlier they had selected him from photographs shown them by the police more than a year after the crime.

Chapple's lawyer tried to introduce expert psychological testimony on the accuracy of such identification. The judge refused to permit it on the grounds that the testimony would pertain only to matters "within the common experience" of jurors. The high court disagreed, maintaining that expert testimony would have provided scientific data on such pertinent matters as the accuracy of delayed identification, the effect of stress on perception and the relationship between witness confidence and accuracy. "We cannot assume," the court added, "that the average juror would be aware of the variables concerning identification and memory" about which the expert would have testified. Chapple's conviction was reversed, and he has been granted a new trial.

Like lawyers and judges, psychologists disagree on whether expert testimony is a good solution to the eyewitness problem.

Two of the most outspoken critics are Michael McCloskey and Howard Egeth of The Johns Hopkins University. These experimental psychologists offer four reasons why they believe that expert testimony on eyewitness reliability is a poor idea. They say that there is no evidence that such testimony is needed; that there is no evidence that it does any good or that is can provide much beyond the intuitions of ordinary experience; that the data base on which the expert must rely is not sufficiently well-developed; and that conflicting public testimony between experts would tarnish the profession's image. Given this sorry state of affairs, they argue, psychologists may do more harm than good by intruding into judicial proceedings.

Obviously, many psychologists disagree with this assessment and believe that both the law and psychology gain from mutual interaction. In the area of eyewitness testimony, information supplied by psychologists to lawyers has stimulated responses that have suggested a number of important ideas for future research.

For example, psychologists need to learn more about the ideas that the rest of us have about the operation of human perception and memory. When these ideas are wrong, psychologists need to devise ways to educate us so that the judgments we make as jurors will be more fully informed and more fair. Only through this give-and-take, and occasional biting controversy, will progress be made. It is too late to help William Jackson, or Steve Titus, or Aaron Lee Owens, but it is not yet too late for the rest of us. ◆

Discussion Questions

1. Why do jurors place so much faith in eyewitness testimony?

2. What are some of the factors that influence witness accuracy?

3. Are police officers more accurate witnesses than ordinary citizens? What's the evidence?

4. What can be done to give juries a better understanding of eyewitness testimony?

5. What are the four arguments against using expert testimony regarding eyewitnesses?

6. Do you think that expert testimony regarding memory and identification should be allowed in a trial? Defend your position.

How to...Uh...**Remember!**

◆ *Gordon H. Bower*

I'll never forget dear old what's his name.

The fact that we forget things important to us is a source of embarrassment and irritation, to say nothing of inefficiency. Forgetting has also been a source of some irritation to psychologists, who are only slowly beginning to understand it.

Hermann Ebbinghaus completed the first studies of forgetting just before the end of the 19th century. Using himself as a subject. Ebbinghaus investigated how much we forget over a period of time. In order to slow down the learning and to void unwanted associations with familiar language, Ebbinghaus would learn a series of nonsense syllables (meaningless consonant-vowel-consonant combination), and then try to recall them after varying periods of time. His famous forgetting curve showed large amounts of forgetting over the first few hours after learning, followed by progressively less loss over ensuing days and weeks.

Ebbinghaus' classic research demonstrated that forgetting occurred in a reliable, orderly fashion. A practical question was how to prevent forgetting, or at least slow it down. Ebbinghaus also had some suggestions there. His main prescription, supported by his evidence, was that forgetting could be reduced by over-learning the ma-

terial originally, beyond the point of mastery; he also prescribed reviving and rehearsing the material every now and then before its final use. These prescriptions are clearly well taken and underlie most school study guides, which cite the need for periodic reviews for refreshing one's memory.

A second practical question is whether memorizing is a skill that can be improved by special means. Research suggests that the ability to remember is indeed a skill, one on which individuals differ reliably and consistently, and that there are a few clearly specifiable components or sub-skills to this overall ability. People can be taught some of these skills. As an elementary example, one component of the skill of learning people's names during introductions is that we must first explicitly attend to and register the name clearly as it is told to us. Most of

> **Research suggests that the ability to remember is indeed a skill, one on which individuals differ reliably and consistently, and that there are a few clearly specifiable components or sub-skills to this overall ability.**

us fail at this initial and most elementary step because we are preoccupied with the other tasks demanded by the occasion—shaking hands, smiling, planning the conversation ahead, or anticipating the next person to be met. In

our preoccupation, the name fails to register clearly. So a first prescription would be that if you want to learn names, then you've got to reshuffle your "cognitive priorities" at the time of introduction and attend clearly to the name and repeat it aloud or to yourself. That at least is a beginning. A second component in remembering names, as in remembering many other types of information, is to embellish or elaborate the material to be learned into meaningful terms and then to associate items. Some features suggested by the name would be elaborated into a bizarre association with a distinctive feature of the face or person to the name. Mr. *Carpenter* can be visualized hammering that long spiked nose of his into the wall; Miss *Lockhart* can be visualized with a huge *padlock* going through her *heart* and wrapped around her chest; and so on.

From Olympus to Oculomotor

This second component, of elaboration and visualization to aid in associating materials to be learned, has been investigated recently under the title of "mnemonic strategies" or simply "mnemonics." Most of us already use elementary forms of mnemonics. Our principal is spelled "pal" because he was our pal, but some of us remembered him as the man without princi*ple*. Similarly we spell "conceive" that way because we learned the rule "i before e except after c."

One problem people have is remembering the right *order* of a set of familiar items. Specially coined phrases or coined words are helpful here. Biology students learn the ordering of the 12 cranial nerves by memorizing the lines "On old Olympus' towering top, a fat-assed German vaults and hops." The first letter of each word is also the first letter of one of the major cranial nerves. The "coined-word" procedure consists of taking the first letter of words to be remembered and making a new word from them. Thus the ordering of colors of the spectrum is suggested by the name Roy G. Biv for red, orange, yellow, etc. If we can remember the coined word or phrase, we can order the items correctly. These particular mnemonics fail in the long run because they do not maintain the actual items in memory. Biology students may recall the limerick long after they have forgotten the names of the cranial nerves. A better mnemonic would contain hints for remembering the items themselves as well as their order. For example, using key words that sound like the names of the nerve, they could remember the following story: "At the *oil factory* (olfactory nerve) *the optician* (optic) looked for the *occupant* (oculomotor) of the *truck* (trochlear). He was searching because *three gems* (trigeminal) had been *abducted* (abducents) by a man who was hiding his *face* (facial) and *ears* (acoustic). A *glossy photograph* (glossopharyngeal) had been taken of him, but it was too *vague* (vagus) to use. He appeared to be *spineless* (spinal accessory) and *hypocritical* (hypoglossal)."

One mnemonic technique is particularly useful whenever two or more things are to be associated. Examples include the principal products of a country, foreign-language vocabulary items, and definitions of new concepts. The method consists simply of searching for or elaborating some vivid connection between the two items. One way to establish a connection is to imagine the two elements interacting in some way. To remember the meaning of the word *porte*, one might picture a huge bottle of *port* wine dangling from a *door*. Thus the word's meaning—door—will be called forth by the image.

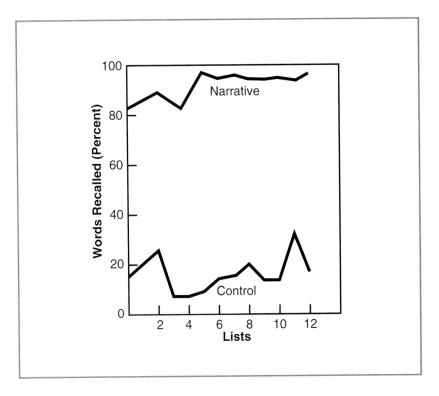

Consider learning a series of word pairs such as DOG-HAT, MAN-PENCIL, CLOCK-WOMAN, SOFA-FLOOR, and PIPE-CLOWN. People usually learn a list such as this by rapidly repeating each pair as often as possible in the allotted time. The method is reasonably satisfactory for short lists and over short retention intervals. But extend either the length of the list or the retention interval, and the rehearsal method falters seriously. People who have learned to use mental imagery to relate the items of a pair perform much better. They visualize a dog wearing a hat, a man resting a large pencil on his shoulder like a rifle, a woman wearing a clock on a chain around her neck, a section of floor resting on a sofa, and a clown smoking a pipe. When provided with one word of each pair, they can call to mind the interactive image they had formed, and can name the other object in the image. This procedure can improve recall by as much as 100 to 150 percent.

> *The value of relating items to each other in a thematic way shows up clearly when one concocts narrative stories as an aid to serial learning.*

Spinning Stories

The value of relating items to each other in a thematic way shows up clearly when one concocts narrative stories as an aid to serial learning. In one study of this "chaining method," Michal Clark and I instructed college students to make up a story around a list of 10 unrelated nouns which were to be remembered. It usually took a student about one or two minutes to construct his story. Each student studied 12 different lists of words in a period of 30 to 40 minutes. Our control subjects learned the lists using any method they chose; they were allowed to study for a time comparable to that taken by the students composing stories. Following presentation of the last list, we tested retention by giving

Memory Freaks I Have Known

In the popular mind, mnemonic devices are associated with magic, memory tricks, chess wizardry, lightning-fast calculations, and other Olympiad feats of mental gymnastics. Being a naive scientist, I vigorously disbelieved such popular dogma. I pictured instead lawyers, doctors and engineers using mnemonics to lighten the memory load of their jobs. To unmask the poppycock, I went to meet some professional mnemonists in the flesh at the first and only convention of a national mnemonics association in the Spring of 1968 in Hollywood, where else. To my chagrin, I discovered that the popular notion is true. The mnemonists I met were usually entertainers doing shows of magic and trickery. Some were simply zany characters who got their kicks from performing spectacular mental gyrations that leave the rest of us dumbfounded and awe-struck. Mnemonists love to entertain and dazzle one another even more than they do a naive audience. Like a reunion of comedians, each mnemonist loves to "top" the other one, with a new trick or new mental skill. They made a charming crowd for a convention: slightly pixilated, wild, madcap, and surprising in their unexpected mental skills.

Arriving at the convention, I saw some 30 people scattered in small conversation groups. My first surprise came when I registered and received a *name tag*. The small conversation groups turned out to be mnemonists comparing notes on how best to do some memory trick. One group was discussing several variants of the "perpetual-calendar" system, which enables the user to calculate rapidly, in his head, the day of the week on which any date fell. The system will tell you that February 12, 1809 was a Sunday and July 15, 1922 was a Saturday. Other groups were discussing schemes for fast memorization of the Morse code, or the order of cards in a shuffled deck, or ways to fool an audience into believing you'd memorized a thousand eight-digit numbers or the entire Los Angeles telephone directory. It was amazing guile but trickery nonetheless.

The convention program consisted principally of performances by these talented people. There was a 96-year-old man who memorized 50 three-digit numbers shouted out to him by the audience. Another participant had memorized the powers of 2 up to 2^{100}, which is a very large number indeed. He did it by recalling a key sentence associated with pegword N, the sentence composed of words which were a phonetically coded translation of successive digits in 2. These coding techniques are explained in my article. The two most spectacular performances were turned in by John Stone, and Willis N. Dysart, whose stage name was Willie the Wizard.

At age 66, Stone had taught himself several complex skills allowing him to carry out nearly simultaneously several activities which, for most people, would interfere with one another. In one of these performances, he would begin with four six-letter words shouted out at random by the audience, from which he proceeded to write rapidly and upside-down a complexly transformed word salad. For instance, given the words GEORGE, STOLEN, MARKER, and ARMPIT, Stone would quickly write a sequence such as:

$$\text{G N W T E Ǝ V I O Ꞁ Я ꟼ R O K M G I Ǝ Я E S Я A}$$

The pattern of the sequence can be shown by selective erasure or by rearranging letters vertically as follows:

$$\text{G E O R G E}$$

$$\text{N Ǝ Ꞁ O Ꞁ S}$$

$$\text{W A Я K E Я}$$

$$\text{T I ꟼ M Я A}$$

The four words appear on each line, either properly ordered, reversed, upside-down (turn page), or a combination.

The amazing feature was the rapidity with which Stone could reel off these letters, writing them upside-down, all the while reciting "The Shooting of Dan McGrew." He was like a one-man band of mental instruments, a walking counterexample to the "limited channel capacity" hypothesis of cognitive psychologists. Seeking to unlock the secrets of the cognitive universe, I asked Stone what went on in his mind as he did this trick. His answer was totally unrevealing: "I practiced it so long that my hand just automatically knows what to do as my eye looks at successive letters of the key words." Such answers, to the dismay of cognitive psychologists, are also about what we get if we ask a pianist or one-man band to explain how he does his "trick." It's like asking the common man how he can understand rapid speech. He doesn't know; he just can do it.

Willie the Wizard was a lightning-fast mental calculator who could multiply and divide very long numbers at a startling speed. He was led through his paces by his manager, a sort of carnival barker who would announce Willie's next feats, solicit problems from the audience, keep track of problems on a blackboard, and call for applause. The general class of problems Willie liked to work on were freaks of the following form: "If a flea jumps two feet, three inches every hop, how many hops must it take to go around the world, the circumference begin 25,020 miles? Also, how long would it require for the journey if the flea takes one hop per second?" Almost before such questions were finished, Willie would have started rattling off the answer, "It would take 58,713,600 hops, requiring one year, 314 days, 13 hours, and 20 minutes." Like most mental calculators, Willie had memorized a vast array of arithmetic facts (e.g., products of all three-digit numbers): he also used many shortcuts which speed up mental calculations. Such skills are poorly understood. As person, Willie was shy, with few interests beside arithmetic; higher math like calculus held no interest for him. He was somewhat of an innocent pixie regarding human relations. His business manager helped shield him from people who would exploit that innocence.

The evening following the conference a banquet was held in a private club for magicians, with haunted-house decor straight out of the Addams family. Throughout dinner we were entertained by conferees doing card tricks and memory tricks. I recall one stunt in which the mnemonist looked briefly through a shuffled deck of cards, then recited from memory the order of the 52 cards. As another trick, after shuffling and dealing you one or more cards, he could inspect the remaining deck and tell you which cards you'd taken. For these stunts, he used a prememorized code word (and image) for each of the 52 cards in conjunction with the pegword system explained in my article.

Such tricks kept us entertained throughout the evening. The only memory failures I noticed in the crowd were some late arrivals who had mistaken the time and place of the banquet and two conferees who forgot where they'd parked their cars. As the evening ended, one stage mnemonist shook my hand with that direct, sincere look and said, "It's been a pleasure knowing you, Dr. Flowers."

the first word of each list and asking the student to recall the other items in that list in order. Students who had constructed stories recalled about seven times as many correct items as the control subjects did.

The narrative chaining method is a good mnemonic because the person provides an overall theme by which to organize the critical words. A second mnemonic for learning lists of items is the method of loci ("locations"): it works not by relating the items to be remembered to one another but rather by relating them to a standard list of known locations. One of the first references to this mnemonic system was made by Cicero, who tells the story of a man named Simonides. While attending a large banquet, Simonides was called outside and during his absence the roof of the hall collapsed, killing all of the revelers. The bodies of the victims were so mangled that they could not be identified by their relatives. Simonides, however, was able to identify each of the corpses by recalling where each person sat before the tragedy. He did this by visualizing the room and mentally walking about, "seeing" who had been seated in each chair. This feat so impressed him that he came to believe that all memory worked by placing objects or ideas into definite locations. The mnemonic is known as the method of loci because it depends on pigeon-holing items to be remembered into a series of "locations."

To use the method of loci, you must first establish a list of "memory snapshots" of locations taken from along a familiar route, such as a walk through your house. (A building, campus, or city would serve as well.) You must be able to see clearly and to recite the different distinctive locations on your list. To learn any new list of items you simply take a "mental walk" through your list of loci, placing successive items in your imagination at successive locations along your familiar route. You should connect the items to their locations by visualizing some vivid interaction between the item and the things at a given location. When you need to recall the items, you simply take another mental walk along your familiar route and see what items have been deposited there. For example, suppose that you need to buy many items at the grocery, including milk, bread, bananas and cigarettes as the first four. The first-four snapshots of your pre-memorized list of locations might be your front hallway closet, the kitchen refrigerator, your favorite easy chair, and the living-room fireplace. To learn the first four items of your shopping list, you should visualize a vivid image of quarts of milk stacked up and bursting in your hallway closet, then a dagger-like loaf of bread piercing the refrigerator door, then large bunches of bananas piled up in your easy chair, and in the fireplace a large pack of cigarettes with several of them sticking out of the pack and smoking. A long list of items to be learned would require a long list of familiar locations in memory. As each object to be learned is studied, it is placed in imagination at the next location on your list of familiar loci. You should try to visualize a clear mental picture of the object "doing something interesting" at the location where it is placed. Later, in the grocery store, you can recall your shopping list by an imaginary walk through your house, pausing to "look at" what you've placed earlier at the standard locations in your route.

This system provides a series of memory hooks on which you can snag items and keep them from getting away. The number of loci can be expanded indefinitely according to one's needs. The system does more than just connect an item to something that is already known. It provides a series of permanent hooks or memory pegs to which you already have reliable access. Since the peg-list doesn't change, the pegs provide cues that can stimulate recall of the needed items.

A man who developed the method of loci to a fine art was the subject of Alexander R. Luria's book, *The Mind of a Mnemonist*. Known simply as *S*, this man performed remarkable feats of memory, recalling long lists of words without effort, and often retaining material many years.

There is also experimental evidence that the method of loci improves memory. Sometimes subjects who use this system are able to recall two to four times as much material as control subjects. In a study by John Ross and Kerry A. Lawrence, students studied a list of 40 nouns using the loci method. Immediately after each student studied the list, he tried to recall it in correct order. The next day the subject returned and again recalled the list before learning a

new list of 40 items. Each student learned several lists this way. The average number of words recalled immediately after presentation of the list was 38 out of 40 in correct order. The average recall of words studied a day before was 34 out of 40 in correct order. This performance is vastly superior to that of students who use rote learning techniques.

Shopping with Mnemonics

In a direct comparison of the methods, David Winzenz and I had college students study five successive "shopping lists" of 20 unrelated words. They were allowed five seconds to study each word; they tried to recall each list immediately after studying it, and at the end of the session they tried to recall all five lists (100 items). Some subjects learned using the mnemonic or slight variations on it, while our control subjects were left to learn by their own devices (which typically consisted of rote rehearsal). The subjects using the mnemonic recalled the words far better than the controls on both the immediate test and the end-of-session test. At this end-of-session

---

There is also experimental evidence that the method of loci improves memory. Sometimes subjects who use this system are able to recall two to four times as much material as control subjects.

---

test, the mnemonic subjects remembered an average of 72 items out of 100, whereas the controls remembered only 28. Furthermore, the items recalled by subjects using the mnemonic were usually assigned to the right position on the right list, whereas the control subjects were very poor at remembering the position and list of the few scattered items they did recall.

A second mnemonic, called the "peg-word system," seems in most respects to be entirely equivalent to the method of loci. Where the method of loci uses mental snapshots of locations as memory pegs, the pegword system uses a familiar list of names of simple, concrete objects. A typical pegword list is one composed of rhymes of the first 20 or so integers. For instance, the pegwords for the first five integers might be 1-bun, 2-shoe, 3-tree, 4-door and 5-hive. The pegs should be names of concrete objects which you can visualize. This pegword list should be well learned so that it can be recited readily (the rhymes help at this stage) before it can be put to use in learning any new set of items.

To memorize a new set of items, you then use the pegwords during study much as you used the locations. You associate each item to be learned with a peg by imagining the two objects interacting in some way. For example, for our earlier grocery list, you would imagine pouring *milk* all over a soggy hamburger *bun*, then a *shoe* kicking and breaking a large stick of French *bread*, then bunches of bananas hanging from a *tree*, then a *door* puffing on a *cigarette* stuck in its keyhole. You can make up any bizarre image you like in order to link the pegword to the item to be learned. When recall is desired, you simply run through your familiar list of pegs and try to call to mind the image you formed earlier associated with each peg.

This system helps whenever the material to be learned is already familiar, but when the items are relatively unrelated, so that the problem is one of reminding yourself of all of them. Typical applications are to memorizing lists of errands, shopping items, geographical facts (e.g., the principal products of Brazil), unrelated sets of scientific laws, the sequence of points in a speech or sets of arguments you are to deliver, of main events in a play or history or novel you want to remember, and so on.

Since each pegword is attached to a number, you can recall a particular item without running through the entire list as you must do with the method of loci. If asked to recall the ninth item, you simply call to mind your pegword for number nine ("nine is wine") and this will cue recall of the ninth item. Going in the reverse direction, you can also identify the serial position of any item; from knowledge that an *orange* was last visualized drink-

---

Both methods, of course, produced recall far superior to that of control subjects who were not using either mnemonic.

---

ing a bottle of *wine*, you know that *orange* was the ninth item on your list.

The numerical mnemonic is obviously very similar to the method of loci; the difference is that images of concrete objects rather than images of familiar locations are used as pegs, and that the pegs are numbered. Judith S. Reitman and I compared recall by student using the two mnemonics, and found them to be entirely equivalent so long as the student was asked only to recall the test items in the order he'd studied them.

Both methods, of course, produced recall far superior to that of control subjects who were not using either mnemonic. The equivalence of the two methods is understandable if one notes that a "location" (such as my chair, my fireplace) is really nothing more than a coherent collection of "objects," like those prescribed for the numerical pegword system.

The same pegs or loci can be used over and over again to learn new lists of items. No particular difficulty is created by such multiple usages so long as you're interested only in remembering the most recent set of items you've stuck on your peg. Typically we can forget about arbitrary lists once we've used them: shopping lists are used but once, legal arguments before a jury are gone through but once, and a waitress has to remember only once that the current customer sitting on the left in the third booth gets the ham sandwich on rye. In such cases, the person has no need or desire to retain earlier lists.

Multiple Learning

But problems do crop up whenever the pegword system is used to learn many similar lists in succession, and the person needs to remember all of them later. One example might be learning on Sunday all of your hourly appointments for the coming week; another would be learning multiple shopping lists of things to buy at the grocery, the hardware store, the garden shop, and the drug store. In the experiment Reitman and I did, we simulated this kind of memorizing task by having

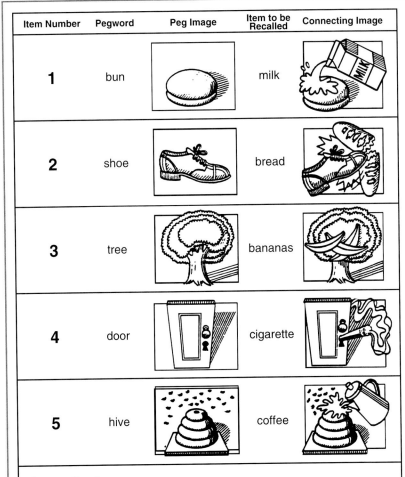

Item Number	Pegword	Peg Image	Item to be Recalled	Connecting Image
1	bun		milk	
2	shoe		bread	
3	tree		bananas	
4	door		cigarette	
5	hive		coffee	

Connecting Images:
1 *Milk* pouring onto a soggy hamburger *bun*
2 A *shoe* kicking and breaking a brittle loaf of French *bread*
3 Several bunches of *bananas* hanging from a *tree*
4 Keyhole of a *door* smoking a *cigarette*
5 Pouring *coffee* into top of a bee *hive*.

some subjects use a pegword system and others a loci system to study five lists of 20 words presented once each. They were tested for ordered recall of each list immediately after they'd studied it. They were also tested unexpectedly for recall of all five lists at the end of the hour's session and again seven days later. We told some subjects to learn the items on each new list by calling to mind a separate, distinctly different version (and vision) of the pegword and to link that to the appropriate item. Thus, if the first pegword was 1-*bun*, they should visualize a small cloverleaf dinner roll for associating to the first item in the first list, a large hamburger roll for the first item on the second list, and so on. They were also told not to call to mind earlier imagers associated to the peg, but to study each list as a distinctly separate set. Other subjects received just the opposite instructions—to use exactly the same image for the peg-word and to progressively elaborate grand imaginal scenes in which the peg was interacting in some way with all the prior objects-to-be-remembered at that list position. Suppose, for example, that the second words in the first four lists were *dog, hat, bicycle,* and *cigar.* Then the peg 2-*shoe* would be elaborated successively over lists as follows: a *dog* wearing *shoes,* that *dog* wearing a *top hat* and those *shoes,* that *dog* riding a *bicycle* while wearing that *top hat* and those *shoes,* and finally that *dog* smoking a *cigar* while riding that *bicycle* and wearing that *top hat* and those *shoes.* Our college students had no difficulty concocting such progressive elaborations, even though they had no more time than those doing the "separate" imagery method.

Although these two conditions gave the same high level of immediate recall after studying each list

(86 percent vs. 87 percent), a huge advantage for the progressive-elaboration procedure appeared at the later tests. On the end-of-session test, the progressive elaborators recalled about 70 percent compared to 38 percent for the separate imagers. At the one-week

---

I once knew a 96-year-old man who could memorize a new list of 50 three-digit numbers shouted out to him by an audience one at a time every five or 10 seconds.

---

test, the scores were 54 percent versus 12 percent, a fourfold difference.

The problem seemed to be that as the separate imagers learned each new peg-to-item association they tended to *unlearn* the prior associations from that peg. Consequently, on the end-of-session test, these subjects were good at recalling the last list they'd learned, but did progressively worse at recalling the earlier lists of the session. The progressive elaborators, on the other hand, learned each new item by first recalling and rehearsing their "peg scene" containing the prior items and then adding a new elaboration of that scene. By this means, later uses of a peg caused revival and strengthening rather than unlearning of earlier items attached to the peg. As a result, at the one-week test, these subjects did best on the first list they'd learned and worst on their final list.

Overloading the Pegs

The practical prescription is obvious: if many similar lists are to be retained simultaneously using the same pegword list, then you frequently have to revive and rehearse earlier lists as you learn new lists. There are two other obvious ways to avoid the interference and forgetting caused by

learning multiple lists. One way is to use a very long list of pegs (say, 100) and segregate items so that List-1 items (e.g., Monday's appointments) go onto pegs 1–20, List-2 items (Tuesday's appointments) go onto pegs 21–40, and so on. A second way to learn multiple lists but still avoid overloading a peg is to have multiple pegword lists at your command. Along with your rhyming pegwords, you might have three lists of 20 loci corresponding to locations along a familiar route inside your house, down the street outside your house, and through the place where you work. Then you can use different peg lists to learn the several similar lists you have to keep in mind. With a little ingenuity, you can even work out a higher-order peg system to remember

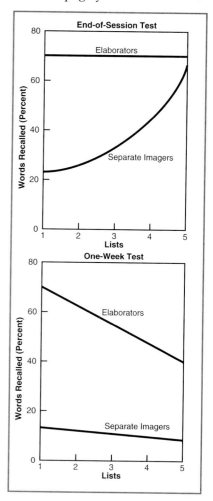

which class of items have been associated to which set of pegwords. Man's memory (or mind) seems quite at ease dealing with such superordinate hierarchies of units, since each hierarchy is built up according to a basic principle—namely, that a symbol can stand for an entire wet of units but that symbol itself can enter into further associations.

As effective as such pegword systems can be, they are of no value in learning meaningless materials like numbers, which cause one of the biggest memory nuisances. We would like to remember telephone numbers, social-security numbers, license plates, room or locker numbers; we need to recall birth dates, anniversaries, addresses and ages; students must remember historical dates and the populations of countries; businessmen need to know production figures and budget allotments. A mnemonic system that is particularly helpful with this kind of material is a number-to-sound coding system.

Meet in Havok

One first assigns consonant sounds to the numbers zero through nine. For example, the numbers zero through nine might be assigned the letters b, c, n, v, r, h, s, k, l, and t. (More elaborate codings can be used.) Once the code has been learned, then a number can be replaced by its assigned letters. Thus the number 537 becomes HVK. These letters can then be made into a word by adding vowels wherever they are needed, as in HAVOK. And so we recall that we are to meet in HAVOK—that is, in room 537.

Dates, appointment times, and other numbers can be coded and learned in the same fashion. Very long numbers typically have to be broken up into a series of words,

to make a phrase. Of course, like learning to play a piano (which requires coding or "translation" from visual score to finger movements), the code needs to be practiced if it is to be effective. You have to become very proficient at rapidly replacing digits by code letters and these by words. However, once the code has been learned, it takes little effort to maintain, much less than the time we ordinarily spend in trying to remember—or look up—important numbers.

Two or more mnemonics can be combined to produce a spectacular performance. I once knew a 96-year-old man who could memorize a new list of 50 three-digit numbers shouted out to him by an audience one at a time every five or 10 seconds. Not only could he recall the list without error, but he could tell you what the 37th item was and that the number 259 was the 18th item. Since he was partly deaf, his main trouble wasn't in remembering the numbers, but in hearing them correctly in the first place. He achieved his mnemonic feat by combining the peg-word system and the number coding system. He had concrete images as pegs for the first 50 numbers. He also had a coded conversion word with a concrete image for each of the first 1,000

> *Whether we like it or not, we all have a great many things to remember. We ought then to acquire those skills that would make memorization less painful and more efficient. Our schools should teach memory skills, just as they teach the skills of reading and writing.*

numbers. When given a number, he converted it to its code word and formed an image to connect that code word to the pegword for the first item. For instance, if the third number to be learned was

546, he would convert that to its code word, say, for example, HORSE. If his pegword for the third item was tree, then all he had to do was form an image of a horse leaning up against a tree, or kicking a tree.

Teaching Memory Skills

Most of us feel no compelling urge to learn long lists of three-digit numbers. Such feats make for interesting conversation and may prove entertaining at parties, but are themselves useless. However, the methods underlying such feats can be put to many practical uses. Whether we like it or not, we all have a great many things to remember. We ought then to acquire those skills that would make memorization less painful and more efficient. Our schools should teach memory skills, just as they teach the skills of reading and writing. Although teachers typically describe educational goals in such lofty terms as teaching their students to be critical, insightful, curious, and deeply appreciative of the subject matter, these are usually only extra requirements beyond the learning of basic facts that is demanded as a minimum. Any geography student who thinks Istanbul is in France, or any art-history student who thinks Salvador Dali painted the Sistine Chapel, is going to flunk his exams if he pulls such boners often enough. The point is that we do demand that students learn a lot of facts just as we are constantly required to do in our daily life. You can get a feel for this if you try to carry on an intelligent conversation about some current event, say, the Nixon Administration's war on inflation, without having learned some facts abut the topic. But the solution to the problem is probably at hand. By systematically applying the knowledge that we now have about learning, we should be able to improve our skills so that we spend less time memorizing facts. By the strategic use of mnemonics, we might free ourselves for those tasks we consider more important than memorization.

We ought to take advantage of what we know about memory, forgetting, and mnemonics, and we ought to do it soon. You are already beginning to forget the material you just read. ◆

Discussion Questions

1. Describe Hermann Ebbinghaus' forgetting curve.

2. What are some of the suggestions given to help remember someone's name?

3. Describe the "chaining method" and how it works.

4. Describe the "method of loci" and how it works.

5. Make a list of "memory snapshots." Once you are familiar with them, apply the method of loci to something that you need to memorize. Did it work? Record your results here.

6. Describe the "peg word system."

Mood AND **Memory**

◆ *Gordon H. Bower*

An American soldier in Vietnam blacked out as he stared at the remains of his Vietnamese girlfriend, killed by Vietcong mortar fire. Vowing revenge, he plunged into the jungle. Five days later an American patrol discovered him wandering aimlessly, dazed, disoriented. His memory of the preceding week was a total blank. He had no idea where he'd been or what he'd been doing for that period. Even after his return to the U.S., he could not recall the blackout period.

Several years later, a psychiatrist treating him for depression put him under hypnosis and encouraged him to reconstruct events from his combat days, both before and during the blackout. He calmly recalled earlier events, but when he neared the traumatic episode, he suddenly became very agitated, and more memories came pouring out. He began to relive the trauma of seeing his girlfriend's body and felt again the revulsion, outrage, and lust for revenge. Then, for the first time, he remembered what had happened after the mortar attack. He had commandeered a jeep, traveled alone for days deep into Vietcong territory, stalked Vietcong in the jungles, and set scores of booby traps with captured weapons before stumbling upon the American patrol. Curiously, after awakening from his hypnotic trance, the patient could remember only a few incidents singled out by the psychiatrist. But further treatments, described in the book *Trance and Treatment* by psychiatrists Herbert ad David Spiegel, enabled him to bring more details into consciousness.

This case illustrates an extreme memory dissociation; the blackout events could be recalled in one state (of hypnotic agitation) but not in another (normal consciousness). Hypnosis helped the person return to the psychic state he was in when the blackout started; at that point, the emotional feelings returned, as did memories of the details of the blacked-out events. Psychoanalysts might call this a case of severe repression, which

> **State-dependency refers to the difficulty in recovering, while we're in one emotional state, memories acquired in a different emotional state.**

refers to the avoidance of anxiety-provoking memories. I believe such a label equates an observation with an explanation that may or may not be correct. Instead, I believe the soldier's case is an example of state-dependent memory, a more encompassing theory that refers to people's difficulty in recovering during one psychological state any memories acquired in a different state. State-dependency and repression are competing theories of forgetting. Each offers an explanation of why the soldier's blacked-out memories re-

turned as he relived his trauma. But repression could not explain why a happy person can find happy memories easier to recover than sad ones.

The idea of studying the efficiency of memory during different psychological states—for example, while in hypnosis, under the influence of drugs, or after sensory deprivation—has been around for more than 50 years. However, previous investigations have been limited both in method and scope. While many clinical examples of state-dependency occur—for instance, violent "crimes of passion" are often blocked out but hypnotically recoverable by the assailant—such cases are really too rare, inconvenient, and complex for an adequate scientific analysis. In an earlier article in *Psychology Today*, Roland Fischer described several examples and conjectured that memories are bound up with specific levels of physiological arousal. But my research shows that arousal level is not nearly as critical as the type of emotion felt—whether fear, depression, anger, or happiness. The most common laboratory method in previous studies of state-dependency used rats, learning with or without an injection of a drug like Amytal and later tested in either a drugged or nondrugged state.

As as experimentalist, I was challenged to produce state-dependent memory in the laboratory, using normal people and trying to evoke commonly occurring emotions as "states." Two of my students, Steve Gilligan and Ken Monteiro, and I were especially interested in trying to produce such learning using different emotions, such as depression, joy, fear, and anger. This turned into a more ambitious project when we found evidence not only of state-dependent memory but also of related emotional influences on thinking, judging, and perceiving. First, I'll describe our work on state-dependent memory.

The technique we employed for inducing moods used our subjects' imaginations, guided by hypnotic suggestion. College students who were very hypnotizable volunteered for our study. After hypnotizing them, we asked them to get into a happy or sad mood by imagining or remembering a scene in which they had been delightfully happy or grievously sad. Often the happy scene was a moment of personal success or of close intimacy with someone; the sad scenes were often of personal failure or the loss of a loved one. We told them to adjust the intensity of their emotion until it was strong but not unbearable—it was important for them to function well enough to learn. After getting into a mood state, the subjects performed a learning experiment for 20 or 30 minutes, after which they were returned to a pleasantly relaxed state before debriefing. (These procedures are harmless and our subjects have willingly volunteered for further experiments.)

After some pilot work, we found that strong mood state-dependent memory could be produced by teaching people two sets of material (such as word lists)—one while happy, the other while sad—and then asking them to remember one set in a happy or a sad mood. In one study, groups of hypnotized subjects learned List A while happy or sad, then learned List B while happy or sad, and then recalled the List A while happy or sad. The lists were 16 words long; memory was always tested by free recall. The groups can be classified into three conditions. In the first, control subjects learned and recalled both lists in a single mood, happy for half of

them and sad for the other half. In the second condition, the subjects learned List A in one mood, learned List B in a different mood, and recalled List A in their original mood; these subjects should have recalled more than the control subjects because their different learning moods helped them to isolate the two lists, thus reducing confusion and interference from List B when they tried to recall List A. The third, interference condition was just the reverse; those students tried to recall List A when they were in their second, List B mood. Their recall of List A should have suffered, because the recall mood evokes memories of the wrong List B rather than the target List A.

When we returned subjects to their original moods, we did so by having them call up scenes different from their original ones. For example, if a woman originally induced happiness by reliving a scene of herself scoring the winning goal in a soccer match, we would instruct her to return to the happy mood by imagining a different scene, such as riding a horse along the beach. We had subjects use a second imagined situation so that any memory advantage obtained for same-mood testing would be due to overlap of moods, not to overlap of imaginary scenes.

A person's retention score was calculated as the percentage of originally learned items that were recalled on the later test. The results are in the chart on page 64; there is an obvious state-dependent effect. People who were sad during recall remembered about 80 percent of the material they had learned when they were sad, compared with 45 percent recall of the

Lab subjects who were put in a sad mood remembered 80 percent of the words they had learned previously while in a sad mood.

material they had learned when they were happy. Conversely, happy recallers remembered 78 percent of their happy list, versus 46 percent of their sad list. The state-dependent memory effect shows up in the crossover of these lines on the chart. A good metaphor for this is to suppose that you have one bulletin board for happy moods and another for sad moods. On each board you post the messages you learn while in that mood. You will be able to read off your messages from the happy bulletin board best if you first get into a happy mood, and the messages on the sad bulletin board best when you get into a sad mood.

Aside from the state-dependent effect, I am often asked whether people learn better when they are happy or when they are sad. others have found that clinically depressed patients are often poor learners. However, in all of our experiments with word lists, we never have found a difference in overall learning rate or later retention that was due to the subject's mood. I suspect this reflects our control over the hypnotic subjects' motivation to do as well as possible in the learning task despite their happy or sad feelings.

We next addressed the issue of whether state-dependency would occur for recall of actual events drawn from a person's emotional life. We enlisted some volunteers who agreed to record such emotional events in a daily diary for a week. We gave these subjects a booklet for recording emotional incidents and discussed what we meant by an emotional incident. Examples would be the joy they experienced at a friend's wedding or the anger they experienced in an argument at work. For each incident they were to record the time, place, participants, and gist of what happened and to rate the incident as pleasant or unpleasant on a 10-point scale.

Conscientious diary-keeping is demanding, and we dropped nearly half of our subjects because they failed to record enough incidents in the proper manner consistently over the week. We collected usable diaries from 14 subjects and scheduled them to return a week later. At that one-week interval they were hypnotized; half were put into a pleasant mood and the other half into an unpleasant mood, and all were asked to recall every incident they could remember of those recorded in their diaries the week before.

The percentages of recall showed the expected results: people in a happy mood recalled a greater percentage of their recorded pleasant experiences than of their unpleasant experiences; people in a sad mood recalled a greater percentage of their unpleasant experiences than of their pleasant experiences.

Suspects in some crimes of passion are not able to recall their actions until they return, under hypnosis, to the same intense emotional state.

Remember that when subjects originally recorded their experiences, they also rated the emotional intensity of each experience. These intensity ratings were somewhat predictive: recall of more intense experiences averaged 37 percent, and of less intense experiences 25 percent. The intensity effect is important, and I will return to it later.

After subjects had finished recalling, we asked them to rate the current emotional intensity of the incidents they recalled. We found that they simply shifted their rating scale toward their current mood: if they were feeling pleasant, the recalled incidents were judged as more pleasant (or less unpleasant); if they were feeling unpleasant, the incidents were judged more unpleasant (or less pleasant) than originally. That should be familiar—here are the rose-colored classes of the optimist and the somber, gray outlook of the pessimist.

Is it possible that recording incidents in a diary and rating them as pleasant or unpleasant encourages subjects to label their experiences in this manner and in some way gives us the results we want? Perhaps. To avoid such contaminants, in our next experiment we simply asked people to recall childhood incidents. We induced a happy or sad mood in our subjects and asked them to write brief descriptions of many unrelated incidents of any kind from their pre-high school days. Subjects were asked to "hop around" through their memories for 10 minutes, describing an incident in just a sentence or two before moving on to some unrelated incident.

The next day, we had the subjects categorize their incidents as pleasant, unpleasant, or neutral while unhypnotized and in a normal mood (so that their mood would not influence how pleasant or unpleasant they rated an event). The few neutral incidents recalled were discarded, and the chart below shows the main results. Happy subjects retrieved many more pleasant than unpleasant memories (a 92 percent bias); sad subjects retrieved slightly more

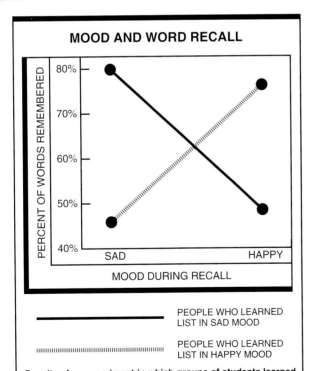

MOOD AND WORD RECALL

PERCENT OF WORDS REMEMBERED

80%
70%
60%
50%
40%

SAD — HAPPY

MOOD DURING RECALL

——————— PEOPLE WHO LEARNED LIST IN SAD MOOD

|||||||||||||||||||||||||||||||||||||||||||||||||| PEOPLE WHO LEARNED LIST IN HAPPY MOOD

Results of an experiment in which groups of students learned a list of words while in one mood and later tried to recall as many as they could while in the same mood or a different mood. They were able to remember a much larger percentage when their learning mood matched their recall mood. This "state-dependency" effect is seen in the big difference between scores in the two recall situations, dramatized by the steep incline of the two lines connecting them. (The black dots show average percentages for both groups.)

unpleasant than pleasant memories (a 55 percent bias in the reverse direction).

What the subjects reported was enormously dependent on their mood when recalling. That is state-dependent memory: the subjects presumably felt pleasant or unpleasant at the time the incidents were stored, and their current mood selectively retrieves the pleasant or the unpleasant memories.

What kind of theory can explain these mood-state dependent effects? A simple explanation can be cast within the old theory that memory depends upon associations between ideas. All we need to assume is that an emotion has the same effect as an "active idea unit" in the memory system. Each distinct emotion is presumed to have a distinct unit in memory that can be hooked up into the memory networks. The critical assumption is that an active emotion unit can enter into association with ideas we think about, or events that happened, at the time we are feeling that emotion. For instance, as the ideas recording the facts of a parent's funeral are stored in memory, a powerful association forms between these facts and the sadness one felt at the time.

Retrieval of some contents from memory depends upon activating other units or ideas that are associated with those contents. Thus, returning to the scene of a funeral, the associations activated by that place may cause one to reexperience the sadness felt earlier at the funeral. Conversely, if a person feels sad for some reason, activation of that emotion will bring into consciousness remembrances of associated ideas—most likely other sad events.

This theory easily explains state-dependent retrieval. In the first experiment, for example, the words of List A became associated both with the list A label and with the mood experienced at that time. Later, the words from List a can be

retrieved best by reinstating the earlier List A mood, since that mood is a strongly associated cue for activating their memory. On the contrary, if a person had to recall List A while feeling in a different (List B) mood, that different mood would arouse associations that competed with recall of the correct items, thus reducing the memory scores. The same reasoning explains how one's current mood selectively retrieves personal episodes associated originally with pleasant or unpleasant emotions.

Beyond sate-dependent memory, the network theory also helps to explain a number of influences of emotion on selective perception, learning, judgment, and thinking. When aroused, an emotion activates relevant concepts, thoughts, and frameworks for categorizing the social world. We have confirmed, for example, that people who are happy, sad or angry produce free associations that are predominantly happy, sad or angry, respectively. Similarly, when asked to fantasize or make up an imaginative story to pictures of the Thematic Apperception Test (TAT), they produce happy, sad, or hostile fantasies, depending on their emotional state. If asked for top-of-the-head opinions about their acquaintances, or the performance of their car or TV, they give highly flattering or negative evaluations, according to their mood. Also, their mood causes them to be optimistic or pessimistic in prognosticating future events about

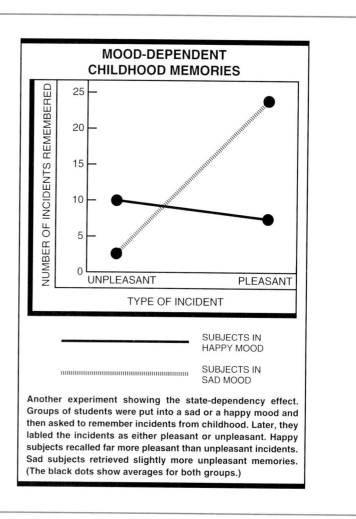

Another experiment showing the state-dependency effect. Groups of students were put into a sad or a happy mood and then asked to remember incidents from childhood. Later, they labled the incidents as either pleasant or unpleasant. Happy subjects recalled far more pleasant than unpleasant incidents. Sad subjects retrieved slightly more unpleasant memories. (The black dots show averages for both groups.)

themselves and the nation. These influences can be seen as veiled forms of state-dependent retrieval of either the positive or negative memories about the person, event or object.

Mood affects the way we "see" other people. Social interactions are often ambiguous, and we have to read the intentions hidden behind people's words and actions. Is that person being steadfast in arguing his position or is he being pig-headed and obstructive? Was his action courageous or reckless? Was that remark assertive or aggressive? In reading others' intentions the emotional premise from which we begin strongly influences what we conclude. Thus the happy person seems ready to give a charitable, benevolent interpretation of social events, whereas the grouch seem determined to find fault, to take offense, or to take the uncharitable view. We find that these effects appear just as strongly when people are judging themselves on competence or attractiveness as well as when they're judging others. For example, when our subjects were in a depressed mood, they tended to judge their actions moment-by-moment in a videotaped interview as inept, unsociable, and awkward; but if they were in a happy mood, they judged their behaviors as confident, competent, and warmly sociable. Thus, social "reality" is constructed in the eye of the beholder, and that eye is connected to the emotions.

The network theory further predicts that an emotion should act as a selective filter in perception, letting in signals of a certain emotional wavelength and filtering out others. The emotional state adjusts the filter so that the person will attend more to stimulus material that agrees with or supports the current emotion. An analogy is that our feelings are like a magnet that selects iron filings from a heap of dust, attracting to itself whatever incoming material it can use.

Emotional effects can be demonstrated in attention and perception as well as learning. Thus, a sad person will look at pictures of sad faces more than happy faces; a happy person will dwell longer on happy faces. People who are happy from having just succeeded at an intelligence task have lower thresholds for seeing "success" words; subjects who've failed have lower thresholds for "failure" words.

The main work we've done on this salience effect concerns selective learning. In one of our experiments, subjects were made happy or sad by a posthypnotic suggestion as they read a brief story about two college men getting together and playing a friendly game of tennis. André is happy—everything is going well for him; Jack is sad—nothing is going well for him. The events of the two men's lives and their emotional reactions are vividly described in the story, which is a balanced, third-person account. When our subjects finished reading the story, we asked them to tell us who they thought the central character was and who they identified with. We found that readers who were happy identified with the happy character, thought the story was about him, and thought the story contained more statements about him; readers who were sad identified with the sad character and thought there were more statements about him.

Our subjects tried to recall the test the next day while in a neutral mood. Eighty percent of the facts remembered by the sad readers were about the sad character; 55 percent of the facts remembered by the happy readers were about the happy character. This is a mood-congruity effect; readers attend more to the character whose mood matches their own. Since all recallers were in a neutral mood, their differing recall results from their selective learning; it is not a state-dependent effect, since that

requires varying subjects' mood during recall as well as during learning.

How is the mood-congruity effect explained? Why is mood-congruent material more salient and better learned? Two explanations seem worth considering.

The first hypothesis is that when one is sad, a sad incident in a story is more likely than a happy incident to remind one of a similar incident in one's life; vice versa, when one is happy. (Note that this is simply the state-dependent retrieval hypothesis.) An additional assumption is that the reminding is itself an event that enhances memory of the prompting event. This may occur because the old memory allows one to elaborate on the prompting event or to infuse it with greater emotion. In other studies, we have found that people remember descriptions of event that remind them of a specific incident in their lives far better than they recall descriptions that don't cause such reminiscence. To summarize, this hypothesis states that the mood-congruity effect is produced by selective reminding.

The second hypothesis, which complements the first, is that the mood-congruity effect comes from the influence of emotional intensity on memory. We demonstrated this idea in a study in which subjects were put in a sad or happy mood during hypnosis and then asked to read a story that went from a happy incident to a sad incident to a happy incident, and so on. Although our hypnotized subjects in several experiments tried to maintain steady moods, they reported that a mood's intensity would wane when they read material of the opposite quality. Thus happy subjects would come down from their euphoria when they read about a funeral or about unjust suffering; those topics intensified the sad subjects' feelings.

But why are intense emotional experiences better remembered? At present, there are many explanations. One is that events that evoke strong emotional reactions in real life are typically events involving personally significant goals, such as attaining life ambitions, elevating self-esteem, reducing suffering, receiving love and respect, or avoiding harm to oneself or loved ones. Because of their central importance, those goal-satisfying events are thought about frequently and become connected to other personal plans and to one's self-concept.

Intense experiences may also be remembered better because they tend to be rare. Because they are distinctive, they are not easily confused with more numerous, ordinary experiences; they tend to be insulated from interference.

The explanation of the mood-congruity effect that fits our lab results best is that mood-congruous experiments may be rehearsed more often and elaborated or thought about more deeply than experiences that do not match our mood. Thus sad people may be quickly able to embroider and elaborate upon a sad incident, whereas they don't elaborate on happy incidents. Because their sad incidents are elaborated and processed more deeply, sad people learn their sad incidents better than their happy ones. The same principle explains why happy people learn happy incidents better.

Having reviewed some evidence for mood-congruity and mood-dependency effects, let me speculate a bit about the possible implications for other psychological phenomena.

One obvious phenomenon explained by mood dependency is

> *Like a magnet that selects the iron filings from a pile, our feelings attract to themselves whatever incoming material they can use.*

mood perpetuation—the tendency for a dominant emotion to persist. A person in a depressed mood will tend to recall only unpleasant events and to project a bleak interpretation onto the common events of life. Depressing memories and interpretations feed back to intensify and prolong the depressed mood, encouraging the vicious circle of depression. One class of therapies for depression aims at breaking the circle by restructuring the way depressed people evaluate personal events. Thus patients are taught to attend to and rehearse the positive, competent aspects of their lives and to change their negative evaluations.

State-dependent memory helps us to interpret several other puzzling phenomena. One is the impoverished quality of dream recall shown by most people. Most people forget their dreams, which is surprising considering that such bizarre, emotionally arousing events would be very memorable had they been witnessed in the waking state. But the sleep state (even the REM state of dreaming)

> *After taking amphetamines, subjects can remember material they learned while high on the drug in the past better than when they're not high on it.*

seems psychologically distinct from the waking state, and dream memories may thus not be easily transferred from one state to the other.

State-dependent retention may also explain the fact that people have very few memories from the first year or two of their lives. In this view, as infants mature, their brains gradually change state, so

that early memories become inaccessible in the more mature state. The problem with this hypothesis is that it leads to no novel predictions to distinguish it from the plethora of competing explanations of infantile amnesia, which generally range from Freud's repression theory to the theory that the infant's and adult's "languages of thought" mismatch so badly that adults can't "translate" records of infant memories.

State-dependent memory has been demonstrated previously with psychoactive drugs like marijuana, alcohol. amphetamines, and barbiturates. For example, after taking amphetamines, subjects remember material they have learned while high on the drug in the past better than when they are not high on it. Since such substances are also mood-altering drugs, a plausible hypothesis is that they achieve their state-dependent effect by virtue of their impact on mood.

To summarize, we have now found powerful influences of emotional states upon selective perception, learning, retrieval, judgments, thought, and imagination. The emotions studied have been quite strong, and their temporary psychological effects have been striking. What is surprising to me is that the emotional effects on thinking uncovered so for seem understandable in terms of relatively simple ideas—the notion that an aroused emotion can be viewed as an active unit in an associative memory and that it stimulates memories, thoughts, perceptual categories, and actions. perhaps this is as it should be—that theories developed in one field (memory) aid our understanding of phenomena in another field (for example, emotional fantasies in the psychiatric clinic). Certainly that is the goal of all basic science.   ◆

Discussion Questions

1. What is state-dependent memory?

2. According to the author, do people learn better when they are happy or when they are sad?

3. What is the network theory?

4. Describe one of the studies that support the network theory.

5. Describe how mood can affect how we perceive other people and social interactions.

6. What is the mood-congruency effect?

7. Have you ever experienced the state-dependent-memory effect? If so, what happened?

Name: _____

Date: _____

Part 7: Memory

1. I believe that my memories of my early childhood experiences are accurate.

   | Agree | ① | ② | ③ | ④ | ⑤ | Disagree |

2. I think that memories can be repressed and later recovered through hypnosis or therapy.

   | Agree | ① | ② | ③ | ④ | ⑤ | Disagree |

3. I believe that people carry memories of past lives and that such memories can be recovered through hypnosis or therapy.

   | Agree | ① | ② | ③ | ④ | ⑤ | Disagree |

Without looking at the real bill, draw the front side of a one-dollar bill below in as much detail as possible. When you have drawn as much as possible, make a second drawing of a dollar bill, this time with a real bill in front of you. How much do the two drawings differ? You have seen a dollar bill thousands of times. If the first drawing is much poorer than the first, what does this suggest about human memory?

Below, record five events from your early childhood that you remember clearly. Then ask one of your parents about the accuracy of each recollection. How well were your memories corroborated? Is it possible to carry clear, strong memories of events that never took place?

PART 8

INTELLIGENCE

23 ▸ **The Seven Frames of Mind: A Conversation with Howard Gardner**

24 ▸ **How Sex Hormones Boost—or Cut—Intellectual Ability,**
by Doreen Kimura

25 ▸ **The Differences Are Real,** by Arthur Jensen

26 ▸ **Differences Are Not Deficits,** by Theodosius Dobzhanshy

In the 1800s, Francis Galton—still Darwin's first cousin—set about to study and catalogue individual differences in just about everything: strength, speed, breathing ability, you name it. He also catalogued differences in intelligence, which is usually defined as a person's ability to think clearly and logically. Galton was an advocate for "eugenics"—selective breeding to improve human abilities, and he hoped that his testing program would help find the best breeding stock. We do it with animals, after all.

Early in the 1900s, at the request of the French government, Alfred Binet and Théodore Simon constructed tests that allowed tracking of school children according to intelligence level; the goal was to provide more efficient education. And in World War I, the American psychologist Lewis Terman was asked by the U.S. Army to develop an intelligence test to help select competent soldiers; the goal was to build a more effective army. Terman envisioned a world in which, some day, properly designed tests would also be used to allow people to select their perfect mates.

People differ from one another. The goal of intelligence testing is to identify certain differences—especially those related to thinking ability—in order to improve education, performance, or, in Galton's case, the human race. While these may be noble causes, intelligence testing has virtually always proved to be controversial and divisive for two very simple (and perhaps obvious) reasons: First, individuals who score poorly will often oppose testing because of the possibility that their scores will be used to penalize them in some way. Second, just as racial and ethnic groups often differ from each other in average height, build, and eye color, they also often differ from each other in their average scores on intelligence tests. Groups with low scores will naturally be opposed to testing, fearing discrimination. Basically, no one wants to know that he or she is inferior to anyone else or that his or her group is inferior to another group, no matter what the noble causes of the testers.

Add to that the curious Western political doctrine that all people are "created equal" (which is supposed to mean "equal in the eyes of the law" but which is often interpreted more broadly), and you can see that intelligence testing—or any testing, for that matter, that identifies individual differences—is bound to make people angry.

While Harvard's Howard Gardner rejects the traditional concept of intelligence in favor of a broad concept that throws in everything from musical ability to self-knowledge, he's not opposed to testing. In the first article in this section, Gardner seems to suggest that children should be tracked according to every strength and weakness they have; I think that even Alfred Binet would be appalled.

In "How Sex Hormones Boost—or Cut—Intellectual Ability," distinguished biopsychologist Doreen Kimura cites controversial data suggesting that women's hormonal fluctuations affect their intellectual abilities. I value my life, so I'll withhold comment.

In the following article, Arthur Jensen defends his controversial assertion that racial differences in IQ scores are probably genetic, following which geneticist Theodosius Dobzhansky criticizes Jensen's position. This issue gets replayed every few years. The most recent debates center around a book called *The Bell Curve*, by Herrnstein and Murray.

Keep in mind that differences between individuals and average differences between groups are very real and sometimes very large. The debate is usually not about whether differences exist but about what these differences mean or, sometimes, about whether we should even dare to measure them. In a world of finite resources, I doubt that the debate will ever end. When differences—especially intellectual differences—are at issue, clear thinking takes a hike. See the irony?

The *Seven* Frames *of* **Mind:** A *CONVERSATION* with Howard ***Gardner***

◆ *James Ellison*

James Ellison: *Frames of Mind* embraces a theory of multiple intelligences. Can you explain that theory in relatively simple terms?

Howard Gardner: Most people in our society, even if they know better, talk as if individuals could be assessed in terms of one dimension, namely how smart or dumb they are. This is deeply ingrained in us. I became convinced some time ago that such a narrow assessment was wrong in scientific terms and had seriously damaging social consequences. In *Frames of Mind*, I describe seven ways of viewing the world; I believe they're equally important ways, and if they don't exhaust all possible forms of knowing, they at least give us a more comprehensive picture than we've had until now.

Ellison: Linguistic and logical-mathematical intelligence are the two we all know about.

Gardner: Most intelligence tests assess the individual's abilities in those two areas. But my list also includes spatial intelligence. The core ability there is being able to find your way around an environment, to form mental images and to transform them readily. Musical intelligence is concerned with the ability to perceive and create pitch patterns and rhythmic patterns. The gift of fine motor movement, as you might see in a surgeon or a dancer, is a root component of bodily-kinesthetic intelligence.

Ellison: That leaves the interpersonal and intrapersonal, which would seem to be controversial categories.

Gardner: They are. But then my entire theory breeds controversy, particularly among those who have a narrow, largely Western conception of what intelligence is.

Ellison: How would you define the interpersonal and intrapersonal as intelligences?

Gardner: Interpersonal involves understanding others—how they feel, what motivates them, how they interact with one another. Intrapersonal intelligence centers on the individual's ability to be acquainted with himself or herself, to have a developed sense of identity.

Ellison: I can see where your critics would grant that language and logic are intelligences, and they'd probably throw in spatial, grudgingly. But they might balk at your other four measures as not being strictly mental activities.

> *My entire theory breeds controversy, particularly among those who have a narrow, largely western conception of what intelligence is.*

Gardner: What right does anyone have to determine a *priori* what the realm of the mind is and is not? Some of my critics claim that I'm really talking about talents, not intelligences, to which I say, fine, if you'll agree that language

and logical-mathematical thinking are talents, too. I'm trying to knock language and logic off a pedestal, to democratize the range of human faculties.

Ellison: Democratize?

Gardner: Forget about Western technological society for a moment and think about other societies. In the Caroline Islands of Micronesia, sailors navigate among hundreds of islands, using only the stars in the sky and their bodily feelings as they go over the waves. To that society, this ability is much more important than solving a quadratic equation or writing a sonnet. If intelligence testers had lived among the Micronesians, they would have come up with an entirely different set of testing methods and a wholly distinct list of intelligences.

Ellison: And reading would have been low on the totem pole for these people.

Gardner: Five hundred years ago in the West, a tester would have emphasized linguistic memory because printed books weren't readily available. Five hundred years from now, when computers are carrying out all reasoning, there may be no need for logical-mathematical thinking and again the list of desirable intelligences would shift. What I object to is this: Decisions made about 80 years ago in France by Alfred Binet, who was interested in predicting who would fail in school, and later by a few Army testers in the United States during World War I, now exercise a tyrannical hold on who is labeled as bright or not bright. These labels affect both people's conceptions of themselves and the life options available to them.

Ellison: Isn't it true that high SAT and I.Q. scores predict superior social and economic results?

Gardner: In the short run, these tests have decent predictive value, at least in schools. Children who do well in the tests tend to get good grades in school, for schools also reward quick responses to short-answer questions. Interestingly, though, the tests don't have good predictive value for what happens beyond school.

Ellison: Are there statistics in support of that conclusion?

Gardner: Well, the best studies I know of were done by sociology professor Christopher Jencks of Northwestern University. He and his associates have shown that I.Q. tests have only a modest correlation with success in professions.

I'm essentially trying to knock language and logic off a pedestal.

Ellison: How can you possibly test something like interpersonal intelligence?

Gardner: You can't, in the usual sense of testing. But let me tell you about a plan that some colleagues and I would like to get funded. We're interested in monitoring intellectual capacity in the preschool years. We want to set up what we call an enriched environment, filled with materials that children can interact with freely on their own. How children interact with these materials over a period of time would serve as a much better indicator of their strengths than any short-term measure.

Let's say we're looking in the area of spatial intelligence. One of the things we would want to do is to give children blocks of various sorts and observe what and how they build. We would show them games involving more complex structures and see if they pick up principles of construction. In the area of music we would give them Montessori bells and simple computer toys that allow children to create their own melody. Schools can be equipped with these aids. To assess personal intelligences, we'll have the children enact different roles in play or work cooperatively on a project. The point is that, in a few weeks or months, you could

see the developmental steps children go through, as well as the richness and depth of their play.

Ellison: I take it you feel this is a better method to use than standard testing.

Gardner: Yes. First of all, it relates much more to children's natural way of doing things, which is exploring, testing themselves with materials. Second, if a child had an off day or didn't like the experimenter, we would simply go on to the next day. A child would be monitored for six months or a year, and at the end of the year we would come up with a profile of intellectual propensities somewhere between an I.Q. score and an annotated report card. We would observe intelligences and combinations of intelligences for a year. Then we would have descriptions a page or two long that say in plain English what the child's strengths and interests are, along with his areas of weakness and how they could be strengthened.

Ellison: Evidently, then, you still feel that some kind of score is necessary.

Gardner: It's more efficient for the professional to be able to quantify, but I'm ambivalent about sharing scores with nonspecialists. We actually hope to develop four kinds of tests. One we call a test of core ability. For example, in the area of music we would look at the child's pitch and rhythm ability. But rather than assess sensitivity to pitches in isolation (as in traditional musical tests), we would teach children a song and code how quickly they learn it and how accurate the pitch and rhythm are. The second test is developmental. We would provide children with materials and give them ample opportunity to explore, to get deeper and deeper into the process, to invent their own products.

The third test, a multiple-intelligence measure, involves taking children to a movie, a museum, perhaps a zoo. Afterwards, children would be asked to recreate the experience, talk about it, sing it, draw it. We would look at how children choose to encode the experience, whether in their recreations, they focus on spatial, musical, linguistic or some combination.

Ellison: You mentioned a fourth test.

Gardner: Yes, an incidental-learning measure. We would supply something in the environment that children have to no idea they're ever going to be asked about. We want to see what they would pick up spontaneously, without ever attending explicitly.

Ellison: Can you give an example?

Gardner: Say the child enters a classroom and there's a certain song playing, each day the same song. One day we simply say to the child, "Can you sing the song you hear in the morning?" This is how you discover what kids pick up incidentally. It has a lot to do with how intelligences work. A person does not have a high intelligence because he works very hard at something. On the contrary, having a high intelligence means that you naturally, without effort, pick up certain kinds of things.

Ellison: What about the practicality of administering these sorts of tests? It obviously would involve a tremendous amount of time and energy.

Gardner: First, you have to decide if the whole thing is feasible. If it is, we move to the question of practicality. Clearly, to be done adequately would involve several hours of monitoring spread out through the year. But if you take into account the amount of time a teacher spends determining the grades for a report card, the monitoring wouldn't take that much more time. And most important, when you consider the social value of assessing an individual's talents, the costs become trivial. A relatively small amount of time and money can make a huge difference for the person and for the society.

Ellison: Do you think there is a chance of changing the way testing is used in the united States today?

Gardner: Once people appreciate the perils, change will follow. There's treachery in labeling and over quantifying. This is true of I.Q. tests and also applies to SAT scores. SATs, after all, are basically I.Q. tests. More people probably know their SAT scores than their own Social Security numbers. I'm delighted that some of the best universities are now questioning the need for an SAT, and I'll do whatever I can to come up with a more humane and pluralistic way of assessing humankind.

Ellison: A way that spans the seven intelligences.

Gardner: Let me put this in personal terms for a moment. I've certainly gotten ahead by virtue of some of those intelligences that are valued in society. Moreover, I leaned early in life to use those intelligences to supplement things that I couldn't do as well. For example, I'm not particularly gifted in the spatial area, but if I'm given a spatial test, I can usually use logical means to figure out the right answer. Also, I think I was "saved" because I've always been very interested in the arts. They are every bit as serious and cognitive as the sciences, and yet because of various prejudices in our society, the arts are considered to be mainly emotional and mysterious. Our culture confuses being a scientist with being smart and se-

> *More people probably know their S.A.T. scores than their own social security numbers.*

rious. I came to realize that we really had to rethink the whole notion of what cognition is all about.

Ellison: In school, the science kids have always been marked as the intellectual whizzes, haven't they? Evidently the attitude that science kids grow up to be our intellectual elite persists in the general adult culture.

Gardner: They are the high priests. And yet the cognitive complexity of Henry James's or Proust's structure of knowledge is every bit as involved and sophisticated as the structural complexities of a physics theory. Granted, it's a different kind of complexity, but I think it's worth noting that someone can be incredibly good as a scientist and have no sense of what's going on in a Henry James novel.

Ellison: Once these various intelligences are identified, how can they be translated into a cohesive educational experience?

Gardner: Let's say you have a child with strong spatial abilities, as assessed by block play or by finding the way around a new environment. And let's say the school doesn't have teachers who work in that area. There certainly are other people in the community

> *I'm in favor of dissolving the boundaries between school and the rest of the community. I think it has to happen in this country, and I'm convinced it will happen.*

with those kinds of gifts, and it should be the school's role to help children and parents find them. I'm in favor of dissolving the boundaries between school and the rest of the community. I think it has to happen in this country, and I'm convinced it will happen.

Also, the apprenticeship system should be reconstituted. The child who's gifted in the spatial area ought to be working in an architect's office or in mapmaking. Apprenticeship ensures the transmission of skills to individuals in a position to use them. We need to motivate people toward things they're good at. Those who are gifted in math like doing it because it provides a lot of satisfaction and they make a lot of progress. But why stop with math? Apprentice the musical kid to a piano tuner. God knows, we need good piano tuners.

Ellison: Are you saying we shouldn't invest energy in areas where our aptitude isn't high?

Gardner: I believe that, up to a point. But still, an effort to understand other subjects has to be made.

Ellison: But why? The students who are whizzes in English and can't solve a geometric problem on pain of death—why should they keep trying?

Gardner: One of the major things that prompted my work was a recognition that in the real world people have different abilities and disabilities. Take someone with a poor prognosis in the spatial area. What should we do? I think it's crucial to try to diagnose that early because everything we know from neuroscience suggests that the earlier an individual has a chance to work intensely with the relevant materials, the more rapidly he or she will develop in that area. And it makes no difference how meager their potential is, it should be developed.

Ellison: Then in a sense you disagree with my idea that we should ignore areas of low aptitude.

Gardner: Areas of low aptitude should be detected early in life, and they can be bolstered by what we might call prostheses for an intelligence. Let's assume I have a poor visual memory and can't remember forms. Today we have all sorts of aids to make the forms perfectly visible. What if I can't transform an image in my mind? We now have a simple computer program that transforms it for me on demand. Culture, you see, can create instruments to supplement lacks in intelligences.

Ellison: How well do we understand these lacks in others, though? Can the skilled linguist who can't carry a tune appreciate the world of the jazz trombonist who can barely read the newspaper?

Gardner: I think the theory of multiple intelligences helps you to understand how people relate, and fail to relate, to one another. We all know that sometimes opposites attract. And if you think about this not in terms of hair color but of intelligences, it's quite intriguing. Often somebody who can't do music worth a damn is attracted to somebody who thinks well musically but has no personal skills and admires the person who's gifted interpersonally. However, problems may arise. One person thinks very spatially but has trouble trying to describe how to get somewhere. The spouse has no spatial ability or has to think of everything linguistically. This can cause considerable conflict, with each person thinking the other stupid, whereas, in fact, their minds are simply working in different ways, displaying contrasting intelligences.

Ellison: Let's move to the personal intelligences. Can you really teach someone to interact well with others? Isn't that an art, a gift, in a sense, inborn?

Gardner: It can be taught. I think a lot can be done through different kinds of media. For example, you can tell stories to children and see what they understand about the motivations of different characters.

Or let them act the characters. Show them film and have them look closely at the interactions of characters in the films. We must always be alert for settings in which children can develop in productive ways. It is harmful to put children who are shy and afraid of other people in an environment where everyone is much older and more sophisticated. But put them in game room with younger children, and you'll enhance their interpersonal understanding.

Ellison: Sometimes individuals are blocked for psychodynamic reasons. Do you see therapy as a possible teaching tool, as a way to promote the personal intelligences?

Gardner: Therapy is our society's way of helping individuals use whatever intrapersonal knowledge they have in a more effective way. in the East you have Hindu, yoga and other kinds of religious philosophies that develop their own sense of what it means to be knowledgeable about the self.

Ellison: Wouldn't you say that the intra- and interpersonal intelligences communicate with each other constantly?

Nothing would make me happier than if society were to stop measuring people in terms of some unitary dimension called 'intelligence.'

Gardner: Certainly they enhance each other. The more you understand about other people, the more potential you have for understanding yourself, and vice versa. Nonetheless, there are people highly skilled in understanding other people and manipulating them—certain politicians and celebrities come to mind—and they show no particular intrapersonal understanding. By the same token, there are people in the artistic areas who seem to understand themselves while routinely miss-

ing cues in other people. An important part of my theory is that each intelligence has its own operation, and one can be strong in one intelligence while weak in others.

Still, there are many activities that involve blends of intelligences, where, as you put it, they communicate. If you look at a society where certain activities use a combination of intelligences, each intelligence will tend to buoy the other. Take those with strong logical-mathematical intelligence. Once they begin to study science, they discover that if they can't write abut their findings, they aren't really scientists. They have to be able to publish. That often means finding a collaborator who writes well. As a result of such collaborations, many scientists go from being wretched writers to becoming decent ones.

Ellison: I assume from *Frames of Mind* that the neural organization of the brain determines the strength of the various intelligences

Gardner: As you know, when somebody has a stroke or an injury to the head, not all skills break down equally. Instead, certain abilities can be significantly impaired while others are spared. A lesion in the middle areas of the left hemisphere will impair somebody' linguistic abilities while leaving musical, spatial and interpersonal skills largely undamaged. Conversely, a large lesion in the right hemisphere will compromise spatial and musical abilities, leaving linguistic abilities relatively intact. Probably the unique feature of my list of intelligences, compared with those of other researchers, is that I claim independent existences for the intelligences in the human neural system. And my chief source of information is how they function following brain damage. There is impressive evidence that each of the seven intelligences has its own special neurological organization.

Ellison: If *Frames of Mind* were to leave the reader with one point, what one would you choose?

Gardner: Nothing would make me happier than if society were to stop measuring people in terms of some unitary dimension called "intelligence." Instead, I would like us to think in terms of intellectual strengths. I'd like to get rid of numbers entirely and simply say that an individual is, let's say, relatively stronger in language than in logic, even though he or she might be well above the norm in both. Because after all, the norm is irrelevant. If you manage to change the way people talk about things, parents and teachers may begin to think and talk about intellectual proclivities rather than just how "smart" a child is. And if we begin to accept these new terms, we can stop labeling one another as smart or dumb. ◆

Discussion Questions

1. According to Howard Gardner, what are the seven intelligences?

2. How can standard intelligence tests misguide us, according to Gardner?

3. How does the concept of intelligence vary from one culture to another?

4. How might the idea of multiple intelligences change the way people view each other?

5. What are some of the reasons for testing children in these seven areas?

6. Relate these seven areas of intelligence to yourself. What are your strong areas? In which areas are you weakest? How could this knowledge help you in life?

How *Sex* **Hormones** **BOOST**—*or Cut*— INTELLECTUAL ABILITY

◆ *Doreen Kimura*

Most people accept the idea that hormones influence how we behave in explicitly sexual situations, and even that they can affect our moods. But evidence is growing that sex hormones influence a wider range of behaviors, including problem-solving or intellectual activities. Some of the observed male-female differences in cognitive ability appear to be determined by sex hormones working on brain systems.

Much of what we know about hormonal control of behavior has been discovered in nonhuman animals, mostly rats and mice. The parallel between human and animal mechanisms has been good enough that we can often fill in the knowledge gaps about human beings by looking at studies in rodents. They tell us that fetal hormones not only determine whether male or female sexual genitalia will be formed, but also whether the adult will act sexually like a male or female. Merely having an XY (male) or XX (female) chromosome does not in itself ensure male or female development. If no male sex hormones (androgens) are present in the fetal life of an XY individual, or if there is a serious abnormality of androgen systems, a female will be formed.

Similarly, we may have XY individuals who do not merely look like females, but appear to have many "sex-typical" female behavioral characteristics, show female play preferences, and the like. In another kind of hormonal anomaly, XX individuals may be mildly androgenized by early exposure to natural or synthetic androgens. Even if they are raised as girls, report Melissa Hines at UCLA and June Reinisch at the Kinsey Institute in Indiana, such individuals are tomboyish, engage in rough and tumble play, and show masculine preferences in toys and other matters. This illustrates the general principle that early exposure to sex hormones has lifelong effects on behavior of both men and women. This type of influence is referred to as an "organizational" effect, in contrast to "activational" effects— the short-term influence of fluctuations in hormones.

One way to observe organizational effects on cognitive function is to look at the differences which exist, on average, between men and women. Men excel on certain spatial tasks, especially those requiring accurate orientation of a line or pattern, imaginal rotation, or discerning a figure embedded in a background pattern. Men are also better on tests of mathematical reasoning. Women, on the other hand, are better at certain verbal tasks, particularly verbal fluency and articulation as well as some fine manual skills. They also appear to be faster in scanning a perceptual array, especially to make an identity match.

Men excel on certain spatial tasks, especially those requiring accurate orientation of a line or pattern, imaginal rotation, or discerning a figure embedded in a background pattern. Men are also better on tests of mathematical reasoning. Women, on the other hand, are better at certain verbal tasks, particularly verbal fluency and articulation as well as some fine manual skills. They also appear to be faster in scanning a perceptual array, especially to make an identity match.

How Hormones Affect Average Gender Differences

One problem with attributing these differences to early hormonal influences is that men and women are also treated differently all their lives. Many people would argue vociferously that the cognitive differences are not large, that they can be diminished by intensive training, and that there is great overlap between men and women in each ability. Without denying any of this, it is nevertheless true that sex hormones have been shown to influence cognitive function in ways not readily explained by differential experience.

For example, Daniel Hier and William Crowley in Chicago found that males in whom puberty did not develop at normal age—a condition related to abnormally low testosterone levels and reduced testicular size—were poor on spatial tasks. The researchers compared them to a group of males who had developed puberty normally, but who subsequently suffered lowered testosterone levels as a result of disease. The males with early testosterone deficiency performed worse on tasks of spatial construction and orientation, and on disembedding. The groups were equal on several verbal intelligence tests.

Rat studies offer direct evidence that manipulating the hormonal environment can affect spatial problem-solving ability. Christina Williams and her coworkers at Barnard College found that in running a radial-arm maze, male rats used only geometry cues while females employed both geometry and landmark cues. In rats, sex hormones can still alter brain organization in the immediate postnatal period, when the genitals have already been formed.

Williams found that castrating males during this period, so that gonadal hormones could no longer affect the brain, caused the males when adults to adopt a more "female" strategy on mazes. Since the rats were neither reared differently by their parents nor exposed differently to mazes, hormones clearly had a powerful, lasting effect on a nonreproductive behavior.

Hier and Crowley's study might appear to suggest that the higher the androgen levels, the higher the spatial ability, but keep in mind that they were comparing normal and subnormal levels. Within the normal range of androgens, it appears that males with lower levels actually perform better on spatial tasks. Valerie Shute and coworkers at the University of California, Santa Barbara, found that, comparing men in the bottom and top 25% in terms of testosterone levels, those with lower levels scored higher on spatial tests. We have recently confirmed this in our laboratory.

Findings from these and other studies suggest a curvilinear rather than a direct relationship between androgen levels and spatial ability. This is consistent with the finding that in females—who of course have lower levels of testosterone than males—those with higher levels of testosterone score higher in spatial ability. The situation is complicated by the fact that testosterone is probably converted to estradiol in the brain before it affects the nervous system. Helmuth Nyborg of the University of Aarhus in Denmark has proposed that estrogen actually is the critical determinant of spatial ability.

Does Ability Fluctuate During Menstrual Cycles?

All these studies were probably sampling the organizational (chronic) effects of sex hormones among groups of people. About six years ago, I decided to examine the possibility that fluctuations in hormones *within* an individual might also be reflected in cognitive changes. The most readily available subjects for this approach were women—young women undergoing natural fluctuations in the course of the menstrual cycle, and older post-menopausal women who wee taking hormone replacement therapy.

To maximize the likelihood of finding intellectual changes, we selected tests that measured either abilities favoring males or those favoring females. We assumed that higher levels of female sex hormones (estrogen and progesterone) might enhance "female" abilities, such as verbal fluency and manual skill, but have no effect, or even a negative effect, on "male" abilities such as spatial skill.

The menstrual-cycle study was done with Elizabeth Hampson, a doctoral student in my laboratory. Initially, we did not have the capacity to analyze blood from our subjects, so we picked periods in the menstrual cycle which could be identified without such assays—the midluteal, about 7 to 10 days before onset of menstruation, when both estrogen and progesterone were high; and days 3 to 5 after onset of menstruation, when levels of all sex hormones are low. (Days 1 and 2 were avoided because some women experience physical discomfort then.) Half the women (we studied 45 in all) were tested first in the high or midluteal phase, and half in the low, or menstrual phase. About 6 weeks elapsed between the two test periods.

We used tests that had previously shown sex differences, either in overall score or in brain organization: spatial tasks, perceptual speed tasks, verbal fluency (saying as many words as possible beginning with a particular letter), rapid articulation and speeded manual learning tasks (see illustration opposite page). I had found that the latter two, although dependent on the left hemisphere in both men and women, showed a different intrahemispheric organization in the two sexes. We also administered a mood inventory, since it is known that there are some mood changes throughout the month, though these are usually greatest in the immediate premenstrual period, which we deliberately avoided.

Female Hormones Make "Female" Skills Better, "Male" Skills Worse

The results were definitive. Comparing women with themselves on tests usually done better by women than men, they did significantly better in speeded articulation and manual skill tasks in the high or midluteal phase than in the low phase. Verbal fluency and perceptual speed were also generally better in the high phase.

In contrast, performance on the spatial tests, in which men are usually better, showed the reverse trend: The women did better in the low phase than in the high. This effect was significant for the Rod-and-Frame test, in which the subject simply makes a judgment about whether a rod is vertical or not. Since practice effects from the first to the second session sometimes obscured the finding, Hampson then looked only at the first test-session results of individuals who were in either the high or low phase. This produced a clearer difference between tests favoring males and tests favoring females: The paper-and-pencil spatial tests now also showed a significant enhancement in the low phase.

The fact that scores went in opposite directions on the two types of tasks suggests very strongly that we are seeing more than a generalized change in ability during one phase or the other. The same was true of the mood inventory. We saw no significant changes in mood between the two phases, and only one significant correlation between any of the mood components—which sample, among other things, depression, fatigue and vigor, and performance on the various tasks.

These were exciting findings, but we were concerned that the spontaneous fluctuations of hormones during the menstrual cycle might be secondary effects; perhaps the cognitive changes were due to concomitant fluctuations in other systems.

The Effects of Hormone Therapy

Fortunately, I had already begun to look into the possible effects of exogenous hormones in post-menopausal women. With them, sex hormones don't fluctuate spontaneously but are administered on a regular basis to relieve discomfort during or after menopause and lessen the risk of osteoporosis. Most of the various regimes of hormone therapy now include progesterone along with estrogen. This treatment can raise plasma estradiol levels into the midluteal range of the natural menstrual cycle, and often improves the feeling of well-being— but we know almost nothing of its intellectual effects.

The 33 women we studied were all over 50 years of age and had not menstruated for at least a year. Twenty-two of them were on estrogen alone, the rest on combined estrogen and medroxyprogesterone. They all took estrogen alone (orally) for at least the first 15 days of the month. Some then took progesterone as well for 5 to 10 days. For the rest of the month they took nothing.

We tested them twice, once 10 days after they had begun estrogen (but before any progesterone was taken), and again when they

---

We found that estrogen affected the motor skills strongly: In the manual task and to a lesser degree the tongue twister, performance was significantly better under the "on estrogen" condition than in the off period.

---

had been off all medication for at least 4 days. To reduce the effect of practice, we tested half of the women first in the "on" phase, and half in the "off" phase, with approximately 6 weeks between testing. Any effects we saw should have been due primarily to estrogen, since the few who took progesterone took it immediately before the off period.

We again gave a variety of tests, including vocabulary to provide a measure of general intelligence; a manual skill task in which a sequence of hand movements had to be carried out quickly on a Manual Sequence Box (see below); an articulatory task— a tongue twister; perceptual speed tests; and two spatial tasks.

The Selective Effects of Estrogen

We found that estrogen affected the motor skills strongly: In the manual task and to a lesser degree the tongue twister, performance

was significantly better under the "on estrogen" condition than in the off period. On the perceptual speed tasks, one of the comparisons showed improvement under estrogen; on the other there was no effect. On the spatial tasks, there were no significant changes related to hormonal status. The results of these studies confirmed that the effects of estrogen, even when administered orally, were selective, in that not all the speeded tasks were improved, but we did not replicate all the findings from the menstrual study.

One reason for the differences might be that, since exogenous estrogen in post-menopausal women is detectable in plasma even several weeks after treatment has ended, the difference in estrogen level between our so-called on and off phases may be quite small. It may be too small to produce changes in spatial ability, though clearly large enough to produce changes in motor and articulatory skill. That suggests that motor programming skills are more sensitive to fluctuating estrogen levels than is spatial skill. We have some indications from the menstrual study as well that this might be the case.

Another reason for the difference might be that older and younger women have different baseline levels of spatial ability, in which case changes in sex hormones would not have the same effects. Unfortunately, we didn't use identical spatial tests, so we couldn't compare our two samples.

How Hormones Affect the Brain

We can only guess what mechanism enhances motor skill during high estrogen states, since we have no direct information on what is happening in the brain then. Here again, however, the animal literature is suggestive. Jill Becker and coworkers at the University of Michigan in Ann Arbor found that female rats were better at walking a narrow plank in the estrus phase of their cycle, when estrogen and progesterone levels are high. She also found that implanting estradiol directly into the basal ganglia enhanced performance. The precise mechanism for this change has still to be worked out, but Becker suggested that estrogen might induce changes in the firing of dopamine neurons. And estrogen may affect other brain areas as well.

In our human studies, estrogen seems to have a strongly positive effect on functions which we know depend critically on the left hemisphere. Performance on the Manual Sequence Box and on speech articulation tasks requires an intact left hemisphere. What's more, these functions are carried out differently in the left hemisphere of males and females: The left anterior part of the brain is more critical in females, suggesting that estrogen somehow facilitates activity of the frontal regions, of the left hemisphere, or of both.

Further evidence that the left hemisphere may be favored by high estrogen levels comes from Hampson's finding that the right-ear superiority on dichotic listening is increased during the preovulatory estrogen surge that occurs in normally cycling women. We are currently also investigating the possibility that frontal and posterior regions of the brain are differently affected by estrogen levels.

People often ask why hormonal changes affect adult abilities, since such effects would seem to serve no useful function. We don't really know the answer, but it seems reasonable that, whatever hormonal mechanism origi-

nally establishes these individual variations, it may simply continue to be sensitive to changes in the critical hormones throughout life. Although the fluctuations may merely be ripples on a preestablished baseline, they are sufficient to suggest that the adult human brain continues to be sensitive to such influences.

Hormones Affect Men as Well as Women

The question of how androgens and estrogen interact, both in originally organizing male and female behaviors, and in their adult effects, is being studied extensively. Roger Gorski of the University of California, Los Angeles, has shown that estradiol produces some aspects of brain sexual differentiation related to perinatal testosterone. Bruce McEwen at Rockefeller University, however, points out that estrogen can have different effects in male and female brains. Perhaps different programs are activated by the same hormone.

We need a great deal more information about the basic action of sex hormones before we can work out their specific contributions to cognitive patterns. For example,

People often ask why hormonal changes affect adult abilities, since such effects would seem to serve no useful function. We don't really know the answer, but it seems reasonable that, whatever hormonal mechanism originally establishes these individual variations, it may simply continue to be sensitive to changes in the critical hormones throughout life.

knowing the current blood levels of testosterone in either men or women is just one step in a chain of information which ultimately mush include how much testosterone reaches the brain, what pro-

portion is converted to estradiol, where the estradiol has its effects, and so on.

How Important Are These Differences?

What do our studies on the apparent fluidity of certain abilities mean for the day-to-day functioning of women? While the fluctuations we find are interesting and significant—they tell us something about how cognitive ability patterns are formed—they are not large. Also, up to now they seem most consistent for the kinds of things women already do well. So for most women, they aren't an important factor. of course, women vary widely in their sensitivity to these influences. For some, the changes may make them feel clumsier at some periods of the month than at others.

It's important to remember that we studied women because it was easy to do. It turns out that men also undergo hormonal fluctuations, both daily and seasonal. We are looking into both types, encouraged by a study of wild voles by Steven Gaulin at the University of Pittsburgh and Randy FitzGerald at Montclair State College. They have found that sex differences on a maze task appear only in polygynous species of these rodents where males must roam a larger territory to find females. This sexually dimorphic type of vole has seasonal fluctuations in territorial range, with the range being larger in the mating season. If there is a parallel effect in humans, we might be able to detect seasonal variations in men for certain spatial abilities. This would give us another important link in understanding how individual differences in abilities evolved. ◆

Discussion Questions

1. What evidence is reported in this article to support the hypothesis that sex hormones influence cognitive function?

2. What were the results of the study using menstruating women?

3. What were the results of the study using menopausal women?

4. How have the studies presented in this article influenced your views on sex differences in intelligence?

The *Differences* Are REAL

◆ *Arthur Jensen*

In 1969, in the appropriately academic context of *The Harvard Educational Review* I questioned the then and still prevailing doctrine of racial genetic equality in intelligence. I proposed that the average difference in IQ scores between black and white people may be attributable as much to heredity as environment. Realizing that my views might be wrongly interpreted as conflicting with some of the most sacred beliefs of our democracy, I emphasized the important distinction between individual intelligence and the average intelligence of populations. Moreover, I presented my research in a careful and dispassionate manner, hoping that it would stimulate rational discussion of the issue as well as further research.

Much to my dismay, however, my article set off an emotional furor in the world of social science. Amplified by the popular press, the furor soon spread beyond the confines of academia. Almost overnight I became a *cause célèbre*, at least on college campuses. I had spoken what Joseph Alsop called "the unspeakable." To many Americans I had thought the unthinkable.

Science vs. the Fear of Racism

For the past three decades the scientific search for an explanation of the well-established black IQ deficit has been blocked largely, I feel, by fear and abhorrence of racism. In academic circles doctrinaire theories of strictly environmental causation have predominated, with little or no attempt to test their validity rigorously. The environmentalists have refused to consider other possible causes, such as genetic factors. Research into possible genetic influence on intelligence has been academically and socially

> *Almost overnight*
> *I became a cause célèbre,*
> *at least on college campuses.*
> *I had spoken what Joseph Alsop called*
> *"the unspeakable." To many Americans*
> *I had thought the unthinkable.*

taboo. The orthodox environmental theories have been accepted not because they have stood up under proper scientific investigation, but because they harmonize so well with our democratic belief in human equality.

The civil-rights movement that gained momentum in the 1950s "required" liberal academic adherence to the theory that the environment was responsible for any individual or racial behavioral differences, had the corollary belief in genetic equality in intelligence. Thus, when I questioned such beliefs I, and my theories, quickly acquired the label "racist." I resent this label, and consider it unfair and inaccurate.

The Real Meaning of Racism

Since the horrors of Nazi Germany, and Hitler's persecution of the Jews in the name of his bizarre doctrine of Aryan supremacy, the well-deserved offensiveness of the term "racism" has extended far beyond its legitimate meaning. To me, racism means discrimination among persons of the basis of their racial origins in granting or denying social, civil or political rights. Racism means the denial of equal opportunity in education or employment on the basis of color or national origin. Racism encourages the judging of persons not each according to his own qualities and abilities, but according to common stereotypes. This is the real meaning of racism. The scientific theory that there are genetically conditioned mental or behavioral differences between races cannot be called racist. It would be just as illogical to condemn the recognition of physical differences between races as racist.

When I published my article in 1969, many critics confused the purely empirical question of the genetic role in racial differences in mental abilities with the highly charged political-ideological issue of racism. Because of their confusion, they denounced my attempt to study the possible genetic causes f such differences. At the same time, the doctrinaire environmentalists, seeing their own position threatened by my inquiry, righteously and dogmatically scorned the genetic theory of intelligence.

Thankfully, the emotional furor that greeted my article has died down enough recently to permit sober and searching consideration of the true intent and substance of what I actually tried to say. Under fresh scrutiny stimulated by the controversy, many scientists have reexamined the environmentalist explanations of the black IQ deficit and found them to be inadequate. They simply do not fully account for the known facts, in the comprehensive and consistent manner we should expect of a scientific explanation.

The Black IQ Deficit

First of all, it is a known and uncontested fact that blacks in the United States score on average about one standard deviation below whites on most tests of intelligence. On the most commonly used IQ tests, this difference ranges from 10 to 20 points, and averages about 15 points. This means that only about 16 percent of the black population exceeds the test performance of the average white on IQ tests. A similar difference of one standard deviation between blacks and whites holds true for 80 standardized mental tests on which published data exist [see chart, page 189].

A difference of one standard deviation can hardly be called inconsequential. Intelligence tests have more than proved themselves as valid predictors of scholastic performance and occupational attainment, and they predict equally well for blacks as for whites. Unpleasant as these predictions may seem to some people, their significance cannot be wished away because of a belief in equality. Of course, an individual's success and self-fulfillment depends upon many characteristics *besides* intelligence, but IQ does represent an index, albeit an imperfect one, of the ability to compete in many walks of life. For example, many selective colleges require College Board test scores of 600 (equivalent to an IQ of 115) as a minimum for admission. An average IQ difference of one standard deviation between blacks and whites means that the white population will have

about seven times the percentage of such potentially talented persons (i.e., IQs over 115) as the black population. At the other end of the scale, the 15-point difference in average IQ scores means that mental retardation (IQ below 70 will occur about seven times as often among blacks as among whites.

The IQ difference between blacks and whites, then, clearly has considerable social significance. Yet the environmentalists dismiss this difference as artificial, and claim it does not imply any innate or genetic difference in intelligence. But as I shall show, the purely environmental explanations most commonly put forth are faulty. Examined closely in terms of the available evidence, they simply do not sustain the burden of explanation that they claim. Of course, they may be *possible* explanations of the IQ difference, but that does not necessarily make them the *most probable*. In every case for which there was sufficient relevant evidence to put to a detailed test, the environmental explanations have proven inadequate. I am not saying they have been proven 100 percent wrong, only that they do not account for *all* of the black IQ deficit. Of course, there may be other possible environmental explanations as yet unformulated and untested.

Arguments for the Genetic Hypothesis

The genetic hypothesis, on the other hand, has not yet been put to any direct tests by the standard techniques of genetic research. It must be seriously considered, however, for two reasons: 1) because the default of the environmentalist theory, which has failed

in many of its most important predictions, increases the probability of the genetic theory; 2) since genetically conditioned physical characteristics differ markedly between racial groups, there is a strong *a priori* likelihood that genetically conditioned behavioral or mental characteristics will also differ. Since intelligence and other mental abilities depend upon the physiological structure of the brain, and since the brain, like other organs, is subject to genetic influence, how can anyone disregard the obvious probability of genetic influence on intelligence?

Let us consider some of the genetically conditioned characteristics that we already know to vary between major racial groups: body size and proportions; cranial size and shape; pigmentation of the hair, skin and eyes; hair form and distribution; number of vertebrae; fingerprints; bone density; basic-metabolic rate; sweating consistency of ear wax; age of eruption of the permanent teeth; fissural patterns on the surfaces of the teeth; blood groups; chronic disease; frequency of twinning; male-female birth ratio; visual and auditory acuity; colorblindness; taste; length of gestation period; physical maturity at birth. In view of so many genetically conditioned traits that do differ between races, wouldn't it be surprising if genetically conditioned mental traits were a major exception?

The Heritability of Intelligence

One argument for the high probability of genetic influence on the IQ difference between blacks and whites involves the concept of *heritability*. A technical term in quantitative genetics, heritability refers to

An educational psychologist who found his name linked by rhetoric to racism tries again to make clear what he believes and does not believe.

the proportion of the total variation of some trait, among persons within a given population, that can be attributed to genetic factors. Once the heritability of that trait can be determined, the remainder of the variance can be attributed mainly to environmental influence. Now intelligence, as measured by standard tests such as the Stanford-Binet and many others, does show very substantial heritability in the European and North American Caucasian populations in which the necessary genetic studies have been done. I don't know of any geneticists today who have viewed the evidence and who dispute this conclusion.

No precise figure exists for the heritability of intelligence, since, like any population statistic, it varies from one study to another, depending on the particular population sampled, the IQ test used, and the method of genetic analysis. Most of the estimates for the heritability of intelligence in the populations studied indicate that genetic factors are about twice as important as environmental factors as a cause of IQ differences among individuals.

I do not know of a methodologically adequate determination of IQ heritability in a sample of the U.S. black population. The few estimates that exist, though statistically weak, give little reason to suspect that the heritability of IQ for blacks, when adequately estimated, should differ appreciably from that for whites. Of course the absence of reliable data makes this a speculative assumption.

What implication does the heritability within a population have concerning the cause of the difference *between* two populations? the fact that IQ is highly heritable within the white and probably the black population does not by itself constitute formal proof that the difference between the popula-

tions is genetic, either in whole or in part. However, the fact of substantial heritability of IQ within the populations does increase the *a priori* probability that the population difference is partly attributable to genetic factors. Biologists generally agree that, almost without exception throughout nature, any genetically conditioned characteristic that varies among individuals within a subspecies (i.e., race) also varies genetically between different subspecies. Thus, the substantial heritability of IQ within the Caucasian and probably black populations makes it likely (but does not prove) that the black population's lower average IQ is caused at least in part by a genetic difference.

> No precise figure exists for the heritability of intelligence, since, like any population statistic, it varies from one study to another, depending on the particular population sampled, the IQ test used, and the method of genetic analysis.

What about the purely cultural and environmental explanations of the IQ difference? The most common argument claims that IQ tests have a built-in cultural bias that discriminates against blacks and other poor minority groups. Those who hold this view criticize the tests as being based unfairly on the language, knowledge and cognitive skills of the white "Anglo" middle class. They argue that blacks in the united States do not share in the same culture as whites, and therefore acquire different meanings to words, different knowledge, and a different set of intellectual skills.

Culture-Fair vs. Culture-Biased

However commonly and fervently held, this claim that the

black IQ deficit can be blamed on culture-biased or "culture-loaded" tests does not stand up under rigorous study. First of all, the fact that a test is culture-*loaded* does not necessarily mean it is culture-*biased*. Of course, many tests do have questions of information, vocabulary and comprehension that clearly draw on experiences which could only be acquired by persons sharing a fairly common cultural background. Reputable tests, called "culture-fair" tests, do exist, however. They use nonverbal, simple symbolic material common to a great many different cultures. Such tests measure the ability to generalize, to distinguish differences and similarities, to see relationships, and to solve problems. They test reasoning power rather than just specific bits of knowledge.

Surprisingly, blacks tend to perform relatively better on the more culture-loaded or verbal kinds of tests than on the culture-fair type. For example, on the widely used Wechsler Intelligence Scale, comprised of 11 different subtests, blacks do better on the culture-loaded subtests of vocabulary, general information, and verbal comprehension than on the nonverbal performance tests such as the block designs. Just the opposite is true for such minorities as Orientals, Mexican-Americans, Indians, and Puerto Ricans. It can hardly be claimed that culture-fair tests have a built-in bias in favor of white, Anglo, middle-class Americans when Arctic Eskimos taking the same tests perform on a par with white, middle-class norms. My assistants and I have tested large numbers of Chinese children who score well above white norms on such tests, despite being recent immigrants from Hong Kong and Formosa, knowing little or no English, and having parents who hold low-level socioeconomic occupations. if the tests have a bias toward the white, Anglo, middle-class, one might well wonder why Oriental children should outscore the white Anglos on whom the tests were originally standardized. Our tests of Mexican-Americans produced similar results. They do rather poorly on the culture-loaded types of tests based on verbal skills and knowledge, but they do better on the culture-fair tests. The same holds true for American Indians. All these minorities perform on the two types of tests much as one might expect from the culture-bias hypothesis. Only blacks, among the minorities we have tested, score in just the opposite manner.

Intelligence Tests Are Colorblind

Those who talk of culture bias should also consider that all the standard mental tests I know of are colorblind, in that they show the same reliability and predictive validity for blacks and whites. In predicting scholastic achievement, for example, we have found that several different IQ tests predict equally well for blacks and whites. College-aptitude tests also predict grades equally well for blacks and whites. The same equality holds true for aptitude tests which predict job performance.

We have studied culture bias in some standard IQ tests by making internal analyses to see which kinds of test items produce greater differences in scores between blacks and whites. For example, we made such an item-by-item check of the highly culture-loaded Peabody Picture Vocabulary Test, on which blacks average some 15 points lower than whites. The PPVT consists of 150 cards, each containing four pictures. The examiner names one of the pictures and the child points to the appropriate picture. The items follow the

order of their difficulty, as measured by the percentage of the children in the normative sample who fail the item.

California vs. England; Boys vs. Girls

To illustrate the sensitivity of this test to cultural differences in word meanings, we compared the performance of white schoolchildren in England with children of the same age in California. Although the two groups obtained about the same total IQ score, the California group found some culture-loaded words such as "bronco" and "thermos" easy, while the London group found them difficult. The opposite occurred with words like "pedestrian" or "goblet." Thus the difficulty of some items differed sharply depending on the child's cultural background. A similar "cultural" bias shows up when comparing the performance of boys and girls, both black and white. Though boys and girls score about equally well over all, they show significant differences in the rank order of item difficulty; specific items, e.g. "parachute" versus "casserole" reflect different sexual biases in cultural knowledge.

Yet when we made exactly the same kind of comparison between blacks and whites in the same city in California, and even in the same schools, we found virtually no difference between the two groups in the order of items when ranked for difficulty, as indexed by the percent failing each item. Both groups show the same rank order of difficulty, although on each item a smaller percentage of blacks give the correct answer. In fact, even the differences between

adjacent test items, in terms of percent answering correctly, show great similarity in both the black and white groups.

If this kind of internal analysis reflects cultural bias between different national groups, and sexual bias *within* the same racial group, why does it not reflect the supposed bias *between* the two racial groups? If the tests discriminate against blacks, why do blacks and whites make errors on the same items? Why should the most and least common errors in one group be the same as in the other?

Another way internal analysis can be used to check for bias involves looking for different patterns of item inter-correlations. For example, if a person gets item number 20 right, he may be more likely to get, say, item 30 right than if he had missed item 20. This follows because the test items correlate with one another to varying degrees, and the amount of correlation and the pattern of inter-correlations should be sensitive to group differences in cultural background. Yet we have found no significant or appreciable differences between item inter-correlations for blacks and whites.

In summary, we have found no discriminant features of test items that can statistically separate the test records of blacks and whites any better than chance, when the records are equated for total number correct. We could do so with the London versus California groups, or for sex differences within the same racial group. Thus, even when using the PPVT, one of the most culture-loaded tests, black and white performances did not differ as one should expect if we accept the culture-bias explanation for the black

> *If the tests discriminate against blacks, why do blacks and whites make errors on the same items? Why should the most and least common errors in one group be the same as in the other?*

IQ deficit. I consider this strong evidence against the validity of that explanation.

The Effect of the Tester

What about subtle influences in the test situation itself which could have a depressing effect on black performance? It has been suggested, for example, that a white examiner might emotionally inhibit the performance of black children in a test situation. Most of the studies that have attempted to test this hypothesis have produced no substantiation of it. In my own study in which 9,000 black and white children took a number of standard mental and scholastic tests given by black and white examiners, there were no systematic differences in scores according to the race of the examiners. What about the examiner's language, dialect, or accent? In one study, the Stanford-Binet test, a highly verbal and individually administered exam, was translated into black ghetto dialect, and administered by a black examiner fluent in that dialect. A group of black children who took the test under these conditions obtained an average IQ score less than one point higher than the average IQ score of a control group given the test in standard English.

The Question of "Verbal Deprivation"

To test the popular notion that blacks do poorly on IQ tests because they are "verbally deprived," we have looked at studies of the test performances of the most verbally deprived individuals we know of: children born totally deaf. These children

> *The racial difference clearly does not involve all mental abilities equally. It involves mainly conceptual and abstract reasoning, and not learning and memory.*

do score considerably below average on verbal tests, as expected. But they perform completely up to par on the nonverbal culture-fair type of tests. Their performances, then, turns out to be just the opposite of the supposedly verbally deprived blacks, who score higher on the verbal than on the nonverbal tests.

If one hypothesizes that the black IQ deficit may be due to poor motivation or uncooperative attitudes of blacks in the test situation, then one must explain why little or no difference in scores occurs between blacks and whites on tests involving rote learning and memory. Such tests are just as demanding in terms of attention, effort and persistence, but do not call upon the kinds of abstract reasoning abilities that characterize the culture-fair intelligence tests. We have devised experimental tests, which look to pupils like any other tests, that minimize the need for reasoning and abstract ability, and maximize the role of nonconceptual learning and memory. On these tests black and white children average about the same scores. Therefore, the racial difference clearly does not involve all mental abilities equally. It involves mainly conceptual and abstract reasoning, and not learning and memory.

Another factors often cited as a possible explanation for the black IQ deficit is teacher expectancy—the notion that a child's test score tends to reflect the level of performance expected by his or her teacher, with the teacher's expectation often based on prejudice or stereotypes. Yet numerous studies of teacher expectancy have failed to establish this phenomenon as a contributing factor to the lower IQ scores of blacks.

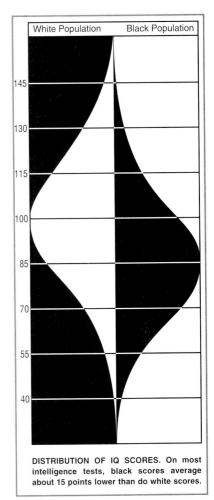

DISTRIBUTION OF IQ SCORES. On most intelligence tests, black scores average about 15 points lower than do white scores.

Testing the Environmental Hypothesis

To test the environmentalist hypothesis, we have examined the results of those tests that most strongly reflect environmental sources of variance, and they turn out to be the very tests that show the least difference between blacks and whites in average scores. The greatest difference in scores between the two racial groups occurs on the tests we infer to be more strongly reflective of genetic variance. If the cultural-environmental hypothesis were correct, just the opposite would be true.

The "Sociologist's Fallacy"

In an attempt to disprove the genetic hypothesis for the black IQ deficit, environmentalists frequently cite studies that compare IQs of socioeconomically matched racial groups, and find considerably less difference in test scores than the usual 15-point difference between races. Here we have a good example of the "sociologist's fallacy." Since whites and blacks differ in average socioeconomic status (SES), the matching of racial groups on SES variables such as education, occupation, and social class necessarily means that the black group is more highly selected in terms of whatever other traits and abilities correlate with SES, including intelligence. Therefore the two groups have been unfairly matched in terms of IQ.

Those who cite the socioeconomic matching studies also fail to take account of the well-established genetic difference between social classes, which invalidates their comparison. For example, when the two races are matched for social background, the average skin color of the black group runs lighter in the higher SES groups. This difference indicates that genetic characteristics do vary with SES. Thus, SES matching of blacks and whites reduces the IQ difference not only because it controls for environmental differences, but because it tends to equalize genetic factors as well.

Variables That Don't Behave

A host of other environmental variables don't behave as they ought to according to a strictly environmentalist theory of the black IQ deficit. For example, on practically all the socioeconomic educational, nutritional and other health factors that sociologists point to as causes of the black-white differences in IQ and scholastic achievement, the American Indian

population ranks about as far below black standards as blacks do below those of whites. The relevance of these environmental indices can be shown by the fact that within each ethnic group they correlate to some extent in the expected direction with tests of intelligence and scholastic achievement. Since health, parental education, employment, family income, and a number of more subtle environmental factors that have been studied are all deemed important for children's scholastic success, the stark deprivation of the Indian minority, even by black standards, ought to be reflected in a comparison of the intelligence and achievement-test performance of Indians and blacks. But in a nationwide survey reported in the Coleman Report, in 1966, Indians

Let me stress that none of the research I have discussed here allows one to conclude anything about the intelligence of any individual black or white person.

scored *higher* than blacks on all such tests, from the first to the 12th grade. On a nonverbal test given in the first grade, for example, before schooling could have had much impact, Indian children exceeded the mean score of blacks by the equivalent of 14 IQ points. Similar findings occur with Mexican-Americans, who rate below blacks on socioeconomic and other environmental indices, but score considerably higher on IQ tests, especially on the nonverbal type. Thus the IQ difference between Indians and blacks, and between Mexican-Americans and blacks, turns out opposite to what one would predict from purely environmental theory, which of course, assumes complete genetic equality for intelligence. No testable environmental hypothesis has as yet been offered to account for these findings.

Does Malnutrition Affect Intelligence?

What about malnutrition, another factor frequently cited by the environmentalists to disprove the genetic hypothesis? Malnutrition has indeed been found to affect both physical and mental development in a small percentage of children in those areas of the world that suffer severe protein deficiencies: India, South America, South Africa, and Mexico. But few blacks in the U.S. show any history or signs of severe malnutrition, and I have found no evidence that the degree of malnutrition associated with retarded mental development afflicts any major segment of the U.S. population.

Nor do I know of any evidence among humans that maternal malnutrition, by itself, can have pre- or postnatal effects on a child's mental development. The severe famine in the Netherlands during the last years of World War II provided an excellent case study of such a possibility. Thousands of men conceived, gestated, and born during the period of most severe famine, were later tested, as young adults, on Raven's Standard Progressive Matrices, a nonverbal reasoning test. Their scores did not differ significantly from the scores of other Dutch youths of the same age who had not been exposed to such maternal nutritional deprivation.

If further research should definitely establish the existence of genetically conditioned differences in intelligence between certain races, what would be the practical implications? It would take several articles to consider the question adequately, but the only morally tenable position in human relations would remain unchanged: that all persons should be treated according to their own individual characteristics, and not in terms of their group identity. Let me stress that none of the research I have discussed here allows one to conclude anything about the intelligence of any individual black or white person.

Equality of rights and opportunities is clearly the most beneficial condition for any society. Acceptance of the reality of human differences in mental abilities would simply underline the need for equality of opportunity in order to allow everyone to achieve his or her own self-fulfillment. In order to take account and advantage of the diversity of abilities in the population, and truly to serve all citizens equally, the public schools should move beyond narrow conceptions of scholastic achievement. they should offer a much greater diversity of ways for children of whatever aptitude to benefit from their education.

Environment vs. Genetics: Still an Open Question

I have tried to emphasize the uncertainty of our knowledge of the causes of race differences in mental abilities. I do not claim any direct or definite evidence, in terms of genetic research, for the existence of genotypic intelligence differences between races or other human population groups. I have not urged acceptance of a hypothesis on the basis of insufficient evidence. I have tried to show that the evidence we now have does not support the environmentalist theory, which, until quite recently, has been accepted as scientifically established. Social scientists have generally accepted it without question, and most scientists in other fields have given silent assent. I have assembled evidence which, I believe, makes such complacent assent no longer possible, and reveals the issue as an open question, calling for much further scientific study.

Politicizing a Scientific Issue

Most of the scientists and intellectuals with whom I have discussed these matters in the past few years see no danger in furthering our knowledge of the genetic basis of racial differences in mental or behavioral traits. Nor do they fear general recognition of genetic differences in such traits by the scientific world, if that should be the eventual outcome of further research. They do see a danger in politicizing a basically scientific question, one that should be settled strictly on the basis of evidence.

Most of the attempts to politicize the issue, I have found, come from the radical left. True liberals and humanists, on the other hand, want to learn the facts. They do not wish to expend their energies sustaining myths and illusions. They wish to face reality, whatever it may be, because only on the level of reality can real problems be effectively confronted. This means asking hard questions, and seeking the answers with as much scientific ingenuity and integrity as we can muster. It means examining all reasonable hypotheses, including unpopular ones. It means maintaining the capacity to doubt what we might most want to believe, acknowledging the uncertainties at the edge of knowledge, and viewing new findings in terms of shifting probabilities rather than as absolute conclusions. ◆

Discussion Questions

1. What is Jensen's definition of racism?

2. What are the two reasons Jensen gives for testing the genetic hypothesis?

3. What is the difference between "culture-biased" and "culture-loaded"?

4. Why, according to Jensen, is the argument that IQ tests are "culturally biased" not a valid reason for dismissing racial differences in test scores?

5. Jensen states that teacher expectancy cannot explain the lower IQ scores of blacks. How might Rosenthal's research on the "self-fulfilling prophecy" contradict Jensen's assertion?

6. Has Jensen proved that racial differences in IQ are genetic? What support, if any, has he provided for this assertion?

7. Jensen claims that merely identifying racial differences is not in itself a form of racism. Do you agree? Defend your viewpoint.

Differences Are **NOT** Deficits

◆ *Theodosius Dobzhansky*

The doctrine that all men are created equal is widespread in much of the modern world. We take equality for granted in American tradition, spell it out in the Declaration of Independence, but the idea frequently bogs down in misunderstanding and apparent contradictions. Equality is often confused with identity, and diversity with inequality.

Even some reputable scientists claim biology demonstrates that people are born unequal. This is sheer confusion; biology proves nothing of the sort. Every person is indeed biologically and genetically different from every other. Even identical twins are not really identical; they are recognizably separate persons who may engage in different occupations and achieve unequal socioeconomic status. But this phenomenon is biological diversity, which has nothing to do with human inequality.

Human equality and inequality are sociological designs, not biological phenomena. Human equality consists of equality before the law, political equality and equality of opportunity. These are human rights that come from religious, ethical or philosophical premises, not from genes. The United Nations recognized this fact in its 1952 UNESCO statement on race: "Equality of opportunity and equality in law in no way depend, as ethical principles, upon the assertion that human beings are in fact equal in endowment."

We may grant equality to all members of the human species or to only a small segment of the population, but we cannot brush away genetic diversity; it is an observable fact. And later in this article I will indicate how a society of equality of opportunity is most propitious for human self-fulfillment.

The reader may question whether genetic diversity has a social significance. At first thought, the answer seems to be no. With the exception of some pathological variants, one's form of enzyme or

> *Human equality and inequality are sociological designs, not biological phenomena. Human equality consists of equality before the law, political equality and equality of opportunity. These are human rights that come from religious, ethical or philosophical premises, not from genes.*

blood group seems to make no difference socially but genes may have effects that modify several characteristics. One cannot rule out the possibility that apparently neutral genetic variants may produce physiological or mental changes. For example, some scientists claim that B, A and O blood groups have something to do with resistance to plague, small pox and syphilis respectively. The validity of this claim is still under scrutiny.

It has been established, however, with varying degrees of certainty, that many human traits which unquestionably matter to their possessors and to society, are genetically conditioned. Intelligence, personality, and special abilities are all susceptible to modification by genetic as well as environmental factors. And recent sensational and inflammatory pronouncements about the genetic basis for racial and socioeconomic differences in IQ make mandatory a critical consideration of the subject.

The Blank Slate

The underpinnings of human intelligence are still somewhat unclear. The most extreme environmentalists say we enter the world with a blank slate upon which circumstance writes a script. Strict hereditarians, on the other hand, believe that parental genes dictate our abilities.

A moderate form of the blank-slate doctrine appeals to many social scientists, who believe we are born with essentially equal potentialities, and become different primarily through upbringing, training and social position. They say that cultural and socioeconomic differences can explain the disparity in intelligence scores between races and classes.

Even a tempered view of genetic predisposition is distasteful in a competitive society. It seems hardly fair that some persons should start life with an advantage over others, and particularly repugnant to think that one race or class is superior to another. But dislike of a theory does not prove or disprove anything.

A third, and more likely, explanation exists for individual and group differences in IQ. Both environment and genetic conditioning may be at work. In this explanation, the bone of contention is not environment versus heredity, but how much environment and how much heredity.

For a clear understanding of the matter, we must define what we mean by IQ. An intelligence quotient is not a measure of the overall quality or worth of an individual. Someone with a high IQ may be vicious, selfish, lazy and slovenly, while someone with a lower score may be kind, helpful, hard-working and responsible. Even psychologists disagree about the mental and psychophysical traits an IQ test measures. Sir Cyril Burt was one of those who claimed that "we may safely assert that the innate amount of potential ability with which a child is endowed at birth sets an upper limit to what he can possibly achieve at school or in afterlife." He believed IQ measures this supposedly innate ability. Others deny that intelligence testing provides any valid information, and see it merely as a device that the privileged use to maintain their status over the less advantaged. Further, there is always the danger that IQ tests are biased in favor of the race, social class, or culture of those who devised the tests. Certainly all existing intelligence tests fall short of being culture-free or culture-fair [see "I.Q.: The Conspiracy" by John Garcia, PT, September 1972].

The Unknown Heritability Factor

It is undeniable, however, that there are significant statistical correlations between IQ scores and success in schooling, advances in the existing occupational structure, and prestige in Western societies.

Researchers have also securely established that *individual* differences in scores are genetically as well as environmentally conditioned. The evidence comes from more than 50 independent studies in eight countries. But how much of this variation is due to genetics, or heritability as scientists call it, is unknown. The best estimates come from studies on twins and other close relatives reared together and apart. Arthur Jensen has carefully reviewed these data, and his analysis has indicated that approximately 80 percent of individual differences in IQ are inherited. This degree of heritability is high compared to the genetic components of other traits in different organisms. It is much higher than that of egg production in poultry or yield in corn, yet animal and plant breeders have substantially improved

---

Because people misunderstand the significance of the high heritability of IQ, we should clarify what it does and does not mean.
To begin with, it does not mean that genes alone condition IQ.

---

these characteristics through genetic selection. In insects, artificial selection has induced spectacular changes for traits that are only half as genetically conditioned as human IQ.

Because people misunderstand the significance of the high heritability of IQ, we should clarify what it does and does not mean. To begin with, it does not mean that genes alone condition IQ. A possessor of certain genes will not necessarily have a certain IQ. The same gene constellation can result in a higher or lower score in different circumstances. Genes *determine* the intelligence (or stature or height) of a person only in his particular environment. The trait that actually develops is *conditioned* by the interplay of the genes with the environment. Every person is unique and non-recurrent, and no two individuals,

except identical twins, have the same genes.

Studies of Twins

Marie Skodak and Harold M. Skeels showed the influence of environment on IQ in their study of identical twins raised together and apart. They found a consistently lower IQ correlation between twins raised apart compared to that between twins reared together. Because identical twins have identical genes, the greater IQ differences in twins raised apart, compared to those reared together, must be due to their different environments.

Now let us consider people in general rather than a particular person…Genes really determine reaction ranges for individuals with more or less similar genes. Genetic traits emerge in the process of development as one's genetic potential is realized. Similar genes may have different effects in unlike environments, and dissimilar genes may have similar effects in like environments.

But it is not useful to say that genes determine the upper and lower limits of intelligence, since existing environments are endlessly variable and we constantly add new ones. To test the reactions of a given gene constellation in all environments is obviously impossible. For example, how could one discover the greatest height I could become in some very propitious environment, or the shortest stature I could have in another environment and still remain alive? It is even more far-fetched to forecast stature in environments that may be engineered in the future, perhaps with the aid of some new growth hormone.

More importantly, heritability is not an intrinsic property of IQ, but of the population in which it occurs. Consideration of limiting cases makes this obvious. If we had a population of genetically identical persons, all individual differences in IQ would be environmentally determined. There would be *no* genetic influence affecting the *differences* in IQ that developed among them. Alternately, if all members of the population lived in the same environment, all IQ differences would be genetic. Therefore, we must confine our estimates of the heritability of IQ to the population under study and to the time we collected the data.

Research Across Race and Class

When we look at estimates of heritability, we must keep in mind the genetic and environmental uniformity or heterogeneity of the population studied. Most of the information on IQ comes from studies on white, middle-class populations. The most abundant data pertain to research on twins and siblings raised together. Children in the same family do not grow up in identical environments, but their surroundings are certainly more alike on the average than those across socioeconomic classes or races. Estimating heritability of IQ differences in one population is beset with pitfalls. Crossracial and crossclass research is even more difficult.

Scientists have documented differences in average IQ for various socioeconomic classes. This is neither surprising nor unexpected, since we know that educational and other opportunities are unequal for members of different social classes. Burt summarized data on 40,000 parents and their children in England. He gathered information on higher professional, lower profession, clerical, skilled, semiskilled and unskilled workers. Fathers in the higher professional

category had an average IQ of about 140. This score was about 85 percent for the unskilled laborers. Children's average IQs ranged from about 121 for the higher professional group to about 93 in the unskilled sample. The children of the high professionals scored lower than their fathers while the children of the unskilled workers

No amount of money can buy a black person's way into a privileged upperclass white community, or buy off more than 200 years of accumulated racial prejudice on the part of the whites...

scored higher than their fathers. This is the well-known phenomenon called regression toward the mean. Regardless of whether the IQ differences between occupational classes are mainly genetic or environmental, children do not fully inherit the superior or inferior performance of their parents.

The Jensen Research

The situation is analogous with human races. Researchers have found a consistent 10 to 20 point disparity in average IQ scores between blacks and whites in the U.S. And because races, unlike socioeconomic groups, are usually physically recognizable, this disparity is often blamed on inferior black genes. But persons who belong to different races, whether they live in different countries or side by side, do not always have equal opportunities for mental development. Nobody, not even racists, can deny that living conditions and educational opportunities are disparate in races and classes.

After psychologist Arthur Jensen explicitly recognizes that heritability of individual differences in IQ cannot be used as a measure of average heritability across populations, he tries to do just that. In fairness to Jensen, he presents a detailed analysis of the environmental factors that could account for the discrepancy, but

then he concludes that none of these factors or their combinations can explain the difference in average black and white IQ scores. He appeals to studies which try to equate black and white environments by comparing populations of equal socioeconomic status. This diminishes the IQ difference between the two races, but it does not erase the difference. Jensen takes this as evidence that a strong genetic component is operating. I remain unconvinced.

W.F. Bodmer and L.L. Cavalli-Sforza have pointed out the inadequacies of equating similar socioeconomic status with similar total environment. In their words: "It is difficult to see, however, how the status of blacks and whites can be compared. The very existence of a racial stratification correlated with a relative socioeconomic deprivation makes this comparison suspect. Black schools are well known to be generally less adequate than white schools, so that equal number of years of schooling certainly do not mean equal educational attainments. Wide variation in the level of occupation must exist within each occupational class. Thus one would certainly expect, even for equivalent occupational classes, that the black level is on the average lower than the white. No amount of money can buy a black person's way into a privileged upperclass white community, or buy off more than 200 years of accumulated racial prejudice on the part of the whites...It is impossible to accept the idea that matching for status provides an adequate, or even substantial, control over most important environmental differences between blacks and whites."

Average vs. Individual

The controversy over the relative influence of nature and nurture on racial differences in IQ has grown hotter since scientists documented the high heritability of *individual* IQ. Racists try to gain maximum propaganda mileage from this fact, but the different race and class *averages* may be less genetically conditioned than individual variations in IQ.

Sandra Scarr-Salapatek shows evidence of this proposition in her study of twins in Philadelphia schools. She attacks the presumption that the influence of genetics and environment is simply additive, and suggests that the two factors may operate dependently and in different ways. She hypothesizes that genetic differences show up more in persons who mature in favorable surroundings, but remain hidden or unused in individuals from adverse or suppressive environments. If her assertion is correct, the heritability of IQ should be lower among disadvantaged groups (both social and racial) than among privileged classes. On the other hand, if genetic and environmental influences simply add together, heritability should be uniform in all groups.

Scarr-Salapatek tested the two hypotheses in her study of intelligence and scholastic-aptitude test data on 1,521 pairs of twins attending public schools in Philadelphia. She compared test scores across races and across socioeconomic levels and found that differences between upper and lower class blacks were much smaller (5.3 points) than those between whites of similar classes (16.1 points). More importantly, for both blacks and whites, test scores varied more among advantaged than among disadvantaged children. She con-

cludes: "From studies of middle-class white populations, investigators have reached the conclusion that genetic variability accounts for about 75 percent of the total variance in IQ scores of whites. A closer look at children reared under different conditions shows that the percentage of genetic variance and the mean scores are very much a function of the rearing conditions of the population. A first look at the black population suggests that genetic variability is important in advantaged groups, but much less important in the disadvantaged. Since most blacks are socially disadvantaged, he proportion of genetic variance in the aptitude scores of black children is considerably less than that of white children..."

Scarr-Salapatek's work lends further support to the possibility that we can explain at least a part of racial and socioeconomic differences in IQ with environmental reasons. But nothing I have said excludes the possibility that there is also a genetic component in such differences. We simply don't

---

It is accurate to say that whenever a variable human trait, even an apparently learned habit such as smoking, has been studied genetically, some genetic conditioning has come to light.

---

know. The available data are inadequate to settle the question.

Care and Tutoring

Suppose, for the sake of argument, that the average intelligence of some class or race is lower than the average for other classes or races in the environments that now exist. This still would not justify race and class prejudice since one could still induce important changes in manifested intelligence by intensive care and tutoring of

children. Perhaps it may even be possible to nullify or to reverse the disparity of group averages by altering environments and practices of child rearing.

We have seen that individual variability within classes and races is both genetically and environmentally conditioned. This is true of IQ as well as scholastic aptitude and achievement. We should keep in mind that IQ is not a unitary trait determined by a single gene, but rather it is a composite of numerous genetic components. IQ surely is not the only genetically conditioned trait. Less detailed but still substantial evidence suggests that many personality characteristics and special abilities, from mathematics to music, have genetic components. It is accurate to say that whenever a variable human trait, even an apparently learned habit such as smoking, has been studied genetically, some genetic conditioning has come to light. In any case, genetic conditioning, no matter how strong, does not preclude improvement by manipulation of the environment, as we have shown in our discussion of race, class and IQ.

Let us return to my original thesis that we can maximize the benefits of human diversity in a society where all individuals have truly equal opportunities. It is utterly unlikely that the incidence of all genetically conditioned traits will remain uniform throughout all socioeconomic classes. While genes for a particular trait, such as IQ, eyesight or stature, may be more common in class A than in class B, this does not mean that all A persons and no B individuals will possess these genes. Since only gene frequencies are involved, an individual's potentialities are determined by his own genetic endowment, not by his class or race. So only in a society of equal opportunity for all, regardless of race or class, will every individual have a chance to use his fullest potential.

Scholastic ability and achievement are important determinants of social mobility in a society with equality of opportunity. Schools and universities are principal ladders for socioeconomic rise. Insofar as achievement is genetically conditioned, social mobility is in part a genetic process. In "Genetics and Sociology," Bruce K. Eckland writes" ...talented adults rise to the top of the social hierarchy and the dull fall or remain on the bottom. Therefore, as the system strives to achieve full equality of opportunity, the observed within-class variance among children tends to diminish while the between-class variance tends to increase on selective traits associated with genetic differences. "Some may be chagrined to learn that increasing equality of opportunity *increases*, rather than decreases, genetic differences between socioeconomic classes. But I intend to show that if we had true equality of opportunity, the classes as we know them now would no longer exist.

The Benefits of Diversity

We can maximize the benefits of human diversity without creating a meritocracy in which the genetic elite concentrate in the upper socioeconomic classes. With anything approaching full equality, those most genetically and environmentally fit for each trade, craft or profession will gravitate to that occupation. But these aggregations of genetic aptitudes will not result in socioeconomic classes or castes. I believe they will develop into new social phenomena, barely foreshadowed at present.

These aptitude aggregations will differ from our present socioeconomic classes primarily by their fluidity. Aggregations will gain

new members who are not descended from old members. These gains will be offset by losses of some of the progeny of old members who will join other occupational groups. Some gains and losses may come to pass when individual occupations become more or less attractive or socially important. Others will be genetically conditioned and hence genetically significant. They result from the segregation of trait genes and must not be frustrated by the impulses of

---

We must not brand people or professions as elite or common. To compliment equality of opportunity we need equality of status.

---

parents either to make their offspring follow in their own occupational footsteps, or to propel them to more privileged job categories.

But it is unlikely that every member of, say, the musicians aggregation, would have the gene for music, even if such a gene really existed. More likely the genetic basis of musical talent is a constellation of several genes, and possibly of different genes in different persons. Some children in the group will lack this genetic predisposition toward musical talent, and move on to other aggregations. Conversely, some talented musicians will be born in other aggregations, and will pass into the aggregation of musicians. This is to some extent analogous to present social-class mobility, but it is more closely tied to human genetics. While socioeconomic mobility is only vertical, aggregate mobility is horizontal and vertical.

Genes for various aptitudes exist in all social strata and professional aggregations, but propinquity and assortive mating will greatly increase the number of marriages between individuals who carry genes for similar aptitudes. This will not necessarily

yield a bumper crop of geniuses, but it enhances the possibility.

Differences, Not Deficits

It is not surprising that not everybody welcomes the prospect of equality. Even a few biologists have concocted horrendous tales of its genetic consequences. They say equality has drained the lower classes of genetic talents, and only worthless dregs remain. We can dispel this fantasy by pointing out that a former untouchable is a cabinet minister in India's government, and that after most of the aristocracy was destroyed during the Russian revolution, able individuals from the former lower classes took over the functions of government.

On the other hand, it may not seem realistic to envisage an entire society consisting of elite aggregations. Maybe one large aggregate will be left with no particular aptitudes. To this I can only say that I agree with Scarr-Salapatek. Differences between humans "can simply be accepted as differences and not as deficits. If there are alternate ways of being successful within the society, then differences can be valued variations of the human theme regardless of their environment or genetic origins." We must not brand people or professions as elite or common. To compliment equality of opportunity we need equality of status. Manual labor is not intrinsically inferior to intellectual labor, even though more of us may be more adept at the former than at the latter. The presence of rare abilities need not detract from appreciation of more common ones. Though this may be hard to accept for individuals who grew up in a class society, I feel it is ethically desirable. Moreover, history is moving in this direction. ◆

Discussion Questions

1. What are the three explanations given by Dobzhansky for individual and group differences in IQ?

2. What does high heritability of IQ mean?

3. How do the IQ scores of identical twins reared apart compare with twins reared together? What does this say about environmental influence on IQ?

4. How does Dobzhansky criticize Jensen's position?

5. What did Sandra Scarr-Salapatek find in her study of twins in Philadelphia schools, and how does Dobzhansky interpret this result?

Name: _____

Date: _____

Part 8: Intelligence

1. Jensen's arguments about racial differences in intelligence are convincing.

Agree	①	②	③	④	⑤	Disagree

2. I am opposed to the widespread use of intelligence tests.

Agree	①	②	③	④	⑤	Disagree

3. I am comfortable with my own level of intelligence.

Agree	①	②	③	④	⑤	Disagree

How do you think you measure up on Gardner's seven scales of intelligence? Rate yourself in each category on a scale of 1 to 10, with 10 being most intelligent. Are you satisfied with your scores? How might you boost them?

1) Linguistic intelligence:

2) Logical-mathematical intelligence:

3) Spatial intelligence:

4) Musical intelligence:

5) Fine-motor intelligence:

6) Interpersonal intelligence:

7) Intrapersonal intelligence:

Write a brief critique of Arthur Jensen's paper on racial differences in intelligence.

PART 9
COGNITION AND LANGUAGE

Thinking and language are usually merged into the same chapter in Introductory Psychology courses because they have much in common. Human cognition is highly verbal, for one thing, and language seems to require a great deal of thinking. Human language and cognition are orders of magnitude more sophisticated than comparable functions in non-human animals. It's language and cognition that make us king of the evolutionary hill, without doubt. The huge cerebral cortex that distinguishes the human brain seems to be largely occupied with these high-order functions.

The articles in this section deal with select issues within this huge topic area. In the first piece, "Capturing Creativity," I discuss my two decades of research on the creative process and introduce you to Generativity Theory, a formal, predictive theory of creativity. My research has convinced me (and a few close friends) that creativity is an orderly process, that the generative mechanisms that underlie creativity are universal, and that, with the right skills, *anyone* can be as creative as Mozart or Picasso. I discuss four specific techniques for accelerating and directing personal creativity.

In "Automated Lives," Harvard's Ellen Langer discusses an all-too-common attention deficit known as "mindlessness," along with its better half, which Langer call "mindfulness," which is also the title of her excellent book on the subject. In "What I Meant To Say," Michael T. Motley reviews several theories of verbal slips and makes a strong case for "spreading activation theory" to explain such slips, including both the Freudian kind and the more mundane. The section ends with an in-depth interview of Rutgers' Howard Gruber, conducted by Howard Gardner. Gruber talks about his analysis of the creativity of famous individuals, including Charles Darwin (if you're thinking that's Francis Galton's cousin, you're correct.)

Cap*turing* **Creativity**

◆ *Robert Epstein*

When it comes to creativity, there's good news and very good news. The good news is that the mysteries of the creative process are finally giving way to a rigorous scientific analysis. The very good news is that, with the right skills, you can boost your own creative output by a factor of 10 or more. Significant creativity is within everyone's reach—no exceptions.

I make these claims based on nearly 20 years of laboratory research on the creative process, conducted with animals, with impaired and normal children, and with normal adults (well, college students). In recent years I've also successfully applied some of the lessons of the laboratory in real-life settings with children, teachers, and parents, as well as with executives at some of the nation's largest corporations.

An explosion of creative forces is at hand, and it could make the accomplishments of the Renaissance look like a ride on a stationary bicycle.

Myths and Mysticism

If creativity is so accessible, what's holding back the flood? When I say to a group of a hundred people, "Please raise your hand if you consider yourself to be creative," why do only 10 hands go up? Why are corporate leaders, government officials, politicians, crime fighters, teachers, and parents all starving for new ideas?

Why are art, music, and literature in the hands of a tiny fraction of the population—while the rest of us are mere spectators?

Two answers suggest themselves, and each is disturbing. First, our creative potential is virtually shut down by early schooling. Teachers are the first to admit this. A kindergarten teacher told me recently, "I can't believe I get paid to have so much fun every day—before the kids get ruined." Ruined? "Well," he said, "in the first grade the kids have to work all the time. There's no more time for fun, because there's so much they've got to learn. They're not even allowed to daydream any more. It's a wonder that any of them ever grow up to be artists or inventors. In kindergarten, on the other hand, all the kids are artists and inventors."

There's another reason why creativity seems to be in short supply: Myths about creativity are deeply entrenched in our culture. Myths have enormous power to shape everyday behavior, often to people's detriment. When people believe the world is flat, for example, they're unlikely to venture out to sea very far, and "lands away" remain undiscovered.

When it comes to creativity, myths keep most people firmly shorebound. *Only artists have creativity* and *creativity is rare,* we're

Significant creativity is within everyone's reach— no exceptions.

told. *Creativity is mysterious and magical and divine,* people say. *It's in your right brain,* the headlines swear.

None of these beliefs is true. The brain hemisphere distinction is based largely on clinical studies of about 40 "split-brain" patients—people whose brains were severed surgically in order to treat seizures or other neurological problems. The initial studies of such patients, conducted in the 1960s, seemed to show significant functional differences between the left and right cerebral hemispheres. In the 1980s, however, scientists began to reinterpret the data. The problem is that split-brain patients all have abnormal brains to begin with.

As a practical matter, the right-hemisphere myth is nonsense because virtually no one has a split brain. The two halves of our brain are connected by an immense structure called the corpus callosum, and the hemispheres also communicate through the sense organs. Creativity has no precise location in the human brain, and people who promise to reactivate your "neural creativity zones" are just yanking your chain.

Pigeon Power

Enough about myths. What about science?

In the 1970s, in animal studies I began at Harvard with behaviorist B. F. Skinner, I became intrigued—well, perhaps "obsessed" is a better word—with the fact that much of the interesting behavior we observed in our subjects had never been trained. We would provide certain training, and then new, often very complex, behavior would emerge. Perhaps more important, I eventually realized that the new behavior wasn't random but that it was in fact related in orderly ways

Fun and Games

Over the years, for various audiences and university classes, I've developed many exercises and games that both spur creativity and illustrate how generative processes work. Here are a few of my favorites:

Capturing a Daydream. You can perform this exercise in a group or on your own—right now, If you like. Just close your eyes and let your mind wander freely for a few minutes. You might drift off to the stars; you might see things you've never seen before. Just let your thoughts wander without deliberately guiding them. Okay, relax and get started...

Did you leave the room? Did you leave the earth? Did you see or hear or experience anything that's impossible to experience in reality? Given enough time and an absence of distraction, everyone answers yes to each of these questions. Behavior is generative—even the covert perceptual behavior that we call "thought." This simple exercise is especially powerful because it can quickly convince anyone that everyone has enormous creative potential and that capturing skills are essential to unlocking that potential.

I've conducted this exercise all over the world, but I've been most deeply moved by its effect on audiences in Japan. Even bright, professional Japanese people believe that the Japanese are not a creative lot—this, in spite of the fact that Japanese patents now dominate many categories of invention worldwide. But after a few minutes of capturing daydreams, Japanese audiences report daydreams every bit as bizarre and rich as Salvador Dali's: "I saw you, the teacher, small, in my hand, and you turned gray and you shrank and disappeared." (What would Freud say about that? Who cares?) "I flew to the top of the building next door, and I saw this building crumble to the ground while I ate a sandwich." (IBM was located next door. Was this fellow hoping for a better job?)

Building a Better Capturing Machine. Ask a group of people to invent machines that will help them become better inventors. Specifically, give them five minutes in which to invent a device that will allow them to capture good ideas on the fly. They can use any materials at hand, including odd items you may supply, except traditional writing implements (pens, crayons, paper, computers, etc.).

At a club one evening, I was faced with one of those challenges that every single person dreads. An appealing woman offered me her telephone number, but I couldn't locate anything with which to write! I grabbed a napkin, tore off one corner to indicate my starting point, and then made a pattern of small tears around the edge to capture the number. First seven tears and a space, then two tears and a space, and then—the rest is none of your business.

The Shifting Game. Generativity Theory suggests that some of the common methods now used to promote creativity have limited value, at best. Brainstorming, for example, works to some extent because it exposes team participants to multiple social stimuli (a "surrounding" technique). But it also inhibits creativity by exposing individuals to disapproval. Participants may try to withhold signs of disapproval, but eyebrows are still raised, and most people hold back a wealth of good ideas.

The Shifting Game uses a team optimally to increase creative output. Two teams are selected from the larger audience. One is instructed to stay together for a 20-minute brainstorming session. The second team is instructed to "shift" twice from five-minute private work sessions to five-minute team meetings. Each team must generate names for a new soft drink, and each has a total of 20 minutes in which to accomplish a task.

The "shifting" group typically generate twice as many ideas as the brainstorming group. Why? Because creativity is always an individual process, and social disapproval is the major deterrent to creativity our entire lives. Groups are far better at *selecting* good ideas than at *generating* them.

to the behavior that had been trained.

Over the years, my students, colleagues, and I, became increasingly adept at providing certain minimal training that would inexorably lead to the generation of a specific, complex, new performance—one that could conceivably be called "creative." For example, in an article published in *Nature* in 1984, we reported that we could get lowly pigeons to solve the classic "box-and-banana" problem in a human-like way.

Trained (a) to push a box toward targets at ground level, and (b) to climb onto a box and peck a toy banana directly overhead, what will a pigeon do the first time the banana is suspended out of reach and the box is placed on the ground a foot away from the position of the banana?

Faced with this new situation, a pigeon looks "confused" at first. It stretches toward the banana repeatedly and looks back and forth from the box to the banana. After twenty or thirty seconds, the pigeon starts to push the box toward the banana, clearly *sighting* the banana as it pushes. When the box is beneath the banana, the pigeon stops pushing, climbs, and pecks the banana. A typical performance takes about a minute.

Non-solutions and partial solutions are easy to generate with different pigeons simply by varying the training histories. For example, if a bird has learned to push but not to climb, it will push the box toward the banana, stop pushing in the right place, and then stretch repeatedly toward the banana without climbing on the box. One bird confronted with this situation stumbled onto the box at one point and then immediately fell off without ever pecking the banana.

The point is that *previously established behavior manifests itself in new situations in new, yet orderly ways.* Novel behavior is truly new, but the particular novel behavior that emerges in a new situation depends on the particular behaviors that were established previously— that is, on the "prior knowledge" of the organism. In other words, creativity is an extension of what you already know.

To be more specific, new behaviors (or "ideas") emerge as old behaviors interact, and the process by which behaviors interact is or-

> *Creativity, in short, is not something mystical; it's an extension of what you already know.*

derly. With animal subjects, it's easy to show how two, three, or even four or more "repertoires" of behavior interact and merge to produce new performances. In 1987, for example, I published a study in which a single pigeon had received five different types of training: It had learned (1) to climb onto a box (but never to peck anything overhead), (2) to peck at a toy banana when it was suspended within the pigeon's reach, (3) to ignore the banana when it was suspended out of the pigeon's reach, (4) to open a transparent door, and (5) to push a box toward targets placed at ground level.

In a test situation, the box was placed behind the transparent door, and the banana was suspended out of reach about a foot away from the doorway. In just four minutes, the pigeon "solved the problem": It opened the door, pushed the box toward the banana, stopped pushing when the box was beneath the banana, climbed onto the box, and pecked the banana.

If a pigeon can do that, just think about the potential the rest of us have.

Generativity and Creativity

Behavior is "generative," by which I mean that it's inherently and continuously novel, like the surface of a fast-flowing river. We never repeat the same action or have the same thought twice, at least not when you look closely enough. We brush our teeth a slightly different way each morning; we think new thoughts and say new sentences each waking hour; we dream new dreams each night. Even when it seems like we're repeating some action, we're not. If you say the "dog" twice, a spectrograph will easily distin-

guish between the two sounds. Behavior flows, and it never stops changing.

Occasionally, some new thing that we say or write or do gets labeled "creative," but the language of creativity is imprecise. "Creative" is an everyday term, not a scientific one. Novel behavior is labeled creative when it has some special value to the community. Alas, communities are extremely inconsistent in their use of the language of creativity. Jackson Pollock would not have been dubbed "creative" in fourteenth-century Europe; he would have been burned at the stake.

From a scientific perspective, it's not creativity itself that's of interest—"creativity" is just a fragile label, after all—it's that flow of novel behavior that sometimes inspires the label that's important. How can we account for and understand that flow? Where does novel behavior come from? How does the "creative process" work?

Generativity Theory is a formal, mathematical theory of the creative process. Put simply, it states that a number of processes act simultaneously on the neural determinates of many different behaviors and that novel behavior is generated continuously by this complex and dynamic process. To put this another way, those "repertoires of behavior" that we trained in the pigeons can be represented mathematically, and, what's more, the way these behaviors interact over time can be modeled with a computer.

In the early 1980s I began to extend the animal research to humans, and the results have been every bit as remarkable as they were with pigeons (well, one should hope so!). With humans, it would be unethical to do true simulation research; that is, you can't isolate your subjects and restrict their experiences. So I've utilized other research strategies, such as the *post hoc simulation.*

Here's the basic idea. We give people a problem to solve and various materials with which to solve the problem. By definition, we've put them in a new situation, one where we expect novel, "creative" behavior to occur. We videotape each performance and then code the tape in a way that allows us to create a special graph called a "frequency profile." Each profile consists of a set of overlapping curves that capture the essence of a unique, novel performance by an individual subject—just as the curves of an electrocardiogram capture a unique performance by your cardiovascular system.

Then we simulate the performance on a computer, using equations that describe how behaviors interact over time. The computer simulation generates another kind of graph, called a "probability profile," which, like the frequency profile, consists of a set of overlapping curves. Do the two profiles look alike? In other words, can a computer-generated probability profile simulate what people actually do? The computer simulations describe real human behavior fairly well, which suggests that Generativity Theory is "valid."

In recent years, I've had subjects solving problems directly on a computer touch-screen, which allows us to simulate the performances in real-time, updating and improving our predictions as the performance proceeds. Real-time simulation of this sort is routinely used in predicting the weather or the flight path of a space ship. Using this technology, we're getting better at predicting unique, novel performances in individual subjects moment-to-moment in time, further suggesting that the creative process is quite orderly—not mysterious at all.

Four Techniques to Boost Creativity

Generativity research suggests four distinct strategies for increasing creative output. Each can be implemented in different situations in different ways, sometimes in multiple ways.

Capturing

New ideas are like rabbits streaking through consciousness; they're fleeting. If you don't grab them quickly, they're usually gone forever. Just a few minutes go, while taking care of nature's business (more about that later), a catchy title for an article about our need for mild stressors—something like "What Would My Dog Do Without Her Fleas?"—popped into my head. Alas, by the time I got back to my desk, the exact title was gone, and I'm unable to get it back.

The main thing that distinguishes "creative" people from the rest of us is that the creative ones have learned ways to *pay attention to* and then to *preserve* some of the new ideas that occur to them. They have *capturing* skills.

The scientist Otto Loewi had struggled for years with a problem in cell biology. One night, a new approach to the problem occurred to him in his sleep. In the dark, he grabbed a pen and pad, recorded his new ideas, and went back to sleep. Come morning, he couldn't read his writing. Had he imagined this great solution, or was it real? The next night he was blessed by the same flash of insight. This time, he took no chances; he pulled on his clothes and went straight to his lab. He won the Nobel Prize for the work he began that night.

People who are serious about exploring their creative side develop and practice various methods of capturing new ideas. Artists carry sketchpads. Writers and advertisers carry notepads or pocket computers. Inventors make notes on napkins and candy-bar wrappers—especially inventors of new foods!

Salvador Dali, the great surrealist, used to grab ideas for paintings from the very fertile semi-sleep state we call the hypnagogic state. He'd lie on a sofa and hold a spoon in one hand, balancing it on the edge of a glass placed on the floor. Just as he'd drift off to sleep, he'd release the spoon, and the sound of the spoon hitting the glass would awaken him. Immediately, he'd sketch the bizarre hypnagogic images he was seeing. *Anyone* can do this. We *all* have bizarre perceptual experiences in those moments before we fall fully asleep. Dali simply developed a way to seize some of them.

Capturing skills can be taught to young children, to high school kids, to adults, to top executives. Teachers, parents, and managers can boost the creative output of a group manyfold simply by providing some simple training and the right materials.

Capturing is easier in certain settings and at certain times, so we improve our catch by identifying the settings and times that work best for us. For some people, the Three Bs of Creativity—the Bed, the Bath, and the Bus—are particularly fertile, especially if you keep writing materials handy in those locations (obviously, today I failed to do so). Others need to sit by a pool or on a cruise ship or in a lonely cabin in the woods. Years ago I gave a talk on creativity at the Rowland Institute, a private research center built by Edwin Land, the millionaire inventor of the Polaroid "Land" camera. Land designed the entire institute to be a giant idea-capturing machine. Inside, a serene Japanese garden runs the length of the building, with skylights overhead. He wanted himself and fellow researchers to be able to "hear themselves think" as they walked, slowly and peacefully, through the magnificent indoor garden—literally, a garden of new ideas.

Challenging

One way to accelerate the flow of new ideas is by challenging yourself—that is, by putting yourself in difficult situations in which you're likely to fail to some extent. A challenging situation is like an "extinction" procedure in the behavioral laboratory. We extinguish behavior when we withdraw the reinforcers that usually maintain that behavior. In challenging situations, a great deal of behavior goes unreinforced; it just doesn't work.

When a behavior is unsuccessful, typically it gets weaker. We feel frustrated and upset, and, most important for creativity, there is a "resurgence" of behaviors that used to be effective. We begin trying out every other behavior that ever worked for us in the past under similar conditions. That gets many behaviors competing vigorously, which greatly enhances the generative process. (Our feelings of frustration and confusion are largely byproducts of this stiff competition.)

Say you start to turn a door knob that has always turned easily. It won't budge. At first, you start to turn the knob harder; then perhaps you pull up on the knob or push if down. Then maybe you wiggle it. Eventually, you shove the door with your shoulder or kick it with your foot. What you do will *depend on your history* with doors. Eventually, you'll shout for help—maybe even call out for

---

Here's the great news: Generativity research shows that everyone has creative abilities.

"mommy," even if your mother is no longer among the living.

It's possible to take advantage of this robust process to spur creativity. For example, from time to time we can give students and employees open-ended problems to solve—problems that have an infinite number of solutions. Rather than saying, "Please give me three names for our company new widget," try saying, "Please give me as many names as possible for the widget." You'll get two or three times as many proposals from which to make a final selection.

"Ultimate problems"—challenging problems that have *no* solution—can also be used to accelerate creative output. With children or friends or colleagues, try spending 15 minutes a week solving one of these:

- ◆ You have 24 hours in which to bring about world peace. How do you do it?
- ◆ You have one year in which to clean up all of the pollution on earth and make sure that people never pollute the planet again. What's your plan?
- ◆ Aging is a real drag. Eliminate it.

You shouldn't expect to find a real solution, but you'll certainly stimulate a lot of interesting new ideas. This is an example of using a "controlled failure system"—a structured challenge that makes

people feel reasonably safe—to stimulate new ideas without causing those annoying myocardial infarctions.

Do we really want to place ourselves in situations in which we know we're going to feel frustrated and confused? Emphatically, yes! If you're feeling frustrated, you're in the company of the greatest poets, composers, and inventors of all time, and, more likely than not, you're on the verge of a new idea. Failure is not something to fear; properly managed, it's a great wellspring of creativity.

Broadening

Here's a deceptively simple fact: for repertoires of behavior to contribute to the generative process, they must first exist. In other words,the more training you have and the more diverse that training is, the greater the potential for creative output. Letting kids float around a classroom from one "activity center" to another is not the way to go; when we're on our own, we gravitate toward a very narrow range of learning opportunities. The creative process is spurred on by multiple well-established repertoires of behavior. Traditional, structured, aggressive methods of teaching and training have special value in laying a foundation for creativity.

A contradiction? Didn't I say that first-grade teachers were monsters who stifled creativity by doing too much teaching? The problem with traditional education is not that it teaches diverse subjects or subjects that lack apparent utility; the problem is that it doesn't allocate any time and training for creativity as such. Kids need to learn things that they don't want to learn—not just to become good citizens, but also to become more creative people.

If you want to enhance your own creativity, take courses in subjects you know nothing about. Once a year, at least, take a course at a local college in the last thing you'd ever want to know about. Land's own breakthrough invention came about because of training he had in crystallography, chemistry, and other fields. The invention of Velcro, the modern theory of electron spin, and countless other advances were made possible because their creators had training in diverse fields.

Surrounding

Finally, you can enhance your creativity by surrounding yourself with diverse stimuli—and, even more important, by changing those stimuli regularly. Diverse and changing stimuli promote creativity because, like resurgence, they get multiple behaviors competing with each other. If you put a Mickey Mouse hat and pliers on your desk in the morning, your thinking will move in odd directions during the day. Call these items distractions, if you like; they are great reservoirs of creativity.

Here's the great news: Generativity research shows that *everyone* has creative abilities. The generative mechanisms that underlie the creative process operate all the time in each of us. Every one of us has the creative potential of Mozart or Picasso or Edison or Einstein. To boost your creative output, capture your new ideas as they occur, challenge yourself in order to get ideas competing, broaden your training so that many new repertoires of behavior will be available to compete, and surround yourself as much as possible with diverse and ever-changing stimuli.

Anyone can master these creative strategies. They're all that stand between you and the most creative people in history. ◆

Discussion Questions

1. How creative are you? Please explain your answer.

2. Give at least two reasons why most people believe that they are not creative.

3. What is wrong with the theory that creativity is in the right hemisphere of the brain?

4. How is creativity based on prior knowledge?

5. Define generativity and explain its relationship to creativity.

6. Give some examples of how teachers can encourage creativity in students.

7. What is a controlled failure system? How does it promote creativity?

8. Why isn't brainstorming an effective method for creating creativity?

9. How would you have characterized creativity before reading this article? After reading this article?

10. List at least four techniques you can use to increase your creative output, and give one or more examples of how to use each technique.

Automated Lives

◆ *Ellen J. Langer*

Why is it that we frequently do not know details of our friends' appearance, like the color of their eyes? Why is it that people who become extremely skilled at some complex task, such as driving a car or solving Rubik's Cube, often cannot explain how they do it? How can something innocently learned in childhood about grandparents influence our behavior toward our own aging a half-century later? How is it that we can treat meaningless explanations as if they contained meaningful information—for example, complying with the request of someone in a supermarket checkout line who says, "Can I get ahead of you? I'd like to pay for this"?

All these are examples of a phenomenon that I call mindlessness, a condition in which people unwittingly respond to the world as if they were automatons. Technically speaking, mindlessness is a state of reduced cognitive activity in which a person responds to the environment without considering its potentially novel elements and instead relies on old distinctions rather than creating new categories. Mindlessness should not be confused with merely withholding attention from one activity to give it to another—doing something in a routine manner so as to think about something else—or closing one's awareness to tiresome or unpleasant events. In mindlessness, people operate as if they were paying attention to the details of a given situation and weighing an appropriate response when in fact they are not.

Mindlessness points to a new and very important view of mental activity—that not only what one thinks but the way one processes information can significantly affect one's psychological, social, and physical well-being. In an extensive series of continuing experiments, my colleagues and I have found that mindlessness occurs in many more situations and is much more pervasive in our lives than people realize. Indeed, it may be a fundamental aspect of human behavior. We have found that mindlessness can be self-damaging, especially in new situations to which people apply information they unknowingly had accepted in an unthinking way. There is even evidence that

> **We have found that mindlessness can be self-damaging, especially in new situations to which people apply information they unknowingly had accepted in an unthinking way.**

mindlessness may lead to a shorter life span for the elderly.

Because mindless and mindful behavior outwardly look the same, and because people cannot directly know when they are being mindless (they would be mindful if they did), we have had to devise experiments that allow us to observe mindlessness indirectly. Many of them take place in real-life situations.

In the experiments that initiated our study of mindlessness (my mindful colleagues on the project were psychologists Arthur Blank and Benzion Chanowitz), we wanted to see whether it was possible for a person to make a decision about a nonroutine matter without thinking about it. All the experiments in this series began with asking someone a favor, and in posing the favor, we carefully distinguished between the way it was presented—its form or structure—and its content—the sense it made. Thus, we formulated a favor in both novel and familiar ways and worded it so that it sometimes made sense and sometimes did not. We predicted that as long as we put the request in a familiar way, people would comply with it, even if the request essentially made no sense. Such compliance would reveal mindlessness—a response that unwittingly disregarded the very particulars to which it presumably was responding.

In one of the experiments, a confederate in a university library approached people at a copying machine and asked them whether they would interrupt their work to let the intruder use the machine.

In this setting, such a request typically included both the request and a reason for it. We devised two such formulations, one sensible ("Excuse me, may I use the Xerox machine because I'm in a rush?") and one senseless ("Excuse me, may I use the Xerox machine because I have to make copies?" Why else would one want to use a copying machine?). We also devised a novel formulation, which omitted any reason ("Excuse me, may I use the Xerox machine?") and so, in terms of its meaning, was equivalent to the familiar but senseless formulation.

The results supported our prediction. As long as the request had the accepted familiar form of a request and a reason, people complied with it, even when it made no sense. The rates of compliance to both the sensible and senseless familiar requests were virtually identical—94 and 93 percent, respectively. Had people been paying attention to the contents of the request rather than to its form, the senseless familiar request should have received roughly the same lower rate of compliance achieved by the senseless novel request—60 percent.

In another experiment in this series, we tested whether the findings would hold for a written request. We sent a memo to 40 secretaries of various departments at a university in New York, asking them to do something manifestly foolish: to return the memo to another room. In this university, memos that sought a response were typically framed as requests, not demands, so we sent equal number of two versions of the text—one in the familiar form of a request ("I would appreciate it if you would return this paper immediately to Room 238 through interoffice mail"— that was all the memo said!) and the other in the novel form of a demand ("This paper is to be returned immediately to Room 238 through interoffice mail"). Memos typically were not signed, so we signed half of each version. This meant that the form of one memo was familiar (the unsigned request) and the forms of the other three were novel (the signed request, the signed demand, and the unsigned demand).

Again, a familiar form undermined the respondents' awareness of what the favor actually asked. The unsigned request brought a 90 percent rate of compliance, while the novel memos all brought significantly lower rates: 70 percent for the signed request, 60 percent for the signed demand, and 50 percent for the unsigned demand.

In both these experiments, then, and in others like them, whether the exchanges between people were face-to-face or established through written communications, whether the requests that we posed did or did not make sense, when the situations were in a form familiar to the participants, they behaved in ways that appeared mindless. It is as if people look to the broad cues that define an event—in these instances, the form of the requests—and once they identify the cues as similar to cues from events in the past, they no longer observe the details that follow.

It might be argued that in all these situations, the participants really were thinking, but for one reason or another—say, the very familiarity or inconsequential character of the situation—they simply skimmed over the details.

In a series of experiments directed to this issue, my colleagues and I have shown that being mindless and being mindful are qualitatively distinct processes,

---

Mindlessness is a state of reduced mental activity in which people respond to a situation without considering its novel elements.

---

and more than simply higher or lower points on the same continuum of thought. When people are mindless—when they know something so well that they no longer need to think while doing it—they become relatively incapable of breaking down their understanding into the separate elements out of which it has been built. In effect, they no longer *can* think about what they know so well.

In one experiment conducted with Cynthia Weinman, a doctoral

© 1998 PhotoDisc, Inc.

student in psychology at the City University of New York, our associates spoke with 120 people at an employment office in Boston, explaining that we wanted to tape their voices for a study on voice quality. We asked half to speak for a minute on a familiar subject (why it was difficult to find a job in Boston) and half to speak on a novel subject (why is was difficult to find a job in Alaska). Then, for a portion of each group, we pretend for about 90 seconds that the tape recorder was not working properly, and told the waiting participants, "You might as well think about the issue if you want while I fix this."

The delays had reverse effects on the groups. On the familiar subject of Boston, the people who spoke immediately were significantly more fluent and had more ideas than those who thought about it. On the exotic subject of Alaska, those who spoke immediately were significantly less fluent and had fewer ideas than the people who thought about it. (We measured fluency by dividing the number of pauses by the number of spoken words in the first 15 seconds of a person's comments.) These differences demonstrate the different properties of mindlessness and mindfulness. The people who spoke about Boston were so familiar with the subject that once they began thinking about it, the integrity it had in their minds became undone. They knew the subject in a way that had reached a level beyond conscious thought and that was not available to conscious thought. The people who spoke about Alaska, on the other hand, did not know their subject, so when we give them time to think about it, they could consider the relevance of different facts and arguments. They could be mindful about it.

Becoming mindless is in many ways analogous to building a house. When you begin construction there are many ways to use the several materials before you. You examine the materials and make your decisions to satisfy some purpose. (Conceivably, you may have made many of these decisions in the blueprint stage.) As the materials are joined, the building takes form, and there are seemingly fewer and fewer choices to be made. The rigid structure develops. Once it is built, the individual parts no longer exist. Were someone to offer you, a homeowner, a great deal of money for, say, a half-dozen window panes, few of us would go to our windows and remove the panes, even though it would be to our financial advantage to do so. For our purposes, they are not individual panes of glass any longer, but parts of a rigid structure, a structure that serves some purposes (to keep us warm) and not others (to earn money). On the other hand, before the house was completely built, when we were mindfully deciding how to use the materials, we would have been happy to take advantage of the generous offer.

The clearest demonstration of how mindlessness cuts one off from the information that originally led

to one's understanding is offered by a study I conducted with Lois Imber, a psychologist at Harvard, on

We often ascribe sense to a meaningless explanation. People at a copying machine may step aside when someone says, 'I have to make some copies.'

how practice can make imperfect. We recruited 126 people from airport lounges in Boston and New York, and told them that we were studying ways to improve the performance of tasks. We explained

that they would code several English sentences into a system consisting of numbers and symbols. We showed them how is was done and let a third of the group code six practice sentences, by the end of which they had mastered the process and no longer needed to refer to the list of letter and symbol equivalents. Another third of the group coded two practice sentences, which made them moderately skilled; the last third had no practice, which of course left them completely unskilled. Having thus established groups with three levels of skills, we

© 1998 PhotoDisc, Inc.

had everyone code one sentence and then asked them to list the individual steps that they could recall taking in order to do it. "For instance," we explained, "you had to look at the letter to be coded."

The striking results almost tell their own story. Both the skilled and unskilled groups recorded significantly fewer steps on the average than did the moderately skilled group. The masters of the task and the neophytes recalled a comparable low number of steps.

Becoming skilled at a task means becoming mindless about it, which means no longer knowing how to do it. One just does it. The better we get at what we do, the less we know how we do it. The irony of being skillful is that when we perform tasks perfectly, we are mindless, passively repeating what we already know; when we perform them imperfectly, we are mindful, actively creating what we are not yet sure of.

The findings I have discussed indicate that mindlessness is not a rarefied phenomenon, but a condition that can occur in anything one does or learns. My most direct confirmation of the everyday presence of mindlessness come from another study with Lois Imber, which shows that people have no clear idea of the normal physical characteristics of the people they know.

We asked seven groups of 16 or 20 students from an introductory psychology class at Harvard to view a videotape of a 23-year-old man reading a *New York Times* editorial. We indirectly encouraged five of the groups and directly encouraged a sixth to observe him with care. To five groups, we gave information that led them to believe that he was, respectively, a millionaire, a homosexual, divorced, a cancer patient, or an ex-mental patient. We asked the sixth group to be especially attentive to

the man's features and physical characteristics. To the seventh and last group, we gave no information or instructions that would lead them to see the reader as anything other than ordinary.

After the students viewed the videotape, we asked them to answer questions about the man's appearance (What was the color of his hair? Was he wearing a ring? Glasses? And so on) and to list any other characteristics they had noticed. As we expected, the six groups that considered the man special identified significantly more features than did the group that regarded him as ordinary. This difference suggests that the students observe the details of a person—look mindfully—only when they consider the person in some way special. Since most people in everyday life are thought of

---

Becoming skilled at a task means becoming mindless about it, which means no longer knowing how to do it. One just does it. The better we get at what we do, the less we know how we do it.

---

as ordinary, it follows that the students are likely to look at them in a mindless way.

We also asked the students to compare the man's features with those of "most people they knew" and estimate whether his characteristic were common or uncommon. The groups that considered the man special consistently ranked his characteristics as less common than did the group that thought the man ordinary. Clearly, it was not awareness of the people they knew that led to these assessments but rather the students' fix on the man. If he was ordinary, so were his characteristics; if he was special, his characteristics were too. The students apparently had no solid sense of the appearance of the peo-

ple they knew. Did they wear glasses? What was the color of their hair? The students did not know. They looked mindlessly at the people who populated their lives.

How does this happen? Over time, after hundreds of exposures to people, one builds up a general notion of a physically normal person. The actual physical details disappear and are no longer available to the conscious mind, just as, to the skilled coders in the previous experiment, the individual steps of the coding process were no longer available. Just as the familiar forms of a request blinded the participants of the first experiments to the details of the request, so the generalized familiar form of a normal person blinds one to details of most people one sees.

Mindlessness does not develop only from repeated exposures to an experience. It can also develop after a single exposure to an experience or a piece of information—and in this form it contains perhaps its greatest potential for harm.

"One-trial" mindlessness can occur when people are presented with information that has no immediate relevance to them. Without critically examining the information, they may simply accept it as true, and subsequently treat it with the same mindlessness they accord to a generalized truth or representation they have built up over time. In short, they have committed themselves prematurely to an idea that has no depth of experience behind it and that they have not scrutinized. We call this structured information a "premature cognitive commitment."

Whether such a commitment produces ill effects depends on the circumstances of one's life. For instance—a wealthy young man, who has no reason to believe that he will lose his fortune, is told that poor people are without hope or value. He accepts this information uncritically. If he maintains his fortune, the information will have no untoward effects on him (aside, perhaps, from poisoning his relationships, should he have any with poor people). But if he loses his money, and the information becomes personally relevant, he may draw the conclusion that he is hopeless and worthless and begin to behave that way.

Benzion Chanowitz and I created the following experiment to demonstrate these ideas. We provided 64 students with pamphlets about two benign perceptual disorders (inventions of Chanowitz and myself) that, like color blindness, were not apparent to the individual. One was a visual disorder in which, we said, individuals see the environment as a "whole field and cannot distinguish or pick out certain things that are 'hidden' in the field." The other was a hearing disorder in which individuals "are unable to break down the sounds into parts or...distinguish differences within the sounds that are in the environment." Half of the pamphlets said that the defects were present in 80 percent of the population; the other half said that they were present in only 10 percent of the population. We then asked half of each group to consider possible strategies for coping with the problems. Thus,

---

When a situation looks like similar situations in the past, it induces mindlessness, leading people to stop thinking about it.

---

we had four groups, three of which were likely to examine the information with care—mindfully—either because we asked the people to think about coping strategies or because they were told that the problems were widespread; the fourth group, which learned that the problems were rare and received no urging to think about them, was likely to absorb the information mindlessly without examining it—that is, to make a premature cognitive commitment.

We "tested" our subjects for the two fictitious disorders, and arranged the score sheet to show that all the participants had the vision problem. We thereby set the stage for comparing the responses of people who had accepted information uncritically and then abruptly discovered that it was relevant to them with the responses of people who had scrutinized the information when first exposed to it. We asked our groups to take a follow-up test to discover the severity of the defect, and the results were dramatic: The people who had mindlessly absorbed the information did only half as well as the people who had grappled with it mindfully; they had a far worse "case" of the nonexistent condition.

To comprehend the possible real-life consequences of such premature cognitive commitments, one need only consider the kind of medical information that typically reaches the general public. For instance, the first thing many people learn about cancer is that it is a killer that initially occurs in one part of the body or another. An informal investigation has shown us that many people never learn anything else about the disease—for example, that there is an appreciable rate of recovery. Should they discover that they have cancer, these people would probably think that they were going to die from it. Like the mindless sufferers of our fictitious perceptual disorders, such knowledge could severely undermine them.

Several researchers and I have explored how ideas about again and alcoholism thoughtlessly accepted in childhood can affect the way people later deal with these conditions. Childhood is a time when people are highly disposed to commit themselves prematurely to an idea: A child usually receives only one version of a piece of information and rarely has reason to question it. When such information

© 1998 PhotoDisc, Inc.

is conveyed by the presence of a person—say, an elderly adult or an alcoholic—this person then becomes the basis for the child's view of old age or alcoholism.

From the residents of old-age homes in metropolitan Boston, we recruited 39 subjects averaging 79 years old who were willing to talk to us about their initial exposure to old age. We specifically focused on whether they had lived with a grandparent when they were very young. We reasoned that if they had, the grandparent, though old to the child, was still relatively young and thus presented the image of an aging adult who was alert and active. This image then became the child's idea of aging and influenced the person's behavior when he or she became old.

Our expectations were confirmed. Independent judges, blind to our reasoning, rated the slightly less than one-third of our subjects who had lived with a grandparent when they were very young as more alert, more active, and less dependent than the two-thirds who had presumably learned about aging in the typically negative fashion that emphasizes its debilitating effects. The positive conception of aging gained by the people who had lived with a grandparent was strong enough to withstand not only a lifetime of varied experience but also the dulling effects of the homogenizing institutions in which many of them currently lived.

Our studies on alcoholism (conducted with clients at the Alcohol Clinic of Peter Bent Brigham and Women's Hospital in Boston) also showed the effects of such cognitive commitments made in childhood. Briefly, alcoholics who had known only one alcoholic in their childhood were less likely to be helped by therapy than were those who, as children, had observed several types of alcoholics. Those

who had known one alcoholic had mindlessly accepted the behavior of the person as the unvarying truth about alcoholism. Because the other alcoholics had known different versions of alcoholism, they could see more easily that alcoholism was amenable to change.

In old-age homes, elderly people who engaged in tasks that demanded mindful attention lived longer than people who did not.

The ultimate harm of mindlessness is that it may actually shorten one's life span. In several investigations, we created situations that allowed nursing-home residents to be more mindful. Among other things, we encourage them to engage in active decision making, and we gave each resident a plant for which he would be fully responsible. In follow-up studies we found that significantly fewer of the mindful residents had died—in one study, 15 percent as compared with 30 percent of the other residents; in another study, 14 percent as compared with 47 percent.

A finding on senility lends further support to the conclusion that mindfulness and longevity are connected. Our studies suggest that what some people consider senility may be a kind of mindfulness, perhaps even an attempt to adapt to an environment whose excessive routines induce mindlessness. A group of nursing-home residents who were considered at least mildly senile by their social workers was compared with a group that was not. We asked all the residents to describe and itemize the uses of three objects: a glass measuring cup, the inner metal part of a lamp that holds the bulb and on which the shade sits, and a set of bicycle clips. Forty undergraduates who knew nothing about our subjects rated the an-

swers for creativity and intelligence on a six-point scale. As a group, the "senile" residents were comparable in intelligence to the nonsenile residents. But they were significantly more creative, and, interestingly, the most creative response to each of the objects came from a senile resident.

Taking these findings as evidence that senility is a kind of mindfulness, however atypical and inappropriate it may be, we next examined the records of a group of nursing-home residents who had died of heart disease and compared the ages of those whose records carried the diagnosis of senility with the ages of those who had not been so diagnosed. The results are straightforward. The mean age of death for the nonsenile group was 83.28; for the senile group, it was 89.80. Those subjects who heart disease was accompanied by a diagnosis of senility lived longer than those who had the disease alone.

Taken as a whole, then, the mindless/mindful distinction is so far relevant for understanding individual behavior, interpersonal relations, feelings of mastery, physical health, successful aging, and possibly longevity. Thus, it is clear that even though there is no way that one can consider everything in the environment mindfully, it is to everyone's advantage always to be mindfully considering something.

But the nature of mindlessness makes it impossible to establish a rule that will generate such consistent mindfulness. The more we follow a prescription to generate mindfulness, the less we think about it and the more we lose our awareness of the individual parts out of which we construct our understanding and behavior. We need to be mindful, but all of us must create and constantly change our own mindful ways of doing it.

◆

Discussion Questions

1. Define mindlessness.

2. When can mindlessness be dangerous?

3. What is a confederate?

4. Describe the main factor necessary for people to do tasks mindlessly.

5. What characteristic is required in a person for others to be mindful of him or her?

6. When are people more likely to be mindless? Why?

7. What are cognitive commitments?

8. How do cognitive commitments made during childhood affect people when they are older?

9. Explain how mindlessness might shorten a person's life.

10. Compare senility to intelligence, and explain how senility is related to mindlessness.

11. What is mindfulness?

WHAT I **Meant** *to Say*

◆ *Michael T. Motley*

It happens quite often. Right before an exam a student calls to ask for a postponement, giving one of several familiar excuses. It is easy to be skeptical when this happens, but I recall one occasion when my doubt was underscored with a curious slip of the tongue. The student said that she wanted the postponement because"...last night my grandmother lied—I mean died!"

How should I have interpreted her verbal slip? One possibility is that she had fabricated the excuse, and that her awareness of the lie prompted the error. Another possibility is that she was telling the truth but was afraid I might think that she was lying. Yet another is that she might have been feeling repressed guilt about a lie she once told her grandmother. On the other hand, the slip may have had nothing to do with lies; perhaps it was an innocent slip of the tongue in which the first "d" in "died" simply got replaced by an "l" as the result of some sort of linguistic confusion or articulatory fluke.

These interpretations hint at the wide range of explanations that psychologists, linguists and others have given for verbal slips during nearly a century of study. Almost all researchers who have examined the phenomenon agree on one thing, however: Since slips of the tongue, which we all experience from time to time, represent breakdowns in the normally

efficient and error-free process of speech, they might provide a sort of window on the mind.

Linguists and cognitive psychologists investigate verbal slips for insights into how the mind processes information (including spoken language) and controls behavior. One discovery has been that slips of the tongue often seem to be the result of competition between similar verbal choices. These aren't conscious and deliberate choices, such as those that accompany delicate social situations, but are the more automatic and instantaneous choices of casual speech. A colleague, for example, once introduced a point with "Is this a rhetorical question perchaps?" when either "perchance" or perhaps" would have fit his intention.

Almost any time we wish to express a thought, we must choose from several roughly equivalent verbal possibilities. Sometimes

Since slips of the tongue, which we all experience from time to time, represent breakdowns in the normally efficient and error-free process of speech, they might provide a sort of window on the mind.

competition between these choices, or indecision about them, results in a slip of the tongue. This explanation has an intuitive appeal, at least in the case of some errors.

At a political event a few years ago, for instance, the featured speaker was introduced as being "as American as mother pie and applehood." Presumably, indecision over two equal choices, "apple pie and motherhood" and "motherhood and apple pie," caused the error. It is easy to imagine verbal competition as the source of numerous slips, such as "hairible" instead of "terrible" or "horrible" and "hairline crackture" instead of "hairline fracture" or "hairline crack."

One reason for such slips could be a lapse in the mental attention normally devoted to resolving competition. Slips of the tongue are more frequent, for example, when we are speaking in public, being interviewed or are confronted with other uncomfortable communication situations. Slips at these times are probably instances of our attention being diverted enough to allow alternate verbal choices to replace intended ones.

There are several ways that verbal competition could cause slips. Some are purely linguistic. When speakers begin to utter one of the choices, they may decide to switch to another after they have passed the point of no return or have uttered a fraction of the first choice. For example, an acquaintance who said "moptimal productivity" might have switched her decision from "maximum" to "optimal" after it was too late to abort the initial "m" of "maximum." But this explanation seems somewhat limited.

A theory known as "spreading activation" offers a more versatile explanation of verbal competition. According to this theory, a person's lexicon, or mental dictionary, is organized so that each word in it is interconnected with other words associated by meaning, sound or grammar—somewhat like the interconnection of points in a com-

plex spider web. When we prepare to speak, the relevant parts of the web are activated, causing reverberation within the system. Activation spreads first to the most closely related words, then to words associated with them and so on. Each word activates an alternate path through the web. The cumulative activation for each word is tallied by checking how often each "point" in the web "vibrates," and the word with the highest accumulated activation (the most vibration, in our web analogy) is selected. Verbal slips would be explained as the result of competing choices that have equal or nearly equal activation levels.

For example, I recently told a colleague who needed information for her son Aaron that she could get it by phoning my wife. I suggested that she "wait for about an hour, because [my wife] is running an Aaron." According to the spreading activation theory, my mental dictionary was receiving activation on the word "Aaron," because he was one of the subjects

of the conversation, on "errand" as a topic of the message and on "Aaron," again, because of its association by sound with "errand." Since "Aaron" got a double dose of activation, it won the cumulative-activation competition, so to speak.

Or consider the slip of an older colleague who identified a motion-picture character as "one of the black women in *The Colored Purple* instead of *The Color Purple*. It is easy to imagine that in this person's mental dictionary, "colored" received activation both as a variation of "color" and as an archaic synonym for "black." Thus, its cumulative activation might have been greater than that of the intended word.

Thus far, spreading activation theorists have not considered the possibility that competing words might be related by something other than meaning, sound or grammar. Sigmund Freud, howev-

er, long ago introduced the idea that verbal slips represent the hidden motives and anxieties of the speaker. We can still call them "Freudian slips," and, as with the cognitive explanation, there is an intuitive sensibility to Freud's notion, at least for some verbal slips. For example, it would explain a mistake I once made when introduced to a competitor at a job interview. Intending to say "Pleased to meet you, " I slipped and said instead, "Pleased to beat you."

Until recently, however, Freud's explanation of verbal slips had been dismissed by most contemporary researchers. The relatively few slips that appear to be related to hidden thoughts were said to be linked by mere coincidence.

There were two arguments against the Freudian explanation. First, there was no known cognitive mechanism by which Freudian slips might operate. It is easy to imagine hidden thoughts that might prompt a local newscaster to proclaim to his voluptuous coanchor that "Bill Cosby is one of the breast bite lights on television," but it is quite difficult to explain the mental operations by which his hidden thoughts could have affected his originally intended utterance "best bright lights." Since it was difficult for many of those interested in the subject to imagine how Freudian slips might occur, it was difficult to believe that they did.

The second criticism of Freud's notion of verbal slips was that his theory was untestable. We can hypothesize, for example, that certain hidden thoughts caused a slip I once heard about a camping trip: "Ron often perks Jackie" instead of "Ron often packs jerky." But it has always seemed difficult to devise methods for testing such hypotheses objectively.

> **Sigmund Freud long ago introduced the idea that verbal slips represent hidden thoughts and anxieties.**

Both of these arguments have been tempered, however, with the development, over the past several years, of laboratory methods for studying slips of the tongue and Freudian hypotheses in particular.

Freud claimed that hidden thoughts can influence our choice of words, even in everyday speech without verbal slips. To test this claim, my colleagues and I asked men to read aloud and complete a series of fill-in-the-blank sentences. Half of them did this while being mildly sexually aroused—an attractive and provocatively attired woman administered the experiment—while the other half read and completed the sentences in the presence of a man.

In line with Freud's suggestion, word choices that related to sex as well as completed the sentence were almost twice as frequent for men who were sexually aroused. For example, to complete the sentence, "The old hillbilly kept his moonshine in big...," most men in the nonarousal group answered "vats," "barrels" or "jars," while "jugs" was the overwhelming answer of the aroused group. In another example, given the sentence, "Tension mounted at the end, when the symphony reached its...," most of the men in the nonaroused group responded "finale," "conclusion" or "peak," while those in the aroused group were much more likely to answer "climax."

Spreading activation of hidden thoughts could account for these results. Both groups of men probably experienced activation on words that would complete the sentences, but it seems that in the aroused group another set of items—words related to sex and sexy women—was also activated. For those who were aroused, the double-entendre words, "jugs" and "climax," received double doses of activation and were selected. This suggests that hidden thoughts can activate our mental dictionary, much as Freud suggested.

If hidden thoughts can compete to influence deliberate word choices, might they also create competition that leads to slips of the tongue? It is possible to produce slips of the tongue by asking people to read silently pairs of words that are flashed on a screen at one-second intervals, after being instructed that if a buzzer sound, they are to pronounce aloud the word pair then on the screen. This process can yield very interesting results. After seeing "let double" and "left decimal," for example, an attempt to say "dead level" will sometimes result in the slip "led devil."

My colleagues and I have used a variation of this procedure to test Freud's claim about verbal slips. One group of men performed the word-pair task believing that they were going to receive an electric shock at some pint, while another group of men performed the task

There is an intuitive sensibility to Freud's notion, yet until recently it had been dismissed by many researchers.

with mild sexual arousal—again in the form of a provocative female experimenter. For both groups, the lists and the words to be spoken loud were identical. Each list contained an equal number of words that could result in slips related to electric shocks or to sexy women.

As Freud might have predicted, the two groups made quite different kinds of mistakes. The men expecting an electric shock were much more likely to make slips such as "damn shock" instead of "sham dock," and "cursed wattage" instead of "worst cottage." Those tested in the presence of the female experimenter were more likely to make slips such as "fast passion" instead of "past fashion," and "nude breasts" instead of "brood nests." Also, men who had been found to be more anxious in general about sexual matters made an especially high number of sex-related slips if they were aroused.

Experiments such as these have given support to Freud's claim that hidden thoughts and anxieties can influence verbal slips. Even more importantly, they are consistent with the spreading activation theory that explains competition between cognitively and linguistically similar choices. Apparently, choices can be activated in the network, whether they originate from the message we intend or from hidden thoughts.

While experiments ad to our understanding of slips, another issue remains to be settled: Freud claimed that virtually all slips of the tongue derive from unconscious hidden thoughts. If this were true, however, hidden motives would be responsible not only for slips such as that made by a neighbor who approached a female cocktail-party guest saying, "I don't' believe we've been properly seduced yet—I mean introduced yet," but for more innocuous slips, such as saying "chee kanes" instead of "key chains," or "coregaty" instead of "category."

Just as the results of experiments make it unreasonable to insist that no slips are Freudian, the spreading activation theory makes it unreasonable to insist that they all are. For many slips of the tongue, the hidden-motive interpretation seems needlessly circuitous. For example, one of three professors at a recent meeting proposed that funding for a special seminar might be available "once we get underground—I mean under way." One might argue that

---

Just as the results of experiments make it unreasonable to insist that no slips are Freudian, it also seems unreasonable to insist that they all are.

---

the "underground" slip shows some sort of guilt or surreptitiousness in the speaker's attitude toward the groups objectives. But one might argue, just as easily, the interpretation that "underground" was the innocuous outcome of competition between "once we get under way" and the colloquial "once we get off the ground," with an extra boost on "underground" coming from similarity to a third alternative "once we're on solid ground," for example.

It seems likely then that the explanation for slips of the tongue lies between the two extremes of those who insist on Freudian interpretations and those who completely exclude them. Most slips probably are the result of verbal competition, with hidden thoughts as the source of the competition in some cases and simple message alternatives providing the competition in others. There is no need to posit hidden motives for slips such as "comprinter puteout" instead of "computer printout," or "offewsional" instead of "occasional." With enough imagination, one might hypothesize hidden thoughts behind these slips, but simpler explanations can be found: "Computer printout" probably competed with "printer output" while "occasional" vied with "few."

On the other hand, hidden motives seem much more likely for slips such as that committed by a lecturer who announced his topic as "Fraud's theories" instead of "Freud's Theories," or the embarrassing reference to an engagement ring as a "garish cheapsake" in lieu of "cherished keepsake." One might dream up competing message choices for these slips, but the most straightforward explanation is competition from hidden thoughts.

For some slips, the derivation will be impossible to determine. I remember being in an especially in elegant diner, for example, and ordering a "chilled grease sandwich" when I meant to order a "grilled cheese sandwich." While I assumed that the slip came from competition with an alternative verbal choice, "cheese sandwich," the waitress assumed that It had originated with a hidden thought, "greasy spoon diner." Which interpretation is correct? All that can be said is that both are reasonable possibilities.   ◆

Discussion Questions

1. Why do linguists study verbal slips?

2. What have psychologists discovered about why verbal slips occur?

3. What is a lexicon?

4. Describe spreading activation theory.

5. Discuss at least two reasons why Freud's explanation for verbal slips has not been accepted.

6. How, if at all, does Freud's theory explain everyday speech errors?

7. Give personal examples of verbal slips, and explain why each may have occurred.

8. Which theory of verbal slips does Motley support and why?

BREAKAWAY MINDS:
A CONVERSATION WITH
HOWARD **Gruber**

◆ *Howard Gardener*

Howard Gardner: Your approach to the study of creativity is quite different from that of other researchers. Will you explain how?

Howard Gruber: Some researchers, influenced by Freud or by personality theory, have looked for the personal characteristics of creative people, qualities like nonconformity or sublimated sexuality. That's important and interesting, but it does not explain the development of a person's special scholarly or artistic or scientific contribution, which is what I'm looking for. A few researchers have been interested in the cognitive aspects of creativity, as I am, but almost without exception they have looked for a particular cognitive trait—tolerance of ambiguity, for example, or "divergent thinking"—and then tried to find that trait in individuals deemed creative—for example, successful architects.

Gardner: And your method?

Gruber: I start with an individual whose creativity is beyond dispute—a Charles Darwin or a Jean Piaget. And then I try to map, as carefully as I can, what was going on in that person's mind over a period in which creative breakthroughs were occurring. Unlike the historian or biographer, I—and psychologists like me—try to build a model to figure out the underlying changes in thought and to uncover the path followed in solving problems.

Gardner: Can you give me an example?

Gruber: In my book on Darwin, my inquiry was aimed at mapping the changes in Darwin's thought during the 18 months that began when he returned to London from the *Beagle* voyage. It was a period of intense theoretical work, done very privately and recorded in his marvelous *Transmutation Notebooks*. In scientific circles, young Darwin was then a celebrity and much sought after, yet he found the quiet time to think the momentous thoughts that produced the theory of evolution.

Gardner: Could you explain more specifically how you work? How, for example, did you use Darwin's notebooks?

Gruber: The notebooks are a grab bag, with much of the writing in Darwin's own idiosyncratic terminology, abbreviations, and private language. I proceeded like an explorer in a new territory, reading the notebooks through, over and over again, figuring out what he was focusing on, what his cryptic

---

I try to map what was going on in a person's mind during the period of intense activity before a breakthrough.

---

notes meant, trying to recreate his thought processes from one day to the next. I tried to freeze the current of his thinking at crucial points. One discovery I made was

how long it takes to think through a new idea.

Gardner: Did anyone think otherwise?

Gruber: Of course they did, and still do. One of the best-known books about creativity is Arthur Koestler's *The Act of Creation*. The title alone gives the picture: the *act*. Koestler claims that the essential event in developing new ideas is "bisociation"—the sudden coming together of two things that had never been combined. He never, by the way, says why it's only two. Another example of instantaneous new ideas is the sudden reorganizations that are the favorites of Gestalt theory. The process is quite different, but the speed element is the same.

Gardner: Can you take us through some of the steps in Darwin's thought during the period you studied? For example, did Darwin have a theory of evolution when he began his notebooks?

Gruber: Oh yes. Quite a strange one from a modern point of view. In early 1837, Darwin came to believe that there were separate elementary forms, called monads, which sprang into life spontaneously. A monad—Lamarck also used the term—was a hypothetical elementary living form. Once created, monads began to evolve in the manner of an irregularly branching tree, with species proliferating upon each branch. But Darwin soon ran into a problem: how did certain species become extinct?

Gardner: Did he have an answer?

Gruber: Only an unsatisfactory one. He drew a parallel between an individual and a species: perhaps a species' life span depended on the monad from which it sprang; then, when the monad's time was up, life would be over for the various species that it had evolved into. Presumably, there would be a mass "death" of species in the geological record.

Gardner: I assume the record didn't show that.

Gruber: No, it didn't. But lack of evidence wasn't the only problem. Darwin had just finished five years of mental struggle against so-called catastrophist theories of earth history. He no longer believed the Biblical story of the flood, and he was skeptical that any permanent phenomena came about by sudden disasters on a global scale.

Gardner: So the monad theory collapsed of its own weight?

Gruber: Yes, giving rise to his "becoming" theory. Later in 1837, Darwin had the notion that certain older species might just give rise to newer ones. That was important, because the fossil record in fact showed that old species sometimes survived and sometimes did not. But he still needed a way of deciding *which* species would survive and which would give way to offspring.

Gardner: He needed the mechanism of selection.

Gruber: Correct. And probably the most important clue to the solution of that mystery came to Darwin when in September of 1838 he happened to be reading—"for amusement," he said—Malthus's essay on population. Given the struggle for existence that Malthus described, it struck Darwin that favorable variations of a species would tend to be preserved and unfavorable ones destroyed. And the result of that would be the emergence of a new species. But another few months went by before Darwin arrived at the principle of natural selection. So you can at least glimpse something of the lengthy, complex pondering that led to Darwin's great theory. It didn't happen in a magical moment.

Gardner: You are not the only psychologist to think in terms of slow growth processes of the mind.

Gruber: No, of course not, and that's what is exciting about my finding. Piaget, working with children, found that the growth of their ideas is a process spread over years. Now that we are learning about adult creative work in this new way, we can compare two radically different developmental processes that have some important points in common. Each will illuminate the other.

Gardner: Your method for studying creativity is the case study, an intensive examination of the workings of a single mind. It's hard to make empirically valid generalizations with an *n* of only one.

Gruber: I like quantitative research, but only when it's the right thing to do. If your task is to understand structure—for example, the emergence of a highly organized theory—measuring isolated variables may lead you down blind alleys. The most important element in developing the theory of evolution turned out to be an image—the irregularly branching tree of nature. That was the first diagram Darwin drew in connection with the theory. And he revised it over and over again. In a highly evolved form, that diagram is the only one in the *Origin of Species*. I've tried to collect all the tree diagrams Darwin made over the years. Each one is a little different and makes some special point. If I had been focusing on only one variable—for example, his references to a special topic like hybridization—I would have been unable to see the evolving structure of is argument.

Gardner: Are these Darwinian trees well known?

Gruber: No. Of course, everyone knows the one in the *Origin*. But most of the others are buried in the manuscript collection. My friend Martin Rudwick has written that his colleagues in the history of science, like most psychologists, tend to be too verbal—they aren't interested in the visual language of science. The neglect of Darwin's trees is a good case in point. I call this kind of visualization an "image of wide scope."

Gardner: Are such images common in creative breakthroughs?

Gruber: They are probably essential. When Einstein was 16, he imagined himself riding a beam of light. This empathetic image of the observer traveling with the thing observed was carried over into his mature theory of relativity.

Gardner: Do only creative people have such images?

Gruber: I imagine everyone has them. The difference is that creative people make new ones and then use them persistently in their work. Images of wide scope are not only tools of expression. The same image may enter into a number of different metaphorical explanations. Take the image of a compressed gas in a closed container. It can be used in understanding all sorts of explosive situations: volcanoes, social revolution, or sexual expression. If we are trying to understand Freud's thinking, for example, we would want to see just how and where he uses this volcano imagery.

Gardner: You've not just immersed yourself in the long-term studies of Darwin and Piaget but have also reviewed the lives of many other creative people in the sciences and the arts. What characteristics distinguish highly creative people?

Gruber: Well, the one thing you can be sure of is that each one is different. What attracts us to each is the special thing he or she accomplished. Why, then, should we expect them to be alike? We might say that Piaget grew increasingly abstract, while Darwin, having reached his maximum degree of abstractness early in life, remained

> **Creative people have a 'network of enterprises'— seemingly unrelated activities that they juggle with ease.**

at that level of abstraction from then on or even grew somewhat more concrete toward the end. Not only did they work in very different ways, their developmental curves were different.

Gardner: Does that mean creative individuals have nothing in common?

Gruber: No, no. There are certainly some general characteristics. For one thing, to be creative you need to know a lot and cultivate special skills. Darwin studied barnacles for eight years and came to know more about them than anyone else. Leonardo drew a thousand hands.

Gardener: They sound very determined.

Gruber: Yes. The most stable generalization about the creative life is that you work hard, probably for a long time. Of course, in working you transform yourself, and what would be hard for others becomes easy for you. Freeman Dyson, the physicist, describes how as an adolescent he discovered the calculus and spent the whole summer working like a madman, solving every problem in a big calculus textbook. After that, the calculus seemed to be almost instinctive.

Gardner: You make this hard work sound like fun.

Gruber: Yes, that's another characteristic. For the creative person, the greatest fun is the work. I think you have to take notice when Darwin says he read Malthus "for amusement."

Gardner: So creative people combine a zest for work with a capacity for play. They're not just workaholics?

Gruber: George Santayana once said that a fanatic is a person who redoubles his efforts when he loses sight of his objective. The people we are talking about do not lose sight of their objectives. Ergo, they are not fanatical workaholics.

Gardner: Psychoanalysts writing about creativity stress the role of unconscious motives. But your remarks imply a conscious "sense of purpose."

Gruber: Yes, the people I've studied all tend to be strong, robust, energetic. They have an overall sense of purpose, a feeling of where they are and where they want to go. That goal-directedness guides the choice of a whole set of enterprises and dictates which enterprise to focus on at a given time. Creative people have a network of enterprises. They become the sort of people who can easily handle seemingly different but intimately related activities. They become highly skilled jugglers. Of course, it's not all entirely conscious, but a great deal of it is.

Gardner: Can you give me an example of "enterprise juggling?"

Gruber: Take Bertrand Russell. Over a very long life he pursued one set of interests in mathematical philosophy and another set of interests in world politics, especially pacifism and, later, nuclear disarmament. They were not specific projects with end points, but ongoing, permanent enterprises. And he managed to orchestrate them quite skillfully. Toward the end of World War I, he was im-

> *At 16, Einstein imagined himself riding a beam of white light. The image led into relativity theory.*

> *Creative people have a sense of problem bracketing. That is, they know that when an issue is fundamental but cannot be settled, they must put it aside—bracket it— at least for a while, and concentrate on the work that can be done.*

prisoned by the British government for his antiwar writings. He wrote a number of philosophical articles in jail, as well as the *Introduction to Mathematical Philosophy,* That's juggling!

Gardner: Does every creative person have a network of enterprises as wide as Russell's or the other giants you have studied?

Gruber: We are just beginning to get a feel for that subject. I don't suppose that all creative networks are so wide. They probably differ in many ways—in their width and complexity, their interconnectedness, the duration of the projects, and so on. So far, the people we've looked at have rather complex and enduring sets of purposes.

Gardener: Do they have a technique for putting one enterprise "on hold" while dealing with another?

Gruber: I think so. Creative people have a sense of problem bracketing. That is, they know that when an issue is fundamental but cannot be settled, they must put it aside—bracket it—at least for a while, and concentrate on the work that can be done.

Gardner: Is such bracketing a useful habit for everyone?

Gruber: It's useful, yes, but it might be risky to make a habit of it. You may bracket something carelessly, something that would turn out to be the heart of the matter and something you could have handled had you not put if on hold. But scientists are working near the borders of what we know, so for them bracketing often has a special urgency. In Newton's case, when he postulated the existence of gravity he had to assume that bodies could act on other bodies at a distance, a strange idea that he didn't like any more than anyone else did. He suspected the cause would have something to do with the inner structure of matter, but it was too early to find out—not enough was known at the time about the structure of matter. So, in effect, he bracketed the problem.

Darwin had a similar difficulty in developing the theory of evolution. He had to make assumptions about heredity, but there was no theory of genetics that was of very much use at the time—Mendel's work wasn't known until later.

Gardner: One psychologist, Phillip Johnson-Laird, has suggested that scientists need a "destruction machine" to eliminate from their consideration problems on which they might get hung up for years and still not solve.

Gruber: Darwin didn't do that, exactly. Instead of destroying the genetics problem, he bracketed it over and over, and then he'd have another whack at it. The practice of glancing occasionally at these treacherous topics reminds me of a medieval map whose unexplored areas are marked with the enticing phrase "unknown seas," or, "here be dragons."

Gardner: They weren't enticing to medieval sailors!

Gruber: That suggests another very important aspect of creative people. When most of us encounter a problem or difficulty, we have a tendency to shut our eyes, to mark it as "unknown." The creative people I've suited favor a course of daring, of challenging the world. Though Darwin is often depicted as a cautious and sickly man, it took great physical courage to travel for five years on the *Beagle*. And it took great intellectual courage to publish a theory that was certain to bring down the wrath of his family and friends, not to say the religious establishment of England.

Gardner: That touches upon a somewhat sensitive issue. Can you have creative people in societies that impose sever sanctions against breaking away? Some Japanese, for example, have been obsessed with the question of why so few of their scientists win Nobel Prizes. One explanation is that the Japanese put so much value on not getting out of line with the group that a single individual is wary abut showing too much initiative. So while you have great technological progress in Japan through the work of teams, you don't get the solitary Faustian figure of Western science.

Gruber: There are really two parts to that question. One is about the solitary Faustian figure. I don't think there are many of them. For example, even when Einstein was deeply immersed in the most abstract topics, he had people he could talk to—and some of them he talked to a lot. The second question is whether too much conformity is possible in society. I don't know much about Japan, but no society is all that monolithic, even when it wants to be. It's possible that in Japan, the conformity pressure you're talking about combines with a view of nature that is different from the Western perspective. Suppose you have a view of man as a participant in nature rather than a master of it, the usual Western notion. For the intellectual tasks we've had up to now, that may not be a very fruitful approach. But I leave open the possibility that a gentler attitude toward nature my turn out to be more illuminating and more fruitful in meeting our future needs.

The people I've studied tend to be strong, robust, energetic. Their work is a high for them, like sex.

Gardner: I'm surprised to hear you question the idea that creative people tend to be isolated.

Gruber: That idea is usually exaggerated. Darwin and Piaget were both extremely skillful in collaborating with others. Newton may be the most extreme case of scientific isolation that we know. And even he had important, fruitful scientific relationships with his peers.

Gardner: How do creative people interact with their peers, then? They don't just work within established peer groups, do they?

Gruber: That's a good point. Creative people must use their skills to devise environments that foster their work. They must invent new peer groups appropriate to their projects. Being creative means striking out in new directions and not accepting ready-made relationships, which takes stamina and a willingness to be alone for a while.

Gardner: Thee's a clear element of courage, then, in being creative?

Gruber: Yes, and not only to say the new and possibly dangerous things that need saying but also the courage to refashion one's personal world.

Gardner: How does that courage develop?

Gruber: Sometimes it doesn't come until late in life, when a person's work matures to the point where an individual and unique voice is required. Sometimes it emerges early. When Bertrand Russell was 15, he began to write about his religious doubts, which gave him much pain. He recorded his thoughts in a very private notebook. In fact, he took the trouble to invent a secret notation consisting of Greek letters and a phonetic spelling of English. He did not have the courage to tell his family that he no longer believed in the existence of an immortal soul. But he did have the courage to think thoughts that were most painful to him. And when he was a grown man 50 years later, he had the courage to defend these views publicly, which cost him his job at the City College of New York.

Gardner: Courage, hard work, juggling open-ended enterprises. In spite of what you've said about play, it sounds overwhelming.

Gruber: Taking a step into the unknown is serious business, but exhilarating, too. Over and over again, I discover that creative people love their work and would not dream of doing anything else. They have very high levels of aspiration, and it excites them to feel that they are doing great things. It's a high for them, like sex.

Gardner: That's a hard line to follow. But I want to put one more question to you. Would you name two or three artists or scientists whose thinking you would like to explore from the standpoint of its creativity?

Gruber: I'm interested in the interpenetration of different levels of experience and in the relations among different modalities of thought. That makes me want to look at people who worked in more than one medium or whose modalities of thought were particularly interesting. The artist-poet William Blake is one example. The inventor-theoretician Thomas Edison is another. His conceptual framework is still be be unearthed, but it will surely be fascinating.

Gardner: Is there any final point you want to make?

Gruber: Yes. We know far too little about how people work together. There are some beautiful collaborations. Marx and Engels, Russell and Whitehead, Wordsworth and Coleridge, Helen Keller and Anne Sullivan, Picasso and Braque, Inhelder and Piaget, Marie and Pierre Curie. The way that people retain their individuality while combining their efforts and talents in something that transcends them both—understanding that is vital to the survival of humanity.

Gardner: Why do you say this?

Gruber: Inventing the capacity we now have to destroy our environment and ourselves—through all sorts of pollution, but especially through thermonuclear war—took years of patient collaborative work among many creative people. This process of self-destruction is moving very rapidly now. We need the most creative and manysided effort the world has ever known to invent and implement new solutions. This is not a task for lonely genius. The solution must be a new way of thinking and acting. This is a social invention and making it must therefore be a social process.   ◆

◆ **Discussion Questions**
_____

1. What is a "network of enterprises?"

2. Explain the term "bracketing."

3. Compare Freud's theory of creativity to Howard Gruber's conception of creativity.

4. How does Gruber try to discover the creative process of an individual?

5. What is Koestler's concept of "bisociation," and how does Gruber criticize it?

6. What is time course for the development of a creative idea?

7. Compare Gruber's creativity theory to Piaget's developmental theory.

8. What role does visualization play in creativity?

9. Describe at least three characteristics of a creative person.

10. What type of environments do you think Gruber would consider ideal for fostering creativity? Include both physical and social environments.

Name: _____

Date: _____

Part 9: Cognition and Language

1. I believe I am a highly creative person.

Agree ① ② ③ ④ ⑤ Disagree

2. Creativity is rare, and it certainly cannot be taught.

Agree ① ② ③ ④ ⑤ Disagree

3. I believe in Freud's view that verbal slips indicate important things about the unconscious mind.

Agree ① ② ③ ④ ⑤ Disagree

List four methods for improving creativity from Epstein's article, "Capturing Creativity." For the next two days, practice using these techniques, and record as many of your new ideas as possible, even if the ideas don't seem to have immediate value. Were the techniques helpful? How so?

Methods:

New ideas:

Check your list after a week. Has the apparent value of any of the ideas changed? How so?

Pick one of the new ideas from your list, and see if you can trace the process by which the new ideas arose, using Howard Gruber's methodology.

PART 10

CHILD DEVELOPMENT

As an undergraduate I took a semester course on Jean Piaget—probably the most influential developmental psychologist in history—in which context I tried to read two of his books. Even though I was reading English translations of the original French, and even though I am a native English speaker, I found the writing to be nearly incomprehensible. Yet I had heard from my professor that Piaget was witty and clear in person. The first article in this section proves the point. In this 1970 interview, published about 10 years before his death, Piaget states his basic views on child development with clarity and charm.

In the next piece, an early article by Lewis P. Lipsitt, we learn that newborns (or "neonates") are sensitive to a variety of environmental stimuli and, more important, that they are capable of significant learning. Because babies have these capabilities, Lipsitt implies that infants need some sort of special training or stimulation in order to achieve normal or superior development, but recent research disputes that.

In "Dreams of Innocence," David Foulkes debunks the notion that children's dreams are cesspools of Freudian fears, finding instead that children's dreams are fairly mundane. Finally, in "Play Is Serious Business," Jerome Bruner talks about play in both monkeys and human children and makes a strong case for the importance of play for later problem solving and creativity.

A CONVERSATION with Jean Piaget

◆ *Elizabeth Hall*

Jean Piaget: I must warn you that I cannot understand English when it is pronounced properly. If you will say *zis* and *zat* and *zhose,* I will be able to follow you.

Elizabeth Hall: And if you promise to speak French wretchedly, I might understand you. But luckily we have Guy Cellerier here to solve our language problems.

You and Sigmund Freud are regarded as the two giants of 20th-Century philosophy. If Freud has changed our thinking about personality, you have certainly changed our thinking about intelligence, yet a great deal of confusion surrounds your work. Whenever someone tries to explain your theories to the rest of us, he succeeds only in obscuring them.

Piaget: Yes, I've seen that done. Perhaps we will do better today.

Hall: It is interesting that both Fred Skinner and D.O. Hebb intended to become novelists.

Piaget: Is that so?

Hall: I was surprised myself when I first heard it. They regard intelligence empirically, while you began as a natural scientist and look at intelligence philosophically.

Piaget: First we must agree on what you mean by philosophical. All the problems I have attacked are epistemological. All the methods I have used are either experimental or formalizations that Americans would also regard as empirical.

Hall: Psychology was originally a part of philosophy; William James was a philosopher. You have raided the field of philosophy again and captured the area of epistemology.

Piaget: It is true that I have taken epistemology away from philosophy, but I have not taken it only for psychology. It belongs in all the sciences; they are all concerned with the nature and origin of knowledge.

Hall: What caused you to turn from biology and the study of mollusks to epistemology?

Piaget: I began to study mollusks when I was 10. The director of the Museum of Natural History in Neuchâtel, who was a mollusk specialist, invited me to assist him twice a week. I helped him stick labels on his shell collection and he taught me malacology. I began publishing articles about shells when I was 15.

Hall: That's quite young to be publishing scientific papers.

Piaget: Specialists in malacology are rare. Because I was so young, I had to decline invitations from foreign specialists who wanted to meet me. My first paper—a one-page report of a part-albino sparrow I had seen—was published when I was only 10. It was about the time that I began to publish articles on shells that I found a book on philosophy in my father's library. My new passion for philosophy was encouraged when my godfather introduced me to Henri Bergson's creative evolution. Sud-

denly the problem of knowledge appeared to me in a new light. I became convinced very quickly that most of the problems in philosophy were problems of knowledge, and that most problems of knowledge were problems of biology. You see, the problem of knowledge is the problem of the relation between the subject and the object—how the subject knows the object. If you translate this into biological terms, it is a problem of the organism's adapting to its environment. I decided to consecrate my life to this biological explanation of knowledge.

Hall: With your interest in the relation between the subject and the object, I am surprised that you did not become Gestalt psychologist.

Piaget: If I had come across the writings of Max Wertheimer and of Wolfgang Köhler when I was 18, I would have. But I was reading psychology only in French, so I was unacquainted with their work.

Hall: In your autobiography, you said that your natural-history background provided protection against the demon of philosophy.

Piaget: The demon of philosophy is taking the easy way out. You believe that you can solve problems by sitting in your office and reasoning them out. Because I was a biologist, I knew that deductions must be made from facts.

> *I always preferred the workings of the intellect to the tricks of the unconscious.*

Hall: But after you establish the facts, then you go back to your office and work out the problem.

Piaget: Yes. Now, if you don't have a philosophical outlook, you probably won't be a good scientist. Abstract reflection is fundamental to seeing problems clearly. But the error of philosophy—its demon—is to believe that you can go ahead and solve the problem you formulated in the office without going into the field and establishing the facts.

Hall: You once wrote that you detested any departure from reality.

Piaget: That was because of my mother's poor mental health. At the beginning of my studies in psychology, I was interested in psychoanalysis and pathological psychology because of her. But I always preferred the workings of the intellect to the tricks of the unconscious.

Hall: Does your dislike of unreality extend to literature?

Piaget: Oh, no. I read many novels—and I even wrote a philosophical novel many years ago. Novels are not pathological.

Hall: I understand that your study of intelligence came about when you tried to standardize reasoning tests at Alfred Binet's laboratory school in Paris.

Piaget: It was Binet's school, but I was not working on Binet's test. My task was to standardize Cyril Burt's tests on the children of Paris. I never actually did it. Standardization was not at all interesting; I preferred to study the errors on the test. I became interested in the reasoning process behind the children's wrong answers.

Hall: Has anyone tried to develop an intelligence test based on your research?

Piaget: That kind of research is going on in two places right now. Here at the University of Geneva, Vinh Bang—a Vietnamese psychologist—is working on a test. And Monique Laurendeau and Adrien Pinard, two psychologists at the University of Montreal, have been using my experimental methods and giving all the various tests to a single child. Just now they are back-checking to see if their experiments and mine produce similar results, and they are publishing volumes on different aspects of the experiments.

Hall: Would such a test have to be an individual test, or could it be given to a group of children at one time?

Piaget: The hope is that we will have a battery of tests that can be

Jean Piaget

given to a group of children together. The risk is that we will get deformed answers.

Hall: Isn't a group test more likely to run aground on the same shoals that wreck the standard tests—a reliance on the answer instead of the method of reasoning?

Piaget: The difference will be that the clinical method will already have been used in studying the reasoning of children at each stage

of development. We will have a background to help interpret the answers. It will have advantages that the I.Q. test lacks because the method of reasoning is unknown.

Hall: Your research—especially in conservation—revealed that children did not understand things that adults assumed they knew.

Piaget: It's just that no adult ever had the idea of asking children about conservation. It was so obvious that if you change the shape of an object, the quantity will be conserved. Why ask a child? The novelty lay in asking the question.

I first discovered the problem of conservation when I worked with young epileptics from 10 to 15. I wanted to find some empirical way of distinguishing them from normal children. I went around with four coins and four beads, and I would put the coins and beads in one-to-one correspondence and then hide one of the coins. If the three remaining coins were then stretched out into a longer line, the epileptic children said they had more coins than beads. No conservation at all. I thought I had discovered a method to distinguish normal from abnormal children. Then I went to work with normal children and discovered that all children lack conservation.

Hall: Isn't it fortunate that you checked?

Piaget: A biologist would have to verify; a philosopher would not have checked.

Hall: When you say that the young child is egocentric, just what do you mean?

Piaget: That term has had the worst interpretations of any word I have used.

Hall: That's why I asked the question.

Piaget: When I refer to the child, I use the term egocentric in an epistemological sense, not in an effective or a moral one. This is why it has been misinterpreted. The egocentric child—and all children are egocentric—considers his own point of view as the only possible one. He is incapable of putting himself in someone else's place, because he is unaware that the other person has a point of view.

Hall: Would this be analogous to man's original belief that the universe revolved around the earth?

Piaget: That is precisely the example I was going to give. It is a nat-

ural tendency of the intelligence and it becomes corrected very slowly as the child matures. Many children, you know, believe that the sun and the moon follow them as they walk. A more prosaic example is the way a young child makes up a new word and assumes that everyone knows exactly what he means by it.

The egocentric child— and all children are egocentric— considers his own point of view as the only possible one. He is incapable of putting himself in someone else's place, because he is unaware that the other person has a point of view.

Hall: Then morality doesn't enter the picture until the child is aware of other viewpoints and disregards them. At one time you did extensive work on the way children develop a sense of right and wrong.

Piaget: That was 40 years ago and I haven't gone back to it. But we can talk about it if you like.

Hall: I believe you said that the child's sense of moral judgment is largely independent of adult influence.

Piaget: You must distinguish between two periods in the development of moral judgment. In the first period, a child accepts his rules from authority and the ideas of adults are important to him. In the second period, he is independent of adults. Solidarity grows between children and a morality develops, based on cooperation.

Hall: As more mothers work, children are placed in nursery schools at earlier ages, and communal methods of life, like those in the kibbutz, are becoming more common. Suppose adults did not impose standards of right and wrong upon children who were reared in kibbutz. Would the children de-

velop this sense of moral justice and cooperation anyway?

Piaget: It would happen even earlier. And if the adults are ready to discuss matters seriously with the children they will form a system of cooperation with the adults.

Hall: Would the morality that developed under this cooperative system be likely to lessen the conflict between the generations?

Piaget: I would think so. Children often must discover the idea of justice at the expense of their parents. From about the age of seven or eight, justice prevails over obedience. But this theory should be studied experimentally.

Hall: You would have to go out into the field and test it.

Piaget: I have other pies in the oven.

Hall: I'm interested in the implications for education of the pies you've already baked. In the United States we have a concept called reading readiness. Some educators say that a child cannot learn to read until he has reached a mental age of six years and six months.

Piaget: The idea of reading readiness corresponds to the idea of competence in embryology. If a specific chemical inductor hits the developing embryo, it will produce an effect if the competence is there, and if it is not, the effect will not occur. So the concept of readiness is not bad but I am not sure that it can be applied to reading. Reading aptitude may not be related to mental age. There could easily be a difference of aptitude between children independent of mental age. But I cannot state that as a fact because I have not studied it closely.

Hall: In recent years the new mathematics has come into American schools. Along with a new vocabulary we introduced new concepts like set theory.

Piaget: Seven years would be perfectly all right for most operations of set theory because children have their own spontaneous operations that are very akin to those concepts. But when you teach set theory you should use the child's actual vocabulary along with activity—make the child do natural things. The important thing is not to teach modern mathematics with ancient methods.

As for teaching children concepts that they have not attained in their spontaneous development, it is completely useless. A British mathematician attempted to teach his five-year-old daughter the rudiments of set theory and conservation. He did the typical experiments of conservation with numbers. Then he gave the child two collections and the five-year-old immediately said those are two sets. But she couldn't count and she had no idea of conservation.

Hall: But she had the vocabulary.
Piaget: That's the point. You cannot teach concepts verbally; you must use a method founded on activity.
Hall: If you had the power in your hands, would you make any changes in the school curriculum?
Piaget: We spend so much time teaching things that don't have to be taught. Spelling is a good example. One learns to spell much better just by reading; teaching spelling is a waste of time. And history. We should reduce the amount of time we spend making people disgusted with history. We should concentrate on giving them a taste for reading history—which is not the same thing at all.

There is one addition I would like to make to the curriculum. So far as I know the experimental method is not taught in any school and it is a way of checking your hypotheses. If we can teach this method to children they will learn that it is possible to check their thoughts.
Hall: How would you go about teaching this?

Piaget: In the experimental method you have the problem of what causes a given effect. A certain number of factors intervene and—in order to discover the cause—you must keep all factors constant except one.
Hall: As when you gave the children five flasks of colorless liquid and asked them to produce yellow.
Piaget: That's right. One of the flasks contained only water, another flask contained bleach, and the other three liquids that when

---

Blindly to accelerate the learning of conservation concepts could be even worse than doing nothing.

---

mixed together turned yellow. We showed the child the color but not how to make it. The child also had to determine just what sort of liquid was in the flasks that held bleach and water. Not until a child reachers the age of 12 does he test all possible combinations of fluids and solve the problem.
Hall: What if the teacher were to demonstrate this experiment to the class?
Piaget: It would be completely useless. The child must discover the method for himself through his own activity.
Hall: That sounds very much like John Dewey's concept of learning by doing.
Piaget: Indeed it does; John Dewey was a great man.
Hall: Now that we've mentioned an American educator, may I ask what you have called "the American question"? Is it possible to speed up the learning of conservation concepts?

John Dewey was a great man.

Piaget: In turn may I ask the counter-question? Is it a good thing to accelerate the learning of these concepts? Acceleration is certainly possible but first we must find out

whether it is desirable or harmful. Take the concept of object permanency—the realization that a ball, a rattle or a person continues to exist when it no longer can be seen. A kitten develops this concept at four months, a human baby at nine months; but the kitten stops right there while the baby goes on to learn more advanced concepts. Perhaps a certain slowness is useful in developing the capacity to assimilate new concepts.

We also know that the ease of learning varies with the developmental level of the child. In the same number of learning sessions children who have reached an advanced stage make marked progress over younger children. It appears that there is an optimum speed of development. If you write a book too slowly it won't be a good book; if you write it too fast it won't be a good book either. No one has made studies to determine the optimum speed.
Hall: But wouldn't the optimum speed vary with the person? Some people naturally write faster than others—and write just as well.
Piaget: That's highly possible. We know the average speed of the children we have studied in our Swiss culture but there is nothing that says that the average speed is the optimum. But blindly to accelerate the learning of conservation concepts could be even worse than doing nothing.
Hall: I think we ask the American question because the ever-increasing length of education troubles us. Many of us would like to find some way to shorten those years that go into professional preparation.
Piaget: It is difficult to decide just how to shorten studies. If you spend one year studying something verbally that requires two years of active study, then you have actually

lost a year. If we were willing to lose a bit more time and let the children be active, let them use trial and error on different things, then the time we seem to have lost we may have actually gained. Children may develop a general method that they can use on other subjects.

Hall: And we come back to learning by doing. Some of your experiments with the child's concept of space indicate that children come to a Euclidian world view very slowly. Does this same conception of space evolve in all peoples, or is it a feature of Western culture?

Piaget: I wouldn't say that Euclidian geometry is cultural. You know, historically scientific geometry began with Euclidian metric geometry. Projective geometry followed and only later did we develop topology. But so far as theory goes, both projective and metric geometry can be derived from topology. Now if you examine the way a child develops his idea of space, you will see that he first develops topological intuitions, so that the child's ideas are closer to mathematical theory than to history. To get back to your question, any group—if they develop that far—would certainly acquire a Euclidean geometry, because once you have the topological intuitions and actual measurement, it is the simplest geometry.

Hall: Then you do not believe that our language determines the way we see the world?

Piaget: There is a very close relationship between language and thought, but language does not govern thoughts or form operations. It is language that is influenced by operations and not our operations that are influenced by language.

Dr. H. Sinclair has made some interesting experiments along this line. She had two groups of children; one group had conservation, the other group did not. She took the group of children that did not understand conservation and taught them the language used by the children who understood the concept. They learned to use "long" and "short" and "wide" and "narrow" in a consistent way.

There is a very close relationship between language and thought, but language does not govern thoughts or form operations.

She wanted to see if the concepts would come once the language was learned. They did not. If a ball of clay was pulled into a sausage, the children could describe it as "long" and "thin." But hey did not understand that the clay was longer but thinner than the ball and therefore the same quantity.

Hall: What if the language does not express a concept?

Piaget: The thing that changes with different languages is the way we partition reality—the way we break the world into composing parts. But this translation of concepts into their parts is not essential to thought.

Hall: Jerome Bruner has studied child development extensively and he is one of your respectful critics. Could you explain to me the difference between your theoretical approach and that of Bruner's?

Piaget: It is very difficult to explain the difference between Bruner and me. Bruner is a mobile and active man and has held a sequence of different points of view. Essentially Bruner does not believe in mental operations while I do. Bruner replaces operations with factors that have varied through his different stages—Bruner's stages, not the child's. Bruner uses things like language, like image. When Bruner was at the stage of strategies he used to say that his strategies were more or less Piaget's operations. At that time our theories were closest. Since then he has changed his point of view.

Hall: Might we say that one day Bruner may reach the operational stage?

Piaget: The answer to your question is that Bruner is an unpredictable man—this is what makes his charm.

Hall: Can we learn about man only by studying man? Or can we go into the laboratory and study rats and primates?

Piaget: Comparative studies are necessary but one must not make the mistake of believing that a rat is sufficient. Many theories of some schools that I will not name are based on the rat. It is not enough for me.

Hall: But I can mention a school of psychology. Could you describe your differences with behaviorism?

Piaget: That's too broad a term. Let's talk instead about behaviorist empiricalism; I think that's what you're really asking about. Empiricism implies that reality can be reduced to observable features and that knowledge must limit itself to those features. Biologists have shown that the organism constantly interacts with this environment; the view that it submits passively to the environment has become untenable. How then can man be simply a

---

Many theories of some schools that I will not name are based on the rat. It is not enough for me.

---

recorder of outside events? When he transforms his environment by acting upon it he gains a deeper knowledge of the world than any copy of reality ever could provide. What is more empiricism cannot explain the existence of mathematics which deals with unobservable features and with cognitive constructions.

In biology the exact counterpart of behaviorist empiricism is the Lamarckian theory of variation and evolution—a long-abandoned doctrine. When we look at the famous stimulus-response schema we find that behaviorist psychologists have retained a strictly Lamarckian outlook. The contemporary biological revolution has passed them by. If we are to get a tenable stimulus-response theory we must completely modify its classical meaning. Before a stimulus can set off a response the organism must be capable of providing it. We talked earlier about the idea of competence in embryology. If this concept applies in learning—and my research indicates that it does—then learning will be different at different developmental levels. It would depend upon the

---

Too often psychologists make practical applications before they know what they are applying.

---

evolution of competences. The classical concept of learning suddenly becomes inadequate.

Hall: Does this mean that individual development is all innate?

Piaget: Not at all. Each man is the product of interaction between heredity and environment. It is virtually impossible to draw a clear line between innate and acquired behavior patterns.

Hall: Are there any pitfalls to trap the unwary psychologist?

Piaget: The danger to psychologists lies in practical applications. Too often psychologists make practical applications before they know what they are applying. We must always keep a place for fundamental research and beware of practical applications when we do not know the foundation of our theories.

Hall: How do you see the future of psychology?

Piaget: With optimism. We see new problems every day. ◆

Discussion Questions

1. What is epistemology?

2. What does Piaget mean by the "demon of philosophy?"

3. What kind of intelligence test does Piaget talk about developing?

4. What does Piaget mean by "conservation," and what did Piaget learn about his ability in normal and abnormal children?

5. What does Piaget mean when he claims that children are "egocentric?"

6. Describe the two stages of moral judgment that Piaget mentions.

7. How would Piaget change the school curriculum, and why?

8. Discuss Piaget's concept of object permanence.

9. How does Piaget criticize Jerome Bruner's work?

Babies: They're a LOT Smarter Than They Look

◆ *Lewis P. Lipsitt*

Fifty years ago psychological learning theory applied to man and beast, but not to little babies. The newborn was a model of helplessness, unable to learn from experience in his first months. William James described the plight of the child who, "assailed by eyes, ears, nose, skin and entrails, feels that all is one great blooming, buzzing confusion."

The newborn infant was also a model of frustration. The mere physical design of a baby was enough to tax all but a mother's love. G. Stanley Hall, the father of American child psychology, described the plight of a researcher assailed by the buzzing confusion of a baby with "its monotonous and dismal cry, with its red, shriveled parboiled skin...squinting, cross-eyed, potbellied and bow legged."

Faith

Soviet pediatrician and physiologist N.I. Krasnogorsky, who applied Pavlov's classical conditioning techniques to children in the early part of this century, found that at least some of the older infant's behavior is caused by stimulation that is essentially identical to the kind that determines learning in lower animals. But it was also Krasnogorsky, perhaps over-impressed by the way learning speed increased with age, who extrapolated to the newborn and pronounced him incapable of learning. (Another Russian, N.I. Kasatkin, kept the faith; his studies of the behavior of newborn babies were keys to present understanding of the newborn's precocity. he showed in 1935 that infants less than 30 days old can develop differential sucking responses to tones varying by two octaves.)

Most early child-development research was devoted to devising test instruments to document the behavior status of the child. Parents and teachers wanted to know how a child compared to other children. Psychologists responded with the concept of I.Q. and mental age. This approach tended to emphasize the child's accomplishment of milestone behaviors, rather than the processes by which the child reached those milestones.

Child psychologists recognized that an infant's behavior changed with increasing chronological age, but they attributed the development to inherent biological factors. Experience did not shape behavior in the very young. In 1929, Arnold Gesell asserted that "There is no convincing evidence that the fundamental acceleration of development can be readily induced by either pernicious or enlightened methods of stimulation."

Walk

Because most children can walk by the time they are 14 months old, no matter what you do with them, psychologists did not bother much to study the conditions that cause a child to enter the walking stage. Researchers did not consider that differences between early walkers and late walkers might be the result of environmental factors that include specific training procedures. This oversight produced a generation of professionals, eager and able to diagnose retardation or other aberrations of development but quite disinterested in environmental or behavior modification.

If a four- or five-year-old child could not perform matching-to-sample tasks, or could not pick out the one object different from the rest, he was simply "not ready to read." He presumably suffered from some condition that limited his potential. No one ever suggested that the necessary conditions for acquiring the behavior had not been made available to the child.

Fourteen years ago my colleagues and I began an intensive study of the effect of the environment on the behavior of babies less than a month old. Evidence contradicts the old view that the very young child is an unresponsive vegetable that looks like every other member of the species at that age—an organism that can do nothing except breathe and eat. The new baby learns much the same way an adult learns, from the very first day of his life.

He arrives with all of his sensory systems functioning and he is clearly capable of communicating at least some of his perceptions and abilities to the watchful observer. He tells us what he hears and feels in the same way that any other inarticulate organism does—through systematic responses to stimulating events. The changes in

> **The new baby learns much the same way an adult learns, from the very first day of his life.**

behavior that result from such learning can help us understand the child's neurological status, the style in which he relates to his mother (and vice versa) and his eventual intellectual and psychomotor performance.

Touch

One of the basic phenomena of behavior change induced by the environment is habituation, the process by which an organism becomes accustomed to a particular set of circumstances. Our first encounter with the habituation response in newborn infants was in a series of classical conditioning experiments, specifically a withdrawal-learning study. We lightly stimulated the toe of an infant, who would withdraw his leg to escape the touch. We wanted to teach the infant that a tone, sounded just before (and continuing with) the touch, signaled the onset of the touch. If conditioning took place, the baby would withdraw his leg when he heard the tone.

We found that the infant's threshold for response to touch gradually increased: he became accustomed to it and stopped jerking his foot away. To continue the study of that type of learning, the intensity of the toe touch would have had to be increased considerably, just to maintain the unconditioned response.

At the same time, we realized that classical conditioning would be difficult to document in the newborn infant, particularly when we used a withdrawal-learning situation far removed from the face, which is the real business end of the infant. We suspected that learning would proceed most rapidly and gracefully under conditions that capitalized on the well-developed sensory and motor functions in the head region. In further studies we focused on the face and on the neural equipment associated with feeding.

Smell

With Trygg Engen and Herbert Kaye, I documented the process of habituation in newborn infants, using smells as the stimulant. Previous researchers had observed that babies respond to different smells, and that the vigor of the response corresponds to the intensity and quality of the stimulant. We wanted to see how an infant would react to repeated exposure to a given smell, and what change there would be in his response if we suddenly confronted him with a different smell.

At one-minute intervals we held a cotton swab saturated with anise oil (a licorice smell) or asafetida (a boiling-onionlike smell) in front of the infant's nose.

A polygraph recorded his bodily movements, respiration, and heart rate. When he first detected the smell, the baby moved his limbs, his breathing quickened, and his heart rate increased, but he gradually developed a disregard for the stimulant. Presumably he realized that the odor was not a threat. The level of the infant's respiration and body reaction declined gradually and reliably during the 10 trials.

After the first round of trials, we administered the alternate odor. The infant immediately showed interest in the novel stimulus, and repeated his initial pattern of response. The increased activity signaled that the child detected the change in stimulants. A new odor had replaced the old, and he was no longer bored. Thus

he communicated his ability to discriminate between two different stimulus events.

We repeated this experiment using a mixture of the two smells. After the baby had become accustomed to the mixture, we exposed him to one of the components. He reacted to this as if it were a new odor.

The newborn infant is a complicated information-processing creature. The change in behavior reveals more than a singular test for the presence of a smell. Habituation and the rapidity with which it occurs reflect the neurological condition of the baby. For example, a brain-damaged infant can smell, but studies have shown his capacity for change in response to repeated stimulation is impaired. And newborn babies who have undergone severe stress during birth or the prenatal period habituate much more slowly than normal babies do. Other studies indicate that the rate of habituation of a newborn child seems to relate to other measures of alertness at later ages.

> *The newborn infant is a complicated information-processing creature. The rate of habituation seems to relate to other measures of alertness at later ages.*

Suck

In other experiments we studied the sucking or food-taking behavior of the newborn child. Kaye and I found that the rate of sucking may increase or decrease depending on the sensory feedback at the time. We compared the behavior of infants who sucked on a nipple, a plain tube, or an alternating sequence of nipple and tube. We found that babies sucked faster at an ordinary commercial nipple than at a less-flexible, rounded tube. The immediate previous experience with the tube reduced the rate of nipple-sucking, while previous experience with the nipple increased tube-sucking.

The role of the shape and texture of the nipple, even in breast feeding, is very important. Mavis Gunther, an English pediatrician, has observed that newborns who do not seem to suck properly may be "instructed" to latch on more effectively through oral manipulation by the mother. Gunther has also suggested that adverse sucking experiences may cause the newborn child to reject the bottle or breast on later occasions. The infant is affected by the conditions that surround feeding. His reactions indicate that learning does occur at this age. If you stroke a newborn baby's face at the corner of the mouth, approximately 25 percent of the time the baby will turn his head in the direction of the touch. The so-called rooting reflex can be treated as a "controlled" operant, with the expectation that associating a reward with it will enhance its occurrence on subsequent occasions. Hanuš Papoušek of Prague found that he could reinforce the response systematically by feeding the infant for turning its head in the appropriate direction and not rewarding any trial in which the infant failed to turn his head properly.

Einar Siqueland and I elaborated on Papoušek's techniques in a series of experiments with babies two to four days old. We rested each baby's head in a swivel-cradle that automatically recorded any movement. Two auditory stimuli served as positive and negative cues for reinforcement of head-turns to the right. We divided 16 infants into two groups. When a baby in one group turned his head to the right in response

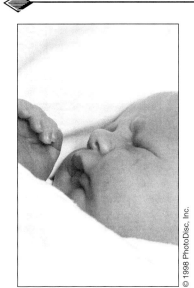

© 1998 PhotoDisc, Inc.

to Tone A, followed by a touch to the baby's cheek, we immediately gave him a bottle of formula and allowed him to eat for several seconds. We did not feed the baby for turning his head in response to Tone B plus touch. For the other group, Tone B was positive and Tone A was negative. We presented a stimulus every 30 seconds, and returned the baby's head to the midline position after each trial. In these conditions, responses to the positive stimulus increased rapidly. The group average increased from 25 percent to 70 percent within the half-hour training period. Response to the nonreinforced tone-touch stimulus changed negligibly.

Hear

Immediately after this training, we reversed the tone stimuli for both groups. The previously negative tone became positive and vice versa. We continued training. The infants altered their head-turning behavior, and turned more to the previously negative, now positive, stimulus than they did to the previously positive, now negative stimulus.

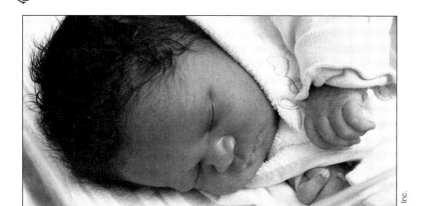

© 1998 PhotoDisc, Inc.

In a later study with newborn children, Siqueland showed that the head-turning response may even act as a free-operant. He increased the frequency of the response by rewarding the infant whenever he turned his head, and did not use any specific stimulus to elicit the response. He demonstrated, moreover, that the newborn infant's behavior follows the pattern well established in adults and in lower animals. A baby who has been fed each time he makes a desired response will stop responding when the reward is withdrawn much sooner than a baby who has been rewarded only part of the time.

Blink

Earlier, I suggested that our studies of the conditioning processes of the young infant progressed when we shifted from the study of an aversive response (leg-withdrawal) to the exploration of food-taking and associated behaviors. But recently, Arlene Little completed a study of classical eyelid conditioning in newborn infants. The eye-

blink response is universal in newborn children. It develops into a conditioned response (like flinching) in older children. The ability to acquire a conditioned eyeblink, as one type of aversive reaction, seems to be especially significant in terms of the infant's neurological integrity and capacity for self-protection. It is not unlikely that infants who are incapable of this type of learning will have other deficiencies as well.

In our orphanage laboratory, where infants can be studied from about five days of age, Little recorded the eyeblink response on a polygraph through a photoelectric device sensitive to light changes caused by the blinking lid. She used a tone as the conditioning stimulus and a mild puff of air near

---

A baby who has been fed each time he makes a desired response will stop responding when the reward is withdrawn much sooner than a baby who has been rewarded only part of the time.

---

the eyelid as the unconditioned or initially effective stimulus. She

trained three groups of infants, 10-, 20-, and 30-days old. She retested them with the identical procedure 10 days later. Training consisted of 50 paired presentations of the tone and air puff, along with 20 interspersed test trials. Little found that babies in all three age groups began to blink when they heard the tone, thus establishing that even a 10-day-old child can learn. Her control group, which received the same stimuli, but in a random fashion, showed no conditioning whatever. Babies in this group blinked only in response to the puff of air.

Little trained half of the babies with a short (half-second) interval between the tone and the air puff, and half with a longer interval (one and one half seconds). The long-interval infants learned, but those trained under the short interval (the optimal interval for adults) did not. This was true for each of the three age groups. These and other results suggest that learning does occur in the very young child, but that it requires rather special conditions.

Cry

It is not possible here to review all of our experiments that point to the considerable plasticity of infant behavior. A normal newborn baby will naturally open his mouth when pressure is applied to his palms (the Babkin response), but consistent events preceding the pressure can be made to produce the response on a conditioned basis. Studies show that the crying behavior of the young infant is affected considerably by the proximity of another crying baby, and that crying is influence by rocking—as mothers have known for generations. What mothers may not have known is that their response to the crying baby may cause learned alterations in the baby's crying. Siqueland has found that premature babies who live in a stimulus-rich environment until they are discharged from the hospital learn more quickly at four months of age than premature babies who live in a normal hospital environment.

Recent studies also suggest that the newborn infant has a keen sense of taste. Sweet substances tend to increase sucking rates in contrast to nonsweet. For example, if plain water is presented to the infant immediately after he has been fed a sweet solution, and the amount of fluid he gets depends upon his sucking rate, water-sucking rates fall below the level found when the infant gets only water. This type of contrast behavior, added to other findings, shows that the infant adapts his behavior to accord with the perceived reinforcement value of his experiences. The infant, at least to some extent, controls his environment.

> **The infant, at least to some extent, controls his environment.**

Taste

In one of our studies Kaye, Theodore Bosack and I fed one group of infants a dextrose solution through a tube, so that these babies got a sweet taste when they sucked. A control group sucked on the tube but did not get its dextrose in association with such sucking. We gave them their dextrose through a dropper. The first group, which was reinforced for tube-sucking, increased their sucking at the tube, while the control group showed increasing disinterest in the tube. Later, when the first group got no further dextrose through the tube, their tube-suck-

ing diminished and they showed the same lack of interest in the tube that babies in the control group displayed.

Affect

The newborn child and the mother, each with congenital and learned-response tendencies, affect each other in a continuously interacting emotional and cognitive bond. The mother stimulates certain congenital reactions in her offspring, while her baby's reactions may elicit reciprocal behaviors from her. Her responses in turn produce further changes in the infant. In spite of the considerable homogeneity of child-rearing practices within cultures, it is unlikely that any two infants would ever experience the same environmental stimulation, even within the first few days of life.

All learning depends on the presence of already-existing sensory systems. In turn, experience alters the baby's inherited behavior. It does not make sense to speak of any given behavior as *either* inherited *or* learned. It is futile to try to measure the relative contributions to the behavioral functioning of a single child of heredity and experience, or maturation and learning. It is impossible at present to tell what an individual child *would* have been like had he not undergone a given experience, or had he experienced different circumstances. At best we may be

> **All learning depends on the presence of already-existing sensory systems.**

able to describe the conditions that seem to be most conducive to optimal development and learning in children. That should be our goal.

Think

Much of the environmental control of a child's behavior is quite inadvertent or, at best, is implemented with inadequate knowledge. The improvement of a child's environment is a matter of concern to humanists and to behavioral engineers. As we learn more about the capabilities of infants, society will face new decisions. Are we prepared, for example, to administer to premature infants an extensive program of in-hospital stimulation, if it turns out that such experience markedly changes the baby's present condition and later learning capacity? Are we prepared to provide presumably beneficial educational experiences to children at much younger age levels than we now do, particularly if such experiences are discovered to be critical in laying down life-long learning styles? Are we prepared, indeed, to condone traumatic or upsetting experiences for children if it turns out that adversity in childhood seems to be an important aspect of the life-histories of creative persons? The evidence we now have suggests that such developments are probable.

But before our society can consider these questions thoughtfully, we need to know how much more about the origins of human behavior in childhood experience. ◆

Discussion Questions

1. Early child psychologists believed that children developed on a strict biological timeline. According to Lipsitt, what factor did they fail to take into consideration?

2. List several reasons why some children may learn to walk at a younger age than other children do.

3. Can infants distinguish odors? How can a researcher determine this?

4. Explain the following phrase, "Habituation and the rapidity with which it occurs reflect the neurological condition of the baby."

5. Can very young children learn? Explain.

6. How did Arlene Little demonstrate classical conditioning in young infants?

7. What has research shown about infants' sense of taste?

8. What are some of the major problems with studying infants and very young children?

9. Lipsitt suggests that because young infants can learn, it's important to expose them to enriched environments in order for them to develop optimally, or perhaps even for normal development to occur. What type of evidence did he present to support this assertion, and how strong was this evidence?

Dreams of INNOCENCE

◆ *David Foulkes*

"What little knowledge we have of children's dreams suggests that their dreams are much more complex and much more dreadful than has previously been thought."

—Calvin Hall,
The Meaning of Dreams,
1966

"Children's dreams are very simple: wishes are fulfilled and anxieties are given tangible form....Particularly before school age, the child has to struggle continually to prevent the pressure of his desires from overpowering his total personality—a battle against the powers of the unconscious which he loses more often than not."

—Bruno Bettelheim,
The Uses of Enchantment,
1976

According to widely accepted psychological theory, children, when alone in bed, see the reality of their situation: powerlessness in an often brutal and awesomely complex world. Their ensuing dreams are thought to be terrifying, overwhelming. But perhaps the traditional Freudian-Jungian view is mistaken.

Results of a five-year-long study at my laboratory contradict these assumptions. The study suggests that young children's dreams are, generally, rather simple and unemotional. The study further suggests that, as with other mental skills, the making of elaborate, imaginative, an even frightening dreams is a developmental accomplishment that is "perfected" only as we reach maturity.

Freud said that dreams are the "royal road to the unconscious." He expected to find buried in the dreams of childhood clues to infantile biology, the "pregenital sexual instincts." In my view, the dreams of children are the royal road to understanding their own mental constructions—their developing ideas of themselves and the world.

To evaluate my study, it is important to understand why the view that children's dreams are complex and often traumatic has been so prevalent. Part of the evidence for the traditional view may lie in our own recollections of some of our earliest nightmares—which we seem to recall more readily than our pleasant dreams. Our children's spontaneous accounts of scary dreams, as they hurriedly seek refuge in our beds, also help to convince us of this view. Part of the theoretical justification is in Freudian dream and developmental theory. Predating the growth of logical ("secondary process") thought, Freud imagined an impulse-driven, irrational mental organization ("primary process"), outside the limits of voluntary control. Most adults fully "regress" to this primitive form of thought only in sleep. For young children, however, primary-process thinking is supposed to be more potent and pervasive. Thus, children's dreams should reflect infantile, irrational feelings in relatively bizarre imagery. Jung, too, ascribed great imagination to the child in sleep. He believed that children's dreams establish contact with a mythological world outside the boundaries of ordinary waking experience (exotic animals, monsters, and other archetypes from human prehistory).

On reflection, however, there are some serious problems with both the theoretical and the observational bases of the traditional view. The theories seem to propose that children's thinking in sleep is vastly more complex than we believe it to be in wakefulness. Careful descriptive analysis of the early waking development of the child's mind, by Jean Piaget and other child psychologists, suggests that only in later childhood is thought genuinely organized and sustained in its pursuit of any goal.

In what Piaget called the "preoperational" phase (beginning roughly at age two), children do think symbolically. That is, they form and use inner representations—images, words—of persons and objects. Presumably, they can dream. Not until about five or six, however, do children start to demonstrate the ability to purposefully organize symbols. Their thought is not yet "operational," not yet systematic in its ordering of symbols in the pursuit of some coherent mental plan. How, then, can the dreams of very young children be driven by narrative operations of a sort that waking evidence suggests is not yet available to them?

> **Dream animals in homelike contexts suggest family themes transposed, as in fairy tales or cartoons.**

Moreover, we now have considerable reason to doubt the kind of dream evidence upon which such theories rest. Spontaneously recalled dreams cannot tell us much about the *typical* workings of the child's mind in sleep. Rapid-eye-movement (REM) sleep is the state in which both adults' and children's most vivid and memorable dreams occur. REM periods of 10 to 30 minutes' duration occur regularly, about four to six times a night, throughout childhood. Yet children very seldom tell us the next day, unless asked, about the dreams that accompany these REM periods. In one study, for example, we were able to estimate that on their own, our six- to seven-year-olds sleeping at home reported only one dream for every 463 of these REM periods.

If the dreams that children recall spontaneously are an extremely limited sample, there is also the strong likelihood that those dreams that they do recall are a biased sample of their dream life. Children are most likely to become aware of dreams that are atypical—dreams that are unusually frightening or vivid, for instance. Our recollections of our own childhood dreams (perhaps we remember only a dream or two from 10 or 15 years of our lives!) obviously constitute an even more incomplete and potentially biased sample. Those recollections, moreover, have probably undergone much elaboration and revision since the dreams first occurred. The same tendency to rework one's memory of a dream must also affect children's spontaneous recollection. Their dream reports may emerge only at the breakfast table or at some later point during the day. At such times, there often seems to be deliberate embellishment so as to produce some effect in the listener (I had a *really funny* dream last night") or gain attention in competition with peers ("If you think

that dream was scary, wait till you hear mine!").

There is an even larger risk of bias if we rely, as dream theory often has, upon the spontaneously reported dreams of persons being treated fro behavioral disorders. Both for adults and for children, there is a positive association between waking behavioral disturbance and sleeping mental dis-

---

Children are most likely to become aware of dreams that are atypical— dreams that are unusually frightening or vivid, for instance.

---

organization. That is, disturbed children have more bizarre and unpleasant dreams than normal children do, and their dreams, therefore, are a particularly poor data base for understanding a child's mind during sleep.

So it is perhaps not so clear, after all, what children's dreams are really like. As theoretically plausible and empirically consistent as it first seems, the view of young children's dreams as complex and often frightening mental fantasies is open to serious doubt. To form a more representative picture, we need to know what sort of dreams normal children are having during those many REM periods from which they ordinarily do not report dreams. We would like these dreams to be told as soon as possible after they are experienced, in a situation that minimizes the incentive to deliberately change the dream in the telling. We would like, at least initially, some simple descriptive account of those dreams, of their "raw" rather than "interpreted" contents.

Raw Data on Dreams

My study of children's dreams was designed to meet those objectives, and I have recently completed some provisional analyses of the results. In the study, 26 children slept at a sleep laboratory eight or nine nights a year for five consecutive years. The nights were not consecutive, but were spread evenly throughout each year. The children were in two groups: 14 children (seven boys and seven girls) were studied from ages three to eight; 12 children (seven girls and five boys) were studied from ages nine to 14. An additional 17 children (nine boys and eight girls) were studied for one or more years, but not for the full five years. Only four children withdrew from the study, in each case because of a family move. The primary dream observations were collected in the study's first, third, and fifth years.

On each experimental night during those years, the children were "wired up" for the recording of eye movements and brain-wave activity; they were awakened three times (most often, but not always, during REM sleep) to tell any dreams they could remember. Over the course of those years, 1,500 awakenings were made during REM periods and 788 dream reports were obtained. REM dream recall increased from ages three and four to ages nine and 10 (from 27 percent to 66 percent), but remained relatively constant thereafter. (Non-REM awakenings produced a significantly lower incidence of dream recall at all ages.) The children's dreams were content-analyzed—for different classes of characters, settings, activities, motives, feelings, and outcomes—and rated on scales—for such qualities as pleasantness, unpleasantness, dreamer active role vs. passive role, distortion of setting and characters, visual vs. conceptual quality.

At no age was the typical child's REM dream particularly frightening or overwhelming. Little direct evidence could be

© 1998 PhotoDisc, Inc.

found, at any age, for a peremptive role of primitive impulses or fantasies in the organization of children's dreams. Little or no evidence could be found, at any age, for the hypothesis that children's dreams bring them into contact with a symbolically complex world of archetypal, primitive myths. At all ages, children's REM dreams were—given that dreams almost never are simple literal memories of one's waking life—reasonably faithful replicas of some of the circumstances, concerns, and interests of their waking lives. Furthermore, we found no evidence to indicate that children's REM-dream thinking is, at any point in early development, more cognitively complex than their waking thinking. In fact, the development of a child's competence as dream-maker seems closely to parallel her or his developing competence as a waking thinker.

These conclusions may be briefly documented by considering typical children's REM dreams at the separate ages we studied. At ages three and four, their dream reports are quite brief (a sentence or two) and notably lacking both in dynamic, interactive quality and in feeling accompaniment. Dream events tend to take place in home or outdoor settings, or more often, to have no particular, well-described locus of action. Dream characters often include the self and sometimes family members, but there are practically no human strangers. As noted in other studies of children's dreams, animals are relatively dominant dream characters, but the child's dream animals tend to come from domesticated or other familiar species (for example, rabbits) rather than from mythical or exotic ones. They generally appear in homelike contexts, suggesting that human familial themes have simply been transposed, as they often are in fairy tales and cartoons, to the animal world. For example, one preschool girl, "Colleen," reported a dream in which chickens were drinking milk for their breakfast. Motivational themes tend to be related to body functions (thirst, hunger, and, interestingly, sleep), rather than to interpersonal interaction. Thus, a preschool boy, "Dean," dreamed that he was sleeping at a Coca-Cola stand.

The young child's dreams seem clearly "preoperational," in Piaget's sense. That is, they are episodic and distractible rather than sustained, and what organization they have derives from a momentarily appearing body stimulus or a discrete memory from the previous day (Freud's "day residue"). Children's dreams at ages three and four are not altogether lacking in organization or inner coherence, but, in general, they cannot be called terribly (much less terrifyingly imaginative.

By five and six, children's dream reports have more than doubled in length and have become markedly more dynamic and interactive in their content. One can speak, for the first time, of most dreams as having definite, if generally simple, story lines. Typical characters are nuclear family members, known persons, human strangers (who generally act in the familiar ways that known persons do), and animals (again from species directly known to the dreamer). Home and recreational settings are common. Here, as elsewhere through the grade-school years, play activities often are portrayed (play as the "business" of childhood). Most dream activities are, at these ages, initiated by characters other than the dreamer. Indeed, one of the more impressive developmental accomplishments seen across the whole dream series is the dreamer's assumption, through middle and late childhood, of an increasingly active role in her or his own dream. This finding indicates the

> **By five and six, children's dream reports have more than doubled in length and have become markedly more dynamic and interactive in their content.**

Dream Symbols and Syntax

"What does it mean?" is a question we often ask about something we have dreamed. Freud's early method of free association still provides the most reasonable way to address the question. With his method, we can also develop plausible models, related to those for waking thought processes, to explain how dreams are constructed.

In my recent book, *A Grammar of Dreams* (Basic Books, 1978), I presented detailed sets of rules for understanding people's reports of their dreams in terms of their associations to those dreams. The theory is that dreams, like language, have both superficial and deeper levels of organization, and that the final choice of dream symbols is determined by rules governing the transformation between a dream's deep and surface forms. Free associations can be used to identify a dream's deep structure and suggest the transformations it undergoes as it comes to surface representation. Following the rules for organizing free associations, different observers can reach reasonable agreement as to the probable meanings and processes at work.

In Freud's method, the dreamer begins by recalling dream images and then reports, in a relaxed and uncritical way, whatever associations come to mind. The method is appropriate for determining meanings because it uses the dreamer's own responses to generate a meaningful context for those images. It returns to the same mind that dreamed the dream, and to the same semantic memory from which its images must have derived. Moreover, in free association, the context is elicited in waking conditions that at least partially mimic those of REM sleep (for instance, relative freedom from concern abut organizing thoughts in a logical way).

Let us imagine that a man dreams that he crushed a rose. His associations to the dream are: "My mother's name is Rose. I often feel angry at her." It is possible to separate out those associations that are of motivational significance ("I often feel angry at her") from those with merely connective value ("My mother's name is Rose"). This example, is, of course, a simple one, and the result is intuitively obvious. But most dreams cannot be reliably interpreted just by intuition.

Let us further imagine that the dreamer goes on to say, "But don't get me wrong. I really love my mother." Here, the formalized association technique permits a reliable identification of an underlying conflict: the dreamer, as subject, is linked to his mother, as object, by two specifiably different sorts of interpersonal motives, anger and love. Again, the result seems obvious. But most associations are not so unequivocal; for those less obvious (but more numerous) cases, a grammar of dreams should provide a more reliable guide to interpretation than does intuition.

Freud showed that the waking mind could provide some clues to the way the dreaming mind works. If we assume that the motives and conflicts revealed in free association were, in fact, the sources of the dream, then we can describe ways in which these sources might have contributed to, and been transformed in, the construction of the dream. In the example given, for instance, we might see the hostility to mother as having been "displaced," in the presence of simultaneous affection for her, to a floral symbol. The grammar of dreams, of which the process of displacement is one element, provides a structured framework in which one can characterize different transformations that the dreaming mind may impose upon memories and motives.

No procedure for organizing free associations can guarantee that it will unerringly reveal "true" dream meanings. In fact, if such meanings exist, they never can be determined accurately. Free associations can be helpful, however, in making our dreams more intelligible. In fact, there is good reason to believe that our most immediate puzzlement, on waking from a relatively bizarre dream, is not "I wonder what I meant by that?" but rather "I wonder how I could have come to think something like that?" The dream doesn't fit. In other words, it isn't what we expect from our experience in waking life. Free association can put any particularly "inexplicable" dream into a more familiar and comprehensible context. More generally, it can also give us an economical way of thinking about—of "modeling"— how we might come to dream the sorts of things we do.

Nor can any procedure for organizing free associations guarantee that it accurately describes how the dream really works. But dream psychology does not stand alone in trying to characterize processes that are not directly observable. Neither in sleep nor in wakefulness do we observe mental processes directly. Nevertheless, we have made substantial progress in understanding the waking mind, and we should be able to do the same in studies of the sleeping mind. Although we never can say that any model for the sleeping or waking mind is absolutely correct, we can evaluate its relative adequacy. A good model is an economical one. It explains known data, and it both generates and explains new observations. It should also be useful in explaining a wide range of phenomena. We should be unhappy, for instance, if two totally different models were developed for the mental processes of speaking and listening, which presumably share a common linguistic base.

In my formalizations of Freud's free-association method; I have attempted to draw upon current models of the waking mind. For instance, Noam Chomsky has shown us the infinite creativity of linguistic expression, and the necessity, therefore, of explaining language behavior with an underlying set of rules governing formation and transformation—a transformational-generative grammar. In dreams, humans are also infinitely creative. We constantly surprise ourselves with what we dream. It seems plausible, then, to imagine that dreams can also be explained by a set of underlying rules—a formational and transformational "dream grammar." In fact, there are some reasons for thinking that the two grammars must be similar to one another.

The past two decades have seen an exciting expansion in knowledge about the higher symbolic processes of the waking mind. We now have full-fledged disciplines of cognitive psychology, transformational-generative grammar, psycholinguistics, and neuropsychology. All of those disciplines have developed models relevant to the study of the dreaming mind. Contemporary theorists of dream processes must move toward integrating their work with the insights of those related disciplines. In return, it is not unreasonable to expect researchers concerned with the waking mind to show interest in what the mind does in sleep.

fidelity with which dreams reflect contemporary waking development. It also suggests that the content of children's dreams, like that of much of their waking play behavior, functions as a vicarious rehearsal for appropriate developmental roles.

At ages five and six, the period of transition from "preoperational" to "operational" thinking, dreams, too, seem to be in transition. They no longer have the flat, static, and prosaic quality of three- and four-year-olds' dreams; they are, rather, more like vignettes, or imaginary "slices of life," but they are not yet fully elaborated fantasies. There is enough dream integration to permit some single line of activity to unfold, but only rarely is it tied into other activities through an overall narrative. During this age span, "Dean" dreamed, for instance, of looking at a cabin and playing with a friend up in the mountains, of running a race against a slightly older boy, and of "driving" toy cars across a bridge he had built with toy blocks. But none of these activities was woven into a real plot.

Piaget would consider that seven- and eight-year-olds generally have achieved an internally integrated, "operational" organization of their waking thoughts. Their dreams, too, seem to have gained markedly in formal organization by this age. Subplots are nicely balanced off against one another. Dream scenarios as a whole begin to reflect clear narrative intentions, and enduring childhood concerns begin to organize dream content in relatively complex and personally meaningful ways.

The most prevalent of these concerns seems to be the child's wish to become a competent female adult or male adult. Sometimes these themes are enacted in relatively realistic imagery of everyday play behavior. On other occasions, however, the child begins to invent relatively novel situations in which we might see such concerns plausibly being portrayed. For instance, at eight years, "Dean" once dreamed of going out with a group of boys his own age and planting a tree. They returned the next day to find the tree fully grown. They then proceeded to plant a whole forest of these trees. The trees survived a forest fire. Some men began to chop them down for firewood, but found that they wouldn't burn. The state police were consulted, and informed the men that the boys had planted nonflammable trees.

Formally, this dream does not seem like a mere vignette. There is evidence of "editing" of the sort that produces feature films rather than home-movie footage. A common theme links together discretely different moments of imagined time. In terms of its manifest content, this dream also reflects the boy's clear progress in the capacity to elaborate imaginative story lines.

Adolescent Dreams

Such "symbolic" narratives, which, as we have seen, both popular opinion and some psychological theory would assign to very young children, in fact seem to occur only after the child has become an "operational" daytime thinker. The narratives apparently are relatively advanced cognitive achievements, and not the product of some primitive form of prelogical thought. It is interesting to speculate that the sort of motive-driven fantasies that Freudians ascribe to young children can only begin to effectively organize children's experience at later stages of cognitive development. In the preschool years, probably neither nocturnal nor daytime thought has sufficient "pattern" to be as complexly organized or imaginative as many personality theorists believe.

By late preadolescence (ages 11 and 12), children's formal powers of dream organization have become well consolidated, and the content of their dreams has become as purposeful, realistic, and affectively benign as it probably ever will be. Although each dream seems to contain at least one kernel that is bizarre or contextually inexplicable, there generally is sex-specific plausibility for each overall scenario. Girls, for instance, are focusing on female dream characters and on sex-typed feminine activities. One preadolescent girl, "Emily," dreamed of attending a party with several of the adult female characters of the then-popular TV series "Bewitched."

> **The content of children's dreams, like their play, may be rehearsal for the next developmental roles.**

Preadolescent girls' dreams contain significantly less overt aggression initiated by other characters than do preadolescent boys' dreams. It is perhaps a mark of the generally good impulse control that children exercise over their nocturnal fantasies that at all ages studied, both boys and girls less often initiated aggressive acts themselves than did other dream characters. As a further note, neither boys nor girls were generally the recipients of the aggressive acts of others in their own dreams.

In early adolescence (ages 13 to 14), there are signs that dream imagery is becoming thematically more obscure and formally more complex. Continuing a trend begun late in preadolescence, family characters and settings are less prominent than formerly (particularly for boys). More generally, there is less literal usage of familiar people and places in con-

> **Children will get better at crazy, dreamlike thinking as they develop in cognitive ability.**

structing dream scenarios, and the scenarios contain fewer instances of concretely enacted "physical" activity. While manual and locomotor activity are still most important in sustaining dream themes, the role of speech is growing at this age (development that parallels the increased capacity for abstract waking thought at these ages). For instance, "Terry" reported a dream in early adolescence about a blind man with a British accent who said to another man, "You can't go on like this, Mead." The dream took place in "some kind of garage or mechanic's shop."

Certain classes of "positive" and "negative" feelings, motives, and outcomes show shifts consistent with the hypothesis that adolescence is a developmental

> **Even in adolescence, social-approach themes occur more often than social-attack themes, and dreamers are more likely to receive friendly than hostile acts initiated by others.**

"disturbance." At this age, for example, the number of dreams in which characters approach one another socially decreases significantly. However, dreams are still competently managed fantasy excursions. Even in adolescence, social-approach themes occur more often than social-attack themes, and dreamers are more likely to receive friendly than hostile acts initiated by others. Girls do have more pleasant dreams during this period than boys, a distinction that may perhaps reflect their different paths in sex-role development.

In adolescence, both REM and non-REM reports begin to include dreams of relatively contextless, discretely imaged objects. For instance, "Emily" had a REM dream of a green, retractable, pipelike pen with a hidden inner mechanism, and a non-REM dream of a package of green paper napkins. From context, such dreams can be plausibly interpreted as symbolizing increased interest in the "machinery" of the body. It is interesting that dreams focusing on objects-without-context, which are sometimes reported by adults from non-REM sleep, appear later in development than dreams with integrated story lines. Formally, they apparently reflect a type of analytic thought that requires greater cognitive skill than is necessary for the synthesis of coherent narratives.

More generally, the children's dream series suggests that dream-making is a mental skill that is subject to the same developmental patterning as any waking mental skill. "Crazy," dreamlike thinking is something young children are not able to execute very well, but they will get successively and predictably better at it as they pass through stages of cognitive development. There can be little doubt that the content of at least some dreams symbolizes issues in the child's current psychosexual development, in a way Freudian and other "symbolic" dream interpreters would have predicted. But it is very important to note that cognitive development places many constraints on the nature of such symbolism. Children's dreams indicate that their ability to conceptualize external reality and their own feelings undergoes definite developmental elaboration.

Testing Dream Meanings

The reader probably has wondered how children might have been affected by sleeping away from home and family, and by all those wires on their scalps and faces. We wondered about that, too. We found that, in general, our children slept normally in the laboratory, except, of course, for the awakenings. We also found, in a study conducted during the second year of the project, that when dreams were sampled in the same way at home and in the laboratory (at a fixed time of morning arousal), there were no general or substantial differences between them.

Skeptics may say it is possible that young children have very complicated and fantastic dreams, but simply can't recall or report them very well. Under this view, the developments in dreaming competence I have described would be seen as developments in recall or report competence. This hypothesis does not seem very plausible to me, for it imagines that young children have an adultlike competence at dream-making but revert to being small children when asked to recall and describe their dreams.

What are we to make, then, of those few occasions when children's dreams do seem to have those properties conventionally ascribed to them—when they definitely are frightening, for example? Night terrors, in which children awaken in a delirium accompanied by great fear, seem primarily to occur in non-REM sleep. The children are often unable to describe a mental context for their feeling. When they can, it is gen-

erally not cognitively complex: they put it simply, maybe with a single word, as, say, in expressing a revulsion to "bugs." the explanation of night-terror episodes may lie in physiology; they may be a kind of unconscious "panic" response to the slowing of life functions—heart rate, blood pressure, respiration—that occurs during the profound non-REM state.

Night terrors, in which children awaken in a delirium accompanied by great fear, seem primarily to occur in non-REM sleep.

Children also can experience anxiety dreams, in which REM mental drama gets "out of hand." Our evidence suggests that such dreams occur in proportion to children's difficulties in managing their waking lives. It also suggests, however, that anxiety dreams are not typical of any developmental stage, and that the capacity to generate unpleasant as well as pleasant dream scenarios actually increases in step with waking cognitive development.

How can we determine, or ever be sure, what children's dreams "mean"? (For a general discussion of the meaning of dreams, see box on page 82.) Since children, especially young children, are not very

adept at free-associating to their own dreams, there are special problems in assigning meanings to their dreams. The children in the study described here were not asked to free-associate to their own dreams. They were, however, asked for regular accounts of their waking lives, and we collected many observations of their behavior and gave them many psychological tests. There also are well-described regularities in the literature of childhood development that are helpful in assigning contextual meanings to particular dreams. From other studies of adolescence, for instance, we have some sense of its special stresses and its new intellectual potentials.

In addition, as Jung and Calvin Hall among others have insisted, each dream in any extended series from a given dreamer finds context in the other dreams of that series. The whole series provides a way of testing hypothetical meanings ascribed to any single dream within it. Finally, our task is made easier by the fact that children's dreams are, relative to our own, somewhat more straightforward. This is why, as Freud saw, studying them should tell us much about why all of us have the dreams we do. ◆

Discussion Questions

1. Explain the traditional Freudian view of children's dreams.

2. What is the author's perspective on children's dreams?

3. Why do people believe that children's dreams are complex and traumatic?

4. What are the problems with the theoretical and observational basis of the traditional view of children's dreams?

5. How does Piaget's research on dreams contradict the theories of Freud and Jung?

6. What did the author discover about children's dreams?

7. According to the author, what do 3- to 4-year old children dream about? 5- to 6-year-olds? 7- to 8-year-olds?

8. Describe the gender differences in childhood dreams.

9. What's typical of adolescent dreams?

10. How does the author react to the criticisms of his work?

Play Is *Serious* Business

◆ *Jerome S. Bruner*

Experimental psychologists are a rather sobersided and tough-minded breed. They prefer to study topics that are scientifically manageable and precisely defined. No surprise, then, that when they began to study early human development, they steered clear of so antic a phenomenon as play. Everyone recognizes play when he sees it, but one cannot frame it into a single, impeccable definition. Play encompasses a motley, very unsober set of activities, from childish punning, to cowboys-and-Indians, to the construction of building block towers.

Fortunately, the progress of research is subject to accidents of opportunity and the availability of data. A decade ago, while the methodologically vexed were still rejecting play as an unmanageable laboratory topic, primate ethologists began to raise new questions about the nature and role of play in primate evolution. On closer inspection, play turned out to be less diverse a phenomenon than had been thought, particularly when observed in its natural setting. Nor was it all that antic in its structure, if analyzed properly.

Most important, primatologists found that play seems to serve a crucial function during immaturity, a function that increases in importance as one moves up the evolutionary scale from Old World monkeys, through great apes, to man. Play, they found, is a precursor of adult competence.

Some of the pioneering observations came from Jan van Lawick-Goodall and her colleagues, who studied free-ranging chimpanzees at the Gombe Stream Reserve in Tanzania. They found that during the first four or five years of life, a chimp is in close contact with his mother, and is her only offspring. Unlike the offspring of Old World monkeys, who are supplanted by new progeny within a year, young chimpanzees have plenty of time to observe adult behavior and incorporate what they observe into their play.

Termites with Relish

Van Lawick-Goodall reported a striking example of how this early observation together with play leads to skilled adult behavior. Adult chimps develop a very skilled technique for catching termites. They wet stripped sticks in their mouths, insert the sticks into the opening of a termite hill, and wait a bit for the termites to adhere to the sticks. Then they remove the fishing instruments with the termites on them and devour the insects with great relish.

Young chimps learn the art of termiting by trying it out in play. Seated by the mother, buffered from external pressures, they learn the individual acts that make up termiting. Though they do not obtain the usual reward of food, they nonetheless learn to play with sticks, strip leaves from twigs, and pick the right length of twig for

getting into different holes. The chimps perform these steps, which eventually must combine into the final act, in all kind of antic episodes of play.

Merlin, a young chimp who lost his mother in his third year and was raised by older siblings, did not learn to termite as well as the others, reported Van Lawick-Goodall. He lacked the opportunity to observe an adult closely, and probably did not get the buffering from distraction and pressure that a mother normally provides. As a result, at four and a half years he was still inept and ill-equipped for the task.

Observations like this one suggest that play does not merely provide practice of instinctive behavior relevant to survival. Rather, it makes possible the playful practice of subroutines of behavior that later come together in useful problem solving. What appears to be at stake is the chance to assemble and reassemble sequences of behavior that lead to skilled action. At least, that is one function of play.

More generally, play seems to reduce or neutralize the pressure that comes from having to achieve. There is a well-known rule in the psychology of learning, the Yerkes-Dodson Law, that states that the more complex a skill is, the lower the optimum level of motivation required to learn it. That is, too much motivation arousal can interfere with learning. By deemphasizing the importance of the goal, play may serve to reduce excessive drive and thus enable young animals and children to learn more easily the skills they will need when they are older.

Playful Solutions

With my colleagues Kathy Sylva and Paul Genova at Harvard University, I studied the effects of play on the problem-solving abilities of three- to five-year olds. The children's task was to fish a prize from a box that was out of reach. The only tools available were two short sticks and a clamp. The solution was to extend the sticks by clamping them together to make a pole.

We gave the children various kinds of training before they tried to solve the problem themselves. Some of them watched an adult demonstrate the principle of clamping sticks together, others practiced fastening clamps on single sticks, and a third group watched the experimenter carry out the entire task. A fourth group of children received no special training, but had an opportunity to play with the materials, while a fifth group had no exposure to the materials at all.

The play group did as well on the problem as those who saw the complete task demonstrated, and did significantly better than the other three groups. The chart summarizes the differences in performance, in terms of the number of solutions spontaneously achieved without help from the experimenter.

We were quite struck by the tenacity with which the children in the play group stuck to the task. Even when their initial approach was misguided, they ended by solving the problem because they were able to resist frustration and the temptation to give up. They were playing.

There are comparable experimental results for primates below man. One technique for removing the pressure to achieve a goal is semidomestication; the experimenter puts out food in the animals' natural habitat, and thus relieves them of the necessity to search out their own sustenance. This has the effect of increasing innovation.

> **Even when their initial approach was misguided, they ended by solving the problem because they were able to resist frustration and the temptation to give up. They were playing.**

In Japanese studies of semi-domestication, macaque monkeys have taken to washing yams, and have learned to separate maize from the sand on which it has been spread by dropping a handful of the mix into sea water and letting the sand sink. Once in the water, the younger animals begin to play, learn to swim, and finally migrate to nearby islands.

In all of these activities, it is the playful young who are most involved, even though they are not always the innovators of the new "technologies." The young are game for change, and their gameness predisposes the troop as a whole to change its ways. The full-grown males are often most resistant, or at least most out of touch, since the new enterprises get a first tryout in the groups that play around the mother monkeys, and adult males are not part of these groups. However, French primatologist Jean Claude Fady has shown that even ordinarily combative adult males will learn to cooperate with each other to move heavy rocks under which food has been hidden, when pressure is removed through semidomestication.

Play also has other functions that are less utilitarian but equally important. Erik Erikson recently reported that in a 30-year follow-up of people who had been studied as children, those subjects who had the most interesting and fulfilling lives were ones who had managed to keep a sense of playfulness at the center of things. And Corinne Hutt of the University of Keele has shown that the opportunity for play affects a child's later creativity.

Hutt designed a supertoy for children three to five years old. The toy consisted of a table with a lever, buzzers, bells and counters attached. Different movements of the lever caused buzzers to sound, bells to ring, etc.

When children encounter this toy, they first explore its possibilities, tentatively trying things out, and then, having contented themselves, they go on to richer, more combinatorial play. Hutt rated the children on how inventive they were in their play, and divided them into nonexplorers, explorers, and inventive explorers. The latter group went from initial exploration to full-blown play.

Unplayful and Tense

Four years later, when the children were seven to 10 years old, Hutt gave them a number of personality tests, including one for creativity. The more inventive and exploratory the children had been in their previous play with the supertoy, the higher their originality scores were four years later. In general, the nonexploring boys viewed themselves as unadventurous and inactive, and their parents and teachers felt they lacked curiosity. the nonex-

ploratory and unplayful girls turned out to be rather unforthcoming in social interactions, as well as more tense than their more playful comrades.

As we examine play and its functions more closely, we are discovering that even the simplest play activities, far from being "random," are structured and governed by rules. In subhuman primates, play is always preceded by certain physical signals. These include a "play face," a particular kind of open-mouthed gesture that signals the message "this is play," as well as a slack but exaggerated gait and galumphing movements.

When Stephen Miller and I analyzed Irven DeVore's films of juvenile play in East African Savanna baboons, we quickly discovered that if one young animal failed to notice the play signal of another who sought to play-fight with him, a real fight broke out. But once the signal was perceived by both parties, the fight changed into the clownish ballet of monkeys feigning a fight. They obviously knew how to do it both ways.

New studies by psycholinguist Catherine Garvey show how three- to five-year-old children, playing in pairs, manage even in their simplest games to create and recognize implicit rules and expectancies, all the while distinguishing sharply between the structure of make-believe and the real thing.

For instance, one common rule is to respond to your playmate by copying what he says. A violation of the rule evokes a reprimand:

Child one: *Bye Mommy*
Child two: *Bye Mommy*
Child one: *Bye Mommy*
Child two: *Bye Daddy*
Child one: *You're a nut.*

At other times, a complement rule prevails, and the expected response to *"Bye Mommy"* is *"Bye Daddy."*

© 1998 PhotoDisc, Inc.

The rules also specify the situation in which the play takes place. These rules may be subject to some discussion and negotiation:

Child one: *I have to go to work.*
Child two: *You're already at work.*
Child one: *No I'm not.*

Young children are usually well aware of the line between fantasy

> **We quickly discovered that if one young animal failed to notice the play signal of another who sought to play-fight with him, a real fight broke out.**

and reality. In the following exchange, the first child is seated on a three-legged stool that has a magnifying glass at its center:

Child one: *I've got to go to the potty.*
Child two: *Really?*
Child one: (Grins) *No, pretend.*

These simple exchanges have a concise, almost grammatical quality, and reveal an extraordinary sensitivity to violations of implicit

expectancies. In them, children work out variations and combinations according to unspoken rules. The combination of elements is an essential feature of language, and one wonders, though we can never know, whether play has some deep connection with the origins of language in man.

Play certainly has a part in a child's first mastery of language. In our studies at Oxford, we have observed how, in exchange games such as "peek-a-boo," young children learn to signal and recognize certain expectancies. They delight in the primitive rules that come to govern their encounters with other children. And they learn to manipulate features of language that they must later put together in complicated ways.

An episode from one study illustrates how play can serve as a vehicle for language acquisition. At nine months, Nan begins to play an exchange game with her mother; she offers her mother an object, withdraws it excitedly, then hands it over and says "Kew," her version of "Thank you." She does not say "Kew" when she herself receives an object. Nan has not yet learned the adult language code for giving and receiving.

Three months later, "Look" has replaced "Kew" in the giving phase of the game, and "Kew" has moved to its correct position in the receiving phase. Nan has used the order of steps in the game to sort out the proper order for the language she uses now in play and will use later to communicate.

Play certainly has a part in a child's first mastery of language. In our studies at Oxford, we have observed how, in exchange games such as "peek-a-boo," young children learn to signal and recognize certain expectancies.

We have come a long way since Piaget's brilliant observation that play helps the child assimilate experience to his personal schema of the world, and more research on play is underway. We now know that play is serious business, indeed, the principle business of childhood. It is the vehicle of improvisation and combination, the first carrier of rule systems through which a world of cultural restraint replaces the operation of childish impulse.   ◆

Discussion Questions

1. Why is play so important for children?

2. How do young chimpanzees learn to catch termites?

3. What is the Yerkes-Dodson Law?

4. What were the results of the study conducted by Bruner, Sylva, and Genova? What do the results suggest about the importance of play?

5. Discuss the relationship between early playfulness and later creativity.

6. What have researchers learned by watching young primates play?

7. Give at least two examples of what children can learn from playing peek-a-boo.

8. How might play allow a child to solve a problem that he or she initially failed to solve?

Exercises

Name: _____

Date: _____

Part 10: Child Development

1. I believe that good parenting can make an enormous difference in the way we develop.

Agree   (1)   (2)   (3)   (4)   (5)   Disagree

2. I believe that my parents are responsible for my psychological problems.

Agree   (1)   (2)   (3)   (4)   (5)   Disagree

3. I think peers have a greater impact on development than parents do.

Agree   (1)   (2)   (3)   (4)   (5)   Disagree

Write a brief history of your childhood up to age 10. Include any major milestones or discoveries you can remember.

Analyze some aspect of your childhood using one or more theories from developmental psychology.

PART 11

ADOLESCENCE AND ADULTHOOD

Occasionally a student asks me, "How come virtually all of the research in developmental psychology has bee conducted with young children? Do we stop developing at age 12?" Not long ago, many textbooks on developmental psychology would have had you believing just that. But, as Bob Dylan once sang, the times they are a-changin', mainly because of the increasing proportion of old people in the American population. As of a few years ago, there were more than 12,000 Americans over the age of 100, and recent estimates suggest at least half of the people who are currently age 50 will reach the century mark. That means that a few decades from now there will be *millions* of Americans over age 100.

The changing demographics have not escaped the notice of the ever-vigilant (and ever-aging) developmental psychologist, who has been scurrying about in recent years to try to devise full-blown "life-span" theories of development. But psychoanalyst Erik Erikson was teaching such a theory at Harvard back in the 1960s. The first article in this section is an extensive interview with this remarkable man, published about a decade before his death in 1994.

In "Those Gangly Years," psychologist Anne C. Petersen discusses survey and interview data that shed light on adolescence—or at least adolescence in the suburbs. Petersen says that reports of turmoil in adolescence have been exaggerated, but perhaps she was looking for turmoil in all the wrong places.

Finally, in "Marriages Made to Last," a husband-and-wife psychology team survey over 300 successful, long-term couples to find out what makes marriages last in our society of quick-and-easy divorces. Their findings—especially about love and sex—are surprising.

A CONVERSATION with
Erik Erikson

◆ *Elizabeth Hall*

Elizabeth Hall: Professor Erikson, over the past 30 years your theory of human development has come to dominate our view of the life cycle. Now that you've reached the eighth and final stage of the cycle, has your own experience changed your view of human development?

Erik Erikson: It undoubtedly has. But in *The Life Cycle Completed* I am offering a review of my views, and I emphasize primarily their inner logic. Of course, 30 years ago I lacked the capacity for imagining myself as old, and the general image of old age was different then. Certainly, the theory has not yet taken into account all the recent changes in society. Consider the thousands and thousands of old people alive today who would not have been alive 30 years ago. But I've always emphasized historical relativity in the study of human beings.

Hall: How does the increase in the number of old people affect the experience of old age?

Erikson: Thirty years ago, we spoke of "elders," the handful of wise old women and men who faced death with dignity. But a society can have only relatively few elders. So our large group of well-preserved old people leads us to speak now of "elderlies." The existence of this group means that we need to rethink the role of old age. Being old is of course a part of life, but—perhaps because we stress youthfulness in our culture—people keep talking about

"later adulthood" as if being old were funny or bad.

Hall: Has the large group of elderlies made you consider inserting another stage into the life cycle between middle adulthood and old age?

Erikson: The various life stages are not equal in length, so you can always make one stage longer and describe a transitional stage, although it gets a little odd to talk about a transitional stage at the end of life. I think that the biggest change in the last stage of life would be that old people will be allowed to remain involved in matters that have always been considered too much for them. The stage of middle adulthood, of course, is the stage of generativity, and the question is, how, and how long, can old people remain generative?

Hall: Generativity means a concern with the next generation. How can old people be generative?

Erikson: I've described generativity as including procreativity, productivity, and creativity. Of course, old people can no longer procreate, but they can be productive, and they can be creative; the creative potential of old people has probably been very much underestimated. Only a few elders have

> **The stage of middle adulthood, of course, is the stage of generativity, and the question is, how, and how long, can old people remain generative?**

been presented as examples of special worth.

Hall: People like Pablo Casals and Picasso and Georgia O'Keeffe.

Erikson: Exactly. But they may be special examples of what more old people can represent. This changing experience of old age doesn't call for a new stage, but perhaps the transition leading to senescence will be longer. People will one day be expected to work longer. And even after they retire, old people can be useful to one another and to the younger generations.

Hall: Are you talking about volunteer work?

Erikson: That depends. Many volunteer projects take on the same quality as the word "elderly." The work is not considered "real" work, and—even if working conditions are adjusted somewhat—it's very important to maintain the quality of real work.

Hall: You mean that if I were doing some volunteer job and I thought that people were just keeping me busy and out of the way, I wouldn't feel good about myself?

Erikson: That's it, exactly. Old people can be generative in another way, too. They can be good grandparents, and not only to their own grandchildren. I'm convinced that old people and children need one another and that there's an affinity between old age and childhood that, in fact, rounds out the life cycle. You know, old people often seem childlike, and it's important that we be permitted to revive some qualities that we had as children.

Hall: Do you mean to look at things afresh with the inexperienced eye of the child, as if you were seeing them for the first time?

Erikson: Yes, something like that. You know, Einstein used the word "wonder" to describe his experience as a child, and he was considered childlike by many people. And I think he claimed that he was able to formulate the theory of relativity because he kept asking the questions that children ask. So when I say old people think like children, I do not mean childishly, but with wonder, joy, playfulness—all those things that adults often have to sacrifice for a while.

When I say old people think like children, I do not mean childishly, but with wonder, joy, playfulness—all those things that adults often have to sacrifice for a while.

Hall: Because they have duties.

Erikson: Things to take care of. The Hindus call it the maintenance of the world. Technology has obviously interfered with this relationship between the old and young, because it concentrates people in communities for economic reasons. That becomes obvious when old people move into a place that just takes care of old people. But technology has also made it possible for the old and young to get together over long distances—you can fly, drive.

Hall: And you can always phone. So technology both breaks the cycle and makes it possible to mend it. How will this extension of vigorous life change our expectations of the life cycle? What happens when the 25-year-old can expect 60 years of married life?

Erikson: Marriages have changed, too. It may not be coincidence that to be married several times is becoming acceptable.

Hall: Do you think that the culture's recent realization that sexuality may be an important part of old age is changing the experience of aging?

Erikson: I certainly would think so. The old attitude was that sexuality in old age either doesn't exist or ought not to be. The new attitude permits choice. Sexuality in old age is a potential to be enjoyed, not an obligation. In old age, fertility is over, so the question is, "What remains and what is important for life?" I call it generalized sensuality, which has something to do with play and the importance of the moment, getting us back again to the potentially childlike quality in old age.

Hall: If I were writing this up for a human sexuality text, I'd say that you were talking about playful sexuality that may or may not culminate in genital intercourse.

Erikson: That's right, but let's note that the genital engagement can be longer than was once assumed. Of course, sexuality does imply closeness and playfulness. It is recreational by nature when the time for procreation is over.

Hall: The time and the responsibility, and perhaps the fear, are eliminated. But what about the current stress on recreational sex for all ages?

Erikson: We make a distinction between "intimacies" and "Intimacy"—with a capital "I." Sex that is purely recreational involves intimacies. But obviously Intimacy means more for the whole person than intimacies.

Hall: You see the stage of young adulthood as centering on the struggle between Intimacy and isolation. Do you think the culture's fascination with purely recreational sex could affect our capacity for Intimacy?

You could have a highly active sex life and yet feel a terrible sense of isolation.

Erikson: It could. You see, that situation has come about in part because of a misunderstanding of psychoanalysis: the idea that you mustn't repress anything, but must always act it out, so that the most important thing becomes genital recreation. When we speak of the development of Intimacy, we emphasize mature mutuality. Mere intimacies can occupy a period in a person's life—even repeated periods—but they cannot be the final aim of sexuality.

Hall: So purely recreational sex is okay, say, during late adolescence or after divorce....

Erikson: Well, if you bring in "okay," then the question is, "In what environment?" And it depends entirely on what kind of a person somebody is. Some people can cultivate the side issues of the life cycle. The main point is whether they are mature enough to handle the main conflict of each period. For example, some people today may fool themselves in their so-called recreational sexuality and actually feel quite isolated because they lack mutuality—real Intimacy. In extreme cases, you could have a highly active sex life and yet feel a terrible sense of isolation because you're never there as a person; you're never perceiving your partner as a person.

Corbis

Erik Erikson

Hall: And that could lead to an increase in sexual activity in an attempt to get rid of the isolation, because you didn't realize what was causing it.

Erikson: Real Intimacy includes the capacity to commit yourself to relationships that may demand sacrifice and compromise. The basic strength of young adulthood is Love—a mutual, mature devotion.

Hall: In your new book you've moved beyond Freud by proposing a stage of generalized sensuality in old age. His psychosexual stages ended with mature genitality in early adulthood.

Erikson: According to Freud, in the young stage sexuality culminated in genitality, which essentially means mutual genital enjoyment. We've proposed two additional psychosexual stages: procreativity in adulthood and generalized sensuality in old age. But please note that on my chart of the life cycle I put them both into parentheses, because they haven't been fully discussed in psychoanalytic theory. You see, I believe that there is a procreative drive: There is an instinctual wish to have children, and it's important the we realize that.

Hall: What happens to someone who decides *not* to have children?

Erikson: Since we're in a period of history when the number of births has to be reduced, many people will be making that decision. But it's important that people who decide to remain childless know what they are *not* doing. The danger is that they will repress the sense of frustration and loss that comes with the rejection of procreativity, so that a new kind of unconscious repression develops in place of the sexual repression of the Victorian age.

Hall: By "repression," you mean to push it completely out of mind, so that if someone said, "Don't you sometimes regret having children?" a person could honestly reply, "No." Now what happens when someone who's chosen not to have children wakes up one morning at age 45 or 50 and says, "What have I done?"

Erikson: *Not* done. Well, you don't keep prescriptions ready for such cases; you don't say, "It's easy to handle your problem, you simply have to sublimate." But "subli-

---

The "Inventor" of the Identity Crisis Remembers His Own

As the rain drummed steadily down from the gray California skies, Erik Erikson, who has been called the "closest thing to an intellectual hero" in the United States, spoke quietly and reflectively about his view of human development.

Unlike most psychoanalytic theorists, Erikson went beyond evidence from disturbed people and drew on his studies of healthy adolescents and of the Sioux and Yurok Native American tribes when building his ideas. Always he has argued that society and history are potent forces in individual development, and he invented the field of psychohistory to demonstrate the point. His book *Young Man Luther* showed that the sympathetic application of psychoanalysis could lead to an understanding of the way in which "the historical moment" and a human life might mesh to affect an entire society. *Gandhi's Truth*, which won both the Pulitzer Prize and the National Book Award, gave similar insights into the development of militant nonviolence.

Erikson was born in Frankfurt-am-Main in 1902 and grew up in the home of his mother and stepfather, a German pediatrician. His father, a Dane, had abandoned his mother before Erik was born. Erik's close sympathy with young people may be in part he result of his own troubled youth. This man who coined the phrase "identity crisis" went through his own intense adolescent crisis, so severe, he says, that at times it brought him near the borderline between neurosis and adolescent psychosis.

He had studied art and intended to become an art teacher, but in Vienna he met Sigmund Freud and other psychoanalysts and, while in his 20s, began to study at the Vienna Psychoanalytic Institute, where he was trained by Anna Freud. In 1933, he was graduated from the institute and came to the United States. Besides maintaining a private practice, he has taught at the Yale School of Medicine, at the University of California, and at Harvard University.

At age 81, Erickson says that he is "pretty much retired." But he is still seeing a few patients, writing, making occasional appearances, and conducting research into aging with Joan Erikson, his wife. The Eriksons have always worked closely together, especially in the gradual formulation of the stages of life and of the life cycle as a whole. A dancer and craftswoman, author and educator, she has edited all of her husband's books.

On the second day of our conversation, the skies cleared and we walked down the steep hillside to a restaurant beside the bay for lunch. Over a glass of German beer, Erikson admitted that he had a large project in the back of his mind—a book about Jesus. It seemed only fitting that the student of Luther and Gandhi should now be probing the words and life of the man who inspired them both.

mate" is the right word; Freud made this very clear many years ago. The procreative urge does need to be directed into socially fruitful channels. Instead of having clear prescriptions, it's better to work out the social structure so that people who never have children of their own will, in the normal course of events, help to take care of all the world's children. You must have noticed how the changes in marriage patterns have led many people to care for children who are not theirs—and do it very well. This is a new trend. Only a few decades ago a child was considered more of a personal possession, and it was very important whose child it was.

Hall: And now we have "his," "hers," and "ours" in many families, as well as the adoption of war orphans from places like Vietnam. The procreative urge is, of course, closely related to generativity, which you regard as a basic tendency of adulthood. Does the urge have to be satisfied by working directly with children?

Erikson: That's why I call it generativity—in order to go beyond procreativity, once we've fully accepted *that*. It can be sublimated into creativity or productivity.

Hall: It's easy for me to see how a childless artist or a writer or a teacher can sublimate generativity in their work. Now how does a plumber do it?

Erikson: Don't underestimate the generative contributions of a good plumber. Also, he or she may be a church member who can do something for all the children in his community. And he or she is still a voter.

Hall: Then the urge to care for future generations can be satisfied by helping to maintain a generative social system?

Erikson: Exactly. That's again why I like so much that Hindu term "the maintenance of the world."

Hall: When you discuss generativity, you contrast it with self-absorption or stagnation as opposing trends during adulthood. If generativity triumphs, a person develops the basic strength of "Care." Generativity also has a regular "dystonic" counterpart: It is "rejectivity."

Erikson: I want to emphasize that those two things belong together. Generativity shouldn't be treated as an achievement that permanently overcomes stagnation. You have both, mostly. If you study the lives of very creative people you'll find that at times they have a terrible sense of stagnation. And the interaction of such opposites is characteristic of every stage of the life cycle.

If you study the lives of very creative people you'll find that at times they have a terrible sense of stagnation.

Hall: If the crisis of a stage is successfully resolved, the defeated quality doesn't disappear; instead, the balance changes so that there is a preponderance of the positive quality?

Erikson: It's exactly a matter of balance, but we avoid the terms "positive" and "negative." Sometimes what we call the "dystonic tendency" can have positive aspects. For example, during old age the life crisis involves the conflict between integrity and despair. How could anybody have integrity and not also despair about certain things in his own life, about the human condition? Even if your own life was absolutely beautiful and wonderful, the fact that so many people were exploited or ignored must make you feel some despair.

Hall: So people shouldn't expect that if their lives are lived according to Eriksonian theory, they'll go through eight rosy stages. Can a person develop what you call the "syntonic" quality of each life

stage without the accompanying dystonic quality? Can you develop generativity without stagnation? Or trust without distrust?

Erikson: Let's take the last one, which describes the psychosocial crisis of infancy. A basic sense of trust means both that the child has learned to rely on his (or her) caregivers to be there when they are needed, and to consider himself trustworthy. But just imagine what somebody would be like who had no mistrust at all.

Hall: Gullible, to say the least. We'd probably think such a person wasn't very bright.

Erikson: Out of the conflict between trust and mistrust, the infant develops hope, which is the earliest form of what gradually becomes faith in adults. If you say that an adult has hope, I'd say, "Well, I hope so," but if you said that a baby has faith, I'd say, "That's quite a baby." Real faith is a very mature attitude.

Hall: So the various strengths take different forms in old age, because they're all tempered by the strength of old age, which is "wisdom."

Erikson: Yes, old age is when a certain wisdom is possible and even necessary, as long as you don't make it too darn wizard-like.

Hall: Perhaps the prayer of St. Frances of Assisi describes what you mean: changing what you can change and not changing what you can't hope to change, but wise enough to know the difference.

Erikson: Absolutely, although one hesitates to make it all too simple.

Hall: If you consider life as a tapestry, as Mrs. Erikson has done, woven with a different color for each strength, the final pattern would be different for each person. But can one successfully handle the crisis of old age—the struggle between integrity and despair—without having resolved the previous stages favorably?

Erikson: You couldn't possibly imagine a person who has resolved all seven previous crises equally well—in fact, I never hope to meet such a person. At the end of life you attempt to consolidate an existential identity. That sounds stilted, but the existential identity has to emerge from the psychosocial identity.

Hall: I'd think that for people like you, who can carry on your profession as long as you like, there'd not be the same questioning of identity as there is in someone who works until 65 and then retires and loses part of his identity. You're no longer a plumber. Or you're no longer a brain surgeon because you lack the coordination.

Erikson: You notice that you're referring to men exclusively.

Hall: A woman can be a brain surgeon—or a plumber.

Erikson: Yes, and that's certainly going to become more common. The reason that men die earlier than women may be purely biological, or it may have much to do with the fact that so far, man's psychosocial existence has depended so much on his occupation.

Hall: But let's look at the traditional woman. When such a woman is widowed, she loses the identity of "wife," yet she continues to outlive the men around her.

Erikson: In many cultures, "widow" is also an identity. And the surviving wife also has a grand-maternal role, depending on the culture. In China, for example, the role of grandmother has been deeply embedded in tradition.

Hall: And the role of grandmother has traditionally been stronger than the role of grandfather, so it would provide a basis for identity. I guess we solved that problem.

Erikson: Even with this extended life, it's still relatively rare for a couple to grow old together. You know how many more widows than widowers we have.

Hall: Husbands are still generally older than their wives. So if a woman expects to become a widow at 70 instead of at 60, it would mean that we're postponing that experience of old age by expanding the earlier period.

Erikson: That's right, which shows that you don't just prove or disprove a life-cycle theme, but learn to observe the changes and then decide whether the terms you first

> *Old age is when a certain wisdom is possible and even necessary, as long as you don't make it too darn wizard-like.*

chose to name the strengths or weaknesses are the right words. Incidentally, we once called the strengths of each stage "virtues"; then we realized that virtue comes from the Latin word *virtus*, which implies manliness. The linguistic implication could be that virtues are male qualities, so I had to change it to "strengths."

Hall: Speaking of women, how does the task of forming an identity differ for adolescent boys and adolescent girls?

Erikson: The task itself doesn't differ; the main stages, strengths, and risks do not differ for men and for women. Rather, they help sexual differences to complement one another. Children do have to learn to become boys and girls, but unless there is very strong sex-typing going on, both sexes have a certain freedom. A little boy can behave a little like a girl, and it's considered charming, or a girl like a boy. It all depends on what the culture makes of it. But essentially, whatever strength has to develop in a certain stage must appear in both boys and girls. Like willpower, for example, or industry. Or identity.

Hall: So the specific tasks of each age are the same for boys and girls, but the content of what they deal with would be somewhat dif-

ferent in different societies, different at different times in the same society, different depending upon both biology and the way the culture brings out the tasks.

Erikson: You sound as if you're ready to teach a course.

Hall: Not yet. Let's go on. A culture can also change the length of time it allows for a stage of life. Take adolescence, when identity is being formed. There is supposed to be a moratorium, when the young person doesn't have the responsibility of adulthood, but in a lot of cultures the official recognition of that period may be only a few weeks, or just puberty rites. When society pays so little attention to a stage, does it affect the way the stage is met?

Erikson: Compressing adolescence into such a short span of time doesn't mean that society cares less. You said in a rather offhand way, "just puberty rites." But take the drama of puberty rites and the enormous existential experience a kid goes through. The transition may take a shorter time, but it may be terribly intense.

Hall: And if society gives you few choices as to what you're going to do afterward, there's no need for all that time to select a future. But let's go back to technological societies. You've pointed out that during identity formation, the adolescent can fall into "totalism," a rigid self-concept that can leave a person susceptible to totalitarian movements. How does the totalism of the 40-year-old member of the Ku Klux Klan differ from the totalism of the adolescent?

Erikson: I don't believe I ever regarded totalism as only an aspect of adolescent thinking. It's an aspect of ideology, which finds easy access to young thinking, but that doesn't mean that there is no totalism after adolescence.

Hall: Would the totalism of a middle-aged Nazi or terrorist be likely to reflect an unsuccessfully resolved adolescent identity crisis? **Erikson:** If you study a case history, you may find that the person didn't resolve something earlier. But it can happen to a whole group, as it did to the young Germans after World War I. Because of historical and economic conditions, they could never settle down to adulthood, and so ideological totalism began to dominate them.

Hall: Let's discuss another aspect of identity: its relation to society. You've always stressed the importance of the historical moment when discussing the life cycle.

Erikson: The way a national or communal identity develops depends a lot on the extent to which the national or political or religious ideology strengthens the sense of "I."

Hall: So that in George Orwell's *1984*, there would have been a very limited sense of "I." What about Hitler's Germany?

Erikson: In such a society, the Führer is the one who stands under a thousand banners and says "I" and everybody identifies with that; it gives them a sense of "I." Marching in unison becomes the act of being oneself.

Hall: Joseph Adelson's research showed that German children—not American or English youngsters—said that everybody needs a strong leader.

Erikson: "Everybody needs it" means that everybody needs it for his or her sense of "I." But a historical period can also be host to a most genuine voice of faith. At the time of Jesus, Jewish history was particularly catastrophic for a national sense of "I." In spite of Jehovah's ("I AM") overlordship, the homeland had been in continuous danger of invasion, occupation, and exile. This,

I think, helped to open some ears to Jesus' great existential message.

Here I cannot help thinking of how nuclear weapons have done away with the boundaries of whole continents, and how, with their threat of global destruction, they call for the recognition of man's indivisible "specieshood."

> **Nuclear weapons have done away with the boundaries of whole continents.**

Hall: Both in *Young Man Luther* and in *Gandhi's Truth*, you showed how the attempts of an exceptional man to solve his personal difficulties benefited the whole group. If Luther and Gandhi had each resolved the previous five stages of life in the best possible way, would they have been so content that they would have lacked the urge to make such great changes?

Erikson: I couldn't say. What I tried to show in each book was not only that an exceptional man had the right conflicts, but that he lived in a period that needed just that man, while the historical period needed to resolve collectively what couldn't be resolved personally. As I said in one of the books, he solved for his period in history and for his own people what he could not resolve in his private life. And that makes a leader.

Hall: So it requires the right personal conflict in the right kind of person at the right moment among people who are ready for this conflict. Four elements, all of which are necessary.

> **Gandhi had a strange and unique mixture of maternal and paternal traits.**

Erikson: Yes, it so happened that in each historical situation, the man and his time complemented each other.

Hall: Since the film *Gandhi* was released, there's been renewed interest both in the man and in your book about him. Speaking of generativity, it seemed to me that Gandhi was more concerned with other people than with his own family.

Erikson: He turned into the father of his nation, and he extended his paternal feelings to mankind. Obviously, he acted for the species. Incidentally, Gandhi had a strange and unique mixture of maternal and paternal traits.

Hall: But isn't that characteristic of most creative people?

Erikson: Yes, because the emphasis is not on your personal procreativity, but on your creativity. People are always asking me how I liked the movie. The film is very different from my book, because I was writing a psychoanalytic book, in which I tried to show the relationship of the hero's personal conflicts to his historical deeds. My aim was to show how Gandhi fitted into that period—the historical moment—and what nonviolence—his truth—meant to him. I couldn't possibly expect to find in the movie a reflection of my developmental point of view.

Hall: Do you feel that anything important was left out?

Erikson: Only one thing—the impression that these nonviolent people made on some of the armed troops. I understood that in several places British soldiers found that they could not resist their nonviolent attackers, and so they threw their weapons away. Perhaps these are just stories, but I'd have liked to see some such reaction in some of the soldiers. For I don't think that all the British were as unfeeling and unresponsive as they were portrayed.

Hall: When Gandhi's followers were lined up five abreast and kept marching toward the clubs, I looked at the soldiers, and they were Indians. And I thought, "What must they be feeling?"

How long can you hit somebody without feeling revulsion at what you're doing?

Erikson: In order for nonviolent behavior to be effective it must be shocking—it has to shake up the violent opponent peacefully. In that situation, what is more important? That you are an Indian? That you are a soldier? That you are an officer? That you are a human being? It has to come to the point where suddenly these other people become human to you. Then you can no longer keep hitting them. Incidentally, it's amazing how American audiences are taking to the movie. Aren't you a little surprised?

Hall: If you consider that everybody is terribly concerned right now with the possibility of nuclear war, it's not so surprising. And people are impressed. During the intermission, instead of noise, talking, and a great rush to the snack bar, there's quiet. People are thinking about what they've seen.

Erikson: And these are not intellectuals. The movie about a great man's use of nonviolent resistance reaches people who do not belong to special peace organizations, and it makes them thoughtful. That's why it's such an important film. I honestly believe that it focuses on something our Judeo-Christian culture has not yet quite understood and has not used, and will probably have to face: the invention of nonviolent tactics to get out of the nuclear dilemma.

Hall: That dilemma gets us into rejectivity—the trend that opposes generativity in adulthood. How can it be dangerous?

Erikson: In our scheme, rejectivity is an unwillingness to include certain persons or groups within your

---

In order for nonviolent behavior to be effective it must be shocking— it has to shake up the violent opponent peacefully.

---

generative concern. Human beings spend an awful lot of their imagination on defining just which others they *don't* care for—in the generative sense. The danger in rejectivity, that is, the rejecting of other people, other groups, or other nations, is that it leads to what I have called "pseudospeciation." People lose the sense of being one species and try to make other kinds of people into a different and mortally dangerous species, one that doesn't count, one that isn't human.

Hall: To the Greeks, everybody else was a barbarian, and the Navajos call themselves "the people"—not "a" people.

Erikson: Many other tribes do the same thing. Other groups are considered to be a different species, and for the sake of decent humanity, you may have to subdue them or get rid of them. You can kill them without feeling that you have killed your own kind.

Hall: If "pseudo" has the connotation of "almost a lie," it indicates

that you know what you're doing. But when people do this, they're not really conscious of it, are they?

Erikson: That's exactly the point, and that's why it's so dangerous. The paradox is that pseudospecies-hood as a sense of representing the best in mankind binds a group together and inspires loyalty, heroism, and discipline.

Hall: So without pseudospeciation we wouldn't have loyalty and devotion and self-sacrifice. The problem is to keep the positive aspects while getting rid of the negative ones.

Erikson: The very existence of humanity depends on the solution of that paradox.

Hall: If I read you right, this has to be done in a way that enables you to keep your own identity as a group so that there's a culture to hand down.

Erikson: Yes, but what's important is a conviction that one's culture and "system" can go on living in a world that includes one's former enemies.

Hall: Would you like to make odds on our chances of developing an identity that encompasses the whole species? Do you think the odds are better than they were 15 years ago?

Erikson: Absolutely. After all, we *are* one species.   ◆

Discussion Questions

1. According to Erikson, what are three features of generativity in adulthood? Can old people be generative?

2. Why is historical relativity important to the study of human beings?

3. What is psychohistory?

4. On whose theories did Erikson base his own, and how is this different from other psychoanalysts?

5. How does Erikson describe real intimacy?

6. What are the two additional psychosexual stages proposed by Erikson?

7. What are the differences between boys and girls in identity forming?

8. What factors determine how long a stage of life will last?

9. According to Erikson, what four elements must be in place for a great leader (such as Gandhi) to emerge?

10. What is rejectivity?

11. What is pseudospeciation?

THOSE **Gangly** *Years*

◆ *Anne C. Petersen*

"How can you stand studying adolescents? My daughter has just become one and she's impossible to live with. Her hormones may be raging, but so am I!" A colleague at a cocktail party was echoing the widespread view that the biological events of puberty necessarily change nice kids into moody, rebellious adolescents. The view has gained such a foothold that some parents with well-behaved teenagers worry that their kids aren't developing properly.

They needn't worry. My research, and that of many others, suggests that although the early teen years can be quite a challenge for normal youngsters and their families, they're usually not half as bad as they are reputed to be. And even though the biological changes of puberty do affect adolescents' behavior, attitudes and feelings in many important ways, other, often controllable, social and environmental forces are equally important.

One 14-year-old, for example, who tried to excuse his latest under-par report card by saying, "My problem is testosterone, not tests," only looked at part of the picture. He ignored, as many do, the fact that, because of a move and the shift to junior high school, he had been in three schools in as many years.

My colleagues and I at Pennsylvania State University looked at a three-year span in the lives of young adolescents to find out how

a variety of biological and social factors affected their behavior and their feelings about themselves. A total of 335 young adolescents were randomly selected from two suburban school districts, primarily white and middle- to upper-middle-class. Two successive waves of these kids were monitored as they moved from the sixth through the eighth grade. Twice a year we interviewed them individually and gave them psychological tests in groups. When the youngsters were in the sixth and eighth grades, we also interviewed and assessed their parents. Just recently we again interviewed and assessed these young people and their parents during the adolescents' last year of high school.

We followed the children's pubertal development by asking them to judge themselves every six months on such indicators as height, pubic hair and acne in both boys and girls; breast development and menstruation in girls; and voice change and facial-hair growth in boys. We also estimated the timing of puberty by finding out when each youngster's adolescent growth spurt in height peaked, so we could study the effects of early, on-time or late maturing.

Although we have not yet analyzed all the data, it's clear that puberty alone does not have the

> *I didn't like being early, but by eighth grade, everyone wore a bra and had their period. I was normal.*

overwhelming psychological impact that earlier clinicians and researchers assumed it did (see "The Puzzle of Adolescence," this article). But it does have many effects on body image, moods and relationships with parents and members of the opposite sex.

Being an early or late maturer (one year earlier or later than average), for example, affected adolescents' satisfaction with their appearance and their body image—but only among seventh- and eighth-graders, not sixth-graders. We found that among students in the higher two grades, girls who were physically more mature were generally less satisfied with their weight and appearance than their less mature classmates.

A seventh-grade girl, pleased with being still childlike, said, "You can do more things—you don't have as much weight to carry around." A girl in the eighth grade, also glad to be a late maturer, commented, "If girls get fat, they have to worry about it." In contrast, an early-maturing girl subsequently commented, "I didn't like being early. A lot of my friends didn't understand." Another girl, as a high school senior, described the pain of maturing extremely early: "I tried to hide it. I was embarrassed and ashamed." However, her discomfort ended in the eighth grade, she said, because "by then everyone wore a bra and had their period. I was normal."

We found the reverse pattern among boys: Those who were physically more mature tended to be more satisfied with their weight and their overall appearance than their less mature peers. One already gangling seventh-grade boy, for example, said he liked being a "a little taller and having more muscle development than other kids so you can beat them in races." He conceded that developing more slowly might help "if you're a jockey" but added, "Really, I can't think of why [developing] later would be an advantage." In reflecting back from the 12th grade, a boy who had matured early noted that at the time the experience "made me feel superior."

For seventh- and eighth-grade boys, physical maturity was related to mood. Boys who had reached puberty reported positive moods more often than their pre-pubertal male classmates did. Pubertal status was less clearly and consistently related to mood among girls, but puberty did affect how girls got along with their parents. As physical development advanced among sixth-grade girls, their relationships with their parents declined; girls who were developmentally advanced talked less to their parents and had less positive feelings about family relationships than did less developed girls. We found a similar pattern among eighth-grade girls, but it was less clear in the seventh grade, perhaps because of the many other changes occurring at that time, such as the change from elementary to secondary school format and its related effects on friendship and school achievement.

The timing of puberty affected both school achievement and moods. Early maturers tended to get higher grades than later maturers in the same class. We suspect that this may stem from the often documented tendency of teachers to give more positive ratings to larger pupils. Although early maturers had an edge academically, those who matured later were more likely to report positive moods.

As we have noted, among relatively physically mature adoles-

cents, boys and girls had opposite feelings about their appearance: The boys were pleased, but the girls were not. We believe that, more generally, pubertal change is usually a positive experience for boys but a negative one for girls. While advancing maturity has some advantages for girls, including gaining some of the rights and privileges granted to maturing boys, it also brings increased limitations and restrictions related to their emerging womanhood. One sixth-grade girl

Parents let boys go out later than girls because they don't have to worry about them getting raped.

stated emphatically, "I don't like the idea of getting older or any of that. If I had my choice, I'd rather stay 10." Or, as one seventh-grade boy graphically explained the gender differences, "Parents let them [boys] go out later than girls because they don't have to worry about getting raped or anything like that."

Differences in the timing of puberty also affect interactions with members of the opposite sex. But is takes two to tango, and in the sixth grade, although many girls have reached puberty and are ready to socialize with boys, most boys have not yet made that transition. Thus, as one girl plaintive-

Shifting schools exposes teens to new extracurricular activities— licit and illicit.

ly summed up the sixth-grade social scene, "Girls think about boys more than boys think about girls."

In the seventh and eighth grades, the physically more mature boys and girls are likely to be pioneers in exploring social rela-

tions with members of the opposite sex, including talking with them on the phone, dating, having a boyfriend or girlfriend and "making out." We had the sense that once these young people began looking like teenagers, they wanted to act like them as well.

But puberty affects the social and sexual activity of individual young adolescents both directly and indirectly; the pubertal status of some students can have consequences for the entire peer group of boys and girls. Although dating and other boy-girl interactions are linked to pubertal status, and girls usually reach puberty before boys do, we found no sex differences in the rates of dating throughout the early-adolescent period. When the early-maturing kids began socializing with members of the opposite sex, the pattern quickly spread throughout the entire peer group. Even prepubertal girls were susceptible to thinking and talking about boys if all their girlfriends were "boy crazy."

The physical changes brought on by puberty have far-reaching effects, but so do many other changes in the lives of adolescents. One we found to be particularly influential is the change in school structure between the sixth and eighth grades. Most young adolescents in our country shift from a relatively small neighborhood elementary school, in which most classes are taught by one teacher, to a much larger, more impersonal middle school or junior high school (usually farther from the child's home), in which students move from class to class and teacher to teacher for every subject. This shift in schools has many ramifications, including disrupting the old peer-group structure, exposing adolescents to different achievement expectations by teachers and providing opportunities for new extracurricular activities—licit and illicit.

Both the timing and number of school transitions are very important. In our study, for example, students who changed schools earlier than most of their peers, as well as those who changed schools twice (both experiences due to modifications of the school system), suffered an academic slump that continued through eighth grade. Therefore, early or double school transition seemed stressful, beyond the usual effects of moving to a junior high school.

Puberty and school change, which appear to be the primary and most pervasive changes occurring during early adolescence, are often linked to other important changes, such as altered family relations. Psychologist Laurence Steinberg of the University of Wisconsin has found that family relationships shift as boys and girls move through puberty. During mid puberty, he says, conflict in family discussions increases; when the conflict is resolved, boys usually become more dominant in conversations with their mothers. (Psychologist John Hill of Virginia Commonwealth University has found that family conflict increases only for boys.) Other research,

---

The Puzzle of Adolescence

At the turn of the century, psychologist G. Stanley Hall dignified adolescence with his "storm and stress" theory, and Anna Freud subsequently argued influentially that such storm and stress is a normal part of adolescence. Ever since, clinicians and researchers have been trying—with only limited success—to develop a coherent theory of what makes adolescents tick.

Psychoanalytic theorist Peter Blos added in the late 1960s and 1970s that adolescents' uncontrolled sexual and aggressive impulses affect relationships with their parents. He suggested that both adolescents and their parents may need more distant relationships because of the unacceptable feelings stimulated by the adolescents' sexuality.

Research conducted in the 1960s showed that not all adolescents experience the storm and stress psychoanalytic theory predicts they should. Many studies, including those of Roy Grinker; Joseph Adelson and Elizabeth Douvan; Daniel Offer; and Albert Bandura, demonstrated that a significant proportion of adolescents make it through this period without appreciable turmoil. These findings suggest that pubertal change per se cannot account for the rocky time some adolescents experience.

Other theories of adolescent development have also been linked to pubertal change. For example, in his theory of how children's cognitive capacities develop, Swiss psychologist Jean Piaget attributed the emergence of "formal operational thought," that is, the capacity to think abstractly, to the interaction of pubertal and environmental changes that occur during the same developmental period.

Some researchers have linked the biological events of puberty to possible changes in brain growth or functioning. Deborah Waber, a psychologist at Boston Children's Hospital, has shown that the timing of pubertal change is related to performance differences between the right- and left-brain hemispheres on certain tasks and to the typical adult pattern of gender-related cognitive abilities: Later maturers, including most men, have relatively better spatial abilities, and earlier maturers, including most women, have relatively better verbal abilities.

It has also been suggested that pubertal change affects adolescent behavior through the social consequences of altered appearance. Once young adolescents look like adults, they are more likely to be treated as adults and to see themselves that way, too.

Coming also from a social psychological perspective, psychologist John Hill of Virginia Commonwealth University, together with former Cornell University doctoral student Mary Ellen Lynch, have proposed that pubertal change leads parents and peers to expect more traditional gender-role behavior from adolescents than from younger children; they suggest that both boys and girls become more aware of these gender stereotypes in early adolescence and exaggerate their gender-related behavior at this age.

Despite all these theories, most studies that look at how puberty affects adolescent development are finding that puberty per se is not as important as we once thought. Puberty does specifically affect such things as body image and social and sexual behavior, but it does not affect all adolescent behavior, and it affects some adolescents more strongly than others. In fact, many studies, like our, are revealing that other changes in early adolescence, particularly social and environmental ones, are at least as important as biological ones.

however, suggests that adolescents wind up playing a more equal role relative to both parents.

In our study, the parents of early-maturing girls and late-maturing boys reported less positive feelings about their children in the sixth and eighth grades than did parents of boys and girls with other patterns of pubertal timing. (These effects were always stronger for fathers than for mothers.) The adolescents, however, reported that their feeling about their parents were unrelated to pubertal timing.

The feelings of affection and support that adolescents and their parents reported about one another usually declined from the sixth to the eighth grades, with the biggest decline in feeling between girls and their mothers. But importantly, the decline was from very positive to less positive—but still not negative—feelings.

Early adolescence is clearly an unusual transition in development because of the number of changes young people experience. But the impact of those changes is quite varied; changes that may challenge and stimulate some young people can become overwhelming and stressful to others. The outcome seems to depend on prior strengths and vulnerabilities—both of the individual adolescents and their families—as well as on

---

The vast majority of early teens we studied were trouble-free or had only intermittent problems. Only 15 percent were plagued by trouble and turmoil.

---

the pattern, timing and intensity of changes.

Youngsters in our study who changed schools within six months of peak pubertal change reported more depression and anxiety than those whose school and biological transitions were more separated in time. Students who experienced an unusual and negative change

at home—such as the death of a parent or divorce of parents—reported even greater difficulties, a finding that supports other research. Sociologists Roberta Simmons and Dale Blyth have found that the negative effects of junior high school transition, especially in combination with other life changes, continue on into high school, particularly for girls.

Many of the negative effects of transitions and changes seen in our study were tempered when adolescents had particularly positive and supportive relationships with their peers and family. The effects of all these early-adolescent changes were even stronger by the 12th grade than in 8th grade.

Overall, we found that the usual pattern of development in early adolescence is quite positive. More than half of those in the study seemed to be almost trouble-free, and approximately 30 percent of the total group had only intermittent problems during their early teen years. Fifteen percent of the kids, however, did appear to be caught in a downward spiral of trouble and turmoil.

Gender played an important role in how young adolescents expressed and dealt with this turmoil. Boys generally showed their poor adjustment through external behavior, such as being rebellious and disobedient, whereas girls were more likely to show internal behavior, such as having depressed moods. But since many poorly adjusted boys also showed many signs of depression, the rates of such symptoms did not differ between the sexes in early adolescence.

By the 12th grade, however, the girls were significantly more likely than the boys to have depressive symptoms, a sex difference also found among adults. Boys who had such symptoms in the 12th grade usually had devel-

© 1998 PhotoDisc, Inc.

oped them in the sixth grade as well; girls who had depressive symptoms as high school seniors usually had developed them by the eighth grade.

For youngsters who fell in the troubled group, the stage was already set—and the pathways distinguishable—at the very beginning of adolescence. There is an overall tendency for academic decline in the seventh and eight grades (apparently because seventh- and eighth-grade teachers adopt tougher grading standards than elementary school teachers do). But the grades of boys with school behavior problems or depressive symptoms in early adolescence subsequently declined far

more than those of boys who did not report such problems. Thus, for youngsters whose lives are already troubled, the changes that come with early adolescence add further burdens—and their problems are likely to persist through the senior year of high school.

One 12th-grade boy who followed this pathway described the experience: "My worst time was seventh to ninth grade. I had a lot of growing up to do and I still have a lot more to do. High school was not the 'sweet 16' time everyone said it would be. What would have helped me is more emotional support in grades seven through nine." In explaining that particularly difficult early-adolescent

period, he said, "Different teachers, colder environment, changing classes and detention all caused chaos in the seventh to ninth grades."

We did not find the same relationship between academic failure and signs of emotional turmoil in girls as in boys. For example, those seventh-grade girls particularly likely to report poor self-image or depressive symptoms were those who were academically successful. Furthermore, when these girls lowered their academic achievement by eighth grade, their depression and their self-image tended to improve. These effects occurred in many areas of girls' course work but were particularly strong in stereotypically "masculine" courses such as mathematics and science. Like the pattern of problems for boys, the girls' pattern of trading grades to be popular and feel good about themselves persisted into the 12th grade. (Some girls, of course, performed well academically and felt good about themselves both in junior high school and high school.)

We think that for certain girls, high achievement, especially in "masculine" subjects, comes with social costs—speculation supported by the higher priority these particular girls give to popularity. They seem to sacrifice the longer-term benefits of high achievement for the more immediate social benefits of "fitting in." Other studies have revealed a peak in social conformity at this age, especially among girls, and have shown that many adolescents reap immediate, but short-term, social benefits from many types of behavior that adults find irrational or risky.

Our most recent research is focused on exploring further whether the developmental patterns established during early adolescence continue to the end of high school. We are also trying to integrate our observations into a coherent theory of adolescent development and testing that theory by seeing whether we can predict the psychological status of these students at the end of high school based on their characteristics in early adolescence. Other key concerns include discovering early warning signs of trouble and iden-tifying ways to intervene to improve the course of development.

The biological events of puberty are a necessary—and largely un-controllable—part of growing up. but we may be able to understand and control the social and environmental forces that make ado-lescence so difficult for a small but troubled group of youngsters. The adolescents' journey toward adult-hood is inherently marked by change and upheaval but need not be fraught with chaos or deep pain.   ◆

Discussion Questions

1. What nonbiological factors influence adolescent behavior?

2. List the biological indications of puberty.

3. What psychological factors does puberty influence?

4. Describe the impact of being an early and a late maturing girl.

5. Describe the impact of being an early and a late maturing boy.

6. How does the timing of puberty affect parent-child relations?

7. Who reaches puberty at a younger age, boys or girls, and what impact does this have?

8. Which factors reduce the negative effects of puberty?

9. What are the behavioral differences between boys and girls who do not adjust well to puberty?

10. According to Petersen, what percent of teens are plagued by serious problems? What percent of teens seem to be trouble-free?

Marriages **Made** to L a s t

◆ *Jeanette Lauer and Robert Lauer*

Americans are keenly aware of the high rate of marital breakup in this country. More than a million couples a year now end their expectations of bliss in divorce; the average duration of a marriage in the United States is 9.4 years. The traditional nuclear family of husband, wife and children is less and less common. Indeed, it seems at times that no one out there is happily married. But in the midst of such facts and figures, another group tends to be overlooked: those couples who somehow manage to stay together, who allow nothing less than death itself to break them up.

Social scientists have long been concerned about the causes of marital disruption. There are numerous works that tell us why people break up. But as J.H. Wallis wrote in his 1970 book, *Marriage Observed*, "we have still not quite come to grips with what it is that makes marriages last, and, enables them to survive." His conclusion remains valid. The books that tell couples how to construct a lasting and meaningful marriage tend to be based either upon the clinical experiences of those who have counseled troubled and dissolving marriages, or upon the speculations of those who believe that they have found the formula for success.

We recently completed a survey of couples with enduring marriages to explore how marriages survive and satisfy in this turbulent world. Through colleagues and students we located and questioned 351 couples, 300 said they were happily married, 19 said they were unhappily married (but were staying together for a variety of

> *"Commitment means a willingness to be unhappy for a while," said a man married for more than 20 years. "I wouldn't go on for years and years being wretched in my marriage. But you can't avoid troubled times."*

reasons, including "the sake of the children"); and among the remaining 32 couples only one partner said he or she was unhappy in the marriage.

Each husband and wife responded individually to our questionnaire, which included 39 statements and questions about marriage—ranging from agreement about sex, money and goals in life to attitudes toward spouses and marriage in general. We asked couples to select from their answers the ones that best explained why their marriages had lasted. Men and women showed remarkable agreement on the keys to an enduring relationship (see box).

The most frequently named reason for an enduring and happy

> **Fewer than 10 percent of the spouses thought that good sexual relations kept their marriage together.**

marriage was having a generally positive attitude toward one's spouse: viewing one's partner as one's best friend and liking him or her "as a person."

As one wife summed it up, "I feel that liking a person in marriage is as important as loving that person. Friends enjoy each other's company. We spend an unusually large amount of time together. We work at the same institution, offices just a few feet apart. But we still have things to do and to say to each other on a positive note after being together through the day."

It may seem almost trite to say that "my spouse is my best friend," but the couples in our survey underscored the importance of feeling that way. Moreover, they told us some specific things that they liked about their mates—why, as one woman said, "I would want to have him as a friend even if I weren't married to him." For one thing, many happily married people said that their mates become more interesting to them in time. A man married for 30 years said that it was almost like being married to a series of different women: "I have watched her grow and have shared with her both the pain and the exhilaration of her journey. I find her more fascinating now than when we were first married."

A common theme among couples in our study was that the things they really liked in each other were qualities of caring, giving, integrity and a sense of humor. In essence, they said, "I am married to someone who cares about me, who is concerned for my well-being, who gives as much or more than he or she gets, who is open and trustworthy and who is not mired

What Keeps A Marriage Going?

Here are the top reasons respondents gave, listed in order of frequency.

Men	Women
My spouse is my best friend.	My spouse is my best friend.
I like my spouse as a person.	I like my spouse as a person.
Marriage is a long-term commitment.	Marriage is a long-term commitment.
Marriage is sacred.	Marriage is sacred.
We agree on aims and goals.	We agree on aims and goals.
My spouse has grown more interesting.	My spouse has grown more interesting.
I want the relationship to succeed.	I want the relationship to succeed.
An enduring marriage is important to social stability.	We laugh together.
We laugh together.	We agree on a philosophy of life.
I am proud of my spouse's achievements.	We agree on how and how often to show affection.
We agree on a philosophy of life.	An enduring marriage is important to social stability.
We agree about our sex life.	We have a stimulating exchange of ideas.
We agree on how and how often to show affection.	We discuss things calmly.
I confide in my spouse.	We agree about our sex life.
We share hobbies and interests.	I am proud of my spouse's achievements.

points, which are very few. Her strong points overcome them too much."

A second key to a lasting marriage was a belief in marriage as a long term commitment and a sacred institution. Many of our respondents thought that the present generation takes the vow "till death us do part" too lightly and is unwilling to work through difficult times. Successful couples viewed marriage as a task that sometimes demands that you grit your teeth and plunge ahead in spite of the difficulties. "I'll tell you why we've stayed together," said a Texas woman married for 18 years. "I'm just too damned stubborn to give up."

Some of the people in the survey indicated that they would stay together no matter what. Divorce was simply not an option. Others viewed commitment somewhat differently. They saw it not as a chain that inexorably binds people together despite intense misery but rather as a determination to work through difficult times. You can't run home to mother when the first sign of trouble appears," said a woman married for 35 years.

"Commitment means a willingness to be unhappy for a while," said a man married for more than 20 years. "I wouldn't go on for years and years being wretched in my marriage. But you can't avoid troubled times. You're not going to be happy with each other all the

down in a somber, bleak outlook on life." The redemption of difficult people through selfless devotion may make good fiction, but the happily married people in our sample expressed no such sense of mission. Rather, they said, they are grateful to have married someone who is basically appealing and likable.

Are lovers blind to each other's faults? No, according to our findings. They are aware of the flaws in their mates and acknowledge the rough times, but they believe that the likable qualities are more important than the deficiencies and the difficulties. "She isn't perfect," said a husband of 24 years. "But I don't worry about her weak

© 1998 PhotoDisc, Inc.

time. That's when commitment is really important."

In addition to sharing attitudes toward the spouse and toward marriage, our respondents indicated that agreement about aims and goals in life, the desire to make the marriage succeed and laughing together were all important. One surprising result was that agreement about sex was far down the list of reasons for a happy marriage. Fewer than 10 percent of the spouses thought that good sexual relations kept their marriage together. Is sex relatively unimportant to a happy marriage? Yes and no.

Although not many happily married respondents listed it as a major reason for their happiness, most were still generally satisfied with their sex lives. Seventy percent said that they always or almost always agreed about sex. And indeed for many, "satisfied" seems too mild a term. A woman married for 19 years said: "Our sexual desire is strong, and we are very much in love." One man said that sex with his wife was like "a revival of youth." Another noted

that for various reasons he and his wife did not have sex as frequently as they would like, but when they do "it is a beautiful act of giving and sharing as deeply emotional as it is physical."

While some reported a diminishing sex life, others described a

A common theme among couples in our study was that the things they really liked in each other were qualities of caring, giving, integrity and a sense of humor.

relatively stable pattern and a number indicated improvement over time. "Thank God, the passion hasn't died," a wife said. "In fact, it has gotten more intense. The only thing that has died is the element of doubt or uncertainty that one experiences while dating or in the beginning of a marriage."

On the other hand, some couples said they were satisfied despite a less-than-ideal sex life. A number of people told us that they were happy with their marriage even though they did not have sex as frequently as they would like. Generally, men complained of this

more than women, although a number of wives desired sex more than did their husbands. There were various reasons for having less sex than desired, generally involving one partner's exhaustion from work or family circumstances ("We are very busy and very involved," reported a husband, "and have a teenager who stays up late. So we don't make love as often as we would like to.").

Does this dissatisfaction with sex life lead to affairs? We did not ask about fidelity directly, but the high value that most of our subjects placed on friendship and commitment strikes us as incongruous with infidelity. And in fact only two of those we questioned volunteered that they had had brief affairs. One husband's view might explain the faithfulness of the group: "I get tempted when we don't have sex. But I don't think I could ever have an affair. I would feel like a traitor."

Such treason, in fact, may be the one taboo in enduring relationships. A wife of 27 years said that although she could work out almost any problem with her husband given enough time, infidelity "would probably not be something I could forget and forgive." The couples in our sample appear to take their commitment to each other seriously.

Those with a less-than-ideal sex life talked about adjusting to it rather than seeking relief in an affair. A woman married 25 years rated her marriage as extremely happy even though she and her husband had had no sexual relations for the past 10 years. "I was married once before and the marriage was almost totally sex and little else," she said. "So I suppose a kind of trade-off exists here—I like absolutely everything else about my current marriage."

Many others agreed that they would rather be married to their spouse and have a less-than-ideal sex life than be married to someone else and have a better sex life. As one wife put it, "I feel marriages can survive and flourish without today's emphasis on sex. I had a much stronger sex drive than my husband and it was a point of weakness in our marriage. However, it was not as important as friendship, understanding and respect. That we had lot of, and still do."

We found a few beliefs and practices among our couples that contradict what some therapists believe is important to a marriage. One involves conflict. Some marriage counselors stress the importance of expressing feelings with abandon—spouses should freely vent their anger with each other, letting out all the stops short of physical violence. According to them, aggression is a catharsis that gets rid of hostility and restores harmony in the marital relationship. But some social scientists argue that intense expressions of anger, resentment and dislike tend to corrode the relationship and increase the likelihood of future aggression.

Happily married couples in our survey came down squarely on the side of those who emphasize the damaging effects of intensely expressed anger. A salesman with a 36-year marriage advised, "Discuss your problems in a normal voice. If a voice is raised, stop. Return after a short period of time. Start again. After a period of time both parties will be able to deal with their problems and not say things that they will be sorry about later."

Only one couple said that they typically yelled at each other. The rest emphasized the importance of restraint. They felt that a certain calmness is necessary in dealing constructively with conflict.

Another commonly held belief that contradicts conventional wisdom concerns equality in marriage. Most social scientists note

© 1998 PhotoDisc, Inc.

the value of an egalitarian relationship. But according to the couples in our sample, the attitude that marriage is 50-50 proposition can be damaging. One husband said that a successful marriage demands that you "give 60 percent of the time. You have to be willing to put in more than you take out." A wife happily married for 40 years said she would advise all young couples "to be willing to give 70 percent and expect 30 percent."

In the long run, the giving and taking should balance out. If either partner enters a marriage determined that all transactions must be equal, the marriage will suffer. As one husband put it, "Sometimes I give far more than I receive, and sometimes I receive far more than I give. But my wife does the same. If we weren't willing to do that, we would have broken up long ago."

Finally, some marriage experts have strongly advocated that spouses maintain separate as well as shared interests. It is important, they argue to avoid the merging of identities. But those in our survey with enduring, happy marriages disagree. They try to spend as much time together and share as many activities as possible. "Jen is just the best friend I have," said a husband who rated his marriage as extremely happy. "I would rather spend time with her, talk with her, be with her than with anyone else."

"We try to share everything," said another. "We even work together now. In spite of that, we often feel that we have too little time together."

We did not detect any loss of individuality in these people. In fact, they disagreed to some extent on many of the questions. Their intense intimacy—their preferences for shared rather than separate activities—seems to reflect a richness and fulfillment in the relationship rather than a loss of identity. "On occasion she has something else to do, and I enjoy the time alone. But it strikes me that I can enjoy it because I know she will be home, and we will be together again."

Our results seem to underscore Leo Tolstoy's observation that "Happy families are all alike." Those who have long-term, happy marriages share a number of attitudes and behavioral patterns that combine to create an enduring relationship. For them, "till death do us part" is not a binding clause but a gratifying reality. ◆

◈ Discussion Questions

1. How many married couples did the Lauers study, and what method did they use to conduct their research?

2. How does commitment impact a marriage?

3. List at least three factors that contribute to a strong marriage. What seems to be the most important factor?

4. How important is sex for keeping a relationship strong? Explain.

5. List four of the qualities spouses liked most about each other.

6. How important are a spouse's faults in causing marital discord?

7. How did the husbands' replies differ from those of the wives?

8. How important is romantic love for keeping a marriage strong? Explain.

9. Did the Lauers' findings surprise you in any way? How so?

10. What do most young people (and perhaps most single people of any age) believe to be the most important factors for a successful marriage? How do these common beliefs conflict with the Lauers' findings?

Name: _____

Date: _____

Part 11: Adolescence and Adulthood

1. Most of the teenagers I know or have known are highly troubled.

   Agree   (1)   (2)   (3)   (4)   (5)   Disagree

2. I think that love is the most important ingredient for the long-term success of a relationship.

   Agree   (1)   (2)   (3)   (4)   (5)   Disagree

3. I believe that most significant development occurs during childhood.

   Agree   (1)   (2)   (3)   (4)   (5)   Disagree

List the significant people in your life from puberty onward. Then rank each person according to the extent that he or she influenced your life (1 being most influential). Write a brief account of how the top five individuals influenced your life.

PART 12

MOTIVATION AND EMOTION

Stendhal, obviously in a cynical mood, once wrote, "Speech was given man so that he might hide his thoughts." As you'll see, psychological research shows that the truth is even worse than that. We communicate with other people not just through verbal language but also through gestures and facial expressions, and the three modes of communication are not always in sync. We may be hiding our true thoughts and feelings through any of these modes, or as is more common, we may be saying one thing while our facial expression and gestures are saying something quite different. We've all dealt with the store clerk, for example, whose words are, "Thanks so much for shopping here today" but whose body is saying "I hate this stupid job, now please go away."

In the first article in this section, Ernst G. Beier reveals some of the mechanisms of nonverbal communication, especially in marriage. In "The Emotional Brain" Laurence Miller speculates about possible emotion centers in the brain, and in "The Universal Smile," Paul Ekman reviews a variety of cross-cultural data that suggest that certain facial expressions may be universally tied to certain emotional states.

How We Send Emotional Messages

◆ Ernst G. Beier

People are forever saying one thing and meaning another. A husband says to his wife, "I love you." According to the dictionary, the man is expressing his affection. He cherishes his wife. He is attracted to her. His life is bound to hers. There are times when she excites him sexually and other times when he would risk his life to protect her. The wife replies coldly, "Go to hell!" and stamps out of the room, slamming the door behind her.

Absurd? Let me add a few details to this imaginary scene.

The man has just returned home at nine p.m. for the 50th night in a row. He smells like a brewery and looks sullen. He sits down without a word, crosses his legs tightly, and starts reading the paper. His wife asks him how his day went. He answers with a grunt.

She says, "I want a divorce." He says, "Where's dinner?" She says, "I'm serious. I've had enough of you. I treat you well and you treat me like a servant. I don't *like* you anymore."

The man looks up from his distractions. There's a look of incomprehension on his face. He needs his wife. He's obviously afraid now. He doesn't want her to leave.

"Give me one reason why I shouldn't walk out of here tonight," she demands.

Perspiration has appeared on his upper lip. He starts to say something but lights a cigarette instead. He avoids her stare, and his eyes dart around the room as if searching for an answer. Then he clears his throat and says with a grin, "I love you."

The Eloquence of Action

Dialogues like this one—exaggerated and even comic as it may seem—take place all the time. The man's actions spoke louder than his words. He was communicating with his face and posture, with his intonation and choice of words, with the way he placed himself in the room. The lexical meaning of "I love you" amounted to a stupid joke in the context of his evident lack of interest.

And yet there is another level to this scene. When confronted with his wife's anger, the man sits up and listens. He communicates his fear of losing her as accurately as he communicated his distaste.

What are we to make of this man's style of communication? We may think of him as unattractive, neurotic, confused, weak, childish; but we wouldn't say that he had much trouble communicating his feelings. He was communicating perfectly. First he communicated indifference, and later he communicated panic. His messages were discordant yet full of meaning. We can assume, moreover (since this is an imaginary scene), that his words of love had often paid off in the past. They are sweet words, and he himself probably believed them. It couldn't be helped that the discrepancy between one of his messages and all the others seemed so blatant that his wife finally decided to believe his behavior alone.

I have been investigating nonverbal communication for several years, both clinically and experimentally. I am interested in some of the same human behaviors that Robert Rosenthal and his colleagues described. But whereas Rosenthal measured the sensitivity of many different receivers to one standardized sequence of nonverbal cues, I am more concerned with the *senders* of emotional information. Specifically, I would like to know how married couples communicate well-being or unease to each other. I also want to elucidate some of those common human transactions in which one person sends another person a clear emotional message of which the sender is unaware but which is nevertheless intended.

Vibes—Good and Bad

Not long ago, the word "vibrations" entered American slang. "Vibes" are feelings that one person arouses in another by supposedly unobservable means. According to popular usage, one person sends vibes and others get them. The term is a metaphor for the communication of emotion. In another sense, vibes are more than a simple message; they're an emotional climate, and like any emotional climate, particularly those evoked by first impressions, they tend to be categorized by receivers as beneficial or dangerous.

It is plausible that vibes may result from certain kinds of nonverbal communication. If so, then the communication of well-being, security, affection and similar feelings would cause good vibes, while messages of hostility, insecurity and anxiety would cause bad vibes. In any case, whether you think of the word "vibes" as a term with definite behavioral cor-

© Digital Vision

relates or simply as a suggestive metaphor, the fact remains that a person can create beneficial and/or dangerous emotional environments through body movements and tones of voice.

Daniel P. Sternberg and I conducted an experiment with 50 newlywed couples in an attempt to learn if they used body language to communicate cues of martial conflict and harmony. Our newlyweds were all between the ages of 18 and 24 and had been married only a few weeks. We gave each couple a questionnaire designed to tell us how much conflict there was in their marriage. Many of them, it turned out, were already experiencing serious problems. We also interviewed the couples and asked them to take turns telling about themselves, about their expectations and disappointments, and about various other aspects of their short lives together. Meanwhile, we videotaped each couple in order to record their nonverbal behavior.

Look at the Eyes

Once we had assessed the relative closeness, stability and harmony of each couple's relationship, we ran the videotapes for several trained judges on nonverbal behavior, who rated each couple purely on the basis of nonverbal interactions. The judges were looking specifically for eye contact, laughing, talking, touching (of the self or of the spouse), and also for the way they held their arms and legs, either open or closed.

It became clear when we analyzed the data that nonverbal cues express a person's feeling very accurately. The happy couples would sit closer together, look more frequently into each other's eyes, would touch each other more often than themselves, and would talk more to their spouses. The happier couples, in short, were able to create for each other a more comfortable and supportive bodily environment.

The couples who were experiencing the most conflict sent out

The happier couples, in short, were able to create for each other a more comfortable and supportive bodily environment.

more distant vibrations. They tended to cross their arms and legs, had less eye contact, and touched themselves more frequently than they touched each other.

We further analyzed the data by dividing all the couples into four groups: 1) those who were equally dissatisfied with the relationship; 2) those where the husband had more complaints; 3) those where the wife had more complaints; and 4) those where both had a minimum of complaints. When we measured the emotional climates that these four types created, we found, as expected, that the couples who had the most serious conflicts were also communicating the most distance. The second most serious conflict group was the one in which the woman complained more than the man.

To have a dissatisfied woman apparently makes a couple far unhappier than the presence of a dis-

satisfied male, at least as can be measured by distance values obtained through nonverbal communication.

A follow-up study, conducted nine months later, indicated that the style of being together which marriage partners initiate seems to maintain itself over time. Those couples who had great dissatisfaction with each other remained dissatisfied; those who lived in reasonable peace with each other managed to preserve that peace, possibly because they consistently communicated harmony without the use of words.

We made another interesting discovery in comparing the complaint scores of husbands and wives. The husbands as a group maintained their complaint score at a medium level, while females increased their complaint scores as the marriage went on. We concluded from this observation that women typically expect a great deal from marriage but don't get much, whereas males typically expect little in the first place and are therefore not let down.

We Make Our Own Environments

The study of newlyweds lends support to the common intuition that people can, and do, communicate by means of moods. These moods, when received, are more than bits of information; for no matter how perceptive and cool-headed someone may be, he or she is still liable to be influenced by the communication of someone else's emotional expression. Most of us are probably aware of this already. We know that our own moods somehow bounce off and make demands of those around us, especially people who are very close to us. Communication by moods can be quite simple, as when laughter sets off a similar laughter in everyone.

Or, it can be complex and of great importance to the nature of human relationships. When we send out listening or caring cues that allow people to feel deeply understood, then people respond quite differently than if we had sent out cues that are seen to be controlling. By using such cues, consciously and unconsciously, we determine to a large extent the human world around us, and we are more responsible for the reactions we obtain from other people than we dare realize. This situation may add credence to the old moral that says we should look carefully at our own behavior before complaining about the behavior of those we live with.

I ran into some striking examples of just how people restrict their emotional environments during a recent experiment involving some of our newlyweds. My students and I were trying to learn more about the nature of emotional expressions, particularly about the frequent discordance between intended expressions and those that are actually—but unconsciously—portrayed.

Angry, Angry, Angry

We asked several people to act out six different moods on videotape. The moods were anger, fear, seductivity, indifference, happiness and sadness. Then we let our subjects review their portrayals and eliminate any that they felt were unrepresentative. The chosen portrayals, in other words, were emotionally authentic in the eyes of their creators.

When we played these videotapes to large audiences to discover if they could decode the moods intended, we found that most senders were able to project accurately only two of the six moods. The particular moods, of course, varied from sender to sender, but in general we were surprised to learn that everyone appears to send out misinformation. Their portrayals often failed to represent their intentions. This finding lent strength to the hypothesis that the discordance between our emotional expressions and our intentions may represent conflicting impulses. It is possible, admittedly, that our audiences were unusually poor judges of nonverbal behavior; our senders, moreover, may have been better actors in less artificial settings. But at least we found evidence for the notion that there are many people whose emotional intentions and self-images are out of harmony with their actual behavior.

We found evidence for the notion that there are many people whose emotional intentions and self-images are out of harmony with their actual behavior.

I shall never forget two examples of this discordance. One girl, who tried like everyone else to appear angry, fearful, seductive, indifferent, happy and sad—and who subsequently edited her own performances for authenticity—appeared to her judges as angry in every case. Imagine what a difficult world she must have lived in. No matter where she set the thermostat of her emotional climate, everyone else always felt it as sweltering hot. Another girl in our experiment demonstrated a similar one-dimensionality; only in her case, whatever else she thought she was doing, she invariably impressed her judges as seductive. Even when she wanted to be angry, men whistled at her.

Compromise Behaviors

The whole question of how people encode and decode emotional signals is extremely complex, and we're fortunate that many psychologists today are investigating nonverbal communication. Yet despite the complexity of emotional expressions, the principle of discordance seems to persist. We may say, for example, that we want another person to like us, and we absolutely believe what we say; yet we send out information, through facial expressions,

posture, tone of voice, and many other cues, that we don't like that person. Perhaps we made an error in communication, or perhaps the other person misinterpreted our meaning. A simpler explanation, particularly if such discordant behavior persists, is that we really wanted to communicate two different feelings at the same time. And so we compromised. We maintained the self-image of a person who wants to show liking, but at the same time we managed to communicate *dis*like, without feeling responsible. The transmission of discordant cues is a way of having our cake and eating it.

Such behavior is common among intimates. Without a doubt, some of the newlyweds who sat with their legs and arms together, touching themselves but rarely touching their spouse, had often spoken words of love and closeness, aloud and to themselves.

Meanwhile they kept their distance without really knowing it and also told their spouse to stay away. The man who told his wife, "I love you," although he probably meant something of substance, did not support his statement with his body. The obvious discordance in these cases, although imperfectly understood by the actors, paid off in definite advantages. Or at least they were supposed to pay off; there are times, inevitably, when such compromise behaviors become transparent, and the motivations behind them are recognized as confused and destructive.

I accept Freud's proposition that many of our acts spring from hidden desires. What I have tried to do is find evidence for this notion in the contradictions between one's intentions and one's actual behavior. We can measure nonverbal cues, therefore, as expressions of unconscious motivations. The evidence, I think, suggests that we often create our own problems by stimulating the world around us without knowing what we're doing. Our nonverbal behavior often serves ends that are obscure to nearly everyone, especially to ourselves.

© Digital Vision

Discussion Questions

1. According to Beier, what are "vibes"?

2. What nonverbal cues communicated the most conflict in the newlywed study?

3. How, according to Beier, can we change the emotional environment that surrounds us?

4. What are discordant behavioral cues?

5. Describe an awkward communication experience that you have had. Besides the semantics, how did nonverbal communication play a role in the interaction?

THE *Emotional* BRAIN

◆ *Laurence Miller*

The idea that the brain's left and right hemispheres are specialized for different kinds of thinking is a familiar one, backed by lots of research. Now it's beginning to look as if the hemispheres are also specialized for different emotional experiences. It's not as simple as, say, a sad side and a happy side, but there's growing evidence that parts of the two hemispheres play different roles in our emotions and moods.

Support for this idea comes from research on some people with brain disorders and on some with apparently perfectly functioning brains. The research is still controversial and sketchy. But the picture that's emerging is intriguing and may lead to new ways of helping people whose emotional lives are out of control.

One line of evidence comes from research on people with neurological problems such as epilepsy, in which storms of abnormal electrical activity occur in certain parts of the brain. If the seizures happen in areas involved in movement, twitches and convulsions may result; if sensory areas are involved, patients may feel tinglings, see flashes or hear strange noises. But if the seizures affect the brain structures involved in emotions and memory, patients may feel rage or fear, have déjà vu sensations or dreamy states or even have mystical experiences.

In most people who suffer seizures, the abnormal electrical ac-

tivity only occurs within one hemisphere. But this was not true of a woman we'll call Mary, who had a trouble spot in each hemisphere. At 33 she suffered her first seizure and thereafter began having what she described as "mild spells" in which she felt "fullness" in her head. For 20 years anticonvulsive medication kept her seizures under control, but she then appeared at a Canadian neuropsychiatric clinic complaining that her head again felt full. She also had bizarre sensations of movement and pressure that made her fear she was going crazy. The clinic staff found her to be depressed and suicidal, although she lacked some of the classic symptoms of major depression such as disturbed appetite. She also had periods of almost manic elation.

A team of clinicians headed by the University of British Columbia's Trevor A. Hurwitz, a psychiatrist, recorded Mary's brain waves with an electroencephalograph (EEG) and her behavior with videotapes. They found that her depression was part of the seizure syndrome itself, not just a reaction to her upsetting symptoms. Moreover, the seizures in each hemisphere produced different psychological and emotional symptoms.

Following left-hemisphere attacks, Mary became depressed and agitated, suffered from insomnia and considered suicide. Voices were telling her she was bad, and her radio kept saying "googli

googli." After right-sided attacks, her mood became manic and her behavior flighty; she danced on her bed and behaved seductively toward the hospital staff. It was as if the left side of her brain had a different mood, even a different personality, from the right.

Studies of people who have had strokes or head injuries suggest a similar emotional division of labor between the hemispheres. Unlike epileptics, who suffer from abnormal bursts of activity in intact parts of the brain, those with strokes or brain injury have lost actual brain tissue.

Early in this century, neurologists noted that when people had left-hemisphere damage severe enough to impair their speech and movement, their reactions were often depressive, even aggressive. Unable to talk coherently to express their frustration, such patients would frequently cry, yell, curse and sullenly refuse to cooperate with those who tried to help them.

By contrast, patients with comparable right-hemisphere injuries (which rarely affect speech but can devastate sensation and movement) were often strangely indifferent to their disability. In extreme cases, patients would even deny that their paralyzed limbs belonged to them and might try to walk on nonfunctioning legs or make their way through the hospital wards even though they were neurologically blind.

These clinical findings have been confirmed by well-controlled studies of patients with one-sided (left or right) brain damage. But such research leaves many questions unanswered: How much brain tissue has to be destroyed before emotional changes are seen? And where, exactly, does the injury have to occur? Since the front and back parts of each hemisphere are also specialized for handling different functions (front mostly for movement and action, and back mostly for awareness

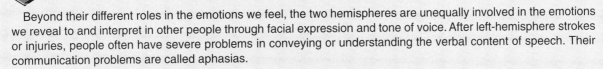

Aphasias and Aprosodias

Beyond their different roles in the emotions we feel, the two hemispheres are unequally involved in the emotions we reveal to and interpret in other people through facial expression and tone of voice. After left-hemisphere strokes or injuries, people often have severe problems in conveying or understanding the verbal content of speech. Their communication problems are called aphasias.

People with right-hemisphere damage are not usually aphasic, but they often have a different cluster of communication problems known as aprosodias. They have difficulty in dealing with prosody, that aspect of speech that enables a listener to tell if a particular statement (for example, "You're the boss") is meant to be a statement of fact or a question, serious or sarcastic, happy or sad, bland or passionate.

Neurologist Oliver Sacks, in his book *The Man Who Mistook His Wife for a Hat*, gives a vivid account of how aphasics and aprosodias differed as they listened to a Presidential speech on TV. The aphasics were, in a sense, like people trying to follow someone talking in a foreign language they didn't know. But since they couldn't grasp the speech's verbal content, they were especially sensitive to its emotional tone and its studied sincerities; they laughed derisively at the Great Communicator's prosodic posings. Sacks speculates that in this sense, "one cannot lie to an aphasic."

The aprosodic patients brought just the opposite skills to the speech. Emily D., a former English teacher whose usual passion for correct grammar, semantics and organization had been heightened by her inability to pick up emotional tone, was visibly disturbed by the speech. Did the President's words, if not his manner, win over such a prosody-deaf but linguistically astute person? No chance. The President "is not cogent," she remarked. "He does not speak good prose. His word use is improper. Either he is brain-damaged or he has something to conceal." Cases such as these remind us that the normal organization of our faculties into intact wholes may sometimes be a disadvantage, hindering our comprehension of the "hidden agenda" behind others' messages.

Patients with injuries to the left or right hemisphere have different communication problems, but both groups often have their feelings and behavior misunderstood—even by health professionals. Robinson and his colleagues have found that people with left-hemisphere damage may continue to feel depressed for up to two years after a stroke, a fact that can be doubly troubling. The depression derails their motivation to participate in rehabilitation programs that might help them recover. And since many rehabilitation professionals focus on physical disabilities and neglect emotional ones, Robinson says, they may view such patients as "difficult" or "resistant" and not give them all the help they need.

Surprisingly, such depressed patients are also likely to get short shrift when it comes to getting mental-health care. According to a study by physicians Richard Rosse and Charles Ciolino of the Georgetown University Medical Center, they are less likely to be seen in psychiatric and counseling services than are people with right-side damage. Rosse and Ciolino point out that because people with left-sided damage have difficulty expressing their feelings verbally, treatment-team members may underestimate the severity of their depression.

The depressive feelings of some aprosodic patients may also be misinterpreted, but for different reasons. Their facial expressions and vice inflection are often strangely blank—almost robotic. Elliott Ross, a neuropsychiatrist at the University of Texas Southwestern Medical Center at Dallas, notes that when aprosodic patients say such things as, "I feel like hell, I wish I were dead," in a flat, deadpan manner, they may not be taken seriously because the comment "lacks feeling."

and evaluation), does it also matter emotionally if the injury occurs toward the front or the back of a given hemisphere?

Neuropsychiatrist Robert Robinson of the Johns Hopkins School of Medicine has concentrated on pinpointing the actual brain mechanisms that produce mood changes after a stroke injures the brain. In one study, his research team put patients whose stroke sites were identified by CAT scan through a comprehensive series of physical, neuropsychological, psychiatric and mood tests. "We found that not only the hemisphere but the specific site of the injury was important," Robinson says. The most severe depressive reactions were seen in patients with lesions in the front parts of the left hemisphere. "The closer the injury was to the frontal areas, the more likely was the emotional effect." Damage toward the front of the right hemisphere also produced the most intense reactions: undue cheerfulness and an apathetic attitude toward the disability.

These studies of people with neurological problems raise a further question: Are the hemispheres specialized for different emotions in brains free of seizures or injury? Researchers Geoffrey Ahern and Gary Schwartz of Yale University believe the answer is yes, at least in the front parts. After hooking up 33 healthy col-

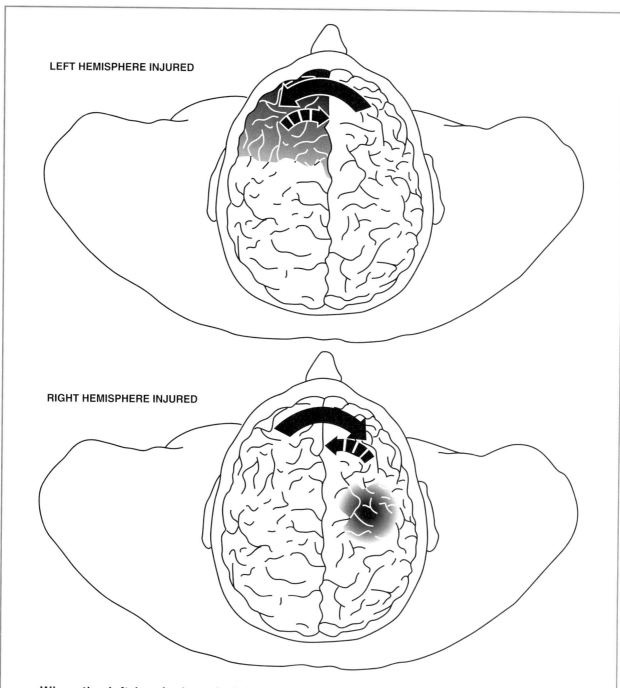

LEFT HEMISPHERE INJURED

RIGHT HEMISPHERE INJURED

When the left hemisphere is injured, depression often results. Injury to the right hemisphere often produces indifference or euphoria. Why? Some researchers propose that in normal states, the left and right hemispheres mutually control one another's emotional tone; disturbance of one hemisphere allows the opposite hemisphere's emotional bias to predominate, thus coloring the person's whole mood.

lege students to an EEG apparatus that measured electrical activity in various parts of the brain, the researchers asked them 60 questions designed to evoke a variety of moods and tap into verbal or spatial thinking as well. Ahern and Schwartz found that when people experienced positive emotions, the left hemisphere was more active than the right but only in the frontal lobes. Conversely, the right-hemisphere frontal lobes were particularly active during negative emotions.

The emotions studied in these experiments were brief and artificially induced. How do the hemispheres behave during emotions that happen naturally, such as feeling depressed? Yale graduate student Carrie Schaffer, while working with colleagues at the State University of New York at Purchase, gave the Beck Depression Inventory to a group of College students. When the researchers then compared the EEG's of students who scored as most characteristically depressed with those of nondepressed students, the depressed students had more electrical activity in the brain's right frontal region. In this case, too, the right hemisphere seemed to play a special role in depressed feelings.

To some researchers, these and other studies are beginning to fit together into a coherent picture but not necessarily the same one (see "The Emotional Brain in Three Dimensions," this article). Neuropsychologist Harold Sackeim of Columbia University's College of Physicians and Surgeons believes that the two sides of the brain control emotion through what he calls "reciprocal inhibitory control"—a system of hemispheric checks and balances. In his view, each hemisphere's activity helps keep the other's in check. Disturbances in mood occur when one hemisphere's functioning gets too strong or two weak and overrides

The Emotional Brain in Three Dimensions

Robert Robinson's group at the Johns Hopkins School of Medicine has recently been studying patients with injury to both cerebral hemispheres, with results that conflict with Harold Sackeim's mutual-watchdog theory about how the brain regulates emotions. "If reciprocal inhibitory control is the rule, the effects of injury to both hemispheres should cancel each other out," Robinson says. In other words, a patient with such damage shouldn't seem appreciably happier or sadder than before the injury. But Robinson's team found that such patients became depressed, as if only the injury on the left side counted.

Neuropsychologist Don Tucker of the University of Oregon has another model of how the brain exerts its control over the emotions—one more complex than Sackeim's. As Tucker sees it, "The main division of the brain may be a front-back one," rather than the right-left one. He reasons that since the frontal lobes are the chief brain system involved in regulating behavior as a whole, they probably regulate emotional behavior as well.

But there's more complexity still. Tucker points out that the brain "is a complex of control mechanisms in tight balance." Emotional control may depend not only on the balance of left-right and front-back components but also of bottom-top components: how the top of the brain works with many structures lower down that are also involved in emotions.

It's tempting to think about the hemispheres as opposites: happy versus sad, positive emotions versus negative ones. but Tucker believes their differences may have more to do with activation (being moved to act on the world) versus arousal (being passively aware of the world). These differences stem from the ways each hemisphere is hooked up preferentially to other parts of the brain. The left hemisphere, he speculates, may activate what we do through its stronger links to the frontal lobes and structures near the base of the brain. The right hemisphere may keep us aroused and aware through its stronger links to posterior and topmost brain regions.

As Tucker sees it, either hemisphere can be involved in pleasant or unpleasant emotions, but each has its own characteristic emotional repertoire due to its special linkages. Thus, the left hemisphere is involved in emotional states tinged with alert expectation—positive ones such as happy anticipation or negative ones such as anxious trepidation. The right hemisphere is involved in more reflective emotional states—positive ones such as relaxed awareness and negative ones such as depression.

or gives way to the other hemisphere's control.

An observation by Canadian psychiatrist Hurwitz, who studied Mary, the epileptic patient described earlier, supports this view. He suggests that seizures in Mary's left hemisphere allowed the right hemisphere's naturally

gloomy style to dominate her emotional life. When seizures zapped the right hemisphere, the left's manic-like emotional tendencies took over.

Sackeim speculates that under normal circumstances, internal and environmental factors combine to keep mood fluctuations fairly consistent with what is happening in our lives. But anything that jars the neural system—such as injury to the brain, the biochemical disruptions of a depressive illness or losing a loved one or job—is likely to release negative emotions.

People who develop depressive illness, he suggests, don't necessarily feel sadder about life's barbs than the rest of us. They just have a harder time inhibiting the depressive reaction once it starts. "Depressives," he says, "have faulty brakes."

Sackeim thinks that in the near future, a new breed of clinician-researchers will be able to pinpoint a variety of mood-disorder syndromes and link them to different patterns of cerebral disorganiza-

---

People who become depressed have faulty brakes; they can't stop the sadness.

---

tion. This, in turn, will lead to more effective therapies, custom-tailored for each specific case.

Research on how the brain hemispheres are involved in emotion is in its infancy, says Sackeim. But as theories and techniques im-prove, such studies promise to help us understand both normal and disordered emotional states. Studies of the link between brain function and emotions—whether in healthy states, mild and severe mood disorders, the neuronal storms of epilepsy or in the traumatic aftermath of strokes and head injuries—may aid in discovering ways to restore balance to the hemispheres and the emotions they regulate. Such research may reveal not just how we speak and reason but also how we love, hate and yearn.   ◈

Discussion Questions

1. "Mary" suffered seizures on each side of her brain. How was she affected by seizures of the left side? On the right side?

2. How is brain damage related to emotional difficulties?

3. What did Robinson's study of stroke injuries suggest about the relationship between brain damage and emotional difficulties?

4. Describe Ahern and Schwartz's study of healthy college students. What were the results?

5. What does Sackeim mean when he says that depressives have "faulty brakes?"

The *Universal* Smile: FACE MUSCLES Talk *Every* Language

◆ *Paul Ekman*

Symbolic gestures vary with culture as languages do. Tibetans stick out their tongues to symbolize friendly greeting, and Bulgarians signal agreement by wagging their heads right-to-left instead of up-and-down. A person could get confused, and sometimes killed, by doing the wrong thing in the wrong place. We could use a Berlitz book for gestures.

On the other hand, many facial expressions of emotion are universal. If you meet a native in New Guinea or your old boss in a Manhattan bar, you will be able to interpret their facial expressions easily, knowing how they feel—or how they want you to think they feel. You'll be able to do this from the particular pattern of facial wrinkles and movements that evolution has associated with the primary emotions.

People who believe that everything is relative, and that everything is learned, maintain that emotions and their form of expression are unique to each culture. Charles Darwin, by contrast, argued that the facial expressions of human beings, and other primates, were biologically based, through the process of evolution, and hence universal. I side with Darwin, and now Wallace Friesen and I have the evidence to support him. Our purpose was to show that the same facial appearances express the same emotions regardless of culture, and that there are more common expressions than just the simple distinction between happiness and unhappiness.

First we showed photographs of different facial expressions to college students in five literate cultures, crossing four language groups—Japan, the United States, Brazil, Chile and Argentina. To select the pictures, we examined over 3,000 photos, checking each one to see if it had all the muscular movements that we postulated as showing a particular emotion. We

> **People are not only similar in labeling emotional expression, but also in recognizing its intensity.**

did this for pictures of adults and children, mentally retarded and normals, posed expressions and spontaneous ones. We ended up with 30 pictures of 14 different persons, representing six emotions—happiness, sadness, anger, fear, surprise and disgust.

If facial expressions of emotion are unique to each culture, or if specific muscle movements are not associated with each emotion, then people in the five countries should have judged the pictures differently.

Tight Emotional Words

But they didn't. The great majority of observers in each country agreed on the emotion that each picture expressed, and observers in all five countries agreed with each other as well. The Japanese students were the least accurate in recognizing anger (63 percent), but they weren't far behind the Americans (69 percent).

We also asked the students to rate each picture for its *intensity* of emotion, for example, from slight anger to extreme anger. The stereotypes, after all, suggest that cultures differ greatly in the intensity of emotion that they permit to be expressed. If that were true, what appears as extreme emotion to Americans might seem to be mild feeling to the "passionate" Latins. But the ratings were almost identical across cultures. People are not only similar in labeling emotional expression, but also in recognizing its intensity.

C.E. Izard, unbeknownst to us, did a similar experiment with students of nine cultures. He used pictures of faces with posed expressions, which American observers had agreed represented eight primary emotions. He gave each student a list of eight pairs of emotion words, a high-intensity and low-intensity word in each pair: interest-excitement, enjoyment-joy, surprise-startle, distress-anguish, disgust-contempt, anger-rage, shame-humiliation, and fear-terror. Then he asked students to match the correct word pair with each facial expression.

In all nine cultures, the majority chose the right picture for each word pair, strong evidence that facial expressions transcend culture or language. Two groups, however, the Africans and the Japanese, showed a lower percentage of agreement on several emotions, notably shame and anger. But this lessened agreement may not have been due to differences in culture. Unlike other participants, Africans were not tested in their native country and their native tongue, and our translators considered the

	Happiness	Fear	Surprise	Anger	Disgust Contempt	Sadness
Japan	87	71	87	63	82	74
Brazil	97	77	82	82	86	82
Chile	90	78	88	76	85	90
Argentina	94	68	93	72	79	85
United States	97	88	91	69	82	73

Judgments of Emotion in Five Literate Cultures (Percentage correct)

EVERYONE AGREES ON WHAT FACES SAY. This chart indicates the percentage of people in each culture who correctly identified facial expression.

Japanese translations used by Izard to be awkward and dated.

John Wayne's Angry Face

Some critics argued that the strong agreement we found concerning facial expressions turned up because we studied cultures that are literate and share visual experience, thanks to mass media and the arts. Perhaps watching John Wayne's angry face, not evolution, was responsible for the seeming universal recognition of facial expression. To demonstrate our hypothesis conclusively, we had to show that visually isolated, nonliterate people interpret facial expressions as we do.

So we embarked on another series of experiments. In the first, with the help of E. Richard Sorenson, we showed photographs of facial expressions to people in two preliterate cultures, Borneo and New Guinea. We had trouble using our old procedure with them, however. We couldn't very well ask them to choose an emotion word from a list and match it to a photograph, because these people could not read and because our faulty knowledge of their language made us doubt our transla-

tions. In fact, our first efforts failed; these people had more trouble than any group we had tested agreeing about the emotions expressed in each photo. Now we were in a quandary: we couldn't tell whether their disagreement meant that we were mistaken, and that facial expressions simply are not universal, or whether the fault lay in our cumbersome method.

We returned to New Guinea a year later with a new system. This time we showed each person three photographs of Caucasian men or women, showing different expressions, such as happiness, anger and fear. We would then read a story and ask the person to select the face that fit the story. For example, the tale about fear ran:

© 1998 PhotoDisc, Inc.

She is sitting in her house all alone and there is no one else in the village; and there is no knife, ax, or bow and arrow in the house. A wild pig is standing in the door of the house and the woman is looking at the pig and is very afraid of it...the pig won't move away from the door and she is afraid the pig will bite her.

We worked with 189 men and women and 130 boys and girls from the Fore group of the South East Highlands of New Guinea. The people we chose had been as isolated as possible from Western missionaries, government workers, traders and scientists. They had never seen a movie, neither spoke nor understood English or Pidgin, and had never worked for a Caucasian.

Fear in New Guinea

This time we found high levels of agreement, among both adults and children, about the emotion that characterized each picture. For example, when we read a happiness story to the Fore adults ("His friends have come and he is happy"), 92 percent chose the smiling, happy face of the three. The only emotion on which the Fore tended to disagree with Westerners was fear, which the Fore couldn't distinguish from surprise—perhaps because in the environment of this culture fearful events tend also to be surprising.

Next we asked other New Guineans to demonstrate how *they* would look if they were the person in an emotion story. We videotaped their facial poses and showed them later to American college students. These culture-bound students, who had never seen New Guinea tribesmen, had no trouble accurately judging our actors' efforts at portraying anger, disgust, happiness and sadness. But just as the Fore had done, the Americans tended to confuse fear and surprise.

It would be hard to argue that our isolated New Guineans agreed on the expression of the basic emotions because they had had contact with Westerners. First of all, it was highly improbable that they had learned "foreign" facial expressions so well that they could not only recognize them but act them out. Second, the people we tested who *did* have contact with Westerners—who had been to mission schools and spoke English—did no better than the most isolated New Guineans. Third, the women, who typically have less contact with Westerners than the men, did just as well in recognizing the emotions.

Dispelling All Doubt

Karl and Eleanor Heider, an anthropologist and a psychologist, did an independent study that verified our conclusions. Their work dispels lingering doubts and counters the possibility that we had biased our results by unconsciously giving cues to the participants. The Heiders worked with the Grand Valley Dani, a tribe who live in the Central Highlands of New Guinea and didn't give up stone axes and tribal warfare until the 1960s. The Heiders doubted that the Dani would judge the photographs the way that members of other cultures had, particularly because the Dani don't even have words for the six emotions we studied. Yet their results were virtually identical to ours with the Fore.

Preliterate, visually isolated people have the same facial expressions and recognize the same facial emotions that we do.

Critics might still argue, however, that *posed* facial expressions simply aren't the same as *spontaneous* expressions. Posed grins and grimaces may simply be a conventional, nonverbal language that has nothing to do with emotion. This argument is plausible, though it doesn't explain why people in New Guinea and New Hampshire learn the same arbitrary facial expressions. So we turned to experiments based on spontaneous expression in a joint study with Richard S. Lazarus and Masatoshi Tomita.

We compared the facial movements of Japanese and Americans in two contexts as they watched a stressful film—provoking, for example, anger or disgust—and a neutral one. We were curious about the popular Western notion that the Japanese are inscrutable. In our terms, this would mean simply that the Japanese are less likely to express emotions publicly or will mask their expressions in public, but they should still show the same facial expressions privately.

Twenty-five students from Tokyo and 25 from Berkeley participated in the study. An investigator from their own culture explained the experiment as a study of physiological response to stress, connected up some wires to

measure heart rate and other reactions, and left the student alone to watch the films. A concealed camera recorded pictures of each person's face.

The investigator then returned to interview the student about his or her feelings, and continued the interview while the student watched more stress films. We interpreted the videotape records with our Facial Affect Scoring Technique (FAST), which allows us to isolate each observable movement of the face and its duration.

Private and Public Faces

When photographed by themselves, the Japanese and Americans reacted to the stress film with strikingly similar facial expressions. But when they were being interviewed about their reactions as they watched the same material, the Japanese tended to mask their disgust or anger with polite smiles. They responded more positively, whereas the American were more apt to express their negative feelings.

This one study, therefore, demonstrates both the universality of some facial expressions and the differences that are specific to each culture. Americans and Japanese, Fore and Dani all show disgust

	United States	English	German	Swedish	French	Swiss	Greek	Japanese	African
				(Percent choice of the correct emotion)					
Interest–Excitement	84	79	82	83	77	77	66	71	52
Enjoyment–Joy	97	96	98	96	94	97	93	94	68
Surprise–Startle	90	81	85	81	84	85	80	79	49
Distress–Anguish	74	74	67	71	70	70	54	67	32
Disgust–Contempt	83	84	73	88	78	78	87	56	55
Anger–Rage	89	81	83	82	91	92	80	57	51
Shame–Humiliation	73	59	72	76	77	70	71	41	43
Fear–Terror	76	67	84	89	83	67	68	58	49

JUDGMENTS OF EMOTIONAL INTENSITY. Across nine literate cultures there was agreement on both the identity and the intensity of facial expressions.

MATCHING FACES AND EMOTIONS. Even the non-literate Fore of New Guinea could accurately identify photographs of most emotional expressions.

Emotion described in story	(Percent choice of the correct emotion)	
	Adults	Children
Happiness	92	92
Sadness	79	81
Anger	84	90
Disgust	81	85
Surprise	68	98
Fear from anger, disgust or sadness	80	93
Fear from surprise	43	not asked

NOTE: The higher figures for the children probably reflect the fact that they were asked to choose from a pair of photographs rather than sets of three.

Our theory holds that all human beings share the same neural programing, which links facial muscles with particular emotions. The specific events that activate an emotion and the rules for managing the display of the emotion are learned and culturally variable, but, basically, Darwin was right.

and delight with the same facial expressions, but *when* they express them and *with whom* they express them varies in each culture.

Evidence for the universality of human facial expressions of the primary emotions now comes from comparable results in 13 literate cultures—Argentina, Brazil, Chile, England, France, Germany, Greece, Hawaii, Japan, Sweden, Turkey, the United States, and African nations—and in two remote, preliterate cultures, the Fore and the Dani of New Guinea. Of course, we still do not know *why* these expressions are universal, or why particular facial movements are associated with particular emotions. Why don't we press our lips tightly together and frown when we're happy?

© 1998 PhotoDisc, Inc.

Discussion Questions

1. How much do symbolic gestures vary from culture to culture?

2. What head movements do Bulgarians use to signal agreements?

3. What was the purpose of the research conducted by Paul Ekman and Wallace Friesen?

4. What were the results of the study by Ekman and Friesen?

5. Why did the researchers have to repeat their tests with "visually isolated, non-literate" populations?

6. What were the results of the author's investigations in Borneo and New Guinea?

7. What is Ekman's theory of facial expression?

8. Do you believe his theory is supported by his data? Why or why not?

9. Look out a window at people talking. Can you guess from their facial expressions how they are feeling? Does that support Ekman's hypothesis? Why or why not?

Exercises

Name: _____

Date: _____

Part 12: Motivation and Emotion

1. I can tell when someone is lying by paying attention to his or her gestures or facial expressions.

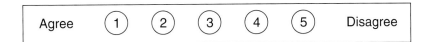

Agree   (1)   (2)   (3)   (4)   (5)   Disagree

2. I believe that my words, gestures, and facial expressions are always conveying the same message.

Agree   (1)   (2)   (3)   (4)   (5)   Disagree

3. I believe that emotions can be controlled and that failure to control one's emotions is a sign of weakness.

Agree   (1)   (2)   (3)   (4)   (5)   Disagree

Study the nonverbal communication of one person. What messages is he or she conveying to you (a) with words, (b) with body language, and (c) with facial expressions? Are there inconsistencies in the message being sent? How do you interpret these inconsistencies?

Team up with a friend, and study each other's verbal and nonverbal messages in a short conversation. Record the feedback you've received from your friend about messages you're sending (a) in words, (b) in gestures, and (c) in facial expressions.

PART 13

HUMAN SEXUALITY AND GENDER

41 **A Conversation with Masters and Johnson**

42 **Male Brain, Female Brain: The Hidden Difference,** by Doreen Kimura

43 **Adrenaline Makes the Heart Grow Fonder,** by Elaine Walster and Ellen Berscheid

44 **The Orgasm Wars,** by F. Bryant Furlow and Randy Thornhill

Try as we might in the behavioral sciences to put Sigmund Freud behind us, in one area he was the master. Issues of sexuality dominate much of human existence, no matter how vigorously Republicans may deny that. In Victorian Europe, sexuality was hidden from public view, but Freud insisted that it was there, seething beneath the surface of everyday life, motivating both the mundane and the bizarre. Freud's focus on sexuality paved the way for the first systematic investigations of sexual behavior, including the landmark surveys of Alfred Kinsey and the laboratory studies of William H. Masters and Virginia Johnson. Before such investigations, our knowledge of sexual behavior was governed mainly by folklore (which, as you know from the "Folk Wisdom" chapter in Part 2, is highly unreliable.)

Here's a historical tidbit for you. There's credible evidence that John B. Watson, the founder of behaviorism, was conducting secret laboratory research on female sexual behavior at Johns Hopkins University before he was dismissed from the university in 1920 (perhaps for that very reason); this was decades before Masters and Johnson came on the scene. Apparently, he also convinced a Hopkins student named Karl Lashley—who later became an eminent physiological psychologist, by the way—to conduct the first sex surveys. Staying one step ahead of the sheriff, Lashley went from one Southern town to another asking people to reveal intimate details about their sexual behavior. Apparently the threat of incarceration or worse was too much for young Lashley, so he quit the survey business, but not before convincing a young biologist named Alfred Kinsey to carry on. Kinsey's books on sexual behavior, published in 1948 and 1953, reported the results of more than 18,000 such surveys and constituted the first large-scale empirical studies of sexual behavior anywhere in the world. Kinsey found surprisingly high degrees of premarital sex, extramarital sex, and homosexuality, dispelling myths that had reigned for centuries. So any sexual knowledge or sexual freedom you have today you owe, indirectly, to Sigmund Freud, the inventor of psychoanalysis, and John B. Watson, the founder of behaviorism.

Masters and Johnson speak for themselves in the first selection in this section—a candid interview with these pioneering sex researchers at the height of their careers. In "Male Brain, Female Brain," neuroscientist Doreen Kimura talks about some of the lesser-known anatomical differences between males and females. Even more disparities have been discovered since this 1985 article, including large differences in brain weight (what males *do* with the extra brain matter remains a complete mystery, however).

In "Adrenaline Makes the Heart Grow Fonder," social psychologists Elaine Walster and Ellen Berscheid apply Schachter and Singer's theory to love and romance: In the right situation, *any* kind of stimulation might fool you into thinking you're in love; that could certainly explain a whole heap of problems. Finally, in "The Orgasm Wars," F. Bryant Furlow and evolutionary biologist Randy Thornhill offer, at long last, a reasonably sound explanation for the function of the female orgasm.

A CONVERSATION with Masters and Johnson

◆ *Mary Harrington Hall*

Mary Harrington Hall: Let me begin by saying that I found *Human Sexual Response* extremely difficult reading. **William H. Masters:** It is hard reading on purpose. We were writing a medical textbook and wanted to avoid any suggestion of pornography. We even rewrote the book to make it as obtuse as possible.

Virginia Johnson: We had to rewrite it. We are both intensely emotional people and when we feel intensely enough, we talk and write in the same fashion. Each of us went through the manuscript and killed the other's sacred cows. Some of the original lines sounded flamboyant and suggestive in the context of the book.

Hall: Can you remember a single line and a change you had to make?

Masters: No, but there was the prostitute's story.

Johnson: Bill wanted to describe a situation where a prostitute was being paid to control her response on a regular work-a-day evening.

Masters: Over a six-hour period, she entertained 27 clients, and we checked her every hour for pelvic congestion. She was grossly uncomfortable. Finally we allowed her to masturbate and her congestion disappeared within a minute or two.

Johnson: His scientist's soul believes in depicting things in specifics and that's just the way he wrote it.

Masters: We described the scene, the situation, the number of clients, the whole sequence. By the time we finished, you could certainly call it pornography, and so it had to come out. But we promised the medical writers that we would write our next textbook in English. And if we ever revise this first text, we'll put it back into English.

Hall: Your research has exploded a number of myths that found their way into marriage manuals and gynecological textbooks.

Johnson: In an area where nothing was known, medicine had to draw from the social lore. A textbook on psychosomatic gynecology published in 1957 stated that women had neither the interest in nor the capacity for orgasmic response.

Masters: When I reviewed the literature in 1954, everything said about female orgasm was written

---

*There is no quarrel at all
with mutual orgasm
if it happens naturally,
but to strive for it and to feel frustrated
if you don't attain it—
that's a bad hang-up.*

---

by males. Suddenly it occurred to me, "How in hell do they know?" That's one of the reasons Gini is such an essential part of this research.

Hall: And as a result of your research, instead of pretending to be nonorgasmic women, or women

who can have one orgasm, we can delight in being multi-orgasmic.

Masters: The human female is naturally multiorgasmic. Now this doesn't mean that all women experience multiple orgasms, but while the male generally loses the ability to ejaculate more than once after the age of 30, the female is still potentially multiorgasmic in her 70s.

Hall: Men really should take this into consideration.

Masters: The average male approach is that if I'm a one-shot man, you must be a one-shot woman. Otherwise I have to admit that you are better than I am. The other side of the coin is that he doesn't even think of the possibility of multiple orgasm in women.

Hall: Until your research was published, he didn't know it.

Johnson: Oh, it's been no secret. Men have more or less suspected it, apparently, for centuries.

Hall: What about the lore of the marriage manual—the mutual orgasm?

Johnson: As a goal, that's probably the most divisive, distress-producing factor I can think of for a sexual relationship. The orgasmic experience is so self-oriented—consuming—that awareness of a partner's response is not fully enjoyed at the time. To strive for mutual orgasm, considering anything else inadequate, produces a pressure of performance and limits the experience.

Masters: It's a complete body phenomenon—total body involvement. There is no quarrel at all with mutual orgasm if it happens naturally, but to strive for it and to feel frustrated if you don't attain it—that's a bad hang-up.

Johnson: If the manuals are taken as written, as technical guides, they can be harmful. Most people who consult them are not seeking variation but knowledge of how it

Virginia Johnson and William H. Masters

is. Concentration on technical expertise precludes spontaneity.

We like to define sexuality as a dimension of the personality and sex as a specific physical activity.

Hall: And the technical approach hinders that. What about the couple with a good relationship who make a big thing of adding new dimension to their sex life?

Johnson: They become preoccupied with watching their partners to time themselves and with altering their own response. If you let this quest for the mutual orgasm become the primary goal, it is like talking a relationship to death—intellectualizing it to the point where it has no living quality.

Hall: If we judge from the sale of marriage manuals, there are a lot of people really lousing themselves up.

Johnson: Terribly. Sex by direction rather than by understanding is not satisfying. It is the give-to-get that makes real response.

Hall: Remember the devastating article by Leslie Farber, "I'm Sorry, Dear." At the time he was actually attacking you, but looking back, he was talking about so many couples who are so crushed

when one does not feel the same thing at the same time as the other. Sex is not mechanical reaction or direction.

Johnson: That's it, of course. Why do people think they have to keep mental notes as a moment-to-moment exercise of what is happening?

Masters: Whenever you do that, you are dissecting and removing and depersonalizing the whole sexual experience.

Hall: But some psychologists are saying that we have been overemphasizing the importance of the orgasm for women, that women can be perfectly happy in a sexual relationship without experiencing orgasm.

Johnson: On any given occasion, I am sure that this is perfectly possible. Bill has even suggested that the '60s will be called the decade of orgasmic preoccupation. But we feel that this is a natural overswing of the pendulum. It expresses the depth of the need to be free of the double standard.

Hall: And still a lot of so-called experts say that orgasm is not an important function for the female.

Masters: Those experts are males talking. I can't conceive of a female with a sense of her own identity taking that stand. Again, it's the male in our culture describing what happens to the female— telling her what must happen.

Johnson: It's the male viewpoint with a vengeance, put forth either in ignorance of women or in rejection of woman as a sexually needful entity.

Masters: Unless you regard coitus as solely for reproductive purposes, it would be just as fair to say that ejaculation isn't important to the male. It just ain't true.

Johnson: If you asked him why the male should ejaculate, he would say, "Oh, for physical reasons—my health, my tension. I would be uncomfortable." Of course, similar mechanisms can produce much the same feelings on the part of females, but concern for *her* need is rarely admissible in the court of sexual justice.

Hall: One of your findings that has received the widest possible publicity is that a clitoral orgasm and an orgasm through thrust are the same.

Johnson: I get so emotionally unhinged trying to talk about that one that I usually turn it over to Bill. The fact is that one can be conditioned to respond to stimulation of any kind, from any place, in any manner, provided it is endowed with sexual meaning for a particular individual.

Masters: Since we published our book, we have found three women who can fantasy themselves into recordable orgasm. We had one girl who became orgasmic by rubbing the small of her back. So you could say we have a small-of-the-back orgasm, a clitoral orgasm, a vaginal orgasm, a fantasy orgasm—but they're all the same kettle of fish. Physiologically, they're identical. Freud assumed—erroneously— that they were different.

The female experiences a greater variation in intensity and

duration than the male does. She may have a very mild orgasmic experience or she may have an overwhelming orgasm. Supposing some continuity of sexual expression, the male orgasm is more a-rose-is-a-rose-is-a-rose sort of thing. Now a thing of beauty is a joy forever, but it is still a rose. The female goes all the way from poppies to orchids.

Johnson: Many men have challenged him on the rose-is-a-rose-is-a-rose bit, and I always shudder when he says it.

Masters: I have been challenged by some attractive guy in the audience who says, "But I enjoy orgasmic intercourse more with one woman than another." And I say, "But I am not talking about what you enjoy. I am talking about what you experience in terms of intensity and duration of experience." That is entirely different.

Johnson: O.K., I can't answer you because I'm not a male.

Hall: There are many males on psychiatric couches all over the country being taught to live with a problem. They are convinced that their penises are too small to stimulate a woman to orgasm.

Masters: First let me say that the size of a man's physical frame has absolutely no relation to the size of his penis. Those males on the psychiatrists' couches really don't have a problem. But the myth is perpetuated by the behaviorists and the biologists of the country who support the concept by treating men for a nonexistent problem.

Great variation in penis size exists only among flaccid penises. The smaller penis engorges much more than the larger one. At the moment of truth, there just isn't that great differential in size.

Besides, whatever the size of the erect penis, under sexual tension the vagina will expand in a completely involuntary manner to accommodate the penis—*and no more*. (This presumes that there is no physical, residual obstetrical trauma.) So there are two reasons why penis size makes no crucial difference. Gini, you make the third point.

Johnson: Woman is the counterpoint.

Hall: You could make a pun there.

Johnson: If a female believes that a large penis is the most exciting and stimulating thing for her, then it is. Perhaps she's told this, perhaps she picks it up from popular lore, perhaps a past pleasurable experience has conditioned her to believe this. But the difference can be real in her mind. It may even be used by her to provide the crucial difference when her own response to a partner is less than she would like.

If a female believes that a large penis is the most exciting and stimulating thing for her, then it is.

Hall: In that case, the problem is really the woman's, not the man's.

Masters: We've been criticized for not stating the average size of the penis in its flaccid state.

Hall: Is there such a thing?

Johnson: If you measure a thousand penises, you certainly are going to come up with an average.

Masters: We won't ever tell. It's our contribution to the security of mankind. No matter what we said, every male would reach for a tape measure the moment we published the statistics.

We won't ever tell. It's our contribution to the security of mankind. No matter what we said, every male would reach for a tape measure the moment we published the statistics.

Johnson: We get four or five letters a week asking what can be done about the size of a penis.

Masters: One man wanted to know what I thought about silicone treatments.

Hall: The same treatments used to enlarge breasts?

Johnson: He was talking about the very same kind of thing. Speculate on that for just a moment.

Masters: I wrote back, "If you have no concern about perpetual erection, be my guest." Can you imagine trying to get your pants on?

Hall: Your work is as much concerned with psychology as it is with physiology.

Masters: Infinitely more. There is no such thing as the pure physiology of sexual response, except as a textbook concept. From a functional point of view, the correct terminology is the psychophysiology of sexual response.

Hall: I have read that your next book will be called *Human Sexual Inadequacy*. It must concentrate on psychology.

Masters: We've completed 10 years of behavioral therapy with cases of impotence, premature ejaculation and female nonorgasmism.

Johnson: There is only passing resemblance to behavior therapy, as that form of psychotherapy is practiced.

First of all, we use male-female therapist teams. The definitions and interpretations of both sexes are very pertinent.

Masters: Second, we see people on a daily basis to provide continuity of communication. And third, we have the advantage of knowing something of the physiology of sexual behavior.

Johnson: We use a unique kind of reorientation of behavior patterns. But we cannot talk about the techniques of our therapy yet.

Masters: When we publish our findings, we will have five years of follow-up after the termination of the acute phase of therapy. So far as we know this has never been done before. Most of the statistics we encounter have to do with the effectiveness of therapy at the termination of its acute stage. This statistic is relatively unimportant. Only your rate of failure should be reported at this stage. No one is qualified to report treatment success until at least five years have passed since therapy was terminated. Our premise is that it matters not how effective your techniques are at reversing distress, but how well the distress remains reversed.

Hall: I understand that you refuse to treat the husband unless the wife also enters therapy.

Masters: We treat the sexual problem within the marriage rather than the individual. There is no such thing as a nontraumatized partner in a marriage where there is a complaint of sexual inadequacy. The couple spends two weeks with us in intensive therapy.

Hall: You can effect cures in only two weeks?

Masters: I wouldn't phrase it that way. We reverse symptoms in 10 days to two weeks. At first we tried a three-week program and discovered that we didn't need that much time. Every week we potentially can start three new couples in the program; we've now worked with more than 350 marriages.

That's a small number for so long a research program, but with good reason. One, we wanted to work in depth; two, it's totally an experimental program; and three, we take only couples who are referred to us by professionals.

Hall: Every couple in your program is a referral?

Masters: We needed help in evaluating those who wanted to come. You need screening to keep the lunatic fringe out of any program of research in sexual behavior.

Johnson: Screening by an interested physician or therapist is very

effective a good percentage of the time.

Hall: To many, the cost of that two-week course—the $2,500 fee—is surprising.

Masters: That money covers two weeks of intensive therapy and five years of follow-up. But we fit the cost of the program to the pocketbook. Roughly half the people pay the full fee, one quarter pay an adjusted fee and one quarter are treated free. The foundation covers the costs of the adjusted fee and the no-cost people. As a matter of fact, there was no charge made for the first five years of the program. We felt it totally unfair to charge for an admittedly experimental program until we had significant experience.

Hall: One of the major forms of inadequacy referred to you must be impotency.

Masters: The potent male is a male who can achieve and maintain an erection sufficient for the mounting process. Now as we define it, there are two different types of impotency. The primarily impotent male fails to achieve and or maintain an erection at his first mounting opportunity, and he continues to fail every time thereafter.

The secondarily impotent male didn't fail for the first time—or maybe the first thousand times. But a male rarely just suddenly becomes impotent. He goes down in stages.

Hall: How does this process begin? I would assume that fatigue and alcohol have some bearing on it.

Johnson: The terms fatigue and preoccupation have become clichés around here. They're both important. But alcohol is a powerful influence. Shakespeare summed it up in *Macbeth*…

Hall: …In the drunken porter scene. The porter tells Macduff that drink: "…provokes the desire, but it takes away the performance: therefore, much drink may be said to be an equivocator with lechery:

it makes and it mars him; it sets him on, and it takes him off, it persuades him, and disheartens him; makes him stand to, and not stand to…"

Johnson: Shakespeare reflected a rare awareness of other people's problems.

Masters: Usually the first failure for the secondarily impotent man occurs when he is really drunk. His fear develops after that. He fails a couple of times with a lot of alcohol, then he begins to worry and will fail without it.

Johnson: Again, we have the horrible contribution of lore, or the absence of correct information within the lore.

Hall: What effect does the aging process have on secondary impotence?

Johnson: Age is not the crucial factor in response.

Hall: That is marvelous to hear, because I feel very old today.

Masters: But being female, you will feel younger tomorrow. The failing male talks himself into impotence. The male in his 50s keeps saying, "Gee, I can't get the job done any more." In truth, he doesn't believe this and he doesn't think anybody around him believes, but he talks himself into it. Because our culture says that the male is going to fail in his 60s and 70s. That just isn't true.

Presuming some continuity, the only thing the male or female needs for effective sexual functioning is a reasonably good state of general health and an interested partner.

Johnson: I'd like to tag on an "interesting partner." You must be attracted to your partner or to the situation that he or she shares. It may not matter *who* it is, but it matters that you have a need in that particular circumstance.

Hall: The other male complaint you get is premature ejaculation.

Johnson: Any learning opportunity that produces performance pressure can lead to premature ejaculation.

Masters: In the old days of the cat house it was hurry up, hurry up. The faster the girls worked, the more money they made. The males hardly had a chance to get their pants off. If a young man learned that way—and at one time most of them did—it carried over to his marriage.

Today it often begins in the back seat of a parked car. Again, it's hurry up and get the job done. The back seat of a car hardly provides an opportunity for the expression of personality.

Hall: Has the problem of premature ejaculation proved to be difficult to treat?

Johnson: No, not with our well motivated population.

Masters: Certainly any marital unit that wants to control premature ejaculation can do it. It's no longer a problem.

Hall: Let's talk about frigidity.

Masters: There is practically no such thing as a sexually unresponsive woman. I suppose the most acceptable definition of frigidity would be the woman who does not achieve orgasm from any form of sexual stimulation.

The male whose wife is only orgasmic twice a week when he thinks she should be orgasmic five times may call his wife frigid. But she is not.

Hall: Let's stick to your terms, orgasmic and nonorgasmic. It will simplify the discussion.

Masters: Don't look at me. No male has any right to talk about the extent of female response, because he can't have the vaguest idea of what he is talking about.

Johnson: We consider all women in adequate physical condition potentially responsive to sexual stimulation. However, we have encountered women who, through

their histories, intensely reject opportunity for, or the fact of, their own sexual response. Usually victims of rape, incest or some other attitudinal conditioning that

> *And then there's the woman who has been taking the pill for 18 months to three years and finds herself losing effective sexual function.*

makes acceptance of sexual feeling unbearable. But these women are not typical.

Masters: And then there's the woman who has been taking the pill for 18 months to three years and finds herself losing effective sexual function.

Hall: That will strike terror into the heart of the American female.

Masters: It's well established as a complication of the pill. We just don't have the perfect contraceptive yet.

Johnson: Only a small percentage of women taking the pill react this way. It's not a lack of interest or a loss of receptivity; it's like a silken curtain that a woman cannot break through to reach orgasm.

> *There is practically no such thing as a sexually unresponsive woman.*

Hall: But if we stop taking the pill....

Masters: That's our recommendation for such women. Stop taking the pill.

Johnson: The sad ones we have seen tend to fall into the group that say to their doctors, "I'm just not interested any more." It reflects fear of performance. The disappointment of not responding breeds avoidance of involvement.

Masters: Just like the male who is becoming progressively more impotent and avoids exposure.

Hall: What about women who have never been traumatized and who are not taking the pill?

Johnson: I think we can generalize and say that it's an attitudinal problem—psychosocial. It's drawn from the role that sexuality plays in a society, born of the residual Victorian puritanical influence.

Hall: Mama says sex is dirty.

Johnson: That's right. Too many people give sex a dishonorable role in our society.

Masters: Let's put it this way. All of us are to a major degree the product of our environment. It's the continuation of the double standard: there are nice girls and bad girls, but there are no bad men. Roués maybe, but they're not bad. Only women are called promiscuous.

Hall: What about the Don Juan theory, that the man who flits from bed to bed is really afraid that he is not male.

Masters: True for some men, but generally speaking, no. He just enjoys going to bed. And until he has trouble finding cooperative partners, he exists in a delightful haze.

Johnson: That Victorian attitude even helped determine the traditional restriction on sexual activity during the last stages of pregnancy. The doctor was giving the poor girl a few more months of peace and protection from having to do that horrible thing.

Masters: After all, she was coming close to the sainted state of Motherhood.

Hall: I was always told there was danger of infection in the last six weeks.

Masters: Only if the membranes are ruptured. Ruptured membranes, pain and bleeding are the only contraindications to intercourse right up to the time of labor.

Hall: There's a big barrier of reticence and prudery even in your own discipline.

Johnson: Physicians are men and women first. Like all men and women, they are products of their lives and times. They will always be so.

Masters: After all, the very first course in sexual response ever taught in American medicine was taught in 1960. Half the medical schools, possibly, still don't teach the course. If a medical student has never had a proper course on the subject, how can he treat it with objectivity?

Hall: But because of your work, more and more medical schools are teaching sexual behavior.

Masters: That is a flattering and common misconception. Harold Lief, who is a professor of psychiatry at the University of Pennsylvania, has done more to orient medical schools toward the teaching of sexual behavior than anyone else.

Johnson: Our work is just the peak of the iceberg. Society is reconstructing its attitudes.

Hall: Are we reconstructing fast enough for our young people? Will they get over the Victorian hang-up?

Johnson: They can, but they have to remember that they are also products of all the influences in their lives. As long as we of the previous generation are around with our doubts and our hang-ups and our fears, they are going to have a few hang-ups, in spite of our hopes—and don't forget, they are going to have some of their own hang-ups, too.

Masters: Potentially, the healthier generation will be *their* children.

Johnson: We can be hopeful that the bright, young people will develop some objective concepts of sex and sexuality during their lifetimes so that their children will have a healthy outlook on sex.

Masters: We firmly believe that below the age of 30 there is no real interest in or demand for the double standard. Today there is a freedom and desire to establish meaningful interpersonal relationships.

Johnson: The missing factor remains *how* to establish those important sexual relationships.

Hall: I wonder if sex education, in addition to the sex experience itself, is going to do this. You need an attitudinal change.

Masters: The greatest form of sex education is Pop walking past Mom in the kitchen and patting her on the fanny and Mom obviously liking it. The kids take a good look at this action and think, "Boy, that's for me."

Johnson: In a setting like that, you can impose any kind of control within reason. If your word means anything, you can be believed…you are believable.

Hall: If your word is an extension of what you are living.

The greatest form of sex education is Pop walking past Mom in the kitchen and patting her on the fanny and Mom obviously liking it. The kids take a good look at this action and think, "Boy, that's for me."

Masters: How you live is far more important than what you say.

Hall: But the generation you are talking about has seen so many divorces.

Masters: Divorce isn't of necessity a poor sex education.

Johnson: Divorce usually represents poor choices of partners by two people or it is circumstantial…the result of economic struggle, in-law intrusion…in other words, the result of the overwhelming odds.

Hall: Is there any evidence that the new morality has produced extensive changes in patterns of human sexual behavior?

Johnson: The new morality is seeking to find more meaning in a way of life. It may manifest itself in rather far-out ways, but for now let's not deal with the specific manifestations. There is so much more concern with the meaning of

actions and the worth of ideas and thoughts and far more realism in handling the results. Does it always come out well for those who try? It's never going to come out well for everyone!

Masters: We have the greatest respect for new attitudes, but we really don't know enough about attitudes we have not studied. One of the problems with past attitudes is that sex has been pigeon-holed as a physical function, instead of valued as an expression of personality—as enhancement of the individuals involved—as sexuality.

Hall: Is it correct that you were advised to get thoroughly established before you began research into sexual functioning?

Masters: Quite correct. I was a third-year medical student at the time, and I was advised that first, a certain amount of chronological seniority was in order; second, that the work should be done within a university certainly, and a medical school preferably; and finally, that the nominal research head should have a reputation for accomplished research in an unrelated field.

So we began to work in steroid replacement in the menopause and post-menopausal years. It was the first laboratory research ever reported in the area, and that helped to establish our research reputation in unrelated fields.

Hall: And you are a gynecologist.

Masters: I'm a gynecologist by trade. Though I still call myself that, we're somewhat removed from the mainstream of gynecology. My own prejudiced opinion is that sexual functioning should be important to gynecology.

Everyone here at the research foundation has a teaching appointment with Washington University, either in the medical school or on the campus. We confine ourselves essentially to reproductive biology, which means conceptive physiology and its clinical applications to conceptive inadequacy, contraceptive physiology with application to population control, and human sexual physiology with application to the treatment of sexual inadequacy.

Hall: And when did Virginia Johnson join your work?

Masters: We began our program in July 1954, and Gini joined me in January 1957. We just celebrated our 12th birthday together.

Hall: I understand, Virginia, that you just went in and applied for a job at Washington University.

Johnson: That's essentially what happened. I had been married to a student here and I applied to the university placement bureau for work when I went back to school. I had been a music major, but I wanted to change my major to sociology and work in that department to help make up for lost time. However, the opportunity to join Bill in the department of obstetrics and gynecology was too interesting to pass up.

Hall: Bill, what made you choose Gini from among all the applicants?

Masters: We were convinced that we couldn't study the physiology and psychology of sexual behavior without having both sexes represented at all times. As a poor male, I constantly need an interpreter, and I have a sneaking suspicion that women occasionally need an interpreter, too.

We picked Gini from all the other women because she has an incredible facility for handling and working with people, she has an active curiosity, and she had a few of the things that were vital to the program: she knew where babies come from, because she had had a couple, she had been married; and she was willing to work her head off.

Hall: Why did you insist on a married woman?

Masters: The nonmarried female inevitably is a professional virgin,

and I couldn't deal with someone who doesn't find sex a totally comfortable subject. If there ever had been evidence of the slightest judgmental attitude, personal embarrassment or lack of objectivity, research in this area would never have been done.

Hall: Your research technique that caused the biggest stir was the artificial phallus.

Masters: People forget that the plastic phallus was designed for research—not as a sex-stimulation technique. As a matter of fact, we used the artificial phallus in three ways: to learn the physiology of the vaginal function; to study the intravaginal distribution of chemical contraceptives; and to create artificial vaginas without surgery.

> *The terms fatigue and preoccupation have become clichés around here. They're both important. But alcohol is a powerful influence. Shakespeare summed it up in Macbeth....*

Women occasionally are born without vaginas. At one time gynecologists had to construct vaginas surgically, but with this equipment we can create an artificial vagina just by gradually increasing the pressure of the artificial phallus and pocketing the skin.

Hall: How did you use it in the study of contraception?

Masters: The plastic phallus was originally designed for contraceptive work. We could use it to evaluate intravaginal chemical or mechanical contraceptives without ever exposing people to pregnancy. The traditional way is to distribute a new contraceptive to the Puerto Rican underprivileged and then count the number of pregnancies. We think it's inhuman to promise somebody a contraceptive and then when the pregnancies turn up say, "Gee, that's a poor statistic."

Hall: Did the use of the artificial phallus prove stimulating?

Johnson: Very few of our women found the artificial phallus very exciting. So they were allowed to use their own automanipulative preference along with it.

Masters: It didn't really make any difference. You know, in my wisdom I had decided that the female would be much more difficult to work with in a project of this kind. I couldn't have been more wrong. The male has much more difficulty functioning effectively under any form of pressure. About 80 percent of all failures to reach orgasm in this laboratory were by males.

Hall: Do you have an explanation?

Masters: I think our culture is responsible. If the male fails to achieve erection, he is under social pressure, because in our frame of reference sexual activity is male performance. After all, the female can't perform unless she performs against something. This the male must provide. Any time two people move toward a bed, the male is under the pressure of performance. If the female simply rolls over she is potent, because the male can carry out the sex act without active participation on her part.

Hall: Your new book will be on sexual inadequacy. What other plans do you have for research?

Masters: One of the fascinating things we are going to do now that our 10-year period of patient follow-up is over is to alternate therapists, not only between male and female, but different therapists over the course of treatment. We are primarily interested in avoiding the depth of transference. The white coat of authority is quite sufficient to inspire confidence. Now we are not talking about eliminating transference; we are channelizing it. If there is going to be an interpersonal orientation, we want it to be between husband and wife.

Hall: I've heard that you are also studying homosexuality.

Masters: Most research has been devoted to the male homosexual. For that reason, we've moved into the female side and are studying lesbianism. But there will be no lesbianism in the 1970 book. We have been studying it only five years, so it will be the mid-'70s before we have anything to say.

Hall: Are there more lesbians than people think?

Masters: We're not sociologists, so we're not qualified to say. There is a very constant, very real level of female homosexual orientation, probably much higher than was believed in the past—at least as a passing commitment.

Hall: Do you mean that the female moves into and out of lesbianism?

Masters: That is an established fact. Probably a higher percentage of women than men move back and forth between the two worlds.

Johnson: The female can maintain a dual commitment with much greater social convenience. But we can't say anything more about the study at this time.

Masters: It takes us at least 10 years to feel at all secure in any area of sexual behavior.

Hall: What do we know abut sexual activity for the damaged heart?

Masters: We don't know a thing about it. As far as I know the subject has never been investigated in depth.

The pleasantest kind of response comes from the open, flowerlike face that can belong to any woman from 23 to 69. In an incredulous, gentle voice, it always says, "How wonderful that you are doing this work. But are there really people who need it?"

Hall: That's terrible!

Masters: I agree with you. But it's expensive research. Before we can move into that area, we'll have to reconstitute our physiology laboratory.

Hall: What kind of reaction do you get from the public?

Johnson: The pleasantest kind of response comes from the open, flowerlike face that can belong to any woman from 23 to 69. In an incredulous, gentle voice, it always says, "How wonderful that you are doing this work. But are there really people who need it?"

Masters: My answer to them is "How marvelous for you."

It's like the little lady and man celebrating their 50th wedding anniversary. The eldest son, a surgeon, is late for the anniversary dinner. He comes in from an emergency and his mother asks, John, dear, what sort of surgery did you do?" And John says very quietly, "Well, Mother, it had to do with a man's penis." Mother says, "Oh, did you have to take the bone out?" And the whole party stands up and drinks a toast to the host.   ◆

Discussion Questions

1. Before 1954, what was the problem with the literature regarding female orgasm?

2. What is the most distressing factor for a sexual relationship, according to William Masters?

3. According to Masters, who is saying that orgasm is not an important function for a woman?

4. How does Masters contrast the male and the female orgasm?

5. What are the two reasons given that penis size does not matter? What is the one reason given for penis size to matter?

6. What is the male sexual problem associated with alcohol?

7. Explain what is meant by sexuality being a personality.

Male Brain, Female Brain: The Hidden Difference

◆ *Doreen Kimura*

The idea that male and female brains are organized differently has been around for a long time. After all, since men and women are dissimilar in size, appearance and sexual role, why shouldn't their brain organization differ too? Research has documented in the past 25 years that there are intellectual differences in the way the two sexes solve problems: On average, women do better in certain verbal skills and men in spatial and mathematical skills.

The notion that men's and women's brains are differently organized began to take hold in earnest as a result of experiments spanning the 1960s and 1970s. It began with the work of psychologist Herbert Lansdell, who studied neurosurgical patients. Others before him had found that, in general, removing the brain's left temporal lobe interfered with verbal skill, while removing the right impaired nonverbal skills. Lansdell found that although such injuries caused a similar overall pattern of impairment in women and men, women were less severely affected than men.

These preliminary findings were confirmed and given support by people working in my laboratory and in other laboratories. Studies of both brain-damaged and normal people revealed that while men and women tend to use one hemisphere more than the other for certain verbal tasks, such as recognizing spoken or seen words, women seem to rely less strongly on a single hemisphere than men do. Particularly striking was a finding by psychologist Jeanette McGlone, then a graduate student in my laboratory, that damage to the left hemisphere (the one usually dominant for language) caused less aphasia (language disorder) in women than in men.

These findings led to what seemed to be an obvious conclusion: Certain thinking skills are more lateralized—more dependent on one hemisphere—in the male brain than in the female. Or, putting the comparison the other way, women's brains are more diffusely organized than men's.

A number of explanations were

The older view: women's brains are more diffusely organized than men's.

---

offered for this apparent sex difference: Women were more verbal, meaning that both their hemispheres were given up to speech; women developed more quickly and lateralization required slower development; women were just as lateralized as men but used verbal strategies more often; connections between the hemispheres were stronger in women and, therefore, the asymmetrical organization of their brain was less detectable. And so on.

Anatomical studies began to suggest that there were structural differences between men's and women's brains, but results were inconsistent regarding the question of men's greater lateralization. After neurologist Norman Geschwind and coworker Walter Levitsky at Harvard Medical School had found that a verbal part of the brain was generally larger on the left than the right side, neuroscientist Juhn Wada reported that these anatomical differences were smaller in women. In addition, biologist Christine de Lacoste-Utamsing, working with anthropologist Ralph Holloway at Columbia University, claimed that part of the corpus callosum, the major connection between the hemispheres, was slightly larger in women.

The problem with viewing men's brains as more lateralized than women's was that it left a lot of questions unanswered. Why, for example, are women more often right-handed than men? Even among right-handers, more women are purely right-handed, suggesting that, if anything, women rely more on one hemisphere than do men. And why was there no evidence that speech disorders occur more often in women following right-hemisphere brain damage, as one would expect if they, unlike men, depended on both hemispheres for speech?

In the course of looking at how damage to specific regions of one hemisphere affects speech and related functions, I came across some unexpected findings that, I believe, help to clarify some of these issues. One of the difficulties in doing research on neurological patients is finding enough people with various kinds of brain damage to study—enough women, for example, with damage limited to particular regions of one hemisphere. It took me 10 years to gather enough data on brain-damaged patients to

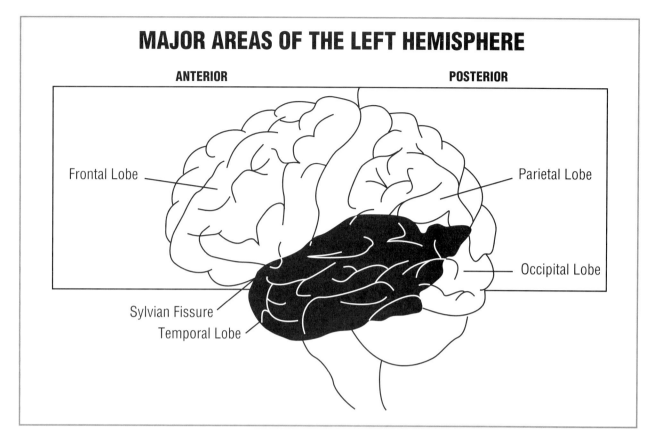

MAJOR AREAS OF THE LEFT HEMISPHERE

ANTERIOR **POSTERIOR**

Frontal Lobe

Parietal Lobe

Occipital Lobe

Sylvian Fissure
Temporal Lobe

make meaningful comparisons. But an important and surprising sex difference emerged.

I was looking at people whose brain damage was restricted to either the front (anterior) or back (posterior) sections of the brain. I found that left-hemisphere damage could cause aphasia in both men and women, but different sites within that hemisphere were involved in the two sexes. Men were equally likely to have a severe speech disorder with anterior or posterior damage, in keeping with the classical picture of "speech areas" in the left hemisphere. Women, however, were much less likely than men to become aphasic after restricted posterior damage, and so far, in all women with damage to the posterior area, the left temporal lobe was affected. No woman has lost her capacity for speech because of damage to the left parietal lobe, but several men have.

This seemed to suggest that the brain area involved in women's speech is, if anything, more localized than in men, at least in the left hemisphere. This idea was so radical that it took me some time to accept it. After all, according to the prevailing wisdom, speech was supposed to be more broadly represented in the female brain than

---

The view now:
**women's brains may be organized like men's for some tasks,
more or less diffusely for others.**

---

in the male. But there was support for this idea from another type of research evidence: a study of how speech is affected when the cortex is electrically stimulated in awake patients during brain surgery.

Since the brain itself cannot feel pain, patients do not need a general anesthetic during brain surgery: local anesthesia to the scalp and skull will suffice. Catherine Mateer, a neuropsychol-

ogist who worked with neurosurgeon George Ojemann at the University of Seattle, found that electrical stimulation in the brain area near the Sylvian fissure interfered with a picture-naming task, but the particular brain areas responsible for such interference differed in men and women. In men, stimulation almost anywhere in the vicinity of the Sylvian fissure resulted in naming difficulties, while in women the pattern was more restricted. In particular, posterior parietal stimulation in women did not result in any naming problems, while it did in men. Thus, both my own data on brain damage and Mateer's on stimulation suggested that speech was not as believed, more diffusely organized in women's left hemisphere than in men's.

What's more, the right hemisphere does not seem to contribute to speech any more in women than in men. Reviewing our own series of right-handed cases with damage restricted to the right hemisphere, we found that aphasic disorders after such damage are very rare (1 to 2 percent of cases), and there is absolutely no difference between men and women in this respect. So we are left with the very strong probability that speech is organized differently within women's left hemisphere compared with men's. It looks as though in women's brains—but not men's—speech favors anterior systems and avoids the parietal region.

Why, then, is aphasia less common after left-hemisphere damage in women? Presumably, it's just a matter of odds: If speech is localized in a more restricted area of women's left hemisphere, and we look at a random series of patients with left-hemisphere damage, the speech systems are simply less likely to be hurt in women and aphasia is less likely to occur.

The different representations of speech functions within the left hemisphere might also partially explain why normal women are slightly less dependent on a single hemisphere than men in dichotic listening tests (see "Listening in to the Hemispheres" box). (In the 1970s psychologists Richard Harshman and Philip Bryden found independently that women have a less pronounced advantage in the right ear, that is, in the left hemisphere, on these tests.) In women, the left auditory cortex may be less directly connected to the speech centers than it is in men because the speech areas are differently located. It's also possible that by having a greater number of fibers in the corpus callosum, women have more effective transmission from the less-favored left ear to the left hemisphere.

Whatever the explanation, our findings that basic speech functions are quite focally organized in women mean that we have to give up the idea that women's brains are generally more diffusely orga-

---

What Are Little Boys and Girls Made Of?

One of the most fascinating facts of biology to emerge in the past few years is that sex is not determined by the genetic makeup of a person in any simple, direct way. An individual can be born with an XY genetic makeup (the male chromosomal pattern), yet grow up to have female genitals and look and behave like a woman. Another individual may have XX chromosomes (the female pattern) and become a man.

What determines whether a group of cells carrying XY or XX chromosomes will turn into a male or female human being is the presence of critical sex hormones early in fetal life. The Y chromosome appears to be necessary for converting the gonads into testes. The testes, in turn, are responsible for secreting androgens, male hormones, which result in the development of a penis rather than a vagina. If no Y chromosome is present, the gonads become ovaries.

But curiously, no hormones are needed to develop the female reproductive tract. If there are no hormones, or if female hormones are present, a vagina rather than a penis develops. This means that we have a biological bias toward being female. It also means that through variations in fetal and perhaps even pubertal hormones, it is possible to have somewhat wider biological variations in "maleness" and "femaleness" than we previously suspected.

Psychologist June Reinisch of the Kinsey Institute in Indiana has shown that girls who have had a higher-than-usual exposure to androgens before birth tend to be tomboyish. And researcher Günther Dorner's work in East Germany suggests that even some instances of homosexuality may reflect variation in fetal hormones. These examples may mean that, although the two sexes differ sharply in genital appearance, each has a range of potential behavior broad enough to defy characterizing behavioral patterns as exclusively limited to one sex or the other.

---

nized than men's. But this could still be true, if not for speech, at least for other functions.

We have, in fact, found some verbal functions more related to abstract verbal ability than to speech production, such as defining words and using them appropriately, that do seem to be more bilaterally organized in women than in men, as several people had earlier suggested.

In particular, Harshman and I found, on analyzing data from people with damage to only one hemisphere, that regardless of which hemisphere was injured, women's vocabulary—the ability to define words—was impaired. I then found this was true whether I

looked at anterior or posterior damage in either hemisphere, suggesting that defining words is a function of the whole brain in women. Men had problems in defining words only after left hemisphere damage. So for this kind of thinking at least, women's brains do indeed seem to be more diffusely organized.

I found different patterns of brain organization using other verbal tests, ones in which people were asked either to generate words beginning with a certain letter or to describe what they should do in various social situations. Other people have found that damage to the left anterior part of the brain causes the most difficulty

Kimura's Model of Dichotic Listening

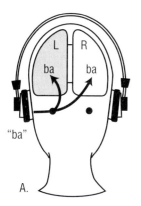

A.

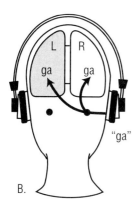

B.

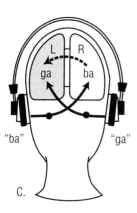

C.

A. Syllable ("ba") sent to left ear goes to right and left hemispheres by different pathways. Subjects report syllable accurately. B. Syllable ("ga") sent to right ear also goes to both hemispheres by different pathways and is reported accurately. C. "Ba" sent to left ear and "ga" to right ear simultaneously. "Ga" goes only to the left (speech) hemisphere and "ba" to the right. So "ga" is usually reported more often and more accurately than "ba."

in performing such tasks. I found this to be true for both men and women. So for this task, men's and women's brains were quite similarly organized.

In short, we are finding that, depending on the particular intellectual function we're studying, women's brains may be more, less or equally diffusely organized compared with men's. No single rule holds for all aspects of thinking. When it comes to speaking and making hand movements that contribute to motor skill, the brain seems to be very focally organized in women compared with men. This may relate to the fact that girls generally speak earlier, articulate better and also have better fine motor control of the hands. Also, a larger proportion of women than men are right-handed, and unequivocally so. But when it comes to certain, more-abstract tasks, such as defining words, women's brains are more diffusely organized than men's, although men and women don't differ in overall vocabulary ability.

> *When it comes to speaking and making hand movements that contribute to motor skill, the brain seems to be very focally organized in women compared with men.*

I have been describing the average state of affairs. But there is reason to believe that there is a lot of variation in brain organization from person to person. We know, for example, that the brains of left-handers and right-handers are organized somewhat differently, yet on average they function quite similarly.

In addition to individual variations, there are some interesting combined effects. Harshman and his colleagues at the University of Western Ontario found, for example, when they looked separately at people with above-average reasoning ability that sex and hand preference interacted. Left-handed men with above-average reason-

ing ability showed poorer scores on certain spatial tests, as well as other tests, than did right-handed men; but left-handed women were better at these tests than were right-handed women. When Harshman and coworkers looked at people with below-average reasoning ability, just the opposite happened: Now the left-handed men performed better than right-handed men on spatial tasks, but left-handed women did worse than the right-handed women.

What does this confusion suggest? It must mean that brain organization for such problem-solving abilities is related not only to sex and hand preference but also to overall intelligence level. And more to the point, it indicates that we have probably not one or two types of brain organization but several.

How are these different patterns of brain organization determined? There have been several suggestions in recent years that they may be related to the organism's rate of development both before and after birth. Biopsychologist Jerre Levy of the University of Chicago suggested some time ago that the two halves of the body, including the brain hemispheres, might grow at different rates in boys and girls, even before birth. The left hemisphere may develop more quickly in girls, and the right hemisphere in boys, thus favoring verbal skills in girls and spatial skills in boys. This idea has persisted in modified form in much of the literature on sex differences.

A recent report by biologist Ernest Nordeen and psychobiologist Pauline Yahr of the University of California at Irvine on the effect of injecting hormones into the brain of newborn rats suggested that

BRAIN ORGANIZATION: MEN AND WOMEN COMPARED

FUNCTION	BRAIN LOCATION		SUMMARY	
	Men	Women	Men and women same	Men and women different
Producing speech	Left hemisphere, front and back	Left hemisphere, mostly front		X Women more focal
Hand movements for motor skill	Left hemisphere, front and back	Left hemisphere, mostly front		X Women more focal
Vocabulary–defining words	Left hemisphere, front and back	Both hemispheres, front and back		X Women more diffuse
Other verbal tests (Naming words beginning with certain letters; describing appropriate social behavior)	Left hemisphere, front	Left hemisphere, front	X	

even the hypothalamus, a very basic regulating system, is asymmetrically organized for sexual behavior; injections on the left or right side affected sex-typical behavior differently. So although it may seem a bit far-fetched at first, there do appear to be basic asymmetries in the developing organism and these asymmetries may well have far-reaching repercussions for later differences between the sexes.

Functions such as speech and spatial ability traditionally have been thought to depend primarily on the cerebral cortex. Although we should not dismiss the idea that deeper brain structures contribute something to these abilities as well, it would be particularly interesting if there were sex-related differences in the structure of the cortex.

Neuropsychologist Marian Diamond of the University of California at Berkeley, comparing cortical thickness in male and female rats, did find that the right cortex is thicker in males at most ages, while the left cortex is thicker in females but only at some ages. Also very suggestive is her finding that, when ovaries are removed at birth, the female rat develops a pattern of hemispheric dominance more like that of the male.

These studies on anatomical asymmetries in the brain are in a very early stage, of course, but they indicate quite strongly that the biological sex differences in brain organization are probably

> **The fact seems inescapable that men and women do differ genetically, physiologically and psychologically.**

dynamic, rather than a crystallized pattern that is laid down entirely by the genes. At various periods in life, different brain structures may be undergoing more- or less-rapid growth, and patterns of brain organization will vary from time to time as a result. This may very well go on throughout a person's life, in fact, since hormonal environments are in lifelong flux.

The role of sex hormones in prenatal development is quite dramatic and profound (see "What Are Little Boys and Girls Made Of?" box). It may also be appreciable in adult life, even affecting cognitive abilities in men and in women. While hormonal changes occur in both sexes over a variety of short and long cycles, the changes in women during stages of the menstrual cycle have been most thoroughly studied. For example, there is some evidence that spatial ability in women may vary

Listening in to the Hemispheres

Before the early 1960s, people interested in the differing roles of the left and right hemispheres depended almost entirely on evidence drawn from animal research, from studies of neurological patients with one-sided brain damage or from patients who had had their corpus callosum, the conduit connecting the two hemispheres, surgically severed. But I found that it was possible to detect which brain hemisphere was most involved in speech and other functions in normal people by having them listen to two different words coming to the two ears at the same time. This became known as the "dichotic listening" procedure. When several word pairs are given in a row, people are unable to report them all, and most right-handers prefer to report—and report more accurately—words given to their right ear. This seems to be related to the fact that signals from the right ear, although sent to both hemispheres, are preferentially sent to the left hemisphere, which controls speech. People who have speech represented in the right hemisphere, a very unusual occurrence even in left-handed people, more accurately report what their left ears hear.

In contrast to the right-ear (left-hemisphere) advantage for speech, there is generally a left-ear (right-hemisphere) advantage for another type of auditory signal: music. When right-handed people listen to melodic patterns, which neuropsychologist Brenda Milner at the Montreal Neurological Institute has shown depend more on the right hemisphere, they report them better from the left ear.

monthly as natural levels of sex hormones in the bloodstream change; it may be best during the phase when the level of the female sex hormone estrogen is lowest.

In contrast to these findings, Elizabeth Hampson, one of my graduate students, has found that women perform best on tests of motor skill when their female sex hormones are at their highest level. So, as in brain organization, the pattern we see may very well depend on the particular function that we study.

What do all these findings tell us about the inherent capabilities of the two sexes? And what can we, as a result, deduce about the abilities of an individual man or woman? The fact seems inescapable that men and women do

> ***We can predict very little about an individual's mental abilities based on his or her sex.***

differ genetically, physiologically and in many important ways psychologically. This should not be surprising to us, since as a species we have a long biological history of having two sexual forms and

have had a sexual division of labor dating back perhaps several million years. Men and women probably have been evolving different advantages for a wide range of activities for at least hundreds of thousands of years. In short, given two genetically different sexes, we can expect differing behavioral capabilities extending even beyond directly sexual roles.

But having said all that, I also have a number of important caveats. First, biological sex itself has turned out to be much more variable and dynamic than we ever imagined. And brain-organization patterns are even more variable from person to person, and probably even within the same person at different times. Further, on most tests of cognitive ability there is enormous overlap of men and women. We strain to look for differences and, of course, tend to emphasize the few we find.

Given these facts, it follows that while genital sex is related to our mental capabilities, it is going to be a very poor screening device for intellectual assessment. Numerous environmental events interact with our genetic heritage from prenatal development onward, and the human brain is extraordinarily malleable and variable. Thus, we can predict very little about an individual's mental capabilities based on his or her sex. A number of men and women can and do excel in activities that, on average, favor the other sex. There may be no inherent characteristics unique to the brains of either sex that necessarily limit the intellectual achievements of individual men or women.

Discussion Questions

1. What were the initial findings that lead to the conclusion that women's brains are more diffusely organized than men's are?

2. What were the surprising sex differences that Kimura found?

3. What did Catherine Mateer and George Ojemann find during brain surgery?

4. For what kind of thinking is a woman's brain more diffusely organized, according to Kimura?

5. How many types of brain organizations does Kimura suggest?

6. What are Kimura's important caveats?

ADRENALINE Makes the *Heart* GROW Fonder

◆ *Elaine Walster and Ellen Berscheid*

A frightened man is a potentially romantic man. So is an angry man, a jealous man, a rejected man or a euphoric man. Anyone, in fact, who experiences the physical arousal that accompanies strong human emotion is a potentially romantic person in that he has already fulfilled one of the two essential conditions for love and is a step ahead of the person whose emotions are in a quiescent stage. If he should meet an unusually desirable woman while he is in this state, he is likely to be more intensely drawn to her than he would be in normal circumstances.

To love passionately, a person must first be physically aroused, a condition manifested by palpitations of the heart, nervous tremor, flushing, and accelerated breathing. Once he is so aroused, all that remains is for him to identify this complex of feelings as passionate love, and he will have experienced authentic love. Even if the initial physical arousal is the result of an irrelevant experience that usually would produce anger, or even if it is induced in a laboratory by an injection of adrenaline, once the subject has met the person, been drawn to the person, and identified the experience as love, it is love.

This is not to say that passionate love can be induced easily in a laboratory setting. However, recent experiments have shown that physical arousal, as a pre-condition to love, can be

so induced. Research also demonstrates that in settings that foster interpersonal attractions, the aroused subject is likely to respond with more affection than is the unaroused subject.

Taboo

For years, the subject of love has been ignored by psychological researchers. A multitude of scientists have conducted experiments on "liking," which is defined as "a positive attitude toward another, evidenced by a tendency to approach and interact with him." Most theorists simply assume—without evidence—that passionate love is nothing more than very intense liking.

"Love" and "sex" have long been taboo words for psychologists. Foundations and government agencies have been reluctant to grant funds for studies on these subjects and psychologists themselves have considered experimenters on the topic of love to be

> To love passionately, a person must first be physically aroused, a condition manifested by palpitations of the heart, nervous tremor, flushing, and accelerated breathing.

"soft-headed," "unscientific" or possessed of a flair for the trivial.

Psychologists have tended to assume that in the laboratory one can

study only mild and quickly developing phenomena. Although poets have proclaimed that love can occur at first sight, psychologists have had less confidence that one can generate passionate love in a two-hour laboratory experiment. Thus, many researchers erroneously assumed that passionate love could be studied only in the field.

Lab

With Masters and Johnson's impressive research, indicating that sex could be studied in the laboratory, the situation quickly reversed itself. In the last five years more psychologists have begun to study romantic love than in the entire history of the science.

The problem now is not with the respectability of such studies, but with the accumulation of facts. When they are asked for information about love and sex today, chagrined psychologists must admit they know very little. However, we believe that by applying an existing theoretical framework that is concerned with human emotion generally, to the specific emotion of passionate love, our understanding of love will be increased.

X

Friendship, or liking, even when it is unusually intense, is an easily predictable phenomenon, a sensible emotion, because it invariably follows the rules. One can predict quite well how much a person will like another if one knows to what extent his companion rewards or punishes him. Reward has so predictable an impact on liking that Donn Byrne has proposed an exact correspondence between reinforcement and liking. "Attraction toward X," he ways, "is a positive linear function of the proportion of positive reinforcements received from X or expected from X."

Love, on the contrary, seems to operate in accordance with the reinforcement rules only part of the time. Some practical persons have been known to fall in love with those beautiful, wise, entertaining and kind persons who offer affection and material rewards to them. Generally, however, love does not seem to fit so neatly into the theory of reinforcement. Individuals do not always feel passionate about the person who provides the most rewards with the greatest consistency. Passion sometimes develops in conditions that would seem more likely to provoke aggression and hatred than to permit love to flower. When we reinforcement theorists state that "we like those who like us and reject those who dislike us," we forget that individuals may intensely love those who have rejected them. A woman experiences pain and jealousy, to be sure, when she discovers that her husband is seeing another woman. But the experience causes some women to realize how much they love their husbands.

Hurdle

Those who argue that "frustration always breeds aggression" likewise ignore the opinions of clinicians who claim that inhibited or frustrated sexuality is a foundation for romantic feelings. Freud noted that "some obstacle is necessary to swell the tide of libido to its height; and at all periods of history whenever natural barriers in the way of satisfaction have not sufficed, mankind has erected conventional ones in order to enjoy love."

The observation that passionate love sometimes flourishes in settings that would seem to thwart its development has always been puzzling to scientists. Poets attribute such inexplicable phenomena to the essential illogic of love. Psychologists, who refuse to ac-

knowledge that anything is inexplicable, do not have such an easy way out. Fortunately, there is an existing theoretical framework—

> *The observation that passionate love sometimes flourishes in settings that would seem to thwart its development has always been puzzling to scientists.*

one devised for the study of human emotions generally—into which this "illogical" phenomenon of passionate love fits neatly and becomes both explicable and predictable.

One-Two

On the basis of an ingenious series of experiments, Stanley Schachter proposed a paradigm for understanding human emotional response. It is from the theory he developed that we believe the specific emotion of passionate love can be clarified. Schachter suggests that in order for a person to experience emotion two factors must be present: 1. The individual must be physiologically aroused, as described above; and 2. It must be reasonable to interpret his stirred-up state in emotional terms. He argues that neither physiological arousal nor mere labeling alone would be sufficient to produce an emotional experience.

Up

In testing this hypothesis experimentally, it is possible to manipulate an individual's physiological arousal in the laboratory. The drug adrenaline replicates the discharge of the sympathetic nervous system. Shortly after one receives an injection of adrenaline, systolic blood pressure increases markedly, heat rate increases somewhat, cutaneous

blood flow decreases, muscle and cerebral blood flow increase, and blood-sugar and lactic-acid concentrate increase, and respiration rate increases slightly. The individual who has had the injection undergoes palpitation, tremor and sometimes flushing and accelerated breathing. These reactions are identical to the physiological reactions that accompany a variety of natural emotional states.

The adrenaline, however, does not engender a true emotion or emotional response in a person. After having been injected with adrenaline, subjects who are asked to report on their experiences will say frequently that there is no emotional response. Sometimes they will report feeling "as if" they might be experiencing some emotion. They make statements such as "I feel as if I were afraid." They perceive that something is not quite authentic about their reactions, that they are not true emotional experiences.

Schachter says the missing ingredient is an appropriate interpretation for the physiological reactions being experienced. If the subject could be led to attribute his stirred-up state to some emotion-arousing event, rather than to the adrenaline injection, Schachter says, his experience would constitute a true emotional state.

Suproxin

To test the hypothesis Schachter had to find a way of manipulating the two components—physiological arousal and appropriate interpretation—separately. In 1962, in his classical experiment with J.E. Singer, he conceived of a way to do just that.

Schachter and Singer recruited volunteers and told them they were to take part in an experiment to investigate the effects on vision of a new vitamin compound, Suproxin.

He told them that they all would receive injections of the drug.

Suproxin was actually a fictitious name. Half of the students had injections of an adrenalinelike drug that causes the physiological reactions described earlier. The other half received placebo injections. The physiological arousal, thus, was in the control of the experimenter.

To gain control of the other element—the appropriate interpretation of the physiological state—Schachter explained to some of the subjects the exact bodily reactions they could expect. He theorized that this group, as they experienced the reaction to the drug, would properly attribute their stirred-up state to the injections. Whatever activities they were engaged in at the time the reactions began would not be blamed for their physical state. Another group, however, was deliberately manipulated so that members would not attribute their reactions to the adrenaline injections.

Some got no information about the effects of the drug. Others got incorrect information about what they might expect, so that when the symptoms appeared these subjects would not easily recognize them. The experimenters hoped that subjects with either incorrect information or no information would attribute their stirred-up states to whatever activities they were engaged in when the symptoms appeared.

Schachter further subdivided the group to get further control of the interpretation component of the experiment. He left some in the presence of fellow subjects (actually trained experimenters) who had been instructed to generate excitement by mischievous and humorous activity. Then Schachter left other subjects in the presence of persons trained to make them angry. These *provocateurs* complained, called the questionnaire they had been asked to fill out "stupid," and finally left the room in a show of anger.

Mood

The experimenters, who watched through one-way mirrors, first determined to what extent each subject had caught the excited or angry mood of his room partners; then they asked the subject to describe his moods and to estimate his own degree of excitement or anger.

Before conducting the experiment, Schachter predicted that subjects who had received adrenaline injections would have stronger emotional reactions than would those who had received placebos or who had received adrenaline, but who were warned what symptoms to expect.

Two components are necessary for a passionate experience: arousal and interpretation.

The data supported these hypotheses. The experiment thus supported the contention that both physiological arousal and appropriate interpretations are indispensable components of a true emotional experience. The experiment seemed to indicate that almost any sort of intense physiological arousal, properly interpreted, will precipitate an emotional experience.

Key

It was intriguing to attempt to apply this theory to the specific emotions, particularly to passionate love. Up to this point, researchers had been busy trying to explain love in terms of reinforcement—one's love for another is a function of the reinforcements the other provided— a theory successfully applied to the emotion of friendship, or liking, but not to passionate love. With the reinforcement theory, it was impossible to explain what one could see easily—that negative experiences often led to increased rather than decreased love.

A sudden insight solved our dilemma and allowed us to apply Schachter's general theory of emotions to the emotion of love. Two components are necessary for a passionate experience: arousal and interpretation. What if the negative experiences function not in the interpretive realm, as had been supposed, but in the realm of arousal? Perhaps negative experiences are effective in inducing love because they intensify one's physiological arousal.

It would follow that the manner in which one produces an agitated state in a lover may be insignificant. What is significant is the fact of heightened physiological arousal. Stimuli that usually produce sexual arousal, gratitude, anxiety, guilt, loneliness, hatred, jealousy or confusion can all increase one's physiological arousal, and thus intensify his emotional experience.

Spark

Some early observers noticed that any form of strong emotional arousal can breed love (although, of course, they did not interpret this relationship in Schachterian terms). H.T. Finck, an early psychologist, concluded: "Love can only be excited by strong and vivid emotion, and it is almost immaterial whether these emotions are agreeable or disagreeable. The Cid wooed the proud heart of Diana Ximene, whose father he had slain, by shooting one after another of her pet pigeons. Such persons as arouse in us only weak emotions or none at all, are obviously least likely to incline us toward them....Our aversion is most likely to be bestowed on individuals who, as the phrase goes, are neither 'warm' nor 'cold'; whereas impulsive, choleric people, though they may readily offend us, are just as capable of making us warmly attached to them."

As long as the subject attributes his agitated state to passionate love, he should experience love.

There is almost no evidence that directly supports this contention. However, a few studies designed to test other hypotheses provide minimal support. Generally, they are concerned with experiments designed to test liking, or friendship, and their application to love may be invalid. Is the frightened man cited at the beginning really a passionate man? To be sure, frightening a person is a very good way to produce intense physiological arousal.

In one study, J. W. Brehm and his associates led one group of men to believe they would receive three "pretty stiff" electrical shocks. Later the experimenters told half of them that there had been an error and they would not receive the shocks. The experimenters never discussed the possibility of electrical shocks with a control group. The experimenters introduced each of the men to a young girl and asked later how much each liked her. Those who were still expecting the electrical shock and those who had been told initially to expect one, but later were told none would be forthcoming, exhibited more liking for the girl than did the control group.

The experimenters concluded that the fear, though it is irrelevant to the emotion of liking, facilitated the attraction. Likewise, the relief from fear—which was a strong emotional experience in itself—seemed to facilitate the attraction.

A passage in Bertrand Russell's autobiography illustrates the point. He reports that an irrelevant, frightening event—World War I—intensified his passion for Collette, a mistress:

"We scarcely knew each other, and yet in that moment there began for both of us a relation profoundly serious and profoundly important, sometimes happy, sometimes painful, but never unworthy to be placed alongside of the great public emotions connected with the War. Indeed, the War was bound into the texture of this love from first to last. The first time that I was ever in bed with her (we did not go to bed the first time we were lovers, as there was too much to say), we heard suddenly a shout of bestial triumph in the street. I leapt out of bed and saw a Zeppelin falling in flames. The thought of brave men dying in agony was what caused the triumph in the street. Colette's love was in that moment a refuge to me, not from cruelty itself, which was unescapable, but from the agonizing pain of realizing that that is what men are…"

Socrates, Ovid, Terence, the Kamasutra and Dear Abby are all in agreement on one point: the person whose affection is easily won will inspire less passion than the person whose affection is hard to win.

Nay

What of the emotional experience of rejection? Could it also, under certain conditions, engender love? In one test, experimenters asked male students to take a series of personality tests. Later, a psychologist interpreted the results to the students in such a manner that half received flattering personality profiles while the other half received insulting reports.

Soon thereafter, it was arranged for a young female college student to make the acquaintance of each of the males. She had been trained to treat each boy initially in a warm, accepting way. Under these conditions, the men who had received the critical evaluations were far more attracted to her than were their more confident counterparts. It could be concluded that the previous arousal engendered by the rejection facilitated the later display of affection.

When the girl was cold and rejecting, there was a dramatic reversal. The previously rejected men disliked the girl more than did their confident counterparts. In summary, it seems that an irrelevant, painful event can inspire strong emotional reactions toward others. Depending on how he labels his feelings, the individual may experience either intense attraction or intense hostility.

Accord

Socrates, Ovid, Terence, the *Kamasutra* and Dear Abby are all in agreement on one point: the person whose affection is easily won will inspire less passion than the person whose affection is hard to win.

Vassilikos poetically elucidated the principle that frustration flames passion while continual gratification weakens it:

"Once upon a time there was a little fish who was a bird from the waist up and who was madly in love with a little bird who was a fish from the waist up. So the Fish-Bird kept saying to the Bird-Fish: 'Oh, why were we created so that we can never live together? You in the wind and I in the wave. What a pity for both of us.' And the Bird-Fish would answer: 'No, what luck for both of us. This way we'll always be in love because we'll always be separated.'"

Gain

Some support for the contention that the hard-to-get person

© Digital Vision

mands physiological arousal, and all of these experiences are certainly arousing.

Error

Thus far the experiments cited have dealt with a negative component as a factor in heightening passionate love. Yet, positive reinforcements—such as sexual gratification, excitement, companionship, discovery and joy—can generate arousal as intense as that stirred by fear, frustration or rejection. It follows that these positive reinforcements can likewise facilitate passionate love.

Even the erroneous belief that one has been sexually aroused by a member of the opposite sex will facilitate a real attraction for that person. Stuart Valins recounts an experiment in which male college students viewed 10 photographs of seminude women. They were told that as they looked at the pictures, their heartbeats would be monitored. In reality, the "monitoring device" was manipulated by the experimenter in a systematic manner that was not influenced by the subject's actual heartbeat. The men were told that certain of the photographs had caused their hearts to beat faster and that some of the pictures had produced little or no physiological reaction. The men then showed marked preference for the photographs that they believed they had reacted strongly to.

Need

The positive emotional reaction of need fulfillment likewise seems capable of facilitating passion, as is the common experience of us all. We have a wide variety of needs, and at any stage of life many of them are unsatisfied. When an unsatisfied need is finally met, the emotional response that accompanies such reinforcement can provide fuel for passion.

may engender unusual passion in the eventually successful suitor comes from Elliot Aronson and Darwyn Linder, who tested the hypothesis that "a gain in esteem is a more potent reward than invariant esteem." They predicted that a person would be better liked if his positive regard were hard to get.

In the test, subjects talked during seven separate meetings with another subject, who was actually a confederate of the experimenters. After each meeting the subjects learned how the confederates regarded them. The experimenters systematically varied these estimations. In one segment, the confederates began by expressing negative impressions of the subjects, gradually modifying their reports until, finally, they appeared to like the subjects. In all the remaining segments, the con-

federates expressed, right from the beginning, only positive opinions about the subjects.

As predicted, the subjects liked the confederates whose affections appeared to be hard to win better than they liked those who appeared to like them from the beginning.

This experiment is consistent with our suggestion that a hard-to-get girl should provoke more passion than the constantly rewarding girl. The aloof girl's challenge may excite the suitor; her momentary rejection may frustrate him. Such arousal may intensify his feelings toward her.

The preceding analysis underscores the contention that the juxtaposition of agony and ecstasy in passionate love is not entirely accidental. Loneliness, deprivation, frustration, hatred and insecurity may, in fact, supplement a person's romantic experiences. Passion de-

The adolescent boy who has been babied at home for many years might react most favorably to the girl who acknowledges his maturity and masculinity. Again, the typical hard-working father whose day-to-day activities are generally limited to breadwinning and family routine may be captivated when an alert lady makes him feel like a reckless lover.

Label

All these experiments serve to validate the contention that Schachter's two-component theory can be applied to passionate love. They all demonstrate that physiological arousal is a crucial component of love, and that fear, pain, frustration, delight and sexual gratification can all deepen the passionate experience under certain conditions.

Yet the experiments also reveal that, according to the two-component theory, the individual so aroused will not actually be experiencing passionate love unless conditions are right for him to label the experience as love.

The American culture strongly encourages individuals to interpret a wide range of confused feelings as love. Ralph Linton makes this point in a somewhat harsh observation: "All societies recognize that there are occasional violent emotional attachments between persons of the opposite sex, but our present American culture is practically the only one which has attempted to capitalize on these and make them the basis for marriage. The hero of the modern American movie is always a romantic lover, just as the hero of an old Arab epic is always an epileptic. A cynic may suspect that in any ordinary population the percentage of individuals with capacity for romantic love of the Hollywood type is about as large as that of persons able to throw genuine epileptic fits."

A physiologically aroused person is more likely to conclude that he is "in love" when cultural pressures encourage him to interpret his mixed feelings in this way than when they do not.

As an example, while the delightful experience of sexual intercourse can be frankly labeled as "sexual fun" by a man, it is more difficult for a girl to interpret her feelings in this way. Culturally, a girl is expected to experience sex only when she is "in love." Thus girls are probably more likely than boys to label sexual feelings in romantic terms.

Green Eyes

In our culture, jealousy is manifested in a variety of petty ways. Margaret Mead said: "Jealousy is not a barometer by which the depth of love may be read. It merely records the degree of the

When an unsatisfied need is finally met, the emotional response that accompanies such reinforcement can provide fuel for passion.

lover's insecurity. It is a negative, miserable state of feeling, having its origin in a sense of insecurity and inferiority." But when the jealous person can convince himself that this emotion is a manifestation of love, he need not regard it as petty. The spurned husband who treats his wife as a chattel may in reality be insecure, yet might interpret his jealousy as a lofty form of love.

Besides the cultural implantations, each individual acquires a set of self-images that also can determine to what extent he is likely to label a physiological arousal as love. The individual who thinks of himself as a nonromantic person should fall in love less often than should an individual who assumes that love, for him, is inevitable. The nonromantic person may experience the same feelings that the romantic does, but he will code them differently.

A girl with a great deal of self-confidence, who considers herself attractive, may induce a normally unreceptive man to label his feelings for her as love. The insecure girl who complains that her boyfriend doesn't love her, who even itemizes for him evidence of his neglect, may effect an actual lowering of his esteem for her.

The examples, of course, are not meant as solid evidence that Schachter's two-component theory can explain passionate love. The consistency of available data with our argument suggests, however, that we should conduct laboratory experimentation to test the thesis that both physiological arousal and proper labeling of the aroused state as passionate love are basic to the human emotion of passionate love. Psychological research is now free of the taboos that prevented such experimentation for many years.

Discussion Questions

1. What do Elaine Walster and Ellen Berscheid say are the ingredients for love?

2. According to Stanley Schachter, what two factors must be present for a person to experience a specific emotion?

3. Describe the experiment that Schachter and Singer designed to test their hypothesis.

4. How can rejection lead to feelings of love?

5. List the negative components that can heighten passionate love.

6. List the positive components that can heighten passionate love.

7. According to the authors, why would women be more inclined to label a sexual experience in romantic terms?

8. Think about a current or past relationship that you have had. Were there any extraneous arousing factors present at the time that you felt attracted to the other person?

THE *Orgasm* **Wars**

◆ F. Bryant Furlow and Randy Thornhill

Ever since Alfred Kinsey and Masters and Johnson made the subject of human sexual response safe for respectable scientists, laboratory studies of the physiologic "hows" of sexual arousal have flourished. Volunteers have been prodded, filmed, tape-recorded, interviewed, measured, wired, and monitored, quantifying for the annals of science the shortened breath, arched backs and feet, grimacing faces, marginally intentional vocalizations, and jumping blood pressure of human orgasm.

While physiological details abound, fewer scientists have attempted to answer the "why" questions about human orgasm. To those who view human behavior in an evolutionary framework, which we believe adds an invaluable perspective, male orgasm is no great mystery. It's little more than a physiologically simple ejaculation that is accompanied by a nearly addictive incentive to seek out further sexual encounters. The greater the number of inseminations a male achieves, the better his chances of being genetically represented in future generations.

Compared with the more frequent and easily achieved orgasm men experience, women's sexual climax has remained a mystery. After all, women do not need to experience orgasm in order to conceive. So what is the function of orgasm in females?

Darwinian theorists who made early attempts to address female orgasm proposed that orgasm keeps a woman lying down after sex, passively retaining sperm and increasing her probability of conception. Others suggested that it evolved to create a stronger pair bond between lovers, inspiring in women feelings of intimacy and trust toward mates. Some reasoned that orgasm communicates a woman's sexual satisfaction and devotion to a lover.

Most recently, evolutionary psychologists have been exploring the

Women's romantic attachment does not increase the frequency of orgasm! Nor does experience.

proposition that female orgasm is a sophisticated adaptation that allows women to manipulate—even without their own awareness—which of their lovers will be allowed to fertilize their eggs.

Male Nipples?

The diversity of evolutionary hypotheses reflects one general attitude: that the quickened breath, moaning, racing heart, muscular contraction and spasms, and nearly hallucinatory states of pleasure that orgasm inspires constitute a complex physiologic event with apparently functional design. But critics of adaptationist hypotheses have long argued that evolution is more slipshod than purposeful. A few, including Harvard evolutionist Stephen Jay Gould, have insisted that female orgasm probably doesn't *have* a function.

Instead, Gould argues, female orgasm is incidental, caused by an anatomical peculiarity of embryonic development. In embryos, the undifferentiated organ that later becomes the penis in males becomes the clitoris in females. Antiadaptationists like Gould—whose thinking uncannily parallels Freud's belief that women spend their life in penis envy—hold that the clitoris is, biologically speaking, an underdeveloped penis; it can let women mimic male orgasm, but it has no functional relevance or evolutionary history of its own.

Well known for his emphasis on chance events and structural constraints as major players in the evolutionary process, Gould sees the supposed functionlessness of female orgasm as a classic illustration why scientists ought not automatically assume that a trait has adaptive significance. He criticizes other evolutionists for overemphasizing natural selection and functionality, and concludes that female orgasm is like the male nipple—nothing more than developmental baggage.

Many evolutionists have rejected Gould's notion that women's orgasms are developmentally contingent on men's. Unlike a male nipple, adaptationists have pointed out, the female orgasm *does* something. It inspires strong emotions that can affect bonding and sexual preferences, making women more likely to prefer the company of one mate over another.

Only during the past few years have studies begun to yield evidence that may resolve the baggage-versus-adaption debate over women's orgasms.

Sperm Competition, with Women Judging

Clues for a reasonable adaptation hypothesis were readily available by the late 1960s, when *The British Medical Journal* published an exchange of letters about the muscular contractions and uterine suction associated with women's orgasm. In one letter, a doctor reported that a patient's uterine and vaginal contractions during sex with a sailor had pulled off his condom. Upon inspection, the condom was found in her cervical canal! The doctor concluded that female orgasms pull sperm closer to the egg as well.

Yet, it was only three years ago that two British biologists, Robin Baker and Mark Bellis, tested the so-called upsuck hypothesis. They were building upon ideas articulated by evolutionary biologist Robert Smith, who suggested that since women don't have orgasms every time out, female orgasm favors some sperm over others. Baker and Bellis sought to learn just how female orgasms might affect which of a lover's sperm is used to fertilize a woman's eggs.

They asked volunteers to keep track of the timing of their orgasms during sex, and, after copulation, to collect male ejaculates from vaginal flowback—a technical term denoting a distinct form of material that emerges from the vagina several hours after sex (scientists have devised a way to collect it). The team counted sperm from over 300 instances of human copulation.

They discovered that when a woman climaxes any time between a minute before to 45 minutes after her lover ejaculates, she retains significantly more sperm than she does after nonorgasmic sex. When her orgasm precedes her mate's by more than a minute, or when she does not have an orgasm, little sperm is retained. Just as the doctors' letters suggested decades earlier, the team's results indicated that muscular contractions associated with orgasm pull sperm from the vagina to the cervix, where it's in better position to reach an egg.

Baker and Bellis proposed that by manipulating the occurrence and timing of orgasm—via subconscious processes—women influence the probability of conception. So while a man worries about a woman's satisfaction with him as a lover out of fear she will stray, orgasmic females may be up to something far more clever—deciding which partner will sire her children.

Good Men Are Hard to Find

Meanwhile, other researchers were making discoveries about the nature of male attractiveness. Behavioral ecologists had noted that female animals, from scorpion flies to barn swallows, prefer males with high degrees of bilateral body symmetry, called developmental stability in the parlance of science.

Development, or the translation of genes into parts of the body, can be perturbed by stresses such as disease, malnutrition, or genetic defects. One measure of develop-

---

As uncomfortable as it may make many of us men, a woman's orgasm appears to be a more complex and discriminating comment about her lover's merits than are our own.

---

mental *in*stability is deviation from bilateral symmetry in traits like hands, eyes, and even birds' tail feathers. Males whose immune systems are strong, and who forage well, develop with high sym-

metry, so females who choose symmetrical suitors are securing good genes for their offspring.

Evolutionary biologist Randy Thornhill and psychologist Steve Gangestad at the University of New Mexico in Albuquerque have tested whether humans also share this preference. And indeed they do! In their studies, women consistently identify as most attractive males whose faces (and other body parts) are most symmetrical.

But this, it turns out, is more than a matter of mere aesthetics. A large and growing body of medical literature documents that symmetrical people are physically and psychologically healthier than their less symmetrical counterparts.

Thornhill and Gangestad reasoned that if women's orgasms are an adaptation for securing good genes for their offspring, women should report more orgasms with relatively symmetrical mates. Collaborating for a second time, the two, along with graduate student Randall Comer, devised some very interesting studies to test this idea.

First they enrolled 86 sexually active heterosexual couples from among the undergraduates. The average age of the partners was 22 and the couples had been together an average of two years. Then the researchers had each person privately—and anonymously—answer questions about his or her sexual experiences.

The researchers took facial photographs of each person and analyzed the features by computer; they also had them graded for attractiveness by independent raters blind to the study. They measured various body parts to assess bilateral symmetry—the width of elbow, wrist, hand, ankle, and foot bones, and the length of the second and fifth fingers. Earlier studies had suggested all of these were associated with health.

Indeed, the hypothesized relationship between male symmetry and female orgasm proved to be true, the researchers recently reported in the journal *Animal Behavior*. From data on sexual behavior provided by the women, those whose partners were most symmetrical enjoyed a significantly higher frequency of orgasms during sexual intercourse than did those with less symmetrical mates. Even the data on sexual experience provided by the men showed the women had more orgasms with the most symmetrical men.

Of course, symmetry is a relative thing, and a relative rarity at that. No one is perfectly symmetrical, and very high symmetry scores were few and far between in this sample, as in others. In consolation, Thornhill and Gangestad point out that the differences they are measuring are subtle, and most require the use of calipers to detect.

What's Love Got to Do with It?

It's important to note what did not correlate with female orgasm during sex. Degree of women's romantic attachment did not increase the frequency of orgasm! Nor did the sexual experience of either partner. Conventional wisdom holds that birth control and protection from disease up orgasm rates, since they allow women to feel more relaxed during intercourse. But no relationship emerged between female orgasm and the use of contraception.

Nor can the study results be explained by the possibility that the symmetrical males were dating especially uninhibited and orgasmic women. Their partners did not have more orgasms during foreplay or in other sexual activities. Male symmetry correlated with a high frequency of female orgasm *only during copulation.*

Explosive Findings!

If we use his study's findings to understand how we humans are designed to behave in the sexual domain, says Randy Thornhill, Ph.D., then we are better equipped to deal with problems that arise in relationships. He points to the following results as among those we should take to heart:

- A woman's capacity for orgasm depends not on her partner's sexual skill but on her subconscious evaluation of his genetic merits.

- Women's orgasm has little to do with love. Or experience.

- Good men are indeed hard to find.

- The men with the best genes make the worst mates.

- Women are no more built for monogamy than men are. They are designed to keep their options open.

- Women fake orgasm to divert a partner's attention from their infidelities.

The findings support evolutionary psychologists' "good genes" hypothesis: Women have orgasm more often with their most symmetrical lovers, increasing the likelihood of conceiving these men's children. Well, that's how it would have worked for millennia, before condoms and the Pill.

And it is for the precontraceptive stone age that our brains seem to be built; the agricultural and industrial revolutions are flashes in the geological pan, far too recent in evolutionary terms to have fundamentally changed the way we experience emotions or sex. To argue, as may champions of chance like Gould, that sexual attraction has remained completely arbitrary throughout evolution seems increasingly unwarranted.

Cheating Hearts

Here's the cruelest part of Thornhill and Gangestad's findings: The males who most inspire high-sperm-retention orgasmic responses from their sexual partners don't invest more in their relationships than do other men. Studies show that symmetrical men have the shortest courtships before having sexual intercourse with the women they date. They invest the least money and time in them. And they cheat on their mates more often than guys with less well-balanced bodies. So much for the beleaguered bonding hypothesis, which wants us to believe that women with investing, caring mates will have the most orgasms.

The women who took part in the study were no saints, either. They sometimes *faked* orgasm. Their fakery was not related to male symmetry. Faking, however, was more common among women who reported flirting with other men. Clearly earlier theories were not too far off the make when they proposed that a man looks for cues of sexual satisfaction from his mate for reassurance about her fidelity. Faking orgasms might be the easiest way for the woman with many lovers to avoid the suspicions of her main partner.

Baker and Bellis found that when women do engage in infidelity, they retain less sperm from their main partners (their husbands, in many cases), and more often experience copulatory orgasms during their trysts, retaining semen from their secret lovers. Taken together, these findings suggest that female orgasm is less about bonding with nice guys than about careful, subconscious evaluation of their lovers' genetic endowment.

Exhibit B

Patterns of female orgasm point to one important conclusion about our evolutionary past—that sexual restraint did not prevail among women. But that's only part of the evidence. Exhibit B is male ejaculation.

Baker and Bellis found that the number of sperm in men's ejaculate changes, and it varies according to the amount of time that romantic partners have spent apart. The longer a woman's absence, the more sperm in her husband's ejaculate upon the couple's reunion. Males increase ejaculate size, it seems, to match the increased risk that a mate was inseminated by a competitor.

In an ancestral environment of truly monogamous mating, there would have been no need for females to have orgasm or for men to adjust ejaculate size. Both are adaptations to a spicy sex life.

Male Bias

Darwin proposed that female animals' preferences have shaped male ornaments such as peacocks' tails. But his audience—largely male scientists—laughed off his theory of sexual selection on the grounds that females (human or otherwise) are too fickle to exert the necessary selection pressure.

Today, evolutionary biology is no longer so completely a male discipline. But many male evolutionists nevertheless carry old biases. The notion that female orgasm is anything other than a developmental legacy leaving females able to imitate "the real thing" will be difficult for some to accept. But as uncomfortable as it may make many of us men—including male scientists—a woman's orgasm appears to be a more complex and discriminating comment about her lovers' merits than are our own. ◆

> *Female orgasm is less about bonding with nice guys than subconscious evaluation of their lovers genetic endowment. Women have orgasm more often with men whose bodies are most symmetrical.*

Discussion Questions

1. What does Stephen Jay Gould say about female orgasms?

2. Describe the baggage-versus-adaptation debate.

3. What is the "upsuck hypothesis?"

4. According to Baker and Bellis, how does the female orgasm influence the probability of conception?

5. Why, according to the authors, do women prefer men who are more symmetrical?

6. In Thornhill and Gangestad's study, what were the factors that did not correlate with female orgasm during sex?

7. What increases the number of sperm a man ejaculates?

Name: _____

Date: _____

Part 13: Human Sexuality and Gender

1. Freud was right in his assertion that sexual urges explain a great deal of human behavior, both normal and abnormal.

| Agree | (1) | (2) | (3) | (4) | (5) | Disagree |

2. Behavioral, intellectual, and emotional differences between males and females are learned, not inherited.

| Agree | (1) | (2) | (3) | (4) | (5) | Disagree |

3. I would like gender role differences to be reduced or eliminated.

| Agree | (1) | (2) | (3) | (4) | (5) | Disagree |

How consistent is your personal experience with Walster and Berscheid's theory about affection? List occasions on which you have felt affection or attraction. In each case, could extraneous sources of arousal have accounted for your feelings?

Design an experiment that you could perform with friends to test the Walster and Berscheid hypothesis.

PART 14

Personality Theory and Assessment

45 **The Decline and Fall of Personality,** by Kenneth J. Gergen

46 **Are You Shy?,** by Bernardo J. Carducci with Philip G. Zimbardo

47 **Does Personality Really Change After 20?,** by Zick Rubin

The term "personality" is part of the vernacular, one of many such terms psychologists have borrowed from the layperson. And there, I think, is the rub. Early studies of personality adopted the lay concept and sought to validate it. According to common belief, people have fixed traits (generosity, aggressiveness, prudence, and so on), which together comprise a fixed "identity" or "self." For decades personality research confirmed this with paper-and-pencil tests and sophisticated statistics. In recent decades, however, psychologists have looked more carefully at how people behave in various settings and situations, and they've also taken a more careful look at the way behavior changes with age. The closer one looks, the more variability one sees. So much for borrowing concepts from the vernacular.

In "The Decline and Fall of Personality," Kenneth J. Gergen reassesses the perspective he took on personality twenty years ago. In the 70s, he took the traditional concept of personality seriously; now he rejects the idea that a fixed identity exists, and he insists that this is good news, especially for women.

In "Are You Shy?" Bernardo J. Carducci and Philip G. Zimbardo review two decades of research on shyness, drawing the surprising and somewhat depressing conclusion that shyness is on the increase, driven in part by modern technology. Finally, Brandeis professor Zick Rubin offers a cautious defense of the concept of personality, citing evidence that personality remains fairly stable during adult life.

There are inconsistencies in these perspectives, but they're resolvable if you pay close attention. The problem, as I mentioned, is that we started with a fuzzy concept. Look carefully at the data collected and the methodology used to collect those data, and clarity will emerge.

The *Decline* and **Fall** OF PERSONALITY

◆ *Kenneth J. Gergen*

We listen to George Bush's speech, but know it was produced by a team of experts. We watch the presidential hopefuls, so earnest and well poised, but we are aware of the hours of coaching necessary to produce the images. We wonder about their private lives and how long it will take before startling revelations hit the press. On the talk shows we hear the stars "telling all"; yet we are conscious that even their sorriest secrets are calculated for career advancement. When we listen to the executive officer address the annual meeting, we know that every garment is geared for impact, every syllable designed to sell. As we observe the professor give a lecture, we are aware that even the casual dress and informal manner are carefully crafted.

Many of us believe that somewhere behind these masks lies the real person, that all this role playing is so much sham. We may also believe that for the sake of society and ourselves we should drop the roles and be what we truly are. Yet if by chance you are beginning to doubt that there is a factual self beneath the fake, and feel the mask *may* just be the genuine article, that "image is everything," you are entering the new world of postmodern consciousness.

Twenty years ago I was privileged enough to write a cover story for *Psychology Today* in which

I described the multiple masks we must wear in meeting the demands of everyday life. Rather than finding inconsistency and incoherence in personality a cause for alarm—possibly a reason to seek therapy—I championed its positive possibilities. Rather than admonishing people to seek a firm and fixed identity, I saw such identities as limiting and in many ways incapacitating. It seemed to me that people who demonstrated a protean elasticity were healthier and more fulfilled.

The article was provocative; it was reprinted numerous times

> **Slowly we are losing confidence that there is a coherent, identifiable substance behind the mask. The harder we look, the more difficult it is to find "anyone at home."**

both in the Unites States and abroad, and was even the topic of a television special. Clearly I was touching sensitive issues, questioning the traditional value of a firm sense of identity, of knowing where one stands and to whom one is committed. At the same time, many readers were curious or relieved; many felt the limitations of the old virtues of coherence and authenticity.

Because the implications of these issues for our ways of life are broad and significant, I have con-

tinued to ponder them. On the one hand, by favoring the fixed identity, one also opts for orderly and predictable ways of life, trustworthiness, long-term commitments, and a sense of security and tranquility. One shudders to think of their disappearance. Yet we no longer live in the world that imparted such high value to these ways of life, and, even if painful, we must continuously question the adequacy of past traditions for the demands of the present. It is now, with the benefit of hindsight, that I see my concerns of 20 years ago as part of a broader cultural story—a single chapter of a tale in which we all participate.

That tale is one of cultural change, now reaching staggering proportions, and from which there is little chance of escape. It is also a tale in which we are all losing our identities and the coherent and committed lives that go with it. But just possibly, if we are wise and fortunate, we can still create a story with a happy ending. In it, we gain the security that comes from discovering our essential relatedness with others.

To begin, let us consider the ingredients required for a centered identity. What is it that holds the personality together, giving it determined direction? It is difficult to understand such a question in a vacuum— cut away from a cultural language of self-understanding. Rather, we have little choice but to rely for answers on the accumulated wisdom of the past. Here, it seems to me, we stand today as the beneficiaries of two primary traditions. Both are highly respected, both give us a sense of strong and stable identity, and both are now in jeopardy.

The first is the *romantic* tradition, which reached its pinnacle in the last century. It is largely from the romantic tradition that we derive our beliefs in a profound and stable center of identity—a center which harbored the vital spirit of life itself. Poets such as Shelley, Keats, and Byron; composers such as Beethoven, Brahms, and Chopin; and a host of philosophers, painters, architects, theologians, and the like, all created a vivid portrait of the romantic self. It was a compelling account of powerful forces buried beneath the surface of consciousness, in the deep interior of one's being.

These forces once defined the individual, furnishing the essential reason for being. For some, the forces were identified as the soul; others saw them as fiery passions; and still others felt they were dark and dangerous. Invariably, however, the forces were wondrous, and their expression (in committed love, loyalty, and friendships) was fulfilling if not heroic. Because of the power of these passions, one could experience profound grief at the loss of a loved one, and a sense of longing or remorse so intense that suicide could be an attractive option. The deep interior was also held to be the source of inspiration, creativity, genius, moral courage—even madness.

Romanticism continues to be a pervasive cultural presence. It is alive in everyday life—in our popular songs, television "soaps," and epic films. The romantic vocabulary is essential to most courtships, weddings, and funerals. And if ever asked what makes our lives worth living, most of us will talk about these deep and vital forces.

Romantic views also remain robust in psychotherapeutic groups. The theories of Freud and Jung, for example, are the children of the romantic tradition. Without their poetic and artistic forebearers, Freud's belief in unconscious dynamics and Jung's search for primordial archetypes would seem nonsensical. And when contemporary therapists speak of self-actualizing tendencies, primal screams, catharsis, defense mechanisms, and rebirthing, they are keeping romanticist flames alive. They are making real the self's deep interior.

Yet for most people the romance with romanticism has cooled. For, as most cultural com-

> *For romanticists, love could be all-consuming; it was a reason to live (or to die), it was unpredictable, and for its sake one might pledge a lifetime— or an eternity—of commitment.*

mentators agree, romanticism has been replaced by perspectives, ways of life, and a conception of the self that we now call *modernist*. As a cultural movement, modernism can be traced largely to industrialization, the world wars, and major advances into science.

In each case, fascination turned from the deep interior of the individual to the demands and opportunities made possible by technology. It was time to "get down to business" and "enter the fast track of progress." It also appeared that scientists were beginning to master the fundamental order of the universe—harnessing energies, mastering flight, curing illnesses, and filling homes with marvelous conveniences. With such mastery, one could truly begin to imagine creating a Utopian world.

Fired by such optimism, philosophers set about to generate the rules of procedure by which such progress could be achieved across the cultural spectrum. A rational search for fundamentals enabled composers to cast aside popular conventions in favor of tonal experimentation, invited choreographers to abandon ballet

> *No longer is our social existence tied to a small town, a suburban community, or an urban neighborhood.*

in search of elemental movements (now termed modern dance), and stimulated poets to emphasize formal properties over sentiment in their verse. Modern architecture was preoccupied with reducing design to its most functional elements, while modern art abandoned the decorative in search for the essentials of form and color.

Through modernism, the self was slowly being redefined. The emphasis shifted from deep and mysterious processes to human consciousness in the here and now. The deep interior of the romanticist no longer seemed so important; indeed talk of souls, passions, moral courage, and inspiration began to seem quaint, ill-suited to life in the material world. To survive in a complex world, the modernist needed conscious capability for keen observation and careful reason. Such capacities allow us to make progress.

Where the romanticists placed drama, passion, and intensity at the center of existence, modernists valued efficacy of action, smooth and stable functioning, and progress toward a goal. The difference in attitude toward love is emblematic. For romanticists, love could be all-consuming; it was a reason to live (or to die), it was unpredictable, and for its sake one might pledge a lifetime—or an eternity—of commitment. The modernist attempts to develop a technology of mate selection through the use of computerized software. Questionnaire compatibility replaced love by thunderbolt.

Modernist views of the self now dominate the profession of psychology. Most research is lodged in the assumption that psychologists can use their powers of observation and reason to master the fundamentals of human functioning. There are, by definition, no mysterious reservoirs, souls, inspirations, and evil forces deep within the individual.

Rather, for contemporary psychologists, people are much like input/output machines—what they do depends on what goes into them. The critical psychological ingredient of the self is thought, or cognition. And cognition, too, is machine-like, functioning much as a computer. With increased abilities to predict and control human behavior, it is believed, programs can be developed to change and repair the individual. Good personalities, like motor cars, can be properly manufactured through social engineering. Should individuals go astray, therapists, like mechanics, can put them right. Both behavior modification and cognitive therapy—primary technologies for repair—define the self in the modernist idiom.

Yet there is good reason to believe that modernism, while dominant, is now slowly crumbling as a cultural movement. New cultural conditions have emerged which many characterize as post-modern. Not only do soul, passion, and creativity become suspicious as centers of human existence, but so does rational thought and the efficient control of one's own actions. Slowly we are losing confidence that there is a coherent, identifiable substance behind the mask. The harder we look, the more difficult it is to find "anyone at home."

What is the driving force behind this shift to postmodernism? In my view, the central ingredient is technology, more specifically a range of technologies that shower us with social relationships both direct and vicarious. The telephone, automobile, radio, television, motion pic-

tures, mass publication, Xerox, cassette recordings, urban mass transportation, the national highway system, jet transportation, satellite transmission, VCR, the computer, fax, and the mobile telephone—all have emerged within the past century, most within the past 50 years. All have grown by leaps and bounds, becoming standard equipment for a normal life.

And all expand the range of our social life. No longer is our social existence tied to a small town, a suburban community, or an urban

> *Through countless exposure to others, we rapidly increase the range of appreciations, understandings, and action possibilities available to us.*

neighborhood. Rather, as we wake to *Good Morning America*, read the papers, listen to radio talk shows, travel miles to work, meet people from around the globe, answer faxes and electronic mail, drive children to cross-town games, check the answering machine, phone long distance, visit with old friends from out of town, order air tickets to the Caribbean, and take a late evening graze through cable-TV channels, we consume and are consumed by a social world of unbounded proportion. We are exposed to more opinions, values, personalities, and ways of life than was any previous generation in

> *Where am I? Hollywood? The Soaps? A teenage novel? With countless repetition of images, reality becomes rhetoric. Substance slowly becomes style.*

history; the number of our relationships soars, the variations are enormous: past relationships remain (only a phone call apart) and new faces are only a channel away.

There is, in short, an explosion in social connection.

What does this explosion have to do with our sense of selves, who we are, and what we stand for? How does it undermine beliefs in a romantic interior or in a rational center of the self?

First, there is a *populating of the self*, that is, an absorption of others into ourselves. Through countless exposure to others, we rapidly increase the range of appreciations, understandings, and action possibilities available to us. Through friends, acquaintances, family members, the media and so on, we come to see and to feel myriad possibilities for being—along with their opposites.

We come to appreciate the possibility of homosexuality, and yet to understand reasons against it; we are encouraged to feel heterosexual longings, and yet to consider ourselves capable of homosexual urges, along with homophobic reactions. Standing alongside these multiple tendencies we also come to see the rationality of androgyny—expressing characteristics of both genders—and the many arguments against any gender differences in the first place. Each of us becomes populated with dozens of potentials, all reasonable and good by some criterion, in some relationship, in some context. Where in the mix is the genuine self, the true feelings, or the rational core?

To paraphrase the poet Walt Whitman, "We contain multitudes."

The sense of a centered self also begins to collapse under the *demands of multiple audiences*. In one of the most rousing scenes from the film *Bugsy*, the infamous gangster (played by Warren Beatty) races desperately from one room of his mansion to another. Breathlessly he plays the affable host for his daughter's birthday party, abandons her to plead for the affection of his doubting wife, reappears with swagger and gusto to impress his gangster cronies in the adjoining room, only to race away again to his daughter's failing party. As we laugh, pity, and loathe this poor figure, we are simultaneously reacting to our own lives. For the socializing technologies are constructing an enormous mansion of conflicting demands for each one of us.

Consider the poor man of today; who must simultaneously demonstrate professional responsibility; soft and romantic sensitivity, macho toughness, and family dedication; he must have expertise in sports, politics, software, the stock market, mechanics, food, and wine; he must have a circle of friends, a fitness program, the right CDs, interesting vacation plans, and an impressive car—that is, if he is to survive in an increasingly complex world. So, like Bugsy Seigel, he races from one situation to another, shifting demeanors, clothing, intensities, views, and values. Where in the chaos of competing personas is he to locate the true and the real man behind the masks?

The third way in which the socializing technologies undermine confidence in deep or essential selves is through the *repetition of images*. The countless reproductions of our ways of life slowly sap them of authenticity. Consider the case of romance. By traditional standards, expressions of love, passion, and desire should be spontaneous eruptions of one's basic self—energetic impulses that suddenly burst into the open. Now consider the number of times you have been exposed to such expressions—on television from your fourth year to the present, in film, books, and magazines, in friends' accounts, and indeed in your own life. You know all the words, all the movements of eyes and mouth, all the gestures and postures.

And with these countless repetitions, authenticity begins to wear thin. Substance slowly becomes style. One loses trust in romantic expressions: the words are stifled in the throat. "Where am I? Hollywood? The soaps? A teenage novel?" And so it is with all our cherished expressions—religious devotion, grief, happy enthusiasm,

> To stuff one's own face, seek one's own riches, be exclusively concerned with one's own image, cuts one away from the very wellsprings of one's potentials.

political remonstrance. With continued repetition, reality becomes rhetoric.

Is this just another disgruntled commentary on the sorry state of contemporary life? Not entirely. Yes, there is room for lament, as we cease to believe in inner mysteries, passions, or inspiration; when we no longer seem to be the authors of our lives, knowing who we are, what we stand for, or where we are going; when reason no longer leads in any particular direction; when expanding relationships turn quiet days into chaos; when intimacy turns into ritual, and commitment becomes a relic of yesteryear.

Yet, when we complain, we are revealing our own roots in the past. If we did not still retain a romanticist belief in the deep interior, would we care whether passion and inspiration were vanishing ideas? And if we didn't cling to the modernist idea of a rationally organized life, would chaos be a problem?

Our children will scarcely feel the pinch as we do; they will

> America exists as it does because of the relationships of which it is a part.

scarcely understand why anyone would make such a fuss over real, true, or inner selves. And for we who do feel the pinch, there are good reasons for expanding our horizons as well. For the technologies that saturate us with others will hardly be abandoned. There is no reversing the cultural clock. As many scientists proclaim, the socializing technologies are only in their infancy.

As we troop toward the future, let us consider some of the positive possibilities of a postmodern life. For there is in these expanding technologies an enormous increase in the possibilities for human development. Each new relationship is simultaneously an opportunity; an open door to growth of expression, appreciation, and skill.

This is especially noticeable in the lives of young women. A half century ago, there was only one strong model against which women could measure the value of their lives: that of devoted wife and mother. The limitations on expression, exploration, and development were numbingly oppressive. Today that image is simply one of many. And even though daily life may bring a torrent of competing demands, each new wrinkle in personality is also a new dimension. The best of moments may even bring an enormous sense of exhilaration, an awed sense of "look at all that I can do, be, see, feel, and know!" During these moments one scarcely worries about inconsistency and incoherence; one does not question what lies behind the many performances. The games are on, and they are everything.

We experience the satisfaction of continuous and sometimes rapturous engagement. Such engagement not only welcomes new facets of self, but opens the way to recapturing the past. In romanticist and modernist times, one had always to be concerned with the true and the genuine: Is this really what I feel, what I think, who I am? If the answer was "no," certain actions were ruled out for plans abandoned. But if we cease to ask such questions, then nothing is prevented in principle. If we cease to believe that there is any deep and essential criterion, any rule of logic, or any internal essence against which actions must be compared, then we are liberated to play the many games offered by this culture, as well as by others.

In the example of romanticism, talk of souls, passions, and inspirations has lost much of its vitality during the modernist age; for the rational and objective mind, such talk is so much folklore. The socializing technologies have further reduced our beliefs in these dimensions of self. Romantic passions are as quaint as old movies. Yet, from the postmodern standpoint, such actions are also essential parts of some of our most valued traditions. We can be romantic not because it is a true reflection of our inner core, not as a life-or-death matter, but because it is one way for us to participate in a special form of relationship our culture offers to us. We can sing in a chorus or play touch football on Sundays not because these actions "reveal the true self." Rather, the actions are themselves part of relationships, and gain their value in just this way.

If postmodern life is more richly expressive, it is also less self-centered. Beliefs in a singular, coher-

ent and stable self can be closely linked with greed, egotism, and selfishness. "If I am a separate self from you," the logic goes, "then better my welfare than yours." But as the socializing technologies expand, beliefs in separate, self-directing individuals decline. We become increasingly aware that all our expressions, beliefs, values, thoughts, and desires are legacies from other persons, little gifts they leave with us in passing.

We may indeed be unique, never repeating these expressions in just the same way. But this uniqueness is not self-determined; rather, it reflects the particular patterns of our relationships. "I am you within me," one realizes, "and you are me within you. We are united." With the dawning of this consciousness, selfishness becomes unrewarding. To stuff one's own face, seek one's own riches, be exclusively concerned with one's own image, cuts one away from the very wellsprings of one's potentials. If it is I *against* you, then I am removed from the sources that fire my enthusiasm, enrich my potentials, and furnish life with value. Left to feed upon the residues of past relationships the "I" would slowly wither.

If our concerns move away from the interior of the self and outward toward relationships, a new sense of optimism is born. We exist in a society where conflict abounds—between racial and ethnic groups, religions, unions and management, men and women, the rich and the poor, pro-choicers and pro-lifers, and more. Much the same picture can be painted at the global level, where Arabs and Jews, Muslims and Hindus, blacks and whites, the

haves and the have-nots, are pitted against each other. These conflicts follow a familiar logic: Each group believes itself to be singular, bounded, and independent, and that it must stick up for its rights, privileges, and well-being in the face of an opposing group. In effect, conflicts among groups are based on much the same thinking that has traditionally colored our perceptions of self.

If the socializing technologies can break down the sense of independent selves, can we look forward to a time when the same can occur at the national and international level? As the technologies increase our contact with those from other walks of life, other value systems, and other cultures, we may continue to expand our range of understanding and appreciation. As we form relationships in business, government, education, the arts, and so on, we may further our sense of interdependence. Have Americans not already absorbed many Japanese points of view, tastes, and appreciations, and vice versa? And is our economy not dependent on theirs and vice versa? To this extent, there is no distinctly American identity. America exists as it does because of the relationships of which it is a part.

So in the end, as the socializing technologies continue their expansion, we can move from a self-centered system of beliefs to consciousness of an inseparable relatedness with others. Perhaps then our postmodern selves will contribute to making the globe a better place for living. ◈

Discussion Questions

1. What are the two primary traditions that Kenneth Gergen describes? What are the origins of these traditions?

2. How does the romantic tradition contribute to the modern concept of personality?

3. How did modernism alter the concept of self?

4. Why does Gergen believe that modernism is now "crumbling as a cultural movement"?

5. What does Gergen mean by the post-modern "populating of the self," "demands of multiple audiences," and "repetition of images"? How does each of these ideas relate to the decline of personality?

6. Why, says Gergen, is the death of personality especially advantageous for women?

7. How does the author suggest that the postmodern life can be better?

ARE You *Shy?*

◆ *Bernardo J. Carducci with Philip G. Zimbardo*

In sharp contrast to the flamboyant lifestyle getting under way at dance clubs across the country, another, quieter, picture of Americans was emerging from psychological research. Its focus: those on the sidelines of the dance floor. In 1975 *Psychology Today* published a groundbreaking article by Stanford University psychologist Philip Zimbardo, Ph.D., entitled "The Social Disease Called Shyness." The article revealed what Zimbardo had found in a survey conducted at several American colleges: An astonishing 40 percent of the 800 questioned currently considered themselves to be shy.

In addition to documenting the pervasiveness of shyness, the article presented a surprising portrait of those with the condition. Their mild-mannered exterior conceals roiling turmoil inside. The shy disclosed that they are excessively self-conscious, constantly sizing themselves up negatively, and overwhelmingly preoccupied with what others think of them. While everyone else is meeting and greeting, they are developing plans to manage their public impression (*If I stand at the far end of the room and pretend to be examining the painting on the wall, I'll look like I'm interested in art but won't have to talk to anybody*). They are consumed by the misery of the social setting (*I'm having a horrible time at this party because I don't know what to say and everyone seems to be staring at me*). All the while their hearts are

pounding, their pulses are speeding, and butterflies are swarming in their stomach—physiological symptoms of genuine distress.

The article catalogued the painful consequences of shyness. There are social problems, such as difficulty meeting people and making new friends, which may leave the shy woefully isolated and subject to loneliness and depression. There are cognitive problems; unable to think clearly in the presence of others, the shy tend to freeze up in conversation, confusing others who are trying to respond to them. They can appear snobbish or dis-

interested in others, when they are in fact just plain nervous. Excessively egocentric, they are relentlessly preoccupied with every aspect of their own appearance and behavior. They live trapped between two fears: being invisible and insignificant to others, and being visible but worthless.

The response to the article was overwhelming. A record number of letters to the editor screamed HELP ME!, surprising considering that then, as now, PT readers were generally well-educated, self-aware, and open-minded—not a recipe for shyness.

The article launched a whole new field of study. In the past 20 years, a variety of researchers and clinicians, including myself, have been scrutinizing shyness. To celebrate the 20th anniversary of PT's epochal report, we decided to spotlight recent advances in understanding this social disease:

◆ Research in my laboratory and elsewhere suggests that, courtesy of changing

---

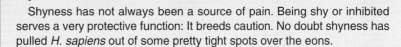

The Natural History of Shyness

Shyness has not always been a source of pain. Being shy or inhibited serves a very protective function: It breeds caution. No doubt shyness has pulled *H. sapiens* out of some pretty tight spots over the eons.

Originally, shyness served as protective armor around the physical self. After all, only after an animal has fully acquainted itself with a new environment is it safe to behave in a more natural, relaxed manner and explore around. The process of habituation is one of the most fundamental characteristics of all organisms.

As conscious awareness has increased, the primary threat is now to the psychological self—embarrassment. Most people show some degree of social inhibition; they think about what they are going to say or do beforehand, as well as the consequences of saying or doing it. It keeps us from making fools of ourselves or hurting the feelings of others.

According to Wellesley psychologist Jonathan Cheek, Ph.D., situational shyness "can help to facilitate cooperative living; it inhibits behaviors that are socially unacceptable." So, a little bit of shyness may be good for you and society. But too much benefits no one.

cultural conditions, the incidence of shyness in the U.S. may now be as high as 48 percent—and rising.

◆ Most shyness is hidden. Only a small percentage of the shy appear to be obviously ill at ease. But all suffer internally.

◆ Some people are born with a temperamental tilt to shyness. But even that inheritance doesn't doom one to a life of averting others' eyes. A lot depends on parenting.

◆ Most shyness is acquired through life experiences.

◆ There is a neurobiology of shyness. At least three brain centers that mediate fear and anxiety orchestrate the whole-body response we recognize as shyness. Think of it as an over-generalized fear response.

◆ The incidence of shyness varies among countries. Israelis seem to be the least shy inhabitants of the world. A major contributing factor: cultural styles of assigning praise and blame to kids.

◆ Shyness has huge costs to individuals at all ages, especially in Western cultures.

◆ Shyness does have survival value.

◆ Despite the biological hold of shyness, there are now specific and well-documented ways to overcome its crippling effects.

Shy on the Sly

How is it possible that 40 to 50 percent of Americans—some of your friends, no doubt—are shy? Because while some people are obviously, publicly shy, a much larger percentage are privately shy. Their shyness, and its pain, is invisible to everyone but themselves.

Only 15 to 20 percent of shy people actually fit the stereotype of the ill-at-east person. They use every excuse in the book to avoid social events. If they are unlucky enough to find themselves in casual conversation, they can't quite manage to make eye contact, to reply to questions without stumbling over their words, or to keep up their end of the conversation; they seldom smile. They are easy to pick out of a crowd because their shyness is expressed behaviorally.

The other 80 to 85 percent are privately shy, according to University of Pittsburgh psychologist Paul Pilkonis, Ph.D. Though their shyness leaves no behavioral traces—it's felt subjectively—it wreaks personal havoc. They feel their shyness in a pounding heart and pouring sweat. While they may seem at ease and confident in conversation, they are actually engaging in a self-deprecating inner dialogue, chiding themselves for being inept and questioning whether the person they are talking to really likes them. "Even though these people do fairly well socially, they have a lot of negative self-thought going on in their heads," explains Pilkonis. Their shyness has emotional components as well. When the conversation is over, they feel upset or defeated.

"There are a lot of people who have private aspects of shyness who are willing to say they are shy but don't quite gibe with the people we can see trembling or blushing," notes Pilkonis.

Shyness can lurk in unlikely hosts—even those of the talk show variety. Take David Letterman, king

> *There are a lot of people who have private aspects of shyness who are willing to say they are shy but don't quite gibe with the people we can see trembling or blushing.*

of late-night TV. Although his performance in front of a live studio audience and countless viewers seems relaxed and spontaneous, Letterman is known to be relentless in the planning and orchestration of each nightly performance down to the last detail. Like Johnny Carson, he spends little time socializing outside a very small circle of friends and rarely attends social functions.

Letterman is the perfect example of what Zimbardo calls the shy extrovert: the cool, calm, and collected type whose insides are in fact churning. A subset of the privately shy, shy extroverts may be politicians, entertainers, and teachers. They have learned to act outgoing—as long as they are in a controlled environment. A politician who can speak from a prepared script at a mass political rally really may get tongue-tied during a question-and-answer period. A professor may be comfortable as long as she is talking about her area of expertise; put in a social gathering where she may have to make small talk, she clams up.

Zimbardo's short list of notable shy extroverts: funny lady Carol Burnett, singer Johnny Mathis, television reporter Barbara Walters, and international opera star Joan Sutherland. These stars are not introverts, a term often confused with shyness. Introverts have the conversational skills and self esteem necessary for interacting successfully with others but prefer to be alone. Shy people want very much to be with others but lack the social skills and self-esteem.

What unites the shy of any type is acute self-consciousness. The shy are even self-conscious about their self-consciousness. Theirs is a twisted egocentricity. They spend so much time focusing on themselves and their weaknesses, they have little time or inclination to look outward.

Wired for Shyness?

According to developmental psychologist Jerome Kagan, Ph.D., and colleagues at Harvard University, up to a third of shy adults were born with a temperament that inclined them to it. The team has been able to identify shyness in young infants before environmental conditions make an impact.

In his longitudinal studies, 400 four-month-old infants were brought into the lab and subjected to such stimuli as moving mobiles, a whiff of a Q-Tip dipped in alcohol, and a tape recording of the human voice. Then they were brought back at a later age for further study. From countless hours of observation, rerun on videotapes, Kagan, along with Harvard psychologists Nancy Snidman, Ph.D., and Doreen Arcus, Ph.D., have nailed down the behavioral manifestations of shyness in infants.

About 20 percent of infants display a pattern of extreme nervous-system reactivity to such common stimuli. These infants grow distressed when faced with unfamiliar people, objects, and events. They momentarily extend their arms and legs spastically, they vigorously wave their arms and kick their legs, and, on occasion, arch their backs. They also show signs of distress in the form of excessive fretting and crying, usually at a high pitch and sustained tension that communicates urgency. Later on, they cling to their parents in a new play situation.

In contrast, 40 percent of all infants exposed to the same stimuli occasionally move an arm or leg but do not show the motor outbursts or fretting and crying typical of their highly reactive

---

Helping Others Beat Shyness

You may not be shy, but one out of two people are. Be sensitive to the fact that others may not be as outgoing and confident. It's your job to make others comfortable around you. Be a host to humanity.

◆ Make sure no one person at a social gathering—including yourself—is the focus of attention. That makes it possible for everyone to have some of the attention some of the time.

◆ Like the host of any party, make it your job to bring out the best in others, in any situation. At school, teachers should make it a point to call on kids who are reluctant to speak up. At work, bosses should seek out employees who don't comment in meetings; encouragement to express ideas and creativity will improve any company. At parties, break the ice by approaching someone who is standing alone.

◆ Help others put their best foot forward. Socially competent people feel comfortable because they tend to steer conversation to their own interests. Find out what the shy person next to you is interested in; introduce the topic.

◆ Help others keep the conversation going. Shy people often don't speak up in ongoing conversations. Ask a shy person his or her opinion next time you are in a lively discussion.

---

brethren. When the low-reactive infants do muster up a crying spell, it is nothing out of the ordinary.

Lab studies indicate that highly reactive infants have an easily excitable sympathetic nervous system. This neural network regulates not only many vital organs, including the heart, but the brain response of fear. With their high-strung, hair-trigger temperament, even the suggestion of danger—a stranger, a

Shyness is un-American. We are, after all, the land of the free and the home of the brave. Personal attributes we esteem are assertiveness, dominance, risk-taking. Think Madonna.

new environment—launches the psychological and physiologic arousal of fear and anxiety.

One of the first components of this reaction is an increased heart

rate. Remarkably, studies show that high-reactive infants have a higher-than-normal heart rate—and it can be detected even before birth, while the infant is still *in utero*. At 14 months, such infants have over-large heart rate acceleration in response to a neutral stimulus such as a sour taste.

Four years later, the same kids show another sign of sympathetic arousal—a cooler temperature reading in their right ring finger than in their left ring finger while watching emotionally evocative film clips. Too, as children they show more brain wave activity in the right frontal lobe; by contrast, normally reactive children display more brain wave activity in the left frontal area. From other studies it is known that the right side of the brain is more involved in the expression of anxiety and distress.

© 1998 PhotoDisc, Inc.

the melatonin may act on cells to create the hyperaroused, easily agitated temperament of the shy.

Further evidence of a biological contribution to shyness is a pattern of inheritance suggesting direct genetic transmission from one generation to the next. Parents and grandparents of inhibited infants are more likely to report being shy as children than the relatives of uninhibited children, Snidman found in one study. Kagan and company are looking for stronger proof—such as, say, an elevated incidence of panic disorder (acute episodes of severe anxiety) and depression in the parents of inhibited children. So far he has found that among preschool children whose parents were diagnosed with panic attack or depression, one-third showed inhibited behavior. By contrast, among children whose parents experience neither panic disorder nor depression, only about five percent displayed the inhibited reactive profile.

Are inhibited infants preordained to become shy adults? Not necessarily, Doreen Arcus finds. A lot has to do with how such children are handled by their parents. Those who are overprotected, she found from in-home interviews she conducted, never get a chance to find some comfortable level of accommodation to the world; they grow up anxious and shy. Those whose parents do not shield them from stressful situations overcome their inhibition.

Snidman, along with Harvard psychiatrist Carl Schwartz, M.D., examined the staying power of shyness into adolescence. They observed 13- and 14-year olds who were identified as inhibited at two or three years of age. During the laboratory interview, the adolescents with a history of inhibition tended to smile less, made fewer spontaneous comments, and reported being more shy than those who were identified as uninhibited infants.

The infant patterns point to an inborn variation in the response threshold of the amygdala, an almond-shaped brain structure linked to the expression of fear and anxiety. This neural hypersensitivity eventually inclines such children to avoid situations that give rise to anxiety and fear—meeting new people or being thrown into new environments. In such circumstances they are behaviorally inhibited.

Though it might sound strange, there may even be a reason for shyness—specifically early fall. Kagan and Harvard sociologist Stephen Gortmaker, Ph.D., have found that women who conceive in August or September are particularly likely to bear shy children. During these months, light is waning and the body is producing increasing amounts of melatonin, a hormone known to be neurally active; for example, it helps set our biological clocks. As it passes through the placenta to the developing fetal brain, Kagan surmises,

We Shall Overcome

1. Overcoming the Anxiety: To tame your racing heart and churning stomach, learn how to relax. Use simple breathing exercises that involve inhaling and exhaling deeply and slowly.

You can ride out the acute discomfort by staying around for a while. If you give into your distress and flee a party after only five minutes, you guarantee yourself a bad time. Stick around.

2. Getting Your Feet Wet: Nothing breeds success like success. Set up a nonthreatening social interaction that has a high probability of success and build from there. Call a radio show with a prepared comment or question. Call some sort of information line.

3. Fact to Face: Then tackle the art of very, very small talk face-to-face. Start a casual, quick exchange with the person next to you, or the cashier, in the supermarket checkout line. Most people in such situations would be very responsive to passing the time in light conversation. Since half the battle is having something to say, prepare. Scan the newspaper for conversation topics, and practice what you are going to say a few times.

4. Smile and Make Eye Contact: When you smile you project a benign social force around you; people will be more likely to notice you and smile back. If you frown or look at your feet, you don't exist for people, or worse, you project a negative presence. Once you have smiled and made eye contact, you have opened up a window for the casual "This elevator is so slow"—type comment. Always maintain eye contact in conversation; it signals that you are listening and interested.

5. Compliment: The shortest route to social success is via a compliment. It's a way to make other people feel good about themselves and about talking to you. Compliment someone every day.

6. Know How to Receive Compliments: Thank the person right away. Then return the compliment: "That's great coming from you, I've always admired the way you dress." Use this as a jumping-off point for a real conversation. Elaborate, ask him where he gets his ties or shops for suits.

7. Stop Assuming the Worst: In expecting the worst of every situation, shy people undermine themselves—they get nervous, start to stutter, and forget what they wanted to say. Chances are that once you actually throw yourself into that dreaded interaction it will be much easier than you thought. Only then will you realize how ridiculous your doomsday predictions are. Ask your workmate if he likes his job. Just do it.

8. Stop Whipping Yourself: Thoughts about how stupid you sound or how nobody really likes you run through your head in every conversation. No one would judge your performance as harshly as you do. Search for evidence to refute your beliefs about yourself. Don't get upset that you didn't ask someone to dance; focus on the fact that you talked to a woman you wanted to meet.

Don't overgeneralize your social mishaps. Say you start to stutter in conversation with someone at a party. Don't punish yourself by assuming that every other interaction that night or in your life will go the same way.

9. Lose the Perfectionism: Your jokes have to be hilarious, your remarks insightful and ironic. Truth is, you set standards so impossible they spawn performance anxiety and doom you to failure. Set more realistic standards.

10. Learn to Take Rejection: Rejection is one of the risks everyone takes in social interaction. Try not to take it personally; it may have nothing to do with you.

11. Find Your Comfort Zone: Not all social situations are for everybody. Go where your interests are. You might be happier at an art gallery, book club, or on a volleyball team than at a bar.

12. Comfort Is Not Enough: The goal in overcoming shyness is to break through your self-centeredness. In an interaction, focus on the other person. Make other people's comfort and happiness your main priority. If people think to themselves, "I really enjoyed being with her," when they leave you, then you have transformed your shyness into social competence. Congratulations.

Taken over a lifetime, gender doesn't figure much into shyness. Girls are more apt to be shy from infancy through adolescence, perhaps because parents are more protective of them than boys, who are encouraged to be more explorative. Yet in adolescence, boys report that shyness is more painful than do girls. This discomfort is likely related to sex-role expectations that boys must be bold and outgoing, especially with girls, to gear up for their role as head of family and breadwinner. But once into adulthood, gender differences in shyness disappear.

Bringing Biology Home

If only 15 to 20 percent of infants are born shy and nearly 50 percent of us are shy in adulthood, where do all the shy adults come from? The only logical answer is that shyness is acquired along the way.

One powerful source is the nature of the emotional bond parents forge with their children in the earliest years of life. According to Paul Pilkonis, children whose parenting was such that it gave rise to an insecure attachment are more likely to end up shy. Children form attachments to their caregivers from the routine experiences of care, feeding, and caressing. When caretaking is inconsistent and unreliable, parents fail to satisfy the child's need for security, affection, and comfort, resulting in insecure bonds. As the first relationship, attachment becomes the blueprint for all later relationships. Although there are no longitudinal studies spotlighting the development of shyness from toddlerhood to adulthood, there is research showing that insecure early attachment can predict shyness later on.

"The most damnable part of it is that this insecure attachment seems to become self-fulfilling," observes Pilkonis. Because of a difficult relationship to their parents, children

The Shy Brain

We all take time to get used to (or habituate to) a new stimulus (a job interview, a party) before we begin to explore the unfamiliar. After all, a novel stimulus may serve as a signal for something dangerous or important. But shy individuals sense danger where it does not exist. Their nervous system does not accommodate easily to the new. Animal studies by Michael Davis, Ph.D., of Yale University, indicate that the nerve pathways of shyness involve parts of the brain involved in the learning and expression of fear and anxiety.

Both fear and anxiety trigger similar physiologic reactions: muscle tension, increased heart rate, and blood pressure, all very handy in the event an animal has to fight or flee sudden danger. But there are important differences. Fear is an emotional reaction to a specific stimulus; it's quick to appear, and just as quick to dissipate when the stimulus passes. Anxiety is a more generalized response that takes much longer to dissipate.

Studies of cue conditioning implicate the amygdala as a central switchboard in both the association of a specific stimulus with the emotion of fear and the expression of that fear. Sitting atop the brain stem, the amygdala is crucial for relaying nerve signals related to emotions and stress. When faced with certain stimuli—notably strangers, authority figures, members of the opposite sex—the shy associate them with fearful reactions.

In contrast to such "explicit" conditioning is a process of "contextual" conditioning. It appears more slowly, lasts much longer. It is often set off by the context in which fear takes place. Exposure to that environment then produces anxiety-like feelings of general apprehension. Through contextual conditioning, shy people come to associate general environments—parties, group discussions where they will be expected to act socially—with unpleasant feelings, even before the perceived feared stimulus is present.

Contextual conditioning is a joint venture between the amygdala and the hippocampus, the seahorse-shaped cell cluster near the amygdala, which is essential to memory and spatial learning. Contextual conditioning can be seen as a kind of learning about unpleasant places.

But a criticial third party participates in contextual conditioning. It's the bed nucleus of the stria terminalis (BNST). The long arms of its cells reach to many other areas of the brain, notably the hypothalamus and the brain stem, both of which spread the word of fear and anxiety to other parts of the body. The BNST is principally involved in the generalized emotional-behavioral arousal characteristic of anxiety. The BNST may be set off by the neurotransmitter corticotropin releasing factor (CRF).

Once alerted, the hypothalamus triggers the sympathetic nervous system, culminating in the symptoms of inner turmoil experienced by the shy—from rapid heartbeat to sweaty paleness. Another pathway of information, from the amygdala to the brain stem, freezes movement of the mouth.

The shy brain is not different in structure from yours and mine; it's just that certain parts are more sensitive. Everyone has a "shyness thermostat," set by genes and other factors. The pinpointing of brain structures and neurochemicals involved in shyness holds out the promise that specific treatment may eventually be developed to curb its most debilitating forms.

internalize a sense of themselves as having problems with all relationships. They generalize the experience—and come to expect that teachers, coaches, and peers won't like them very much.

These are the narcissistically vulnerable—the wound to the self is early and deep, and easily evoked. They are quick to become disappointed in relationships, quick to feel rejection, shame, ridicule. They are relentlessly self-defeating, interpreting even success as failure. "They have negative perceptions of themselves and of themselves in relation to others that they hold onto at all costs," says Pilkonis. The narcissistically vulnerable are among the privately shy—they are seemingly at ease socially but torture themselves beneath the surface. Theirs is a shyness that is difficult to ameliorate, even with psychotherapy.

Shyness can also be acquired later on, instigated at times of developmental transition when children face new challenges in their relationships with their peers. For instance, entering the academic and social whirl of elementary school may leave them feeling awkward or inept with their peers. Teachers label them as shy and it sticks; they begin to see themselves that way—and act it.

Adolescence is another hurdle that can kick off shyness. Not only are adolescents' bodies changing but their social and emotional playing fields are redefining them. Their challenge is to integrate sexuality and intimacy into a world of relationships that used to be defined only by friendship and relatives. A complicated task!

Nor are adults immune. Shyness may result from tail-spinning life upheavals. Divorce at mid-life might be one. "A whole new set of problems kick in with a failure of a relationship, especially if you are interested in establishing new relationships," says Pilkonis. For highly successful, career-defined people, being fired from a long-held job can be similarly debilitating, especially in the interviewing process.

Count in the Culture

Biology and relationship history are not the sole creators of shyness. Culture counts, too. Shyness exists universally, although it is not experienced or defined the same way from culture to culture. Even Zimbardo's earliest surveys hinted at cultural differences in shyness: Japanese and Taiwanese students consistently expressed the highest level of shyness, Jewish students the lowest. With these clues, Zimbardo took himself to Japan, Israel, and Taiwan to study college students. The cross-cultural studies turned up even greater cultural differences than the American survey. In Israel, only 30 percent of college-age students report being shy—versus 60 percent in Japan and Taiwan.

From conversations with foreign colleagues and parents, Zimbardo acquired unprecedented insights into how culture shapes behavior in general, and more specifically the cultural roots of shyness. The key is in the way parents attribute blame or praise in the performance of their children. When a child tries and fails at a task, who gets the blame? And when a child tries and succeeds, who gets the credit?

In Japan, if a child tries and succeeds, the parents get the credit. So do the grandparents, teachers, coaches, even Buddha. If there's any left over, only then is it given to the child. But if the child tries and fails, the child is fully culpable and cannot blame anyone else. An "I can't win" belief takes hold, so that children of the culture never take a chance to do anything

Call it the Hugh Grant Effect. Shy men may turn to prostitutes just to avoid the awkwardness of intimate negotiations.

that will make them stand out. As the Japanese proverb states, "the nail that stands out is pounded down." The upshot is a low-key interpersonal style. Kids are likely to be modest and quiet; they do little to call attention to themselves. In fact, in studies of American college students' individuation tendencies—the endorsement of behaviors that will make a person stand out, unique, or noticed—Asian students tend to score the lowest. They are much less likely to speak or act up in a social gathering for fear of calling attention to themselves.

In Israel, the attributional style is just the opposite. A child who tries gets rewarded, regardless of the outcome. Consider the Yiddish expression *kvell*, which means to engage in an outsize display of pride. If a child tries to make a kite, people *kvell* by pointing out what a great kite it is. And if it doesn't fly, parents blame it on the wind. If a child tries and fails in a competitive setting, parents and others might reproach the coach for not giving the child enough training. In such a supportive environment, a child senses that failure does not have a high price—and so is willing to take a risk. With such a belief system, a person is highly likely to develop *chutzpah*, a type of audacity whereby one always take a chance or risk—with or without the talent. Children of such a value system are more apt to speak up or ask someone to dance at a party without overwhelming self-consciousness.

Shyness, then, is a relative, culture-bound label. It's a safe bet that a shy Israeli would not be considered shy in Japan. Nancy Snidman brings the point home. In studying four-month-olds in Ireland and the U.S., she found no differences in degree of nervous system reactivity. But at age five, the Irish kids did not talk as much nor were they as loud as the American kids. The difference lies in the cultural expectations expressed in child-rearing. Using American norms of social behavior as he standard of comparison, the normal Irish child would be labeled shy. But, in their own culture, with their own norms of behavior, they are not. By the same token, American kids may be perceived as boorish by the Irish.

The Scarlet S

Shyness is un-American. We are, after all, the land of the free and the home of the brave. From the first settlers and explorers who came to the New World 500 years ago to our leadership in space exploration, America has always been associated with courageous and adventurous people ready to boldly go where others fear to tread. Our culture still values rugged individualism and the conquering of new environments, whether in outer space or in overseas markets. Personal attributes held high in our social esteem are leadership, assertiveness, dominance, independence, and risk-taking. Hence a stigma surrounding shyness.

The people given the most attention is our society are expressive, active, and sociable. We single out as heroes actors, athletes, politicians, television personalities, and rock stars—people expert at calling attention to themselves: Madonna, Rosanne, Howard Stern. People who are most likely to be successful are those who are able to obtain attention and feel comfortable with it.

What shy people don't want, above all else, is to be the focus of attention. Thus, in elementary

school, the shy child may not even ask the teacher for help. In college, the shy student is reluctant to ask a question in class. In adulthood, the shy employee is too embarrassed to make a formal presentation to those who grant promotions. In every case, shyness undermines the ability to access the attention of others who would increase the likelihood of success. In a culture where everybody loves a winner, shyness is like entering a foot race with lead insoles.

Consider the findings of Stanford Business School professor Thomas Harrell. To figure out the best predictors of success in business, he gathered the records of Stanford B-School graduates, including their transcripts and letters of recommendation. Ten years out of school, the graduates were ranked from most to least successful based on the quality of their jobs. The only consistent and significant variable that could predict success (among students who were admittedly bright to start with) was verbal fluency—exactly what the typically tongue-tied shy person can't muster. The verbally fluent are able to sell themselves, their services, and their companies—all critical skills for running a corporation; think of Lee Iacocca. Shy people are probably those behind the scenes designing the cars, programs, and computers—impressive feats, but they don't pay as much as CEO.

The costs of shyness cut deeper than material success, and they take on different forms over a lifetime.

- A shy childhood may be a series of lost opportunities. Think of the child who wants so much to wear a soccer uniform and play just like all the other kids

The people given the most attention in our society are expressive, active, and sociable.

but can't muster the wherewithal to become part of a group. And if the parents do not find a way to help a child overcome feelings of nervousness and apprehension around others, the child may slip into more solitary activities, even though he really wants to be social. The self-selection into solitary activities further reduces the likelihood of the child developing social skills and self-confidence.

- Shy kids also have to endure teasing and peer rejection. Because of their general disposition for high reactivity, shy children make prime targets for bullies. Who better to tease and taunt than someone who gets scared easily and cries?

- Whether inherited or acquired, shyness predisposes to loneliness. It is the natural consequence of decades spent shunning others due to the angst of socializing. Reams of research show that loneliness and isolation can lead to mental and physical decline, even a hastened death.

- Without a circle of close friends or relatives, people are more vulnerable to risk. Lacking the opportunity to share feelings and fears with others, isolated people allow them to fester or escalate. What's more, they are prone to paranoia; there's no one around to correct their faulty thinking no checks and balances on their beliefs. We all need someone to tell us when our thinking is ridiculous, that there is no Mafia in suburban Ohio, that no one is out to get you, that you've just hit a spate of bad luck.

♦ Shyness brings with it a potential for abusing alcohol and drugs as social lubricants. In Zimbardo's studies, shy adolescents report feeling greater peer pressure to drink or use drugs than do less shy adolescents. They also confide that they use drugs and alcohol to feel less self-conscious and to achieve a greater sense of acceptance.

♦ Call it the Hugh Grant Effect. Shyness is linked to sexual, uh, difficulties. Shy people have a hard time expressing themselves to begin with; communicating sexual needs and desires is especially difficult. Shy men may turn to prostitutes just to avoid the awkwardness of intimate negotiations. When Zimbardo asked them to describe their typical client, 20 San Francisco prostitutes said that the men who frequented them were shy and couldn't communicate their sexual desires to wives or girlfriends. And the shy guys made distinctive customers. They circled a block over and over again in their car before getting the nerve to stop and talk to the prostitute. To shy men, the allure of a prostitute is simple—she asks what you want, slaps on a price, and performs. No humiliation, no awkwardness.

Performance anxiety may also make the prospect of sex overwhelming. And because shy people avoid seeking help, any problems created by embarrassment or self-doubt will likely go untreated.

♦ Another cost—time. Shy people waste time deliberating and hesitating in social situations that others can pull off in an instant. Part of their problem is that they don't live in the present, observes Zimbardo, who is currently focusing on the psychology of time perspective. "Shy people live too much in their heads," obsessed with the past, the future, or both. A shy person in conversation is not apt to think about what is being said at the moment, but about how past conversations have initially gone well and then deteriorated—just as the current one threatens to. Says Zimbardo: "These are people who cannot enjoy that moment because everything is packaged in worries from the past—a Smithsonian archive of all the bad—that restructure the present."

Or shy people may focus all their thoughts and feelings on future consequences: If I say this, will he laugh at me? If I ask him

A shy person in conversation is not apt to think about what is being said at the moment, but about how past conversations have initially gone well and then deteriorated— just as the current one threatens to do.

something simple like where he is from, he'll be bored and think I'm a lousy conversationalist, so why bother anyway? The internal decision trees are vast and twisted. "Concern for consequences always makes you feel somewhat anxious. And that anxiety will impair the shy person's performance," says Zimbardo.

Factoring in past and future is wise, but obsession with either is undermining. Shy people need to focus on the now—the person you are talking to or dancing with—to appreciate any experience. "Dancing is a good example of being completely of the moment," comments Zimbardo. "It is not something you plan, or that you remember, you are just doing it." And enjoying it.

If the costs of shyness are paid by shy people, the benefits of shyness are reaped by others—parents, teachers, friends, and society as a whole.

Yet shy people are often gifted listeners. If they can get over their self-induced pressures for witty repartee, shy people can be great at conversation because they may actually be paying attention. (The hard pat comes when a response is expected.) According to Harvard's Doreen Arcus, shy kids are apt to be especially empathic. Parents of the children she studies tell her that "even in infancy, the shy child seemed to be sensitive, empathic, and a good listener. They seem to make really good friends and their friends are very loyal to them and value them quite a bit." Even among children, friendships need someone who will talk and someone who will listen.

For any society to function well, a variety of roles need to be played. There is a place for the quiet, more reflective shy individual who does not jump in where angels fear to tread or attempt to steal the limelight from others. Yet as a culture we have devalued these in favor of boldness and expressiveness as a means of measuring worth.

The Future of Shyness

To put it bluntly, the future of shyness is bleak. My studies have documented that since 1975 its prevalence has risen from 40 per-

Helping Shy Kids

Infants with a touchy temperament are not necessarily doomed to become shy adults. Much depends on the parenting they receive.

Do not overprotect or overindulge: Although it may sound counterintuitive, you can help your child cope more effectively with shyness by allowing him or her to experience moderate amounts of anxiety in response to challenges. Rather than rush to your child's aid to soothe away every sign of distress, provide indirect support. Gradually expose your child to new objects, people, and places so that the child will learn to cope with his own unique level of sensitivity to novelty. Nudge, don't push, your child to continue to explore new things.

Show respect and understanding: Your children have private emotional lives separate from yours. It is important to show your shy child that you can understand and sympathize with her shyness, by talking with the child about her feelings of nervousness and being afraid. Then talk with her about what might be gained by trying new experiences in spite of being afraid. Revealing related experiences from your own childhood is a natural way to start the ball rolling. Overcoming fears and anxieties is not an easy process; the feelings may remain even after specific shy behaviors have been overcome. Key ingredients are sympathy, patience, and persistence.

Ease the tease: Shy children are especially sensitive to embarrassment. Compared to other children, they need extra attention, comfort, and reassurance after being teased and more encouragement to develop positive self-regard.

Help build friendships: Invite one or two playmates over to let the child gain experience in playing with different kids in the security of familiar surroundings. But allow them as much freedom as possible in structuring play routines. Shy kids sometimes do better when playing with slightly younger children.

Talk to teachers: Teachers often overlook a shy child or mistake quietness and passivity to disinterest or a lack of intelligence. Discuss what measure might be taken in the classroom or playground.

Prepare the child for new experiences: You can help to reduce fears and anxieties by helping your child get familiar with upcoming novel experiences. Take the child to a new school before classes actually start. Help rehearse activities likely to be performed in new situations, such as practicing for show-and-tell. Also role play with the child any anticipated anxiety-provoking situations, such as how to ask someone to dance at a party (if they'll let you, or speak up in a group at summer camp.

Find appropriate activities: Encourage your child to get involved in after-school activities as a means of developing a network of friends and social skills.

Provide indirect support: Ask the child the degree to which he wants you to be involved in his activities. For some kids, a parent cheering in the bleachers is humiliating. Better is indirect support—discussing the child's interests with him and letting him know of your pleasure and pride in him for participating.

Fit not fight: It's not as important to overcome shyness as to find a comfort zone consistent with your child's shyness. Rather than try to make your daughter outgoing, help her find a level of interaction that is comfortable and consistent with her temperament.

Own your temperament: Think how your own personality or interaction style operates in conjunction with your child's. If you aren't shy, understand that your child may need more time to feel comfortable before entering a novel situation or joining a social group. If you are shy, you may need to address your own shyness as a bridge to helping your child with hers.

Bottom line: Talk, listen, support, and love shy children for who they are, not how outgoing you would like them to be.

cent to 48 percent. There are many reasons to expect the numbers to climb in the decades ahead.

Most significantly, technology is continually redefining how we communicate. We are engaging in a diminishing number of face-to-face interactions on a daily basis. When was the last time you talked to a bank teller? Or a gas station attendant? How often do you call friends or colleagues when you know they aren't in just so you can leave a message on their machine? Voice mail, faxes, and E-mail give us the illusion of being "in touch," but what's to touch but the keyboard? This is not a Luddite view of technology, but a sane look at its deepest costs.

The electronic age was supposed to give us more time, but ironically it has stolen it from us. Technology has made us time-efficient—and redefined our sense of time and its value. It is not to be wasted, but to be used quickly and with a purpose.

Office encounters have become barren of social interaction. They are information-driven, problem-oriented, solution-based. No pleasantries. No backs slapped. We cut to the chase: I need this from you. Says Zimbardo, "You have to have an agenda." Some people don't even bother to show at the office at all; they telecommute.

The dwindling opportunities for face-to-face interaction put shy people at an increasing disadvantage. They no longer get to practice social skills within the comfort of daily routine. Dropping by a colleague's office to chat becomes increasingly awkward as you do it less and less. Social life has shrunk so much it can now be entirely encapsulated in a single, near-pejorative phrase: "face time," denoting the time employees may engage in eyeball-to-eyeball conversation. It's commonly relegated to morning meetings and after 4:00 p.m.

Electronic hand-held video games played solo now crowd out the time-honored social games of childhood. Even electronically simulated social interactions can't substitute—they do not permit people to learn the necessary give and take that is at the heart of all interpersonal relationships.

Technology is not the only culprit. The rise of organized sports for kids and the fall of informal sidewalk games robs kids of the chance to learn to work out their own relationship problems. Instead, the coach and the referee do it.

If technology is ushering in a culture of shyness, it is also the perfect medium for the shy. The Internet and World Wide Web are conduits for the shy to interact with others; electronic communication removes many of the barriers that inhibit the shy. You prepare what you want to say. Nobody knows what you look like. The danger, however, is that technology will become a hiding place for those who dread social interaction.

The first generation to go from cradle to grave with in-home computers, faxes, and the Internet is a long way from adulthood. We will have to wait at least another 20 years to accurately assess shyness in the wake of the new electronic age. But to do so, we must find a group of infants—shy and non-shy—and follow them through their life, rather than observe different people, from different generations, in different periods of their lives. Only then will we see the course of shyness over a lifetime. Stay tuned to for PT's next shyness article, in 2015.   ◆

> *In a culture where everybody loves a winner, shyness is like entering a foot race with lead insoles.*

Discussion Questions

1. In Zimbardo's early study, how did shy people say they felt in social interactions?

2. List the progress in understanding shyness.

3. Define a shy extrovert.

4. What brain structure may be involved in shyness?

5. How is season related to shyness?

6. How can parents contribute to shyness?

7. What is the self-fulfilling aspect of shyness?

8. What are the costs of shyness?

9. What, says Carducci, is the future of shyness?

10. Are you shy? Was there a time in your life when you felt shy? Describe what it feels like (or what you think it would feel like).

Does *Personality* Really CHANGE **After 20?**

◆ *Zick Rubin*

"In most of us," William James wrote in 1887, "by the age of 30, the character has set like plaster, and will never soften again." Though our bodies may be bent by the years and our opinions changed by the times, there is a basic core of self—a personality—that remains basically unchanged.

This doctrine of personality stability has been accepted psychological dogma for most of the past century. The dogma holds that the plaster of character sets by one's early 20s, if not even sooner than that.

Within the past decade, however, this traditional view has come to have an almost archaic flavor. The rallying cry of the 1970s has been people's virtually limitless capacity for change—not only in childhood but through the span of life. Examples of apparent transformation are highly publicized: Jerry Rubin enters the 1970s as a screaming, war-painted Yippie and emerges as a sedate Wall Street analyst wearing a suit and tie. Richard Alpert, an ambitious assistant professor of psychology at Harvard, tunes into drugs, heads for India, and returns as Baba Ram Dass, a long-bearded mystic in a flowing white robe who teaches people to "be here now." And Richard Raskind, a successful ophthalmologist, goes into the hospital and comes out as Renée Richards, a tall, well-muscled athlete on the women's tennis circuit.

Even for those of us who hold on to our original appearance (more of less) and gender, "change" and "growth" are now the bywords. The theme was seized upon by scores of organizations formed to help people change, from Weight Watchers to est. It was captured—and ad-

> **Even for those of us who hold on to our original appearance (more or less) and gender, "change" and "growth" are now the bywords.**

vanced—by Gail Sheehy's phenomenally successful book *Passages*, which emphasized people's continuing openness to change throughout the course of adulthood. At the same time, serious work in psychology was coming along—building on earlier theories of Carl Jung and Erik Erikson—to buttress the belief that adults keep on developing. Yale's Daniel Levinson, who provided much of Sheehy's intellectual inspiration, described, in *The Seasons of a Man's Life*, an adult life structure that is marked by periods of self-examination and transition Psychiatrist Roger Gould, in *Transformations*, wrote of reshapings of the self during the early and middle adult years, "away from stagnation and claustrophobic suffocation toward vitality and an expanded sense of inner freedom."

The view that personality keeps changing throughout life has picked up so many adherents recently that it has practically become the new dogma. Quantitative studies have been offered to document the possibility of personality change in adulthood, whether as a consequence of getting married, changing jobs, or seeing one's children leave home. In a new volume entitled *Constancy and Change in Human Development*, two of the day's most influential behavioral scientists, sociologist Orville G. Brim, Jr., and psychologist Jerome Kagan, challenge the defenders of personality stability to back up their doctrine with hard evidence. "The burden of proof," Brim and Kagan write, "is being shifted to the larger group, who adhere to the traditional doctrine of constancy, from the minority who suggest that it is a premise requiring evaluation."

And now we get to the newest act in the battle of the dogmas. Those who uphold the doctrine of personality stability have accepted the challenge. In the past few years they have assembled the strongest evidence yet available for the truth of their position—evidence suggesting that on several central dimensions of personality, including the ones that make up our basic social and emotional style, we are in fact astoundingly stable throughout the course of adult life.

The 'Litter-ature' on Personality

Until recently there was little firm evidence for the stability of personality, despite the idea's intuitive appeal. Instead, most studies showed little predictability from earlier to later times of life—or even, for that matter, from one situation to another within the same time period—thus suggesting an essential lack of consistency in people's personalities. Indeed, many researchers began to question whether it made sense to speak of "personality" at all.

But whereas the lack of predictability was welcomed by advocates of the doctrine of change through the life span, the defenders of stability have another explanation for it: most of the studies are lousy. Referring derisively to the "litter-ature" on personality, Berkeley psychologist Jack Block estimates that "perhaps 90 percent of the studies are methodologically inadequate, without conceptual implication, and even foolish."

Block is right. Studies of personality have been marked by an abundance of untested measures (anyone can make up a new "scale" in an afternoon), small samples, and scatter-gun strategies ("Let's throw it into the computer and get some correlations"). Careful longitudinal studies, in which the same people are followed over the years, have been scarce. The conclusion that people are not predictable, then, may be a reflection not of human nature but of the haphazard methods used to study it.

Block's own research, in contrast, has amply demonstrated that people *are* predictable. Over the past 20 years Block has been analyzing extensive personality reports on several hundred Berkeley and Oakland residents that were first obtained in the 1930s, when the subjects were in junior high school. Researchers at Berkeley's Institute of Human Development followed up on the students when the subjects were in their late teens, again when they were in their mid-30s, and again in the late 1960s, when the subjects were all in their mid-40s.

The data archive is immense, including everything from attitude checklists filled out by the subjects to transcripts of interviews with the subjects, their

---

How much personality changes in adult life depends on what you mean by (a) personality, (b) change and stability, and (c) what you're trying to prove. Meantime, seemingly contradictory findings are sparking debate.

---

parents, teachers, and spouses, with different sets of material gathered at each of the four time periods.

To reduce all the data to manageable proportions, Block began by assembling separate files of the information collected for each subject at each time period. Clinical psychologists were assigned to immerse themselves in individual dossiers and then to make a summary rating of the subject's personality by sorting a set of statements (for instance, "Has social poise and presence," and "Is self-defeating") into piles that indicated how representative the statement was of the subject. The assessments by the different raters (usually three for each dossier) were found to agree with one another to a significant degree, and they were averaged to form an overall description of the subject at that age. To avoid potential bias, the materials for each subject were carefully segregated by age level; all comments that referred to the person at an earlier age were removed from the file. No psychologist rated the materials for the same subject at more than one time period.

Self-defeating dolescents were self-defeating adults, one study found, and cheerful teenagers were cheerful 40-year-olds.

Using this painstaking methodology, Block found a striking pattern of stability. In his most recent report, published earlier this year, he reported that on virtually every one of the 90 rating scales employed, there was a statistically significant correlation between subjects' ratings when they were in junior high school and their ratings 30 to 35 years later, when they were in their 40s. The most self-defeating adolescents were the most self-defeating adults; cheerful teenagers were cheerful 40-year-olds; those whose moods fluctuated when they were in junior high school were still experiencing mood swings in midlife.

'Still Stable After All These Years'

Even more striking evidence for the stability of personality, extending the time frame beyond middle age to late adulthood, comes from the work of Paul T. Costa, Jr., and Robert R. McCrae, both psychologists at the Gerontology Research Center of the National Institute on Aging in Baltimore. Costa and McCrae have tracked people's scores over time on standardized self-report personality scales, including the Sixteen Personality Factor Questionnaire and the Guilford-Zimmerman Temperament Survey, on which people are asked to decide whether or not each of several hundred statements describes them accurately. (Three sample items: "I would prefer to have an office of my own, not sharing it with another person." "Often I get angry with people too quickly." "Some people seem to ignore or avoid me, although I don't know why.")

Costa and McCrae combined subjects' responses on individual items to produce scale scores for each subject on such overall dimensions as extraversion and neuroticism, as well as on more specific traits, such as gregariousness, assertiveness, anxiety, and depression. By correlating over time the scores of subjects tested on two or three occasions—separated by six, 10, or 12 years—they obtained estimates of personality stability. The Baltimore researchers have analyzed data from two large longitudinal studies, the Normative Aging Study conducted by the Veterans Administration in Boston and the Baltimore Longitudinal Study of Aging. In the Boston study, more than 400 men, ranging in age from 25 to 82, filled out a test battery in the mid-1960s and then completed a similar battery 10 years later, in the mid-1970s. In the Baltimore study, more than 200 men between the ages of 20 and 76 completed test batteries three times, separated by six-year intervals. Less extensive analyses, still unpublished, of the test scores of women in the Baltimore study point to a similar pattern of stability.

In both studies, Costa and McCrae found extremely high correlations, which indicated that the ordering of subjects on a particular dimension on one occasion was being maintained to a large degree a decade or more later. Contrary to what might have been predicted, young and middle-aged subjects turned out to be just as unchanging as old subjects were.

"The assertive 19-year-old is the assertive 40-year-old is the assertive 80-year-old," declares Costa, extrapolating from his and McCrae's results, which covered shorter time spans. For the title of a persuasive new paper reporting their results, Costa and McCrae rewrote a Paul Simon song title, proclaiming that their subjects were "Still Stable After All These Years."

Other recent studies have added to the accumulating evidence for personality stability throughout the life span. Gloria Leon and her coworkers at the University of Minnesota analyzed the scores on the Minnesota Multiphasic Personality Inventory (MMPI) of 71 men who were tested in 1947, when they were about 50 years old, and again in 1977, when they were close to 80. They found significant correlations on all 13 of the MMPI scales, with the highest correlation over the 30-year period on the scale of "Social

Neurotics are likely to be complainers throughout life. They may complain about different things as they get older—for example, worries about love in early adulthood, a "midlife crisis" at about age 40, health problems in late adulthood—but they are still complaining.

Introversion." Costa and McCrae, too, found the highest degrees of stability, ranging from .70 to .84, on measures of introversion-extraversion, which assess gregariousness, warmth, and assertiveness. And Paul Mussen and his colleagues at Berkeley, analyzing interviewers' ratings of 53 women who were seen at ages 30 and 70, found significant correlations on such aspects of introversion-extraversion as talkativeness, excitability, and cheerfulness.

Although character may be most fixed in the domain of introversion-extraversion, Costa and McCrae found almost as much constancy in the domain of "neuroticism," which includes such specific traits as depression, anxiety, hostility, and impulsiveness. Neurotics are likely to be complainers throughout life. They may complain about different things as they get older—for example, worries about love in early adulthood, a "midlife crisis" at about age 40, health problems in late adult-

hood—but they are still complaining. The less neurotic person reacts to the same events with greater equanimity. Although there is less extensive evidence for its stability, Costa and McCrae also believe that there is an enduring trait of "openness to experience," including such facets as openness to feelings, ideas, and values.

Another recent longitudinal study of personality, conducted by University of Minnesota sociologist Jeylan Mortimer and her coworkers, looked at the self-ratings of 368 University of Michigan men who were tested in 1962-63, when they were freshmen, in 1966-67, when they were seniors, and in 1976, when they were about 30. At each point the subjects rated themselves on various characteristics, such as relaxed, strong, warm, and different. The ratings were later collapsed into overall scores for well-being, competence, sociability, and unconventionality. On each of these dimensions, Mortimer found a pattern of persistence rather than one of change. Mortimer's analysis of the data also suggested that life experiences such as the nature of one's work had an impact on personality. But the clearest message of her research is, in her own words, "very high stability."

Is Everybody Changing?

The high correlations between assessments made over time indicate that people in a given group keep the same rank order on the traits being measured, even as they traverse long stretches of life. But maybe *everyone* changes as he or she gets older. If, for example, everyone turns inward to about the same extent in the latter part of life, the correlations—representing people's *relative* standing—on measures of introversion could still be very high, thus painting a misleading picture of stability. And, indeed, psychologist Bernice Neugarten concluded as recently as five years ago that there was a general tendency for people to become more introverted in the second half of life. Even that conclusion has been called into question, however. The recent longitudinal studies have found only slight increases in introversion as people get older, changes so small that Costa and McCrae consider them to be of little practical significance.

Specifically, longitudinal studies have shown slight drops over the course of adulthood in people's levels of excitement seeking, activity, hostility, and impulsiveness. The Baltimore researchers find no such changes in average levels of gregariousness, warmth, assertiveness, depression, or anxiety. Costa summarizes the pattern of changes as "a mellowing—but the person isn't so mellowed that you can't recognize him." Even as this mellowing occurs, moreover, people's relative ordering remains much the same—on the average, everyone drops the same few standard points. Thus, an "impulsive" 25-year-old may be a bit less impulsive by the time he or she is 70 but is still likely to be more impulsive than his or her agemates.

The new evidence of personality stability has been far too strong for the advocates of change to discount. Even in the heart of changeland, in Brim and Kagan's *Constancy and Change in Human Development*, psychologists Howard Moss and Elizabeth Susman review the research and conclude that there is strong evidence for the continuity of personality.

People Who Get Stuck

The new evidence has not put the controversy over personality stability and change to rest, however. If anything, it has sharpened

it. Although he praises the new research, Orville Brim is not convinced by it that adults are fundamentally unchanging. He points out that the high correlations signify strong associations between measures, but not total constancy. For example, a .70 correlation between scores obtained at two different times means that half of the variation (.70 squared, or .49) between people's later scores can be predicted from their earlier scores. The apostles of stability focus on this predictability, which is all the more striking because of

---

Even as this mellowing occurs, moreover, people's relative ordering remains much the same— on the average, everyone drops the same few standard points.

---

the imperfect reliability of the measures employed. But the prophets of change, like Brim, prefer to dwell on the half of the variability that cannot be predicted, which they take as evidence of change.

Thus, Costa and McCrae look at the evidence they have assembled, marvel at the stability that it indicates, and call upon researchers to explain it: to what extent may the persistence of traits bespeak inherited biological predispositions, enduring influences from early childhood, or patterns of social roles and expectations that people get locked into? And at what age does the plaster of character in fact begin to set? Brim looks at the same evidence, acknowledges the degree of stability that it indicates, and then calls upon researchers to explain why some people in the sample are changing. "When you focus on stability," he says, "you're looking at the dregs—the people who have gotten stuck. You want to

look at how a person grows and changes, not at how a person stays the same."

Brim, who is a president of the Foundation for Child Development in New York, also emphasizes that only certain aspects of personality—most clearly, aspects of social and emotional style, such as introversion-extraversion, depression, and anxiety—have been shown to be relatively stable. Brim himself is more interested in other parts of personality, such as people's self-esteem, sense of control over their lives, and ultimate values. These are the elements of character that Brim believes undergo the most important changes over the course of life. "Properties like gregariousness don't interest me," he admits; he does not view such traits as central to the fulfillment of human possibilities.

If Brim is not interested in some of the personality testers' results, Daniel Levinson is even less interested. In his view, paper-and-pencil measures like those used by Costa and McCrae are trivial, reflecting, at best, peripheral aspects of life. (Indeed, critics suggest that such research indicates only that people are stable in the way they fill out personality scales.) Levinson sees the whole enterprise of "rigorous" studies of personality stability as another instance of psychologists' rushing in to measure whatever they have measures for before they have clarified the important issues. "I think most psychologists and sociologists don't have the faintest idea what adulthood is about," he says.

Levinson's own work at the Yale School of Medicine has centered on the adult's evolving life structure— the way in which a person's social circumstances, including work and

---

The person is a dynamic organism, in one view, constantly striving to become something more than it is.

---

family ties, and inner feelings and aspirations fit together in an overall picture. Through intensive interviews of a small sample of men in the middle years of life—he is now conducting a parallel study of women—Levinson has come to view adult development as marked by an alternating sequence of relatively stable "structure-building" periods and periods of transition. He has paid special attention to the transition that occurs at about the age of 40. Although this midlife transition may be either smooth or abrupt, the person who emerges from it is always different from the one who entered it.

The midlife transition provides an important opportunity for personal growth. For example, not until we are past 40, Levinson believes, can we take a "universal" view of ourselves and the world rising above the limited perspective of our own background to appreciate the fullest meaning of life. "I don't think anyone can write tragedy—real tragedy—before the age of 40," Levinson declares.

Disagreement Over Methods

As a student of biography, Levinson does not hesitate to take a biographical view of the controversy at hand. "To Paul Costa," he suggests in an understanding tone, "the most important underlying issue is probably the specific issue of personality stability or change. I think the question of *development* is really not important to him personally. But he's barely getting to 40, so he has time." Levinson himself began his research on adult development when he was 46, as part of a way of understanding the changes he had undergone in the previous decade. He is now 60.

Costa, for his part, thinks that

Levinson's clinical approach to research, based on probing interviews with small numbers of people, lacks the rigor needed to establish anything conclusively. "It's only 40 people, for crying out loud!" he exclaims. And Costa doesn't view his own age (he is 38) or that of his colleague McCrae (who is 32) as relevant to the questions under discussion.

Jack Block, who is also a hardheaded quantitative researcher—and, for the record, is fully 57 years old—shares Costa's view of Levinson's method. "The interviews pass through the mind of Dan Levinson and a few other people," Block grumbles, "and he writes it down." Block regards Levinson as a good psychologist who should be putting forth his work as speculation, and not as research.

> **The midlife transition provides an important opportunity for personal growth.**

As this byplay suggests, some of the disagreement between the upholders of stability and the champions of change is methodological. Those who argue for the persistence of traits tend to offer rigorous personality-test evidence, while those who emphasize the potential for change often offer more qualitative, clinical descriptions. The psychometricians scoff at the clinical reports as unreliable, while the clinicians dismiss the psychometric data as trivial. This summary oversimplifies the situation, though, because some of the strongest believers in change, like Brim, put a premium on statistical, rather than clinical, evidence.

When pressed, people on both sides of the debate agree that personality is characterized by *both* stability and change. But they argue about the probabilities assigned to different outcomes. Thus, Costa maintains that "the assertive 19-year-old is the assertive 40-year-old is the assertive 80-year-old...*unless something happens*

to change it." The events that would be likely to change deeply ingrained patterns would have to be pretty dramatic ones. As an example, Costa says that he would not be surprised to see big personality changes in the Americans who were held hostage in Iran.

From Brim's standpoint, in contrast, people's personalities—and especially their feelings of mastery, control, and self-esteem—will keep changing through the course of life...*unless they get stuck*. As an example, he notes that a coal miner who spends 10 hours a day for 50 years down the shaft may have little opportunity for psychological growth. Brim believes that psychologists should try to help people get out of such ruts of stability. And he urges researchers to look more closely at the ways in which life events—not only the predictable ones, such as getting married or retiring, but also the unpredictable ones, such as being fired or experiencing a religious conversion—may alter adult personality.

At bottom, it seems, the debate is not so much methodological as ideological, reflecting fundamental differences of opinion about what is most important in the human experience. Costa and McCrae emphasize the value of personality constancy over time as a central ingredient of a stable sense of identity. "If personality were not stable," they write, "our ability to make wise choices about our future lives would be severely limited." We must know what we are like—and what we will continue to be like—if we are to make intelligent choices, whether of careers, spouses, or friends. Costa and McCrae view the maintenance of a stable personality in the face of the vicissitudes of life as a vital human accomplishment.

Brim, however, views the potential for growth as the hallmark of humanity. "The person is a dynamic organism," he says, "constantly striving to master its environment and to become something more than it is." He adds, with a sense of purpose in his voice, "I see psychology in the service of liberation, not constraint."

Indeed, Brim suspects that we are now in the midst of "a revolution in human development," from a traditional pattern of continuity toward greater discontinuity throughout the life span. Medical technology (plastic surgery and sex-change surgery, for example), techniques of behavior modification, and the social supports for change provided by thousands of groups "from TA to TM, from AA to Zen" are all part of this revolution. Most important, people are trying, perhaps for the first time in history, to change *themselves*.

Some social critics, prominent among them Christopher Lasch in *The Culture of Narcissism*, have decried the emphasis on self-improvement as a manifestation of the "Me" generation's excessive preoccupation with self. In Brim's view, these critics miss the point. "Most of the concern with oneself going on in this country," he declares, "is not people being selfish, but rather trying to be better, trying to be something more than they are now." If Brim is right in his reading of contemporary culture, future studies of personality that track people through the 1970s and into the 1980s may well show less stability and more change than the existing studies have shown.

The Tension in Each of Us

In the last analysis, the tension between stability and change is found not only in academic debates but also in each of us. As

> *Efforts to track people into the 1980s may reveal a pattern of less stability and more change in personality.*

Brim and Kagan write, "There is, on the one hand, a powerful drive to maintain the sense of one's identity, a sense of continuity that allays fears of changing too fast or of being changed against one's will by outside forces…On the other hand, each person is, by nature, a purposeful, striving organism with a desire to be more than he or she is now. From making simple new year's resolutions to undergoing transsexual operations, everyone is trying to become something that he or she is not, but hopes to be."

A full picture of adult personality development would inevitably reflect this tension between sameness and transformation. Some aspects of personality, such as a tendency to be reclusive or outgoing, calm or anxious, may typically be more stable than other aspects, such as a sense of mastery over the environment. Nevertheless, it must be recognized that each of us reflects, over time, both stability and change. As a result, observers can look at a person as he or she goes through a particular stretch of life and see either stabil-

> *Whether a person stays much the same or makes sharp breaks with the past may depend in large measure on his or her own ideas about what is possible and about what is valuable.*

ity or change or—if the observer looks closely enough—both.

For example, most people would look at Richard Alpert, the hard-driving psychology professor of the early 1960s, and Ram Dass, the bearded, free-flowing guru of the 1970s, and see that totally different persons are here now. But Harvard psy-

chologist David McClelland, who knew Alpert well, spent time with the Indian holy man and said to himself, "It's the same old Dick!"—still as charming, as concerned with inner experience, and as power-oriented as ever. And Jerry Rubin can view his own transformation from Yippie to Wall Streeter in a way that recognizes the underlying continuity: "Finding out who I really was was done in typical Jerry Rubin way. I tried everything, jumped around like crazy with boundless energy and curiosity." If we look closely enough, even Richard Raskind and Renée Richards will be found to have a great deal in common.

Whether a person stays much the same or makes sharp breaks with the past may depend in large measure on his or her own ideas about what is possible and about what is valuable. Psychological research on adult development can itself have a major impact on these ideas by calling attention to what is "normal" and by suggesting what is desirable. Now that researchers have established beyond reasonable doubt that there is often considerable stability in adult personality, they may be able to move on to a clearer understanding of how we can grow and change, even as we remain the same people we always were. It may be, for example, that if we are to make significant changes in ourselves without losing our sense of identity, it is necessary for some aspects of our personality to remain stable. "I'm different now," we can say, "but it is me."

As Jack Block puts it, in his characteristically judicious style: "Amidst change and transformation, there is an essential coherence to personality development." ◆

Discussion Questions

1. What is the problem with most studies of personality?

2. What factors made Block's research more valid?

3. What were the results of Block's study on personality?

4. Describe the personality study by Costa and McCrae. What were the results?

5. What aspects of personality change most, according to Brim?

6. If only "half the variation" in personality test scores can be predicted from previous test scores, is personality stable or unstable? Defend your answer. (And be careful: Your answer could be an important clue to your personality!)

7. What is Daniel Levinson's perspective on personality? Why is he critical of paper-and-pencil tests of personality?

8. Contrast the qualitative and the quantitative approaches to personality research which are described in Rubin's article.

9. Do you think your personality has changed over the years? In what ways? In what ways have you stayed the same? Do you think your personality will change as you age? If so, how?

Name: _____

Date: _____

Part 14: Personality Theory and Assessment

1. I believe that personality is formed early in life and that it remains stable throughout life.

Agree　①　②　③　④　⑤　Disagree

2. I am aware of my major personality traits, and I believe that these distinguish me from many other people.

Agree　①　②　③　④　⑤　Disagree

3. I behave in very different ways in different situations.

Agree　①　②　③　④　⑤　Disagree

Kenneth J. Gergen has come to reject the idea of a fixed identity, but Zick Rubin and others still defend the concept of personality, at least to some degree. Analyze yourself, a close relative, and a close friend that you have known for five years or more, and see if you can resolve the debate. What traits in yourself and others have remained stable over a five-year period? What traits, if any, have changed? Do you agree with Gergen's position? Why or why not?

Does stability necessarily mean that personality *cannot* change? Under what conditions might you, your relative, and your friend assume very different personalities?

PART 15

HEALTH, STRESS, AND SELF-CHANGE

48 **On the Real Benefits of Eustress: A Conversation with Hans Selye**

49 **Stress and Health: Exploring the Links,** by Steven F. Maier and Mark Laudenslager

50 **Rx: Biofeedback,** by Neal E. Miller

51 **A Sense of Control: A Conversation with Judith Rodin**

When I teach Introductory Psychology, I always have my students work on self-management projects throughout the course. They pick a troublesome problem—anger control, say, or nail biting—and then use self-change techniques that we learn about in class to solve the problem over a period of a few weeks. If one technique doesn't work, they try another, and when one problem is solved, they move on to the next. For most students, the idea that there are specific skills and techniques that can be used for self-change is completely new. And what a tragedy that is! Psychologists have been cataloguing and studying such techniques for decades. Why aren't these techniques being taught in elementary schools, and, for that matter, why aren't they being taught at home?

Much of the potential people have for personal achievement or peace of mind is lost, I believe, simply because they have never learned self-management skills: skills for meeting deadlines and goals, planning skills, time-management and organizational skills, anger-management skills, advanced breathing techniques, self-monitoring skills, meditation and other relaxation skills, stress-management skills, and so on. We depend, instead, on "will-power"—the Rambo approach to self-change. We simply "will" that we stop smoking or drinking or overeating, and that's supposed to take care of the problem. It rarely does. The effective alternative is to master a broad range of self-management skills to help you achieve virtually any kind of self-change. *Skill, not will*—that's my motto.

I'm leaping down off the soapbox now to talk about this section, which begins with an interview with one of the towering researchers of this century, Hans Selye (pronounced *SEL-yay*), published just four years before his death in 1982. Selye introduced the world to the modern concept of stress (a term he borrowed from physics) in a paper published in 1936, and since that time Selye's studies on stress have been cited in more than 370,000 scientific papers. Specifically, Selye studied how the body (mainly of rats) changes when demands are placed on it—in other words, when it is exposed to what Selye called "stressors." Selye discovered that stressors of almost any sort produce *virtually-identical hormonal reactions* that activate many systems in the body. Short-term, this process prepares the body to fend off the stressors, but if these systems are active for too long, the immune system and vital organs start to deteriorate. In other words, prolonged stress can lead to illness or death.

In the next article, "Stress and Health," Steven F. Maier and Mark Laudenslager present some of the contemporary evidence that ties prolonged stress to illness. In "Rx: Biofeedback," Neal E. Miller, the pioneering inventor of biofeedback, explains how biofeedback, employed in conjunction with other techniques, can alleviate a variety of problems, from anxiety to incontinence to curvature of the spine. The final article is an interview with obesity expert Judith Rodin, who talks about weight, dieting, and ways to keep old people feeling young.

ON THE REAL
Benefits of *Eustress:*
A CONVERSATION WITH
Hans Selye

◆ *Laurence Cherry*

Laurence Cherry: How do you cope with stress?

Hans Selye: By being as busy with my work as I possibly can.

Cherry: How busy is that?

Selye: I almost always put in at least a 10-hour day, and often more. This week, for example, along with receiving visitors to our new International Institute of Stress here in Montreal, attending staff conferences, and writing various papers, I'll be making speeches in cities both inside and outside Canada. And far from being wearied by this typically hectic schedule, I find that I positively flourish on it.

Cherry: Doesn't that contradict all the grim advice we hear about the need to slow down to avoid stress?

Selye: Unfortunately, there's a great deal of confusion about what stress actually is and how we should deal with it. Stress is the body's nonspecific response to *any* demand placed on it, whether that demand is pleasant or not. Sitting in a dentist's chair is stressful, but so is exchanging a passionate kiss with a lover—after all, your pulse races, your breathing quickens, your heartbeat soars. And yet who in the world would forgo such a pleasurable pastime simply because of the stress involved? Our aim shouldn't be to completely avoid stress, which at any rate would be impossible, but to learn how to recognize our typical response to stress and then to try to modulate our lives in accordance with it.

One striking thing we've discovered is that there are two main types of human beings: "racehorses," who thrive on stress, and are only happy with a vigorous, fast-paced lifestyle; and "turtles," who in order to be happy require peace, quiet, and a generally tranquil environment—something that would frustrate and bore most racehorse types. I myself could hardly imagine any torture worse than having to lie on a beach doing nothing day after day; yet, in my travels, I've noticed a great many people whose chief aim in life is to be able to do precisely that.

As you say, we hear a great deal these days about the dangers of overwork and excessive striving, and of being the so-called Type A personality. But I think in many ways this is exaggerated and arouses unnecessary anxiety. To give you a personal example, even though I am a most pronounced racehorse type, at the age of 71 I've never suffered a heart attack or any of the usual stress-linked diseases, and I think it would be far more stressful for me to cut back my schedule—which I certainly have no intention of doing.

If a danger does exist, its main cause is that some people occasionally mistake their own type and push themselves beyond their normal stress endurance.

> *Unfortunately, there's a great deal of confusion about what stress actually is and how we should deal with it.*

And that, of course, should be avoided.

Cherry: How can a person decide to which type he belongs?

Selye: By careful observation. All the stress inventories in common use are somewhat flawed because they fail to give enough weight to individual differences. Each of us is really the best judge of himself, and we can gradually develop an instinctive feeling that tells us whether we are running above or below the stress level that suits us best. There are also revealing body clues. Animals in a stressful situation invariably show an increased amount of body movement, as do humans. You may not be aware that you're under stress, but meanwhile your heart rate has increased, and you are making more gesticulating movements with your hands. Of course, there are also behavioral indicators, such as insomnia or irritability. Deciding on your own type and detecting when and where you are prone to stress isn't very difficult once you've acquired this knack of being more self-aware. After some years of practice, I now know quite well when I've had enough, and then I stop; I don't need any complex scientific test to help me decide. And then I take steps to protect myself.

For example, thanks to my profile, which some have not unfairly compared to that of my compatriot, the Canadian moose, I find myself constantly recognized in airports, restaurants, or on the street. This is flattering, of course, but fame can be stressful, too, particularly when I find myself besieged by well-meaning fans, or have my time taken up by potential patients in search of a free consultation. For years, I wore dark glasses and a wig whenever I took a trip, but finally both proved to be

Hans Selye

insufficient. So, turning to our always-helpful counselor, Nature, I took a tip from the skunk, who always manages to get rid of unwanted intruders without using force. I now travel with a few bulbs of garlic in my pocket, and when cornered, chew them like gum. I happen to like the taste, but sooner or later the other person always mumbles something and departs— leaving me happily to my privacy. I also always fly first class in order to reduce the physical stress of travel, particularly since I've had both of my hips removed in the past few years and sitting uncomfortably can lead to pain. And I stay at deluxe hotels all the time, although I have no real taste for luxury; after all, even a racehorse type eventually learns the value of a comfortable stable and a refreshing, if brief, rest.

Cherry: Wherever one goes these days, one can hardly escape advertisements for various medications to help people cope with stress, as well as a host of various relaxation techniques, such as Transcendental Meditation. How valuable do you think they are?

Selye: The oldest chemical ways of coping with stress, of course, are

drinking something alcoholic or, more recently, taking drugs such as tranquilizers. Neither method really works [except for temporary relief], and all have some undesirable side effects. As for these new "stress capsules" and their like, I consider them practically worthless. Someday there may perhaps be a pill that will totally protect us against the effects of stress—but only perhaps.

For some reason, there seems to be a general impression that I endorse TM as a way of handling stress. Actually, although I've met the Maharishi and find his ideas interesting, I've never even taken his course. As far as I know, TM (like Edmund Jacobson's relaxation exercises and Herbert Benson's "relaxation response") helps some people who suffer from too much stress, but fails to help others. In some instances, it might even be dangerous for individuals to spend too much time on these techniques. There are actually people who suffer from too little stress—hypostress—and they need more external stimuli, more activity in their lives, rather than sitting down and silently meditating; in time, this could become a form of sensory deprivation.

All the stress inventories are flawed because they fail to give enough weight to individual differences.

After some years of practice, I now know quite well when I've had enough, and then I stop; I don't need any complex scientific test to help me decide. And then I take steps to protect myself.

Rather than relying on drugs or other techniques, I think there's another, better way to handle stress, which involves taking a different attitude toward the various events in

our lives. Attitude determines whether we perceive any experience as pleasant or unpleasant, and adopting the right one can convert a negative stress into a positive one— something I call a "eustress," employing the same Greek prefix for "good" that occurs in such words as "euphoria" and "euphonia."

Cherry: So the concept of will enters stress theory. Does positive stress, eustress, also place demands on the body?

Selye: Yes, but for reasons we can't yet explain, far less of a demand. For example, I doubt if anyone, even a person with a naturally high stress threshold, could endure my busy schedule unless he took as favorable a view of the work as I do. In either case, the stress, the schedule, is the same, but for me it has become a eustress. Being the descendant of several generations of dedicated physicians, I was told as I grew up that hard work is both an obligation and, if approached in the right spirit, a pleasure, and I certainly have found that to be true.

I think the cultivation of this attitude toward life was also responsible for helping me in other ways. "Imitate the sundial's ways, count only the pleasant days" was a folk proverb I often heard while growing up in Austria-Hungary, and it made a deep impression on me. I find I've learned to quickly forget unpleasant incidents and that I cannot carry grudges for very long. If wronged by some friend or colleague, as happens to almost everyone at some point in life, I may break off contact with the person out of sheer self-protection, but I bear him little enmity. After all, Nature gives even the most fortunate of us only a limited capital of energy to resist stress, and it would be silly to squander it on quite pointless anger or hatred.

This same attitude helped me very much a few years ago, when my doctor told me I had cancer and only a few months to live. I refused to retreat from life in desperation or to rail at fate, and was determined to keep living and working without worrying about my end. And although I can't prove it, perhaps this attitude helped my body combat the stress of my disease and subsequent operations and recuperations, since, as you see, I am still ticking today—and I might add, ticking quite well.

Cherry: You mention how important your upbringing was in helping you to develop useful attitudes. Do you think today families or teachers fail to show us how to adequately cope with stress, possibly because the stresses themselves have increased? There seems to be a general feeling that we live in a particularly stressful age of anxiety.

Selye: Every era has been an age of anxiety, most old stresses have simply been replaced by similar new ones. There was obviously no threat of nuclear war a few hundred years ago, for example, but there was always the terrible danger of the plague, which quite literally destroyed whole populations. And everything in human life is uncertain and contingent—you may be rich today and poor tomorrow, or healthy or sick; this has been true throughout human history.

But there is one type of social stress that I think has particularly increased in our time. This is a loss of motivation, a spiritual malady that has assumed almost epidemic proportions among the young. And with it, naturally, come desperate

attempts to escape the dilemma by any spastic effort. I believe that a large part, if not the major part, of violence, alcoholism, and drug addiction is due to a loss of the stabilizing support of constructive goals. Science has destroyed the credibility of old beliefs, but many today can find no suitable substitutes for

> *Every era has been an age of anxiety, most old stresses have simply been replaced by similar new ones.*

them. I'm convinced that the formulation of a scientifically acceptable philosophy of behavior by which people could live could do much more for humanity in general than any discovery.

Cherry: Teilhard de Chardin said, "The future is in the hands of those who can give tomorrow's generation valid reasons to live and hope." But it seems most scientists can offer nothing more inspiring than the gloomy picture of a universe ruled by chance.

Selye: Yes. But in order to be valid, any reason for hope, and any code of life, must be firmly grounded in scientific principles. Otherwise, like the traditional religious faiths, it will end up with many no longer taking any of it very seriously.

I first began to consider this problem in true earnest when I noticed its effect on my children and their friends.

> *Adopting the right attitude can convert a negative stress into a positive one— what I call a 'eustress.'*

They seemed to be purposelessly drifting, unsure of what to do with themselves or with their lives—one of the most stressful situations imaginable. Two answers were offered to their dilemma, both of which contain some of the truth, but neither of which contains all of it. The first, possibly the most influential at the moment, is the notion that you should live entirely

for yourself without really giving much thought, if any, to others.

Cherry: The attitude reflected in the host of current best-sellers celebrating the virtues of selfishness and the wisdom of "looking out for Number One."

Selye: Yes. And of course that is wise, up to a point. Human beings, like all organisms, are born egoists—they necessarily have to look out for themselves first. No matter what some of the great sages have said, as long as there's life on this planet, it will have to be egoistic. The fallacy is that people somehow confuse this perfectly natural phenomenon with egotism—the ruthless and exclusive pursuit of one's own ends. I doubt if there could be a more stressful approach to life, since it almost inevitably creates antagonism and enemies all around you. One of the most striking things I've noticed through life is how frighteningly quick rank, fortune, and power can be lost. Pity the poor men and women who, having clawed their way to the top, have created so much ill will around them that they desperately have to remain there—or else.

The other popular answer, that of absolute altruism and endless self-sacrifice, is given by many popular cults and traditions, and it contains its own grain of truth. Just as we're all born egoists, so we're also born altruists. Even the Mafiosi are altruistic: As vicious as they can be to others, they usually subordinate their own good to that of both their genetic family and their crime family.

For more proof, go to any zoo and watch how eagerly people feed the animals there, even though most of them know quite well that the zookeepers make sure they're well fed. They hand out their peanuts and crackers, not expecting any sort of reward, but simply because normal human beings enjoy giving pleasure to others. The danger is that altruism carried to an extreme—constantly putting other people's good before your own—violates our nature, the biological basis of life, and leads, in all cases I've seen, to constant, if not always conscious, stressful frustration and resentment.

I believe the only acceptable answer, paradoxical as it sounds, is altruistic egoism. I saw it practiced in an instinctive way in the Hungarian town in which I grew up. The doctors there might have treated medicine as many do today, as a job rather than a vocation, charging as much as they could and making themselves generally resented and disliked. Instead, they tried hard to improve their skills and do their best for all the local people, whether rich or poor. They did this not really out of a sense of altruism, but from the egoistic awareness that in this way, they were really best protecting themselves. In the periods of particular stress, war and revolution, they found their reward. At a time when many people were starving, the local people never forgot to come to my father's door to present chickens, eggs, homemade sausages, and other foods that seemed to us like miracles.

Later on, as a scientist working in a laboratory, I saw that the balance between altruism and egoism was preserved on even the most primitive levels of life. Individual cells, at some point in the past, gave up their independence to form stronger and more complex beings. Just how important this is can be seen in the growth of a cancer, whose distinguishing characteristic is that it cares only for itself. It feeds on its host until it kills it—and so commits suicide, since a cancer cell cannot live except with the body in which it started its reckless and egocentric development. And going from the simplest level of life to the most

complex, I noticed that most of our patients who were suffering from stress-linked diseases also suffered from a warped code of behavior— one that emphasized either too much selfishness or too much self-sacrifice.

And so, little by little, drawing on my own experience and scientific work, I was able to make a kind of recipe for the best antidote to the stresses of life. The first ingredient, as I told you, is to seek your own stress level, to decide whether you're a racehorse or a turtle and to live your life accordingly. The second is to choose your goals and make sure they're really your own, and not imposed on you by an overhelpful mother or teacher. For example, I truly wanted to be a scientist; otherwise, I'm sure I would have succumbed to the pressures of my work. I've seen too many cases of doctors who re-

---

I've seen too many cases of doctors who really wanted to be musicians, or office clerks who really wanted to be plumbers or carpenters, not to realize how much stress is caused and suffering is involved in trying to live out choices other people have made for you.

---

ally wanted to be musicians, or office clerks who really wanted to be plumbers or carpenters, not to realize how much stress is caused and suffering is involved in trying to live out choices other people have made for you. And the third ingredient to this recipe is altruistic egoism—looking out for oneself by being necessary to others, and thus earning their goodwill. I've always advised my children and students not to worry about saving money or about climbing the next rung on their career ladder. Much more important, they should work at making sure they're useful, by acquiring as much competence in

their chosen fields as they can— their ultimate protection no matter what the future holds in store.

Cherry: But doesn't your advice on how to avoid stress overlook the fact that most of us are *not* indispensable? There are very few Einsteins or da Vincis or Mozarts; how many of us can be so useful to those around us?

Selye: I think all of us can. You needn't discover the equivalent of the theory of relativity; you can work at being a good teacher, a good baker, a good neighbor. And striving to make yourself ever more useful and necessary is an aim you can safely pursue throughout your life, and one that will protect you from the worst of all modern social stresses, purposelessness. I think the response to this idea from people all over the world indicates how great a need there is for this kind of direction to our lives.

Cherry: You must be aware that some of your fellow scientists have criticized you for mixing philosophy with science—less politely put, for treading where you don't belong.

Selye: I know I have the dubious honor of being one of the most frequently attacked medical-research people of our time. My response to such attacks is very simple. If I feel I'm right, I defend my point of view fiercely, I never accept defeat simply because everyone appears to be against me. As I think back over many years of struggling to get the stress concept accepted, it gives me infinite pleasure that several points that were once so violently attacked are now commonplace.

I realized that once I strayed from simply reporting my investigations into the biochemical or histological details of stress, the level of criticism would rise. But almost 50 years ago, the great American physiologist Walter Cannon, who coined the term "homeostasis," expressed his conviction that the philosophy of man could and should be guided by biological research. And actually my attempt to develop a new philosophy of life is only the logical development of my work, since my aim has always been to discover how we can live with stress and make it work for us.

Cherry: At 71, do you feel your final word about stress has been spoken?

Selye: I don't consider my work on stress to be finished at all. I know very well I won't ever see the end of this study, since we're constantly faced with new ways of looking at biological problems. But I feel relieved to know that al-though my "child" stress research, will outlive me, by now it's reached the critical stage of maturity and independence that assures its survival and growth without my help. If it can teach others to be as happy and content as I am when they reach 71, by mastering the different stresses of life, I'll be most satisfied indeed. ◆

Discussion Questions

1. What does Selye say are the best ways to relieve stress?

2. What type of social stress has increased in our time?

3. What are the two personality stress types, according to Selye?

4. How do you find out what type of "stress" type you are?

5. What's wrong, according to Selye, with tests that purport to measure how stressed people are?

6. What is "eustress"?

7. How does Selye distinguish "stress" from "stressors"?

8. List some of the stressors in your life. Now think of alternative ways of looking at them? How might you reduce the stressors in your life, or at least change your attitude toward them?

STRESS AND HEALTH: *Exploring* the **Links**

◆ *Steven F. Maier and Mark Laudenslager*

After his daughter died, the middle-aged doctor could hardly contain his grief. He was disconsolate and felt during the next year as if he were "giving himself cancer." He managed, by denying both her existence and her death, to continue to work for the next few years but had continual infections and a nagging cough.

Three years after her death, anticipating the girl's birthday, the doctor began again to grieve. At the same time, for a three-month stretch, work was particularly stressful.

On the eve of his daughter's birthday, the doctor, barely able to breathe, was admitted to the local hospital's intensive care unit. After a lung biopsy revealed that he had a very rare type of pneumonia, he was given antibiotics and promptly responded. Despite his apparent recovery, his infection had made him suspicious. After researching in his local medical library, the doctor, a bisexual, diagnosed his condition as AIDS, a diagnosis later confirmed by a laboratory workup.

The doctor's true story is a new variation on a very old theme. Whether as folklore or as the anecdotes of today's health professionals, the essence of his story has been repeatedly retold: Disease and even death can follow in the wake of grief, unrequited love, financial losses, humiliation and other emotionally painful events.

We've all heard, for instance, that stress can cause ulcers and heart attacks. Now evidence is mounting that vulnerability to infectious disease—and even cancer—may be affected by how people react to stress.

But only some individuals seem to be vulnerable, and only under certain circumstances. Today's research challenge is to find out what accounts for these differences and, if possible, to find ways to keep more people well despite life's stings and setbacks.

Researchers were once reluctant to associate psychological states with infectious diseases because they could not imagine a physiological connection between them.

Vulnerability to infectious disease—and even cancer—may be affected by how people react to stress in their lives.

But evidence of such connections has grown in the past decades. And researchers in the emerging field of behavioral immunology are beginning to explain how psychological events can affect physical health.

Infectious diseases provide a particularly good example. Since they are caused by exposure to identifiable pathogens such as viruses and bacteria, their origins seem quite simple and biological, not psychological. But that's not the whole story. Only a fraction of those infected with a pathogen become ill, and psychological factors may play a major role in determining who does and does not get sick.

A number of investigators have studied how some life stresses (such as job change, the birth of a child or marital difficulties) are related to the development of infectious diseases by asking sick people to list stressful life changes they went through before the disease. Their responses are compared with those of people who do not have the illness. The results have revealed that high levels of stress frequently precede illness.

Other researchers use a more informative technique, measuring life stress in healthy people, then tracking them to see who develops an infectious disease and how stress is related to that illness. For example, in 1979, Stanislav Kasl, Alfred Evans and James Neiderman at the Yale School of Medicine studied the development of infectious mononucleosis in a class of West Point cadets. All entering cadets were screened for immunity and susceptibility to the disease, caused by the Epstein-Barr Virus (EBV). Those whose blood contained the antibody to EBV were considered immune, while those without the antibody were classified as susceptible. The susceptible cadets had their blood tested periodically. The investigators also studied interview data on the cadets' expectations and family backgrounds, obtained by West Point during routine testing of new cadets.

About one-fifth of the susceptible cadets became infected each year. However, only about one-quarter of the infected cadets developed mono's clinical symptoms. Several psychological factors were involved: Cadets who had described their fathers essentially as "overachievers" were more likely to develop symptoms. Moreover,

Fighting to Stay Well

The immune system is burdened with the momentous task of keeping us healthy by recognizing and destroying foreign materials such as bacteria, viruses, fungi and tumors. Its workhorses are white blood cells—more than a thousand billion of them—which are based in the lymph system and circulate through the bloodstream. These cells belong to two major classes: lymphocytes—B-cells, T-cells, and natural killer (NK) cells—and phagocytes.

In general, the job of lymphocytes is to recognize invaders (antigens) as foreign; to multiply after recognition so more invaders can be identified; and to generate chemicals, such as the antibodies produced by B-cells, that can reach and neutralize or destroy antigens.

Most lymphocytes need the backup of phagocytes, which are attracted to antigens being attacked. The phagocytes then finish off their destruction.

However, some lymphocytes, such as NK cells, can fight their own battles directly with antigens. They can spontaneously destroy tumor and other cells and seem less specific than other lymphocytes. These cells have received a lot of attention recently because they may play a key role in tumor rejection. Recent human studies have suggested that when NK cells are very active, cancers may be less likely to develop. NK cells appear to form part of an early immune surveillance system preventing the growth and spread of tumors, but how is still unclear.

the cadets most likely to become ill most strongly wanted a military career but performed poorly academically, just the ones who ought to be under the greatest stress.

Studies such as these strongly support the idea that psychological factors can influence the development of infectious disease, presumably by altering the immune system, the body's major defense against pathogens (see "Fighting to Stay Well" box).

More than 40 years ago, Hans Selye, a pioneer of stress research, noticed an increase in adrenal-gland activity and a decrease in immune-system activity in response to physical stress. Modern immunology has confirmed Selye's findings. In animal studies, stressors include electric shock, high-intensity sounds, burn injuries and physical restraint. In studies of humans, more complex

psychological stressors, such as a number of life changes, exams and academic pressures, sleep deprivation, bereavement and depression, have been associated with lowered immune system response. Certainly, in both animals and humans, the link between stressors and impaired immune functioning

---

Sometimes, just thinking that control is possible can prevent adverse effects of stress.

---

is quite strong. But why, then, do only some stressed individuals become ill?

When considering how humans react to life events, we must distinguish between exposure to a potential stressor and actual physical and psychological responses to it. Stress does not simply result

from a particular negative event, even a loved one's death. Rather, it results from a complex interaction between the event and a variety of psychological factors, such as the person's expectations and experience and the presence or absence of a network of caring people. Such factors may be important in determining whether a negative event will affect immune functioning and disease.

Research with both animals and humans indicates that an individual's control over an event is particularly important in determining its psychological and physiological effects. Research by psychologist Jay M. Weiss of Duke University School of Medicine has shown, for example, that if animals have control over an unpleasant stimulus, they do not develop ulcers, depressed appetite, sleep disturbances or brain-chemistry changes characteristic of stress responses.

The effects of stressor control on behavior are also striking. Animals that have been in an uncontrollable stressful situation show a variety of disturbances when later confronted with stressors that can be controlled by escape or avoidance. Most importantly, they behave passively and do not learn to avoid the stressors. Such behavioral changes, resulting from exposure to uncontrollable stressors, are part of a syndrome called "learned helplessness" by psychologist Martin Seligman of the University of Pennsylvania and one of us (Maier) when we collaborated in studying this response.

Learned-helplessness effects occur in humans, too, when they lack control over stressful events. But sometimes, just thinking that control is possible, even if it isn't, can prevent adverse stress effects. Essentially, people's beliefs that they can control a stressful event affect how they will react.

In 1972, psychologists David Glass and Jerome Singer gave two groups of people a number of mental tasks to do, while exposing them to loud, unpleasant noises. The first group was not told of any way to stop the noise. People in the second group were told they could turn off the noise by pressing a button, although the experimenter would prefer that they did not. This choice of being able to stop the noise gave the second group a feeling of control. Later both groups were given a second task of proofreading, without any noise disturbance. In this experiment, the group who earlier could not control the noise made more errors than the group who had felt in control.

Clearly, the fact and the belief that stressors can be controlled are important in determining psychological and physiological reactions to stressful situations. But how do these factors affect the immune system and the development of disease?

One clue comes from research done in 1979 that showed that in animals exposed to uncontrollable stressors, implanted tumors grew more rapidly and were less often rejected than in those exposed to stressors they could control.

Tumor growth and rejection are affected by the immune system but also by many nonimmune processes. Thus, we and our colleagues at the University of Colorado at Boulder set out to determine directly whether the ability to control a stressor affects the immune system's activity. We reasoned that if we could show in animals that a purely psychological factor—being able to control a stressor—altered immune function, we could determine which emotional factors were involved,

which immune-system changes occurred and which physiological mechanisms produced them.

We studied this in rats by exposing them to controllable and uncontrollable stressors and comparing their immune-system responses. Rats in the controllable-stressor group were put in a box with a wheel in it. We attached to their tails electrodes that could give a mild, intermittent shock to one tail portion. The apparatus was arranged so that the rats could shut off the shock whenever it occurred by turning the wheel; naturally, they quickly learned the trick.

Rats in the uncontrollable-stressor group were put in an identical set-up, but the shocks were actually controlled by the behavior of the rats in the first group. Nothing the rats in the second group did affected the pattern of the shocks. Two other groups were used for comparison: those exposed to the apparatus without shock, and those unstressed at all.

As a measure of immune-system response, we studied how readily the rats' T-cells (a type of lymphocyte, a key component of the immune system) multiplied when "challenged" by mitogens. Like antigens, the foreign invaders T-cells normally fight in the body, mitogens stimulate these cells to proliferate extensively.

We found that in response to the mitogens, T-cells from rats that could control the shock multiplied as readily as did those from unstressed rats. However, T-cells from rats exposed to identical but uncontrollable shock only multiplied weakly. Thus, the shocks did interfere with the immune response only in rats that could not control them.

We wondered whether our results might extend to another

> **The stress of an infant's grief at separation from its mother can affect its immune system.**

© 1998 PhotoDisc, Inc.

immune-system measure: the tumor-killing ability of natural killer (NK) cells, which play a key role in tumor surveillance. In collaboration with psychologists John Liebeskind and Yehuda Shavit of the University of California at Los Angeles, we removed and studied NK cells from rats exposed to controllable, uncontrollable or no stress. NK cells from unstressed rats or those that could control the stressor killed tumor cells normally, while NK cells from rats exposed to an uncontrollable stressor were less able to kill tumor cells.

These studies are the only ones to manipulate directly the effect of controllability of stressors on immune function. But many other situations involving an uncontrollable stressor have been studied. One is the separation of infants from parents, an especially obvious and potentially important example. In 1982, one of us (Laudenslager), working with psychiatrist Martin Reite of the University of Colorado Health Sciences Center, set out to study whether separating an infant from its mother would alter immune functioning. Since human subjects could not be used, the next-best subject was chosen: the monkey. Two weeks after 6-month old monkeys had been separated from their mothers, the youngsters' im-

© 1998 PhotoDisc, Inc.

Perhaps bereaved people who feel able to control their negative circumstances are more protected than others from depression and lessened immune responses.

A recent study by psychiatrist Steven Locke and his colleagues at Harvard University Medical School supports this sort of argument. Healthy volunteers were given questionnaires on life stresses within the past month and the past year, as well as a checklist of common psychological complaints. A blood sample was taken and NK-cell activity was assessed. Surprisingly, the occurrence of life stresses, even very severe ones, did not predict

NK-cell activity. Many people, despite repeated upheavals, did not show abnormally low levels of NK-cell activity. What was critical, however, was how people reacted emotionally to stressful events. Those who reported many life stresses as well as high levels of anxiety and depression had the lowest NK-cell activity. Those with similarly extensive life stresses but little anxiety and depression showed the highest NK-cell activity, even higher than in people who experienced few life stresses and were low in anxiety and depression.

Locke and his colleagues speculate that people who, despite

mune-system responses were lessened, as indicated by lowered lymphocyte proliferation. Similar separation studies by psychologists Christopher Coe and Seymour Levine at Stanford University in California have shown lowered ability to generate antibodies to specific viral invaders. Thus, stressors do not have to be simple physical events such as noise or shock to suppress immunity. They can be as psychological as an infant's "grief" at being separated from its mother.

Are human reactions similar? It appears that they may be. We can infer from various studies that the immune responses of some people may be suppressed when they cannot control severe negative events. The death of a spouse is perhaps the most potent uncontrollable and negative event for many of us. Roger Bartrop of the University of New South Wales and his colleagues in 1977 monitored several aspects of immunity in 26 people soon after their spouses died. Six weeks after the death, immune function was impaired: Lymphocyte proliferation was lowered.

Other studies have shown that some bereaved people may become seriously depressed, and that some depressed people tend to show less immunity to disease.

The Bridges

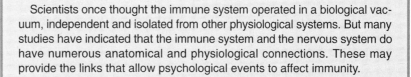

Scientists once thought the immune system operated in a biological vacuum, independent and isolated from other physiological systems. But many studies have indicated that the immune system and the nervous system do have numerous anatomical and physiological connections. These may provide the links that allow psychological events to affect immunity.

We and our colleagues have been particularly intrigued by the potential effects on the immune system of a group of brain chemicals called endorphins, enkephalins and dynorphins. The evidence from our work and others is still sketchy but provocative.

The endorphins are sometimes called natural opiates because, like opiates, they relieve pain and produce euphoria. They also appear to act on neurons as do opiates such as morphine.

One of us (Maier) became interested in natural opiates when studies of learned helplessness with coworkers revealed diminished sensitivity to pain in animals exposed to uncontrollable stressors. These effects did not occur in animals exposed to controllable stressors. Later studies showed that the analgesia probably stems from the release of natural opiates, and that drugs that block the action of such opiates also reverse the analgesic effects associated with uncontrolled stressors.

But do opiates released in response to uncontrolled stressors affect the immune system? There's suggestive evidence that they do. One clue comes from many findings that lymphocytes have opiate receptors on them. In other words, these immune-system cells are equipped to receive "messages" from the opiates that may alter how they behave. Another key clue comes from the work of James W. Lewis at the University of Michigan and colleagues, who have found that chemicals that block opiate action also keep uncontrollable stressors from suppressing immune responses. Perhaps such chemicals can be used to prevent impaired immune function produced by such states as bereavement and depression.

many negative life events, do not react with anxiety or depression can cope well, a psychological characteristic reflected in their very high NK-cell activity. Conversely, those who react with anxiety and depression seem to have poor coping skills, reflected as well in their lowered NK-cell activity.

Psychologist Sandra Levy has reached similar conclusions in her exploratory study of how personality factors are related to NK-cell activity and the spread of cancer to the lymph nodes in women treated for breast cancer. Women who accepted the disease and ad-justed to their condition showed lower NK-cell activity than those who responded with anger and agitation.

Levy argues that acceptance of the cancer and adjustment to the situation may reflect a belief that nothing can be done about the disease, a helpless reaction. In contrast, anger and disturbance may reflect attempts to alter the course of the disease. Thus, beliefs in possible control might have profoundly affected NK-cell activity in these women. When it was high, lymph-node involvement was less likely.

Much of what has been discovered through behavioral immunology still needs to be clarified, verified and more fully explained. Immunology itself is a rapidly developing field, and current understanding of the immune response and ways to measure it is changing daily. We expect the field of behavioral immunology to reveal additional links between behavior and health, yielding more comprehensive approaches to treating illness and new ways to help people maintain good health.   ◆

Discussion Questions

1. What seems to be the relationship between infectious disease and people's reaction to stress?

2. Why don't all people who become infected by a pathogen become sick?

3. What are the two responses to stress that Selye discovered?

4. Give three reasons why people react differently to stress.

5. What is learned helplessness?

6. What is a stressor?

7. Compare the effects of uncontrollable versus controllable stressors on the growth of tumor cells in animals.

8. Would two people experiencing the same amount of stress and with similar immune systems definitely develop the same disease when exposed? Why or why not?

9. Explain at least three psychological factors that seem to lead to impaired immune systems.

10. How do stress, control, depression, coping, and the immune system contribute to the development of disease?

Rx: **Bio***feed*back

◆ *Neal E. Miller*

Imagine trying to learn to shoot basketball foul shots with a blindfold on. Without the visual feedback, you'd never learn to shoot very accurately. Imagine trying to take a coin out of your pocket without sensory information from your fingers telling you what your hand is doing. Without the sensory feedback, you probably couldn't do it. In fact, if you were deprived of the sensations from your hand, you'd probably never use that hand again. Nobel laureate Sir Charles S. Sherrington demonstrated this in 1895 by cutting the sensory nerves that led from an animal's forelimb. The animal never used that limb again, even though the nerves that carried motor impulses to it remained intact.

For years no one even thought of asking whether animals could be trained to resume using such a limb; it was assumed they could not. Then, psychologist Edward Taub and his associates showed in 1969 that simply restraining a monkey's good arm motivates it to use the affected one, and with practice it learns to do even delicate tasks, such as picking up raisins.

Taub's research suggested that patients suffering from brain injury and other forms of nerve damage might have an unsuspected potential for recovery. And that has proved to be the case. Steven Wolf of the Center for Rehabilitation Medicine at the Emory School of Medicine, for example, worked with patients paralyzed on one side. He found that even though they had reached the limits of improvement possible through conventional methods of physical therapy, they could continue to improve if he restrained their good arms and thus encouraged them to learn to use the nonfunctioning arms. One woman who was especially successful explained that the arm restraint helped her realize that her afflicted arm was still capable of performing many of her household chores.

Similarly encouraged by Taub's research, psychologist Bernard Brucker of the University of Miami Medical School worked with a

---

Biofeedback has helped hundreds of patients recover some portion of their lost abilities.

---

man who couldn't walk because a spinal injury had deprived him of all sensory feedback from both of his legs. Brucker taught the man to walk again by providing him with a different type of feedback, using a television monitor and electrodes to individual leg muscles to measure motor signals from the brain to those muscles, signaling them to contract. When the signal gets through to the correct muscle, dots on the TV screen move toward the top of the screen.

This visual information, called biofeedback because it is provided by equipment that measures a biological function, substituted for the missing natural feedback from the leg muscles. The man gradually learned to correctly contract all the leg muscles involved in walking. And once he learned the correct pattern of motor commands, he was able to walk on his own without being attached to the feedback machine.

In addition to biofeedback, the key to this patient's therapy was a process called operant conditioning, instrumental learning or, simply, trial-and-error learning—a flexible technique in which correct responses are rewarded and thereby strengthened, or learned. The reward in this case was seeing the dot move up the TV screen and thus realizing that he was actually controlling a specific muscle. Without the biofeedback, he wouldn't have known that he could move the muscle and probably never would have learned to use it again.

Brucker used similar procedures to treat a young boy who had lost the use of his right hand and arm following brain damage received in a car accident when he was 3 years old. From shortly after the injury until he was 9 years old, the child received continuous and rigorous physical therapy. He made significant gains for the first three years, but after that there was no improvement. His arm, wrist and fingers remained spastic—the muscles were involuntarily and abnormally contracted. Then he was given 10 sessions in biofeedback training during a two-week period. He learned to grasp a glass and lift it to his mouth and to use a fork. Now, he can use his right arm and hand for eating, dressing and other everyday activities.

In addition, John Basmajian of McMaster University in Canada and Joseph Brudny of New York University Medical Hospital have pioneered in the successful treatment of patients suffering from a number of neuro-muscular disorders, ranging from simple nerve and muscle damage to cerebral palsy and paralysis caused by strokes. And recent advances in computer chip and microprocessor technology should lead to better and less expensive devices as well as to new applications, such as the one Barry Dworkin and I recently developed for the treatment of scoliosis, and S-shaped curvature of the spine seen most often in girls, an kyphosis, a forward curvature of the spine.

Scoliosis, which can lead to serious back problems and even to life-threatening complications, is usually treated by one of two methods. In the more severe cases, a steel rod is implanted alongside the spinal column to straighten it by force. If the condition is detected early enough, it often can be treated with a body brace. But for such a brace to be effective, the girl must cooperate with it. It does no good if she just slouches into it and develops thick calluses at pressure points.

Dworkin and I reasoned that these body braces have a behavioral function. That is, by causing discomfort at the pressure points when the wearer is in a bad posture, they motivate her to straighten up. But if calluses thick enough to prevent discomfort develop at the pressure points, they interfere with this reminder.

To obtain a similar behavioral effect, we designed a posture-training device to replace the disfiguring and restraining brace. A nylon fiber sliding through a Teflon tube goes around the vertical axis of the body (see illustration). Straightening the spine, or standing tall, lengthens this harness. But because it can also be lengthened if the wearer takes a deep breath, she wears another harness around the chest that mea-

sures breathing. A small electronic device combines information from both harnesses and indicates when the wearer is standing tall.

Whenever the girl has been in a bad posture for more than 20 sec-

---

Advances in computer chip technology should lead to better devices and new applications.

---

onds, a tone that she can barely hear sounds. If she does not straighten up within 20 seconds, a louder tone sounds. The girl rapidly learns to straighten up and turn off the first tone before the louder one sounds for everyone to hear. As she develops the skill and muscle strength to maintain a better posture, the device is programmed to encourage her to stand even straighter.

This device is not yet commercially available, but it has been proven effective in two studies. Dworkin, our colleagues and I tested it with 12 girls whose curvatures had been increasing to the point where it was probable that they would need braces. During 30 months of treatment, 10 of them were discharged as satisfactorily corrected. Only two needed braces. In another study, Niels Birbaumer and Bernhard Cevey of the University of Tübingen in West Germany worked with 27 patients (19 with scoliosis, 8 with kyphosis) and had similarly encouraging results, especially with kyphosis. They reported that the patients learned the correction response so well that it became almost reflexive.

Biofeedback and instrumental learning can do more than help patients learn to control their skeletal muscles. The same techniques are being used to teach people to control visceral responses, such as those of the heart, blood vessels, gastrointestinal tract and glands, that were once thought to be involuntary and therefore not open to control by in-

strumental learning. It was thought that the autonomic nervous system, which controls these involuntary responses, could be modified only by a simpler form of learning, called classical conditioning—as when Pavlov's dog salivated at the sound of a bell.

Almost 40 years ago, I wondered if this was really the case. I was impressed with the similarities between classical conditioning and instrumental learning and thought they might be basically the same. But people were always saying, "Well, if they are the same, how come you can't control visceral responses with instrumental learning?" I put off the research for years, perhaps because I was afraid I would fail. Then, in the 1960s, as my interests turned more and more to physiological work, I began to use polygraphs and other equipment that enabled me to measure visceral responses and attempt to condition them through instrumental learning.

My main interest at the time was theoretical. I wanted to know in what ways classical and instrumental learning are different or similar and if the autonomic nervous system could be modified by instrumental learning. But I also had a strong interest in the possible clinical applications. A book by the Russian scientist K. M. Bykov, translated in 1957, had shown how many visceral responses could be classically conditioned. I wanted to find out if we could use biofeedback to teach people to control these same responses voluntarily. If so, we could greatly expand the horizons of behavioral medicine.

The research has had its ups and downs. At first, everyone thought it was impossible. But by the late 1960s, after my lab and several others around the country had some successes with animals and humans, more funds and researchers became available. This

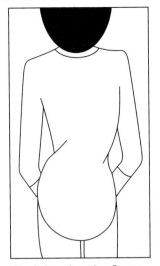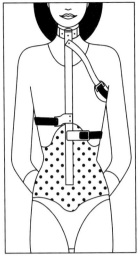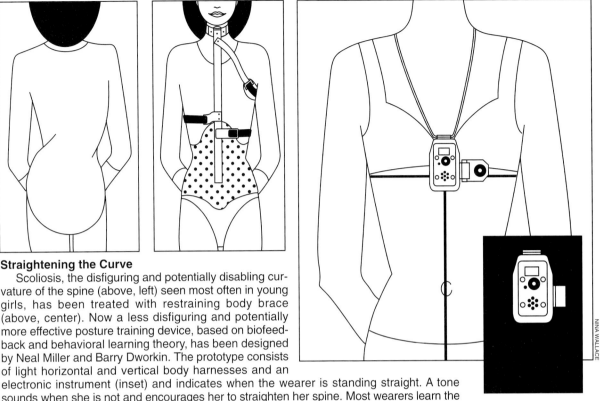

Straightening the Curve
Scoliosis, the disfiguring and potentially disabling curvature of the spine (above, left) seen most often in young girls, has been treated with restraining body brace (above, center). Now a less disfiguring and potentially more effective posture training device, based on biofeedback and behavioral learning theory, has been designed by Neal Miller and Barry Dworkin. The prototype consists of light horizontal and vertical body harnesses and an electronic instrument (inset) and indicates when the wearer is standing straight. A tone sounds when she is not and encourages her to straighten her spine. Most wearers learn the straightening response so well that it becomes almost reflexive and their curvature is gradually corrected.

early success was followed by an initial wave of gross exaggeration and overselling, which led to some skepticism. The field then settled down and we began to make steady progress.

One problem in learning to control visceral responses, such as those responsible for blood pressure, is that most people are unable to detect, unaided, the small changes in responses that take place. Like the blindfolded basketball shooter, they don't get feedback and don't learn to control their responses. But modern measuring equipment can give people moment-to-moment information on many of these small visceral responses and thus remove the blindfold. This is demonstrated in an experiment Brucker and I did with a man whose skeletal muscles were paralyzed from the neck down by damage to his spinal cord.

As a result, whenever the man was helped into a normal sitting position, his blood pressure fell so low that he fainted.

Brucker equipped the man with instruments that measured blood pressure and sounded a tone

> *Biofeedback techniques already available are preventing unnecessary suffering, correcting disabling conditions and helping people regain control of their lives.*

whenever it increased slightly. As the patient learned to increase his blood pressure voluntarily, we raised the level needed to sound the tone. After several weeks of training, he could produce enough of an increase to sit up without fainting. He eventually learned to detect slight changes in blood

pressure and to control it without the measuring equipment.

How did he do it? Since we know that tensing the muscles increases blood pressure, we asked the man to do this as much as possible. Even though he was paralyzed from the neck down, he was able to produce a small (12 millimeters Hg) increase in blood pressure—but only with great difficulty. He showed obvious signs of effort, and measurements revealed high levels of electrical activity in his forehead and neck muscles. When we asked him to raise his blood pressure by the voluntary response learned through biofeedback, he could sit there relaxed, with no signs of muscular activity other than those necessary to balance his head, and increase his blood pressure by more than three times (40 millimeters Hg).

We tested all of the skeletal responses we could think of that he and other patients might have used to produce such large changes and concluded that the changes were not produced indirectly by muscular tension. The patients apparently learned, through biofeedback training, to control their blood pressure directly. Some say they use exciting images at first, but however they started out, most say that eventually they just think about wanting their blood pressure to go up and it does, much as your arm goes up when you want it to.

Unfortunately, we haven't done as well with patients who want to reduce high blood pressure. But through a combination of behavioral procedures, such as training in progressive muscular relaxation, relaxing imagery, deep breathing and various types of biofeedback training, we and others have had moderate success in reducing blood pressure and in lessening dependence on antihypertension drugs. Considering the cost of maintaining a patient on drugs for many years and the known short-term and unknown long-term side effects of these drugs, the further improvement of this and other nondrug techniques for controlling blood pressure is a worthwhile line of research.

Biofeedback, in combination with behavioral treatments, has also been useful in controlling motion and space sickness, migraine and tension headaches, Raynaud's disease (an excessive coldness of the fingers caused by constriction of the blood vessels) and urinary and fecal incontinence. Because incontinence is one of the major reasons people are put in nursing homes, Deputy Surgeon General Faye G. Abdellah estimates that the widespread use of biofeedback techniques to treat incontinence in the institutionalized elderly could save $13 billion a year.

Saving money, of course, is only one measure of the value of biofeedback. When I asked a woman who had been confined to a horizontal position in a hospital for five years what it meant to her to control her blood pressure so that she could sit up, she gave me a beautiful smile and said, "Why, it's opened the door on that bird cage—out into life." The biofeedback and behavioral medicine techniques already available are preventing unnecessary suffering, correcting disabling conditions and helping people regain control of their lives. As better instruments and techniques are devised, they are likely to enhance the remarkable capacity we have to control our bodies.   ◆

Discussion Questions

1. How do natural feedback and biofeedback differ?

2. What possibilities did Taub's research suggest for human patients suffering from brain injury?

3. What other techniques are normally used in conjunction with biofeedback?

4. Explain how biofeedback and operant conditioning have been used in the treatment of scoliosis.

5. Give examples of four abnormal conditions that can be successfully treated with biofeedback and operant conditioning.

6. According to Miller, why is biofeedback advantageous for patients and society?

7. Why, according to Miller, is it important to help people recover without medications or with reduced medication?

8. What is one of the main reasons people are placed in nursing homes? Could biofeedback help some of these people? Why or why not?

9. Describe the different ways that biofeedback has helped in rehabilitation.

A **Sense** of *Control:*

A CONVERSATION WITH

Judith *Rodin*

◆ *Elizabeth Hall*

Elizabeth Hall: You've become the major authority on obesity research among psychologists. What has happened to psychology's view of obesity since you began your research?

Judith Rodin: In the past 10 or 15 years, there's been a dramatic shift in our perception of the causes of obesity. We used to think that psychological causes, such an unhappiness or high responsiveness to external food cues, were primary. Today, we see that obesity, like other behavioral disorders, is really determined by biological factors interacting with psychological and sociocultural factors. Behavior can alter biological factors which, in turn, change our behavior again.

Hall: Your early research, which got a good deal of coverage in the popular press, seemed to indicate that overweight people were compelled to eat by any reminders of food. Put a bowl of potato chips next to them and they were lost.

Rodin: We never meant that, although we were certainly misinterpreted that way. Once, when I was a graduate student, I took the subway the day after *The New York Times* had written up some of my research with Stan Schachter. One woman on the subway turned to another and said, "I'm not fat, I'm external. I can't help it." I'm afraid that we replaced the notion that obese people were being driven by inner forces like unhappiness with the belief that they were compelled to

eat by something in the environment. Actually, we only presented means and statistical probabilities: Confronted with a bowl of potato chips, overweight people, on the average, were more likely to eat them than were normal-weight people. But there were many heavy people who did not show this tendency.

Hall: Are people who are extra-responsive to food cues in the environment extra-responsive in other ways as well?

Rodin: That's been a controversial area of research, so let me put it this way: I've found that many people are externally responsive to food cues. When they are, they are also more responsive to other cues in the environment: They respond more quickly to complex stimuli, have better immediate recall and are more easily distracted by irrelevant stimuli. The tendency toward external responsiveness seems to play a significant role in

---

Women today feel too fat, even if they're five pounds underweight.

---

the development of obesity, although not all people with these characteristics are overweight.

Joyce Slochower and I studied children with no history of being overweight who were attending summer camp. With lots of food around, the kids were regulating their own eating for the first time. The most externally responsive

kids gained the most weight, but some of them began losing at the end of the summer. That's when I first began to understand about biological factors. Although external responsiveness was pushing the kids to overeat, something metabolic or biochemical was holding some of them back.

Hall: It wasn't a matter of saying, "Oh, my shorts are getting tight"?

Rodin: No, we assessed that. It was not conscious restraint. But many people who feel motivated to respond to external cues do consciously restrain themselves, battling to keep environmental food cues from overwhelming their eating habits. And for some, the psychic and biologic costs of all that restraint are quite considerable.

Hall: Don't you think that a majority of women in this country operate under that kind of conscious restraint all the time?

Rodin: Yes, I do, and I have a lot of data to support it. I believe that by virtue of being a woman in this day, you feel too fat, even if you're five pounds underweight. The current body ideal is ridiculously slim, and almost all women aspire to it. It's unfortunate, because women are genetically programmed to be fatter than men, to lay down more fat cells and to store more fat. When you put that genetic program in the context of the pressures on women to be thin, it's not surprising that there's so much erratic eating behavior among women today.

Hall: How do you reconcile the thin body ideal with changes in women's roles and the rejection of woman as sex object?

Rodin: The thin body ideal may have become another competitive area. Some of our research indicates that women who have a high need to be successful also have a great need to control their weight. Other researchers have found that nontraditional women may associate the more ample female body with a wife and mother role.

Hall: Does that account for why so many adolescents are bulimic, going on regular eating binges followed by vomiting or taking laxatives?

Rodin: We don't have data on adolescents, but it's been estimated that from 35 to 60 percent of college women are binge eaters. Psychologists used to think that bulimic women were mentally ill, but nearly all women share their fear of being fat, and most adolescents of normal weight firmly believe that they are fat. You might say that bulimia reflects pathology in society. Bulimic women seem to have carried the typical female reaction to a pathological extreme.

Hall: Is dieting during adolescence particularly harmful?

Rodin: Some of us fear it may destroy the normal processes of weight regulation. Every time you go on a diet, your metabolism slows down as the body tries to protect itself against the loss of fat stores. And when you go off the diet, your metabolism doesn't immediately return to normal, so you gain weight and go on another diet, setting up a vicious cycle. The adolescent girl's metabolism rate is not yet set for adulthood, and the dieting cycle may set it at a lower rate than it would otherwise have been.

Hall: Despite all the pressure on us to stay thin, this is a food-abundant culture. How does anybody escape obesity?

Rodin: One way is by being blessed with very good genes. The genetic contribution to obesity, though not fully understood, is very strong, much stronger than society allows overweight people to believe. Genes may make metabolism more efficient, or increase the number of fat cells or stimulate fat cells to deposit more fat.

The second way to escape obesity is through exercise. No matter what your genetic predisposition, aerobic exercise helps increase your metabolic rate. You might say that

---

Today, we see that obesity, like other behavioral disorders, is really determined by biological factors interacting with psychological and sociocultural factors.

---

overweight people have a metabolism that is simply too efficient.

The third way to escape obesity is by being born male. This cuts through the rest: Men are more likely to exercise, less likely to be genetically predisposed toward fat storage, and they seem to have higher metabolism rates.

Hall: You've made it clear that physiology is important in the development of obesity. How does being fat keep people fat?

Rodin: There are multiple ways: First, your fat tissue changes. With overeating, you can increase the size of your fat cells, so you store more fat. When the cells can't store any more, you can increase the number of fat cells. Unfortunately, the animal data indicate that this can go on forever. It's a one-way street. Filling your existing fat cells to capacity at any time in life can lead to an increase in fat cells, but undereating never reduces their number, it only shrinks them.

Hall: Does losing weight and having all these empty extra fat cells make it easier to put back the fat?

Rodin: The empty fat cells may be hollering, "Feed me, feed me!" But we don't know whether they are truly refilled more easily or whether some other aspect of the body has been altered during the period of obesity. Maybe a body with a lot of empty fat cells finds it easier to store weight than when

---

To escape obesity: have good genes, do aerobic exercise and be born male.

---

fewer cells are pushed to hold more fat.

Hall: Must a person who has lost weight always eat less than one who's never been overweight?

Rodin: I wish we knew the answer. We think that if you do aerobic exercise on a regular basis, probably not. But if you don't, you must watch closely what you eat, at least for the first five years. By that time, your metabolism may have shifted and your new body may have adapted to the new weight level, becoming more permissive. But no one can be certain about this because we don't have good long-term studies with people who have been able to keep weight off. My guess is that there are as many successful strategies for keeping weight off as there are people who have been successful.

Hall: Some of your studies have shown that the sight or smell of food can send insulin levels up. Does this happen to everyone?

Rodin: No, but it's not a function of weight. Our research shows that externally responsive people, obese or not, are more likely to show this response. In fact, there's a whole cascade of responses to the sight and smell of food: changes in salivation, gastric secretions, free fatty acid levels, insulin and so on. And externally responsive people may have higher levels of all of these responses. In general, such responses prepare all of us to digest and metabolize food efficiently. The problem is that, with conditioning, these digestive responses become associated with increased hunger, making people with the largest insulin surges tend to eat more than others.

Let's take the insulin response as an example. Increased insulin levels in response to seeing food make people feel hungry, and they are likely to eat more than people who do not oversecrete insulin when looking at food. Those higher insulin levels also have a significant effect on metabolism. If two people eat exactly the same amount of food, the one with the higher insulin levels stores more of that food as fat. So that person is doubly damned: He's hungrier so he eats more; and even if he eats the same amount, he's more likely to store it as fat.

Hall: Will these people also secrete insulin if they just think about food?

Rodin: Yes. Now think of all the food ads on TV and all the fast-food restaurants along the highway. If our internal imagery also stimulates us to think of food, we have a real problem.

Hall: How does what we eat affect our insulin levels?

Rodin: When we eat complex carbohydrates—cereals, breads, pasta—insulin levels rise and fall off gradually. But when we eat simple sugars—sugar, candy, pastries—insulin levels rise quickly and drop sharply, although it varies depending on the particular food. Glucose levels in the blood are also affected differentially. The net result is that we are more likely to eat again an hour or two after eating simple sugars than after eating complex carbohydrates. And the kind of food we eat at one meal also affects what and how much we eat at the next. A number of hormones are responsive to the content of a meal. They thus affect hunger, perceived pleasantness of food and the amount of food that's consumed later.

Hall: So eating a doughnut or a piece of pie at one meal not only provides the wrong kind of calo-

ries, but sets one up for trouble at the next meal.

Rodin: Correct. People used to argue against the doughnut because it was "empty calories." That's still true, nutritionally, but what I'm now saying is that even if you control for calories, the doughnut is going to have a worse effect on the next meal than will some low-sugar food.

Hall: Then I can have pasta but not pie.

Rodin: Yes. Complex carbohydrates are really all right. Bread, pasta and such things are actually fairly nutritious as well as bulky and satisfying.

Hall: Then if I can't have candy or a doughnut, what about diet snacks?

Rodin: It could be a problem if you have them alone, without any other nutritious food. Our studies have found that artificial sweeteners—at least saccharin, which we studied—boost insulin secretion and don't provide enough calories to satisfy, leaving the system turned on. So the person who has

We said, maybe memory declines because people cease to use it as they grow older.

We believe that by providing choices we changed people's sense of being able to alter their environment. That's a profound psychological state.

just had a saccharin-sweetened snack at two o'clock is more likely to want a piece of cake at four o'-clock.

Hall: What if I use an artificial sweetener as part of a meal, say, on a bowl of oatmeal?

Rodin: That's OK, It's only bad when you are using it as a complete substitute for calories, when you stimulate without satisfying.

Hall: We've been talking primarily about people who are already fat.

Let's consider how we get that way. You and William Kessen have been studying the development of obesity by following children from birth. How old are your subjects now?

Rodin: Between 3 and 5 years old. We're comparing children who had two overweight parents to those with normal-weight parents, so we think we have both ends of the scale. We've found three separate predictors, any one of which makes a baby more likely to be an obese preschooler: family obesity; hyper-responsiveness to visual stimuli on the first day of birth; and hyper-responsiveness to sweet tastes on the first day of birth. Whether a child is fed by bottle or breast, on demand or on a schedule seems to have no effect on later weight.

Hall: Then are some people born to be fat?

Rodin: I think that the genetic contribution interacts with a variety of environmental factors. Certainly early learning experiences, such as a mother's anxiety over her child's eating, figure importantly in the development of obesity.

Hall: Media reports emphasize your obesity research, but you've also done important work in the field of aging. What got you started on that line of research?

Rodin: That was about 10 years ago, when the field of aging was heavily influenced by the medical model, and researchers were attributing too much influence to biological factors that made a decline with age inevitable. As a social psychologist, I was interested in understanding how environmental factors affect older people. It seemed to me that during the later years, the environment is so drastically altered that people must feel restricted, and that might influence their sense of control.

Hall: The changes are certainly enormous: retirement, death of friends and family, altered lifestyle and real changes in physical abilities.

Rodin: Laboratory studies had already shown us that how much choice people perceive they have over important things in their lives influences their happiness, their ability to perform and their sense of well-being. Aging seemed to be the essence of that situation. Psychologist Ellen Langer and I chose to study the effects of perceived choice in a nursing home, where showing improvement in people who were already ill would be much more dramatic than keeping people from becoming sick in the first place.

Hall: I was struck by the huge impact you got with such seemingly trivial environmental changes as allowing them to choose when to see a movie or how to arrange their room. Yet their health and psychological well-being improved, and the death rate dropped.

Rodin: The changes seem trivial to people with a broad range of choices. But against the background of no choice at all, having any choice is dramatic. We believe that by providing choices we changed people's sense of being able to alter their environment. That's a profound psychological state. The residents had a greater sense of efficacy, so they responded to others differently, and that enabled their families and nurses to respond to them more positively. That dynamic process reverberated in all areas of their lives. But in some ways, we found that study less striking than our research with memory.

Hall: The controversy over the inevitability of memory decline with age is still raging on. Some researchers find it and others don't.

Rodin: Langer and I ignored the controversy. We said, "Maybe memory declines because people

cease to use it as they grow older." At retirement, the environment starts to contract, demands shrink

---

Those who had been taught coping strategies had much lower levels of the stress hormone cortisol, even during the follow-up period.

---

and the need to remember things also lessens. So biological loss is exacerbated by an unstimulating environment.

Hall: Just as the younger person who doesn't use a learned foreign language finds that it's slipped away.

Rodin: But if he or she goes to the foreign country, it quickly comes back. That's exactly the conceptual model we used. Thinking that if we could restimulate older people their memories might improve, we gave them a reason to remember, such as rewarding them with poker chips they could exchange for gifts. When we did this, we found clear improvement on standard tests of memory. Environmental factors appear to have important effects on memory, and they are much easier to change than biological factors.

To get another picture of how environment and biology interact, our group here at Yale worked with two major hospitals in the New Haven area, studying everyone older than 62 who entered the hospital.

We have to find ways to keep people from blaming themselves for failures.

We selected at random from a group scheduled to enter a nursing home on discharge and gave half of them an opportunity to participate in the decision. Initially, both groups had similar health status. After one year, those in the group given some control over the decision to enter a nursing home were healthier, and fewer had died than in the group given no choice.

Hall: You've also found an interaction between the way people think about problems and their physical health. Just how does that come about?

Rodin: Our other studies gave us the sense that as the number and variety of their coping resources increase, people have a greater sense of control. So we tried to enhance older people's sense of control by teaching them new and more diverse coping strategies. We taught them positive ways to think about themselves. By "positive," I mean both setting a goal and articulating a strategy for obtaining it. For example, if I feel dreadful because my daughter failed to pay me a promised visit at two o'clock, I can phone her, say I really need to see her today and ask her to come at five o'-clock. The action makes me feel in control, which makes me feel better, and it includes a way to attain my goal. We found that coping-skills training did increase the sense of control in these older adults. Another group given just as much sympathetic attention but no explicit skills training didn't show the same improvement.

A wonderful thing happened while we were running that study. A local newspaper story reported that the government paid $10 a month more to old people in Massachusetts nursing homes than in Connecticut nursing homes. Three of the people in our intervention group bused to Hartford to petition the legislature for changes. What a great demonstration that these people felt a sense of control over their environment. Subjects in the intervention group also felt less stress than the controls. They perceived themselves as having fewer problems and felt better able to cope with the problems they did have.

But the most impressive finding was biological: Those who had been taught coping strategies had much lower levels of the stress hormone cortisol, even during the follow-up period. And their health was better, too. They developed fewer illnesses, and their chronic conditions were less likely to worsen.

Hall: Animal studies by Martin Seligman and by Steven Maier have suggested that lack of control affects the immune system adversely and might affect health. Is that also true for people?

Rodin: We think so, although human studies are obviously harder to do. John Dwyer and I are now studying several hundred elderly people in the community, looking at the relationship between stress, control and immune function. It will require three leaps to demonstrate a relationship: One, does stress really alter the immune system? Two, does control mediate the impact of stress on the immune system? And three, if the answer to both those questions is yes, does the interaction affect the outcome of disease?

Our preliminary data suggest that feelings of unpredictability and lack of control concerning some highly stressful life events are related to diminished efficiency in the immune system. There are fewer of the white blood cells called "helper T cells" available to amplify the responses of the cells that attack foreign substances. In

---

Our preliminary data suggest that feelings of unpredictability and lack of control concerning some highly stressful life events are related to diminished efficiency in the immune system.

---

addition, there are more "suppressor T cells," white blood cells that seem to have the opposite effect, reducing those responses.

We are following these people to see what diseases develop in those whose immune systems show this suppression and how their health compares with other people in the study. We hope to understand which events, mediated by which experiences, lead to what kinds of biological effects and, ultimately, to what kinds of diseases.

Hall: The apparent effect of control on health and cognition leads to another question: Does the sense of perceived control help a person to diet?

Rodin: Yes. In fact, I've used our nursing-home studies as an example for the treatment of obesity. They show how altering people's sense of control and giving them greater coping skills can affect behavior, health, motivation and the sense that "I can do it." Too often, diets are simply prescribed for people, with no room for choice.

Hall: And if they're given a magic little pill to substitute for control, they won't feel that they were responsible for any weight loss.

Rodin: That's right. Instead, let's figure out ways to increase internal psychological self-regulation.

Today there's a tremendous move toward self-regulation as a therapeutic strategy for weight control. I have only one concern, though, and it applies to both aging and obesity: In emphasizing how much events can be controlled, we may be leading people to feel that their failures are entirely their fault. We don't want to create such a profound sense of blame and guilt. We would like to intervene but acknowledge that not everyone is going to succeed. We have to find ways to keep people from blaming themselves for failures. That's difficult, but we're optimistic. ◆

Discussion Questions

1. How, according to Rodin, have psychologists' views on obesity changed in recent years?

2. Are people who are extra-responsive to food cues also extra-responsive in other ways? Explain.

3. How does societal pressure on women to be slim run counter to natural biological tendencies?

4. What percent of college women are binge eaters?

5. Describe three ways to escape obesity.

6. Why is it important for people to feel that they have a sense of control?

7. What effect would giving nursing home residents more choices have on them?

8. What effect does positive reinforcement have on older people's ability to remember?

9. What effect does a choice of diet have on older people?

10. Why is it important to teach people coping skills? Give at least three reasons.

11. What is the relationship between coping strategies and cortisol?

Name: _____

Date: _____

Part 15: Health, Stress and Self-Change

1. I have all the skills I need to cope with stressors in my life.

Agree	①	②	③	④	⑤	Disagree

2. I believe I can use willpower to change myself whenever necessary.

Agree	①	②	③	④	⑤	Disagree

3. I frequently make changes in my environment in order to change my future behavior.

Agree	①	②	③	④	⑤	Disagree

List the major stressors in your life.

Explain how you might be able to cope better with each stressor in the future.

How might you eliminate or reduce the severity of some of these stressors?

List major life events that you believe might cause you stress in the future (e.g., your wedding, the death of a loved one, job failure, or relationship problems). How might you prepare for such events to reduce their negative impact?

PART 16

PSYCHOLOGICAL DISORDERS

Serious depression is characterized by appetite changes, erratic sleep, low energy, and feelings of hopelessness, and it affects more than 17 million Americans each year, some of whom choose to end their lives rather than live with their sadness. Although especially common among women, depression is probably more dangerous in men, because men often turn to alcohol or suicide rather than seek treatment. In "College Blues," a classic article by a pioneer in the treatment of depression, Aaron T. Beck, and his colleague Jeffrey E. Young, you'll learn why depression is so common among college students, along with a variety of ways for beating the college blues.

In "What I Learned from A.D.D.," psychiatrist Edward M. Hallowell, reviews the latest evidence for the existence of and possible biological basis of attention deficit disorder, which, alas, has lately become the symbol of modern times. Although a true believer, even Hallowell admits that the A.D.D. craze has gotten out of hand with media estimates that 25 percent of the population suffers from this disorder (Hallowell says the real figure is probably 5 percent) and with people using A.D.D. to excuse their every failing. Is A.D.D. a robust diagnostic category? Personally, I'm not convinced.

There are very few robust diagnostic categories in the mental health field. The reason for this is explained in the last article in section, a classic piece by Theodore R. Sarbin called "Schizophrenia is a Myth, Born of Metaphor, Meaningless." As Sarbin explains, "diagnoses" of mental "illness" have long been inspired by the "disease model" of mental "illness." It's difficult, as you can see, even to talk about impairments of mood or behavior without using medical terms; that's how entrenched this model has become. But schizophrenia, A.D.D., depression, autism, and other psychological "disorders" (another medical term) are not diseases in the medical sense; they are not produced by specific microorganisms, they cannot be prevented by vaccines, and they cannot be "cured" by the immune system or the right drug. It's true, of course, that psychological impairments have some basis in the brain, but so does *all* behavior and emotion. If someone is highly distractible, the brain is undoubtedly in a special state, but that doesn't mean that distractibility is a disease or in any way analogous to a disease. Nor does it mean that someone should be medicated.

The critical mistake we make in mental "health" is in attaching labels to certain patterns of abnormal mood and behavior and then thinking that these labels have explanatory value. But as Isaac Newton warned centuries ago, a description or property of some phenomenon (such as the viscosity of a liquid) cannot be used to *explain* that phenomenon (as in, "The liquid is moving slowly *because* it is viscous"). Schizophrenia is a crude label for a wide variety of disparate behaviors and affective states, and so is A.D.D. The use of such labels creates the false impression that we understand more about these impairments than we do, and, in some cases, the labels probably keep us from developing effective treatments.

College *Blues*

◆ *Aaron T. Beck and Jeffrey E. Young*

Over the next nine months, as many as 78 percent of the 7,500,800 students enrolled in American colleges may suffer some symptoms of depression—roughly a quarter of the student population at any one time. These figures come from recent studies, such as the one conducted by Joan Oliver, Leo Croghan, and Norman Katz at four unnamed universities, and are echoed by our clinical experience. We cannot be sure how they relate to the depression rate for the population as a whole, because funds have been lacking for definitive studies. Those estimates that do exist are based on very limited samples that are not representative of the entire country. But the incidence of student depression seems quite high; with depression the leading psychiatric disorder on our college campuses.

Triggered by traditional student pressures—including failure to meet personal academic standards, the need to define goals for life and career, and the lack of support systems to fend off loneliness—the depression will be mild or subclinical for about a third of the students who get the campus blues. But for 46 percent of them, however, the depression will be intense enough to warrant professional help. Campus depression will play a role in as many as 500 suicides, which are 50 percent more frequent among college students than among nonstudents of the same age.

Despite the amount of depression around them, however, depressed students often perceive themselves to be alone. One result is that they often have trouble evaluating the seriousness of their problems and whether or not they should consult a psychiatrist or psychologist.

In our work for the past six years at the Mood Clinic of the University of Pennsylvania Hospital's Center for Cognitive Therapy—and in 20 years of previous research—we have found that it is

---

The incidence of student depression seems quite high, with depression the leading psychiatric disorder on our college campuses.

---

often difficult for students to distinguish, for example, between a temporary feeling of sadness and full-blown clinical depression. Frequently, they decide not to seek professional help, which is one reason that statistics on depression in both the college population and the general population are thin.

The confusion is understandable. A student who is just "low" and one who is clinically depressed might both describe themselves as blue, unhappy, empty, sad, and lonely. Both may have difficulty falling asleep at night, feel fatigued, or lose their appetites. The difference between

them lies in the number, intensity, and duration of their symptoms: while merely in a sad mood, for example, an individual may have to exert extra effort to get started at something, while depressed patients often cannot work at all, even when others prod them.

For those students who do decide to approach mental-health clinics for help, the senior author has developed the Beck Depression Inventory to help diagnose their level of depression. Students are asked to fill out a 21-item survey—now used at several clinics and colleges around the country—choosing from among four statements in each category to describe the intensity of their condition (see box, "A Stepladder of Depression," this article). The results then indicate to both therapist and student just how debilitating the student's symptoms are.

The basis of our treatment for depression is an application to students of cognitive therapy. It grows from our finding that students' misperceptions of the world, of the stresses that surround them, may be as important a cause of depression as the stresses are.

Students do not hallucinate their problems—they cope with the real stresses of academic and social adjustment—but they inflate the importance of temporary setbacks and misjudge the severity of rejections; in short, they misperceive their problems. Students who grieve over their lack of friends, for example, may have real problems in social adjustment, yet they usually turn out to have at least some caring and supportive friends. They may also severely overestimate academic difficulties—on the basis of one mediocre grade.

Not all students suffer from mere misperception, of course; their distortions of reality may mask other problems, such as a deep fear of new situations. As we apply cognitive therapy to college students, correcting the errors in thinking and social behavior of those who are lonely and depressed, such phobias, once uncovered, can reveal themselves in treatment.

Stress and Transition

College students may be especially prone to psychological problems because they encounter so many new situations that potentially can be misperceived. They experience simultaneously all the transitions that are major stresses in adulthood: all at once, they lose family, friends and familiar surroundings, with college supplying no ready-made substitutes. They lose their high school "job"—simple student status—and must substitute a career choice with long-term consequences. Going to college may even mean a shift in social or class status. These pressures war with each other for students' time and attention; and, if their competing goals are not balanced successfully, the students are likely to feel deprived.

Students who cannot make career decisions, for example, may feel they are working hard, but to no purpose; those who allot too much time to studying may feel that their future is assured at the price of getting no pleasure from their present lives; students who engage in many extracurricular activities but have not developed an intimate relationship may feel the lack of someone they can confide in. Students who concentrate on one goal to the exclusion of other people and other pursuits may find that they are left without necessary support systems in the event of disillusionment.

Carl's problems were typical of those growing primarily out of academic pressures. He was a 17-year-old freshman at an Ivy League university several hours away from his hometown. He had been a popular student in high school—a member of the student council and the tennis team—and had a close circle of friends. He had also worked hard and obtained high grades. Carl knew he wanted to become a doctor, and wanted to guarantee his admission to medical school as soon as possible.

Carl decided before starting college that if he was going to compete successfully, he would have to devote all his time to studying. By the end of his first week at college, he was spending virtually every waking hour at classes, in the library, or shut in his room alone. Carl knew many of the other students in his dormitory by name, but felt that he could not

---

Students experience simultaneously all the transitions that are major stresses in adulthood.

---

spare too much time for socializing because he might lose his "competitive edge." He decided not to continue with his tennis because he simply could not spare the time required for team practice every afternoon.

When Carl received a C on his chemistry midterm exam, he felt his world crumbling. He believed that he had lost any chance for admission to medical school and that, to make matters worse, nobody else really cared what happened to him. Carl soon developed a severe depression.

Many students like Carl enter college with a past record of successes both academic and social. Although they recognize, rationally, that the selective college-admissions process may throw them together with others from the top 10 or 20 percent of high school students, nonetheless, they still expect

to excel. Never having learned to cope with failure, they attach inordinate importance to each disappointing grade, letting it blot out the memory of other successes. They may come to think they have overestimated their academic potential and will never measure up.

The dissatisfaction and self-reproach may lead to clinical depression that will begin to interfere with their actual performance, creating a vicious spiral: as students misinterpret their academic difficulties as evidence of intellectual deficiencies rather than emotional stress, they become still less able to do well academically, and get still sadder and less motivated.

Students, of course, have worried about grades forever—or at least since college ceased to be the province of Fitzgerald's prep-school princes with their "Gentleman's Cs." But as competition for admission to graduate and professional schools becomes more intense, it becomes more and more likely that mediocre grades *can*, in fact, spell the difference between success and failure; these lapses can break the carefully planned chain that in theory, at least, leads a student from college to professional school to career.

Intensifying this tightrope pressure still further is what we call "obligated success": students on scholarships, for example, may feel an extra obligation to do well in order to justify their special treatment. As college costs increasingly pinch middle-class families, more and more students feel the pressure of obligated success because of their parents' financial sacrifice. This feeling of responsibility to the family—to live out the parents' ambitions or live up to their expectations—may hit especially hard if a student is away from home and family for the first time.

Some students caught in the cycle of "failure" and self-torment decide to leave school, feeling that they are simply "not cut out for college." A study of dropouts by David Luecke and James McClure at Washington University showed that one-third had suffered serious depression just before leaving school, and a majority had not sought out professional help.

Similarly, a recent study at University of Pennsylvania Law School conducted by vice-dean Phyllis Beck and psychiatrist David Burns found that a high proportion of law students who consulted the administration about dropping out of school were also suffering from depression or anxiety.

Here, however, dropping out was dramatically reduced by a system for identifying and treating depression. Students who complained that they did not have the intellectual "equipment," had lost their interest in law, or had made some terrible mistake in choosing law as a profession were helped through guidance and psychotherapy to recognize and vanquish their underlying depression, and could then acknowledge that they did, in fact, have the interest and qualifications to continue in school.

Out of the Nest

Other stressful collegiate situations are primarily social. Jill was the youngest child in a large family, and was always pampered as "the baby." Her older brothers and sisters lavished attention on her. Although everyone else in the family had household responsibilities, Jill was encouraged to "just enjoy herself." When she had problems, she would turn to someone else in the family for help and reassurance. In junior high school, Jill found a circle of older girl friends who "adopted" her, tutored her in her academic work, and told her how to act with boys. During three years of high school, Jill came to depend on Mark, her boyfriend,

for praise and affection. When she entered college and left him and her family, she was fearful about what would happen to her.

Jill soon felt overwhelmed by college. Unable to manage her

time, she began to fall behind in her course work. Nor was she making friends. She waited for other students to come over and introduce themselves, but they all seemed too busy. After a month,

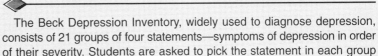

A Stepladder of Depression

The Beck Depression Inventory, widely used to diagnose depression, consists of 21 groups of four statements—symptoms of depression in order of their severity. Students are asked to pick the statement in each group that best describes the way they have been feeling over the previous week. Their answers provide a profile of symptoms. Some sample items:

1. I am not particularly discouraged about the future.
   I feel discouraged about the future.
   I feel I have nothing to look forward to.
   I feel the future is hopeless and that things cannot improve.

2. I do not feel like a failure.
   I feel I have failed more than the average person.
   As I look back on my life, all I can see are a lot of failures.
   I feel I am a complete failure as a person.

3. I don't feel I am any worse than anybody else.
   I am critical of myself for my weaknesses and mistakes.
   I blame myself all the time for my faults.
   I blame myself for everything bad that happens.

4. I don't cry any more than usual.
   I cry more now than I used to.
   I cry all the time now.
   I used to be able to cry, but now I can't cry even though I want to.

5. I am no more irritated now than I ever am.
   I get annoyed or irritated more easily than I used to.
   I feel irritated all the time now.
   I don't get irritated at all by the things that used to irritate me.

6. I can work about as well as before.
   It takes an extra effort to get started at doing something.
   I have to push myself very hard to do anything.
   I can't do any work at all.

7. I can sleep as well as usual.
   I don't sleep as well as I used to.
   I wake up one or two hours earlier than usual and find it hard to get back to sleep.
   I wake up several hours earlier than I used to and cannot get back to sleep.

8. I do not feel sad.
   I feel sad.
   I am sad all the time and I can't snap out of it.
   I am so sad or unhappy I can't stand it.

© 1998 PhotoDisc, Inc.

cases, we have found that the underlying problem was a lifelong fear of going into new environments. In high school, these students generally were able to compensate for their phobia (which therefore went unrecognized) by having a friend along at all times. Deprived of these social supports after entering college, such students would tend to avoid classes and social events. As they progressively withdrew, and fell further behind in their schoolwork, they were deprived of the types of satisfactions to which they had been accustomed, and fell into the cycle of depression.

Jill's underlying social fears were set off by one of the most common triggers for depression: the breakup of an intimate relationship. Here again, misperceptions made the problems worse. College students often do not know how to adjust to a lover's rejection. Deprived of intimacy, companionship, and support, students magnify the long-term importance of the loss. Instead of thinking realistically, "I'm going to miss him, but I'll get over it," they think, "No one cares what happens to me and no one ever will." The distorted interpretation of rejection is often responsible for excruciating feelings of loneliness, which are often the first link in a chain leading to clinical depression.

Dynamics of Loneliness

Loneliness is a major cause of depression, but it can also be a problem on its own or in combination with other emotional states. Loneliness arises from the perceived absence of a desired relationship; and although some forms of relationships can compensate for the lack of others, relationships are certainly not interchangeable. Through a recent study of students at the University of Pennsylvania, the junior author pinpointed several distinct forms of loneliness,

she met Ron. They became very close, and she once again felt secure. But later, when he broke off with her, Jill became depressed. Feeling that she could no longer cope with all the problems in her life, she would sit alone most of the day and cry.

Jill's case demonstrates how students can be devastated by the loss of social support systems. Many high school students have a circle of friends to "party" with; a good friend to confide in; a parent to turn to in times of crisis; and an intimate boyfriend or girlfriend to love. When they enter college, these supports are gone and freshmen have to develop new relationships as substitutes. This may take months or even years, and during the process,

students almost inevitably experience loneliness.

The process of transition was especially difficult for Jill, who had moved from an environment in which other people took care of her to one in which she had to function independently. Unfortunately, like many college freshmen, Jill had never learned to be self-sufficient. Accustomed to having others initiate relationships, Jill had never had to seek out friends. But in college, her passivity left her isolated.

We have seen a number of students who, like Jill, have been popular in the precollege years and who "suddenly" develop fears of going to classes, attending social functions, and making new acquaintances. In most of these each reflecting a particular kind of relationship. Using the Young Loneliness Inventory (modeled on the Beck Depression Inventory), we have identified four types of loneliness:

1. *Exclusion* reflects the belief that one is not part of a group of people to which one would like to belong. This is the feeling students report at a large party when everyone else seems to be having a good time and they feel left out, or the feeling of wanting to belong to a particular dorm clique but not being accepted by its members.

2. *Feeling unloved* may be the most painful form of loneliness, perhaps because the feeling of being loved provides us with a basic sense of security and stability. Students beginning college often miss parents or intimate boyfriends or girlfriends who, in high school, cared about their welfare and could be depended upon during periods of crisis. Naturally, they turn to new relationships, but problems can develop if they rely too heavily on the new relationships to validate their self-worth. Donald, a 22-year-old college junior who visited the Mood Clinic, started out by telling us, "I have never done anything right. I have always let everybody down." He had started to feel depressed, lonely, and suicidal, he said, when his year-long relationship with his girlfriend became punctuated by quarrels.

His opinion of himself had been based on the notion that he had to achieve a degree of academic success in order to be regarded as worthwhile. Both his parents were successful scientists and, although they did not directly set high standards for him, he felt that they expected a great deal of him and could not accept his academic shortcomings. As long as Elaine loved him, he said, "it meant that she loved me for myself. I didn't have to be any-

thing." He could feel totally accepted, regardless of how well he performed. When he and Elaine quarreled, his tendency to evaluate himself harshly became greatly intensified; their relationship could no longer protect him against his savage self-criticisms.

3. *Constriction* is the feeling that one's thoughts and feelings are bottled up inside. Depressed students often report that there is no one they can talk to about their private concerns. Our experience dovetails with a study at Boston University, which found that students who had attempted suicide were much more likely to feel that they did not have confidantes than did students who had suicidal thoughts but had not made an actual attempt. This study used only women, but constriction loneliness may be more of a problem among men. A survey at UCLA demonstrated that students of either sex were generally intolerant of male students' expressing depression, yet showed sympathy for women who expressed the same feelings. This may explain why women seeking help at student mental-health clinics outnumber men two to one. Male students may be

Students beginning college often miss parents or intimate boyfriends or girlfriends who, in high school, cared about their welfare and could be depended upon during periods of crisis.

Transiently lonely people can see later that most of their friendships were actually satisfactory all along.

more reluctant to either acknowledge their depression or talk to others about it because of a fear of social intolerance and disparagement that appears to be realistic.

4. *Alienation* is a form of loneliness in which one feels that he or she is completely different from other people. Some college students who feel they do not share the values and interests of their peers experience pervasive loneliness. A black high school student who grew up in the inner city and enters a college with primarily white, upper-middle-class students, for example, is likely to feel left out. Unless he finds other students "like him," he may come to feel increasingly depressed and isolated. We have seen the same alienation among female students at formerly all-male institutions that have gone coed. Another variation afflicts students who are either dramatically more conservative or more liberal than other students they know. Many college students from conservative backgrounds felt severe alienation during the late 1960s, at a time when many of their fellow students were involved in political protest.

Diagnosing Loneliness

These four types of loneliness can affect students with varying frequency, intensity, and duration. These dimensions of students' symptom levels help us in turn to distinguish chronically lonely, situationally lonely, and transiently lonely students.

Chronic loneliness evolves when an individual is not able to establish satisfactory interpersonal relationships over a period of years. These students, like Jill, may have a phobia about initiating relationships with other people or they may be unable to sustain friendships at a deep level of intimacy for a long-enough period of time. Some of the chronically lonely come to us feeling bitter about people in general and express beliefs like "You can't trust other people" or "People only care about themselves." Their beliefs then sustain their pattern of social isolation.

A second category consists of students who are lonely because of changes in their life situations. More college freshmen initially fall into this category as they try to develop new social contacts to replace the old. Situational loneliness may also involve more serious changes, such as the death of a parent. In this case, a brief period of grieving and depression can be considered normal as the individual learns to accept the loss of a lifelong attachment.

Transient loneliness is probably the most common of the three diagnostic categories and refers to the everyday, garden variety of loneliness, the periodic passing mood that usually disappears as soon as someone comes to talk with us.

Students often fall into this kind of loneliness when they exaggerate the importance of a minor event (such as a quarrel with a friend) and take it as a sign that all of their relationships are deficient; in fact, transiently lonely people can see a day or two later that most of their friendships were actually satisfactory all along.

The process of exaggerating the importance of unpleasant events is called "cognitive distortion." A study we completed last year at the University of Pennsylvania illustrates how these distortions can work to increase loneliness. One hundred and three freshmen and sophomores completed questionnaires: one-third were instructed to answer the questions when they felt happy, one-third when they were sad, and one-third when they were lonely.

Students in sad and lonely moods painted a distinctly more desolate picture of their relationships than did students who were feeling good. They were more likely to report that they had no one to depend on and no one who really cared about them or loved them at school. Lonely students stated more often that there was a group of people who did not like them as much as they would have wanted. They were also more likely to question whether anyone understood them, describing themselves as outsiders who bottled up their feelings. Furthermore, lonely students were more likely to attribute these problems to personal inadequacies and to feel disappointed in themselves. Overall, these students were more pessimistic about the future and less content with their lives.

But the lonely students' feeling that they were living isolated lives, devoid of relationships, was a distortion of reality. Although the lonely students generally agreed with the statement that "there's no one here at school I can really depend on," when asked to list and rate *specific* friends, students who were in lonely moods listed the same number of close friends as did the happy students. Moreover, they were just as likely as the happy group to report that the close friends they listed really cared about them.

Treating Depression and Loneliness

The techniques we use at the Center for Cognitive Therapy emphasize three primary goals: relieving the student's primary symptoms of depression, changing the unrealistic thoughts responsible for the student's negative view of life, and teaching the student new skills for adapting to schoolwork and to relationships. We have found that most students can overcome depression and loneliness relatively quickly, without having to probe into childhood experiences.

Before students can begin actively working to change their thinking or learn new skills, they often need some relief from the most distressing symptoms of depression, especially sadness and fatigue. Because most depressed students report sleeping much of the time and remaining inactive, we encourage them to use a Daily Activity Schedule, planning activities to fill up every hour of the day. We help them select activities that provide them either with a sense of pleasure or a feeling of accomplishment. These seemingly simple activities, such as going to movies with a friend or taking notes in class, are often sufficient to demonstrate to the students that they are not totally incompetent and have not lost the ability to enjoy themselves. To help give students "mental space," we may also intervene with administration or faculty to arrange makeup examinations or postpone paper deadlines, temporarily removing some academic pressure.

One approach we use is to have students fill out a Dysfunctional Thought Record each day. Each time a student experiences an unpleasant emotion such as sadness, he describes the situation, and the underlying irrational thought. With the help of the therapist, he then writes a rational response to the upsetting thought. For example, a student who thinks, "No one

> *These seemingly simple activities, such as going to movies with a friend or taking notes in class, are often sufficient to demonstrate to the students that they are not totally incompetent and have not lost the ability to enjoy themselves.*

loves me," and then feels lonely, could supply the response "Just because my girlfriend left me doesn't mean no one loves me."

As we work with students to correct their misconceptions, we also employ a variety of other behavioral techniques going beyond traditional therapeutic roles. For example, we teach students like Jill better methods for studying and scheduling time efficiently. We school them in making important decisions, rehearsing the process of formulating a problem, thinking of solutions, and deciding which alternative will best fulfill their needs.

For students with social phobias, we employ several behavioral methods for anxiety management. Most of these methods involve graduated exposure to the feared situation. In come cases, students are taught ways to relax while imagining the feared situation or actually confronting it. Lonely students might also be trained to develop and maintain close friendships. This is often done through role-playing, in which the student and therapist rehearse real-life situations in the office. The therapist serves as a director, coaching the student in skills to improve his or her performance in such situations as initiating a conversation with a new acquaintance or handling a problem with a close friend.

For the student experiencing situational loneliness, in crisis because of the abrupt loss of important relationships, treatment is directed, first, at offering support and reassurance so that the student's loneliness does not intensify because he or she has no one to communicate with. We next initiate a preventive approach to help the student anticipate, recognize, and combat such common cognitive distortions as thinking, "I'll never meet anyone." Finally, the therapist advises the student on places and strategies for making new friends. Many students, surprisingly, have never thought of the laundromat or the vending machines at the library as places to meet people.

Techniques like these can be employed not only by clinicians—although in the case of serious depression we urge students to

---

Many students who are reluctant to consult psychologists or psychiatrists, thinking of it as too drastic a step, can be helped through early counseling by faculty or peers.

---

consult professionals—but also by campus paraprofessionals: upperclass, "big brothers" or "big sisters," housemasters, and resident counselors. "Faculty friend" programs at such places as Princeton and Vanderbilt Universities have also proven useful in helping students to cope with psychological, as well as academic, problems.

With recent budget cuts at many universities reducing the availability of mental-health professionals, these paraprofessional alternatives take on added importance. Many students who are reluctant to consult psychologists or psychiatrists, thinking of it as too drastic a step, can be helped through early counseling by faculty or peers.

In fact, one study at Yale University by Andrew Slaby showed that of freshmen seeking counseling help over a five-week period, only 17 percent went to the mental-health service; the others consulted deans, chaplains, and freshmen counselors.

The magnitude of the college depression problem is such, however, that the real remedies can only be institutional. It is unlikely that as a society, we will reconsider the practice of placing heavy pressures of career choice and competition on young men and women, but if such pressures are expected, students can be cushioned against their impact. High schools must provide better training in study techniques, and even in social skills, warning students what to expect from college in terms of competition and isolation. Increased use of independent study projects in high schools, still extremely limited, would help college-bound students get their sea legs before they set off into the academic storm. Colleges, in turn, should strengthen their orientation and transition programs, providing easy access to counselors for all types of problems, real or illusory. Recognizing and treating college depression on an institutional level may be the best hope for curbing the prevalence of this widespread disorder, whose every sufferer feels alone. ◆

Discussion Questions

1. Give five reasons why college students tend to become depressed.

2. Name and describe four types of loneliness.

3. What is cognitive distortion?

4. What steps are used at the Center for Cognitive Therapy to overcome depression?

5. Why is role playing used to treat loneliness?

6. What typically prevents depressed students from seeking professional help?

7. How might young people be better prepared for the challenges of college?

8. What is the leading psychological disorder among college students? Why?

9. How does clinical depression differ from "feeling blue."

10. How might colleges help prevent depression among their students?

What I've LEARNED
from A.D.D.

◆ *Edward M. Hallowell*

When I discovered, in 1981, that I had attention deficit disorder (ADD), it was one of the great "Aha!" experiences of my life. Suddenly so many seemingly disparate parts of my personality made sense—the impatience, distractibility, restlessness, amazing ability to procrastinate, and extraordinarily brief attention span (here-one-moment-gone-the-next), not to mention the high bursts of energy and creativity and an indefinable, zany sense of life.

It was a pivotal moment for me, but the repercussions have been more powerful and wide-ranging than I could have imagined 16 years ago. Coming to understand ADD has been like stepping through a porthole into a wider world, expanding my view of my patients, friends, and family. I now know that many personality traits and psychological problems have a genuine basis in biology—not just ADD, but also depression, learning disorders, anxiety, panic attacks, and even shyness.

That insight has been tremendously freeing, for myself and my patients, and it has also led the mental health field to novel, effective treatments for brain disorders. I use the word "brain" intentionally, to emphasize that in many ways our personality is hardwired. Yet just as important is the fact that biology is only part of the story: We're all born with a set of genes, but how those genes get expressed depends largely on life experience and the way our environment interacts with our biology. If we understand this, we can "manage" our brains more deftly, using methods that range from medicine to lifestyle changes. Diagnosing and treating ADD—in my own life and those of hundreds of patients—has shown me just how remarkable these interventions can be. I have seen more than a few teetering marriages right themselves when the couple understood it was ADD, not bad character, causing their troubles. I

Scores of students have been able to rescue their academic careers after diagnosis and treatment.

have also seen many careers that had been languishing in the bin labeled "underachiever" suddenly take off after diagnosis and treatment of ADD. Scores of students have been able to rescue their academic careers after diagnosis and treatment. It is a powerful diagnosis: powerfully destructive when missed and powerfully constructive when correctly picked up.

ADD has taught me to look at people differently. These days, when I meet someone I often ask myself the question, "What kind of brain does he have?" as a way of trying to understand the person. I've learned that brains differ tremendously from person to person, and that some of the most interesting and productive people around have "funny" (i.e., highly idiosyncratic) brains. There is no normal, standard brain, any more than there is a normal, standard automobile, dress, or human face. Our old distinctions of "smart" and "stupid" don't even begin to describe the variety of differences in human brains; indeed, these distinctions trample over those differences.

Today we know more than ever about the brain—but in learning more we have realized how little we actually know. With sophisticated brain scans that map the activity of networks of neurons we can peer inside the once impenetrable armor of our skulls and learn just how brains act when they are seeing, thinking, remembering, and even malfunctioning. And yet the vast territory of the brain still stretches out before us uncharted, like the sixteenth-century maps of the New World we used to see in our fifth-grade history books. Although we are coining new terms all the time (like emotional intelligence or post-traumatic stress disorder or even attention deficit disorder), although we are discovering new neurotransmitters and brain peptides that reveal new connections and networks within the brain, and although we are revising or throwing out old theories as new ones leap onto our screens, any honest discussion of mental life must begin with the confession, "There's so much we still don't know."

Disorder and Metaphor?

What do these philosophical flights of fancy have to do with ADD and me? A few years ago ADD burst upon the American scene the way psychiatric disorders sometimes do, emerging as a riveting new metaphor for our cul-

Anatomy of A.D.D.

The official definition of ADD is found in the fourth edition of the *Diagnostic and Statistical Manual of Mental Disorders*, published by the American Psychiatric Association in 1994. Keep in mind that ultimately the DSM is a fair attempt to systematize—through extensive empirical fieldwork and data—a field that is almost impossible to systematize. It's also important to remember that ADD is not a condition that you either have or don't have, like pregnancy. It is a condition that, like depression, occurs in varying degrees of intensity. That said, for a patient to be formally diagnosed with ADD the following should be true:

1. Six or more of the following symptoms of inattention have persisted for at least six months to a degree that is maladaptive and inconsistent with developmental level:
   - the patient often fails to give close attention to details or makes careless mistakes in schoolwork, work, or other activities.
   - often has difficulty sustaining attention in tasks or play activities
   - often does not seem to listen when spoken to directly
   - often does not follow through on instructions and fails to finish schoolwork, chores, or duties in the workplace
   - often has difficulty organizing tasks and activities
   - often avoids, dislikes or is reluctant to engage in tasks that require sustained mental effort
   - often loses things necessary for tasks or activities
   - is often easily distracted by extraneous stimuli
   - is often forgetful in daily activities

Alternatively, the patient should have six or more of the following symptoms of hyperactivity and impulsivity, which have persisted for at least six months to a degree that is maladaptive and inconsistent with developmental level:
   - the patient often fidgets with hands or feet or squirms in seat
   - often leaves seat in classroom or in other situations in which remaining seated is expected
   - often runs about or climbs excessively in situations in which it is inappropriate
   - often has difficulty playing or engaging in leisure activities
   - is often "on the go" or often acts as if "driven by a motor"
   - often talks excessively
   - often blurts out answers before questions have been completed
   - often has difficulty awaiting turn
   - often interrupts or intrudes on others

2. Some hyperactive-impulsive symptoms that caused impairment were present before the age of 7:

3. Some impairment from the symptoms is present in two or more settings (such as school, work, home):

4. There is clear evidence of clinically significant impairment in social, academic, or occupational functioning.

tural milieu. In the 1930s we embraced neurasthenia; in the '50s W. H. Auden coined the term "the age of anxiety"; in the '70s Christopher Lasch dubbed us the "culture of narcissism." Now, in the '90s, ADD has emerged as a symbol of American life (see "A Culture Driven to Distraction," this article). This may explain why *Driven to Distraction* and *Answers to Distraction*, two books I wrote a few years ago with Harvard psychiatrist John Ratey, M.D., found a surprisingly wide and vocal audience.

At the same time, there has been some misunderstanding because of the sudden popularity of ADD. Scientists rightly get upset when they see extravagant claims being made that studies cannot justify—claims, for instance, that up to 25 percent of our population suffers from ADD. (The true number is probably around 5 percent.) And ordinary people are annoyed because they feel this diagnosis has become a catchall excuse—clothed in neurological, scientific language—for any inappropriate behavior. ADD can seem to undercut our country's deep belief in the work ethic. "Why didn't you do your homework?" *"Because I have ADD."* "Why are you late?" *"Because I have ADD."* "Why haven't you paid your income tax in five years?" *"Because I have ADD."* "Why are you so obnoxious?" *"Because I have ADD."* But, in fact, once ADD is properly diagnosed and treated, the opposite happens: The sufferer is able to take responsibility more effectively and becomes more productive and patient. The student who always forgot his homework and was constantly penalized for doing so is able to remember his homework—after his ADD is treated. The same is true for the adult in the workplace, who, once his ADD is treated, is finally able to finish the project he has so "irresponsibly" neglected, or the academician who is at last able to complete her Ph.D. dissertation.

So what is this condition, and where has it been all these centuries? Is it just another fad, or is there some scientific basis to ADD?

ADD is not a new disorder, although it has not been clearly understood until recent years, and its definition will become even more refined as we learn more about it. Right now, we are like blind men describing an elephant. The elephant is there—this vast collection of people with varying attentional strengths and vulnerabilities. However, generating a definitive description, diagnostic workup, and treatment plan with replicable research findings still poses a challenge. As long ago as in the 1940s, the term "minimal brain damage syndrome" was used to describe symptoms similar to what we now call ADD. Today, the standard manual of the mental health field, the DSM-IV, defines ADD as a syndrome of involuntary distractibility—a restless, constant wandering of the crucial beam of energy we call attention. That trait is the hallmark of this disorder. More specifically, the syndrome must include six or more symptoms of either inattention or hyperactivity and impulsivity—the latter variant is known as attention deficit disorder with hyperactivity, or ADHD. (See "Anatomy of ADD," this article.)

To define a disorder solely in terms of attention is a true leap forward, since for centuries nobody paid any attention to attention. Attention was viewed as a choice, and if your mind wandered, you were simply allowing it to do so. Symptoms of ADD—not unlike those of depression, mania, or anxiety disorders—were considered deep and moral flaws.

When people ask me where ADD has been all these years, I respond that it has been in classrooms and offices and homes all over the world, right under our noses all along, only it has been called by different names: laziness, stupidity, rottenness, and worthlessness. For decades children with ADD have been shamed, beaten, punished, and humiliated. They have been told they suffered from a deficit not of attention but of motivation and effort. That approach fails as miserably as trying

to beat nearsightedness out of a child—and the damage carries over into adulthood.

It's All in Your Head

The evidence that ADD has a biological basis has mounted over the last 20 years. First, and most moving, there is the clinical evidence from the records of millions of patients who have met the diagnostic criteria and who have benefited spectacularly from standard treatment. These are human stories of salvaged lives. The fact that certain medications predictably relieve target symptoms of ADD means that these symptoms have roots in the physical world.

I recall watching an eighth grader named Noah receive a reward for "Most Improved" at graduation. This boy's mother had been told by an expert that Noah was so severely "disturbed" that she should look into residential placement. He was

> *One seems to inherit a susceptibility to this disorder, which appears to cluster in families just as manic-depression and other mental illnesses do.*

often in trouble at school. From my first meeting with Noah I was struck by his kindness and tenacity: no expert had understood that he suffered from ADD, as well as mild cerebral palsy. Like many ADDers he was intuitive, warm, and empathic. After coaching, teacher involvement, extra structure, and the medication Ritalin, Noah improved steadily, from the moment of diagnosis in sixth grade until graduation from eighth. As I watched him walk up to receive his award, awkward but proud, shake the hand of the principal, then turn and flash us all a grin, I felt inside a gigantic, "YES!" *Yes* for the triumph of this boy, *yes* for the triumph of knowledge and determination over misunderstanding, *yes* for all the children who in the future will not

have to suffer. Standing in the back of the gym, leaning against the wall, I cried some of the happiest tears I've ever shed.

There is also intriguing biological evidence for the existence of ADD. One seems to inherit a susceptibility to this disorder, which appears to cluster in families just as manic-depression and other mental illnesses do. Though no scientist has been able to isolate a single causative gene in any mental disorder—and, in fact, we are coming to understand that a complex interaction of genes, neurotransmitters, hormones, and the environment comes into play in mental illness—there is solid evidence that vulnerability can be passed down through generations. One particularly careful, recent review in *The Journal of The American Academy of Child and Adolescent Psychiatry* supported the heritability of ADD based upon family and twin-adoption studies and analysis of gene inheritance.

Evidence of ADD may even show up in specific areas of the brain. In 1990, Alan Zametkin, M.D., a psychiatrist at the National Institute of Mental Health (NIMH), reported startling findings about the ADD brain in the *New England Journal of Medicine*. Zametkin measured sugar metabolism—a major indicator of brain activity—in the brains of 30 adults who had a childhood history of ADD, along with 30 normal individuals. PET scans (positron emission tomography) allowed Zametkin to determine just how much sugar each participant's brain was absorbing, and in what regions. Sufferers of ADD absorbed less sugar in the areas of the brain that regulate impulse control, attention, and mood. Another study by NIMH researcher

David Hauser, M.D., linked ADD to a rare thyroid condition called generalized resistance to thyroid hormone (GRTH). Seventy percent of individuals with GRTH suffer from ADD—an extraordinarily high correlation. Finally, recent brain scan studies have revealed both anatomical and functional differences in the brains of individuals with ADD—slight but real differences in the size of the corpus callosum (which serves as the switchboard that connects the two hemispheres of the brain), as well as differences in the size of the caudate nucleus, another switching station deep within the brain. These breakthrough studies lay the foundation for promising research, but much more work needs to be done before we may be able to use these findings to actually help us diagnose ADD. They simply point us in the direction of biology—and that pointer is powerful.

A Culture Driven to Distraction

America today suffers from culturally induced attention deficit disorder, or what I call "pseudo-ADD." That's one reason ADD has captured the imagination of so many people, and why the diagnosis has become so seductive that is sometimes seems more like a designer label on a piece of clothing than a real, potentially disabling disorder.

Pseudo-ADD has many of the same core symptoms as true ADD—a high level of impulsivity, an ongoing search for high stimulation, a tendency to restless behavior and impatience, and a very active, fleeting attention span.

It's easy to see how our culture can induce an ADD-like state. When I was a little boy, growing up in the 1950s, television had only recently come into every American's living room, and dial telephones had not yet appeared in my small town. Now we all have access to everyone else, anytime, anywhere, always. A colleague of mine recently received 40,000 pieces of e-mail in a week. Computers, cell and car phones, satellite technology, fax, copy and answering machines, VCRs, cable TV, the Internet, video conferences—all these are now commonplace. We are, as the cliché has it, wired—stimulated and speeded up day and night, constantly sending and receiving messages.

And yet, as we've become hyperconnected electronically, we've become disconnected interpersonally. We no longer sit down and talk, face-to-face, the way we once did. Each connection is briefer, more fleeting, and followed by another as ephemeral. Without a feeling of deep and stable connectedness, people feel at sea: distracted, restless, and hungry for something ever nameless—the very same symptoms we associate with ADD.

Because ADD so resembles the side effects of living in the late-twentieth century, the diagnostician must sometimes ask, "Does this person suffer from attention deficit disorder or just a severe case of modern life?" The answer is usually clear-cut. The symptoms of pseudo-ADD melt away when the individual is taken out of the ADD-ogenic environment. In true ADD the symptoms remain. The treatment for pseudo-ADD is to slow down and connect with what matters to you. Turn off the TV and turn down the answering machine; have dinner together with your family or companions; get to know your neighbors; re-establish contact with your extended family; and learn to say no to some of the endless requests for your time.

This is easier said than done, as a multitude of seemingly irresistible demands press upon the gateways to our minds all the time. How can we live wired but still plugged in, face-to-face? One answer is to shift our society, to reinvent from the ground up structures that used to work for us but don't work well today, such as family, church, social clubs, the small town and the neighborhood. The more practical answer is to take responsibility as individuals and vigorously insist upon a calmer, more connected lifestyle. You'll be fighting the tide of an entire culture, but the reward is a richer, fuller, more meaningful life.

The Pivotal Moment

Nothing matters more in ADD than proper diagnosis. Even today this condition is so misunderstood that it is both missed and overdiagnosed. As the public's awareness of the disorder grows, more and more people represent themselves as experts in ADD. As one of my patients said to me, "ADD has become a growth industry." Not every self-proclaimed expert knows ADD from ABC. For instance, depression can cause someone to be distracted and inattentive (and in many cases depression and ADD even occur together). However, a constant pattern of ADD symptoms usually extends back to early childhood, while depression is usually episodic. Thyroid disease can also look very much like ADD, and only testing by a physician can rule this out. High IQ can also mask or delay the diagnosis of ADD.

If the proper care is taken, a diagnosis of ADD can be made with confidence and accuracy, even though there is no single proof-positive test. Like most disorders,

ADD occurs on a wide spectrum. In severe cases an individual can barely function due to rampant disorganization or uncontrollable impulsivity, not to mention secondary symptoms such as low self-esteem or depression. Yet very mild cases of ADD can be barely noticeable, especially in a bright individual who has adapted well.

To me, the life history is the one, absolutely convincing "test," which is then supported by the criteria of the DSM-IV and by psychological testing. When someone tells me they've been called "space-shot," "daydreamer," and "out in left field" all their lives, I suspect they might have ADD. At our clinic in Concord, Massachusetts, we use an abbreviated neuropsychological battery that helps us confirm a diagnosis. The battery includes standard written tests that measure memory and logic, impulsivity, and ability to organize complex tasks. Score alone does not tell the whole story; the tester needs to watch the client to determine whether he or she becomes easily frustrated and distracted. We even include a simple motor test that measures how quickly a person can tap their finger. (Patients with ADD are very good at this; depressed patients are not.) Though these tests are helpful, they are by no means definitive. A very smart person without ADD may find these tests boring, and become distracted. On the other hand, one of the great ironies of this kind of testing is that three of the best non-medication treatments available for ADD—structure, motivation, and novelty—are actually built into the testing situation, and can temporarily camouflage ADD.

A diagnosis by itself can change a life. My own father suffered from manic-depression, and I used to wonder if I had inherited the same disorder. When I learned I had ADD, that fact alone made a huge difference to my life. Instead of thinking of myself as having a character flaw, a family legacy, or some potentially ominous "difference" between me and other people, I could see myself in terms of having a unique brain biology. This understanding freed me emotionally. In fact, I would much rather have ADD than not have it, since I love the positive qualities that go along with it—creativity, energy, and unpredictability. I have found tremendous support and goodwill in response to my acknowledging my own ADD and dyslexia. The only time talking about this diagnosis will get you in trouble is when you offer it as an excuse.

After a diagnosis of ADD, an individual and his or her family can understand and change behavior patterns that may have been a problem for many years. Treatment must be multifaceted, and includes:

◆ **Educating the individual** and his or her family, friends, and colleagues or schoolteachers about the disorder. Two of the largest national organizations providing this information are CHADD (Children and Adults with Attention Deficit Disorder: call 954-587-3700) and ADDA (Attention Deficit Disorder Association: call 216-350-9595).

◆ **Making lifestyle changes**, such as incorporating structure, exercise, meditation, and prayer into one's daily life. Structural approaches include using practical tools like lists, reminders, simple filing systems, appointment books, and strategically placed bulletin boards. These can help manage the inner chaos of the ADD life, but the structure should be simple. One patient of mine got so excited about the concept of structure he impulsively went out to Staples and spent several thousand dollars on complex organizing materials that he never used. An example of simple structure: I put my car keys in a basket next to my front door so that I do not have to start each day with a frantic search for them. Exercise can help drain off anxiety and excess aggression. Regular meditation or prayer can help focus and relax the mind.

◆ **Coaching, therapy, and social training**. Often ADD sufferers complain that structure is boring. "If I could be structured, I wouldn't have ADD!" moaned one patient. A coach can be invaluable in helping people with ADD organize their life, and encouraging them to stay on track. If a psychotherapist is the coach, he or she needs to be actively involved in advising specific behavioral changes.

Therapy itself can help resolve old patterns of self-sabotage or low self-esteem, and may help couples address long-standing problems. For example, setting up a simple division of labor between partners can prevent numerous arguments. Social training can help those with ADD learn how to avoid social gaffes. And merely understanding the condition can promote more successful interactions.

◆ **Medication**. The medications used to treat ADD constitute one of the miracles of modern medicine. Drugs are beneficial in about 80 percent of ADDers, working like a pair of eyeglasses for the brain, enhancing and sharpening mental focus. Medications prescribed include stimulants like Ritalin or Dexedrine, tricyclic antidepressants like Tofranil and Elavil, and even some high-blood pressure medicines like Catapres.

All of these medications work by influencing levels of key neurotransmitters, particularly dopamine, epinephrine, and norepinephrine. It seems that the resulting change in neurotransmitter availability helps the brain inhibit extraneous stimuli—both internal and external. That allows the mind to focus more effectively. There is no standard dose; dosages can vary widely from person to person, independent of body size.

Ritalin, by far the most popular drug for the treatment of ADD, is safe and effective. Of course, Ritalin and other stimulants can be dangerous if used improperly. But Ritalin is not addictive. Nor is it a euphoric substance—people use drugs to get high, not to focus their minds. For example, you would not cite, "I took Ritalin last night and read three books" as an example of getting high. Using stimulants to cram before exams, however, is as inadvisable as over-dosing on coffee. Students do it, but they should be warned against it. Ritalin should only be taken under medical supervision and of course should not be sold, given away, or otherwise misused.

The diagnosis and treatment of ADD represent a triumph of science over human suffering—just one example of the many syndromes of the brain we are at last learning to address without scorn or hidden moral judgment. As we begin to bring mental suffering out of the stigmatized darkness it has inhabited for centuries and into the light of scientific understanding and effective treatment, we all have reason to rejoice.   ◈

Discussion Questions

1. What is ADD? Describe five common symptoms.

2. According to Hallowell, which is more important in forming our personalities, biology or our social environment? Why?

3. How can ADD affect one's everyday life?

4. What is the current rate of ADD in the U.S.?

5. List the current diagnostic criteria for ADD according to the DSM-IV.

6. What type of evidence suggests that ADD has a biological basis?

7. Describe two anatomical differences in the brains of people with ADD.

8. Explain why ADD is easy to misdiagnose.

9. Explain three effective treatments for ADD besides medication.

10. How can being diagnosed with ADD make a difference in a person's life?

11. What are the most common medications used to treat ADD?

12. List the neurotransmitters that seem to be involved in ADD.

Schizophrenia

Is A Myth, Born Of **Metaphor**,

Meaningless

◆ *Theodore R. Sarbin*

For many years we have believed that there is a disease called schizophrenia. This belief is false. Schizophrenia, once a useful metaphor, is a myth.

But myths die hard, and professionals and laymen alike persist in using a term that is meaningless. Consider this definition, taken from a widely used diagnostic manual:

(Schizophrenia) includes a group of disorders manifested by characteristic disturbances of thinking, mood, and behavior...which are marked by alterations of concept formation which may lead to misinterpretations of reality and sometimes to delusions... mood changes include ambivalent, constricted and inappropriate emotional responsiveness and loss of empathy with others...

Label

Schizophrenia "may" do this and it "sometimes" leads to that. It produces "characteristic" disturbances (unspecified) and "inappropriate" emotional responses (also unspecified). It is therefore not surprising that psychiatrists have notoriously high rates of disagreement in their diagnoses of this illness. Nevertheless, neither the vagueness of the definition nor their inability to agree in diagnosis has kept professionals from applying the schizophrenic label freely. Or from speaking of schizophrenia with unmerited precision.

For example, Loren Mosher, Chief of the Center for Studies in Schizophrenia at the National Institute of Mental Health in Rockville, Maryland, wrote gloomily that more than 200,000 Americans are in hospitals suffering from schizophrenia, and that two to six percent of persons born in 1960 will undergo schizophrenic episodes. Yet Mosher admits that the exact definition of schizophrenia, the process by which it develops, and the most effective treatment "elude adequate solution."

AAAA

The view that schizophrenia is a disease dates back some 60 years to the work of Eugen Bleuler, a Swiss psychiatrist. Bleuler named the disorder, and defined it in terms of The Four As: weak *associations*, inappropriate *affect*, *ambivalence*, and *autism* (preoccupation with oneself). The Four As continue to underlie modern definitions, although Arnold H. Buss's survey of schizophrenia research in 1966 found that most authorities rejected the last two, and there is some doubt about the first two.

To understand how this concept of schizophrenia evolved, we must inquire how deviant behavior (such as talking to nonexistent persons) became a symptom of a disease rather than an example of misconduct (unwanted behavior).

For many centuries, *illness* meant the conjunction between a patient's reported discomforts ("I have a miserable itch") and observable body symptoms (a rash). Misconduct—any behavior that departed from the existing norms—was explained by a demonaical model, codified in the 15th-century *Malleus malleficarum* [*The Witches' Hammer*, regarded as a textbook on witchcraft]. Demons accounted for unusual thoughts, deviant beliefs, and nonconformist behavior; hence the church was responsible for the control and cure of norm-violators. The diagnosis of witchcraft became a fine art, and church specialists in witch-hunting reached a pinnacle of power during the 16th-century Inquisition.

Nuns

A transformation began in the 1600s. The excesses of the Inquisition were softened by the emergence of humanistic philosophy, the rejection of scholasticism, and discovery of the works of the Greek physician Galen and other classical writers. In this atmosphere, Teresa of Avila instigated the shift from the devils to "illness" as the cause of deviant behavior.

A group of nuns were acting out what we would call today a hysterical syndrome. Agents of the Inquisition maintained that the women were possessed by the devil, and attempted to begin exorcism procedures. Teresa kept the Inquisitors at bay by declaring the nuns to be infirm, ill. She invoked the concept of natural causes for their behavior: melancholia (resurrected from Galen's theories), weak imagination, and drowsiness. The unusual conduct, argued Teresa, could be explained by natural causes. The

> *Teresa of Avila instigated the shift from devils to 'illness' as the cause of deviant behavior.*

403

nuns should therefore be considered not evil, but *como enfermas—* as if sick.

Humors

Note her words carefully, *As if sick*. Teresa used the metaphor of *illness* to excuse certain kinds of misconduct or to make them understandable.

However, in the use of metaphor there is a human tendency to drop qualifiers—the *as-ifs*, the *seem-likes*, and so on—that remind us that the term is figurative, not literal. The Renaissance forerunners of today's physicians found it awkward to talk about two kinds of illness: "real" illness and "as if" illness. Eventually, they dropped the as-if modification, so that they could look at deviant behavior as symptomatic of mental pathology, just as they saw body symptoms as symptomatic of physical pathology.

The doctors were able to do this partly because of the dominant medical theory of the time: Galen's concept of humors. The diagnostic problem was to infer the balance of humors inside the person; when the balance was out of kilter, the patient experienced a symptom. Since the mind-body distinction was taken as truth, those diseases not caused by bodily defects had to be caused by mental defects: hence the label *mental illness*.

Tumors

Galen's model survives in modern medicine: but microbes, toxins and tumors have replaced humors. Doctors still look to mechanical, internal factors that "cause" disease, whether of such tangible organs as the liver and heart, or of such intangibles as states of mind.

Thus the 17th century saw two transformations: one that made a metaphorical concept into a literal one, originally to save nonconformists being labeled as witches: a second that grafted deviant behavior onto the existing medical model.

Split

The medical approach to mental illness, then, had existed for some 300 years when Bleuler began his work in the early 1900s. Bleuler was dissatisfied with the then-current concept of *dementia praecox* (literally, "mental deterioration in young people"). For one thing, patients of all ages had it, whatever it was.

Bleuler was operating from an intellectual structure and a set of premises that were popular at that time. Psychology, only recently divorced from philosophy, was

---

Studies consistently have shown that professionals simply are unable to agree in their diagnoses of schizophrenia.

---

based on the existence of *mind*, itself made up of three components: intellect, will and emotions. The brain, psychologists thought, was an organ of mind. The blossoming knowledge of the anatomy and physiology of the brain permitted analogies to the mind. For example, since patients whose *brains* were not whole (because of physiological dysfunction) would act in strange and unpredictable ways, it was assumed that patients who acted in bizarre fashion in the absence of brain pathology would have split *minds*.

Coin

When Bleuler examined a patient, he brought to bear on his analysis three premises based on the scientific paradigm of that era: 1. that people can be sick in the mind; 2. that the mind is com-posed of three parts; 3. that deviant behavior occurs when the three parts are not acting in unison—as in a damaged brain. *It is as if the three parts are not working together*, Bleuler might have thought. So from Greek roots he coined the metaphor: schizophrenia (literally, "splitting-mind"). The term stuck, quickly replacing *dementia praecox*.

But the same thing happened to Bleuler's metaphor that happened to Teresa's: it turned into myth. A term that began as a way of poetically talking about events was transformed into a term that denoted the events themselves.

I define *metaphor* as a word taken from one universe of discourse to describe an event in another: e.g. *a sour note, a bitter disappointment, Frank is a goat*. One may indicate metaphors, as I've mentioned, by the use of conventional modifiers, e.g. it is *as if* the note were sour. I define *myth* as a literal statement, unsupported by empirical evidence, that is used as a guide to action. When the modifier is dropped the metaphor may become reified, thus it is transformed into myth and becomes a directive for behavior. For example, to praise Dorothy's good qualities, we may say—in metaphor—*it is as if she were a saint*. If we then become convinced she *is* a saint, and attempt to convert others to our belief, *she is a saint* has become myth. This process holds regardless of whether the myth serves overtly political ends, such as the myth of Nordic superiority, or scientific ends, such as the myth of mental illness.

Trip

The history of psychology shows that its metaphors or hypothetical constructs tend to become myths. There is a laboratory paradigm of this process. Leonard

Carmichael, H. P. Hogan, and A. A. Walter, in their now-classic 1932 study, presented to their subjects figures that could be described in two ways. In one condition, the experimenter presented two adjacent circles connected by a bar and said "this resembles a dumbbell"; in another condition he would say of the same figure "this resembles eyeglasses". When the subjects later reproduced the figures, they dropped the metaphoric modifier "resembles"—and drew pictures of eyeglasses or dumbbells.

To demonstrate further the metaphor-to-myth transformation that occurs in scientific discovery, Ki-Taek Chun and I did several experiments.

We read aloud to our subjects (college students) four stories in the form of short press releases. One of the press releases, for instance, was about a new psychiatric syndrome. We predicted that when metaphors are opaque (abstract and unfamiliar), they would more quickly turn into myths than when they were transparent (familiar in detail or theme). Accordingly, subjects listened to two opaque stories, and two transparent ones. Each press release contained five *as-if* qualifiers or their equivalents, such as *seemed* or *appeared*.

In addition, some subjects read stories with opaque titles (e.g. "Sinvoluntatia"), others read the same stories with transparent titles (e.g. "the syndrome suggestive of the separation of mind and will"). We asked some subjects to reproduce the stories in writing; others responded *true* or *false* to a number of questions about the press release.

Paring

In general, the experiments demonstrated that people tend to drop the metaphoric qualifiers. They reproduce or recognize verbal descriptions as if they had been uttered as firm, categorical sentences, rather than tentative figurative statements.

Some experimental conditions produced more metaphor-to-myth transformations than others. Opaque titles and reports encouraged oversimplifications: subjects dropped the as-ifs and other qualifiers more often than they did when they dealt with transparent titles and reports. Instead of repeating the tentative "it is as if the patients had no will power," for example, they were more likely to say categorically "the patients had no will power." The metaphor that was most likely to be transformed into myth was the scientific-sounding Latin word *sinvoluntatia*.

Doctrine

When Bleuler defined his patients as schizophrenic, the term was perfectly transparent for him,

> **The labeling of unwanted behavior is a moral enterprise, not a scientific one.**

connecting as it did with his clinical observations. But for Bleuler's followers, most of whom were not bilingual in Greek and English, the term was inaccessible, opaque. For them, it described behavior that was not "as if" the patients had a split mind; it described the split mind, literally. Within his lifetime, Bleuler witnessed the transformation of his own metaphor into myth—a guideline for action and cure. Eventually, he even came to believe it himself, concluding that schizophrenia was indeed a disease.

Official doctrine, then, has stated for some 60 years that schizophrenia, a mental disease, exists. To pursue my argument that it does not, James C. Mancuso and I reviewed every research report on schizophrenia published in the *Journal of Abnormal Psychology* for the period 1959 to 1968, a total of 179 studies.

The basic experimental paradigm for such research is the same for all. There is a hypothesis, usually of the form *compared to normals, chizophrenics will perform poorly on such-and-such an experimental procedure.* The task might be anything from solving logical problems, or completing of sentences or drawings, to assessing manual dexterity. Whatever the task, it derives from the researchers' theoretical model. For example, a theory that regards the loosening of associations as the critical cause of schizophrenia will suggest word-association tests, interpretation of proverbs, concept-formation problems, and the like.

Most of the 179 studies we read showed small differences in favor of the so-called normals. A few reported no differences, and one found the normals doing more poorly than the schizophrenics. The statistics for these experiments, however, were designed to show only that such differences between the average scores of the two groups were not due to chance. They were not intended to locate subjects precisely as belonging to the "schizophrenic" category or the "normal" category. As a result, there were considerable overlaps in the scores of the two groups. Indeed, every study in the review contained a high proportion of cases that ran counter to the expectations of the hypothesis at hand.

Net

The clear conclusion: *most schizophrenics functioned no differently on these tests from most normals.* We cannot, in other words, identify a given person as schizophrenic or normal by his score on any of these tasks.

Further, in more than three fourths of the studies we reviewed, the investigators presented no data to show that their measures were reliable.

And the hypotheses at hand were a diverse and contradictory lot, jockeying for popularity like petulant children. Five kinds of theories emerged in the 10-year time period we studied; each flourished briefly, spat at its nearest competitor, and died at the hands of a younger upstart:

Contemporary researchers have a choice. They may persevere in the search for that elusive factor that will reliably distinguish schizophrenics from normals. Or they may question the disease model of schizophrenia itself, and try to find a better, truly explanatory paradigm.

---

1. A favorite hypothesis, which got its original impetus from Bleuler, was that schizophrenics suffer from loosened associations, which are disrupted by their high drive levels (usually called anxiety). A series of experiments designed to test this assumption worked fairly well. Within five years, other investigators were unable to confirm it.

2. Another hypothesis, introduced in 1957, was that schizophrenics are inordinately sensitive to social criticism. Experiments showed that, indeed, schizophrenics worked better under conditions of mild social censure. Later, two independent researchers published contradictory results: censure or praise had no effect on schizophrenics' performance levels.

3. The most popular hypothesis was that the thought processes of schizophrenics were prelogical, based on their performance in sorting objects, solving problems, and so on. By contrast, controlled studies done in 1964 found that schizophrenics could not be distinguished from normals in their use of nonlogical solutions to these problems.

4. In 1941, Kurt Goldstein and Martin Scheerer promoted the vague hypothesis that schizophrenics cannot function abstractly in classifying objects; rather, they function concretely. The abstractness-concreteness dimension generated a profusion of studies, some of which supported Goldstein and Scheerer, most of which did not. A refinement suggested that two dimensions to the classification task were involved: open vs. closed classes, and public vs. private classes. Schizophrenics were supposed to prefer open and private classes. In 1964, an investigator contradicted the refinement, finding schizophrenics to be no different from normals on any type of classification task.

5. Some hypotheses concerned physiological and biochemical characteristics: the blood, urine, or saliva of schizophrenics was purported to differ from that of normals. Invariably, such discoveries were not replicated. For example, one researcher studied the "mauve spot" in the urine of schizophrenic patients, a sign thought to be helpful in diagnoses. It turned out that the mauve spot was an artifact of the tranquilizers given schizophrenic patients—when the medication stopped, the mauve spot disappeared.

To complicate the picture further, studies consistently have shown that professionals simply are unable to agree in their diagnoses of schizophrenia. One expert will assign this label, a second will disagree and prefer another. Yet 85 percent of the studies we reviewed used the fallible declarations of staff psychiatrists to define schizophrenia. No one seemed to think this would have something to do with the inconsistent findings.

Agents

A successful scientific paradigm generates puzzles. As puzzles are solved, the paradigm is refined or abandoned for a better one. This logical process has not applied to schizophrenia; quite the contrary. The disease paradigm has produced a confusing plethora of supposed causative agents, none of which is substantiated, yet all of which hang on to the original model. Instead of refining the paradigm, researchers have loaded more and more *ad hoc* variations on it. The result is not a lean and useful theory, but one that is fat, cumbersome and unwieldy. We have, in short, a paradigm-in-crisis.

The very foundation of the disease model is that doctors will be able, on the basis of clear symptoms, to identify the disease. Treatment follows on such identification. The process of diagnosis and cure follows directly from the concept of *efficient cause*, i.e. locating the agent that is operative in producing the disease. A bacillus is the efficient cause of tuberculosis; a lack of vitamins is the efficient cause of pellagra.

X & Y

Behavioral scientists imitated the natural scientists in a search for efficient causes. They had, after all, achieved high scientific status by use of the mechanistic models that had guided the natural sciences during the 19th century. And the mechanistically inclined researcher liked statements of the efficient-cause form: that X is the functional antecedent of Y, or that Y is the inevitable consequence of X.

But the efficient cause of deviant behavior is not to be found internally, as is the efficient cause of a physical ailment. Psychiatric practitioners made a grievous error in thinking it was. Deviance does not have efficient causes, but they are to be found at the interface of the person's behavior and in the moral judgments that others make about that behavior. Professional diagnosticians did not see that the candidate for diagnosis came to them *already prejudged* by the police, his neighbors, or worried relatives. They did not see that his behavior is a complex of his actions *and* those of this accusers.

Apple

Such blindness permitted mental-health practitioners to move unwittingly, from making efficient-cause statements to making formal-cause statements, which are traditionally invoked to account for moral transgressions.

Formal-cause paradigms regard statements of correspondence between X and Y to be adequate approximations of the truth; they do not postulate X to be an antecedent of Y. A woman smokes because she is an oral character; a man hates minority groups because he is a Fascist; a schizophrenic behaves as he does because he has the form (identity) of a schizophrenic. Such statements of correspondence are not explanations, and have no more utility than saying that an apple sways in the breeze because it is in the nature and form of the apple to sway in breezes. Yet formal-cause statements have carried the day in the mental-health specialties, disguised as efficient-cause explanations. Patients are labeled schizophrenic; this presumably explains their bad behavior. What is the cause of hallucination? Schizophrenia. What is the cause of violent acts? Schizophrenia. What is the cause of unrestrained religiosity? Schizophrenia.

Judgment

To expose a myth or unfrock a metaphor is not to deny that certain events occur. Some people do act in ways that we think are silly, perplexing, irrational, or dangerous. If their actions are sufficiently threatening to those around them or to society, others will judge the offender as bad and in need of reform. To label strange behavior "sick," invites the intervention of doctors, the use of hospitals, the prescription of drugs. On the other hand, we may interpret the conduct of the offender as a creative effort to make sense out of a complex, crazy world. But in either case, we must recognize such interpretations for what they are: moral judgments. The labeling of unwanted behavior is a moral enterprise, not a scientific one.

Contemporary researchers have a choice. They may persevere in the search for that elusive factor that will reliably distinguish schizophrenics from normals. Or they may question the disease model of schizophrenia itself, and try to find a better, truly explanatory paradigm. Continuing with the old paradigm is—for "schizophrenics" and researchers alike—an exercise in futility. ◆

Discussion Questions

1. Which part of the schizophrenia diagnosis leads Sarbin to believe that the disorder does not exist?

2. Why do clinicians often disagree about schizophrenia diagnoses?

3. Who was Eugen Bleuler?

4. What are the "Four As" of schizophrenia?

5. What does "schizophrenia" mean literally? Who created that name, and why did he feel it was appropriate?

6. Why does the author claim that schizophrenia is a myth?

7. What is the formal-cause paradigm, and how is it related to the diagnosis of schizophrenia?

8. Why is it dangerous to use a description or property of some phenomenon as an *explanation* for that phenomenon?

9. What does the author mean by "the labeling of unwanted behavior is a moral enterprise, not a scientific one"?

10. What is the disease model of schizophrenia, and why does Sarbin reject it?

Exercises

Name: _____

Date: _____

Part 16: Psychological Disorders

1. I occasionally or frequently get depressed.

   Agree ① ② ③ ④ ⑤ Disagree

2. I believe that psychiatric diagnoses such as "schizophrenia," "A.D.D.," "conduct disorder," and so on, are valid, akin to medical diagnoses like "appendicitis."

   Agree ① ② ③ ④ ⑤ Disagree

3. I believe that suicide is a legitimate and understandable way for someone to deal with his or her depression.

   Agree ① ② ③ ④ ⑤ Disagree

You are a counselor at a large university. Design two programs that could help to reduce the amount of depression experienced by the students. One program is for entering freshmen, and the other program is for sophomores, juniors, and seniors.

A female college student in her junior year comes to your office for help. What kind of questions should you ask her, and how should you proceed if you determine she is depressed?

PART 17

THERAPIES

I'm reminded of a joke—the in-house kind that psychologists tell only to other psychologists:

A man who's stranded on a remote island in the Pacific stumbles upon one of those great lamps with a genie inside. He does the usual thing, and the genie grants him one wish.

"I'd like you to build a highway from here to the mainland," says the man.

"Well," says the genie, "I can't really do that one. The mainland is thousands of miles away. It would take hundreds of thousands of pylons and millions of tons of concrete to build such a highway, and the ocean is miles deep along the way. I'm afraid such a highway would also do serious damage to the earth's ecosystem. That's just too tall of an order. Do you have an alternate wish?"

"Yes," says the man. "I'd like you to make psychotherapy effective."

"Did you want two lanes or four?"

Actually, recent studies, including an extensive survey by *Consumer Reports*, suggest that psychotherapy may help many people, especially if the right therapist is matched with the right patient. Unfortunately, we don't yet have a way of matching patients and therapists. Because rapport is essential in psychotherapy, it's also important that patient and therapist get along with each other, but we don't have a way of predicting successful rapport. To further complicate matters, there are *hundreds* of types of therapy, and it's not clear which approach works best for which problem. What's more, no form of psychotherapy has ever been abandoned for lack of effectiveness, which suggests that practitioners adhere to particular therapies with religious zeal, even therapies that are presumably of limited value. (That should make you uneasy. It sure makes *me* uneasy.)

The first article in this section is by Albert Ellis, creator of rational-emotive therapy (RET), a form of therapy that ferrets out irrational beliefs and replaces them with rational ones. Ellis' own effectiveness as a therapist is legendary, and RET is now one of the most popular forms of psychotherapy.

In "The Frontiers of Pharmacology," Larry J. Siever provides a recent overview of the relationship between brain chemistry and various mood and personality problems. His article suggests that considerable understanding has been achieved, but the article that follows, "Prescriptions for Happiness?," by Seymour Fisher and Roger P. Greenberg, will make you think twice. Fisher and Greenberg insist that anti-depressant medications work mainly as placebos—that chemically and medically, they do little or nothing, which suggests that we don't know quite as much about the chemistry of human brains as Siever would have us believe. The final article, "A road to Self-Control," by G. Terence Wilson and Gerald C. Davison, reviews early work in behavior therapy, the form of therapy inspired by B. F. Skinner's work on operant conditioning.

The **No** Cop-Out *Therapy*

◆ *Albert Ellis*

From any conventional viewpoint, Ms. P needed no therapy at all. She had just been offered an exceptionally good job. High-level men had sought her company after her husband's death. She had no problems with her 18-year-old daughter, who was adjusting well to an out-of-town college. Yet, she came to me in an extreme state of panic.

She slept little and fitfully, and vacillated about accepting the new job. These were recent, and she thought surface, manifestations of her anxiety. More importantly, she was afraid of failing on any job, although she had never failed. She believed her husband had lost interest in her before his death, though he had never shown signs of disinterest. And she felt inadequate sexually, despite her sexual partners' protestations about their inadequacies rather than hers.

Instead of feeling better, in light of her recent business and social successes, and after what she called "three highly successful years" of psychoanalysis, she was becoming considerably more anxious and disturbed.

Her previous analyst, a woman well trained in Freudian and Sullivanian methods, had guided her to believe that the basis of her disturbance was her attitude toward men. She had learned through psychoanalysis that she had vainly sought her father's love when she was a child, but had never succeeded in weaning him away from his much greater and obsessive interest in her older brother. Consequently, she unconsciously hated men. She had resolved this problem by forcing herself to compete compulsively with males, to win out over them in the business world. But she had felt it too dangerous to compete with them sexually, since they were always better at having orgasms than she. So she had retreated, according to her analyst, to extravaginal stimulation instead of intercourse.

Awareness of the psychoanalytic explanations for her disturbance was not enough for Ms. P. She decided that her analysis was not progressing, and in desperation decided to try Rational-Emotive Therapy (RET).

RET, which I originated in 1955, goes further than orthodox psychoanalysis and classical behavioristic approaches. It places man at the center of the universe

Albert Ellis

and gives him almost full responsibility for his own fate. It is his choice to make or to refuse to make himself seriously disturbed. Although RET's basic theory of human personality has strong roots in biological and environmental assumptions, it holds that the individual himself can, and usually does, significantly, intervene between his environmental input and his emotional output, and that therefore he—and, of course, she—has potentially, an enormous amount of control over what he feels and does.

The A-B-Cs of RET

RET uses a simple A-B-C approach to human personality and its disturbance. The therapist usually begins with C, the upsetting emotional *Consequence* that the client has recently experienced. Typically, he has been rejected. This rejection can be called A, the *Activating* experience, which the person wrongly believes directly causes C, his feelings of anxiousness, worthlessness and depression. The client learns that an Activating event (A) in the outside world does not, and cannot, cause or create any feeling or emotional Consequence (C). For if it did, the therapist explains, then virtually everyone who gets rejected would have to feel just as depressed as the client. But since this is hardly true, C is really caused by some intervening variable, which is the individual's *Belief* system (B).

When rejection occurs, the healthy individual has a mainly rational set of Beliefs: "Isn't it unfortunate that I was rejected. I will suffer real losses or disadvantages by this rejection. Now, how can I be accepted by this person in the future, or by some other person who will probably bring me almost as much joy?" These Beliefs are rational because they increase a person's happiness and minimize his pain,

and they are related to observable, empirically provable events.

If the individual held rigorously to his (or her) rational Belief about being rejected, he or she would experience profound feelings at point C, but they would not be those that result from an irrational set of Beliefs: anxiousness, worthlessness and depression. Instead, he would have feelings of disappointment, frustration and annoyance. His feelings would then be quite appropriate to the Activating experience or event, since they would motivate him to try to change his life so that he would be accepted in the future and, hence, enjoy himself more.

Ms. P's Beliefs were irrational. If one assumes that she had failed to win her father's love because of his obsessive interest in her older brother, it becomes important to know why she had made those grim facts of life all-important and why she had insisted on letting them affect her for so long. Other females have fathers who favored their older brothers, but unlike Ms. P, they all do not unconsciously hate men forever and compulsively compete with them. A crucial question therefore was: What was her fundamental Belief system or philosophy of life, which she had brought to and derived from her unsuccessful attempts to get her father's love?

Choosing Beliefs

I began to teach Ms. P the A-B-Cs of Rational-Emotive Therapy and to show her why psychoanalysis, which had concentrated on A and C, but not on B, may have given her a misleading or highly superficial explanation of her disturbance.

As we probed, Ms. P began to see that her depression was not a direct result of her father's rejection, but was a consequence of her system of Beliefs. Her C responses, or Consequences, were not

caused by her father's favoring her brother but by her own mediation processes, or what she thought about this favoritism.

She actually gave herself those Consequences by choosing to create certain value assumptions, or Beliefs. She had chosen these Beliefs early in life, and she still clung to them. I explained that she continued to demand that her father (and virtually all males) be devoted to her, and that she would not free herself from anxiety and hatred until she gave up her childish demands.

Although she was able to see, on theoretical grounds, that Activating events do not cause emotional Consequences in people unless their Beliefs about these events are strongly positive or negative, Ms. P did not feel comfortable with this idea. Her strong conviction, shared by most people, that emotions arise out of experiences, helped block her acknowledgement of this RET hypothesis. Also, her ardent allegiance to her previous analyst and to the analytic theory that current events are determined by past history helped increase the blocking. During our fifth session, the therapeutic tide turned. Ms. P started to cry. She told me about her father's death a year ago and about the unveiling of his headstone that was to take place at his grave the following Sunday. I asked why she was crying, since his death, at the age of 55, may have been a waste to him but was not really so "wasteful" as far as she was concerned. She answered that the unveiling made it utterly final: "I still value his love highly, and it's very unfortunate that I'll never in any way be able to get it now."

I demurred. I thought there was more to it than that. If she thought the loss of his love was only unfortunate, she would feel very sad—but not depressed, as she seemed to be.

"Yes, " she agreed. "To be honest, when I was crying there, I was

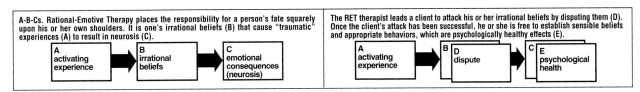

A-B-Cs. Rational-Emotive Therapy places the responsibility for a person's fate squarely upon his or her own shoulders. It is one's irrational beliefs (B) that cause "traumatic" experiences (A) to result in neurosis (C).

The RET therapist leads a client to attack his or her irrational beliefs by disputing them (D). Once the client's attack has been successful, he or she is free to establish sensible beliefs and appropriate behaviors, which are psychologically healthy effects (E).

also feeling depressed. And I guess I still am, whenever I fully face the fact that he's gone, gone forever, and that I'll *never* get from him the love I always craved."

"And that makes you—?" I asked in typical RET fashion.

"A rotten person! A no-good, low-down, rotten person, whose own father never could, and now never will, love her!"

My hunch and my persistence had paid off. Ms. P clearly saw that there was something much more than the loss of her father's love that bothered her and caused her depression—namely her profound Belief that *she* was worthless for losing that love. That turned the therapeutic tide. From that moment she acknowledged that *she* was the cause of her emotional disturbance and that her Beliefs about her father and herself had been irrational.

Changing Beliefs

Ms. P's new insight did not end her therapy. RET has two main purposes. The first is to show the emotionally disturbed person how irrational Beliefs create dysfunctional Consequences. The second, and in some ways the more important, is to teach the individual how to *Dispute* (D) in order to change or surrender these irrational Beliefs. RET overlaps significantly with various "insight" therapies, including Freudian psychoanalysis and Adlerian individual psychology, in regard to the first of these two purposes, but it tends to deviate radically from them on the second. RET espouses confrontational, philosophic and behavioristic attacks on the individual's Belief system.

If the therapist succeeds in leading the individual to Dispute his irrational Beliefs about himself and the world, he then proceeds to E, new and better-functioning *Effects*. He (or she) encourages the client to adopt new philosophies of living, thus losing feelings of anxiety. Eventually, the client will almost automatically stop creating anxiety when he undergoes disappointing Activating experiences.

Ms. P realized that it was not her early childhood experiences that created panic about her new job offer, depression about the supposed loss of her dead husband's love, and feelings of worthlessness about her sexuality. I then helped her to see the main irrational Beliefs that caused her symptoms. Paraphrased, they were:

- ◆ "I must do exceptionally well at work to prove that my father was wrong about favoring my brother over me, and to show that I am a worthwhile person."
- ◆ "In order to show, again and again, that I am a valuable person who can accept myself, I must have 100 percent love and acceptance from any man with whom I am intimately involved. And, since my late husband did not love me completely, he didn't love me at all, and that proves that I am bad."
- ◆ "If I am not regularly capable of having orgasms during intercourse, I am not a woman and that means I am unlovable."
- ◆ "I must not be panicked, depressed and indecisive; and since I am, I'm no good."
- ◆ "Now that I have admitted my problems and gone for

psychotherapy, I must succeed at curing myself in a reasonably short length of time or else I am a hopeless weakling."

To help Ms. P give up these self-deprecating ideas, I first used a rational-cognitive approach. I showed her that her irrational Beliefs about needing competency, love, and freedom from panic, were unrealistic.

Most people tend to believe several unrealistic ideas. They hold to these ideas with dreadful results in terms of their emotions and behaviors. As far as I have been able to determine, all of these beliefs are forms of absolutism. They consist of unqualified demands and needs, instead of preferences or desires. Consequently, they have nothing to do with reality.

The Irrational Trinity

There are perhaps 10 to 15 supreme "necessities" that people commonly impose on themselves and others. These can be reduced to three dictates that cause immense emotional difficulties.

The first dictate is: "Because it would be highly preferable if I were outstandingly competent, I absolutely should and must be; it is awful when I am not; and I am therefore a worthless individual."

The second irrational (and unprovable) idea is: "Because it is highly desirable that others treat me considerately and fairly, they absolutely should and must and they are rotten people who deserve to be utterly damned when they do not."

The third impossible dictate is: "Because it is preferable that I experience pleasure rather than pain, the world absolutely should arrange this and life is horrible, and I can't bear it when the world doesn't."

These three fundamental irrational Beliefs, and their many corollaries and sub-ideas, are the main factors in what we often call neurosis, character disorder, or psychosis. They are not the sole causes of these disorders, since they, in their own turn, have their own origins or "causes." However, the original causes of an individual's main irrational Beliefs are not that important—and that is why psychoanalysis, which stresses such origins, is so unhelpful. For if you believe, as did Ms. P, that your mate *must* completely love you, and you consequently feel insecure, even if you do discover exactly where and when you first got that unrealistic idea, how will the "insight" help you surrender it? What is important, and what philosophers rather than psychologists have tended to see for many centuries, is a concerted uprooting of the disturbed person's irrational Belief system and a replacing of it by a considerably sounder, reality-oriented philosophy.

Ms. P succeeded in attacking and reconstructing her irrational Beliefs. She continued to learn positive approaches to life. I had shown her how to accept reality, give up all magical assumptions, and apply the scientific method to her everyday existence. RET maintains that if one is an empiricist and invents no absolute necessities, it is almost impossible to become emotionally disturbed. One may still feel sad or annoyed, joyful or even ecstatic. "Rational" in Rational-Emotive Therapy doesn't mean unemotional. In fact, the more determined a person is to be self-accepting, hedonistic and self-actualizing by working with

his head and his other faculties, the more emotional and the more in touch with his feelings he tends to be.

I used several other cognitive methods with Ms. P. I gave her information about sex and the fre-

---

Most people tend to believe several unrealistic ideas. They hold to these ideas with dreadful results in terms of their emotions and behaviors.

---

quency of female orgasm during intercourse. I taught her imaging techniques, such as sexual imaging, that helped her become more aroused and climax more intensely. I also had her read a number of RET pamphlets and booklets and listen to some of our tape recordings.

On the emotive level, I used confrontation to help Ms. P combat her irrational thinking and inappropriate emoting. She joined one of my regular therapy groups, where she engaged in various risk-taking exercises. For Example, we induced her to speak up about her own and others' problems, even when she was most reluctant to do so. The members of the group confronted her with her hostility to

---

Efficient therapies that stress the potentialities of the client's control over his emotional processes are in many respects the most humanistic means of personality change.

---

men, which she was at first loath to acknowledge. We used empathy training, particularly through role-playing , in which we asked her to put herself into the "skin" of a man who was trying to relate to her and to satisfy her sexually. She received what Carl Rogers calls unconditional positive regard, and what RET calls undamning accep-

tance, both from me and from other members of the group. She learned to acknowledge and reveal some of her positive emotions, especially by telling some of the male members of the group that she liked them when she was very hesitant to do so.

I also used several behavioral techniques with Ms. P in the course of her RET individual and group sessions. We helped her, through role-playing with other members of the group, to be more assertive with her lover. To help her lose weight, we put her on a self-management schedule, using the principles of self-reward when she followed a reducing diet and self-penalization when she did not. She learned to desensitize herself, by relaxation techniques and by rational-emotive images (REI), so that she lost her extreme fear of making public speeches. In REI, she was induced to fantasize herself in failing situations and practice feeling sorry and frustrated, rather than feeling destroyed and depressed, when she imagined them. She was given homework assignments of accepting a new job offer and working through her panic about it. Also, through her homework, she learned to become emotionally involved with her lover, even though she was afraid he would later reject her.

All the techniques used in RET are designed to do more than change behavior and help the client feel better. They are also used to change basic philosophies and to give him or her specific means of restructuring these philosophies again and again, until he or she rarely reverts to personally sabotaging and other-hating views and actions.

After eight months of RET, mostly in group therapy, Ms. P was remarkably improved. Her state of panic had long since vanished, and she only occasionally became anxious. She was working well on her new job, so well that she had received still another offer. She was able to accept the new position without vacillation and with little help from her therapy group. She was looking forward to taking it even though she knew that she might fail. She felt that if she did, she would feel "sad" but hardly "awful." She still had problems reaching orgasm in intercourse but was not bothered about this difficulty and viewed herself, in fact, as a "very good" sex partner to her lover.

Most importantly, perhaps, Ms. P accepted herself with all her symptoms. When she was anxious, indecisive, compulsively competitive, or failed to reach orgasm, she deplored her behavior but not herself. Therefore, she was able to turn her time and effort toward changing her unfortunate performances, instead of wasting her energy on flagellating and damning herself.

Humanism Means Self-Control

RET is no miracle cure. It requires a considerable amount of effort and practice on the part of the client. Hence, it is hardly the therapy of choice for the individual who wants to be coddled, who thinks he must have immediate gratification within the therapy sessions, who believes that some sudden insight will produce a magic cure, or who refuses to work at helping himself. It is also not the cup of tea for the therapist who primarily wants to gratify himself during therapy.

RET, however, can be used with a large variety of clients. It is cognitive-emotive-behavior therapy. It teaches individuals how to understand themselves and others, how to react differently, and how to change their basic personality patterns. I originally called it rational psychotherapy, since it is more honestly and directly didactic and persuasive than other forms of psychological treatment. After it was only a few years old, however, I began to see that it was in truth a cognitive-affective procedure. Now, my associates and I frequently refer to it as rational-behavior therapy or cognitive-behavior therapy, and acknowledge that it is definitely a form of behavior therapy. However, because it deliberately draws on intellectual processes, RET is unlike B. F. Skinner's operant conditioning or Joseph Wolpe's reciprocal inhibition (desensitization).

People often charge that RET is anti-humanistic and that it is over-intellectualized, mechanistic and manipulative. These accusations are not only mistaken, but they miss an important point. Efficient therapies that stress the potentialities of the client's control over his emotional processes are in many respects the most humanistic means of personality change that have yet been invented. They are usually man-centered, creativity-oriented, and relevant to the maximum actualization of human potential.

Although experientially oriented psychologists, such as Abraham Maslow, Fritz Perls, and Carl Rogers, are outstanding humanists, so too are cognitively oriented therapists, such as Aaron T. Beck, Eric Berne, Charlotte Bühler, George Kelly, Arnold Lazarus, E. Lakin Phillips, and Julian Rotter.

Rational-Emotive Therapy is a comprehensive system of psychotherapy. It is substantiated by research studies that show that the A-B-C theory of emotional disturbance and change is valid, and by other studies that show its main method, RET teaching and the giving of homework assignments, is effective. Basically, RET is a scientific procedure derived from and aiming at maximum humanization, or the more efficient and happiness-producing relating of the individual to himself, to others, and to the world. ◆

Discussion Questions

1. What is Rational-Emotive Therapy (RET) and who developed it?

2. According to Ellis, what role does belief play in emotional disturbance?

3. What does "A-B-C" stand for in Ellis' system, and what do these terms mean?

4. What causes someone to feel anxious or worried?

5. How might RET be superior to psychoanalysis in explaining a woman's anxiety and worries?

6. Name and describe the two main purposes of RET.

7. What is the irrational trinity?

8. Why, according to Ellis, is psychoanalysis ineffective?

9. What type of client would not be helped by RET and why?

10. List at least three criticisms of RET. How does Ellis reply?

The *Frontiers* of PHARMACOLOGY

◆ *Larry J. Siever*

When we think of what makes somebody unique, we not only call forth an image of what he or she looks like—blond hair and blue eyes, for example—but we see this image flavored by that person's particular personality. Some have a dour, pessimistic temperament while others seem perpetually cheerful. Many of us know people who are impulsive, doing things without really thinking about their consequences, while others may seem odd—a bit out of step.

Yet while we're accustomed to thinking of personality as something that is shaped by early experiences, primarily with parents and other caregivers, researchers are now discovering specific genetic and biologic factors that flavor normal personality and may play an important role in the development of personality disorder—just as they do for the color of one's eyes or hair.

The idea of a biology of temperament—that is, the innate tendencies toward how someone relates to their environment—is not a new one. We have now, however, arrived at a point in our understanding of the brain that we can begin to explore the underlying mechanisms that contribute to specific temperamental styles. New tools probe brain chemicals, as well as new imaging techniques to actually visualize how the brain works, allow scientists to get a clearer idea of how individual differences in brain functioning might contribute to differences in personality.

While temperament may be present at birth, personality develops, through ongoing experience, over the course of a lifetime. Personality is a complex constellation of traits, coping strategies, and defenses against seemingly built-in vulnerabilities. Some people struggle through life, for example, because they fly off the handle too easily; others seem to be born already armed with a set of defensive tools to combat life's difficulties.

In our laboratory, we try to identify and evaluate certain traits to discover how they relate to personality and its related disorders and discomforts.

> **Personality is a complex constellation of traits, coping strategies, and defenses against seemingly built-in vulnerabilites.**

Frank was a middle-aged man who came to our evaluation program because his boss suggested he seek psychiatric treatment. He was a good accountant but nevertheless was always passed over for promotion because he couldn't supervise other employees. Quiet and conservative, he rarely made eye contact with colleagues and, when faced with pressure or deadlines, he would perceive coworkers' questions as intrusive and

become angry and abusive. He generally felt misunderstood by others and considered himself a loner.

When he completed the testing program, I reviewed some of the findings with Frank. I explained to him that his ability to organize information seemed to decline rapidly when he was under stress and became upset. At this point he would lash out at what he imagined was the source of his distress, often finding meanings in events or comments where they were not warranted.

In the course of our discussion, Frank began to feel that some of his angry behavior and peculiarities were finally being understood by someone. He also latched on to the idea that a chemical imbalance in his brain may have caused his problem. I explained that much of our research was still preliminary, but that, with proper medication, the disorganization he experienced under stress (which was causing many of his problems with people) might be alleviated.

Three Key Traits

While a knowledge of the biology of the brain and its relation to personality will not allow us to predict an individual's behavior, it may offer us a vocabulary to understand why some people are more prone to outbursts of anger, for instance, while others are painfully shy and fearful of social contact.

In addition, understanding the biologic vulnerabilities to traits such as impulsivity or irritability may also help physicians to identify medications that will reduce these troublesome tendencies. It should also help them find more adaptive solutions to their life dilemmas.

In our program, we focus on three personality traits—impulsivity, emotional reactivity (which can also be thought of as sensitivity or irritability), and eccentricity—in people whose disturbed thoughts, feelings, and/or behaviors are se-

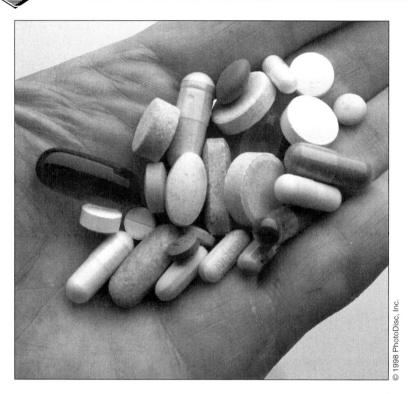

© 1998 PhotoDisc, Inc.

vere enough that they result in problems at work or in their relationships. In their extreme form of expression—when they are not episodic but *characteristic* of how someone relates to the world around them—these traits are analogous to more serious mental disorders: Impulsivity, for example, is related to kleptomania; emotional reactivity to depression; and eccentricity to schizophrenia.

In order to better define the biologic bases of certain personality disorders, we have focused on individual differences in neurotransmitter systems and their relation to these key traits.

The first trait, impulsivity (a tendency to act aggressively rather than reflect), rather consistently appears to relate to brain chemistry. Abnormalities in one of the brain's messenger systems—the release and uptake of serotonin (a neurotransmitter involved in aggression and ambition, among other functions)—have been found

in people who get into trouble because they act without thinking. They may be irritable and get into fights; experience stormy, unstable relationships; or have trouble with alcohol and drugs.

New drugs such as fluoxetine (Prozac) which prolong the effect of serotonin by slowing its reuptake in the brain, might be beneficial in improving not only mood but also the tendency toward impulsive, aggressive, or self-destructive behavior.

The second key trait, emotional reactivity or sensitivity, seems to relate rather strongly to the norepinephrine system. Norepinephrine raises blood pressure, stimulates heart rate, and sharpens perceptual processing in response to new events, especially those that may be threatening or dangerous.

In our preliminary studies, we found that people with overactive norepinephrine systems may be more likely to be the risk-takers of the world, to be irritable or in

other ways overreactive to their environment—seeking novelty and adventure whenever they can. Lower levels of norepinephrine activity often lead to depression and detachment from life.

The third trait, eccentricity, may lead people to appear somewhat odd and experience reality in a peculiar fashion. Some may feel, for example, that they are constantly being watched because they are "bad"; some may be suspicious or wary of the motivations of others. In these people, increases in the brain chemical dopamine, which is important in initiating and regulating thoughts and behaviors, may be involved. Here, drugs that block the activity of dopamine may mute the suspiciousness and distorted perception of more paranoid individuals, including schizotypal patients—that is people with disturbances in thinking and perception.

In our program at Mt. Sinai, we have developed and are in the process of implementing several specialized tests designed to evaluate people who are troubled by these feelings of impulsivity, emotional reactivity, and/or eccentricity—people who have altered perceptions of the world around them and difficulty connecting with others. We use a variety of psychophysiologic, information-processing, neuropsychologic, brain-imaging, and neurochemical tests—as well as complete diagnostic, psychologic, and family history evaluations to better understand the biologic roots of these personality traits.

Serotoinin and Impulsivity

At the National Institute of Mental Health (NIMH), in the lab of researcher Dennis Murphy, I worked on a study of hormone responses to a medication called fenfluramine, an anti-obesity agent that causes the brain to release serotonin. This serotonin release in turn stimulates production of a hormone called prolactin. By measuring levels of prolactin in blood samples taken before and after fenfluramine is given, we may get a reflection of serotonin activity in the brain.

In the NIMH study, patients who reported feeling depressed showed a reduced prolactin response to fenfluramine, suggesting lower levels of serotonin activity. Later, in our work at Mt. Sinai, my colleague, Emil Coccaro, and I found that both depressed and borderline personality disorder patients—including those who acted impulsively, exhibited angry outbursts, or had made suicide attempts—had the same lowered prolactin response to fenfluramine. In fact, the degree to which the response was blunted, or decreased, was directly proportional to how much the patients exhibited impulsive or aggressive behavior such as getting into fights and losing their temper easily.

These results appear to support our belief that reduced serotonin activity contributes to impulsive and/or aggressive behavior. In fact, low serotonin activity might make it harder for people to actually *learn* from their experiences, especially those with negative consequences, and to turn life's sometimes difficult lessons into positive methods for improvement. Impulsive or antisocial people don't seem to respond to punishment, for example, and have trouble suppressing behaviors that are later punished.

Joey came to our clinic depressed after losing his job and getting divorced. While he did not meet criteria for major depression, he was upset and angry. A scrapper all his life, as a child he was constantly hauled into the principal's office for getting into fights. His parents were divorced and he lived with his mother and six brothers and sisters. As a teenager he joined a gang but was really at the margins of the group because of his erratic behavior and hot temper.

In his early twenties he married and had two children, but drifted from job to job because he was constantly

---

Scientists are now trying to understand what might cause brain-function abnormalities that cause certain personality traits.

---

being fired for getting into arguments with coworkers. Just prior to coming to the hospital for evaluation, he had slammed his fist through a plaster wall. In a rage like this, he reported, he would often throw things, get into fights, or sometimes even take it out on himself by cutting his arm.

On his admission into the hospital for testing, his mood varied widely. In our evaluation program on mood and personality disorders, Joey scored high on rating scales for hostility, aggression, and impulsivity. He also showed one of the most markedly reduced prolactin responses to fenfluramine we had ever seen, indicating very low serotonin activity.

As a result, we started him on fluoxetine. Soon after, his mood improved, his wide fluctuations of emotion were reduced, and he was ultimately discharged from the hospital and followed as an outpatient.

Norepinephrine and Reactivity

Another neurotransmitter that may be related to both impulsivity and emotional reactivity is norepinephrine, which acts on other brain systems to enhance the signal of incoming information. Basically, it serves as an arousal system that says, "Pay attention! This may be important!" It is particularly reactive to events that act as stressors and is quiet during restitutive functions such as sleeping, resting or eating.

Abnormalities in this system have been suggested to play an important role in depression. Decreased efficiency of this neurotransmitter may be in part responsible for the altered states of arousal, sleep, daily activity, and goal-directed behavior of depression. Since norepinephrine enhances information processing—akin to increasing the contrast and intensity of color on a television set—reductions in its activity might contribute to a lack of pleasure and engagement with life, analogous to watching a bland, washed-out picture on TV.

In contrast, increased activity may be associated with impulsivity and seeking stimulation in activities such as gambling or sexual promiscuity.

Like all neurotransmitters, norepinephrine acts in the nervous system by attaching to specific receptors, initiating a cascade of events in the receiving cell. The responsiveness of these receptors appears to be blunted in people who suffer from major depressive episodes.

Here, we test the system by administering clonidine, a medication for high blood pressure. Clonidine acts on one type of norepinephrine receptor to stimulate growth-hormone secretion. By measuring growth hormone in blood samples taken before and after clonidine administration, we may be able to gauge the system's efficiency.

So far, we have found that depressed patients have a more blunted response to clonidine than normal volunteers, while high responses indicate an increase in emotional reactivity or sensitivity.

Carol, another patient who came to our clinic for evaluation, had been moody and volatile for as long as she could remember. Her father had been an alcoholic and her mother was frequently depressed. At age 10 she took an overdose of aspirin, and as a teenager she started abusing drugs and was quite promiscuous.

By her mid-20s, as a divorced mother, she reported feeling "angry and worthless." Her relationships were stormy and unstable, usually ending in a violent argument. In her initial interview in our program, she appeared engaging, almost childlike; however, she became irritable and angry when discussing her boyfriend or child.

When we administered the fenfluramine test, we found her prolactin response was lowered, suggesting she had reduced levels of serotonin. Then, when we gave her the clonidine test, we found that she had an exaggerated growth-hormone response, which suggested increased norepinephrine responsiveness. The combination of the two may have contributed to her difficulty with feelings of impulsivity and irritability—the impulsivity might stem from her low serotonin level and the irritability from her overactive norepinephrine system.

After her evaluation, she was started on sertraline (Zoloft)—a cousin of fluoxetine that leaves some patients feeling less of a "jittery" side effect. After several days her mood brightened up. Soon she no longer felt the need to abuse drugs and alcohol and felt much more comfortable with herself.

Dopamine
and Eccentricity

Scientists are now trying to understand what might cause the abnormalities in brain structure and function that account for person-ality traits such as eccentricity, social isolation, and suspiciousness. Some hypothesize that alterations in the *development* of the brain—for example, the migration of nerve cells to their appointed spots—may somehow go awry. It is also possible that key chemicals are deficient in regions of the brain such as the frontal lobe.

One candidate for such chemical deficiency is dopamine, which seems to be important in the maintenance of "working memory"—that is, in holding information on line for further processing. It is precisely this function that is apparently problematic in people with eccentric personalities who have difficulty processing information.

On the assumption that making more dopamine available in these regions might improve cognitive function, we evaluated patients' performance on an information-processing task called the Wisconsin Card Sorting Test (WCST) after giving them amphetamine—a drug that releases dopamine. The

> *...when we consider the possibility that there are hundreds of neurotransmitter systems working together in the brain, it seems clear that we're wired for certain traits that contribute to the overall sum of who we are and how we act.*

WCST is a kind of solitaire game in which subjects must sort a deck of cards marked with four different colors, numbers, and shapes. They are given no rules as to how to initially sort the cards—in fact, the rules change periodically throughout the test.

Our preliminary results indicated that people with eccentric personality disorders do worse on this test than patients with other personality disorders. In fact, these people actually performed *better* on the WCST after amphetamine was administered than after a placebo, raising the possibility that dopamine or related chemicals might actually improve their cognitive performance. With further experimentation, we may be able to determine whether long-term administration of medications designed to increase dopamine might help improve the social isolation of eccentric personality types.

Paradoxically, too *little* dopamine in the frontal cortex may be the result of too much in the more primitive areas of the brain—those regions regulating emotions. This oversupply may contribute to suspiciousness and distortions in the perception of reality. In fact, people who have taken amphetamines (as a recreational drug) in too high doses for too long a time may become paranoid, fear others are watching them, or focus on repetitive thoughts and behaviors—in effect mimicking those with eccentric disorders.

One might imagine the role of dopamine in these people with subtle alterations in brain structure and processing as akin to the powerful amplifier in a stereo system. The static and noise on an old record is similar to the slippage and errors of cognitive processing in the eccentric person. But when such a record is played on a powerful stereo that amplifies the distortions, the result is a horrendous cacophony of sounds, with much of the music being lost. Medications that block the receptors for dopamine appear to "turn down the noise."

Barry was a man in his early 50s who looked perhaps 10 years older than his real age. His shoulders were stooped, he wore ill-fitting pants, a belt that was only partially buckled, and a shirt with ink stains on the front pocket. He appeared at the same time out of place and forlorn. He lived alone in an apartment, spending the day doing crossword puzzles and watching TV, going out only occasionally to grocery shop.

While Barry never became "clinically" depressed (such that he lost weight, had a poor appetite or trouble sleeping), he derived little pleasure from his life and felt that the rest of humanity was like a passing parade of which he was only an observer. He was wary of others' motives and rarely confided in anybody.

In his initial interview, he showed little emotion and his voice had a flat, monotonous quality. On the WCST, he made numerous errors, but his performance greatly improved after he got amphetamine. It changed little with the placebo. We also performed a spinal lumbar tap to remove and test a sample of cerebral spinal fluid—and found that concentrations of a dopamine breakdown product were slightly low, indicating lowered levels of dopamine.

I explained to Barry that his tests showed he might have some difficulty focusing his attention, as well as holding in and organizing information from his environment. He acknowledged that sometimes he felt "overloaded" and had trouble keeping track of what was happening, and that sometimes, because of this, he worried that others were making fun of him. That was part of the reason, he said, he felt so uncomfortable around people.

Barry's treatment involved taking Wellbutrin, an antidepressant that makes dopamine more available in the brain, in the hopes that increasing his dopaminergic activity might improve his symptoms.

"Flying Lessons"

This model of testing, diagnosis, and treatment, while still hypothetical and based on preliminary evidence, at least illustrates how neurotransmitters—the biologic messengers of the brain—can act in a negative function to create difficulty and dis-

comfort in people with certain personality disorders. It becomes even clearer, in certain patients, how two neurotransmitters might work in tandem to modulate problematic behaviors such as violence or suicide attempts even across different psychiatric categories.

In Carol's case, for example, her feelings of being "angry and worthless" may have stemmed from her overactive norepinephrine system, while a deficit in her serotonin activity may have contributed to her impulsive anger and led her into stormy, sometimes violent relationships.

The two systems working—or *not* working—together, influence

Long-term administration of medications may help improve the feelings of social isolation among eccentric personality types.

---

the behavioral expression of each other. And when we consider the possibility that there are hundreds of neurotransmitter systems working together in the brain, it seems clear that we're wired for certain traits that contribute to the overall sum of who we are and how we act.

For researchers, the trick is to map out the chart of brain wirings and separate the innate from the environmental—and to discover where the "short circuits" are. Newer and newer drugs that act more specifically on a particular "short" are appearing on the market, although further research is needed to test their ability to ease one problem without creating other, more serious discomforts.

In addition to the immediate benefits of relief for the patient, medication might also promote the learning of new, more adaptive and flexible coping strategies. For example, the impulsive individual, who cannot easily reflect upon the consequences of his behavior, may

have difficulty benefiting from psychotherapy alone. Proper medication, though, may permit patients to incorporate more positive ways of interacting—in psychotherapy as well as in relationships.

In addition, while having a "tantrum" when frustrated or upset may have brought them to the attention of their parents as children, it certainly doesn't work for them as adults—and can lead to repeated job loss and divorce. So the calming effects of medication may in fact enable people to learn to reflect upon and talk more about their needs and frustrations without short-circuiting to the often inappropriate action that had previously gotten them nowhere.

Medication may give them the language they need to communicate in a positive, forward-moving fashion, free of the distortions and angry outbursts that clouded their life beforehand. In the words of one patient, "Medication gave me wings; now I need to learn how to fly." Psychotherapy, in this context, can be thought of as "flying lessons."

Understanding = Help

Finally, a simple understanding of the *source* of a patients', underlying temperamental vulnerabilities—such as irritability or aggression—can help the therapist, family members, spouses, and others close to the patient feel more empathy and have more patience with that person's particular struggles. We might learn to understand the outbursts of an impulsive person, for instance, because we know how he has more difficulty weighing the consequences of his behavior before acting than most of us.

We might also have more patience with the knowledge that he is not simply ignoring his punishment—whether it be repeated firings or relationship fights—but that a chemical deficiency makes it difficult for him to *learn* from it: His behavior is not simply malevolent but stems from his difficulty in reflecting. (This does not absolve individual responsibility: He still needs to learn how to compensate for this vulnerability, just as a person with ulcers or diabetes must learn to deal with their illness and watch their diet.)

Similarly, the process of recognizing and identifying someone's underlying temperamental susceptibilities may even help the *patient* understand the vulnerabilities he or she is struggling with, as in Frank's or Barry's case. This understanding alone may be beneficial to the patient's recovery.

As we learn more about the biology of the brain, we may become better able to regulate and alter the neurotransmitters important in mood and personality. Of course, some may ask whether people with even "normal" variations could be in some way "improved" with medication, a question often raised in connection with drugs such as Prozac, which has reportedly "transformed" people. While these drugs may be of enormous benefit to those suffering from depression or prone to impulsivity and other disorders, it is not clear what role they would play in those not experiencing any serious distress from these problems.

The question, however, is complicated by the fact that a large proportion of the population—up to one in five—at one time or another may experience some form of depression. Personality disorders are also not as uncommon as we tend to think: up to 10 percent, according to some studies.

Yes, medications may have an impact on a wider population of people than has been previously imagined. We already know that stimulants such as amphetamine can improve performance and brighten mood in people who may be slightly depressed or fatigued—yet we do not endorse the widespread use of stimulants, nor would they prove appealing to a well-rested, highly functioning person.

As we better understand the ways medications modify the brain and help individuals with specific kinds of problems, there will hopefully be a more consensual set of guidelines for the appropriate use of them. Because of the reduced side effects of newer drugs, however, their potential impact on a wide range of psychological and emotional problems seems great.   ◆

Discussion Questions

1. What is a biological temperament?

2. What three personality traits are the focus of the research described in Siever's article? Briefly describe each trait.

3. Define impulsivity and its related disorder. How are they related?

4. How does Prozac affect the brain? What effects does it have on behavior?

5. How does norepinephrine affect the body? What problems are caused by norepinephrine imbalances?

6. What chemical imbalance may be related to schizophrenia?

7. What are neurotransmitters, and how do they function in the brain?

8. What type of memory does dopamine appear to maintain?

9. How can dopamine activity be increased?

10. Should psychological disorders be treated with drugs alone? What should be used in conjunction with drug treatment? Why?

11. How might an improved understanding of chemical irregularities in the brain help patients and their families?

Prescriptions *for* HAPPINESS?

◆ *Seymour Fisher and Roger P. Greenberg*

The air is filled with declarations and advertisements of the power of biological psychiatry to relieve people of their psychological distress. Some biological psychiatrists are so convinced of the superiority of their position that they are recommending young psychiatrists no longer be taught the essentials of doing psychotherapy. Feature stories in such magazines as *Newsweek* and *Time* have portrayed drugs like Prozac as possessing almost a mystical potency. The best-selling book *Listening to Prozac* by psychiatrist Peter Kramer, M.D., projects the idyllic possibility that psychotropic drugs may eventually be capable of correcting a spectrum of personality quirks and lacks.

As longtime faculty members of a number of psychiatry departments, we have personally witnessed the gradual but steadily accelerated dedication to the idea that "mental illness" can be mastered with biologically based substances. Yet a careful sifting of the pertinent literature indicates the modesty and skepticism would be more appropriate responses to the research accumulated thus far. In 1989, we first raised radical questions about such biological claims in a book *The Limits of Biological Treatments for Psychological Distress: Comparisons with Psychotherapy and Placebo* (Lawrence Erlbaum). Our approach has been to filter the studies that presumably anchor

them through a series of logical and quantitative (meta-analytic) appraisals.

How Effective Are Antidepressant Drugs?

Antidepressants, one of the major weapons in the biological therapeutic arsenal, illustrate well the largely unacknowledged uncertainty that exists in the biological approach to psychopathology. We suggest that, at present, no one actually knows how effective antidepressants are. Confident declarations about their potency go well beyond the existing evidence.

To get an understanding of the scientific status of antidepressants, we analyzed how much more ef-

> *Vivid differences between the body sensations of drug and placebo could signal to patients whether they are receiving an active or inactive agent.*

fective the antidepressants are than inert pills called "placebos." That is, if antidepressants are given to one depressed group and a placebo to another group, how much greater is the recovery of those taking the active drug as compared to those taking the inactive placebo? Generous claims that antidepressants usually produce improvement in about 60 to 70 percent of patients are not infrequent, whereas placebos are said

to benefit 25 to 30 percent. If antidepressants were, indeed, so superior to placebos, this would be a persuasive advertisement for the biological approach.

We found 15 major reviews of the antidepressant literature. Surprisingly, even the most positive reviews indicate that 30 to 40 percent of studies show no significant difference in response to drug versus placebo! The reviews indicate overall that one-third of patients do not improve with antidepressant treatment, one-third improve with placebos, and an additional third show a response to medication they would not have attained with placebos. In the most optimistic view of such findings, two-thirds of the cases (placebo responders and those who do not respond to anything) do as well with placebo as with active medication.

We also found two large-scale quantitative evaluations (meta-analyses) integrating the outcomes of multiple studies of antidepressants. They clearly indicated, on the average, quite modest therapeutic power.

We were particularly impressed by the large variation in outcomes of studies conducted at multiple clinical sites or centers. Consider a study that compared the effectiveness of an antidepressant among patients at five different research centers. Although the pooled results demonstrate that the drug was generally more effective than placebo, the results from individual centers reveal much variation. After six weeks of treatment, every one of the six measures of effectiveness showed the antidepressant (imipramine) to be merely equivalent to placebo in two or more of the centers. In two of the settings, a difference favoring the medication was detected on only one of 12 outcome comparisons.

In other words, the pooled, apparently favorable, outcome data conceal that dramatically different

425

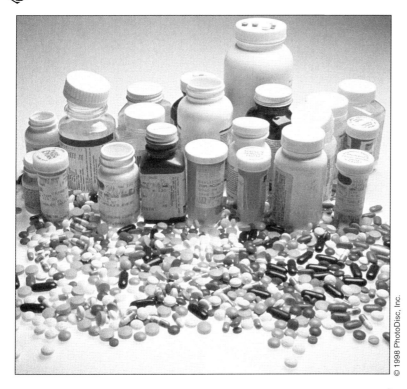

© 1998 PhotoDisc, Inc.

results could be obtained as a function of who conducted the study and the specific conditions at each locale. We can only conclude that a good deal of fragility characterized the apparent superiority of drug over placebo. The scientific literature is replete with analogous examples.

Incidentally, we also looked at whether modern studies, which are presumably better protected against bias, use higher doses, and often involve longer treatment periods, show a greater superiority of the antidepressant than did earlier studies. The literature frequently asserts that failure demonstrate antidepressant superiority due to such methodological failures as not using high enough doses, and so forth.

We examined this issue in a pool of 16 studies assembled by psychiatrists John Kane and Jeffrey Lieberman in 1984. These studies all compare a standard drug, such as imipramine or

amitriptyline, to a newer drug and a placebo. They use clearer diagnostic definitions of depression than did the older studies and also adopt currently accepted standards for dosage levels and treatment duration. When we examined the data, we discovered that the advantage of drug over placebo was modest. Twenty-one percent more of the patients receiving a drug improved as compared to those on placebo. Actually most of the studies showed no difference in the percentage of patients significantly improved by drugs. There was no indication that these studies, using more careful methodology, achieved better outcomes than older studies.

Finally, it is crucial to recognize that several studies have established that there is a high rate of relapse among those who have responded positively to an antidepressant but then are taken off treatment. The relapse rate may be

60 percent or more during the first year after treatment cessation. Many studies also show that any benefits of antidepressants wane in a few months, even while the drugs are still being taken. This highlights the complexity of evaluating antidepressants. They may be effective initially, but lose all value over a longer period.

Are Drug Trials Biased?

As we burrowed deeper into the antidepressant literature, we learned that there are also crucial problems in the methodology used to evaluate psychotropic drugs. Most central is the question of whether this methodology properly shields drug trials from bias. Studies have shown that the more open to bias a drug trial is, the greater the apparent superiority of the drug over placebo. So questions about the trustworthiness of a given drug-testing procedure invite skepticism about the results.

The question of potential bias first came to our attention in studies comparing inactive placebos to active drugs. In the classic double-blind design, neither patient nor researcher knows who is receiving drug or placebo. We were struck by the fact that the presumed protection provided by the double-blind design was undermined by the use of placebos that simply do not arouse as many body sensations as do active drugs. Research shows that patients learn to discriminate between drug and placebo largely from body sensations and symptoms.

A substance like imipramine, one of the most frequently studied antidepressants, usually causes clearly defined sensations, such as dry mouth, tremor, sweating, constipation. Inactive placebos used in studies of antidepressants also apparently initiate some body sensations, but they are fewer, more inconsistent, and less intense as indicated by the fact that they are less often cited by patients as a source of discomfort causing them to drop out of treatment.

Vivid differences between the body sensations of drug and placebo groups could signal to patients as to whether they are receiving an active or inactive agent. Further, they could supply discriminating cues to those responsible for the patient's day-to-day treatment. Nurses, for example, might adopt different attitudes toward patients they identify as being "on" versus "off" active treatment—and consequently communicate contrasting expectations.

The Body of Evidence

This is more than theoretical. Researchers have reported that in a double-blind study of imipramine, it was possible by means of side effects to identify a significant number of the patients taking the active drug. Those patients receiving a placebo have fewer signals (from self and others) indicating they are being actively treated and should be improving. By the same token, patients taking an active drug receive multiple signals that may well amplify potential placebo effects linked to the therapeutic context. Indeed, a doctor's strong belief in the power of the active drug enhances the apparent therapeutic power of the drug or placebo.

Is it possible that a large proportion of the difference in effectiveness often reported between antidepressants and placebos can be explained as a function of body sensation discrepancies? It is conceivable, and fortunately there are research findings that shed light on the matter.

Consider an analysis by New Zealand psychologist Richard Thomsen. He reviewed double-blind, placebo-controlled studies of antidepressants completed be-

tween 1958 and 1972. Sixty-eight had employed an inert placebo and seven an active one (atropine) that produced a variety of body sensations. The antidepressant had a superior therapeutic effect in 59 percent of the studies using inert placebo—but in only one study (14 percent) using the active placebo. The active placebo eliminated any therapeutic advantage for the antidepressants, apparently because it convinced patients they were getting real medication.

How Blind Is Double-Blind?

Our concerns about the effects of inactive placebos on the double-blind design led us to ask just how blind the double-blind really is. By the 1950s reports were already surfacing that for psychoactive drugs, the double-blind design is not as scientifically objective as originally assumed. In 1993 we searched the world literature and found 31 reports in which patients and researchers involved in studies were asked to guess who was receiving the active psychotropic drug and

---

A patient's attitude toward the therapist is just as biological in nature as a patients's response to an antidepressant drug.

---

who the placebo. In 28 instances the guesses were significantly better than chance—and at times they were surprisingly accurate. In one double-blind study that called for administering either imipramine, phenelzine, or placebo to depressed patients, 78 percent of patients and 87 percent of psychiatrists correctly distinguished drug from placebo.

One particularly systematic report in the literature involved the administration of alprazolam, imipramine, and placebo over an eight-week period to groups of patients who experienced panic at-

tacks. Halfway through the treatment and also at the end, the physicians and the patients were asked to judge independently whether each patient was receiving an active drug or a placebo. If they thought an active drug was being administered, they had to decide whether it was alprazolam or imipramine. Both physicians (with an 88 percent success rate) and patients (83 percent) substantially exceeded chance in the correctness of their judgments. Furthermore, the physicians could distinguish alprazolam from imipramine significantly better than chance. The researchers concluded that "double-blind studies of these pharmacological treatments for panic disorder are not really 'blind.'"

Yet the vast majority of psychiatric drug efficacy studies have simply *assumed* that the double-blind design is effective; they did not test the blindness by determining whether patients and researchers were able to differentiate drug from placebo.

We take the somewhat radical view that this means most past studies of the efficacy of psychotropic drugs are, to unknown degrees, scientifically untrustworthy. At the least, we can no longer speak with confidence about the true differences in therapeutic power between active psychotropic drugs and placebos. We must suspend judgment until future studies are completed with more adequate controls for the defects of the double-blind paradigm.

Other bothersome questions arose as we scanned the cascade of studies focused on antidepressants. Of particular concern is how unrepresentative the patients are who end up in the clinical trials. There are the usual sampling problems having to do with which persons seek treatment for their discomfort, and, in addition, volunteer as subjects for a study. But

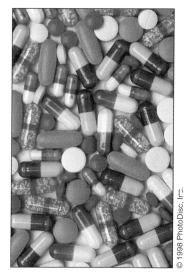

© 1998 PhotoDisc, Inc.

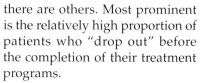

there are others. Most prominent is the relatively high proportion of patients who "drop out" before the completion of their treatment programs.

Numerous dropouts occur in response to unpleasant side effects. In many published studies, 35 percent or more of patients fail to complete the research protocol. Various procedures have been developed to deal fairly with the question of how to classify the therapeutic outcomes of dropouts, but none can vitiate the simple fact that the final sample of fully treated patients has often been drastically reduced.

There are still other filters that increase sample selectivity. For example, studies often lose sizable segments of their samples by not including patients who are too depressed to speak, much less participate in a research protocol, or who are too disorganized to participate in formal psychological testing. We also found decisions not to permit particular racial or age groups to be represented in samples or to avoid using persons below a certain educational level. Additionally, researchers typically recruit patients whose depression

is not accompanied by any other type of physical or mental disorder, a situation that does not hold for the depressed in the general population.

So we end up wondering about the final survivors in the average drug trial. To what degree do they typify the average individual in real life who seeks treatment? How much can be generalized from a sample made up of the "leftovers" from multiple depleting processes? Are we left with a relatively narrow band of those most willing to conform to the rather rigid demands of the research establishment? Are the survivors those most accepting of a dependent role?

The truth is that there are probably multiple kinds of survivors, depending upon the specific local conditions prevailing where the study was carried out. We would guess that some of the striking differences in results that appear in multicenter drug studies could be traced to specific forms of sampling bias. We do not know how psychologically unique the persons are who get recruited into, and stick with, drug research enterprises. We are not the first to raise this question, but we are relatively more alarmed about the potential implications.

Researcher Motivation and Outcome

We recently conducted an analysis that further demonstrates how drug effectiveness diminishes as the opportunity for bias in research design wanes. This analysis seized on studies in which a newer antidepressant is compared (under double-blind conditions) with an older, standard antidepressant and a placebo. In such a context the efficacy of the newer drug (which the drug company hopes to introduce) is of central interest to the researcher, and the effectiveness of the older drug or peripheral im-

port. Therefore, if the double-blind is breached (as is likely), there would presumably be less bias to enhance the efficacy of the older drug than occurred in the original trials of that drug.

We predicted that the old drug would appear significantly less powerful in the newer studies than it had in earlier designs, where it was of central interest of the researcher. To test this hypothesis, we located 22 double-blind studies in which newer antidepressants were compared with an older antidepressant drug (usually imipramine) and a placebo. Our meta-analysis revealed, as predicted, that the efficacy rates, based on clinicians's judgments of outcome, were quite modest for the older antidepressants. In fact, they were approximately one-half to one-quarter the average size of the effects reported in earlier studies when the older drug was the only agent appraised.

Let us be very clear as to what this signifies: When researchers were evaluating the antidepressant in a context where they were no longer interested in proving its therapeutic power, there was a dramatic decrease in that apparent power, as compared to an earlier context when they were enthusiastically interested in demonstrating the drug's potency. A change in researcher motivation was enough to change outcome. Obviously this means too that the present double-blind design for testing drug efficacy is exquisitely vulnerable to bias.

Another matter of pertinence to the presumed biological rationale for the efficacy of antidepressants is that no consistent links have been demonstrated between the concentration of drug in blood and its efficacy. Studies have found significant correlations for some drugs, but of low magnitude. Efforts to link plasma levels to therapeutic outcome have been disappointing.

Similarly, few data show a relationship between antidepressant dosage levels and their therapeutic efficacy. That is, large doses of the drug do not necessarily have greater effects than low doses. These inconsistencies are a bit jarring against the context of a biological explanatory framework.

We have led you through a detailed critique of the difficulties and problems that prevail in the body of research testing the power of the antidepressants. We conclude that it would be wise to be relatively modest in claims about their efficacy. Uncertainty and doubt are inescapable.

While we have chosen the research on the antidepressants to illustrate the uncertainties attached to biological treatments of psychological distress, reviews of other classes of psychotropic drugs yield similar findings. After a survey of anti-anxiety drugs, psychologist Ronald Lipman concluded there is little consistent evidence that they help patients with anxiety disorders: "Although it seems natural to assume that the anxiolytic medications would be the most effective psychotropic medications for the treatment of anxiety disorders, the evidence does not support this assumption."

Biological Versus Psychological?

The faith in the biological approach has been fueled by a great burst of research. Thousands of papers have appeared probing the efficacy of psychotropic drugs. A good deal of basic research has attacked fundamental issues related to the nature of brain functioning in those who display psychopathology. Researchers in these areas are dedicated and often do excellent work. However, in their zeal, in their commitment to

the so-called biological, they are at times overcome by their expectations. Their hopes become rigidifying boundaries. Their vo-

---

Administering a therapeutic drug is not simply a medical, biological act. It is also a complex social act, its effectiveness mediated by the patient's expectations.

---

cabulary too easily becomes a jargon that camouflages oversimplified assumptions.

A good example of such oversimplification is the way in which the term "biological" is conceptualized. It is too often viewed as a realm distinctly different from the psychological. Those invested in the biological approach all too often practice the ancient Cartesian distinction between somatic-stuff and soul-stuff. In so doing

---

While we have chosen the research on the antidepressants to illustrate the uncertainties attached to biological treatments of psychological distress, reviews of other classes of psychotropic drugs yield similar findings.

---

they depreciate the scientific significance of the phenomena they exile to the soul-stuff category.

But paradoxically, they put a lot of interesting phenomena out of bounds to their prime methodology and restrict themselves to a narrowed domain. For example, if talk therapy is labeled as a "psychological" thing—not biological—this implies that biological research can only hover at the periphery of what psychotherapists do. A sizable block of behavior becomes off limits to the biologically dedicated.

In fact, if we adopt the view that the biological and psycholog-

ical are equivalent (biological monism), there is no convincing real-versus-unreal differentiation between the so-called psychological and biological. It *all* occurs in tissue and one is not more "real" than the other. A patient's attitude toward the therapist is just as biological in nature as a patient's response to an antidepressant. A response to a placebo is just as biological as a response to an antipsychotic drug. This may be an obvious point, but it has not yet been incorporated into the world views of either the biologically or psychologically oriented.

Take a look at a few examples in the research literature that highlight the overlap or identity of what is so often split apart. In 1992, psychiatrist Lewis Baxter and colleagues showed that successful psychotherapy of obsessive-compulsive patients results in brain imagery changes equivalent to those produced by successful drug treatment. The brain apparently responds in equivalent ways to both the talk and drug approaches. Even more dramatic is a finding that instilling in the elderly the illusion of being in control of one's surroundings (by putting them in charge of some plants) significantly increased their life span compared to a control group. What could be a clearer demonstration of the biological nature of what is labeled as a psychological expectation than the postponement of death?

Why are we focusing on this historic Cartesian confusion? Because so many who pursue the so-called biological approach are by virtue of their tunnel vision motivated to overlook the psychosocial variables that mediate the administration of such agents as psychotropic drugs and electroconvulsive therapy.

They do not permit themselves to seriously grasp that psychosocial variables are just as biological as a capsule containing an antidepressant. It is the failure to understand this that results in treating placebo effects as if they were extraneous or less of a biological reality than a chemical agent.

Placebo Effects

Indeed, placebos have been shown to initiate certain effects usually thought to be reserved for active drugs. For example, placebos clearly show dose-level effects. A larger dose of a placebo will have a greater impact than a lower dose. Placebos can also create addictions. Patients will poignantly declare that they cannot stop taking a particular placebo substance (which they assume is an active drug) because to do so causes them too much distress and discomfort.

Placebos can produce toxic effects such as rashes, apparent memory loss, fever, headaches, and more. These "toxic" effects may be painful and even overwhelming in their intensity. The placebo literature is clear: Placebos are powerful body-altering substances, especially considering the wide range of body systems they can influence.

Actually, the power of the placebo complicates all efforts to test the therapeutic efficacy of psychotropic drugs. When placebos alone can produce positive curative effects in the 40 to 50 percent range (occasionally even up to 70–80 percent), the active drug being tested is hard-pressed to demonstrate its superiority. Even if the active drug exceeds the placebo in potency, the question remains whether the advantage is at least partially due to the superior potential of the active drug itself to mobilize placebo effects because it is an active substance

that stirs vivid body sensations. Because it is almost always an inactive substance (sugar pill) that arouses fewer genuine body sensations, the placebo is less convincingly perceived as having therapeutic prowess.

Drug researchers have tried, in vain, to rid themselves of placebo effects, but these effects are forever present and frustrate efforts to demonstrate that psychoactive drugs have an independent "pure" biological impact. This state of affairs dramatically testifies that the labels "psychological" and "biological" refer largely to different perspectives on events that all occur in tissue. At present, it is somewhat illusory to separate the so-called biological and psychological effects of drugs used to treat emotional distress.

The literature is surprisingly full of instances of how social and attitudinal factors modify the effects of active drugs. Antipsychotic medications are more effective if the patient likes rather than dislikes the physician administering them. An

---

If a stimulant drug is administered with the deceptive instruction that it is a sedative, it can initiate a physiological response characteristic of a sedative, such as decreased heart rate.

---

antipsychotic drug is less effective if patients are led to believe they are only taking an inactive placebo. Perhaps even more impressive, if a stimulant drug is administered with the deceptive instruction that it is a sedative, it can initiate a pattern of physiological response, such as decreased heart rate, that is sedative rather than arousing in nature. Such findings reaffirm how fine the line is between social and somatic domains.

What are the practical implications for distressed individuals and their physicians? Administer-

ing a drug is not simply a medical (biological) act. It is, in addition, a complex social act whose effectiveness will be mediated by such factors as the patient's expectations of the drug and reactions to the body sensations created by that drug, and the physician's friendliness and degree of personal confidence in the drug's power. Practitioners who dispense psychotropic medications should become thoroughly acquainted with the psychological variables modifying the therapeutic impact of such drugs and tailor their own behavior accordingly. By the same token, distressed people seeking drug treatment should keep in mind that their probability of benefiting may depend in part on whether they choose a practitioner they truly like and respect. And remember this: You are the ultimate arbiter of a drug's efficacy.

How to go about mastering unhappiness, which ranges from "feeling blue" to despairing depression, puzzles everyone. Such popular quick fixes as alcohol, conversion to a new faith, and other splendid distractions have proven only partially helpful. When antidepressant drugs hit the shelves with their seeming scientific aura, they were easily seized upon. Apparently serious unhappiness (depression) could now be chemically neutralized in the way one banishes a toothache.

But the more we learn about the various states of unhappiness, the more we recognize that they are not simply "symptoms" awaiting removal. Depressed feelings have complex origins and functions. In numerous contexts—for example, chronic conflict with a spouse—depression may indicate a realistic appraisal of a troubling problem and motivate a serious effort to devise a solution.

While it is true that deep despair may interfere with sensible problem-solving, the fact is that, more and more, individuals are being instructed to take antidepressants at the earliest signs of depressive distress and this could interfere with the potentially constructive signaling value of such distress. Emotions are feelings full of information. Unhappiness is an emotion, and despite its negativity, should not be classified single-mindedly as a thing to tune out. This in no way implies that one should submit passively to the distress. comfort of feeling unhappy. Actually, we learn to experiment with a variety of strategies for making ourselves feel better, but the ultimate aim is long-term effective rather than a depersonalized "I feel fine."

Discussion Questions

1. What is a placebo?

2. What do reviews of research on anti-depressant medication appear to reveal about the effectiveness of this type of medication?

3. What is a "double-blind" study?

4. What is the difference between an active placebo and an inert placebo? When active placebos are employed in anti-depressant drug studies, how effective do the drugs appear to be?

5. Why is it important that active placebos be used in drug studies? Why are they used so rarely?

6. What is the impact on study results when patients drop out? Which patients are most likely to drop out of a study on depression, and why should this be of concern?

7. If a drug produces clear physical sensations, why might the typical double-blind procedure be inadequate for testing that drug?

8. How, according to the authors, might the placebo effect or even talk therapy be considered "biological" effects?

9. Can a placebo be addictive? Why or why not?

10. What is the impact of patient expectations when taking an active medication?

11. Did the authors convince you that anti-depressant medications are ineffective? Explain your answer.

BEHAVIOR *THERAPY:* A Road to **Self-***Control*

◆ *G. Terence Wilson and Gerald C. Davison*

Fingernails bitten to the quick, eyes puffy from lack of sleep, Mrs. S. told the behavior therapist of a life dominated by anxiety and spells of nervous depression. Waves of acute fear and deep feelings of worthlessness would sweep over her, uncontrollable and unpredictable. Tension headaches, often precipitated by insomnia, brought almost daily stress and pain.

Mrs. S., aged 29, worked part-time in a college library, where the strain of her personal problems was beginning to show. Neither reassurance from friends nor Librium from her physician had helped. After her husband had accused her of being mentally disturbed and threatened to divorce her, she decided to seek professional help.

Traditional psychotherapists, of course are confronted almost daily with such complex clinical problems. It is not generally known, however, that behavior therapists—who are sometimes said to deal only with single-symptom phobias—have been wrestling with the same kinds of challenges.

To help Mrs. S., the behavior therapist, like any professionally trained therapist, spent the first session establishing rapport. Regardless of the methods ultimately used, the patient's trust and cooperation are essential for success.

As the therapist gained her confidence, he began to make a behavioral assessment of the case, a searching analysis of the biological, psychological and sociological factors that were responsible for her distress. He then divided her problems into those resulting from behavioral excesses (such as frequent rages) and those resulting from behavioral deficits (such as underassertiveness). To learn more about her problems, he asked Mrs. S. about her social skills, her personal strengths, her sex life. He identified the specific conditions under which her problem behaviors occurred and charted Mrs. S.'s thoughts about her problems, noting how competent she felt as a wife and whether her personal standards were unrealistically stringent.

The Uptight Mrs. S.

Specificity is the hallmark of behavior therapy. The therapist must find clear instances of behavior that exemplify the client's often vague, subjective impressions. Mrs. S., like most clients, tended to describe her problems in terms too general for a behavioral analysis: "I guess I'm just an uptight person." So the therapist asked her to keep a daily diary in which she was to record important events and her reactions to them. In addition to helping the therapist assess her behavior, this self-monitoring helped Mrs. S. develop her own awareness of the things that were causing her suffering.

After a half-dozen sessions, the behavioral assessment revealed a picture of a woman who had always been underassertive and often anxious in her relations with other people. Mrs. S.'s inability to express her feelings led to her exploitation by others, which in turn bred resentment, hidden anger, intense guilt over her anger, and low self-esteem. Her depression appeared to be tied closely to her negative picture of herself. The therapist also learned that Mrs. S. had never experienced an orgasm. She had tried to hide this fact from her husband, but felt that her lack of response was depriving him of a satisfying sexual relationship and might lead him to extramarital affairs. Such thoughts appeared to exacerbate her anxiety and her low opinion of herself. Since this problem and most of her other problems centered on her marital relationship, Mrs. S. agreed to the therapist's suggestion that they include her husband in the therapy.

While making the behavioral assessment, the therapist was also deciding tentatively on which therapeutic techniques to employ. Unlike many traditional psychotherapists who use an all-purpose treatment, behavior therapists can choose from a variety of methods within a theoretically consistent framework, tailoring the technique to the client rather than fitting the client's problems into a preordained therapeutic regimen. For Mrs. S., as for most complex cases, the therapist forged a multifaceted treatment program.

Early on, Mrs. S. began a program of relaxation training to curb her anxiety. This training shows the client how to tighten and then relax groups of muscles systematically so as to become more aware of the build-up of tension and to acquire the ability to relax at will. This training greatly reduced the severity of Mrs. S.'s insomnia and headaches in addition to damping down her anxiety.

Strategies for Assertiveness

In these same early sessions, the therapist started a program of assertion training. He had Mrs. S. rehears more expressive ways of responding in situations in which she had always been submissive. He modeled appropriate behavior for her and made constructive comments on her efforts to emulate him. After helping her husband adopt a more supportive attitude toward her, the therapist instructed the couple in ways to use assertion strategies at home. In this way Mrs. S. learned to be assertive outside the therapist's office.

The third major facet of treatment was a Masters and Johnson-type program aimed at overcoming Mrs. S.'s lack of orgasm. Bolstered by the cooperation and understanding of her husband, Mrs. S. responded well and, after three weeks of treatment, began to have orgasms. This success, coupled with the assertion training, greatly enhanced the quality of their relationship.

Nevertheless, Mrs. S. still became depressed on occasion and continued to doubt her adequacy as a wife. These reactions appeared to stem from her unnecessarily low opinion of her own abilities, and the excessively negative interpretation she placed on different life situations. For example, rather than viewing as merely unfortunate her failure to meet her husband's train on time one day, she tended to see it as a catastrophe. Accordingly, the therapist used rational-emotive techniques originated by Albert Ellis. He encouraged Mrs. S. to think up and repeat constructive statements about herself that were incompatible with her feelings of worthlessness. After some initial struggling, she gradually acquired better control over her neurotic thought patterns than she had ever had.

Approximately four months after getting in touch with the therapist, Mrs. S. reported a dramatic reduction in anxiety and depression. Moreover, as part of her newfound emotional freedom and self-confidence, she had decided to return to school to work toward an advanced degree.

The Origins of Be Mod

The historical roots of behavior therapy go back to the beginning of this century, but it was not until the 1950s that behavior therapy emerged as an alternative to the prevailing psychodynamic or Freudian approach. One of the most influential pioneer investigators was Joseph Wolpe, whose book *Psychotherapy by Reciprocal Inhibition* appeared in 1958. In it, he introduced the anxiety-relieving technique of systematic desensitization, drawing on the earlier clinical work of Andrew Salter, and based on classical conditioning principles as developed by the Russian behaviorist Ivan Pavlov and the American behaviorist Clark Hull.

Humanists attack behavior therapy as a mechanistic, totalitarian form of control. But it's the client who has the major say about the goals of treatment.

In systematic desensitization, an anxious or fearful client learns to relax completely. Then, while in a relaxed state, he is confronted with or is asked to imagine the situations or objects he fears, beginning with the least stressful and progressing to more and more difficult images. After several repetitions, this relaxed confrontation leads to a reduction in anxiety.

Wolpe's clinical studies in South Africa, as well as the innovative broad-spectrum approach of Arnold Lazarus, laid the groundwork for the contemporary practice of behavior therapy. At Maudsley Hospital in London, Hans J. Eysenck and his students gave important impetus to a scientific treatment of abnormal behavior based on learning theory. In the United States, the influence of B. F. Skinner and the development of operant conditioning helped establish observable behavior as worthy of study in its own right, rather than as a symptom of some underlying pathological illness. The operant approach, with its emphasis on encouraging desirable behavior, was soon extended to the modification of a whole range of psychiatric disorders, particularly those of children and institutionalized adults.

The most sophisticated view of behavior therapy to date is the social-learning framework proposed by Albert Bandura of Stanford University. This approach focuses not only on changing behavior by using the techniques of operant and classical conditioning, but also on the role of thought in developing and maintaining the change. Bandura stresses the importance of vicarious learning, in which one watches another person model appropriate behavior. In contrast to a strict operant viewpoint, in which man is often seen as a passive reactor to external forces, Bandura has emphasized people's capacity for self-directed behavior change. The development of self-control procedures that promise people greater mastery over their own lives represents perhaps the most significant feature of contemporary behavior research and therapy.

Several misconceptions surround the practice of behavior therapy. It is often alleged, for example, that behavior therapy ignores the client's mind. While this allegation may be true of some radicals in the field, therapists who adhere to social-learning theory believe that what goes on inside a person is both a legitimate and necessary target for therapy.

Another misconception is that behavior therapy modifies only symptoms, whereas psychodynamic therapies deal with the real underlying causes of behavior disorders. Actually, the differences stem from different ideas about "underlying causes." Traditional therapists favor the past and the unconscious as determining a person's behavior, while behavior therapists emphasize current factors, such as rewards and punishments that follow behavior, as well as other sources of social influence on that behavior. An inadequate assessment of a client's behavior doubtless will lead to an incomplete treatment program and might well result in rapid relapse or apparent "symptom substitution." But this would be bad behavior therapy. In the case of Mrs. S., for example, simply using relaxation and assertion training would have left important causes of her distress untouched.

The burgeoning evidence from well-controlled clinical research suggests that behavior therapy has been successful in treating the entire spectrum of psychiatric disorders and is clearly the therapy of choice in many areas. It has been especially successful in the treatment of childhood disorders. Bedwetting, for example, can be rapidly eliminated and, far from resulting in symptom substitution, its elimination produces generalized improvement in the child's functioning, both at home and at school. The treatment of autistic children by Ivar Lovaas and his colleagues has produced substantial, often dramatic therapeutic

gains. Other clinicians have made comparable advances with severely retarded children. Studies also have shown the efficacy of behavioral treatment for such problems as social withdrawal, delinquent acts, phobias, aggression, and social disruption.

Systematic desensitization is the most thoroughly researched technique used with adults. In 1969, after reviewing the evidence, Gordon L. Paul concluded that "for the first time in the history of psychological treatments, a specific technique has reliably produced measurable benefits for clients across a broad range of distressing

---

By emphasizing clear-cut goals chosen by the client, behavior therapists try to avoid the covert manipulations and subtle persuasions of less-structured therapies.

---

problems in which anxiety was of fundamental importance."

More recently developed methods such as "flooding," in which the client's avoidance reactions are directly modified in the real world, appear to be even more effective than desensitization. Masters and Johnson's successful, rapid-treatment program for sexual dysfunction uses many procedures that have been a standard part of the behavior therapists's repertoire since Wolpe's and Lazarus' pioneering contributions. Behavior therapy appears to be the preferred treatment for obesity, and progress has also been made in the treatment of smoking and alcoholism.

Although agreement certainly is not unanimous about the overall efficacy of behavior therapy, it is noteworthy that a special task force of the American Psychiatric Association concluded in 1973 that behavior therapy has "reached a stage of development where [it] unquestionably [has] much to

offer informed clinicians in the service of modern clinical and social psychiatry."

Goals and Values

Opponents of behavior therapy, especially the followers of humanistic psychology, have attacked it as a mechanistic, totalitarian form of control that is imposed arbitrarily upon clients. Behavior therapy really is a collection of principles and techniques about *how* to change behavior; it says nothing about *who* should modify *what* behavior, or *why* or *when*. It is the client who has the major say in deciding on therapy goals. Selecting effective techniques with which to change behavior is an empirical question in which the therapist presumably an expert; choosing therapeutic objectives is a matter of value judgments. The therapists's contribution to the latter lies in generating alternative strategies for the client to follow and in analyzing the likely consequences of pursuing different courses of action.

Selecting therapeutic goals is particularly difficult with clients who are in prisons or mental hospitals or who are too young or too mentally impaired to participate in determining the objectives of therapy. In these instances goals should be approved by an independent review committee created to safeguard the individual's civil rights and general well-being. In this connection, a special commission of the American Psychological Association is developing detailed guidelines for the ethical and legal practice of behavior therapy with different kinds of people.

Recent court decisions have argued that residents in correctional and psychiatric institutions possess a set of inalienable rights, and these rulings affect the practice of behavior therapy. For instance, some behavior therapists have offered inmates and patients the amenities of life as reinforcement for constructive changes in behavior. This practice has meant that these amenities were denied inmates at early stages of the program and then restored as the treatment progressed. In keeping with recent court rulings, such programs, predicated as they are upon the initial withholding of rights, seem no longer acceptable. As a result, behavior therapists will have to use increasing ingenuity in their efforts to find meaningful incentives for behavior change.

In a related area, behavior therapists have helped develop incentive systems to increase the productivity of inmates to prison industries and to encourage patients to help maintain hospital wards. The objectives of such systems are to provide rehabilitative experiences and to offer some distraction from the monotony of institutional life. Recent court rulings indicate that the servitude implicit in these programs must be replaced by compensation at or above the Federal minimum wage,

and that participation must be voluntary. This ruling may work to the disadvantage of patients. Institutional directors, interested in maximum efficiency, may call upon outside employees to perform the essential jobs within institutions, thereby denying patients opportunities to acquire skills that could make them able to support themselves upon discharge.

The Politics of Be Mod

It is now widely acknowledged that all forms of therapy involve social influence. By explicitly recognizing this influence process and by emphasizing clear-cut client-defined goals, behavior therapy attempts to avoid the covert manipulations and subtle persuasions inherent in less structured therapies. This approach, in which the sources of behavior control are openly identified and publicly disseminated, is a necessary deterrent to totalitarian control. As representatives of the Association for Advancement of Behavior Therapy argued at a recent conference of the American Civil Liberties Union, to allow these forces to remain be-

yond public scrutiny is to increase the possibility that the few who are skilled in these techniques will manipulate people for potentially antisocial ends.

Behavior therapy is far from being inconsistent with a humanistic philosophy. On the contrary, it is probably the most effective means of promoting personal freedom and individualism because it enhances the individual's freedom of choice. Mrs. S. had been a depressed, dependent woman, unable to express her genuine feelings or assert her right to be treated with respect. Freeing her from her crippling inhibitions and teaching her to be appropriately assertive gave her a sense of human dignity and expanded the courses of action open to her. She was able to assert herself with her husband without experiencing guilt, to obtain sexual fulfillment without embarrassment, and to return to college to pursue her studies. Behavior therapy need not limit creativity or produce conformity; rather, as Mrs. S.'s case illustrates, it can foster diversity, expand personal horizons and facilitate self-fulfillment. ◆

Discussion Questions

1. What is self-monitoring? How did the authors use it as part of therapy for an anxious patient?
2. Describe a method for training assertiveness.
3. Describe systematic desensitization, and give an example of when it might be used.
4. What are the common misconceptions about behavior therapy, and what are the facts?
5. Who decides what behaviors will be changed in behavior therapy?
6. Explain how modeling is used in a therapy session.
7. According to the authors, what type of behavior does Rational Emotive Therapy try to change?
8. How, according to the authors, is behavior therapy consistent with humanistic ideals?

Name: _____

Date: _____

Part 17: Therapies

1. I think that talk therapy is superior to medication in the treatment of psychological disorders.

Agree   ①   ②   ③   ④   ⑤   Disagree

2. My thinking is entirely rational.

Agree   ①   ②   ③   ④   ⑤   Disagree

3. I believe that most psychological problems are the result of bad experiences in childhood.

Agree   ①   ②   ③   ④   ⑤   Disagree

Design a study to test an experimental anti-anxiety drug. Your task is to test the effectiveness of the new drug against existing anti-anxiety medications and placebos.

How would you test the effectiveness of the new drug against behavior therapy and Rational-Emotive Therapy?

In treating mood problems like anxiety and depression, which do you think is more effective: medication or talk therapy? What is the basis for your opinion?

PART 18

SOCIAL PSYCHOLOGY

If you have now made it through the previous seventeen sections of this volume or perhaps through ninety-four percent of an Introductory Psychology course, you may have noticed that psychologists focus their studies almost exclusively on the behavior of individuals who are performing alone or, on occasion, with one other person. But individuals tend to behave in entirely new ways when they're part of groups. Conformity, crowding effects, riots, and other phenomena could probably never be predicted from the study of individuals behaving outside of groups. Hence the need for social psychology, which focuses on the behavior of individuals in group settings. So what, you may be asking, is *sociology?* Sociology and social psychology occasionally overlap, but, generally speaking, sociologists focus on the characteristics of groups per se, whereas social psychologists focus on the characteristics of individuals *in* groups. (It's taken me twenty-five years to figure out these distinctions, so I hope you're paying attention.)

This section opens with an interview with one of social psychology's most prolific and wide-ranging researchers, Elliot Aronson, author of the popular textbook, *The Social Animal.* In the next piece, "Beauty and the Best," Ellen Berscheid and Elaine Walster review disturbing data suggesting that physical appearance has an overwhelming impact on our social and professional lives. And in the final article, "Brainwash," distinguished social psychologist Robert Zajonc explains why the proverb, "Familiarity breeds contempt," is just plain wrong.

A Missionary for Social Psychology:

A CONVERSATION WITH Elliot Aronson

◆ *John Wilkes*

John Wilkes: You've been very involved in policy research, an area that seems to be dominated by economists. What role do you see social psychologists playing there?

Elliot Aronson: We should have a lot more to say than we do now. The problem with economists is that they believe people will behave rationally and do what is most cost-effective. We social psychologists know that a lot of things interfere with rational thinking. Human behavior is complex but not unfathomable. We simply need to take cognitive and social phenomena into consideration when making policy.

Wilkes: What sorts of things are the economists missing?

Aronson: I've been exploring what social psychologists can add to the economic model of how people think and act about conservation. We think we can help policymakers encourage people to make decisions about energy conservation that are in their own self-interest as well as in the national interest. Sadly, people are not making these decisions for reasons we understand better than the economists seem to. For example, most people won't borrow money from utility companies at low interest to insulate their houses, even though that would be cost-effective. Some

economists throw their hands up and say, "People are irrational." We say people aren't irrational, they just have other things to consider—such as their distrust of utility companies.

Wilkes: How, in practical terms, would you go about getting people to conserve energy?

Aronson: I'd like to do an experiment in which a utility company gave me 50 of their energy auditors for one weekend. I would train them how to present the material in a way that was vivid and personally involving. Perhaps I'd

---

If I could train these engineeers to be social-psychology communicators, I'm sure I could get them to be much more effective.

---

show consumers how much money they're losing through energy inefficiency rather than how much they'd gain, because that has more impact. If I could train these engineers in two days to be social-psychology communicators, I'm sure I could get them to be much more effective. My long-range plan is to use these kinds of methods to bring about voluntary energy conservation.

Wilkes: You've been working on questions of attitude change for a long time. About 15 years ago you managed to induce black, Chicano

and white kids to cooperate in an unprecedented way. Why did you stop doing your jigsaw-classroom work?

Aronson: Two related reasons: One is that I just needed to move on. I'd been working the same beat for 10 years. Also, I was frustrated—there's no public policy on education in this country. We were given carte blanche in Austin because the schools were in crisis. But most school administrators are reluctant to change things unless it's absolutely necessary. After Austin, although I could present solid data that the jigsaw classroom worked, and I was offering to train teachers in other cities for free, I had real trouble getting inside the schools. I had to go to a great many before I got one to do jigsaw.

Wilkes: You seem to have an unusual amount of sympathy for kids from nontraditional educational backgrounds.

Aronson: I was one of them myself. I grew up in an uneducated, impoverished Jewish household. I don't remember seeing my mother or father ever reading a book. I went to high school in a lower-class neighborhood where carrying books home was frowned on by most of my peers. Many times I walked home from school without any books, then walked back again to get some, because I didn't want my friends to know that I was actually reading assignments. Even so, I was an indifferent student in high school.

Wilkes: How does an indifferent student get to be a social psychologist?

Aronson: I became a practicing social psychologist—amateur—at 14. I lived near an amusement park, and all my friends and I worked there, for 60 cents an hour. One of my jobs was at the Pokerino table, where you play by rolling five balls down an incline into marked pockets to get a poker hand. One night when we were open late and there were hardly any customers on the boardwalk, the "mike man," the guy who gave the spiel to get people inside to play the game, let me take over on the mike. I was a shy kid. But behind the microphone I grew pretty bold. I went through the whole routine the way he did it, but it was boring, so I began to make things up. I would start announcing winners even though the place was deserted. No one was playing, but people were winning! Some people peered in, out of curiosity. They were amused and began to play the game. Before I knew it, the place was jammed. The owner wandered in and was astonished. I think we had half the people on the boardwalk playing Pokerino. From then on, I had a steady job as a mike man.

Wilkes: So you learned something about human nature?

Aronson: I learned a lot. It became clear that people won't do things unless they think it's an "in" thing to do. Almost nobody wants to be the first person to sit down and participate. The major job of the mike man was to lure the first few people in. Occasionally I could do it with humor. When that failed, I gave my friends a few nickels apiece—out of my own pocket—and had them sit down and play. Soon, others joined in. In college, I learned that social psychologists had a name for this: social influence.

Wilkes: How did you get from the amusement park to college?

Aronson: I was very lucky. I got to go to a first-rate university. Brandeis had just opened a couple of years before I graduated from high school, and its admissions policy was pretty loose. My grades were mediocre, but my SAT scores were high, so I was admitted and even was given a work-study scholarship that enabled me to go.

Wilkes: Did you start right off majoring in psychology?

Aronson: No, economics. Guess why? My father wanted me to go to college because, to him, education meant money. I was so naive, so dumb. I had no idea of what universities were about. So, I ma-

> *It became clear that people won't do things unless they think it's an 'in' thing to do. Almost nobody wants to be the first person to sit down and participate.*

jored in economics. Anyway, I was doggedly pursuing my economics, spending a lot of time at it and being bored, and meanwhile my roommate was taking a course in introductory psychology from Abraham Maslow, father of the human-potential movement. And my roommate kept coming home spouting humanistic psychology and saying things like, "This guy's terrific! He says it's okay to masturbate!" All the humanistic stuff. And here I was, pounding my head against the wall in economics. I was envious, so I took his course the second semester of my sophomore year, and I fell in love—with Maslow and with humanistic psychology. It was an absolute revelation that a great many of the things I had been thinking about ever since I was a kid were actually an academic discipline at a university. I found myself reading faster, looking for new things to read that weren't assigned. Maslow was such a powerful model for me.

Wilkes: Who else influenced your career?

Aronson: My mentor was Leon Festinger. I've never known a smarter, tougher person. It wasn't easy to be his student, but once

> *They say I'm a missionary, and I think there's some truth in that.*

Festinger concluded that I had talent, nobody could talk him out of that. He was a tough bastard, but a warm human being, and he had enormous confidence in his own judgment, so I gained confidence in myself partly through his belief in me.

Wilkes: Festinger's specialty was research. How did he feel about your enthusiasm for teaching?

Aronson: He tried to discourage it. Festinger believed that people who were good at research should not be distracted by other academic pursuits. It was our biggest disagreement. But he came over to my side some 20 years later, in 1980, when I won a distinguished-teaching prize and a distinguished-research prize simultaneously. I had to give a public acceptance speech, and Festinger was asked to introduce me. During a very affectionate, almost schmaltzy, introduction (I loved it!) he admitted that he had tried to discourage me from wasting my time teaching. He conceded that he had been wrong, that I was the only person he knew whose teaching enhanced his research.

Wilkes: As a committed teacher at strongly research-oriented universities, you must have felt as if you were swimming upstream. What impelled you to teach?

Aronson: They say I'm a missionary, and I think there's some truth in that. When I first started teaching a beginning social-psychology course at Harvard, a lot of the students were also taking "hard science" courses such as physiological psychology. I wanted to make the point that social psychology was indeed a science, so I spent a lot of my energy describing social-psychology experiments in detail to show the students that we were rigorous. When I got to Texas, I encountered a lot of racism. I wanted to affect the students, to change them. I wanted people to become more tolerant, thoughtful and introspective, and to get as excited as I was about the notion that our attitudes aren't all locked up by the time we're 14 years old. I wanted them to understand that growth and change are vital parts of the educational experience.

Wilkes: One way of helping people realize that they can change their attitudes is to show them that some of their cherished common sense notions are false. Do the classic experiments in cognitive dissonance theory help you do this?

Aronson: Absolutely. For example, I think the Festinger-Carlsmith experiment is the most important single experiment ever done in social psychology. It made us see human nature differently than we had ever seen it before. To a person steeped in reinforcement theory, the idea that people who tell a lie for $1 end up believing it more fully than people who tell the same lie for $20 is an extremely powerful and counterintuitive notion. Dissonance theory's broader implication is that people are rationalizing animals who strive to make their attitudes line up with their behavior—after the fact. If we don't keep that in mind we are going to make dreadful mistakes by oversimplifying our understanding of how people form attitudes and relate to one another.

Wilkes: Your own work in dissonance theory gained you a considerable reputation early in your career. Which experiment are you most proud of?

Aronson: I'm not sure which one I'm most proud of, but the one I'm fondest of is the very first experiment I ever did, on how a person's allegiance to a group is determined by the severity of the group's initiation. The severer the initiation, the stronger the allegiance. Fraternity hazing is an example. I was exhilarated at being able to set up a situation to test a

> *Textbooks bore me, and I've never read one all the way through. I wrote* **The Social Animal** *as an anti-textbook.*

proposition that had never been tested before. It taught me something new and exciting about human behavior. I don't think I will ever do anything again that could capture the flavor of my initial discovery.

Wilkes: You must be equally fond of your book *The Social Animal*, which by now has been read by

hundreds of thousands of college students. Why did you write that book, and what was it like to write it?

Aronson: I loved writing it because I hate textbooks. Textbooks bore me, and I've never read one all the way through. I wrote *The Social Animal* as an anti-textbook. I wanted the book to grab students, to get them involved. I wrote it in 1970 and '71, during the Vietnam War. Society was falling apart, yet academicians were still writing textbooks as if social psychology had nothing to do with society.

Wilkes: What was different about your book?

Aronson: Before I was a writer I was a reader. I try to write stuff that

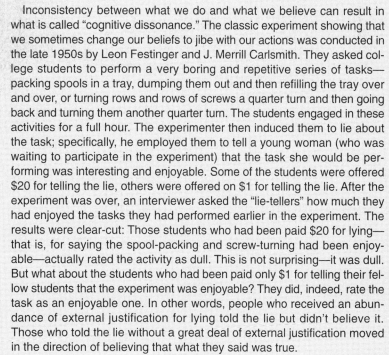

Cognitive Dissonance: Making the Thought Fit the Deed

Inconsistency between what we do and what we believe can result in what is called "cognitive dissonance." The classic experiment showing that we sometimes change our beliefs to jibe with our actions was conducted in the late 1950s by Leon Festinger and J. Merrill Carlsmith. They asked college students to perform a very boring and repetitive series of tasks—packing spools in a tray, dumping them out and then refilling the tray over and over, or turning rows and rows of screws a quarter turn and then going back and turning them another quarter turn. The students engaged in these activities for a full hour. The experimenter then induced them to lie about the task; specifically, he employed them to tell a young woman (who was waiting to participate in the experiment) that the task she would be performing was interesting and enjoyable. Some of the students were offered $20 for telling the lie, others were offered on $1 for telling the lie. After the experiment was over, an interviewer asked the "lie-tellers" how much they had enjoyed the tasks they had performed earlier in the experiment. The results were clear-cut: Those students who had been paid $20 for lying—that is, for saying the spool-packing and screw-turning had been enjoyable—actually rated the activity as dull. This is not surprising—it was dull. But what about the students who had been paid only $1 for telling their fellow students that the experiment was enjoyable? They did, indeed, rate the task as an enjoyable one. In other words, people who received an abundance of external justification for lying told the lie but didn't believe it. Those who told the lie without a great deal of external justification moved in the direction of believing that what they said was true.

Adapted from *The Social Animal* (Freeman)
by Elliot Aronson

I would want to read. I try very hard to write the way I talk and not to become self-consciously "proper" in making the transition between my mouth and my pen. A certain journal editor used to send my research papers back to me and say, "I like the experiment, but you'll have to clean up the slummy writing style." But, actually, I like my slummy style. I like to be colloquial, even in technical writing, as long as it doesn't interfere with precision and understanding of the meaning.

Wilkes: Did writing the book have any effect on you?

Aronson: It got me thinking broadly. I had lived through the '60s, and I had been doing research on interpersonal attraction from about 1964 to 1970. But I was experiencing a paradox: While I was doing experiments on why people like each other, people all around me were getting divorced, or at least having a lot of difficulty relating to one another. And I wondered, what did I know that could help them? The answer was: nothing. So I got interested in encounter groups as a way of increasing effectiveness of communication between people who care about each other. For a few years I was leading a double life. On weekends, Vera and I would have 20 people over at our house for an intensive encounter session. Yet during the week I was doing social-psychological laboratory experiments, which are probably the extreme opposite of encounter. An experiment in social psychology often requires the experimenter to deceive the subject in some way, but encounter doesn't let people cut any corners when it comes to honesty. I was feeling schizophrenic, trying to keep those two categories separate. I think most of my colleagues were a little embarrassed by my activities on weekends. But my strategy was then, and still is today, to follow my heart.

Wilkes: Your continuing interest in encounter and in applied research in public policy suggests that you've cooled off somewhat on your experimental psychology work.

Aronson: Not at all. I think the ex-

We've gotten much more concerned ethically about lying to people while conducting an experiment.

---

perimental method is very important, in both the laboratory and the field. But I've found it increasingly difficult to do the kinds of laboratory experiments we were doing 15 or 20 years ago. For one thing, we've gotten much more concerned ethically about lying to people while conducting an experiment. This limits the kinds of questions we can ask and the realness of the experience we can create in the laboratory.

Vietnam and Watergate made everyone aware that people in high places were lying. We social psychologists found ourselves using similar kinds of deception. We could insist that it was for a good cause, namely, furthering knowledge about human behavior. We could also tell ourselves that we could debrief our subjects an hour later, and that no lasting harm would have been done. Yet,

---

As a society we're doing a terrible job dealing with old people. The current situation for the aged is pretty bleak. One of the worst things that happen to old people is that they are made to feel increasingly useless.

---

some of us couldn't escape feeling implicated by these national events. The zeitgeist made elaborate deception particularly unappetizing. Also, some researchers had been looking into the effectiveness of our debriefings, and they discovered that in some instances, we might not ever be able to completely undo the harm caused by some of the more extreme discomfort produced in experiments.

Wilkes: Do you know yet where you'll be headed after your research on attitudes toward energy conservation?

Aronson: I'm not certain, but the problem I'm beginning to think about is old age. As a society we're doing a terrible job dealing with old people. The current situation for the aged is pretty bleak. One of the worst things that happen to old people is that they are made to feel increasingly useless. I don't think that's necessary, and I'm going to investigate strategies to help old people become useful and feel useful in ways that are meaningful to them.

Wilkes: If you involve yourself next in research on the plight of the aged, you will have pretty firmly located your work in the real world. Do you feel any nostalgia for the old days when you had a laboratory, lots of research hypotheses burning in your brain and a roomful of eager graduate students across the hall to help you test them?

Aronson: I do have some nostalgia for that period of my life, sure. But I like what I'm doing now. It's less buzz-buzz-buzz and more contemplative. You know, I teach a course on the life cycle. And in teaching, it has become increasingly clear to me that I still have the self-concept of a "promising young man," more like 32 than 52. At the same time, I see my interests becoming less specialized—much broader, more settled. So maybe I am 52 after all. My only hope is that I can continue to remain promising. ◈

Discussion Questions

1. What is a "jigsaw" classroom, and how did this help the integration movement?

2. What did Aronson learn about human nature at a Pokerino table?

3. Who were Aronson's role models in college? How did they influence him?

4. What is cognitive dissonance theory? How is it supported by the Festinger-Carlsmith experiment?

5. Why do social psychologists use deception in their research studies? Do you think that their use of deception is justified? Please explain.

6. Aronson asserts that social psychologists should be involved in the making of public policy. What is his rationale? Do you agree? Explain your answer.

Beauty *and the* **Best**

◆ *Ellen Berscheid and Elaine Walster*

A billion-dollar cosmetics industry testifies that the severity of the sentence may depend upon the quality of the skin. We can cold-cream it, suntan it, bleach it, lift it, and paint it—but we cannot shed it. And, unless we are willing to adopt the tactics of the Oregon State student who enclosed himself in a large black bag, our physical appearance is our most obvious personal characteristic.

For the past few years we have investigated the impact of one aspect of appearance—physical attractiveness—upon relationships between persons. Our initial interest in attractiveness was negligible. We shared the democratic belief that appearance is a superficial and peripheral characteristic with little influence on our lives. Elliot Aronson has suggested that social scientists have avoided investigating the social impact of physical attractiveness for fear they might learn just how powerful it is. It may be, however, that we have simply given too much credence to collective assertions that internal attributes are more important determinants of who wins or loses our affections than external appearance is.

Impact

The results of our research suggest that beauty not only has a more important impact upon our lives than we previously suspected, but its influence may begin startlingly early.

Nursery-school teachers often insist that all children are beautiful, yet they can, when they are asked, rank their pupils by appearance. The children themselves appear to behave in accordance with the adult ranking.

Beauty has more impact than we suspected. Its influence may begin startlingly early.

This finding resulted from a study of nursery-school records. Some schools collect information on how students view each other. A teacher will ask a child to select from photographs of his classmates the person he likes most and the person he likes least. The teacher also asks such questions as *Who is teacher's pet?*, *Who is always causing trouble in the class?*, and *Who is most likely to hit other kids?*

The children in our nursery-school sample ranged in age from four to six. We thought that the older nursery-school children, who had had more time to learn the cultural stereotypes associated with appearance, might be more influenced by their classmates' attractiveness than the younger children. To examine this hypothesis, we divided the sample into two age groups. We then studied the children's reactions to their classmates who had been judged to be attractive or unattractive by adults.

We found that boys who had been judged by adults to be relatively unattractive were not as well liked by their classmates as the more attractive boys. This was true regardless of the age of the boy. In contrast, the unattractive girls in the younger group were more popular than the attractive girls. With age, however, the unattractive girls declined in popularity, while the attractive girls gained favor with their classmates.

Fight

We also examined how the children described their classmates' behavior. We found that unattractive boys were more likely to be described by their classmates as aggressive and antisocial than were attractive boys. Children said that the less-attractive boys were more likely to fight a lot, hit other students, and yell at the teacher.

The nursery-school children also thought that their unattractive peers, regardless of sex, were less independent than attractive children. They were seen to be afraid, unlikely to enjoy doing things alone, and as needing help from others.

When the children were asked to name the one person in their class who scared them, they were more likely to nominate an unattractive classmate than an attractive one.

Type

The available data did not reveal whether the unattractive children actually did misbehave more than the attractive children. We do not know if the students' opinions of their classmates were based on factual observation of the behavior, or on adherence to social stereotypes.

© 1998 PhotoDisc, Inc.

It is possible that physical-appearance stereotypes have already been absorbed at this early age. We know that nursery-school children can differentiate among various body types and prefer some to others. For example, fat bodies are already disliked at this age. If a child assumes that nice children are handsome and naughty ones are unattractive, he may notice only those episodes that fit this image.

Whether or not attractive and unattractive children really do behave differently, their classmates think they do and they doubtless act accordingly. Physical attractiveness thus may become a major factor in the social development of the child. It could affect his self-concept and his first social relationship.

Physical attractiveness may even influence which students make the honor roll.

Bias

What if the children's reports of behavioral differences are not the result of distorted perception to fit their stereotype, but are accurate descriptions of their classmates' behavior? What if unattractive nursery-school boys are indeed more aggressive and hostile than handsome boys? Research suggests that such differences might be caused by discriminatory treatment at the hands of parents, teachers and babysitters.

A study by Karen Dion indicates that adults may have a stereotyped image of the moral character of attractive and unattractive children. She found that this image may affect the way adults handle a matter such as discipline for misconduct.

Dion asked young women to examine reports of disturbances created by schoolchildren. To each report she attached a paper that gave a child's name and age, and a photograph that other adults had judged to be attractive, or unattractive. The women believed that the descriptions came from teachers' journals reporting classroom and playground disturbances. Dion asked each woman to evaluate the disturbance and to estimate how the child behaved on a typical day.

Dion hypothesized that the women would interpret the same incident differently depending on whether the naughty child was attractive, or unattractive. The data supported her hypothesis. When the supposed misconduct was very mild in nature, the women did not distinguish between the everyday behavior of unattractive and attractive children. When the disturbance was severe, however, the women assumed that the unattractive boys and girls were chronically antisocial in their everyday behavior.

Cruelty

One young woman made this comment after reading about an attractive girl who had supposedly thrown rocks at a sleeping dog: "She appears to be a perfectly charming little girl, well-mannered, basically unselfish. It seems that she can adapt well among children her age and make a good impression....She plays well with everyone, but like anyone else, a bad day can occur. Her cruelty…need not be taken too seriously."

When a less-attractive girl committed the identical act, another young woman concluded: "I think the child would be quite bratty and would be a problem to teachers....She would probably try to pick a fight with other children her own age....She would be a brat at home....All in all, she would be a real problem."

To a significant degree, the young women expressed the ominous expectation that the unattractive child would be more likely to commit a similar disturbance in the future. To a lesser, nonsignificant degree the women suspected the unattractive child of having misbehaved in the past.

Who

These findings suggest that in cases in which there is some question about who started the classroom disturbance, who broke the vase, or who stole the money (and with children it always seems that there is the question of *who did it?*) adults are likely to identify an unattractive child as the culprit. The women in Dion's study also believed that unattractive children were characteristically more dishonest than their attractive classmates.

Thus, if an unattractive child protests his innocence, his pleas may fall on deaf ears. The long march to the principal's office starts early, and physical unattractiveness may be a silent companion for the marcher. Often the only possible justice is blind justice.

Grades

Contrary to the popular belief that "beauty and brains don't mix," there is evidence that physical attractiveness may even influence which students make the honor roll. In collaboration with Margaret Clifford, we asked 400 fifth-grade teachers to examine a child's report card. The report card itemized the student's absences during the school year, his grades (for six grade periods) in reading, language, arithmetic, social studies, science, art, music, and physical education. It also reported his performance in healthful living, his personal development, and his work habits and attitudes.

Pasted in the corner of the report card was a photograph of a child, one of six boys and girls who previously had been judged to be relatively attractive, or one of six boys and girls judged to be less attractive.

Future

We asked the teachers to evaluate the student's I.Q., his parents' attitudes toward school, his future

© 1998 PhotoDisc, Inc.

educational accomplishment, and his social status with his peers. We predicted that the child's appearance would influence the teacher's evaluation of the child's intellectual potential, despite the fact that the report cards were identical in content. It did.

The teachers assumed that the attractive girl or boy had a higher I.Q., would go to college, and that his parents were more interested in his education. Teachers also assumed that the attractive student related to his or her classmates better than did the unattractive student.

Prophecy

Other researchers have shown that a student is likely to behave in the way a teacher expects him to behave. Robert Rosenthal and Lenore Jacobson gave an I.Q. test to students in grades one through six. They told teachers that the test identified children who were likely to show marked intellectual improvement within the year. The researchers then, at random, chose 20 percent of the children and announced that test scores had identified these children as the special students.

A year later, Rosenthal and Jacobson gave the same I.Q. test to the same children—all of them. The results of the second test revealed that the supposed bloomers showed more improvement in I.Q. than the other youngsters did. The gains were most pronounced for first- and second-graders. Rosenthal and Jacobson speculated that teachers probably were more encouraging and friendly toward those children identified as bloomers. Their expectations acted as a self-fulfilling prophecy.

These studies suggest that physical attractiveness in young

children may result in adult evaluations that elicit special attention. In turn, special attention may confirm teacher predictions of individual accomplishment.

Dating

The preceding findings, which indicate that a child's physical attractiveness may affect a variety of his early social and educational experiences, were somewhat unexpected. That beauty affects one's social relationships during the adolescent dating years comes as less of a surprise. What is disconcerting, however, is the apparently overwhelming importance of appearance in opposite-sex dating.

Physical attractiveness may be the single most important factor in determining popularity among college-age adults. In a series of studies of blind dates, we found that the more physically attractive the date, the more he or she was liked. We failed to find additional factors that might predict how well a person would be liked. Students with exceptional personality features or intelligence levels were not liked more than individuals who were less well endowed.

> *Physical attractiveness may be the single most important factor in determining popularity among college-age adults.*

Match

In these studies of the factors that influence courtship, we tested the hypothesis that persons of similar levels of social desirability tend to pair off in courtship and marriage. Erving Goffman described this matching process in 1952: "A proposal of marriage in our society tends to be a way in which a man sums up his social attributes and suggests to a woman that hers are not so much better as to preclude a merger or a partnership in these matters." To test the matching hypothesis we sponsored a computer dance for college students. We obtained a rough estimate of each student's social attributes from scores on personality, social skill, and intelligence tests. In addition, we rated each student's physical appearance at the time he or she purchased a ticket.

The participants assumed that the computer would select their dates on the basis of shared interests. But we paired the students on a random basis, with only one restriction—the cardinal rule of dating that the man be taller than the woman.

Gap

At intermission we handed out a questionnaire to determine how the students liked their dates. If the matching hypothesis is true, we would expect that students paired with dates from their own levels of social desirability would like each other more than those paired with dates from levels inferior or superior to their own. The results did not confirm the hypothesis. The most important determinant of how much each person liked his or her date, how much he or she wanted to see the partner again, and (it was determined later) how often the men actually did ask their computer partners for subsequent dates, was simply how attractive the date was. Blind dates seem to be blind to everything but appearance.

Subsequent blind-date studies, however, did provide some support for the hypothesis that persons of similar social-desirability levels pair off. Although a person strongly prefers a date who is physically attractive, within this general tendency he or she does seek a person who is closer to his or her own attractiveness, rather

than a person who is a great deal more or less attractive. Apparently, even in affairs of the heart, a person is aware of a credibility gap.

We thought at first that the blind-date studies had exaggerated the importance of physical attractiveness as a determinant of popularity for, after all, blind-date situations do not allow the dates much opportunity to get to know one another. Subsequent evidence indicated, however, that the importance of beauty probably had not been exaggerated.

In one study, for example, Polaroid pictures of a sample of college girls were rated for attractiveness. This rough index of each girl's beauty was compared to each girl's report of the number of dates she had had within the past year. We found an unexpectedly high correlation ($+.61$) between physical attractiveness and the woman's actual social experience. The girls in our sample

Although a person strongly prefers a date who is physically attractive, within this general tendency he or she does seek a person who is closer to his or her own attractiveness, rather than a person who is a great deal more or less attractive.

represented a wide range of personality traits, social skills, intelligence, values and opinions, differences in inclination to date, and so on. Although in natural settings men do have the opportunity to know and appreciate such characteristics, physical attractiveness still had a major bearing on popularity.

Vulgarity

These findings contradict the self-reports of college students. A multitude of studies have asked students to list the characteristics

they find most desirable in a date or mate. Males almost always value physical attractiveness more than women, but both sexes claim that it is less important than such sterling characteristics as intelligence, friendliness and sincerity. What accounts for the discrepancy between the reality and the self-report? Many students seem to believe that it is vulgar to judge others by appearance. They prefer to use such attributes as "soul" or warmth as bases for affection. Their apparent disregard for grooming seems to support their charge that it is only to members of the over-30 crowd that appearance matters.

Traits

Young adults may not be as inconsistent as it appears at first glance. There is evidence that students may prefer physically attractive individuals because they unconsciously associate certain positive personality traits (traits which they value) with an attractive appearance. In a study conducted with Dion, we found that

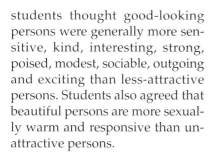

© 1998 PhotoDisc, Inc.

students thought good-looking persons were generally more sensitive, kind, interesting, strong, poised, modest, sociable, outgoing and exciting than less-attractive persons. Students also agreed that beautiful persons are more sexually warm and responsive than unattractive persons.

Lure

In addition to estimating the personality characteristics of attractive and unattractive persons, we asked the students to tell us what lay ahead for each individual. They expected that attractive persons would hold better jobs, have more successful marriages and happier and more fulfilling lives in general than less-attractive persons. They reversed their optimism on only one dimension—they did not believe that attractive individuals made better parents than did unattractive ones.

These findings suggest a possible reason for our nearly obsessive pursuit of suitably attractive mates. If we believe that a beautiful person embodies an ideal personality, and that he or she is likely to garner all the world's ma-

terial benefits and happiness, the substantial lure of beauty is not surprising.

Sex

Is there any truth to these stereotypes? Is it true that attractive persons have better personalities or more successful marriages? It does seem possible that an attractive woman might have a happier marriage than a less-attractive woman. A beautiful woman has a wider range of social activity and consequently has a better chance of meeting a man who has similar interests and values—or any of the factors that appear to lead to stability in marriage.

It also seems possible that physically attractive women are in fact more responsive sexually than less-attractive females. Gilbert Kaats and Keith E. Davis found that good-looking college women were in love more often and had more noncoital sexual experience than girls of medium or low physical attractiveness. They also were more likely to have had sexual intercourse than girls of medium attractiveness. In almost any area of human endeavor, practice makes perfect. It may well be that beautiful women are indeed sexually warmer—not because of any innate difference—but simply because of wider experience.

Reversal

Do attractive coeds actually end up leading happier, more-fulfilling lives than less-attractive coeds? We examined interview data taken from women now in their late 40s and early 50s. We were able to locate early pictures

of most of the women by looking through their college yearbooks. A panel of judges from a group of the same age (who presumably were familiar with the standards of beauty that prevailed 25 years ago) rated the pictures. We found that the physical attractiveness of each woman in her early 20s bears a faint but significant relationship to some of the life experiences she reports over two decades later.

Good looks in college seemed to have significant effect on marital adjustment and occupational satisfaction in older women, but the effect was exactly the opposite of what we expected. The more attractive the woman had been in college, the less satisfied, the less happy, and the less well-adjusted she was 25 years later.

Clifford Kirkpatrick and John Cotton have suggested why things do not go well with beautiful-but-aging women: "Husbands may feel betrayed and disillusioned in various ways and even disgusted with the reliance on charms which have faded with the passing of years." They neglect to mention how aging wives will feel about their once-handsome husbands.

> *The more attractive the woman had been in college, the less satisfied, the less happy, and the less well-adjusted she was 25 years later.*

Criterion

Love at first sight is the basis of song and story, but usually we get around to taking a second look. It is possible that time lessens the influence of our stereotyped images of beautiful persons. However, many of our interactions with other persons are once-only, or infrequent. We have limited exposure to job applicants, defendants in jury trials, and political candidates, yet on the basis of initial impressions we make decisions that affect their lives. In the case of political candidates, our decisions also affect our lives.

Our research indicates that physical attractiveness is a crucial standard by which we form our first impressions. There is reason to believe that Richard Nixon lost his first campaign for President at least in part because he did not have a good make-up man, while John Kennedy did not need one. Public figures eventually have to act, however, and handsome is not always as handsome does. Mayor John Lindsay may well have been the most beautiful man

© 1998 PhotoDisc, Inc.

in New York, but that apparently didn't solve the problems of subway travel, traffic, crime, or any of the other ills that bedevil New Yorkers.

Beholder

Our research has shown some of the ways we react to attractive persons. We still do not know what variables affect our perception of beauty. If we think that a person has a beautiful personality, do we also see him or her as physically more attractive than we ordinarily would? One study suggests that this may be so. Students took part in discussion groups with other students whose political views ranged from radical to conservative. We later asked the students to judge the physical attractiveness of the group members. We found that students thought that the persons who shared their political views were more physically attractive than those who didn't. Perhaps Republicans no longer think that John Lindsay is as beautiful, now that he is a Democrat.

We should point out that in each study we conducted, we used photographs drawn from relatively homogeneous socioeconomic samples, principally from the middle class. We excluded individuals of exceptional physical beauty and

those of unusual unattractiveness, as well as those with noticeable physical handicaps or eyeglasses. Had we included the full range of beauty and ugliness it is possible that the effects of physical attractiveness would have been even more dramatic.

Health

Our research also does not tell us the source of our stereotyped images of beautiful persons. It seems possible that in earlier times physical attractiveness was positively related to physical health. Perhaps it still is. It might be the instinctive nature of any species to want to associate and mate with those who are the healthiest of that species. We may be responding to a biological anachronism, left over from a more primitive age.

Although social scientists have been slow to recognize the implications of our billion-dollar cosmetics industry, manufacturers may be quicker to capitalize upon the additional exploitation possibilities of beauty from early childhood through the adult years. Such exploitation could pour even more of our gross national product into the modification of the skins in which we are all confined—some of us more unhappily than others. ◆

Discussion Questions

1. According to Berscheid and Walster, what do nursery-school children believe about their less attractive peers?

2. What is a possible explanation for aggressive behavior in unattractive children?

3. Describe the study by Karen Dion. What were the results?

4. Describe the report card study. What were the results?

5. What is the most important determinant of popularity for college-age adults?

6. According to the authors, why do people claim that physical attractiveness is not important in choosing mates, even though it is the principle characteristic they actually use to pick mates?

7. The authors suggest that attractive people might actually be better lovers. What is their rationale?

8. The authors suggest that attractive coeds may end up less happy in middle age than their unattractive peers. On what basis did they make this prediction?

9. How do you think your experiences have been shaped by your appearance?

Brain*wash:* FAMILIARITY Breeds *Comfort*

◆ *Robert Zajonc*

The word *nice* comes from the Latin word *ignorant.* By the time it got into Middle English, *nice* meant *foolish;* and in the 17th Century English sentence above it meant *fastidious* or *finicky.* Today, of course, *nice* has a nicer meaning. A similar evolution is true for the word *pretty,* which can be traced to the Old English *praetig*—deceitful or sly. In its Middle English form, *prati* meant *cunning,* a usage which soon gave way to *ingenious.*

A vast number of words have changed their meanings over the centuries to become more positive. This mysterious process can, in some of its aspects, be reproduced in a laboratory in a much shorter period of time—about five minutes. Take a word your subject has never seen before, such as the Turkish word *dilikli.* Show it to the person a number of times and ask him whether it means something good or something bad. The more times the person has seen *dilikli,* the more likely he is to say it means something good. Subjects who have seen the word only once or twice don't like it much at all.

I don't wish to imply that etymology is simply a matter of repetition and that word meanings always improve. There are many words whose meanings have deteriorated over time. But the above example does illustrate a phenomenon that is vastly more universal, and whose consequences are more profound and diverse, than it would at first appear. The proposition holds that the *mere repeated exposure of an unfamiliar stimulus is enough to increase one's attraction to that stimulus.* Repeated exposure makes words more positive, food more appetizing, strangers more acceptable. Repeated exposure will increase the attraction between two people or two animals. I am

> **Repeated exposure makes words more positive, food more appetizing, strangers more acceptable.**

not saying that exposure is always necessary for attraction or attachment to occur. Many other psychological processes are equally efficient in getting people to like each other. But exposure *itself,* under certain conditions, is enough to increase attraction.

The first support for this hypothesis came from semantics—specifically, data on word frequencies. That is, in many languages there are counts of how often certain words occur. E. L. Thorndike and Irving Lorge did such a count for English during the Depression. They determined how often each of 30,000 words appears in a total of 4.5 million. In 1960 R. C. Johnson, C. W. Thomson and G. L. Frincke observed that words with "positive" meaning occur much more frequently than words with "negative" meaning. *Love,* for example, occurs 5,129 times, while *hate* appears only 756 times; *beauty* outscores *ugliness* by 776 to 18; and *happiness* is 25 times as frequent as *unhappiness.* These observations are also true for such innocent members of our vocabulary as prepositions, pronouns and adverbs. We prefer to be *in* rather than *out—up* occurs twice as often as *down,* and *in* five times as often as *out.* And in anticipation of recent modes of entertainment, Thorndike and Lorge counted 1,674 instances of *high* to 1,224 of *low.*

Unfortunately for us, word frequencies are clearly fickle in representing reality. But they are extraordinarily accurate in representing real values: words that stand for good, desirable and preferred aspects of reality are more frequently used. This frequency-value relationship, I suggest, is one case of the exposure effect.

My colleagues and I gave a list of 154 antonym pairs to a large number of subjects and asked them to judge which member of each pair had the more favorable meaning—which word "represented the more desirable object, event or characteristic." The subjects showed remarkable agreement in their preferences. And it is clear, above all, that they preferred the member of the pair that is most frequently used. For instance, 97 of the 100 student subjects thought *on* was more desirable than *off; on* occurs 30,224 times, *off* a mere 3,644.

One interesting exception is the *warpeace* pair. Our students unquestionably preferred *peace,* but the Thorndike-Lorge count (which presumably represents the feelings of the entire population) shows that *war* is favored and occurs more often. I will add that the frequencies of *war* and *peace* in German are about the same as in English. But in French and Spanish, *paix* and *paz* occur much more often than *guerre and guerra.* I shall leave you to draw your own conclusions about national character.

The frequency effect is not limited to the meanings of words. It also applies to a person's attitudes toward what the words stand for. Our subjects' liking for cities and countries, for example, related quite closely to the frequencies with which the names of these places occur in the written language. Their attitudes toward trees, fruits, flowers and vegetables show the same effect.

Since these findings are correlational, one cannot speculate about casual directions. We do not know whether we rate *sweet* more favorably than *bitter* because *sweet* is used more frequently or because it means something more pleasant than *bitter.* We can argue that many roses are grown because people like roses, or we can argue that people like roses because there are many roses around. Still there are some studies that get around this problem.

Ordinarily we do not think of numbers as being pleasant or unpleasant. Yet I have found that contrary to the cultural values of "the bigger the better" and "the more the merrier," it seems that people like smaller numbers best—the numbers that occur most frequently. William Johntz, a mathematics teacher, once asked some children whether they liked even or odd numbers best. The children overwhelmingly preferred the even numbers—and also thought there were many more evens than odds! The frequency effect is true of letters as well as numbers. In 1962, E. A. Alluisi and O. S. Adams found that some letters—the more frequent ones—are consistently better liked than others. Since it would be hard to argue that the letter E and the number 2 occur often because for some peculiar reason they are well-liked, we had best assume that they are well-liked because they occur often. In

this case at least, frequency determines attractiveness.

Good experimental evidence supports these studies. Johnson, Thomson and Frincke were the first to find that the preference ratings of nonsense words can be enhanced if the words are presented repeatedly. My colleagues and I have similar evidence. We exposed

our subjects to a number of three-syllable Turkish words, such as *iktitaf, afworbu* and *jandara.* They saw some of these words frequently (25 times), some occasionally (five or 10 times), others rarely (once or twice). The words were randomized so that each had a different frequency for each subject. We then told them that they had

Preference and Frequency of Antonym Pairs

Preference	Word	Frequency	Preference	Antonym	Frequency
100%	Able	930	0%	Unable	235
99	Good	5,122	1	Bad	1,001
99	Peace	472	1	War	1,118
98	Friend	2,553	2	Enemy	883
98	Love	5,129	2	Hate	756
97	On	30,224	3	Off	3,644
97	Remember	1,682	3	Forget	882
95	Most	3,443	5	Least	1,259
94	Leader	373	6	Follower	49
92	Up	11,718	8	Down	5,534
91	Always	3,285	9	Never	5,715
85	In	75,253	15	Out	13,649
77	Usually	718	23	Unusually	91
63	Answer	2,132	37	Question	1,302
58	Husband	1,788	42	Wife	1,668
52	Play	2,606	48	Work	2,720

(Thorndike and Lorge, 1944)

Preference Rank and Frequency Counts for Ten Countries and Ten Cities

Preference	Country	Frequency	Preference	City	Frequency
1	England	497	1	Boston	255
2	Canada	130	2	Chicago	621
3	Holland	59	3	Milwaukee	124
4	Greece	31	4	San Diego	9
5	Germany	224	5	Dayton	14
6	Argentina	15	6	Baltimore	68
7	Venezuela	9	7	Omaha	28
8	Bulgaria	3	8	Tampa	5
9	Honduras	1	9	El Paso	1
10	Syria	4	10	Saginaw	2

Preference Ratings and Frequency of Fruits and Flowers (from Zajonc, 1968)

Rank	Fruits	Fre-quency	Average Pref. Rating*	Rank	Flowers	Fre-quency	Average Pref. Rating*
1	Apple	220	5.13	1	Rose	801	5.55
2	Cherry	167	5.00	2	Lily	164	4.79
3	Strawberry	121	4.83	3	Violet	109	4.58
4	Pear	62	4.83	4	Geranium	27	3.83
5	Grapefruit	33	4.00	5	Daisy	62	3.79
6	Cantaloupe	1.5	3.75	6	Hyacinth	16	3.08
7	Avocado	16	2.71	7	Yucca	1	2.88
8	Pomegranate	8	2.63	8	Woodbine	4	2.87
9	Gooseberry	5	2.63	9	Anemone	8	2.54
10	Mango	2	2.38	10	Cowslip	2	2.54

*Preference Rating Scale, 0 = dislike, 6 = like

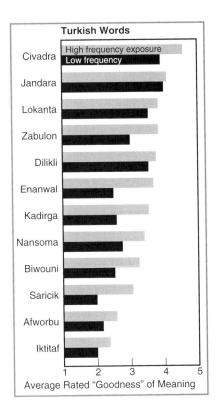

Turkish Words

High frequency exposure
Low frequency

Civadra
Jandara
Lokanta
Zabulon
Dilikli
Enanwal
Kadirga
Nansoma
Biwouni
Saricik
Afworbu
Iktitaf

1 2 3 4 5
Average Rated "Goodness" of Meaning

just seen a list of Turkish adjectives and shamelessly asked them to guess what the words meant. (They were Turkish words indeed, but not all adjectives.) We said we appreciated how nearly impossible this task was, given their unfamiliarity with Turkish, but we insisted that they try. To help, we told them that each adjective meant something good or something bad, and all they had to do was guess which. The results clearly supported the prediction: the more often the subject had seen the word, the more likely he was to think that the word meant something good. We repeated this experiment using Chinese ideographs and men's faces instead and the exposure-liking effect remained.

Don Rajecki and I tried the Turkish-word study in a more natural situation. We printed the same set of words in two college papers, one at the University of Michigan, at Ann Arbor, and the other at Michigan State, at East Lansing. For several weeks these words appeared every day with-

out explanation. We "advertised" some of the words once, others twice, the rest five, 10 or 25 times. Those shown frequently in one paper were shown infrequently in the other. The word appeared in a rectangle one column wide and one inch deep. After the ad campaign we went to several classes with our scales and asked for the same kind of ratings that we took in the lab experiments. We also sent out hundreds of questionnaires by mail to the subscribers of the newspapers. The results confirmed the earlier studies. Readers liked the words that had appeared most often, although they had no idea what the words meant or why they were in the paper.

Why does repeated exposure increase the attractiveness of an object? Albert Harrison suggests an explanation that may be fairly simple. Consider something a person encounters for the first time: obviously he has no ready response to it. But in some ways this new object will be similar to others that he has encountered in the past; the word or face may be unfamiliar,

but he has certainly seen words and faces before. Generalizing from experience, the person will want to respond to the stimulus in several different ways. Some of these response tendencies may be incompatible, and the individual will feel mild stress. Since this stress is associated with the unfamiliar object, the person is not likely to consider the object attractive. But as the stimulus is exposed more, it becomes more familiar; the incompatible responses drop out and the person establishes a stable way of responding. The initial stress and discomfort are reduced greatly and the object becomes more attractive.

Harrison and Margaret Matlin have done independent experiments that support this explanation. Both have shown that novel stimuli elicit several conflicting responses, and that this causes discomfort. As a result, new objects are less well liked than familiar objects to which single responses have been attached. Novelty apparently is associated with uncertainty and with conflict, which are likely to produce tension and neg-

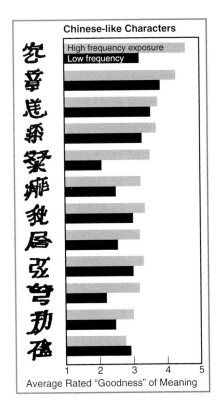

Chinese-like Characters

High frequency exposure
Low frequency

1 2 3 4 5
Average Rated "Goodness" of Meaning

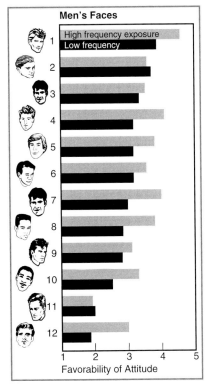

Men's Faces

High frequency exposure
Low frequency

1
2
3
4
5
6
7
8
9
10
11
12

1 2 3 4 5
Favorability of Attitude

ative feelings. Familiarity, on the other hand, is comfortable.

The novelty explanation puts a critical limit on the applicability of the exposure effect. Repeated exposure will enhance liking primarily when we show the person something he has never seen before. Probably the effect won't work at all on familiar objects, such as Aunt Martha. There are two other such limitations.

> *Repeated exposure will enhance liking primarily when we show the person something he has never seen before. Probably the effect won't work at all on familiar objects, such as Aunt Martha.*

1. The effect of exposure on attraction is logarithmic. That is, early exposures produce the strongest effects, while each successive presentation adds less and less to the total attractiveness of the object;
2. The effect of exposure is easiest to demonstrate when the object is a neutral one. If you already have strong feelings about it, the exposure effect will probably be overcome. But you usually do not have strong feelings about new objects.

Even with these qualifications, however, the implications of the exposure phenomenon reach far. Almost every psychological process involves exposure of a new stimulus—for example, acquisition of habits, perceptual and social learning, attachment. Exposure may even help form attitudes. Consider a study of persuasion aimed at changing a person's attitude. Most of these studies attempt to change opinions in a positive direction; the subject hears a lot of arguments designed to make him like chocolate grasshoppers, teaching machines,

or even Spiro Agnew. But for every argument in favor of Agnew there is also an exposure of the name Agnew. In this case the number of arguments works along with increased exposure to produce a more favorable attitude. Theoretically, this should be easier to do than to make attitudes more unfavorable. In that case, every argument given against Spiro Agnew would be counteracted by exposure to his name. And, in fact, studies of persuasion seldom try to effect a negative change.

In one recent study, P. H. Tannenbaum and R. W. Gengel could get only positive shifts of opinion, although they had tried to get negative ones as well. Or recall the AMA's propaganda campaign against Medicare—a compelling case in point. Richard Harris, writing in *The New Yorker* in 1966, concluded that "the medical profession's immense outlay may have brought about precisely what it least wanted—increased public interest in some form of national health insurance."

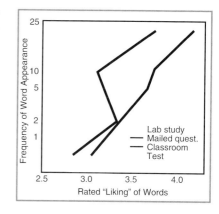

The exposure effect applies not only to human beings, but also to a wide variety of animals. Consider imprinting, a form of attachment of young animals to objects or to other animals, typically the mother.

Imprinting has long been considered the crowning example of the interaction between instinct and learned habit. The process itself, say the ethologists, is generated by an innate disposition; but the target and onset of the process are determined or "triggered" by experience.

However, it is entirely plausible that imprinting is not at all instinctive. In contract to the well-established instinctual bases of mating, nest-building and hoarding, imprinting has not been traced to any specific neuroanatomic structures, to endocrine

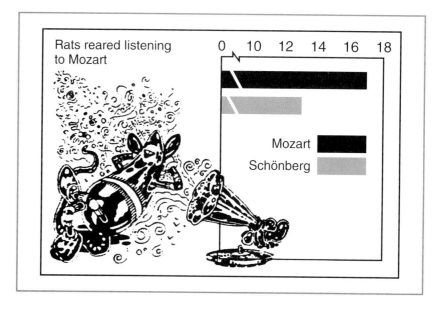

processes or to other physiological functions. These functions may yet be discovered, but for now the evidence for an instinct theory rests on three observations:

1. Imprinting occurs nearly universally among some species;
2. It occurs in a most compelling and dramatic fashion;
3. It is particularly likely to occur during a short time of the animal's life, shortly after birth. (For example, John Scott considers the period between the third and seventh weeks as the only time during which a puppy can become attached to people.)

These facts are not proof that imprinting is necessarily a matter of instinct.

Suppose that imprinting is nothing more than a special case of mere exposure. The young animal likes whatever he sees most often, whether it is his mother, a milk bottle, a cardboard box or a human being. In all cases this attachment can be explained in terms of early social experience alone.

Typically, of course, this experience is with members of the animal's species. The normal Oregon fruitfly, for instance, grows up with other Oregon fruitflies, and at mating time an Oregon male will court an Oregon female in preference to other species. But as M. Mainardi showed, fruitflies raised in isolation do not discriminate between Oregon females and yellow ones. They have not learned the difference.

But mere exposure is enough to attach an animal to members of a different species. R. B. Cairns did an experiment with lambs that had lived for several weeks with their mothers and other lambs. He then separated the lambs from the

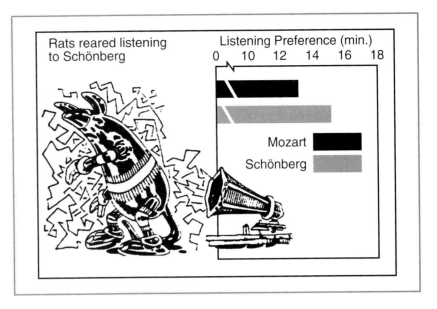

Rats reared listening to Schönberg

Listening Preference (min.)

Mozart
Schönberg

flock and each lamb lived for 71 days with one of four possible companions: a dog in the same cage, a dog in an adjacent cage, an unfamiliar ewe, or a continuously operating television set. At various times during this period Cairns put each lamb in a maze and allowed it to choose between an empty compartment or one containing the companion. Each lamb chose the cohabitant, and this preference increased over time. Dogs, ewes, and television sets were all equally effective in gaining the lambs' affections.

Nine weeks later, Cairns let each lamb choose between his companion and a tethered ewe. Most still chose the companions. Television didn't fare quite as well; lambs raised with the TV sets generally chose the ewe. Still this preference was not overwhelming, and reliably lower than that shown by control animals.

Imprinting is not even limited to animate targets. In fact, almost any object or repeated event will do. Chicks and ducklings have been imprinted to small red boxes, colored balls and sponges, a plastic milk bottle mounted on an electric train, and wooden decoys. (In our own laboratory, David Reimer exposed chicks to four styrofoam shapes for differing

amounts of time. He found a clear exposure effect—the birds later approached the most familiar shapes.) Experience also has a lot to say about food preferences. Gulls raised on cat food will prefer that to worms, a food closer to their natural diet.

Animals can even become attached to sounds. H. A. Cross, C. G. Halcomb and W. W. Matter tried an ingenious musical experiment with three groups of rats. One group grew up with Mozart; 12 hours a day for 52 days, these rats listened to such pieces as the *Violin Concerto No. 5, The Magic Flute* and *Symphonies No. 40 and 41.* The second group heard only Schönberg: *Pierrot Lunaire, Chamber Symphonies No. 1 and 2, Verklarte Nacht,* and so on. The third group was totally deprived of music. After 52 days the experimenters gave all the rats a two-week rest, then tested their musical preferences. They put each rat in a chamber with a floor that was hinged in the center and suspended over two switches, one on each side of the hinge. A rat's weight was enough to push down one side or other of the floor and thus activate a switch. As you might guess, one switch turned on music by Mozart, the other turned on music by Schönberg. Let me

add that Cross and his colleagues used selections that the rats had not heard before.

It is clear from the results that experience with one kind of music led the animals to prefer that kind. But I would like to stress, with some sympathy, that animals reared with Mozart became true Mozart lovers, while the Schönberg group merely learned to prefer Schönberg. And the rats that had grown up with no music at all preferred Mozart. (Incidentally, the Thorndike-Lorge count for Mozart is 8. There is no entry for Schönberg.)

The studies show not only that the rat may have a more tender soul than we have come to believe, but also that it takes little more than mere exposure to produce affection and attachment. But if we consider imprinting as a special case of the exposure effect we must still explain two important findings. First, why are certain critical periods especially favorable for the formation of these attachments? Second, if a lamb can love a TV set, why shouldn't a newly hatched chick become enamored of a nearby twig or rock instead of its mother?

The existence of critical periods is due in part to the maturation process of the animal. For exam-

ple, a three-day old puppy simply cannot see well enough to distinguish between possible objects of attachment. To the extent that the animal cannot make fine discriminations, his behavior toward his surrounding will be very generalized. Only when his senses have developed sufficiently will he be able to imprint. For puppies this development takes about three weeks; for ducklings no more than seven hours.

But sensory development cannot explain why the critical period *ends*. This stage is not as inflexible as we had once thought; it can be restricted or extended. But it always has a clear termination point; animals do not form attachments easily after this period. One explanation is that imprinting, like marriage, exercises a priority right. Once an attachment has been made, others are less likely to form. The tendency to approach new objects will begin to conflict with the affection for the original target.

This explanation must be extended to encompass two additional facts. Animals kept in isolation during the critical period still show a subsequent inability to form attachments. In addition, these inexperienced and isolated animals will prefer members of their own

species even on a first encounter. Both of these occurrences can be explained by assuming self-exposure and self-attachment. That is, consider an animal reared in isolation. This poor fellow will be deprived of social experience and a rich physical environment, but his sensory development is not delayed. So he cannot prevent being exposed to many things about himself. He can hear himself bark or chirp or squeak; he can see his legs or wings or feet or tail; he can smell his own odor and feel his own texture, and so on. There must be thousands of cues associated with his own body and behavior that are obviously like the bodies and behavior of members of his species.

Thus an isolated animal may develop some form of attachment to the only objects and events to which it is exposed; its own body and its own behavior.

The critical period, then, ends when a primary attachment has been made. That attachment, whether it is to the animal itself, to another animal, or to an inanimate object, enjoys the privilege of priority over subsequent objects of liking. If the animal has been raised with others of his species, he will prefer them as targets of imprinting because of their similarity to himself. If he has been reared alone, he may become attached to himself. To the extent that isolation leads to self-imprinting, the likelihood of the animal's forming other attachments is severely curtailed. Given a choice, he may later prefer to associate with others of his species; after all, they have some of his characteristics.

In short, imprinting and attachment can be explained as examples of the effects of mere exposure. We do not need to resort to an instinct theory, for which there is no convincing evidence thus far.

By now it should be obvious that I believe the exposure effect has a wide range of applicability for animals and people alike. No one doubts that human attitudes and attachments are motivated by a complex variety of factors. But it is also clear that some of them are a result of mere exposure.

A few years ago when young men began to grow their hair long, many of us on the other side of the generation gap were aghast. Some treated the phenomenon as a passing fad, a few said it was a protest against the war, others regarded it as a symptom of the utter perversity of the Dr. Spock generation. It simply did not seem proper for honors scholars in our universities to wear the hairstyles of Louis XIV while adorning their feet with moccasins. We were extremely critical. But now more and more of our children look that way, and fewer and fewer adults are appalled. Those of us who still can grow longer hair do so. High schools are rescinding rules on hair length for boys. We have got used to it, you say. We have accepted the inevitable. Or are these the effects of repeated exposure?

Not long ago a mysterious student, totally enveloped in a big black bag, attended a speech class at Oregon State University. Only the professor knew his identity. The professor later said, in describing the feelings of other students in the class, that their attitude changed from hostility toward the Black Bag to curiosity and finally to friendship. The effect of repeated exposure?

High schools are rescinding rules on hair length for boys. We have got used to it, you say. We have accepted the inevitable. Or are these the effects of repeated exposure?

A man by the name of Hal Evry will elect you to office if you can follow his formula. You must not make speeches, not take a stand on issues. In fact, you must not appear at all in the campaign. But his organization guarantees that your name will be as familiar to voters as Tide or Ford. Evry mounted an extensive saturation campaign on behalf of one unknown fellow, by

flooding the city with signs saying *three cheers for Pat Milligan.* That was all. The voters saw those words on billboards, in full-page newspaper ads, on facsimile telegrams sent through the mails. The advertisement of this slogan went on for months, and on election day Pat Milligan was the undeniable winner. What else but the effects of mere exposure?

With this evidence in mind, consider the advertising community. Clearly they believe that effective salesmanship requires exposure of the product, but they aren't convinced that *mere* exposure is enough. They insist on *attractive* exposure. Thus few products appear without a seductive woman. I wonder, however, about the effects of this strategy. Associating so many products with sex gives sex an unprecedented amount of exposure. Does this really increase sales, or does it only make potential customers more interested in sex? ◆

Discussion Questions

1. How does repeated exposure to a stimulus (such as an unfamiliar word) affect a person's feelings toward that stimulus?
2. What did Johnson, Thomson, and Frincke find regarding word preferences?
3. How does Albert Harrison explain why repeated exposure increases preference?
4. List the two reasons why repeated exposure to common objects will not increase attraction.
5. How does imprinting in animals support Zajonc's theory?
6. What is Zajonc's rationale for rejecting an instinct theory of imprinting and attachment? How does he explain these phenomena?
7. What is something that you did not like at first but gradually came to like after repeated exposures?

Exercises

Name: _____

Date: _____

Part 18: Social Psychology

1. I believe that my physical appearance has made an enormous difference in the way other people have treated me throughout my life.

Agree (1) (2) (3) (4) (5) Disagree

2. I consider myself an extreme nonconformist.

Agree (1) (2) (3) (4) (5) Disagree

3. I believe that the use of deception in social psychology experiments is justified.

Agree (1) (2) (3) (4) (5) Disagree

Conduct a simple experiment to test the ideas presented in "Beauty and the Best." For example, wearing old clothes and looking extremely disheveled, ask passers-by in a mall if they will sign a petition. What proportion will agree to sign in 30 minutes? Repeat the procedure looking your very best. Does the portion increase?

Is the procedure above a fair test of the beauty hypothesis? Why or why not? How could you perform a better experiment?

ABOUT THE EDITOR

ROBERT EPSTEIN is University Professor at United States International University in San Diego and the founder and Director Emeritus of the Cambridge Center for Behavioral Studies in Massachusetts. He is also the host of "Psychology Today," a nationally-syndicated radio program sponsored by *Psychology Today* magazine, where he is a contributing editor. Dr. Epstein received his Ph.D. in psychology in 1981 from Harvard University. He is the developer of Generativity Theory, a scientific theory of creativity, and his research on creativity and problem solving has been reported in *Time* magazine, the *New York Times*, and *Discover*, as well as on national and international radio and television. Epstein's recent books include *Creativity Games for Trainers* (McGraw-Hill), *Cognition, Creativity, and Behavior: Selected Essays* (Praeger), *Pure Fitness: Body Meets Mind* (Masters Press, with Lori "Ice" Fetrick of the American Gladiators), *Self-Help Without the Hype* (Performance Management Publications), *Stress-Management and Relaxation Activities for Trainers* (McGraw-Hill), and *Irrelativity* (Astrion). He is also the editor of two books of writings by the eminent psychologist, B. F. Skinner, with whom Epstein collaborated at Harvard. He has taught at Boston University, the University of Massachusetts at Amherst, the University of California San Diego, Keio University (Tokyo), and other universities. He served as Professor of Psychology and Chair of the Department of Psychology at National University and was also appointed that university's first Research Professor. Dr. Epstein maintains a laboratory at the Center for Behavioral Epidemiology at San Diego State University, where he is Adjunct Professor of Psychology. He also directed the Loebner Prize Competition in Artificial Intelligence for five years. He has been a commentator for NPR's "Marketplace" and the Voice of America, and his popular writings have appeared in *Reader's Digest, The Washington Post, Psychology Today, Good Housekeeping, Parenting*, and other magazines and newspapers.

INDEX

bisociation, 225
Bleuler, Eugen, 403–405
Block, Jack, 354, 357
blood pressure, controled by
  biofeedback, 377–378
Blos, Peter, 273
Blum, Kenneth, 73
Bock, Michael, 121
bodily-kinesthetic intelligence, 179
body language, 288–290
body types, differentiated by children,
  447
Bogen, Joseph, 114–115
Bonnet, Michael H., 47
Bower, Gordon, 151
box-and-banana problem, 208–209
boys and girls, behavioral differences,
  45–46
bracketing, problem, 227–228
brain
  aging, 63
  asymmetries, 317
  attention deficit disorder, 397,
    399–400, 402
  daydreaming, 123
  depression, 145
  emotion, 292–296
  enriched environment, 61–65
  hemispheres of, 66–69, 114–116,
    182, 207, 292–296, 313–318
  immune system, 64
  injury, 292–294, 296, 313–315, 375
  "left brain"–"right brain" myths,
    66–69
  left and right–handers, 316
  male and female differences, 64,
    313–318
  organ of mind, 404
  organization, 316
  sex hormones effect on, 186–187,
    273
  unconscious, the, 113–116
breast cancer, and genes, 74
Briddell, Daniel, 53
Brim, Orville G., Jr., 353, 356, 357–358
Brucker, Bernard, 375, 377
Brundy, Joseph, 375
Bruner, Jerome, 233, 239
Bryden, Philip, 315
bulimia, 380
Bykov, K. M., 376

C

Cain, William S., 81
Cannon, Walter, 368
capturing skills, 210–211
Carducci, Bernardo J., 333
Carlsmith, J. Merrill, 443
Carpenter, John, 50
Cartwright, Rosalind, 109
case study method, 226

caudate nucleus, 400
Center for Cognitive Therapy, 389, 394
centered self, 335–338, 339
  technology's effects on, 337–338,
    339
  See also self
Cevey, Bernhard, 376
chaining method, 159, 161
challenging situation, 211
change in personality doctrine,
  353–358
  debate with stability doctrine,
    357–358
channel capacity, for odor quality,
  89–90
Cheek, Jonathan, 341
child abuse, 28, 29, 44, 47
child development, 233, 235–258
child-raising, 3–4
chronic loneliness, 393–394
circadian rhythm patterns, 46–47
Civilization and Its Discontents, 28
clairvoyance, 95, 99
classical conditioning. *See*
  conditioning, classical
Clever Hans, case of, 38
Client-Centered Therapy, 14
client-therapist relationship in
  Rogerian therapy, 11
clinical psychologists, 59
clitoris, 327
clonidine, 421
coding, in learning, 165, 215–216
cognition, human, 205
  self and, 337
cognitive commitment, premature,
  216–218
cognitive dissonance, 443
cognitive distortion, 394, 395
cognitive processes, 68
  in dreams, 247–253
  and drinking, 49, 54, 55
  sex hormones influence, 184–187,
    273, 317
  shyness, 341
  for smell, 88, 93–94
coherence in personality, 335–339
commissures, cerebral, 114, 115
commitment, as a key to a lasting
  marriage, 278–279, 338
communication, of emotion, 287–290
competence, stability of, 355
complaints, in marriage, 288
compromise behaviors, 289–290
conception timing, and shyness, 344
conditioning, classical, 127
  and biofeedback, 376
  in infants, 242–245
confederate, 213, 324
confession (self–disclosure), 44
confidentiality, 28

conflict, 339
  in marriage, 288
"Conflicting Psychologies of
  Learning - A Way Out, The," 21
conscious awarness, 28, 113
consciousness, 105, 107, 113
  levels of, 105, 109–111, 112
consequence, emotional, in RET, 414,
  415
consequences (reinforcers), 4
conservation concepts, 236–237
  accelerate learning of, 238
consistency, in personality, 335–339
*Constancy and Change in Human
  Development*, 353, 356
constriction (type of loneliness), 393
contextual conditioning, 346
contingencies of reinforcement, 4–9
contraception, study of, 311
contraceptive pill, 309
control cases, 30
control groups, 41, 48
controllable stressors, 371–374
controlled failure system, 211
coping, 374, 382–383
Corinth, Lovis, 69
corpus callosum, 59, 67, 207, 313, 315,
  400
corrective feedback, 90–91, 93
cortex, cerebral, 59, 61–64, 86, 87, 205,
  314, 315, 317
corticotropin releasing factor (CRF),
  346
cortisol, 383
Costa, Paul T., 354–355, 356, 357
courts, and token programs, 132–133
Creative Dreaming, 107
creativity, 66, 69, 205, 207–212,
  225–229, 268
  exercises and games involving,
    208
  generativity, 209–212
  myths about, 207
  play affecting, 256
  strategies for increasing, 210–212
  training for, 211–212, 256–258
critical period, imprinting, 458
Croghan, Leo, 389
"crotch hang–ups," 25
crying behavior, infant, 244
culture, shyness and, 347–348
culture-biased tests, 191–192
culture-fair tests, 191–192
culture-loaded tests, 191–192
Curle, Adam, 44–45

D

Dali, Salvador, 210
Darwin, Charles, 225–226, 227, 228,
  297, 330
Davis, Michael, 346